EDITED BY

MORTON W. BLOOMFIELD
Harvard University

ROBERT C. ELLIOTT
University of California, San Diego

GREAT PLAYS

THIRD EDITION

SOPHOCLES TO ALBEE

HOLT, RINEHART AND WINSTON, INC.

NEW YORK   CHICAGO   SAN FRANCISCO   ATLANTA   DALLAS

Library of Congress Cataloging in Publication Data

Bloomfield, Morton Wilfred, comp.
  Great plays, Sophocles to Albee.
  First ed. published in 1951 under title: Ten plays.
  CONTENTS: Sophocles. Antigone.—Shakespeare, W.
Othello.—Molière. The misanthrope. [etc.]
    1. Drama—Collections. I. Elliott, Robert C.,
joint comp. II. Title.
  PN6112.B5   1975   808.82   74-7270
  ISBN 0-03-089464-6

9 · 038   9 8 7 6 5

Preface

Here are thirteen plays selected from the work of some of the greatest playwrights of the world. The plays range in time from the fifth century before Christ to today; they were written for audiences of Plato's Athens, Shakespeare's London, Louis XIV's Paris, Czar Nicholas II's Moscow, and our own Broadway. They vary enormously in theme, in style, in tone, and in the theatrical conventions that govern them. With all this diversity, however, they have this in common: they are superb examples of the dramatic art, and they were written to be acted and to be witnessed. Even the most intense reading is no substitute for seeing these plays performed.

Still, a careful reading may produce a major experience of its own kind, one in which the printed page stimulates and controls the student's imagination so that he will see the action and hear the characters as they speak in the theatre of his own mind. The student becomes, in effect, the producer of the drama. In the classroom, among conflicting interpretations of action, dialogue, style, and structure, he finds the test of his production.

A necessary condition of this experience is that the student understand the language of the plays that historical change may have rendered obscure. The editors have supplied full textual notes to help remove this barrier to comprehension. An introduction to each play contains biographical data about the author, relevant background information, and brief critical remarks on the play itself. Interpretive comment has been kept to a minimum. The editors believe that the major responsibility for interpretation properly belongs to the teacher and the student.

We wish to express our thanks for permission to use the following plays: to Mr. E. F. Watling, translator, and Penguin Books Ltd., publishers, for *Antigone;* to Harcourt Brace Jovanovich, Inc., for *The Misanthrope* (translated by Richard Wilbur); to The Chandler Publishing Co. for *Miss Julie* (translated by E. M. Sprinchorn); to The Society of Authors for *Arms and the Man;* to A. P. Watt & Son for *Three Sisters* (translated by Constance Garnett); to Random House, Inc., for *The Hairy Ape* and *The Glass Menagerie;* to Mr. Eric Bentley for *The Caucasian Chalk Circle* (adapted by Eric Bentley); to Farrar, Straus & Giroux, Inc., for *The Firebugs* (translated by Mordecai Gorelik); and to Coward, McCann & Geoghegan, Inc., for *The American Dream.* We wish to thank Ms. Mary Bischoff for her help in preparing this manuscript.

M.W.B.
R.C.E.

CAMBRIDGE, MASSACHUSETTS
LA JOLLA, CALIFORNIA
DECEMBER 1974

iii

Contents

Antigone

Sophocles

Sophocles

In the fifth century B.C., the city of Athens was blessed with four great dramatists—three tragedians, Aeschylus, Sophocles, and Euripides, and one comedian, Aristophanes. Their preserved plays, too few of the many they wrote, have provided the world with one of its supreme periods in dramatic creation. Of the body of extant plays, we have picked one, *Antigone* (442-441 B.C.) by Sophocles (496-406 B.C.), because of its universal theme and easy accessibility to modern readers. It has been one of the most popular of the Greek plays and has been frequently revived. The new views of state and centralizing power and the growth of a greater sensitivity to individual rights have made its relevance to our times especially strong.

Greek drama arose out of, and was probably always connected with, religion, especially the worship of the god Dionysus. Its plots were well-known stories taken from the early and mythical history of Greece. They dealt with the gods, as the early history of Greece was considered by the ancient Greeks to be of a religious nature; it had, that is, a religious as well as a patriotic significance.

Greek plays were performed at certain annual festivals, the most important of which occurred in the spring. Playwrights submitted their works to a board that weeded out the poorer ones. The remainder were presented to the public, and prizes were given to the best. Attendance at these performances in the open air was somewhat equivalent to a religious duty, and the audience went, not only to amuse themselves, but to participate in worship, from motives akin to those which inspire one today to attend a performance of the Passion play dealing with Jesus' life and crucifixion. To the Greeks, however, a visit to the theatre was not just a pious act, but a kind of public participation in religious worship and celebration of the gods.

The chorus in every Greek drama originally consisted of about fifty members and comprised the whole cast of the play. They danced and chanted to honor the gods or to direct the attention of the audience to certain phases of the story. Later, individual actors were given special roles to speak or act so as to point up and animate the story. Gradually, more roles were evolved and taken away from the chorus, which was reduced in number to about fifteen. In spite of this loss, the chorus always held an important part in Greek drama.

From the observer's point of view, the chorus provides information about the action and comments on its significance. The viewer sees the play at least partially through their eyes and from their vantage point. In effect, they add a new dimension of vision. In *Antigone*, the elders of Thebes, who form the chorus, tell what is necessary about the reactions of the people of Thebes, give clues to the action, take a limited part in the dialogue with the main characters,

4

and, above all, recite several great lyrics, commenting on the eternal meaning of what is unrolling before the audience's eyes.

On the Greek stage, no violent action was permitted—the lack of curtains and elaborate scenery made this type of action difficult to represent anyway—and it was all reported to the audience. Attention was concentrated on the speakers and their reactions. The basic outline of the story was already known, and the absence of direct action allowed for greater concentration on the essence of drama—the emotions and wills of human beings in conflict with each other.

Greek plays usually followed what have been known, since the Renaissance, as the three unities, those of time, place, and action. The drama catches the action at its peak and never covers more time than one day. It never moves about in place and never has more than one plot. It would have been considered inappropriate and unfitting—both adjectives are very characteristic of the Greek view of life—to mingle two plots or to have comic relief as we find it in Shakespeare. Comedy was provided at each performance by a separate satyr play which was a kind of burlesque, often very gross, and frequently related to the theme and subject matter of the principal play or plays. On occasion, of course, there were performances of comedies alone.

Antigone is based on an incident taken from the history of the royal family of Thebes. The tragedy arises from the conflict of two loyalties—loyalty to God (or the gods) and loyalty to the state. Antigone represents the first and Creon the second. Caught between these two forces is Haemon, Creon's son and Antigone's fiancé. He is torn between filial piety and love for his bride-to-be. The tragedy could have been written around him, but that was not the way Sophocles chose. Rather, he turned his back on Haemon's problem to take up the larger intellectual tragic problems.

Actually there is a real question in *Antigone* as to who is the tragic hero. That it must be either Antigone or Creon is clear from the play itself, and the title should lend credence to those who favor Antigone. But it is most likely that the title was used by Sophocles merely to indicate the general subject matter. A stronger case can be made for the theory that *Antigone* is Creon's tragedy. It is his tragic fault of pride (*hybris*) or obstinacy which brings upon him his doom in the deaths of his son and wife. The chorus points this out clearly throughout the play and especially at the end.

> *Of happiness the crown*
> *And chiefest part*
> *Is wisdom, and to hold*
> *The Gods in awe.*
> *This is the law*
> *That, seeing the stricken heart*
> *Of pride brought down,*
> *We learn when we are old.*

Creon pitted himself against the gods who demand that honor be paid to the dead and, in his presumption, he was brought low. The Greeks looked with particular horror at those who refused to allow the dead to be buried properly. Such a deed would still today arouse indignation, but to the Greeks it would be the violation of a religious duty and a true sacrilege. It meant that the shade (or soul) of the unburied would not be allowed to enter Hades, the abode of the dead.

Although Antigone, in our opinion, is not the tragic hero of this play, she does more than serve as a mere foil and as opposition to Creon. She is a majestic and moving figure in her own right. Inflexible and perhaps somewhat arrogant, she nevertheless moves us in her dignity and in her defense of a higher morality than the expedient and the immediate. She is not in love with death, as her grief over her unmarried state shows, but she is willing to die for what she knows is right. She serves as an eternal symbol and warning for all men.

Aristotle in his *Poetics* held that the playgoer, witnessing a great tragedy, undergoes a purgation of soul (catharsis) as he pities the characters and feels terror for their (and his) human lot. Much ink has been spilled trying to explain exactly what catharsis is, and the subject cannot be dealt with here. But the experience should become clear to those who enter into the spirit of this great drama, whose relevance to moral and political issues of our own time is strikingly clear.

The family relationships of the Theban royal house must be visualized in order to understand the play. Thebes was an old Greek city-state, reputedly founded by Cadmus, from whom the rulers claimed descent. The family name is often given as the Labdacidae, taken from the grandson of Cadmus, who was Labdacus, father of Laius.

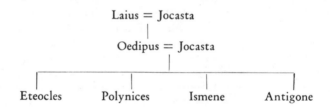

Jocasta was a sister of Creon, both children of Menoeceus.

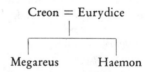

Oedipus is the outstanding and most unfortunate member of the family. He, unwittingly, murdered his father and married his mother, a deed which eventually brought doom upon him and passed on a curse to his family.

Antigone opens just after the two sons of Oedipus have killed each other in a duel, allowing the throne to pass to their uncle (or granduncle), Creon. Polynices, with six champions, had besieged Thebes to take the throne away from his brother Eteocles. This famous expedition is known as the Seven against Thebes and is the subject of a play by Aeschylus. After the death of Polynices, the besieging army withdrew, having failed in its attempt to take the city.

Antigone

Sophocles

TRANSLATED BY E. F. WATLING

CHARACTERS

ISMENE ⎫ *daughters of Oedipus*
ANTIGONE ⎭
CREON, *King of Thebes*
HAEMON, *son of Creon*
TEIRESIAS, *a blind prophet*
A SENTRY
A MESSENGER

EURYDICE, *wife of Creon*
CHORUS *of Theban elders*
KING'S ATTENDANTS
QUEEN'S ATTENDANTS
A BOY *leading Teiresias*
SOLDIERS

SCENE. *Before the Palace at Thebes. Enter* ISMENE *from the central door of the Palace.* ANTIGONE *follows, anxious and urgent; she closes the door carefully, and comes to join her sister.*

ANTIGONE. O sister! Ismene dear, dear sister Ismene!
You know how heavy the hand of God is upon us;
How we who are left must suffer for our father, Oedipus.
There is no pain, no sorrow, no suffering, no dishonour
We have not shared together, you and I.
And now there is something more. Have you heard this order,
This latest order that the King has proclaimed to the city? [1]
Have you heard how our dearest are being treated like enemies?
ISMENE. I have heard nothing about any of those we love,
Neither good nor evil—not, I mean, since the death
Of our two brothers, both fallen in a day.

Antigone by Sophocles, from *The Theban Plays,* translated by E. F. Watling (Penguin Classics, 1947). Copyright © E. F. Watling, 1947. Reprinted by permission of Penguin Books, Ltd. The terms for the performance of this play may be obtained from The League of Dramatists, 84 Drayton Gardens, London, SW 10, to whom all applications for permission should be made.

[1] Creon has just issued an order that the body of Eteocles, his predecessor, be honorably buried and that Polynices' body be left unburied. Anyone violating this order was to be put to death.

The Argive[2] army, I hear, was withdrawn last night.
I know no more to make me sad or glad.
ANTIGONE.   I thought you did not. That's why I brought you out here,
Where we shan't be heard, to tell you something alone.
ISMENE.   What is it, Antigone? Black news, I can see already.
ANTIGONE.   O Ismene, what do you think? Our two dear brothers . . .
Creon has given funeral honours to one,
And not to the other; nothing but shame and ignominy.
Eteocles has been buried, they tell me, in state,
With all honourable observances due to the dead.
But Polynices, just as unhappily fallen—the order
Says he is not to be buried, not to be mourned;
To be left unburied, unwept, a feast of flesh
For keen-eyed carrion birds. The noble Creon!
It is against you and me he has made this order.
Yes, against me. And soon he will be here himself
To make it plain to those that have not heard it,
And to enforce it. This is no idle threat;
The punishment for disobedience is death by stoning.
So now you know. And now is the time to show
Whether or not you are worthy of your high blood.
ISMENE.   My poor Antigone, if this is really true,
What more can *I* do, or undo, to help you?
ANTIGONE.   *Will* you help me? Will you do something with me? Will you?
ISMENE.   Help you do what, Antigone? What do you mean?
ANTIGONE.   Would you help me lift the body . . . you and me?
ISMENE.   You cannot mean . . . to bury him? Against the order?
ANTIGONE.   Is he not my brother, and yours, whether you like it
Or not? *I* shall never desert him, never.
ISMENE.   How could you dare, when Creon has expressly forbidden it?
ANTIGONE.   He has no right to keep me from my own.
ISMENE.   O sister, sister, do you forget how our father
Perished in shame and misery, his awful sin
Self-proved, blinded by his own self-mutilation? [3]
And then his mother, his wife—for she was both—
Destroyed herself in a noose of her own making.
And now our brothers, both in a single day
Fallen in an awful exaction of death for death,
Blood for blood, each slain by the other's hand.
Now we two left; and what will be the end of us,
If we transgress the law and defy our king?
O think, Antigone; we are women; it is not for us
To fight against men; our rulers are stronger than we,
And we must obey in this, or in worse than this.
May the dead forgive me, I can do no other

[2] An adjective meaning "of Argos" or "from Argos."
[3] Oedipus had blinded himself upon learning of his incest.

But as I am commanded; to do more is madness.
ANTIGONE.   No; then I will not ask you for your help.
Nor would I thank you for it, if you gave it.
Go your own way; I will bury my brother;
And if I die for it, what happiness!
Convicted of reverence—I shall be content
To lie beside a brother whom I love.
We have only a little time to please the living,
But all eternity to love the dead.
There I shall lie for ever. Live, if you will;
Live, and defy the holiest laws of heaven.
ISMENE.   I do not defy them; but I cannot act
Against the State. I am not strong enough.
ANTIGONE.   Let that be your excuse, then. I will go
And heap a mound of earth over my brother.
ISMENE.   I fear for you, Antigone; I fear—
ANTIGONE.   You need not fear for me. Fear for yourself.
ISMENE.   At least be secret. Do not breathe a word.
I'll not betray your secret.
ANTIGONE.   Publish it
To all the world! Else I shall hate you more.
ISMENE.   Your heart burns! Mine is frozen at the thought.
ANTIGONE.   I know my duty, where true duty lies.
ISMENE.   If you can do it; but you're bound to fail.
ANTIGONE.   When I have *tried* and failed, I shall have failed.
ISMENE.   No sense in starting on a hopeless task.
ANTIGONE.   Oh, I shall hate you if you talk like that!
And *he* will hate you, rightly. Leave me alone
With my own madness. There is no punishment
Can rob me of my honourable death.
ISMENE.   Go then, if you are determined, to your folly.
But remember that those who love you . . . love you still.
[ISMENE *goes into the Palace.* ANTIGONE *leaves the stage by a side exit.*
Enter the CHORUS *of Theban elders*[4]]
CHORUS.   Hail the sun! the brightest of all that ever
Dawned on the City of Seven Gates, City of Thebes!
Hail the golden dawn over Dirce's river[5]
Rising to speed the flight of the white invaders
Homeward in full retreat!

The army of Polynices was gathered against us,
In angry dispute his voice was lifted against us,
Like a ravening bird of prey he swooped around us
With white wings flashing, with flying plumes,
With armed hosts ranked in thousands.

[4] Here the chorus sings a song of victory, celebrating the defeat of the Seven.
[5] The Dirce flows through the district of Thebes on the west.

At the threshold of seven gates in a circle of blood
His swords stood round us, his jaws were opened against us;
But before he could taste our blood, or consume us with fire,
He fled, fled with the roar of the dragon[6] behind him
    And thunder of war in his ears.

The Father of Heaven[7] abhors the proud tongue's boasting;
He marked the oncoming torrent, the flashing stream
Of their golden harness, the clash of their battle gear;
He heard the invader cry Victory over our ramparts,
    And smote him with fire to the ground.[8]

Down to the ground from the crest of his hurricane onslaught
He swung, with the fiery brands of his hate brought low:
Each and all to their doom of destruction appointed
    By the god that fighteth for us.

Seven invaders at seven gates seven defenders
Spoiled of their bronze for a tribute to Zeus; save two
Luckless brothers in one fight matched together
    And in one death laid low.

    Great is the victory, great be the joy
    In the city of Thebes, the city of chariots.
    Now is the time to fill the temples
    With glad thanksgiving for warfare ended;
    Shake the ground with the night-long dances,
    Bacchus[9] afoot and delight abounding.

    But see, the King comes here,
    Creon, the son of Menoeceus,
    Whom the gods have appointed for us
    In our recent change of fortune.
    What matter is it, I wonder,
    That has led him to call us together
    By his special proclamation?

[*The central door is opened, and* CREON *enters*]

CREON.   My councillors:[10] now that the gods have brought our city
    Safe through a storm of trouble to tranquillity,
    I have called you especially out of all my people
    To conference together, knowing that you

---

    [6] The symbol of Thebes; Cadmus, at Athene's command, sowed dragon's teeth, from which sprang warriors, the ancestors of the chief families of the city.
    [7] Zeus, chief of the gods.
    [8] This is an allusion to Capaneus, one of the attacking Seven, who vowed that he would force his way into Thebes, in spite of Zeus himself. Even as he climbed the ladder he had placed against the wall of the city, Zeus killed him with a thunderbolt for his boasting and impiety.
    [9] God of wine and ecstasy, also known as Dionysus. He was especially favored by the Thebans and was intimately connected with dramatic performances generally.
    [10] The Theban Elders, besides taking the part of the chorus, also act as a kind of council to Creon.

Were loyal subjects when King Laius[11] reigned,
And when King Oedipus so wisely ruled us,
And again, upon his death, faithfully served
His sons,[12] till they in turn fell—both slayers, both slain,
Both stained with brother-blood, dead in a day—
And I, their next of kin, inherited
The throne and kingdom which I now possess.

No other touchstone can test the heart of a man,
The temper of his mind and spirit, till he be tried
In the practice of authority and rule.
For my part, I have always held the view,
And hold it still, that a king whose lips are sealed
By fear, unwilling to seek advice, is damned.
And no less damned is he who puts a friend
Above his country; I have no good word for him.
As God above is my witness, who sees all,
When I see any danger threatening my people,
Whatever it may be, I shall declare it.
No man who is his country's enemy
Shall call himself my friend. Of this I am sure—
Our country is our life; only when she
Rides safely, have we any friends at all.
Such is my policy for our common weal.

In pursuance of this, I have made a proclamation
Concerning the sons of Oedipus, as follows:
Eteocles, who fell fighting in defence of the city,
Fighting gallantly, is to be honoured with burial
And with all the rites due to the noble dead.
The other—you know whom I mean—his brother Polynices,
Who came back from exile intending to burn and destroy
His fatherland and the gods of his fatherland,
To drink the blood of his kin,[13] to make them slaves—
He is to have no grave, no burial,
No mourning from anyone; it is forbidden.
He is to be left unburied, left to be eaten
By dogs and vultures, a horror for all to see.
I am determined that never, if I can help it,
Shall evil triumph over good. Alive
Or dead, the faithful servant of his country
Shall be rewarded.
CHORUS. Creon, son of Menoeceus,
    You have given your judgment for the friend and for the enemy.

[11] See diagram on p. 6, following introduction.
[12] Eteocles and Polynices had agreed to alternate as rulers of the kingdom, each to reign a year. Eteocles' refusal to relinquish his rule precipitated Polynices' revolt and brought about the expedition of the "Seven against Thebes."
[13] Slaughter them.

As for those that are dead, so for us who remain,
Your will is law.[14]
CREON.   See then that it be kept.
CHORUS.   My lord, some younger would be fitter for that task.
CREON.   Watchers are already set over the corpse.
CHORUS.   What other duty then remains for us?
CREON.   Not to connive at any disobedience.
CHORUS.   If there were any so mad as to ask for death—
CREON.   Ay, that is the penalty. There is always someone
Ready to be lured to ruin by hope of gain.
[*He turns to go.* A SENTRY *enters from the side of the stage.* CREON *pauses
at the Palace door*]
SENTRY.   My lord: if I am out of breath, it is not from haste.
I have not been running. On the contrary, many a time
I stopped to think and loitered on the way,
Saying to myself 'Why hurry to your doom,
Poor fool?' and then I said 'Hurry, you fool.
If Creon hears this from another man,
Your head's as good as off.' So here I am,
As quick as my unwilling haste[15] could bring me;
In no great hurry, in fact. So now I am here . . .
But I'll tell my story . . . though it may be nothing after all.
And whatever I have to suffer, it can't be more
Than what God wills, so I cling to that for my comfort.
CREON.   Good heavens, man, what ever is the matter?
SENTRY.   To speak of myself first—I never did it, sir;
Nor saw who did; no one can punish me for that.
CREON.   You tell your story with a deal of artful precaution.
It's evidently something strange.
SENTRY.   It is.
So strange, it's very difficult to tell.
CREON.   Well, out with it, and let's be done with you.
SENTRY.   It's this, then, sir. The corpse . . . someone has just
Buried it and gone. Dry dust over the body
They scattered, in the manner of holy burial.
CREON.   What! Who dared to do it?
SENTRY.   I don't know, sir.
There was no sign of a pick, no scratch of a shovel;
The ground was hard and dry—no trace of a wheel;
Whoever it was has left no clues behind him.
When the sentry on the first watch showed it us,
We were amazed. The corpse was covered from sight—
Not with a proper grave—just a layer of earth—
As it might be, the act of some pious passer-by.
There were no tracks of an animal either, a dog

---

[14] The Elders display little enthusiasm for Creon's new law.
[15] The sentry is not very enthusiastic about his task of bringing bad news, for often such a messenger would be killed in anger.

Or anything that might have come and mauled the body.
Of course we all started pitching in to each other,
Accusing each other, and might have come to blows,
With no one to stop us; for anyone might have done it,
But it couldn't be proved against him, and all denied it.
We were all ready to take hot iron in hand
And go through fire and swear by God and heaven
We hadn't done it, nor knew of anyone
That could have thought of doing it, much less done it.

Well, we could make nothing of it. Then one of our men
Said something that made all our blood run cold—
Something we could neither refuse to do, nor do,
But at our own risk. What he said was 'This
Must be reported to the King; we can't conceal it'.
So it was agreed. We drew lots for it, and I,
Such is my luck, was chosen. So here I am,
As much against my will as yours, I'm sure;
A bringer of bad news expects no welcome.
CHORUS. My lord, I fear—I feared it from the first—
That this may prove to be an act of the gods.
CREON. Enough of that! Or I shall lose my patience.
Don't talk like an old fool, old though you be.
Blasphemy, to say the gods could give a thought
To carrion flesh! Held him in high esteem,
I suppose, and buried him like a benefactor—
A man who came to burn their temples down,
Ransack their holy shrines, their land, their laws?
Is that the sort of man you think gods love?
Not they. No. There's a party of malcontents
In the city, rebels against my word and law,
Shakers of heads in secret, impatient of rule;
They are the people, I see it well enough,
Who have bribed their instruments to do this thing.
Money! Money's the curse of man, none greater.
That's what wrecks cities, banishes men from home,
Tempts and deludes the most well-meaning soul,
Pointing out the way to infamy and shame.
Well, they shall pay for their success.
[*To the* SENTRY] See to it!
See to it, you! Upon my oath, I swear,
As Zeus is my god above: either you find
The perpetrator of this burial
And bring him here into my sight, or death—
No, not your mere death shall pay the reckoning,
But, for a living lesson against such infamy,
You shall be racked and tortured till you tell
The whole truth of this outrage; so you may learn

To seek your gain where gain is yours to get,
Not try to grasp it everywhere. In wickedness
You'll find more loss than profit.
SENTRY. May I say more?
CREON. No more; each word you say but stings me more.
SENTRY. Stings in your ears, sir, or in your deeper feelings?
CREON. Don't bandy words, fellow, about my feelings.
SENTRY. Though I offend your ears, sir, it is not I
But he that's guilty that offends your soul.
CREON. Oh, born to argue, were you?
SENTRY. Maybe so;
But still not guilty in this business.
CREON. Doubly so, if you have sold your soul for money.
SENTRY. To think that thinking men should think so wrongly!
CREON. Think what you will. But if you fail to find
The doer of this deed, you'll learn one thing:
Ill-gotten gain brings no one any good.
[*He goes into the Palace*]
SENTRY. Well, heaven send they find him. But whether or no,
They'll not find me again, that's sure. Once free,
Who never thought to see another day,
I'll thank my lucky stars, and keep away.
                                                    [*Exit*]

CHORUS.[16] Wonders are many on earth, and the greatest of these
Is man, who rides the ocean and takes his way
Through the deeps, through wind-swept valleys of perilous seas
    That surge and sway.

He is master of ageless Earth, to his own will bending
The immortal mother of gods by the sweat of his brow,
As year succeeds to year, with toil unending
    Of mule and plough.

He is lord of all things living; birds of the air,
Beasts of the field, all creatures of sea and land
He taketh, cunning to capture and ensnare
    With sleight of hand;

Hunting the savage beast from the upland rocks,
Taming the mountain monarch in his lair,
Teaching the wild horse and the roaming ox
    His yoke to bear.

The use of language, the wind-swift motion of brain
He learnt; found out the laws of living together

[16] This is the most famous chorus in the play and one of the best-known passages in Greek dramatic literature. Its function dramatically is to allow for the passage of time so that the sentry may find Antigone. Now that Creon is about to discover the culprit and now that the core of the basic conflict between Creon and Antigone is about to be revealed, the chorus also points out the nobility and glory, as well as the pride or *hybris*, of man. Man is great in his potentialities for good or evil.

In cities, building him shelter against the rain
  And wintry weather.

There is nothing beyond his power. His subtlety
Meeteth all chance, all danger conquereth.
For every ill he hath found its remedy,
  Save only death.

O wondrous subtlety of man, that draws
To good or evil ways! Great honour is given
And power to him who upholdeth his country's laws
  And the justice of heaven.

But he that, too rashly daring, walks in sin
In solitary pride to his life's end,
At door of mine shall never enter in
  To call me friend.
[*severally, seeing some persons approach from a distance*]
  O gods! A wonder to see!
Surely it cannot be—
It is no other—
Antigone!
Unhappy maid—
Unhappy Oedipus' daughter; it is she they bring.
Can she have rashly disobeyed
The order of our King?
[*Enter the* SENTRY, *bringing* ANTIGONE *guarded by two more soldiers*]
SENTRY. We've got her. Here's the woman that did the deed.
  We found her in the act of burying him.[17] Where's the King?
CHORUS. He is just coming out of the Palace now.
  [*Enter* CREON]
CREON. What's this? What am I just in time to see?
SENTRY. My lord, an oath's a very dangerous thing.
  Second thoughts may prove us liars. Not long since
  I swore I wouldn't trust myself again
  To face your threats; you gave me a drubbing the first time.
  But there's no pleasure like an unexpected pleasure,
  Not by a long way. And so I've come again,
  Though against my solemn oath. And I've brought this lady,
  Who's been caught in the act of setting that grave in order.
  And no casting lots for it this time—the prize is mine
  And no one else's. So take her; judge and convict her.
  I'm free, I hope, and quit of the horrible business.
CREON. How did you find her? Where have you brought her from?
SENTRY. She was burying the man with her own hands, and that's the truth.

---

[17] This second act of burial has raised some questions, for the Greek burial rite had been fulfilled the first time. What happened afterward (for the soldiers had swept off the earth from the body) would not affect the fact that Polynices had been buried properly. The probable explanation is that when Antigone saw the corpse of her brother exposed again, her feelings, rather than religious need, prompted her to bury him again.

CREON. Are you in your senses? Do you know what you are saying?

SENTRY. I saw her myself, burying the body of the man
    Whom you said not to bury. Don't I speak plain?

CREON. How did she come to be seen and taken in the act?

SENTRY. It was this way.
    After I got back to the place,
    With all your threats and curses ringing in my ears,
    We swept off all the earth that covered the body,
    And left it a sodden naked corpse again;
    Then sat up on the hill, on the windward side,
    Keeping clear of the stench of him, as far as we could;
    All of us keeping each other up to the mark,
    With pretty sharp speaking, not to be caught napping this time.
    So this went on some hours, till the flaming sun
    Was high in the top of the sky, and the heat was blazing.
    Suddenly a storm of dust, like a plague from heaven,
    Swept over the ground, stripping the trees stark bare,
    Filling the sky; you had to shut your eyes
    To stand against it. When at last it stopped,
    There was the girl, screaming like an angry bird,
    When it finds its nest left empty and little ones gone.
    Just like that she screamed, seeing the body
    Naked, crying and cursing the ones that had done it.

    Then she picks up the dry earth in her hands,
    And pouring out of a fine bronze urn she's brought
    She makes her offering three times to the dead.
    Soon as we saw it, down we came and caught her.
    She wasn't at all frightened. And so we charged her
    With what she'd done before, and this. She admitted it,
    I'm glad to say—though sorry too, in a way.
    It's good to save your own skin, but a pity
    To have to see another get into trouble,
    Whom you've no grudge against. However, I can't say
    I've ever valued anyone else's life
    More than my own, and that's the honest truth.

CREON [*to* ANTIGONE]. Well, what do you say—you, hiding your head there?
    Do you admit, or do you deny the deed?

ANTIGONE. I do admit it. I do not deny it.

CREON [*to the* SENTRY]. You—you may go. You are discharged from blame.
                        [*Exit* SENTRY]

    Now tell me, in as few words as you can,
    Did you know the order forbidding such an act?

ANTIGONE. I knew it, naturally. It was plain enough.

CREON. And yet you dared to contravene it?

ANTIGONE. Yes.
    That order did not come from God. Justice,
    That dwells with the gods below, knows no such law.

I did not think your edicts strong enough
To overrule the unwritten unalterable laws
Of God and heaven, you being only a man.
They are not of yesterday or to-day, but everlasting,
Though where they came from, none of us can tell.
Guilty of their transgression before God
I cannot be, for any man on earth.
I knew that I should have to die, of course,
With or without your order. If it be soon,
So much the better. Living in daily torment
As I do, who would not be glad to die?
This punishment will not be any pain.
Only if I had let my mother's son
Lie there unburied, then I could not have borne it.
This I can bear. Does that seem foolish to you?
Or is it you that are foolish to judge me so?
CHORUS.   She shows her father's stubborn spirit: foolish
Not to give way when everything's against her.
CREON.   Ah, but you'll see. The over-obstinate spirit
Is soonest broken; as the strongest iron will snap
If over-tempered in the fire to brittleness.
A little halter is enough to break
The wildest horse. Proud thoughts do not sit well
Upon subordinates. This girl's proud spirit
Was first in evidence when she broke the law;
And now, to add insult to her injury,
She gloats over her deed. But, as I live,
She shall not flout my orders with impunity.
My sister's child—ay, were she even nearer,
Nearest and dearest, she should not escape
Full punishment—she, and her sister too,
Her partner, doubtless, in this burying.
Let her be fetched! She was in the house just now;
I saw her, hardly in her right mind either.
Often the thoughts of those who plan dark deeds
Betray themselves before the deed is done.
The criminal who being caught still tries
To make a fair excuse, is damned indeed.
ANTIGONE.   Now you have caught, will you do more than kill me?
CREON.   No, nothing more; that is all I could wish.
ANTIGONE.   Why then delay? There is nothing that you can say
That I should wish to hear, as nothing I say
Can weigh with you. I have given my brother burial.
What greater honour could I wish? All these
Would say that what I did was honourable,
But fear locks up their lips. To speak and act
Just as he likes is a king's prerogative.
CREON.   You are wrong. None of my subjects thinks as you do.

ANTIGONE.   Yes, sir, they do; but dare not tell you so.

CREON.   And you are not only alone, but unashamed.

ANTIGONE.   There is no shame in honouring my brother.

CREON.   Was not his enemy, who died with him, your brother?

ANTIGONE.   Yes, both were brothers, both of the same parents.

CREON.   You honour one, and so insult the other.

ANTIGONE.   He that is dead will not accuse me of that.

CREON.   He will, if you honour him no more than the traitor.

ANTIGONE.   It was not a slave, but his brother, that died with him.

CREON.   Attacking his country, while the other defended it.

ANTIGONE.   Even so, we have a duty to the dead.

CREON.   Not to give equal honour to good and bad.

ANTIGONE.   Who knows? In the country of the dead that may be the law.

CREON.   An enemy can't be a friend, even when dead.

ANTIGONE.   My way is to share my love, not share my hate.

CREON.   Go then, and share your love among the dead.
    We'll have no woman's law here, while I live.
    [*Enter* ISMENE *from the Palace*]

CHORUS.   Here comes Ismene, weeping
    In sisterly sorrow; a darkened brow,
    Flushed face, and the fair cheek marred
    With flooding rain.

CREON.   You crawling viper! Lurking in my house
    To suck my blood! Two traitors unbeknown
    Plotting against my throne. Do you admit
    To a share in this burying, or deny all knowledge?

ISMENE.   I did it—yes—if she will let me say so.
    I am as much to blame as she is.

ANTIGONE.   No.
    That is not just. You would not lend a hand
    And I refused your help in what I did.

ISMENE.   But I am not ashamed to stand beside you
    Now in your hour of trial, Antigone.

ANTIGONE.   Whose was the deed, Death and the dead are witness.
    I love no friend whose love is only words.

ISMENE.   O sister, sister, let me share your death,
    Share in the tribute of honour to him that is dead.

ANTIGONE.   You shall not die with me. You shall not claim
    That which you would not touch. One death is enough.

ISMENE.   How can I bear to live, if you must die?

ANTIGONE.   Ask Creon. Is not he the one you care for?

ISMENE.   You do yourself no good to taunt me so.

ANTIGONE.   Indeed no; even my jests are bitter pains.

ISMENE.   But how, O tell me, how can I still help you?

ANTIGONE.   Help yourself. I shall not stand in your way.

ISMENE.   For pity, Antigone—can I not die with you?

ANTIGONE.   You chose; life was your choice, when mine was death.

ISMENE.   Although I warned you that it would be so.

ANTIGONE. Your way seemed right to some, to others mine.
ISMENE. But now both in the wrong, and both condemned.
ANTIGONE. No, no. You live. My heart was long since dead,
So it was right for me to help the dead.
CREON. I do believe the creatures both are mad;
One lately crazed, the other from her birth.
ISMENE. Is it not likely, sir? The strongest mind
Cannot but break under misfortune's blows.
CREON. Yours did, when you threw in your lot with hers.
ISMENE. How could I wish to live without my sister?
CREON. You have no sister. Count her dead already.
ISMENE. You could not take her—kill your own son's bride?
CREON. Oh, there are other fields for him to plough.
ISMENE. No truer troth was ever made than theirs.
CREON. No son of mine shall wed so vile a creature.
ANTIGONE. O Haemon, can your father spite you so?
CREON. You and your paramour, I hate you both.
CHORUS. Sir, would you take her from your own son's arms?
CREON. Not I, but death shall take her.
CHORUS. Be it so.
Her death, it seems, is certain.
CREON. Certain it is.
No more delay. Take them, and keep them within—
The proper place for women. None so brave
As not to look for some way of escape
When they see life stand face to face with death.
[*The women are taken away*]
CHORUS.[18] Happy are they who know not the taste of evil.
From a house that heaven hath shaken
The curse departs not
But falls upon all of the blood,
Like the restless surge of the sea when the dark storm drives
The black sand hurled from the deeps
And the Thracian[19] gales boom down
On the echoing shore.

In life and in death is the house of Labdacus[20] stricken.
Generation to generation,
With no atonement,
It is scourged by the wrath of a god.
And now for the dead dust's sake is the light of promise,
The tree's last root, crushed out
By pride of heart and the sin

---

[18] The chorus in this ode now call attention to the tragic history of the "house of Labdacus"; they make clear that those who violate the moral law imbedded in the very structure of the universe and created by the gods will suffer for it. Evil lives on and is a reminder of the littleness of man beside the greatness of Zeus and the gods.

[19] From Thrace, in the northeast.

[20] The royal house of Thebes; see the genealogical table following the introduction.

Of presumptuous tongue.

For what presumption of man[21] can match thy power,
O Zeus, that art not subject to sleep or time
Or age, living for ever in bright Olympus? [22]
To-morrow and for all time to come,
As in the past,
This law is immutable:
For mortals greatly to live is greatly to suffer.
Roving ambition helps many a man to good,
And many it falsely lures to light desires,
Till failure trips them unawares, and they fall
On the fire that consumes them. Well was it said,
Evil seems good
To him who is doomed to suffer;
And short is the time before that suffering comes.

But here comes Haemon,
Your youngest son.
Does he come to speak his sorrow
For the doom of his promised bride,
The loss of his marriage hopes?
CREON.   We shall know it soon, and need no prophet to tell us.
[*Enter* HAEMON]
Son, you have heard, I think, our final judgment
On your late betrothed. No angry words, I hope?
Still friends, in spite of everything, my son?
HAEMON.   I am your son, sir; by your wise decisions
My life is ruled, and them I shall always obey.
I cannot value any marriage-tie
Above your own good guidance.
CREON.   Rightly said.
Your father's will should have your heart's first place.
Only for this do fathers pray for sons
Obedient, loyal, ready to strike down
Their fathers' foes, and love their fathers' friends.
To be the father of unprofitable sons
Is to be the father of sorrows, a laughing-stock
To all one's enemies. Do not be fooled, my son,
By lust and the wiles of a woman. You'll have bought
Cold comfort if your wife's a worthless one.
No wound strikes deeper than love that is turned to hate.
This girl's an enemy; away with her,
And let her go and find a mate in Hades.
Once having caught her in a flagrant act—

[21] An allusion to the vice (or sin) which the Greeks called *hybris* (or *hubris*), insolent pride, a belief in human self-sufficiency. Creon has just given an example of it and will shortly do so again.
[22] The mountain in Thessaly, northern Greece, on which, it was believed, the gods dwelled.

The one and only traitor in our State—
I cannot make myself a traitor too;
So she must die. Well may she pray to Zeus,
The God of Family Love. How, if I tolerate
A traitor at home, shall I rule those abroad?
He that is a righteous master of his house
Will be a righteous statesman. To transgress
Or twist the law to one's own pleasure, presume
To order where one should obey, is sinful,
And I will have none of it.
He whom the State appoints must be obeyed
To the smallest matter, be it right—or wrong.
And he that rules his household, without a doubt,
Will make the wisest king, or, for that matter,
The staunchest subject. He will be the man
You can depend on in the storm of war,
The faithfullest comrade in the day of battle.
There is no more deadly peril than disobedience;
States are devoured by it, homes laid in ruins,
Armies defeated, victory turned to rout.
While simple obedience saves the lives of hundreds
Of honest folk. Therefore, I hold to the law,
And will never betray it—least of all for a woman.
Better be beaten, if need be, by a man,
Than let a woman get the better of us.

CHORUS. To me, as far as an old man can tell,
It seems your Majesty has spoken well.

HAEMON. Father, man's wisdom is the gift of heaven,
The greatest gift of all. I neither am
Nor wish to be clever enough to prove you wrong,
Though all men might not think the same as you do.
Nevertheless, I have to be your watchdog,
To know what others say and what they do,
And what they find to praise and what to blame.
Your frown is a sufficient silencer
Of any word that is not for your ears.
But *I* hear whispers spoken in the dark;
On every side I hear voices of pity
For this poor girl, doomed to the cruellest death,
And most unjust, that ever woman suffered
For an honourable action—burying a brother
Who was killed in battle, rather than leave him naked
For dogs to maul and carrion birds to peck at.
Has she not rather earned a crown of gold?—
Such is the secret talk about the town.

Father, there is nothing I can prize above
Your happiness and well-being. What greater good

Can any son desire? Can any father
Desire more from his son? Therefore I say,
Let not your first thought be your only thought.
Think if there cannot be some other way.
Surely, to think your own the only wisdom,
And yours the only word, the only will,
Betrays a shallow spirit, an empty heart.
It is no weakness for the wisest man
To learn when he is wrong, know when to yield.
So, on the margin of a flooded river
Trees bending to the torrent live unbroken,
While those that strain against it are snapped off.
A sailor has to tack and slacken sheets
Before the gale, or find himself capsized.

So, father, pause, and put aside your anger.
I think, for what my young opinion's worth,
That, good as it is to have infallible wisdom,
Since this is rarely found, the next best thing
Is to be willing to listen to wise advice.
CHORUS. There is something to be said, my lord, for his point of view,
    And for yours as well; there is much to be said on both sides.
CREON. Indeed! Am I to take lessons at my time of life
    From a fellow of his age?
HAEMON. No lesson you need be ashamed of.
    It isn't a question of age, but of right and wrong.
CREON. Would you call it right to admire an act of disobedience?
HAEMON. Not if the act were also dishonourable.
CREON. And was not this woman's action dishonourable?
HAEMON. The people of Thebes think not.
CREON. The people of Thebes!
    Since when do I take my orders from the people of Thebes?
HAEMON. Isn't that rather a childish thing to say?
CREON. No. I am king, and responsible only to myself.
HAEMON. A one-man state? What sort of a state is that?
CREON. Why, does not every state belong to its ruler?
HAEMON. You'd be an excellent king—on a desert island.
CREON. Of course, if you're on the woman's side—
HAEMON No, no—
    Unless you're the woman. It's you I'm fighting for.
CREON. What, villain, when every word you speak is against me?
HAEMON. Only because I know you are wrong, wrong.
CREON. Wrong? To respect my own authority?
HAEMON. What sort of respect tramples on all that is holy?
CREON. Despicable coward! No more will than a woman!
HAEMON. I have nothing to be ashamed of.
CREON. Yet you plead her cause.
HAEMON. No, *yours,* and mine, and that of the gods of the dead.

CREON. You'll never marry her this side of death.
HAEMON. Then, if she dies, she does not die alone.
CREON. Is that a threat, you impudent—
HAEMON. Is it a threat
   To try to argue against wrong-headedness?
CREON. You'll learn what wrong-headedness is, my friend, to your cost.
HAEMON. O father, I could call you mad, were you not my father.
CREON. Don't toady me, boy; keep that for your lady-love.
HAEMON. You mean to have the last word, then?
CREON. I do.
   And what is more, by all the gods in heaven,
   I'll make you sorry for your impudence.
   [*calling to those within*]
   Bring out that she-devil, and let her die
   Now, with her bridegroom by to see it done!
HAEMON. That sight I'll never see. Nor from this hour
   Shall you see me again. Let those that will
   Be witness of your wickedness and folly.

[*Exit*]

CHORUS. He is gone, my lord, in very passionate haste.
   And who shall say what a young man's wrath may do?
CREON. Let him go! Let him do! Let him rage as never man raged,
   He shall not save those women from their doom.
CHORUS. You mean, then, sire, to put them both to death?
CREON. No, not the one whose hand was innocent.
CHORUS. And to what death do you condemn the other?
CREON. I'll have her taken to a desert place
   Where no man ever walked, and there walled up
   Inside a cave, alive, with food enough
   To acquit ourselves of the blood-guiltiness
   That else would lie upon our commonwealth.
   There she may pray to Death, the god she loves,
   And ask release from death; or learn at last
   What hope there is for those who worship death.

[*Exit*]

CHORUS. Where is the equal of Love?
   Where is the battle he cannot win,
   The power he cannot outmatch?
   In the farthest corners of earth, in the midst of the sea,
   He is there; he is here
   In the bloom of a fair face
   Lying in wait;
   And the grip of his madness
   Spares not god or man,

   Marring the righteous man,
   Driving his soul into mazes of sin
   And strife, dividing a house.

For the light that burns in the eyes of a bride of desire
Is a fire that consumes.
At the side of the great gods
Aphrodite[23] immortal
Works her will upon all.
[*The doors are opened and* ANTIGONE *enters, guarded*]
But here is a sight beyond all bearing,
At which my eyes cannot but weep;
Antigone forth faring
To her bridal-bower of endless sleep.

ANTIGONE.   You see me, countrymen, on my last journey,
Taking my last leave of the light of day;
Going to my rest, where death shall take me
Alive across the silent river.[24]
No wedding-day; no marriage-music;
Death will be all my bridal dower.

CHORUS.   But glory and praise go with you, lady,
To your resting-place. You go with your beauty
Unmarred by the hand of consuming sickness,
Untouched by the sword, living and free,
As none other that ever died before you.

ANTIGONE.   The daughter of Tantalus, a Phrygian maid,[25]
Was doomed to a piteous death on the rock
Of Sipylus, which embraced and imprisoned her,
Merciless as the ivy; rain and snow
Beat down upon her, mingled with her tears,
As she wasted and died. Such was her story,
And such is the sleep that I shall go to.

CHORUS.   She was a goddess of immortal birth,
And we are mortals; the greater the glory,
To share the fate of a god-born maiden,
A living death, but a name undying.

ANTIGONE.   Mockery, mockery! By the gods of our fathers,
Must you make me a laughing-stock while I yet live?
O lordly sons of my city! O Thebes!
Your valleys of rivers, your chariots and horses!
No friend to weep at my banishment
To a rock-hewn chamber of endless durance,
In a strange cold tomb alone to linger
Lost between life and death for ever.

CHORUS.   My child, you have gone your way

---

[23] Greek goddess of love, known as Venus to the Romans.

[24] The Styx, river of Hades, across which the dead are ferried.

[25] Niobe, the daughter of Tantalus, was the wife of Amphion, an earlier king of Thebes, and the mother of seven sons and seven daughters. Because she boasted of them to Leto, who had only two children, the gods Apollo and Artemis killed all her children with arrows, as a punishment for her *hybris*. She returned to her home on Mount Sipylus in Lydia (which bordered on and had associations with Phrygia) and wept until she was turned into a weeping stone.

To the outermost limit of daring
And have stumbled against Law enthroned.
This is the expiation
You must make for the sin of your father.

ANTIGONE. My father—the thought that sears my soul—
The unending burden of the house of Labdacus.[26]
Monstrous marriage of mother and son.[27] . . .
My father . . . my parents . . . O hideous shame!
Whom now I follow, unwed, curse-ridden,
Doomed to this death by the ill-starred marriage[28]
That marred my brother's life.

CHORUS. An act of homage is good in itself, my daughter;
But authority cannot afford to connive at disobedience.
You are the victim of your own self-will.

ANTIGONE. And must go the way that lies before me.
No funeral hymn; no marriage-music;
No sun from this day forth, no light,
No friend to weep at my departing.

[*Enter* CREON]

CREON. Weeping and wailing at the door of death!
There'd be no end of it, if it had force
To buy death off. Away with her at once,
And close her up in her rock-vaulted tomb.
Leave her and let her die, if die she must,
Or live within her dungeon. Though on earth
Her life is ended from this day, her blood
Will not be on our hands.

ANTIGONE. So to my grave,
My bridal-bower, my everlasting prison,
I go, to join those many of my kinsmen
Who dwell in the mansions of Persephone,[29]
Last and unhappiest, before my time.
Yet I believe my father will be there
To welcome me, my mother greet me gladly,
And you, my brother, gladly see me come.
Each one of you my hands have laid to rest,
Pouring the due libations[30] on your graves.
It was by this service to your dear body, Polynices,
I earned the punishment which now I suffer,
Though all good people know it was for your honour.

[26] See above, p. 19, note 20.
[27] The sin of her father Oedipus—incest.
[28] When Polynices married Argeia, daughter of Adrastus, king of Argos, it was a sign that he had thrown in his lot with the Argive forces who were to attack Thebes. Hence his marriage may be regarded as a root of all the later trouble, including Antigone's death.
[29] Queen of the netherworld, wife of Hades (or Pluto as he is sometimes known). Hence, here, the underworld.
[30] The pouring of liquid, usually wine, on the ground or altar, as an offering to a deity. Here a general reference to Greek funeral rites.

O but I would not have done the forbidden thing[31]
For any husband or for any son.
For why? I could have had another husband
And by him other sons, if one were lost;
But, father and mother lost, where would I get
Another brother? For thus preferring you,
My brother, Creon condemns me and hales me away,
Never a bride, never a mother, unfriended,
Condemned alive to solitary death.
What law of heaven have I transgressed? What god
Can save me now? What help or hope have I,
In whom devotion is deemed sacrilege?
If this is God's will, I shall learn my lesson
In death; but if my enemies are wrong,
I wish them no worse punishment than mine.

CHORUS.   Still the same tempest in the heart
Torments her soul with angry gusts.

CREON.   The more cause then have they that guard her
To hasten their work; or they too suffer.

CHORUS.   Alas, that word had the sound of death.

CREON.   Indeed there is no more to hope for.

ANTIGONE.   Gods of our fathers, my city, my home,
Rulers of Thebes! Time stays no longer.
Last daughter[32] of your royal house
Go I, *his* prisoner, because I honoured
Those things to which honour truly belongs.

[ANTIGONE *is led away*]

CHORUS.   Such was the fate, my child, of Danae[33]
Locked in a brazen bower,
A prison secret as a tomb,
Where was no day.
Daughter of kings, her royal womb
Garnered the golden shower
Of life from Zeus. So strong is Destiny,
No wealth, no armoury, no tower,
No ship that rides the angry sea

---

[31] The nine lines beginning here are omitted by some editors, although they occur in all mss. of the play as an interpolation. The argument presented weakens the force of Antigone's reasons and seems inconsistent with her general attitude. It is possible, however, that in her last moments, Antigone could have uttered a somewhat ignoble thought. Some have urged that, however weak logically and structurally, the sentiments expressed are dramatically and psychologically correct.

[32] She regards Ismene as having given up her family connections because of her refusal to help bury Polynices.

[33] The chorus sings of three children of kings in Greek myth who were doomed to be confined in prison by cruel fate. Danae, daughter of Acrisius, king of Argos, was shut up in a "brazen bower" by her father so that he could escape an oracle which predicted that he would be killed by his daughter's son. Zeus loved her and entered the tower in a shower of gold. The result of this union was Perseus, who later fulfilled the prediction of the oracle and accidentally slew his grandfather.

Her mastering hand can stay.
And Dryas' son,[34] the proud Edonian king,
Pined in a stony cell
At Dionysus' bidding pent
To cool his fire
Till, all his full-blown passion spent,
He came to know right well
What god his ribald tongue was challenging
When he would break the fiery spell
Of the wild Maenads'[35] revelling
And vex the Muses' choir.[36]
It was upon the side
Of Bosporus, where the Black Rocks stand
By Thracian Salmydessus[37] over the twin tide,
That Thracian Ares[38] laughed to see
How Phineus' angry wife[39] most bloodily
Blinded his two sons' eyes that mutely cried
For vengeance; crazed with jealousy
The woman smote them with the weaving-needle in her hand.
Forlorn they wept away
Their sad step-childhood's misery
Predestined from their mother's ill-starred marriage-day.
She was of old Erechtheid blood,[40]
Cave-dwelling daughter of the North-wind God;
On rocky steeps, as mountain ponies play,
The wild winds nursed her maidenhood.
On her, my child, the grey Fates[41] laid hard hands, as upon thee.
[*Enter* TEIRESIAS,[42] *the blind prophet, led by a boy*]

TEIRESIAS.   Gentlemen of Thebes, we greet you, my companion and I,
Who share one pair of eyes on our journeys together—
For the blind man goes where his leader tells him to.

CREON.   You are welcome, father Teiresias. What's your news?

TEIRESIAS.   Ay, news you shall have; and advice, if you can heed it.

CREON.   There was never a time when I failed to heed it, father.

---

[34] Lycurgus, a king of the Edones, a Thracian people, who persecuted the god Dionysus and was punished by him in return.

[35] Frenzied female votaries of Dionysus.

[36] A reference to the ritual songs in honor of the god Dionysus.

[37] A Thracian kingdom on the shores of the Bosporus.

[38] God of war. His Roman name is Mars.

[39] Eidothea, second wife of Phineas, king of Salmydessus. In a fit of jealousy, she blinded and imprisoned her two stepsons and their mother, Cleopatra, her husband's first wife.

[40] Cleopatra was the daughter of Boreas (the north wind) and Orithyia (daughter of Erechtheus, a legendary king of Athens). The adjective *Erechtheid* is made up from Erechtheus.

[41] The three sisters, known by various names, who, the ancient Greeks believed, controlled each individual's destiny.

[42] A traditional seer and prophet who appears in various Greek works, notably Homer's *Odyssey,* and who, because of his blindness, is usually led by a boy. He is a priest in Thebes and is upset because his auguries and sacrifices show that the favor of the gods has been withdrawn from the city.

TEIRESIAS. And thereby have so far steered a steady course.
CREON. And gladly acknowledge the debt we owe to you.
TEIRESIAS. Then mark me now; for you stand on a razor's edge.
CREON. Indeed? Grave words from your lips, good priest. Say on.
TEIRESIAS. I will; and show you all that my skill reveals.

At my seat of divination where I sit
These many years to read the signs of heaven,
An unfamiliar sound came to my ears
Of birds in vicious combat, savage cries
In strange outlandish language, and the whirr
Of flapping wings; from which I well could picture
The gruesome warfare of their deadly talons.
Full of foreboding then I made the test
Of sacrifice upon the altar fire.
There was no answering flame; only rank juice
Oozed from the flesh and dripped among the ashes,
Smouldering and sputtering; the gall vanished in a puff,
And the fat ran down and left the haunches bare.
Thus (through the eyes of my young acolyte,
Who sees for me, that I may see for others)
I read the signs of failure in my quest.

And why? The blight upon us is *your* doing.
The blood that stains our altars and our shrines,
The blood that dogs and vultures have licked up,
It is none other than the blood of Oedipus
Spilled from the veins of his ill-fated son.
Our fires, our sacrifices, and our prayers
The gods abominate. How should the birds
Give any other than ill-omened voices,
Gorged with the dregs of blood that man has shed?
Mark this, my son: all men fall into sin,
But sinning, he is not for ever lost
Hapless and helpless, who can make amends
And has not set his face against repentance.
Only a fool is governed by self-will.

Pay to the dead his due. Wound not the fallen.
It is no glory to kill and kill again.
My words are for your good, as is my will,
And should be acceptable, being for your good.
CREON. You take me for your target, reverend sir,
Like all the rest. I know your art of old,
And how you make me your commodity
To trade and traffic in for your advancement.
Trade as you will; but all the silver of Sardis[43]

---

[43] Capital of Lydia, in Asia Minor; it was a great and wealthy commercial center in Sophocles' time.

And all the gold of India will not buy
A tomb for yonder traitor. No. Let the eagles
Carry his carcase up to the throne of Zeus;
Even that would not be sacrilege enough
To frighten me from my determination
Not to allow this burial. No man's act
Has power enough to pollute the goodness of God.
But great and terrible is the fall, Teiresias,
Of mortal men who seek their own advantage
By uttering evil in the guise of good.

TEIRESIAS. Ah, is there any wisdom in the world?
CREON. Why, what is the meaning of that wide-flung taunt?
TEIRESIAS. What prize outweighs the priceless worth of prudence?
CREON. Ay what indeed? What mischief matches the lack of it?
TEIRESIAS. And there you speak of your own symptom, sir.
CREON. I am loth to pick a quarrel with you, priest.
TEIRESIAS. You do so, calling my divination false.
CREON. I say all prophets seek their own advantage.
TEIRESIAS. All kings, say I, seek gain unrighteously.
CREON. Do you forget to whom you say it?
TEIRESIAS. No.
  Our king and benefactor, by my guidance.
CREON. Clever you may be, but not therefore honest.
TEIRESIAS. Must I reveal my yet unspoken mind?
CREON. Reveal all; but expect no gain from it.
TEIRESIAS. Does that still seem to you my motive, then?
CREON. Nor is my will for sale, sir, in your market.
TEIRESIAS. Then hear this. Ere the chariot of the sun
  Has rounded once or twice his wheeling way,
  You shall have given a son of your own loins
  To death, in payment for death—two debts to pay:
  One for the life that you have sent to death,
  The life you have abominably entombed;
  One for the dead still lying above ground
  Unburied, unhonoured, unblest by the gods below.
  You cannot alter this. The gods themselves
  Cannot undo it. It follows of necessity
  From what you have done. Even now the avenging Furies,[44]
  The hunters of Hell that follow and destroy,
  Are lying in wait for you, and will have their prey,
  When the evil you have worked for others falls on you.
  Do I speak this for my gain? The time shall come,
  And soon, when your house will be filled with the lamentation
  Of men and of women; and every neighbouring city
  Will be goaded to fury against you, for upon them
  Too the pollution falls when the dogs and vultures

---

[44] Also known as the Erinyes and Eumenides; represented as winged women in Greek mythology, their function was to avenge crimes, especially those against one's kindred.

Bring the defilement of blood to their hearths and altars.[45]
I have done. You pricked me, and these shafts of wrath
Will find their mark in your heart. You cannot escape
The sting of their sharpness.
Lead me home, my boy.
Let us leave him to vent his anger on younger ears,
Or school his mind and tongue to a milder mood
Than that which now possesses him.
Lead on.

                                                        [*Exit*]

CHORUS.   He has gone, my lord. He has prophesied terrible things.
    And for my part, I that was young and now am old
    Have never known his prophecies proved false.
CREON.   It is true enough; and my heart is torn in two.
    It is hard to give way, and hard to stand and abide
    The coming of the curse. Both ways are hard.
CHORUS.   If you would be advised, my good lord Creon—
CREON.   What must I do? Tell me, and I will do it.
CHORUS.   Release the woman from her rocky prison.
    Set up a tomb for him that lies unburied.
CREON.   Is it your wish that I consent to this?
CHORUS.   It is; and quickly. The gods do not delay
    The stroke of their swift vengeance on the sinner.
CREON.   It is hard, but I must do it. Well I know
    There is no armour against necessity.
CHORUS.   Go. Let your own hand do it, and no other.
CREON.   I will go this instant.
    Slaves there! One and all,
    Bring spades and mattocks out on the hill!
    My mind is made; 'twas I imprisoned her,
    And I will set her free. Now I believe
    It is by the laws of heaven that man must live.[46]

                                                        [*Exit*]

CHORUS.   O Thou whose name is many,[47]
    Son of the Thunderer, dear child of his Cadmean bride,
    Whose hand is mighty
    In Italia,
    In the hospitable valley
    Of Eleusis,[48]

---

[45] Apparently Creon had left others of his enemies unburied.

[46] At this point, Creon recognizes his action for what it was. It is the turning point in the tragedy.

[47] The chorus sings a song of joy and relief to Dionysus, a god specially favored of Thebes and a bringer of relief and healing. He is known under many names—Bacchus, Iacchus, Sabazius, etc. He was born of Zeus (the Thunderer) and Semele, daughter of Cadmus. His mother was consumed by the lightning of Zeus, but the unborn child (Dionysus) was saved.

[48] The site of the most famous Greek mystery religions where Demeter, Persephone, and later Dionysus (under the name of Iacchus) were worshipped in secret rites only for the initiated.

And in Thebes,
The mother-city of thy worshippers,
Where sweet Ismenus[49] gently watereth
The soil whence sprang the harvest of the dragon's teeth;[50]

Where torches on the crested mountains gleam,
And by Castalia's stream[51]
The nymph-train in thy dance rejoices,
When from the ivy-tangled glens
Of Nysa[52] and from vine-clad plains
Thou comest to Thebes where the immortal voices
Sing thy glad strains.

Thebes, where thou lovest most to be,
With her, thy mother, the fire-stricken one,[53]
Sickens for need of thee.
Healer of all her ills,
Come swiftly o'er the high Parnassian hills,[54]
Come o'er the sighing sea.
The stars, whose breath is fire, delight
To dance for thee; the echoing night
Shall with thy praises ring.
Zeus-born, appear! With Thyiads[55] revelling
Come, bountiful
Iacchus, King!

[*Enter a* MESSENGER, *from the side of the stage*]

MESSENGER.   Hear, men of Cadmus' city, hear and attend,
Men of the house of Amphion,[56] people of Thebes!
What is the life of man? A thing not fixed
For good or evil, fashioned for praise or blame.
Chance raises a man to the heights, chance casts him down,
And none can foretell what will be from what is.
Creon was once an enviable man;
He saved his country from her enemies,
Assumed the sovereign power, and bore it well,
The honoured father of a royal house.
Now all is lost; for life without life's joys

---

[49] This river flows through the district of Thebes on the east.

[50] The legend connected with the founding of Thebes.

[51] The river or spring on Mount Parnassus, near Delphi, named after a nymph who threw herself into it to escape the attentions of Apollo. Delphi, the site of the famous Greek oracle, was sacred not only to the cult of Apollo, but also to that of Dionysus, to whom this hymn is dedicated.

[52] A mountain, the location of which is not known, but which was claimed by various Greek localities. According to the legend of Dionysus, he was brought up here by nymphs after the death of his mother, Semele. From Nysa, Dionysus is supposed to have come to Thebes to teach men to use wine and to worship him.

[53] Semele; see above, note 47.   [54] From his place of worship at Delphi.

[55] Maenads or bacchantes, female devotees of Dionysus.

[56] An early ruler of Thebes, husband of Niobe (see above, p. 24, note 25).

Is living death; and such a life is his.
Riches and rank and show of majesty
And state, where no joy is, are empty, vain
And unsubstantial shadows, of no weight
To be compared with happiness of heart.

CHORUS.   What is your news? Disaster in the royal house?

MESSENGER.   Death; and the guilt of it on living heads.

CHORUS.   Who dead? And by what hand?

MESSENGER.   Haemon is dead,
Slain by his own—

CHORUS.   His father?

MESSENGER.   His own hand.
His father's act it was that drove him to it.

CHORUS.   Then all has happened as the prophet said.

MESSENGER.   What's next to do, your worships will decide.

[*The Palace door opens*]

CHORUS.   Here comes the Queen, Eurydice. Poor soul,
It may be she has heard about her son.

[*Enter* EURYDICE, *attended by women*]

EURYDICE.   My friends, I heard something of what you were saying
As I came to the door. I was on my way to prayer
At the temple of Pallas,[57] and had barely turned the latch
When I caught your talk of some near calamity.
I was sick with fear and reeled in the arms of my women.
But tell me what is the matter; what have you heard?
I am not unacquainted with grief, and I can bear it.

MESSENGER.   Madam, it was I that saw it, and will tell you all.
To try to make it any lighter now
Would be to prove myself a liar. Truth
Is always best.
It was thus. I attended your husband,
The King, to the edge of the field where lay the body
Of Polynices, in pitiable state, mauled by the dogs.
We prayed for him to the Goddess of the Roads,[58] and to Pluto,[59]
That they might have mercy upon him. We washed the remains
In holy water, and on a fire of fresh-cut branches
We burned all that was left of him, and raised
Over his ashes a mound of his native earth.
That done, we turned towards the deep rock-chamber
Of the maid that was married with death. Before we reached it,
One that stood near the accursed place had heard
Loud cries of anguish, and came to tell King Creon.

---

[57] The goddess Pallas Athene, general protector of Greek cities.

[58] Hecate, who haunted crossroads, and a power in Hades. She would be offended at the treatment meted out to Polynices, who had been deprived of the proper ritual to enable him to enter her realm.

[59] King of Hades. His reaction to Creon's maltreatment of Polynices would be similar to that of Hecate. Both gods had to be propitiated by Creon, who is hastening to undo the ritual damage rather than first releasing Antigone.

As he approached, came strange uncertain sounds
Of lamentation, and he cried aloud:
'Unhappy wretch! Is my foreboding true?
Is this the most sorrowful journey that ever I went?
My son's voice greets me. Go, some of you, quickly
Through the passage where the stones are thrown apart,
Into the mouth of the cave, and see if it be
My son, my own son Haemon that I hear.
If not, I am the sport of gods.'
We went
And looked, as bidden by our anxious master.
There in the furthest corner of the cave
We saw her hanging by the neck. The rope
Was of the woven linen of her dress.
And, with his arms about her, there stood he
Lamenting his lost bride, his luckless love,
His father's cruelty.
When Creon saw them,
Into the cave he went, moaning piteously.
'O my unhappy boy,' he cried again,
'What have you done? What madness brings you here
To your destruction? Come away, my son,
My son, I do beseech you, come away!'
His son looked at him with one angry stare,
Spat in his face, and then without a word
Drew sword and struck out. But his father fled
Unscathed. Whereon the poor demented boy
Leaned on his sword and thrust it deeply home
In his own side, and while his life ebbed out
Embraced the maid in loose-enfolding arms,
His spurting blood staining her pale cheeks red.
[EURYDICE *goes quickly back into the Palace*]
Two bodies lie together, wedded in death,
Their bridal sleep a witness to the world
How great calamity can come to man
Through man's perversity.
CHORUS. But what is this?
The Queen has turned and gone without a word.
MESSENGER. Yes. It is strange. The best that I can hope
Is that she would not sorrow for her son
Before us all, but vents her grief in private
Among her women. She is too wise, I think,
To take a false step rashly.
CHORUS. It may be.
Yet there is danger in unnatural silence
No less than in excess of lamentation.
MESSENGER. I will go in and see, whether in truth
There is some fatal purpose in her grief.

Such silence, as you say, may well be dangerous.
[*He goes in*]
[*Enter Attendants preceding the King*]
CHORUS. The King comes here.
What the tongue scarce dares to tell
Must now be known
By the burden[60] that proves too well
The guilt, no other man's
But his alone.
[*Enter* CREON *with the body of* HAEMON]
CREON. The sin, the sin of the erring soul
Drives hard unto death.
Behold the slayer, the slain,
The father, the son.
O the curse of my stubborn will!
Son, newly cut off in the newness of youth,
Dead for my fault, not yours.
CHORUS. Alas, too late you have seen the truth.
CREON. I learn in sorrow. Upon my head
God has delivered this heavy punishment,
Has struck me down in the ways of wickedness,
And trod my gladness under foot.
Such is the bitter affliction of mortal man.
[*Enter the* MESSENGER *from the Palace*]
MESSENGER. Sir, you have this and more than this to bear.
Within there's more to know, more to your pain.
CREON. What more? What pain can overtop this pain?
MESSENGER. She is dead—your wife, the mother of him that is dead—
The death-wound fresh in her heart. Alas, poor lady!
CREON. Insatiable Death, wilt thou destroy me yet?
What say you, teller of evil?
I am already dead,
And is there more?
Blood upon blood?
More death? My wife?
[*The central doors open, revealing the body of* EURYDICE]
CHORUS. Look then, and see; nothing is hidden now.
CREON. O second horror!
What fate awaits me now?
My child here in my arms . . . and there, the other . . .
The son . . . the mother. . . .
MESSENGER. There at the altar with the whetted knife
She stood, and as the darkness dimmed her eyes
Called on the dead, her elder son[61] and this,

---

[60] Haemon's body, which Creon is carrying. In this action we see vividly the humbling of the proud king.

[61] A reference to Megareus, their elder son, who gave his life for the city to fulfill an earlier prophecy of Teiresias that one of the Theban royal house must die if the city was to be preserved.

And with her dying breath cursed you, their slayer.

CREON. O horrible. . . .
Is there no sword for me,
To end this misery?

MESSENGER. Indeed you bear the burden of two deaths.
It was her dying word.

CREON. And her last act?

MESSENGER. Hearing her son was dead, with her own hand
She drove the sharp sword home into her heart.

CREON. There is no man can bear this guilt but I.
It is true, I killed him.
Lead me away, away. I live no longer.

CHORUS. 'Twere best, if anything is best in evil time.
What's soonest done, is best, when all is ill.

CREON. Come, my last hour and fairest,
My only happiness . . . come soon.
Let me not see another day.
Away . . . away. . . .

CHORUS. The future is not to be known; our present care
Is with the present; the rest is in other hands.

CREON. I ask no more than I have asked.

CHORUS. Ask nothing.
What is to be, no mortal can escape.

CREON. I am nothing. I have no life.
Lead me away . . .
That have killed unwittingly
My son, my wife.
I know not where I should turn,
Where look for help.
My hands have done amiss, my head is bowed
With fate too heavy for me.

[*Exit*]

CHORUS. Of happiness the crown
And chiefest part
Is wisdom, and to hold
The gods in awe.
This is the law
That, seeing the stricken heart
Of pride brought down,
We learn when we are old.

[*Exeunt*]

Othello

William Shakespeare

William Shakespeare

Drama is, in one sense, a manifestation of belief; that is, the manner in which a playwright treats his subject will be in large measure conditioned by the system of beliefs and attitudes held by the society to which he belongs. In *Antigone*, Sophocles' treatment of the problem of conflicting loyalties was in accordance with the system of values of pre-Christian Athenian society. Over two thousand years later William Shakespeare dealt with themes of equal significance but in terms of a considerably different system of beliefs —that of a Renaissance Englishman. Shakespeare lived in an age when the highly integrated life—both spiritual and temporal—of medieval society was breaking down under the impact of the individualistic Renaissance spirit. The conflict in society thus generated was reflected in an equally severe conflict in the minds of men. The struggle was between two seemingly incompatible ways of life—a way which assumed that men must give themselves over to a principle of order and regularity so that society might exist, and a way which assumed that men must realize themselves as fully as possible as unique, free, aspiring individuals. Generally speaking, it was in terms of this basic conflict that Shakespeare dealt with those problems of abiding significance that have concerned thoughtful men of every age.

Shakespeare was born in Stratford-on-Avon in 1564 and in all probability was educated there. When he was nineteen, he married Anne Hathaway and sometime in the eighties moved to London. The motives for this move and his early occupations in the city are not known, but they were probably connected with the theatre, for, by 1592, he had some reputation as an actor and playwright. After this date, there are scattered allusions to him in public and literary records. On the whole, except for these, scholars know little of Shakespeare and certainly cannot penetrate into his personality except through his works, a somewhat hazardous occupation. Because of the Elizabethan system of playwriting and publishing, it is not even possible to know accurately the dates of composition of most of his dramas. Tests of style and meter, and certain other more objective methods, do enable researchers, however, to work out some kind of chronology which is probably correct enough.

In Shakespeare's time, all plays were put on by "repertory" companies. These were small groups of men, organized somewhat after the fashion of the medieval guilds, who stayed together as an acting and producing unit for many years. Shakespeare himself was attached to one of these companies, a group known under various names, the most famous of which is the Lord Chamberlain's Company. He not only acted with the Company but, what is more important, he wrote many plays for them that they produced with notable success. Shakespeare, of course, shared in this success; he was able to become a shareholder in the Globe Theatre, built by the Company in 1599, and grew increasingly wealthy. About 1611 he retired to Stratford and died there on April 23, 1616.

Although Shakespeare was recognized as a great playwright during his lifetime, it was not until after his death that his unparalleled fame was established. People of many lands and of many times have paid homage to a genius almost incredible in the universality of its appeal. His insights into the complexities of the human condition have such brilliance and warmth, and are expressed in language of such surpassing beauty, that the name Shakespeare has become a symbol of that which is greatest in the creation of literature.

Of the four tragedies—*King Lear, Hamlet, Macbeth,* and *Othello*—acknowledged by most critics to be Shakespeare's greatest works, the play printed here is the most concentrated and most realistic in treatment and atmosphere. Its magnificently compact plot is supported by a unity of tone that allows no relaxation as events move with inexorable swiftness to the tragic climax. *Othello* (written probably in 1604) presents the story of an essentially noble and heroic figure who, through his lack of insight into the characters of others and at the instigation of an evil man, brings doom upon his wife and himself.

The four main characters are Othello, the Moorish commander of the Venetian troops in Cyprus; Desdemona, his wife, a Venetian lady who ran away from her father's house to marry an outsider; Cassio, his trusty lieutenant, upon whom the suspicion of cuckolding Othello is thrown; and Iago, his disappointed assistant, whose malignant planning brings about the tragedy. The minor characters are vividly presented, especially Emilia, Iago's wife and Desdemona's lady-in-waiting.

For critics, the chief problem in the play is the character of Iago. The debate usually centers around whether he had sufficient motives for his cruel actions or whether, on the other hand, he is an example of "motiveless malignity." The question cannot be resolved here, nor is it necessary to try to resolve it. Iago, whether because of his disappointment at not having been given Cassio's position, or because of his belief that Othello had cuckolded him, or because of his love of evil for its own sake, is nevertheless a man who has rejected all ties of morality and idealism. He believes in nothing and desires only to destroy. From our own history we know that such men exist. As a result of modern psychological investigation, or from the point of view of traditional religion, it is clear that there is a little of Iago in everyone. Here, on the stage, is a portrait of human evil, perhaps somewhat heightened as is proper to art, but one that all perceptive men may recognize.

Othello's lack of insight, cunningly played upon by Iago, leads to his downfall. And as the full enormity of his deed dawns upon him in the great scene of tragic self-revelation at the end, the audience may perhaps experience catharsis, that purgation of the soul brought about by an almost unbearable pity for him and his victims, and by terror at what human nature is capable of and what pitfalls await us in life. Throughout the play, the audience possesses the information which Iago's victim does not have; the viewers know all along what

Othello does not know. From that omniscient view, they look upon this tortured human being with a strong sense of the irony and tragedy of his position. They want to help him but they cannot, and are helpless, as people must often be in life, to avert the disaster. After Othello's delusion has passed, after his fierce rages and his attempts at judicial calm, he gives a final quiet self-denunciation and objective self-portrait of "one who loved not wisely but too well." The audience then becomes aware that they are witnessing one of the most powerful scenes in all dramatic literature. *Othello* gives a deep insight, in dramatic terms, into life; anyone who reads or sees the play emerges with a heightened awareness of the tragedy of human existence and a sense of having participated in a mighty experience.

It would be useless to list all the performances of *Othello* in recent times. In brief it has been one of Shakespeare's most frequently performed plays in all countries of the world. Its taut structure, its human interest, its plethora of good parts, its poetry, its profundity, all combine to make it a notable and popular theatrical experience.

A Note on Shakespeare's Theatre

The dramatist's art is always conditioned to some degree by the physical characteristics of the theatre in which his plays are to be performed. Shakespeare wrote for a theatre different in many respects from our own. The typical Elizabethan playhouse (the first public theatre in London was built in 1576) was octagonal or circular in shape, with no roof over it. The stage itself consisted of a large, uncurtained platform jutting out into the yard (or pit) where stood the "groundlings," the poorer spectators, who surrounded the platform on three sides. Around the sides of the building were three tiers of galleries seating those who could afford to pay for the privilege. A roof, called "the shadow" or "the heavens," projected over part of the platform stage; it protected the actors from rain, and from it could be lowered certain stage properties. Most of the action in a play took place on the platform itself. No scenery was employed, although the actors sometimes wore elaborate costumes, and specific properties—such as a throne, a bed, a tree—were used to give a symbolic indication of place. The lack of scenery made the stage a kind of neutral territory; it could be any place the playwright wanted it to be: Rome one moment, Alexandria the next, with no interlude necessary for changing sets. If the dramatist wanted the scene (or the time of day or night) localized, he had to describe it in his lines; this necessity gave rise to some of the loveliest descriptive poetry in our language.

At the rear of the platform was an inner stage, separated from the main platform by a curtain; it was called "the alcove" or "the study," and could be set with properties to indicate a bedroom, a study, or some similar area. Above the alcove was the upper stage or "chamber," also cut off by a curtain; this stage served as Juliet's balcony, as the battlement of a castle, or as any other place needing an indication of height.

The use of these three acting areas had certain obvious advantages, and the lack of any attempt to create a specifically localized sense of place gave a fluidity to the Elizabethan stage that our modern theatre has only in recent years tried to recapture.

One further characteristic of the Elizabethan theatre should be mentioned: all women's roles were acted by young boys. Not until the Restoration did actresses appear on the English stage.

Othello

William Shakespeare

CHARACTERS

OTHELLO, *the* Moor
BRABANTIO, *father of Desdemona*
CASSIO, *an honorable Lieutenant*
IAGO, *a villain, 'ancient' or standard-bearer, and third in command to* Othello
RODERIGO, *a gulled gentleman*
DUKE OF VENICE
SENATORS
MONTANO, *Governor of Cyprus*
GENTLEMEN OF CYPRUS

LODOVICO *and* GRATIANO { *two noble Venetians, relative and brother, respectively, of Brabantio*
SAILORS
CLOWN
DESDEMONA, *wife of Othello and daughter of Brabantio*
EMILIA, *wife to Iago*
BIANCA, *a courtesan*
MESSENGERS, HERALD, OFFICERS, MUSICIANS, AND ATTENDANTS

SCENE: *Act I, at Venice; Acts II-V, at a sea-port (Famagosta) in Cyprus*

Act First

SCENE FIRST: *Venice. A Street.*

[*Enter* RODERIGO *and* IAGO]
RODERIGO. Tush! Never tell me! I take it much unkindly
    That thou, Iago, who hast had my purse
    As if the strings were thine, shouldst know of this.[1]
IAGO. 'Sblood,[2] but you will not hear me!
    If ever I did dream of such a matter,
    Abhor me.
RODERIGO. Thou told'st me thou didst hold him in thy hate.

---

[1] Desdemona's elopement with Othello.   [2] 'By God's blood.'

IAGO. Despise me if I do not. Three great ones of the city,
 In personal suit to make me his lieutenant,
 Off-capp'd to him; and, by the faith of man
 (I know my price), I am worth no worse a place.
 But he, as loving his own pride and purposes,
 Evades them with a bombast circumstance[3]
 Horribly stuff'd with epithets of war;
 And, in conclusion,
 Nonsuits[4] my mediators; for, 'Certes,'[5] says he,
 'I have already chose my officer.'
 And what was he?
 Forsooth, a great arithmetician,
 One Michael Cassio, a Florentine
 (A fellow almost damn'd in a fair wife),[6]
 That never set a squadron in the field,
 Nor the division of a battle knows
 More than a spinster,—unless the bookish theoric,[7]
 Wherein the toged consuls[8] can propose[9]
 As masterly as he. Mere prattle, without practice,
 Is all his soldiership; but he, sir, had the election,
 And I (of whom his eyes had seen the proof
 At Rhodes, at Cyprus, and on other grounds
 Christian and heathen) must be be-lee'd and calm'd
 By Debitor-and-Creditor.[10] This counter-caster,[11]
 He, in good time, must his lieutenant be,
 And I—God bless the mark![12]—his Moorship's ancient.[13]
RODERIGO. By heaven, I rather would have been his hangman.
IAGO. Why, there's no remedy. 'Tis the curse of service.
 Preferment goes by letter[14] and affection,
 And not by old gradation,[15] where each second
 Stood heir to the first. Now, sir, be judge yourself,
 Whether I in any just term am affin'd[16]
 To love the Moor.
RODERIGO.   I would not follow him then.
IAGO. O sir, content you.
 I follow him to serve my turn upon him;
 We cannot be all masters, nor all masters
 Cannot be truly follow'd. You shall mark
 Many a duteous and knee-crooking knave,
 That (doting on his own obsequious bondage)
 Wears out his time much like his master's ass,

[3] Fancy phrases. [4] Rejects the requests of. [5] Indeed.
[6] The meaning here has been much debated. Cassio is certainly not married. The *almost* may suggest that Cassio is close to marriage. There is an Italian proverb that one is damned if one has a beautiful wife because she will betray him. "Wife" may, on the other hand, just mean woman.
[7] Except the theory of books. [8] Councillors in their togas (not military dress).
[9] Discuss, talk. [10] Bookkeeper. [11] Calculator.
[12] A mild oath. [13] Ensign, standard bearer. [14] Letters of recommendation, influence.
[15] Seniority. [16] Bound.

For nought but provender, and when he's old,—cashier'd!
Whip me such honest knaves. Others there are
Who, trimm'd in forms and visages[17] of duty,
Keep yet their hearts attending on themselves,
And throwing but shows of service on their lords,
Do well thrive by 'em, and when they have lin'd their coats
Do themselves homage. Those fellows have some soul,
And such a one do I profess myself. For, sir,
It is as sure as you are Roderigo,
Were I the Moor, I would not be Iago.
In following him, I follow but myself;
Heaven is my judge, not I for love and duty,
But seeming so for my peculiar[18] end.
For when my outward action does demonstrate
The native act and figure of my heart[19]
In complement extern,[20] 'tis not long after
But I will wear my heart upon my sleeve
For daws to peck at. I am not what I am.

RODERIGO.   What a full fortune does the thick-lips[21] owe,[22]
If he can carry't thus!

IAGO.   Call up her father.
Rouse him,[23] make after him, poison his delight,
Proclaim him in the street, incense her kinsmen,
And though he in a fertile climate dwell,
Plague him with flies; though that his joy be joy,
Yet throw such chances of vexation on't
As it may lose some color.[24]

RODERIGO.   Here is her father's house. I'll call aloud.

IAGO.   Do; with like timorous[25] accent and dire yell
As when (by night and negligence) the fire
Is spied in populous cities.

RODERIGO.   What, ho, Brabantio! Signior Brabantio, ho!

IAGO.   Awake! what, ho, Brabantio! thieves! thieves! thieves!
Look to your house, your daughter, and your bags!
Thieves! thieves!

[BRABANTIO *at a window, above*]

BRABANTIO.   What is the reason of this terrible summons?
What is the matter there?

RODERIGO.   Signior, is all your family within?

IAGO.   Are your doors lock'd?

BRABANTIO.   Why, wherefore ask you this?

IAGO.   'Zounds,[26] sir, you're robb'd!—For shame, put on your gown!—
Your heart is burst, you have lost half your soul.

[17] Outward appearances.   [18] Private, personal.
[19] The innate actions and inclination of my heart; my true feelings.
[20] Outward equivalence; in external actions.   [21] Othello.   [22] Possess.   [23] Othello.
[24] So that his joy may be tarnished.   [25] Terrifying.
[26] By God's wounds.

Even now, now, very now, an old black ram
Is tupping[27] your white ewe. Arise, arise!
Awake the snorting[28] citizens with the bell,
Or else the devil [29] will make a grandsire of you.
Arise, I say.

BRABANTIO.   What! have you lost your wits?

RODERIGO.   Most reverend signior, do you know my voice?

BRABANTIO.   Not I. What are you?

RODERIGO.   My name is Roderigo.

BRABANTIO.   The worser welcome!
I have charg'd thee not to haunt about my doors.
In honest plainness thou hast heard me say
My daughter is not for thee; and now, in madness,
Being full of supper and distempering[30] draughts,
Upon malicious bravery[31] dost thou come
To start my quiet.

RODERIGO.   Sir, sir, sir!

BRABANTIO.   But thou must needs be sure,
My spirit and my place have in them power
To make this bitter to thee.

RODERIGO.   Patience, good sir.

BRABANTIO.   What tell'st thou me of robbing? This is Venice.
My house is not a grange.

RODERIGO.   Most grave Brabantio,
In simple and pure soul I come to you.

IAGO.   'Zounds, sir, you are one of those that will not serve God if the devil bid
you. Because we come to do you service and you think we are ruffians, you'll
have your daughter covered with a Barbary[32] horse; you'll have your
nephews[33] neigh to you; you'll have coursers for cousins[34] and jennets[35] for
germans.[36]

BRABANTIO.   What profane wretch art thou?

IAGO.   I am one, sir, that come to tell you, your daughter and the Moor are now
making the beast with two backs.

BRABANTIO.   Thou art a villain.

IAGO.   You are—a senator.

BRABANTIO.   This thou shalt answer. I know thee, Roderigo.

RODERIGO.   Sir, I will answer anything. But, I beseech you,
If't be your pleasure and most wise consent
(As partly, I find, it is) that your fair daughter,
At this odd-even[37] and dull watch o' th' night,
Transported with no worse nor better guard
But with a knave of common hire, a gondolier,
To the gross clasps of a lascivious Moor—
If this be known to you, and your allowance,[38]

---

[27] Covering.   [28] Snoring.
[29] Usually visualized as black in the Middle Ages and Renaissance.   [30] Intoxicating.
[31] Bravado.   [32] Moorish.   [33] Grandsons.   [34] Close relatives.   [35] Moorish horses.
[36] Relations.   [37] Around midnight.   [38] Has your approval.

We then have done you bold and saucy wrongs.
But if you know not this, my manners tell me
We have your wrong rebuke. Do not believe
That, from[39] the sense of all civility,
I thus would play and trifle with your reverence.
Your daughter (if you have not given her leave,
I say again) hath made a gross revolt,
Tying her duty, beauty, wit and fortunes
In an extravagant and wheeling[40] stranger
Of here and everywhere. Straight satisfy yourself.
If she be in her chamber or your house,
Let loose on me the justice of the state
For thus deluding you.

BRABANTIO.   Strike on the tinder, ho!
Give me a taper! call up all my people!
This accident is not unlike my dream.
Belief of it oppresses me already.
Light, I say! light!

[Exit]

IAGO.   Farewell, for I must leave you.
It seems not meet nor wholesome to my place
To be produc'd [41] (as, if I stay, I shall)
Against the Moor; for I do know the state
(However this may gall him with some check) [42]
Cannot with safety cast him; for he's embark'd
With such loud [43] reason to the Cyprus wars,[44]
Which even now stand in act,[45] that, for their souls,
Another of his fathom[46] they have not
To lead their business. In which regard,
Though I do hate him as I do hell's pains,
Yet for necessity of present life,
I must show out a flag and sign of love,
Which is indeed but sign. That you shall surely find him,
Lead to the Sagittary[47] the raised search,
And there will I be with him. So, farewell.

[Exit]

[Enter (below) BRABANTIO *in his night gown,[48] and* SERVANTS *with torches]*

BRABANTIO.   It is too true an evil. Gone she is,
And what's to come of my despised time[49]
Is nought but bitterness. Now, Roderigo,
Where didst thou see her? O unhappy[50] girl!
With the Moor, sayst thou? Who would be a father!

---

[39] Ignoring.   [40] Vagabond and roving.   [41] Called as a witness.   [42] Rebuke.
[43] Strong.
[44] Venice was at this time defending the isle of Cyprus against a threatened Turkish attack.
[45] Are actually under way.   [46] Capacity.   [47] Presumably the name of a Venetian inn.
[48] Dressing gown.   [49] The rest of my miserable life.   [50] Unfortunate.

How didst thou know 'twas she? O, she deceives me
Past thought. What said she to you? Get mo[51] tapers!
Raise all my kindred! Are they married, think you?

RODERIGO.   Truly, I think they are.

BRABANTIO.   O heaven! How got she out? O treason of the blood!
Fathers, from hence trust not your daughters' minds
By what you see them act. Is there not charms
By which the property of youth and maidhood
May be abus'd? [52] Have you not read, Roderigo,
Of some such thing?

RODERIGO.   Yes, sir, I have indeed.

BRABANTIO.   Call up my brother. O, would you had had her!
Some one way, some another! Do you know
Where we may apprehend her and the Moor?

RODERIGO.   I think I can discover him, if you please
To get good guard and go along with me.

BRABANTIO.   Pray, lead me on. At every house I'll call;
I may command [53] at most. Get weapons, ho!
And raise some special officers of night.
On, good Roderigo. I'll deserve[54] your pains.

                                                      [*Exeunt*]

SCENE SECOND: *Another Street. Before the Sagittary.*

[*Enter* OTHELLO, IAGO, *and* ATTENDANTS *with torches*]

IAGO.   Though in the trade of war I have slain men,
Yet do I hold it very stuff o' th' conscience
To do no contriv'd [55] murder. I lack iniquity
Sometimes to do me service. Nine or ten times
I had thought t' have yerk'd him[56] here under the ribs.

OTHELLO.   'Tis better as it is.

IAGO.   Nay, but he prated,
And spoke such scurvy and provoking terms
Against your Honor
That with the little godliness I have
I did full hard forbear him. But, I pray, sir,
Are you fast married? Be assur'd of this,
That the magnifico[57] is much belov'd,
And hath in his effect[58] a voice potential
As double as the duke's.[59] He will divorce you,
Or put upon you what restraint and grievance
The law, with all his might to enforce it on,
Will give him cable.[60]

OTHELLO.   Let him do his spite.
My services which I have done the Signory[61]

---

[51] More.   [52] Deceived.   [53] Get supporters to follow me.   [54] Reward.
[55] Premeditated.   [56] Stabbed him [Brabantio].   [57] Venetian nobleman.
[58] Actually.   [59] Influence twice as strong as the doge (or duke) of Venice.
[60] Permission; literally, rope.   [61] The collective rulers of Venice.

Shall out-tongue his complaints. 'Tis yet to know[62]
(Which when I know that boasting is an honor
I shall promulgate), I fetch my life and being[63]
From men of royal siege,[64] and my demerits[65]
May speak unbonneted[66] to as proud a fortune
As this that I have reach'd. For know, Iago,
But that I love the gentle Desdemona,
I would not my unhoused[67] free condition
Put into circumscription and confine
For the sea's worth. But, look! what lights come yond?

IAGO.   Those are the raised father and his friends.
You were best go in.

OTHELLO.   Not I. I must be found.
My parts,[68] my title, and my perfect[69] soul
Shall manifest me rightly. Is it they?

IAGO.   By Janus,[70] I think no.

[*Enter* CASSIO *with lights,* OFFICERS *and torches*]

OTHELLO.   The servants of the duke, and my lieutenant.
The goodness of the night upon you, friends!
What is the news?

CASSIO.   The duke does greet you, general,
And he requires your haste-post-haste appearance,
Even on the instant.

OTHELLO.   What's the matter, think you?

CASSIO.   Something from Cyprus, as I may divine.
It is a business of some heat. The galleys
Have sent a dozen sequent messengers
This very night at one another's heels,
And many of the consuls, rais'd and met,
Are at the duke's already. You have been hotly call'd for;
When being not at your lodging to be found,
The Senate sent above three several quests
To search you out.

OTHELLO.   'Tis well I'm found by you.
I will but spend a word here in the house,
And go with you.

[*Enters the Sagittary*]

CASSIO.   Ancient, what makes he here?

IAGO.   Faith, he to-night hath boarded a land carrack.[71]
If it prove lawful prize, he's made for ever.

CASSIO.   I do not understand.

IAGO.   He's married.

CASSIO.   To who?

IAGO.   Marry,[72] to—

---

[62] It is not yet known.   [63] I am descended.   [64] Rank.   [65] Merits.
[66] With my hat on as to an equal.   [67] Unmarried or unconfined.   [68] Abilities.
[69] Guiltless.   [70] Two-faced deity of the Romans.   [71] A large valuable ship.
[72] By the virgin Mary. A pun on marry-Mary.

[*Re-enter* OTHELLO]

Come, captain, will you go?

OTHELLO. Have with you.

CASSIO. Here comes another troop to seek for you.

IAGO. It is Brabantio. General, be advis'd;
He comes to bad intent.

[*Enter* BRABANTIO, RODERIGO, *and others, with lights and weapons*]

OTHELLO. Holla! stand there!

RODERIGO. Signior, it is the Moor.

BRABANTIO. Down with him! Thief!

[*They draw on both sides*]

IAGO. You, Roderigo! Come, sir, I am for you.

OTHELLO. Keep up[73] your bright swords, for the dew will rust 'em.
Good signior, you shall more command with years
Than with your weapons.

BRABANTIO. O thou foul thief! Where hast thou stow'd my daughter?
Damn'd as thou art, thou hast enchanted her;
For I'll refer me to all things of sense,[74]
If she in chains of magic were not bound,
Whether a maid so tender, fair, and happy,
So opposite to marriage that she shunn'd
The wealthy curled darlings of our nation,
Would ever have (t'incur a general mock)
Run from her guardage[75] to the sooty bosom
Of such a thing as thou—to fear, not to delight.
Judge me the world,[76] if 'tis not gross in sense[77]
That thou hast practis'd on her with foul charms,
Abus'd her delicate youth with drugs or minerals
That weaken motion.[78] I'll have't disputed on.[79]
'Tis probable, and palpable to thinking.
I therefore apprehend and do attach thee
For an abuser of the world, a practiser
Of arts inhibited and out of warrant.[80]
Lay hold upon him. If he do resist,
Subdue him at his peril.

OTHELLO. Hold your hands,
Both you of my inclining and the rest.
Were it my cue to fight, I should have known it
Without a prompter. Where will you that I go
To answer this your charge?

BRABANTIO. To prison, till fit time
Of law and course of direct session[81]
Call thee to answer.

OTHELLO. What if I do obey?
How may the duke be therewith satisfied,

---

[73] Sheathe.   [74] Sensible or rational things.   [75] Guardian.   [76] Let the world judge
[77] Obvious.   [78] Inclination.   [79] Refer it to the authorities.
[80] Prohibited and illegal arts; i.e., magic.   [81] Due course of law, no special trial.

Whose messengers are here about my side
Upon some present[82] business of the state
To bring me to him?
OFFICER.   'Tis true, most worthy signior.
The duke's in council, and your noble self,
I am sure, is sent for.
BRABANTIO.   How? The duke in council!
In this time of the night! Bring him away.
Mine's not an idle cause. The duke himself,
Or any of my brothers of the state,
Cannot but feel this wrong as 'twere their own;
For if such actions may have passage free,
Bondslaves and pagans shall our statesmen be.

                                              [*Exeunt*]

SCENE THIRD: *The Doge's Palace.*

[*Enter* DUKE *and* SENATORS, *set at a table with lights and* ATTENDANTS]
DUKE.   There is no composition[83] in these news
   That gives them credit.
FIRST SENATOR.   Indeed, they are disproportion'd.
My letters say a hundred and seven galleys.
DUKE.   And mine, a hundred forty.
SECOND SENATOR.   And mine, two hundred.
But though they jump[84] not on a just account
(As in these cases, where the aim[85] reports,
'Tis oft with difference), yet do they all confirm
A Turkish fleet, and bearing up to Cyprus.
DUKE.   Nay, it is possible enough to judgment.
I do not so secure me in the error,
But the main article I do approve
In fearful sense.[86]
SAILOR *within.*   What, ho! what, ho! what, ho!
OFFICER.   A messenger from the galleys.
   [*Enter* SAILOR]
DUKE.   Now! The business?
SAILOR.   The Turkish preparation makes for Rhodes.
So was I bid report here to the state
By Signior Angelo.
DUKE.   How say you by this change?
FIRST SENATOR.   This cannot be,
By no assay of reason.[87] 'Tis a pageant

---

[82] Immediate.   [83] Consistency.   [84] Agree.
[85] Conjecture [of the enemy's strength and disposition].
[86] Despite the conflicting reports, I believe, with apprehension, the main point [that a Turkish fleet of whatever size is approaching Cyprus].
[87] Reasonable test.

To keep us in false gaze.[88] When we consider
Th'importancy of Cyprus to the Turk,
And let ourselves again but understand
That as it more concerns the Turk than Rhodes,
So may he with more facile question bear it,[89]
For that it stands not in such warlike brace,[90]
But altogether lacks th'abilities
That Rhodes is dress'd in—if we make thought of this,
We must not think the Turk is so unskilful
To leave that latest which concerns him first,
Neglecting an attempt of ease and gain
To wake and wage[91] a danger profitless.

DUKE.   Nay, in all confidence, he's not for Rhodes.

OFFICER.   Here is more news.

[*Enter a* MESSENGER]

MESSENGER.   The Ottomites,[92] reverend and gracious,
Steering with due course toward the isle of Rhodes,
Have there injointed [93] them with an after[94] fleet.

FIRST SENATOR.   Ay, so I thought. How many, as you guess?

MESSENGER.   Of thirty sail; and now they do re-stem[95]
Their backward course, bearing with frank appearance
Their purposes toward Cyprus. Signior Montano,
Your trusty and most valiant servitor,
With his free duty recommends[96] you thus,
And prays you to believe him.

DUKE.   'Tis certain then, for Cyprus.
Marcus Luccicos is not here in town?

FIRST SENATOR.   He's now in Florence.

DUKE.   Write from us: wish him post-post-haste dispatch.

FIRST SENATOR.   Here comes Brabantio and the valiant Moor.

[*Enter* BRABANTIO, OTHELLO, CASSIO, IAGO, RODERIGO, *and* OFFICERS]

DUKE.   Valiant Othello, we must straight employ you
Against the general enemy Ottoman.
[*To* BRABANTIO] I did not see you. Welcome, gentle signior;
We lack'd your counsel and your help to-night.

BRABANTIO.   So did I yours. Good your Grace, pardon me.
Neither my place nor aught I heard of business
Hath rais'd me from my bed, nor doth the general care
Take hold on me, for my particular grief
Is of so floodgate[97] and o'erbearing nature
That it engluts[98] and swallows other sorrows
And it is still itself.

DUKE.   Why, what's the matter?

BRABANTIO.   My daughter! O my daughter!

ALL.   Dead?

---

[88] Looking in the wrong direction.   [89] Capture it more easily.   [90] Condition of defense.
[91] Arouse and dare.   [92] Turks.   [93] Joined.   [94] Second or reserve.   [95] Retrace.
[96] Informs.   [97] Torrential.   [98] Swallows.

BRABANTIO.   Ay, to me.
    She is abus'd, stol'n from me, and corrupted
    By spells and medicines bought of mountebanks;
    For nature so preposterously to err
    Being not deficient, blind, or lame of sense,
    Sans[99] witchcraft could not.

DUKE. Whoe'er he be that in this foul proceeding
    Hath thus beguil'd your daughter of herself
    And you of her, the bloody book of law[100]
    You shall yourself read in the bitter letter
    After your own sense; yea, though our proper[101] son
    Stood in your action.[102]

BRABANTIO.   Humbly I thank your Grace.
    Here is the man, this Moor; whom now, it seems,
    Your special mandate for the state affairs
    Hath hither brought.

ALL.   We are very sorry for't.

DUKE [*to* OTHELLO]. What, in your own part, can you say to this?

BRABANTIO. Nothing but 'This is so.'

OTHELLO. Most potent, grave, and reverend signiors,
    My very noble and approv'd [103] good masters:
    That I have ta'en away this old man's daughter,
    It is most true; true, I have married her.
    The very head and front[104] of my offending
    Hath this extent, no more. Rude[105] am I in my speech,
    And little bless'd with the soft phrase of peace,
    For since these arms of mine had seven years' pith[106]
    Till now some nine moons wasted,[107] they have us'd
    Their dearest[108] action in the tented field;
    And little of this great world can I speak
    More than pertains to feats of broil and battle,
    And therefore little shall I grace my cause
    In speaking for myself. Yet, by your gracious patience
    I will a round [109] unvarnish'd tale deliver
    Of my whole course of love: what drugs, what charms,
    What conjuration, and what mighty magic,
    (For such proceedings am I charg'd withal)
    I won his daughter.

BRABANTIO.   A maiden never bold;
    Of spirit so still and quiet, that her motion
    Blush'd at herself! And she, in spite of nature,
    Of years, of country, credit,[110] everything,
    To fall in love with what she fear'd to look on!
    It is a judgment maim'd and most imperfect
    That will confess perfection so could err

---

[99] Without.   [100] A reference to capital punishment.   [101] Own.
[102] Were involved by your accusation.   [103] Proved by experience.   [104] Forehead.
[105] Rough.   [106] Marrow.   [107] Ago.   [108] Most important.   [109] Plain.   [110] Reputation.

Against all rules of nature, and must be driven
To find out practices of cunning hell,
Why this should be. I therefore vouch again
That with some mixtures powerful o'er the blood,
Or with some dram conjur'd to this effect,
He wrought upon her.

DUKE.   To vouch this is no proof,
Without more certain and more overt test
Than these thin habits[111] and poor likelihoods
Of modern[112] seeming do prefer against him.

FIRST SENATOR.   But, Othello, speak.
Did you by indirect and forced courses
Subdue and poison this young maid's affections?
Or came it by request and such fair question
As soul to soul affordeth?

OTHELLO.   I do beseech you,
Send for the lady to the Sagittary,
And let her speak of me before her father.
If you do find me foul in her report,
The trust, the office I do hold of you
Not only take away, but let your sentence
Even fall upon my life.

DUKE.   Fetch Desdemona hither.

[Exit two or three]

OTHELLO.   Ancient, conduct them. You best know the place.

[Exit IAGO*]*

And till she come, as truly as to heaven
I do confess the vices of my blood,
So justly to your grave ears I'll present
How I did thrive in this fair lady's love,
And she in mine.

DUKE.   Say it, Othello.

OTHELLO.   Her father lov'd me; oft invited me,
Still [113] question'd me the story of my life
From year to year, the battles, sieges, fortunes
That I have pass'd.
I ran it through, even from my boyish days
To th' very moment that he bade me tell it.
Wherein I spake of most disastrous chances,
Of moving accidents by flood and field,
Of hair-breadth 'scapes i' th' imminent deadly breach,[114]
Of being taken by the insolent foe
And sold to slavery, of my redemption thence
And portance[115] in my traveller's history.
Wherein of antres[116] vast and deserts idle,[117]
Rough quarries, rocks and hills whose heads touch heaven,

---

[111] The insubstantial evidence.   [112] Trivial.   [113] Constantly.
[114] Gap in the wall of city being attacked.   [115] Behavior.   [116] Caves.   [117] Barren.

It was my hint[118] to speak (such was the process[119]),
And of the Cannibals that each other eat,
The Anthropophagi, and men whose heads
Do grow beneath their shoulders. This to hear
Would Desdemona seriously incline;
But still the house-affairs would draw her thence,
Which ever as she could with haste dispatch
She'd come again, and with a greedy ear
Devour up my discourse. Which I observing,
Took once a pliant[120] hour and found good means
To draw from her a prayer of earnest heart
That I would all my pilgrimage dilate,[121]
Whereof by parcels she had something heard,
But not intentively.[122] I did consent;
And often did beguile her of [123] her tears,
When I did speak of some distressful stroke
That my youth suffer'd. My story being done,
She gave me for my pains a world of sighs.
She swore, i' faith, 'twas strange, 'twas passing strange;
'Twas pitiful, 'twas wondrous pitiful.
She wish'd she had not heard it, yet she wish'd
That heaven had made her[124] such a man. She thank'd me,
And bade me, if I had a friend that lov'd her,
I should but teach him how to tell my story,
And that would woo her. Upon this hint I spake.
She lov'd me for the dangers I had pass'd,
And I lov'd her that she did pity them.
This only is the witchcraft I have us'd.
Here comes the lady; let her witness it.
  [*Enter* DESDEMONA, IAGO, *and the rest*]
DUKE.   I think this tale would win my daughter too.
  Good Brabantio,
  Take up this mangled matter at the best.[125]
  Men do their broken weapons rather use
  Than their bare hands.
BRABANTIO.   I pray you, hear her speak.
  If she confess that she was half the wooer,
  Destruction on my head, if my bad blame
  Light on the man! Come hither, gentle mistress.
  Do you perceive in all this noble company
  Where most you owe obedience?
DESDEMONA.   My noble father,
  I do perceive here a divided duty.
  To you I am bound for life and education.
  My life and education both do learn[126] me

---

[118] Occasion.   [119] Proceeding.   [120] Suitable.   [121] Relate in full.   [122] Intently.
[123] Draw from her.   [124] [For] her.   [125] Settle this sorry business as best you may.
[126] Teach.

How to respect you: you are the lord of duty,[127]
I am hitherto your daughter. But here's my husband;
And so much duty as my mother show'd
To you, preferring you before her father,
So much I challenge that I may profess
Due to the Moor my lord.

BRABANTIO.   God be with you! I have done.
Please it your Grace, on to the state affairs.
I had rather to adopt a child than get[128] it.
Come hither, Moor:
I here do give thee that with all my heart
Which, but thou hast already, with all my heart
I would keep from thee. For your sake, jewel,
I am glad at soul I have no other child,
For thy escape would teach me tyranny,
To hang clogs on 'em. I have done, my lord.

DUKE.   Let me speak like yourself and lay a sentence,[129]
Which, as a grise[130] or step, may help these lovers
Into your favor.
When remedies are past, the griefs are ended
By seeing the worst, which late on hopes depended.
To mourn a mischief that is past and gone
Is the next[131] way to draw more mischief on.
What cannot be preserv'd when Fortune takes,
Patience her[132] injury a mockery makes.
The robb'd that smiles steals something from the thief;
He robs himself that spends a bootless[133] grief.

BRABANTIO.   So let the Turk of Cyprus us beguile,
We lose it not so long as we can smile.
He bears the sentence well that nothing bears
But the free comfort which from thence he hears;
But he bears both the sentence and the sorrow
That, to pay grief, must of poor patience borrow.
These sentences, to sugar, or to gall,
Being strong on both sides, are equivocal:
But words are words; I never yet did hear
That the bruis'd heart was pierced through the ear.
Beseech you, now to the affairs of state.

DUKE.   The Turk with a most mighty preparation makes for Cyprus. Othello,
the fortitude[134] of the place is best known to you; and though we have
there a substitute of most allowed [135] sufficiency, yet opinion, a sovereign
mistress of effects,[136] throws a more safer voice on you. You must therefore
be content to slubber[137] the gloss of your new fortunes with this more
stubborn and boisterous expedition.

OTHELLO.   The tyrant custom, most grave senators,

---

[127] According to duty.   [128] Beget.   [129] Proverbial sayings or maxims.   [130] Degree or step.
[131] Nearest.   [132] Fortune's; as a result of Fortune.   [133] Useless, vain.   [134] Fortification.
[135] Admitted.   [136] Reputation, which produces results.   [137] Sully.

Hath made the flinty and steel couch of war
My thrice-driven[138] bed of down. I do agnize[139]
A natural and prompt alacrity[140]
I find in hardness,[141] and do undertake
These present wars against the Ottomites.
Most humbly therefore bending to your state,
I crave fit disposition for my wife,
Due reference[142] of place and exhibition,[143]
With such accommodation and besort[144]
As levels with her breeding.

DUKE.   If you please,
Be't at her father's.

BRABANTIO.   I'll not have it so.

OTHELLO.   Nor I.

DESDEMONA.   Nor I. I would not there reside,
To put my father in impatient thoughts
By being in his eye. Most gracious duke,
To my unfolding[145] lend your prosperous[146] ear,
And let me find a charter[147] in your voice
T'assist my simpleness.

DUKE.   What would you? Speak.

DESDEMONA.   That I did love the Moor to live with him,
My downright violence and storm of fortunes[148]
May trumpet to the world. My heart's subdu'd
Even to the very quality[149] of my lord.
I saw Othello's visage in his mind,
And to his honors and his valiant parts
Did I my soul and fortunes consecrate.
So that, dear lords, if I be left behind,
A moth of peace, and he go to the war,
The rites for which I love him are bereft me,
And I a heavy interim shall support
By his dear absence. Let me go with him.

OTHELLO.   Your voices,[150] lords! Beseech you, let her will
Have a free way. I therefore beg it not
To please the palate of my appetite,
Nor to comply with heat the young affects[151]
In my distinct and proper satisfaction,
But to be free and bounteous to her mind;
And heaven defend [152] your good souls that you think
I will your serious and great business scant
For[153] she is with me. No, when light-wing'd toys[154]
Of feather'd Cupid steel [155] with wanton dulness

---

[138] Thrice sifted.   [139] Confess.   [140] Congeniality.   [141] Hardship.   [142] Assignment.
[143] Allowance.   [144] Attendants.   [145] Revelation, plan.   [146] Favorable.   [147] Sanction.
[148] I.e., my strong and violent action.   [149] Profession, i.e., soldiering.
[150] Favorable votes.   [151] Lust which is characteristic of youth.   [152] Forbid.
[153] Because.   [154] Trifles.   [155] Close up.

My speculative and offic'd instruments,[156]
That my disports[157] corrupt and taint my business,
Let housewives make a skillet of my helm,
And all indign[158] and base adversities
Make head against[159] my estimation! [160]

DUKE. Be it as you shall privately determine,
Either for her stay or going. Th' affair cries haste,
And speed must answer. You must hence to-night.

DESDEMONA. To-night, my lord?

DUKE.   This night.

OTHELLO.   With all my heart.

DUKE. At ten i' the morning here we'll meet again.
Othello, leave some officer behind,
And he shall our commission bring to you;
With such things else of quality or respect[161]
As doth concern you.

OTHELLO.   Please your Grace, my ancient.
A man he is of honesty and trust.
To his conveyance I assign my wife,
With what else needful your good Grace shall think
To be sent after me.

DUKE.   Let it be so.
Good night to every one. [*To* BRABANTIO] And, noble signior,
If virtue no delighted beauty lack,[162]
Your son-in-law is far more fair than black.

FIRST SENATOR. Adieu, brave Moor! use Desdemona well.

BRABANTIO. Look to her, Moor, if thou hast eyes to see:
She has deceiv'd her father, and may thee.

OTHELLO. My life upon her faith!
                [*Exeunt* DUKE, SENATORS, OFFICERS, *&c*]
                          Honest Iago,
My Desdemona must I leave to thee:
I prithee, let thy wife attend on her;
And bring her after in the best advantage.—[163]
Come, Desdemona; I have but an hour
Of love, of wordly matters and direction
To spend with thee. We must obey the time.
                          [*Exeunt* MOOR *and* DESDEMONA]

RODERIGO. Iago!

IAGO. What sayst thou, noble heart?

RODERIGO. What will I do, think'st thou?

IAGO. Why, go to bed, and sleep.

RODERIGO. I will incontinently[164] drown myself.

IAGO. Well, if thou dost, I shall never love thee after it. Why, thou silly gentleman?

---

[156] Faculties of sight (perception) and action.   [157] Amusements.   [158] Unworthy.
[159] Overcome.   [160] Reputation.   [161] Of importance or honor.   [162] If virtue is satisfy-
ingly beautiful in itself.   [163] At the best opportunity.   [164] Immediately.

RODERIGO. It is silliness to live when to live is a torment; and then have we a
prescription to die when death is our physician.

IAGO. O, villainous! I ha' looked upon the world for four times seven years, and
since I could distinguish between a benefit and an injury, I never found a
man that knew how to love himself. Ere I would say I would drown myself
for the love of a guinea-hen, I would change my humanity with a baboon.

RODERIGO. What should I do? I confess it is my shame to be so fond,[165] but it is
not in my virtue[166] to amend it.

IAGO. Virtue! a fig! 'Tis in ourselves that we are thus or thus. Our bodies are
gardens, to the which our wills are gardeners; so that if we will plant nettles
or sow lettuce, set hyssop and weed up thyme, supply it with one gender of
herbs or distract it with many, either to have it sterile with idleness or
manured with industry, why, the power and corrigible[167] authority of this
lies in our wills. If the balance of our lives had not one scale of reason to
poise[168] another of sensuality, the blood and baseness of our natures would
conduct us to most preposterous conclusions. But we have reason to cool our
raging motions, our carnal stings, our unbitted [169] lusts, whereof I take this
that you call love to be a sect or scion.[170]

RODERIGO. It cannot be.

IAGO. It is merely a lust of the blood and a permission of the will. Come, be a
man. Drown thyself? Drown cats and blind puppies. I confess me thy friend,
and I confess me knit to thy deserving with cables of perdurable toughness.
I could never better stead [171] thee than now. Put money in thy purse. Follow
these wars; defeat thy favor with an usurped beard.[172] I say, put money in
thy purse. It cannot be that Desdemona should long continue her love unto
the Moor,—put money in thy purse,—nor he his to her. It was a violent
commencement, and thou shalt see an answerable sequestration.[173] Put but
money in thy purse. These Moors are changeable in their wills. Fill thy purse
with money. The food that to him now is as luscious as locusts,[174] shall be to
him shortly as acerb[175] as the coloquintida.[176] She must change for youth.
When she is sated with his body, she will find the error of her choice. She
must have change, she must. Therefore put money in thy purse. If thou wilt
needs damn thyself, do it a more delicate way than drowning. Make all the
money thou canst. If sanctimony and a frail vow betwixt an erring[177]
barbarian and a super-subtle Venetian be not too hard for my wits and all the
tribe of hell, thou shalt enjoy her: therefore make money. A pox o' drowning! 'tis clean out of the way. Seek thou rather to be hanged in compassing[178]
thy joy than to be drowned and go without her.

RODERIGO. Wilt thou be fast to my hopes if I depend on the issue? [179]

IAGO. Thou art sure of me. Go, make money. I have told thee often, and I tell
thee again and again, I hate the Moor. My cause is hearted:[180] thine hath no
less reason. Let us be conjunctive[181] in our revenge against him. If thou
canst cuckold him, thou dost thyself a pleasure, me a sport. There are many

---

[165] Foolish, here over love.   [166] Manhood.   [167] Correcting.   [168] Counterbalance.
[169] Uncontrolled.   [170] Branch or offshoot.   [171] Help.
[172] Hide your face by a false beard.   [173] Corresponding separation.   [174] A sweet fruit.
[175] Bitter.   [176] A fruit from which a bitter drug was made.   [177] Wandering.
[178] Achieving.   [179] Rely on the outcome.   [180] Deep-seated.   [181] United.

events in the womb of time which will be delivered. Traverse![182] go!
provide thy money! We will have more of this to-morrow. Adieu.

RODERIGO. Where shall we meet i' th' morning?

IAGO. At my lodging.

RODERIGO. I'll be with thee betimes.

IAGO. Go to;[183] farewell. Do you hear, Roderigo?

RODERIGO. What say you?

IAGO. No more of drowning, do you hear?

RODERIGO. I am chang'd. I'll sell all my land.

IAGO. Go to; farewell. Put money enough in your purse.

[*Exit* RODERIGO]

Thus do I ever make my fool my purse;
For I mine own gain'd knowledge should profane,
If I would time expend with such a snipe
But for my sport and profit. I hate the Moor,
And it is thought abroad that 'twixt my sheets
He's done my office. I know not if 't be true,
But I, for mere suspicion in that kind,
Will do as if for surety.[184] He holds me well.
The better shall my purpose work on him.
Cassio's a proper[185] man. Let me see now.—
To get his place, and to plume[186] up my will
In double knavery: how? how? Let's see.—
After some time t'abuse[187] Othello's ear
That he is too familiar with his wife.
He has a person and a smooth dispose[188]
To be suspected, fram'd to make women false;
The Moor a free and open nature too,
That thinks men honest that but seem to be so,
And will as tenderly be led by th' nose
As asses are.
I have't! it is engender'd! Hell and night
Must bring this monstrous birth to the world's light.

[*Exit*]

Act Second

SCENE FIRST: *Famagosta, capital of Cyprus. An open place near the quay.*

[*Enter* MONTANO, *Governor of Cyprus, with two other* GENTLEMEN]

MONTANO. What from the cape can you discern at sea?

FIRST GENTLEMAN. Nothing at all. It is a high-wrought flood;[1]
I cannot 'twixt the heaven and the main
Descry a sail.

---

[182] March.   [183] An interjection. Here, equivalent to "come."   [184] Will act as if it is true.
[185] Handsome.   [186] Gratify, pamper.   [187] Deceive.   [188] Disposition, manner.
[1] Rough sea.

MONTANO.   Methinks the wind does speak aloud at land;
  A fuller blast ne'er shook our battlements.
  If it hath ruffian'd so upon the sea,
  What ribs of oak, when mountains melt on them,
  Can hold the mortise? [2] What shall we hear of this?

SECOND GENTLEMAN.   A segregation[3] of the Turkish fleet;
  For do but stand upon the foaming shore,
  The chidden billow seems to pelt the clouds;
  The wind-shak'd surge, with high and monstrous mane,
  Seems to cast water on the burning bear[4]
  And quench the guards[5] of th' ever-fixed pole.
  I never did like molestation[6] view
  On the enchafed [7] flood.

MONTANO.   If that the Turkish fleet
  Be not enshelter'd and embay'd, they are drown'd.
  It is impossible they bear it out.
  [*Enter a third* GENTLEMAN]

THIRD GENTLEMAN.   News, lads! our wars are done.
  The desperate tempest hath so bang'd the Turks
  That their designment halts. A noble ship of Venice
  Hath seen a grievous wrack and sufferance[8]
  On most part of their fleet.

MONTANO.   How! is this true?

THIRD GENTLEMAN.   The ship is here put in,
  LA VERONESA. Michael Cassio,
  Lieutenant to the warlike Moor Othello,
  Is come on shore; the Moor himself at sea,
  And is in full commission here for Cyprus.

MONTANO.   I am glad on't; 'tis a worthy governor.

THIRD GENTLEMAN.   But this same Cassio, though he speak of comfort
  Touching the Turkish loss, yet he looks sadly
  And prays the Moor be safe, for they were parted
  With foul and violent tempest.

MONTANO.   Pray heaven he be;
  For I have serv'd him, and the man commands
  Like a full soldier. Let's to the seaside, ho!
  As well to see the vessel that's come in
  As to throw out our eyes for brave Othello,
  Even till we make the main and th' aerial blue
  An indistinct regard.[9]

THIRD GENTLEMAN.   Come, let's do so;
  For every minute is expectancy
  Of more arrivance.
  [*Enter* CASSIO]

CASSIO.   Thanks to the valiant of this warlike isle,

---

[2] Remain joined.   [3] Dispersal.   [4] The Great Bear constellation.
[5] The stars in the Little Bear which are in line with the polestar.   [6] Such a disturbance.
[7] Irritated.   [8] Disaster.   [9] Blur.

That so approve the Moor! And let the heavens
Give him defence against the elements,
For I have lost him on a dangerous sea.

MONTANO.   Is he well shipp'd?

CASSIO.   His bark is stoutly timber'd, and his pilot
Of very expert and approv'd allowance.[10]
Therefore my hopes, not surfeited to death,
Stand in bold cure.[11]

MESSENGER [*Within*]   A sail!—a sail!—a sail!

[*Enter a* MESSENGER]

CASSIO.   What noise?

MESSENGER.   The town is empty. On the brow o' th' sea
Stand ranks of people, and they cry, 'A sail!'

CASSIO.   My hopes do shape him for the governor.

[*A shot*]

SECOND GENTLEMAN.   They do discharge the shot of courtesy.
Our friends, at least.

CASSIO.   I pray you, sir, go forth,
And give us truth who 'tis that is arriv'd.

SECOND GENTLEMAN.   I shall.

[*Exit*]

MONTANO.   But, good lieutenant, is your general wiv'd?

CASSIO.   Most fortunately. He hath achiev'd a maid
That paragons description and wild fame;
One that excels the quirks of blazoning pens,[12]
And in th' essential vesture of creation[13]
Does tire the ingener.[14]

[*Enter* SECOND GENTLEMAN]

                          Now, who has put in?

SECOND GENTLEMAN.   'Tis one Iago, ancient to the general.

CASSIO.   He's had most favorable and happy speed.
Tempests themselves, high seas, and howling winds,
The gutter'd [15] rocks, and congregated sands,
Traitors ensteep'd [16] to clog the guiltless keel,
As having sense of beauty, do omit
Their mortal [17] natures, letting go safely by
The divine Desdemona.

MONTANO.   What is she?

CASSIO.   She that I spoke of, our great captain's captain,
Left in the conduct[18] of the bold Iago,
Whose footing[19] here anticipates our thoughts
A sennight's[20] speed. Great Jove, Othello guard,
And swell his sail with thine own powerful breath,
That he may bless this bay with his tall ship,
Make love's quick pants in Desdemona's arms,

---

[10] Tested skill.   [11] Have a good chance to be cured (fulfilled).
[12] Flourishes of praising pens (poets).   [13] Her natural virtues and appearance.
[14] Artistic creator.   [15] Jagged.   [16] Submerged.   [17] Deadly.   [18] Escort.   [19] Landing.
[20] Week's.

Give renew'd fire to our extincted [21] spirits,
And bring all Cyprus comfort!
[*Enter* DESDEMONA, IAGO, EMILIA, *and* RODERIGO, *with* ATTENDANTS]
O! behold,
The riches of the ship is come ashore.
Ye men of Cyprus, let her have your knees.
Hail to thee, lady! and the grace of heaven,
Before, behind thee, and on every hand,
Enwheel [22] thee round!

DESDEMONA.   I thank you, valiant Cassio.
What tidings can you tell me of my lord?

CASSIO. He is not yet arriv'd; nor know I aught
But that he's well, and will be shortly here.

DESDEMONA. O, but I fear! How lost you company?
[*Cry within:* 'A sail!—a sail!']

CASSIO. The great contention of the sea and skies
Parted our fellowship. But hark! a sail. [*Guns heard*]

SECOND GENTLEMAN. They give their greeting to the citadel:
This likewise is a friend.

CASSIO.   See for the news!
[*Exit* SECOND GENTLEMAN]
Good ancient, you are welcome. [*Kisses* EMILIA] Welcome, mistress.
Let it not gall your patience, good Iago,
That I extend my manners.[23] 'Tis my breeding
That gives me this bold show of courtesy.

IAGO. Sir, would she give you so much of her lips
As of her tongue she oft bestows on me,
You'd have enough.

DESDEMONA.   Alas, she has no speech.

IAGO. In faith, too much.
I find it still when I have list[24] to sleep.
Marry, before your ladyship, I grant,
She puts her tongue a little in her heart,
And chides with thinking.

EMILIA. You have little cause to say so.

IAGO. Come on, come on! You are pictures[25] out o' doors,
Bells[26] in your parlors, wild cats in your kitchens,
Saints in your injuries,[27] devils being offended,
Players[28] in your housewifery, and housewives[29] in your beds.

DESDEMONA. O fie upon thee, slanderer!

IAGO. Nay, it is true, or else I am a Turk.
You rise to play and go to bed to work.

EMILIA. You shall not write my praise.

IAGO.   No, let me not.

---

[21] Extinguished.   [22] Encompass.   [23] Go beyond normal courtesy, i.e., by kissing your wife.
[24] Desire.   [25] Painted up.   [26] I.e., always clanging.
[27] Act like saints when you offend others.   [28] Triflers.
[29] Hussies, as the word was then pronounced.

DESDEMONA. What wouldst thou write of me, if thou shouldst praise me?

IAGO. O gentle lady, do not put me to't,
For I am nothing if not critical.

DESDEMONA. Come on; assay.[30] There's one gone to the harbor?

IAGO. Ay, madam.

DESDEMONA. I am not merry, but I do beguile
The thing I am by seeming otherwise.
Come, how wouldst thou praise me?

IAGO. I am about it, but indeed my invention comes from my pate as birdlime
does from frieze.[31] It plucks out brains and all. But my muse labors, and
thus she is deliver'd.

If she be fair and wise.—Fairness and wit:
The one's for use, the other useth it.

DESDEMONA. Well prais'd! How if she be black[32] and witty?

IAGO.

If she be black, and thereto have a wit,
She'll find a white[33] that shall her blackness fit.

DESDEMONA. Worse and worse.

EMILIA. How if fair and foolish?

IAGO.

She never yet was foolish that was fair,
For even her folly help'd her to an heir.

DESDEMONA. These are old fond paradoxes to make fools laugh i' th' alehouse.
What miserable praise hast thou for her that's foul [34] and foolish?

IAGO.

There's none so foul and foolish thereunto
But does foul pranks which fair and wise ones do.

DESDEMONA. O heavy ignorance that praises the worst best! But what praise
couldst thou bestow on a deserving woman indeed? one that, in the authority
of her merits, did justly put on the vouch[35] of very malice itself?

IAGO.

She that was ever fair and never proud,
Had tongue at will [36] and yet was never loud;
Never lack'd gold and yet went never gay,
Fled from her wish and yet said 'Now I may';
She that being anger'd, her revenge being nigh,
Bade her wrong stay and her displeasure fly;
She that in wisdom never was so frail
To change the cod's head for the salmon's tail;[37]
She that could think and ne'er disclose her mind,
See suitors following and not look behind:
She was a wight, if ever such wights were,—

DESDEMONA. To do what?

IAGO.

To suckle fools and chronicle small beer.[38]

---

[30] Try.   [31] Rough cloth.   [32] Brunette.   [33] Pun on wight (person).   [34] Ugly.
[35] Win the approbation.   [36] Was loquacious.
[37] To exchange something worthwhile for something flashy.   [38] Keep household accounts.

DESDEMONA. O most lame and impotent conclusion! Do not learn of him, Emilia, though he be thy husband. How say you, Cassio? Is he not a most profane and liberal [39] counsellor?

CASSIO. He speaks home, madam. You may relish him more in the[40] soldier than in the scholar.

IAGO [*Aside*] He takes her by the palm. Ay, well said,[41] whisper! With as little a web as this will I ensnare as great a fly as Cassio. Ay, smile upon her, do! I will gyve[42] thee in thine own courtship.[43] [CASSIO *speaks to* DESDEMONA *in pantomime*] You say true, 'tis so, indeed. If such tricks as these strip you out of your lieutenantry, it had been better you had not kissed your three fingers[44] so oft, which now again you are most apt to play the sir[45] in. Very good! well kissed! an excellent courtesy! 'tis so, indeed. Yet again your fingers to your lips? would they were clyster-pipes[46] for your sake!

[*Trumpets within*]

The Moor! I know his trumpet.

CASSIO. 'Tis truly so.

DESDEMONA. Let's meet him and receive him.

CASSIO. Lo, where he comes!

[*Enter* OTHELLO *and* ATTENDANTS]

OTHELLO. O my fair warrior!

DESDEMONA.   My dear Othello!

OTHELLO. It gives me wonder great as my content
To see you here before me. O my soul's joy,
If after every tempest come such calms,
May the winds blow till they have waken'd death!
And let the laboring bark climb hills of seas
Olympus-high, and duck again as low
As hell's from heaven! If it were now to die,
'Twere now to be most happy, for I fear
My soul hath her content so absolute
That not another comfort like to this
Succeeds in unknown fate.

DESDEMONA.   The heavens forbid
But that our loves and comforts should increase
Even as our days do grow.

OTHELLO.   Amen to that, sweet powers!
I cannot speak enough of this content.
It stops me here.[47] It is too much of joy;
And this, and this, the greatest discords be   [*They kiss*]
That e'er our hearts shall make!

IAGO [*Aside*] O! you are well tun'd now,
But I'll set down the pegs that make this music,[48]
As honest as I am.

OTHELLO.   Come, let us to the castle.—

---

[39] Licentious.   [40] As a.   [41] Well done.   [42] Fetter, trap.   [43] Courtesy.
[44] A courteous gesture.   [45] Gentleman, gallant.   [46] Syringes.   [47] In my heart.
[48] Put these strings out of tune. Iago is carrying out the musical image first used by Othello in the preceding speech.

News, friends! Our wars are done. The Turks are drown'd.
How does my old acquaintance of this isle?—
Honey, you shall be well desir'd [49] in Cyprus;
I have found great love amongst them. O my sweet,
I prattle out of fashion,[50] and I dote
In mine own comforts. I prithee, good Iago,
Go to the bay and disembark my coffers.
Bring thou the master to the citadel;
He is a good one, and his worthiness
Does challenge much respect. Come, Desdemona!
Once more, well met at Cyprus!

> [*Exit* OTHELLO *and* DESDEMONA *with all except* IAGO *and* RODERIGO]

IAGO [*To* RODERIGO] Do thou meet me presently at the harbor. Come hither. If thou be'st valiant (as they say base men being in love have then a nobility in their natures more than is native to them), list[51] me. The lieutenant tonight watches on the court of guard.[52] First, I must tell thee this: Desdemona is directly in love with him.

RODERIGO. With him? Why, 'tis not possible.

IAGO. Lay thy finger thus,[53] and let thy soul be instructed. Mark me with what violence she first loved the Moor but[54] for bragging and telling her fantastical lies. And will she love him still for prating? Let not thy discreet heart think it. Her eye must be fed; and what delight shall she have to look on the devil? When the blood is made dull with the act of sport, there should be, again to inflame it, and to give satiety a fresh appetite, loveliness in favor, sympathy in years, manners, and beauties; all which the Moor is defective in. Now, for want of these required conveniences, her delicate tenderness will find itself abused, begin to heave the gorge,[55] disrelish and abhor the Moor. Very nature will instruct her in it, and compel her to some second choice. Now, sir, this granted (as it is a most pregnant[56] and unforced position), who stands so eminently in the degree of this fortune as Cassio does? A knave very voluble, no farder[57] conscionable[58] than in putting on the mere form of civil and humane seeming[59] for the better compassing of his salt[60] and hidden affections? Why, none; why, none. A subtle, slippery knave, a finder-out of occasions, that has an eye can stamp and counterfeit advantages,[61] though true advantage never present itself. A devilish knave! Besides, the knave is handsome, young, and hath all those requisites in him that folly and green[62] minds look after. A pestilent complete knave! and the woman has found him already.

RODERIGO. I cannot believe that in her. She's full of most bless'd condition.[63]

IAGO. Bless'd fig's end! The wine she drinks is made of grapes. If she had been bless'd, she would never have loved the Moor. Bless'd pudding! Didst thou not see her paddle with the palm of his hand? Didst not mark that?

RODERIGO. Yes, that I did; but that was but courtesy.

IAGO. Lechery, by this hand! an index and obscure prologue to the history of

---

[49] Loved.   [50] Chatter idly.   [51] Hear.   [52] Cassio is on guard duty tonight.
[53] On your lips, i.e., be quiet.   [54] Only.   [55] Be nauseated.   [56] Evident.   [57] Further.
[58] Conscientious.   [59] Courteous show.   [60] Lewd.   [61] Forge opportunities.
[62] Inexperienced.   [63] She's too blessed in her love.

lust and foul thoughts. They met so near with their lips that their breaths embraced together. Villainous thoughts, Roderigo! When these mutualities[64] so marshal the way, hard at hand comes the master and main exercise, the incorporate[65] conclusion. Pish! But, sir, be you ruled by me: I have brought you from Venice. Watch you to-night. For your command, I'll lay't upon you. Cassio knows you not. I'll not be far from you. Do you find some occasion to anger Cassio, either by speaking too loud, or tainting[66] his discipline, or from what other cause you please which the time shall more favorably minister.[67]

RODERIGO. Well.

IAGO. Sir, he is rash and very sudden in choler,[68] and haply with his truncheon may strike at you. Provoke him that he may, for even out of that will I cause these of Cyprus to mutiny, whose qualification[69] shall come into no true taste[70] again but by the displanting of Cassio. So shall you have a shorter journey to your desires by the means I shall then have to prefer[71] them, and the impediment most profitably removed without the which there were no expectation of our prosperity.

RODERIGO. I will do this, if you can bring it to any opportunity.

IAGO. I warrant thee. Meet me by and by at the citadel. I must fetch his necessaries ashore. Farewell.

RODERIGO. Adieu.

[*Exit*]

IAGO. That Cassio loves her, I do well believe't;
That she loves him, 'tis apt, and of great credit.[72]
The Moor (howbeit that I endure him not)
Is of a constant, noble, loving nature;
And I dare think he'll prove to Desdemona
A most dear husband. Now, I do love her too,—
Not out of absolute lust (though peradventure
I stand accountant[73] for as great a sin),
But partly led to diet[74] my revenge,
For that I do suspect the lusty Moor
Hath leap'd into my seat; the thought whereof
Doth like a poisonous mineral [75] gnaw my inwards.
And nothing can nor shall content my soul
Till I am even'd with him, wife for wife,—
Or failing so, yet that I put the Moor
At least into a jealousy so strong
That judgment cannot cure. Which thing to do,
If this poor trash of Venice, whom I thrash
For his quick hunting,[76] stand the putting-on,[77]
I'll have our Michael Cassio on the hip,[78]
Abuse him to the Moor in the rank garb[79]

---

[64] Intimacies.   [65] Carnal.   [66] Disparaging.   [67] Provide.   [68] Anger.
[69] Appeasement.   [70] Satisfactory condition.   [71] Promote.   [72] Likely and most credible.
[73] Accountable.   [74] Feed.   [75] Drug.   [76] To make a better hunter of him.   [77] Inciting.
[78] Bring Cassio down.
[79] In the grossest manner, i.e., by accusing him of cuckolding Othello.

(For I fear Cassio with my night-cap too),
Make the Moor thank me, love me, and reward me
For making him egregiously an ass
And practising upon[80] his peace and quiet
Even to madness. 'Tis here, but yet confus'd:
Knavery's plain face is never seen till us'd.

[*Exit*]

SCENE SECOND: *A street.*

[*Enter* OTHELLO'S HERALD, *with a proclamation*]

HERALD.   It is Othello's pleasure, our noble and valiant general, that, upon certain tidings now arrived, importing the mere perdition[81] of the Turkish fleet, every man put himself into triumph;[82] some to dance, some to make bonfires, each man to what sport and revels his addiction leads him; for, besides these beneficial news, it is the celebration of his nuptial. So much was his pleasure should be proclaimed. All offices[83] are open, and there is full liberty of feasting from this present hour of five till the bell have tolled eleven. Heaven bless the isle of Cyprus and our noble general Othello!

[*Exit*]

SCENE THIRD: *A hall in the Citadel.*

[*Enter* OTHELLO, DESDEMONA, CASSIO, *and* ATTENDANTS]

OTHELLO.   Good Michael, look you to the guard to-night.
Let's teach ourselves that honorable stop,
Not to outsport discretion.

CASSIO.   Iago hath direction what to do;
But, notwithstanding, with my personal eye
Will I look to't.

OTHELLO.   Iago is most honest.
Michael, good night. To-morrow with your earliest[84]
Let me have speech with you.
            [*To* DESDEMONA]   Come, my dear love.
The purchase made, the fruits are to ensue;
The profit's yet to come 'twixt me and you.
Good night.
                [*Exeunt* OTHELLO *and* DESDEMONA *and* ATTENDANTS]
    [*Enter* IAGO]

CASSIO.   Welcome, Iago; we must to the watch.

IAGO.   Not this hour, lieutenant; 'tis not yet ten o'clock. Our general cast[85] us thus early for the love of his Desdemona,—who let us not therefore

---

[80] Plotting against.   [81] Utter destruction.   [82] Celebrate.
[83] Kitchens where free food and drink would be dispensed.   [84] At the earliest.
[85] Dismissed.

blame. He hath not yet made wanton the night with her, and she is sport for Jove.

CASSIO. She's a most exquisite lady.

IAGO. And, I'll warrant her, full of game.

CASSIO. Indeed, she is a most fresh and delicate creature.

IAGO. What an eye she has! Methinks it sounds a parley of provocation.[86]

CASSIO. An inviting eye, and yet methinks right modest.

IAGO. And when she speaks, is it not an alarum[87] to love?

CASSIO. She is indeed perfection.

IAGO. Well, happiness to their sheets! Come, lieutenant, I have a stoup of wine, and here without are a brace of Cyprus gallants that would fain have a measure to the health of black Othello.

CASSIO. Not to-night, good Iago. I have very poor and unhappy brains for drinking. I could well wish courtesy would invent some other custom of entertainment.

IAGO. O they are our friends. But one cup. I'll drink for you.

CASSIO. I have drunk but one cup to-night, and that was craftily qualified[88] too, and, behold, what innovation[89] it makes here. I am unfortunate in the infirmity, and dare not task my weakness with any more.

IAGO. What, man! 'tis a night of revels. The gallants desire it.

CASSIO. Where are they?

IAGO. Here at the door. I pray you, call them in.

CASSIO. I'll do't; but it dislikes[90] me.

IAGO. If I can fasten but one cup upon him,
With that which he hath drunk to-night already,
He'll be as full of quarrel and offence
As my young mistress' dog. Now, my sick fool Roderigo,
Whom love hath turn'd almost the wrong side out,
To Desdemona hath to-night carous'd
Potations pottle-deep;[91] and he's to watch.
Three lads of Cyprus, noble swelling spirits,
That hold their honors in a wary distance,[92]
The very elements[93] of this warlike isle,
Have I to-night fluster'd with flowing cups,
And they watch too. Now, 'mongst this flock of drunkards,
Am I to put our Cassio in some action
That may offend the isle. But here they come.
If consequence do but approve my dream,
My boat sails freely, both with wind and stream.

[*Enter* CASSIO, MONTANO, *and* GENTLEMEN (BOYS *following with wine*)]

CASSIO. 'Fore God, they have given me a rouse[94] already.

MONTANO. Good faith, a little one. Not past a pint, as I am a soldier.

IAGO. Some wine, ho!

[*Sings*]

---

[86] Invites to love.   [87] Summons.   [88] Diluted.   [89] Disturbance.   [90] Displeases.
[91] To the bottom of the cup.   [92] Who are very sensitive about their honor.
[93] Representative types.   [94] A full drink.

> And let me the canikin clink, clink;
> And let me the canikin clink.
> A soldier's a man;
> O man's life's but a span;
> Why then let a soldier drink.

Some wine, boys!

CASSIO. 'Fore God, an excellent song.

IAGO. I learned it in England, where indeed they are most potent in potting.[95] Your Dane, your German, and your swag-bellied Hollander,—drink, ho!—are nothing to your English.

CASSIO. Is your Englishman so exquisite in his drinking?

IAGO. Why, he drinks you with facility your Dane dead drunk. He sweats not to overthrow your Almain.[96] He gives your Hollander a vomit ere the next pottle can be filled.

CASSIO. To the health of our general!

MONTANO. I am for it, lieutenant; and I'll do you justice.[97]

IAGO. O sweet England!

[*Sings*]

> King Stephen was and—a worthy peer,
>   His breeches cost him but a crown.
> He held them sixpence all too dear,
>   With that he call'd the tailor lown.[98]
> He was a wight of high renown,
>   And thou art but of low degree.
> 'Tis pride that pulls the country down,
>   Then take thine owd [99] cloak about thee.

Some wine, ho!

CASSIO. 'Fore God, this is a more exquisite song than the other.

IAGO. Will you hear't again?

CASSIO. No; for I hold him to be unworthy of his place that does those things. Well, God's above all; and there be souls must be saved, and there be souls must not be saved.

IAGO. It's true, good lieutenant.

CASSIO. For mine own part,—no offence to the general, nor any man of quality, —I hope to be saved.

IAGO. And so do I too, lieutenant.

CASSIO. Ay; but, by your leave, not before me. The lieutenant is to be saved before the ancient. Let's have no more of this; let's to our affairs. God forgive us our sins! Gentlemen, let's look to our business. Do not think gentlemen, I am drunk. This is my ancient; this is my right hand, and this is my left hand. I am not drunk now. I can stand well enough, and I speak well enough.

GENTLEMEN. Excellent well.

CASSIO. Why, very well, then. You must not think then that I am drunk.

[*Exit*]

---

[95] Big drinkers.   [96] German.   [97] I'll keep up with you in drinking.   [98] Lout.
[99] Old.

MONTANO. To the platform,[100] masters. Come, let's set the watch.

IAGO. You see this fellow that is gone before.
He is a soldier fit to stand by Cæsar
And give direction; and do but see his vice.
'Tis to his virtue a just equinox,[101]
The one as long as th' other. 'Tis pity of him.
I fear the trust Othello puts him in,
On some odd time of his infirmity,
Will shake this island.

MONTANO.   But is he often thus?

IAGO. 'Tis evermore the prologue to his sleep:
He'll watch the horologe a double set,[102]
If drink rock not his cradle.

MONTANO.   It were well
The general were put in mind of it.
Perhaps he sees it not, or his good nature
Prizes the virtue that appears in Cassio,
And looks not on his evils. Is not this true?
  [*Enter* RODERIGO]

IAGO [*Aside to him*] How now, Roderigo?
I pray you, after the lieutenant. Go!

                                        [*Exit* RODERIGO]

MONTANO. And 'tis great pity that the noble Moor
Should hazard such a place as his own second
With one of an ingraft[103] infirmity.
It were an honest action to say
So to the Moor.

IAGO.   Not I, for this fair island:
I do love Cassio well, and would do much
                    [*Cry* 'Help! Help!' *within*]
To cure him of this evil. But hark! what noise?
  [*Enter* CASSIO, *driving in* RODERIGO]

CASSIO. Zounds! You rogue, you rascal!

MONTANO. What's the matter, lieutenant?

CASSIO. A knave teach me my duty! I'll beat the knave into a twiggen[104] bottle.

RODERIGO. Beat me?

CASSIO. Dost thou prate, rogue? [*Striking* RODERIGO]

MONTANO. [*Staying him*] Nay, good lieutenant. I pray you, sir, hold your hand.

CASSIO. Let me go, sir, or I'll knock you o'er the mazzard.[105]

MONTANO. Come, come; you're drunk.

CASSIO. Drunk!
  [*They fight*]

IAGO. [*Aside to* RODERIGO] Away, I say! Go out, and cry a mutiny.
                                        [*Exit* RODERIGO]

---

[100] Ramparts.   [101] Exact equivalent.   [102] Stay up for twenty-four hours.   [103] Engrafted.
[104] Wicker.   [105] Head.

Nay, good lieutenant! God's will, gentlemen!
Help, ho! Lieutenant! Sir Montano! sir!
Help, masters! Here's a goodly watch indeed!
[*A bell rung*]
Who's that that rings the bell? *Diablo*,[106] ho!
The town will rise. God's will! lieutenant, hold!
You will be sham'd for ever.
[*Enter* OTHELLO *and* GENTLEMEN *with weapons*]

OTHELLO.   What is the matter here?

MONTANO. Zounds! I bleed still. I am hurt to the death.

OTHELLO. Hold, for your lives!

IAGO. Hold, hold, lieutenant! Sir Montano! gentlemen!
Have you forgot all sense of place and duty?
Hold! the general speaks to you; hold for shame!

OTHELLO. Why, how now, ho! from whence arises this?
Are we turn'd Turks, and to ourselves do that
Which heaven has forbid the Ottomites?
For Christian shame put by this barbarous brawl.
He that stirs next to carve for[107] his own rage
Holds his soul light; he dies upon his motion.
Silence that dreadful bell! it frights the isle
From her propriety.[108] What's the matter, masters?
Honest Iago, that looks dead with grieving,
Speak, who began this? On thy love, I charge thee.

IAGO. I do not know. Friends all but now, even now,
In quarter and in terms[109] like bride and groom
Devesting them for bed; and then, but now
(As if some planet had unwitted men[110])
Swords out, and tilting one at other's breast,
In opposition bloody. I cannot speak
Any beginning to this peevish odds,[111]
And would in action glorious I had lost
These legs that brought me to a part of it!

OTHELLO. How came it, Michael, you were thus forgot? [112]

CASSIO. I pray you, pardon me; I cannot speak.

OTHELLO. Worthy Montano, you were wont be civil.
The gravity and stillness[113] of your youth
The world hath noted, and your name is great
In mouths of wisest censure.[114] What's the matter,
That you unlace your reputation thus
And spend your rich opinion[115] for the name
Of a night-brawler? give me answer to't.

MONTANO. Worthy Othello, I am hurt to danger.
Your officer, Iago, can inform you

---

[106] The devil.   [107] Satisfy.   [108] Natural habits.   [109] At peace.
[110] As if some evil star had deprived men of their reason.   [111] Silly quarrel.
[112] That you so forgot yourself.   [113] Dignified behavior.
[114] Judgment.   [115] Reputation.

(While I spare speech, which something[116] now offends[117] me)
Of all that I do know; nor know I aught
By me that's said or done amiss this night,
Unless self-charity[118] be sometime a vice,
And to defend ourselves it be a sin
When violence assails us.

OTHELLO.   Now, by heaven,
My blood begins my safer guides to rule,
And passion, having my best judgment collied,[119]
Assays to lead the way. Zounds! If I stir,
Or do but lift this arm, the best of you
Shall sink in my rebuke. Give me to know
How this foul rout[120] began, who set it on;
And he that is approv'd [121] in this offence,
Though he had twinn'd with me—both at a birth—
Shall lose me. What! in a town of war,
Yet wild, the people's hearts brimful of fear,
To manage[122] private and domestic quarrels
In night, and on the court and guard of safety!
'Tis monstrous. Iago, who began't?

MONTANO.   If partially affin'd, or leagu'd in office,[123]
Thou dost deliver more or less than truth,
Thou art no soldier.

IAGO.   Touch me not so near.
I had rather have this tongue cut from my mouth
Than it should do offence to Michael Cassio;
Yet I persuade myself, to speak the truth
Shall nothing wrong him. Thus it is, general.
Montano and myself being in speech,
There comes a fellow crying out for help,
And Cassio following him with determin'd sword
To execute upon him. Sir, this gentleman
Steps in to Cassio, and entreats his pause.[124]
Myself the crying fellow did pursue,
Lest by his clamor (as it so fell out)
The town might fall in fright. He, swift of foot,
Outran my purpose, and I return'd the rather[125]
For that I heard the clink and fall of swords,
And Cassio high in oath, which till to-night
I ne'er might say before. When I came back
(For this was brief), I found them close together,
At blow and thrust, even as again they were
When you yourself did part them.
More of this matter can I not report,

---

[116] Somewhat.   [117] Hurts.   [118] Self-love, the desire for self-preservation.   [119] Blackened.
[120] Riot.   [121] Found guilty.   [122] Carry on.
[123] If biased because of your affection or because he is a fellow officer.
[124] Asks him to stop.   [125] Sooner.

But men are men; the best sometimes forget.
Though Cassio did some little wrong to him,[126]
As men in rage strike those that wish them best,
Yet surely Cassio, I believe, receiv'd
From him that fled some strange indignity,
Which patience could not pass.

OTHELLO.   I know, Iago,
Thy honesty and love doth mince this matter,
Making it light to Cassio. Cassio, I love thee;
But never more be officer of mine—
[*Enter* DESDEMONA, *with others*]
Look, if my gentle love be not rais'd up!—
[*To* CASSIO] I'll make thee an example.

DESDEMONA.   What's the matter?

OTHELLO.   All's well now, sweeting. Come away to bed.—
Sir, for your hurts, myself will be your surgeon.
Lead him off.

[MONTANO *is led off*]

Iago, look with care about the town,
And silence those whom this vile brawl distracted.
Come, Desdemona; 'tis the soldiers' life,
To have their balmy slumbers wak'd with strife.

[*Exeunt* MOOR, DESDEMONA, *and* ATTENDANTS]

IAGO.   What! are you hurt, lieutenant?

CASSIO.   Ay, past all surgery.

IAGO.   Marry, God forbid!

CASSIO.   Reputation, reputation, reputation! O! I have lost my reputation. I
have lost the immortal part of myself, and what remains is bestial. My
reputation, Iago, my reputation!

IAGO.   As I am an honest man, I thought you had received some bodily wound.
There is more sense in that than in reputation. Reputation is an idle and
most false imposition,[127] oft got without merit, and lost without deserving.
You have lost no reputation at all, unless you repute yourself such a loser.
What, man! there are ways to recover[128] the general again. You are but
now cast in his mood [129] (a punishment more in policy than in malice),
even so as one would beat his offenceless dog to affright an imperious lion.
Sue to him again, and he is yours.

CASSIO.   I will rather sue to be despised than to deceive so good a commander
with so slight, so drunken, and so indiscreet an officer. Drunk! and speak
parrot! [130] and squabble, swagger, swear, and discourse fustian[131] with one's
own shadow! O thou invisible spirit of wine! if thou hast no name to be
known by, let us call thee devil!

IAGO.   What was he that you followed with your sword? What had he done to
you?

CASSIO.   I know not.

IAGO.   Is't possible?

---

[126] Here Montano.   [127] Artificial addition, i.e., not in nature.   [128] Regain favor with.
[129] Dismissed as the result of a whim.   [130] Gibberish.   [131] Nonsense.

CASSIO.   I remember a mass of things, but nothing distinctly; a quarrel, but nothing wherefore. O God! that men should put an enemy in their mouths to steal away their brains; that we should, with joy, revel, pleasure, and applause, transform ourselves into beasts.

IAGO.   Why, but you are now well enough. How came you thus recovered?

CASSIO.   It hath pleased the devil drunkenness to give place to the devil wrath. One unperfectness shows me another, to make me frankly despise myself.

IAGO.   Come, you are too severe a moraler. As the time, the place, and the condition of this country stands, I could heartily wish this had not so befallen, but since it is as it is, mend it for your own good.

CASSIO.   I will ask him for my place again. He shall tell me I am a drunkard. Had I as many mouths as Hydra,[132] such an answer would stop them all. To be now a sensible man, by and by a fool, and presently a beast! O strange! Every inordinate cup is unblessed and the ingredient is a devil.

IAGO.   Come, come; good wine is a good familiar creature if it be well used. Exclaim no more against it. And, good lieutenant, I think you think I love you.

CASSIO.   I have well approved it, sir. I drunk!

IAGO.   You or any man living may be drunk at some time. I'll tell you what you shall do. Our general's wife is now the general. I may say so in this respect, for that he has devoted and given up himself to the contemplation, mark, and denotement[133] of her parts and graces. Confess yourself freely to her; importune her help to put you in your place again. She is of so free, so kind, so apt, so blessed a disposition, that she holds it a vice in her goodness not to do more than she is requested. This broken joint between you and her husband entreat her to splinter,[134] and my fortunes against any lay[135] worth naming, this crack of your love shall grow stronger than it was before.

CASSIO.   You advise me well.

IAGO.   I protest, in the sincerity of love and honest kindness.

CASSIO.   I think it freely; and betimes in the morning will I beseech the virtuous Desdemona to undertake for me. I am desperate of my fortunes[136] if they check me here.

IAGO.   You are in the right. Good night, lieutenant; I must to the watch.

CASSIO.   Good night, honest Iago!

[*Exit* CASSIO]

IAGO.   And what's he, then, that says I play the villain,
When this advice is free I give and honest,
Probal [137] to thinking and indeed the course
To win the Moor again? For 'tis most easy
Th' inclining Desdemona to subdue
In any honest suit; she's fram'd as fruitful [138]
As the free elements.[139] And then for her
To win the Moor,—were't to renounce his baptism,
All seals and symbols of redeemed sin,
His soul is so enfetter'd to her love,

---

[132] A multiheaded beast slain by Hercules.   [133] Close observation.   [134] Put in splints, heal.
[135] Bet.   [136] Future success.   [137] Probable.   [138] Created as bountiful.   [139] Air.

That she may make, unmake, do what she list,
Even as her appetite shall play the god
With his weak function.[140] How am I, then, a villain
To counsel Cassio to this parallel course
Directly to his good? Divinity of hell!
When devils will their blackest sins put on,[141]
They do suggest[142] at first with heavenly shows,
As I do now; for while this honest fool
Plies Desdemona to repair his fortunes,
And she for him pleads strongly to the Moor,
I'll pour this pestilence into his ear
That she repeals[143] him for her body's lust;
And, by how much she strives to do him good,
She shall undo her credit with the Moor.
So will I turn her virtue into pitch,
And out of her own goodness make the net
That shall enmesh them all.
[*Enter* RODERIGO]
How now, Roderigo?

RODERIGO.   I do follow here in the chase, not like a hound that hunts, but one that fills up the cry. My money is almost spent; I have been tonight exceedingly well cudgelled; and I think the issue will be, I shall have so much experience for my pains; and so, with no money at all and a little more wit,[144] return again to Venice.

IAGO.   How poor are they that have not patience!
What wound did ever heal but by degrees?
Thou know'st we work by wit and not by witchcraft,
And wit depends on dilatory time.
Does't not go well? Cassio has beaten thee,
And thou by that small hurt hast cashiered Cassio.
Though other things grow fair against the sun,
Yet fruits that blossom first will first be ripe.
Content thyself awhile. By the mass, 'tis morning;
Pleasure and action make the hours seem short.
Retire thee; go where thou art billeted.
Away, I say; thou shalt know more hereafter.
Nay, get thee gone.

[*Exit* RODERIGO]

Two things are to be done:
My wife must move for[145] Cassio to her mistress—
I'll set her on—;
Myself awhile to draw the Moor apart,
And bring him jump[146] when he may Cassio find
Soliciting his wife. Ay, that's the way.
Dull not device[147] by coldness and delay.

[*Exit*]

---

[140] Qualities.   [141] Instigate.   [142] Seduce.   [143] Desires his return to favor.
[144] Intelligence.   [145] Urge support for.   [146] Precisely, just.   [147] A scheme or plan.

Act Third

[*Enter* CASSIO *with* MUSICIANS]

CASSIO. Masters, play here, I will content your pains.[1]
    Something that's brief, and bid 'Good morrow, general.'
    [*They play, and enter the* CLOWN]

CLOWN. Why, masters, ha' your instruments been at Naples, that they speak
    i' th' nose thus? [2]

MUSICIAN. How, sir? how?

CLOWN. Are these, I pray, called wind-instruments?

MUSICIAN. Ay, marry, are they, sir.

CLOWN. O! thereby hangs a tail.

MUSICIAN. Whereby hangs a tale, sir?

CLOWN. Marry, sir, by many a wind-instrument that I know. But, masters,
    here's money for you; and the general so likes your music that he desires
    you, for love's sake, to make no more noise with it.

MUSICIAN. Well, sir, we will not.

CLOWN. If you have any music that may not be heard, to't again; but (as
    they say) to hear music the general does not greatly care.

MUSICIAN. We ha' none such, sir.

CLOWN. Then put up your pipes in your bag, for I'll away. Go; vanish into
    air; away!

                                [*Exeunt* MUSICIANS]

CASSIO. Dost thou hear, my honest friend?

CLOWN. No, I hear not your honest friend; I hear you.

CASSIO. Prithee, keep up thy quillets.[3] There's a poor piece of gold for thee. If
    the gentlewoman that attends the general's wife be stirring, tell her there's
    one Cassio entreats her a little favor of speech. Wilt thou do this?

CLOWN. She is stirring, sir. If she will stir hither, I shall seem to notify unto
    her.

CASSIO. Do, good my friend.

                                  [*Exit* CLOWN]

[*Enter* IAGO]

                        In happy time,[4] Iago.

IAGO. You ha' not been a-bed, then?

CASSIO. Why, no. The day had broke
    Before we parted. I ha' made bold, Iago,
    To send in to your wife. My suit to her
    Is that she will to virtuous Desdemona
    Procure me some access.

IAGO.   I'll send her to you presently,[5]
    And I'll devise a mean to draw the Moor

---

[1] Requite your labor.   [2] A reference to the nasal quality of the Neapolitan dialect and a
double-entendre reference to venereal disease (the Neapolitan disease).   [3] Quibbles.
[4] Glad to see you.   [5] Immediately.

Out of the way, that your converse and business
May be more free.

CASSIO. I humbly thank you for't.

[*Exit* IAGO]

I never knew

A Florentine[6] more kind and honest.

[*Enter* EMILIA]

EMILIA. Good morrow, good lieutenant. I am sorry
For your displeasure;[7] but all will soon be well.
The general and his wife are talking of it,
And she speaks for you stoutly. The Moor replies
That he you hurt is of great fame in Cyprus
And great affinity,[8] and that in wholesome wisdom
He might not but refuse you;[9] but he protests he loves you,
And needs no other suitor but his likings
To take the saf'st occasion by the front
To bring you in again.

CASSIO.   Yet, I beseech you,
If you think fit, or that it may be done,
Give me advantage of some brief discourse
With Desdemona alone.

EMILIA.   Pray you, come in.
I will bestow you where you shall have time
To speak your bosom[10] freely.

CASSIO.   I am much bound to you.

[*Exeunt*]

SCENE SECOND: A room in the Citadel.

[*Enter* OTHELLO, IAGO, *and other* GENTLEMEN]

OTHELLO. These letters give, Iago, to the pilot,
And by him do my duties[11] to the Senate.
That done, I will be walking on the works;[12]
Repair there to me.

IAGO.   Well, my good lord, I'll do't.

OTHELLO. This fortification, gentlemen, shall we see't?

GENTLEMEN. We wait upon your lordship.

[*Exeunt*]

SCENE THIRD: The garden of the Citadel.

[*Enter* DESDEMONA, CASSIO, *and* EMILIA]

DESDEMONA. Be thou assur'd, good Cassio, I will do
All my abilities in thy behalf.

---

[6] One of my own countrymen.   [7] Misfortune.   [8] Connections.
[9] He had to relieve you of your position.   [10] Inner thoughts.
[11] Present my loyal compliments.   [12] Fortifications.

EMILIA. Good madam, do. I know it grieves my husband,
    As if the case were his.
DESDEMONA. O that's an honest fellow! Do not doubt, Cassio,
    But I will have my lord and you again
    As friendly as you were.
CASSIO.   Bounteous madam,
    Whatever shall become of Michael Cassio,
    He's never anything but your true servant.
DESDEMONA. O, sir, I thank you. You do love my lord.
    You have known him long; and be you well assur'd
    He shall in strangeness[13] stand no farther off
    Than in a politic distance.
CASSIO.   Ay, but, lady,
    That policy may either last so long,
    Or feed upon such nice[14] and waterish diet,
    Or breed itself so out of circumstances,[15]
    That, I being absent and my place supplied,
    My general will forget my love and service.
DESDEMONA. Do not doubt that. Before Emilia here
    I give thee warrant of thy place.[16] Assure thee,
    If I do vow a friendship, I'll perform it
    To the last article. My lord shall never rest;
    I'll watch him tame,[17] and talk him out of patience;
    His bed shall seem a school, his board a shrift;[18]
    I'll intermingle everything he does
    With Cassio's suit. Therefore be merry, Cassio;
    For thy solicitor shall rather die
    Than give thy cause away.
    [*Enter* OTHELLO *and* IAGO *at a distance*]
EMILIA. Madam, here comes my lord.
CASSIO. Madam, I'll take my leave.
DESDEMONA. Why, stay, and hear me speak.
CASSIO. Madam, not now. I am very ill at ease,
    Unfit for mine own purposes.[19]
DESDEMONA. Well, do your discretion.

                                            [*Exit* CASSIO]

IAGO. Ha! I like not that.
OTHELLO.   What dost thou say?
IAGO. Nothing, my lord; or if—I know not what.
OTHELLO. Was not that Cassio parted from my wife?
IAGO. Cassio, my lord? No, sure, I cannot think it,
    That he would steal away so guilty-like,
    Seeing you coming.
OTHELLO.   I do believe 'twas he.

---

[13] Aloofness.   [14] Fastidious.   [15] Get used to the new conditions, i.e., to doing without me.
[16] Guarantee that the position will be yours again.
[17] A phrase taken from falconry. Falcons were tamed by depriving them of sleep.
[18] Confessional.   [19] In no condition to argue my own case.

DESDEMONA. How now, my lord!
  I have been talking with a suitor here.
  A man that languishes in your displeasure.
OTHELLO. Who is't you mean?
DESDEMONA. Why, your lieutenant, Cassio. Good my lord,
  If I have any grace or power to move you,
  His present reconciliation take;
  For if he be not one that truly loves you,
  That errs in ignorance and not in cunning,[20]
  I have no judgment in an honest face.
  I prithee call him back.
OTHELLO.   Went he hence now?
DESDEMONA. Yes, faith; so humbled,
  That he has left part of his griefs with me.
  I suffer with him. Good love, call him back.
OTHELLO. Not now, sweet Desdemon. Some other time.
DESDEMONA. But shall't be shortly?
OTHELLO.   The sooner, sweet, for you.
DESDEMONA. Shall't be to-night at supper?
OTHELLO.   No, not to-night.
DESDEMONA. To-morrow dinner then?
OTHELLO.   I shall not dine at home.
  I meet the captains at the citadel.
DESDEMONA. Why then, to-morrow night, or Tuesday morn;
  On Tuesday noon, or night; on Wednesday morn.
  I prithee name the time, but let it not
  Exceed three days. I' faith, he's penitent;
  And yet his trespass, in our common reason[21]
  (Save that they say, the wars must make examples
  Out of their best), is not almost a fault[22]
  T' incur a private check. When shall he come?
  Tell me, Othello. I wonder in my soul,
  What you could ask me that I should deny,
  Or stand so mammering[23] on. What? Michael Cassio,
  That came a-wooing with you, and so many a time,
  When I have spoke of you dispraisingly,
  Hath ta'en your part; to have so much to do
  To bring him in! [24] By 'r Lady, I could do much—
OTHELLO. Prithee, no more! Let him come when he will.
  I will deny thee nothing.
DESDEMONA.   Why, this is not a boon.
  'Tis as I should entreat you wear your gloves,
  Or feed on nourishing dishes, or keep you warm,
  Or sue to you to do a peculiar profit
  To your own person. Nay, when I have a suit
  Wherein I mean to touch your love indeed,

[20] Wittingly.   [21] Common sense.   [22] Is hardly a fault.   [23] Hesitating.
[24] Into your favor.

It shall be full of poise[25] and difficulty,
And fearful [26] to be granted.

OTHELLO.   I will deny thee nothing.
Whereon, I do beseech thee, grant me this,
To leave me but a little to myself.

DESDEMONA.   Shall I deny you? No. Farewell, my lord.

OTHELLO.   Farewell, my Desdemona. I'll come to thee straight.

DESDEMONA.   Emilia, come. Be it as your fancies teach you.[27]
Whate'er you be, I am obedient.

[*Exeunt* DESDEMONA *and* EMILIA]

OTHELLO.   Excellent wretch! Perdition catch my soul
But I do love thee! and when I love thee not,
Chaos is come again.[28]

IAGO.   My noble lord,—

OTHELLO.   What dost thou say, Iago?

IAGO.   Did Michael Cassio, when you woo'd my lady,
Know of your love?

OTHELLO.   He did, from first to last. Why dost thou ask?

IAGO.   But for a satisfaction of my thought.
No further harm.

OTHELLO.   Why of thy thought, Iago?

IAGO.   I did not think he had been acquainted with her.

OTHELLO.   O yes; and went between us very oft.

IAGO.   Indeed?

OTHELLO.   Indeed? ay, indeed. Discern'st thou aught in that?
Is he not honest?

IAGO.   Honest, my lord?

OTHELLO.   Honest? ay, honest.

IAGO.   My lord, for aught I know.

OTHELLO.   What dost thou think?

IAGO.   Think, my lord?

OTHELLO.   Think, my lord?
By heaven, he echoes me,
As if there were some monster in his thought
Too hideous to be shown.—Thou didst mean something.
I heard thee say but now, thou lik'st not that,
When Cassio left my wife. What didst not like?
And when I told thee he was of my counsel
In my whole course of wooing, thou criedst, 'Indeed?'
And didst contract and purse thy brow together,
As if thou then hadst shut up in thy brain
Some horrible conceit.[29] If thou dost love me,
Show me thy thought.

IAGO.   My lord, you know I love you.

OTHELLO.   I think thou dost;

---

[25] Weight.   [26] Hard.   [27] As you please.
[28] The world returns to the original chaos out of which it was created.
[29] Notion.

And, for[30] I know thou'rt full of love and honesty,
And weigh'st thy words before thou give 'em breath,
Therefore these stops of thine fright me the more;
For such things in a false disloyal knave
Are tricks of custom,[31] but in a man that's just
They are close delations,[32] working from the heart
That passion cannot rule.

IAGO.   For Michael Cassio,
I dare be sworn I think that he is honest.

OTHELLO.   I think so too.

IAGO.   Men should be what they seem;
Or those that be not, would they might seem none! [33]

OTHELLO.   Certain, men should be what they seem.

IAGO.   Why then, I think Cassio's an honest man.

OTHELLO.   Nay, yet there's more in this.
I pray thee, speak to me as to thy thinkings,
As thou dost ruminate, and give thy worst of thoughts
The worst of words.

IAGO.   Good my lord, pardon me:
Though I am bound to every act of duty,
I am not bound to that all slaves are free to.
Utter my thoughts? Why, say they are vile and false;
As where's that palace whereinto foul things
Sometimes intrude not? who has a breast so pure
But some uncleanly apprehensions
Keep leets and law-days,[34] and in session sit
With meditations lawful?

OTHELLO.   Thou dost conspire against thy friend, Iago,
If thou but think'st him wrong'd, and mak'st his ear
A stranger to thy thoughts.

IAGO.   I do beseech you,
Though I perchance am vicious[35] in my guess
(As, I confess, it is my nature's plague
To spy into abuses, and oft my jealousy[36]
Shapes faults that are not)—I entreat you then,
From one that so imperfectly conjects,[37]
You'ld take no notice nor build yourself a trouble
Out of my scattering and unsure observance.
It were not for your quiet nor your good,
Nor for my manhood, honesty, or wisdom,
To let you know my thoughts.

OTHELLO.   What dost thou mean?

IAGO.   Good name in man, and woman, dear my lord,
Is the immediate[38] jewel of our souls.
Who steals my purse steals trash. 'Tis something, nothing;

---

[30] Because.   [31] Customary.   [32] Secret accusations.   [33] Not to be men at all.
[34] Both phrases mean literally "attend court on the days when it is in session."
[35] Wrong.   [36] Suspicion.   [37] Makes conjectures.   [38] Most precious.

'Twas mine, 'tis his, and has been slave to thousands;
But he that filches from me my good name
Robs me of that which not enriches him,
And makes me poor indeed.

OTHELLO.   By heaven, I'll know thy thought.

IAGO.   You cannot, if my heart were in your hand;
Nor shall not, whilst 'tis in my custody.

OTHELLO.   Ha!

IAGO.   O beware, my lord, of jealousy!
It is the green-ey'd monster which doth mock[39]
The meat it feeds on. That cuckold lives in bliss
Who, certain of his fate, loves not his wronger;
But, O, what damned minutes tells he o'er
Who dotes, yet doubts; suspects, yet strongly loves!

OTHELLO.   O misery!

IAGO.   Poor and content is rich, and rich enough,
But riches fineless[40] is as poor as winter
To him that ever fears he shall be poor.
Good God, the souls of all my tribe defend
From jealousy.

OTHELLO.   Why, why is this?
Think'st thou I'd make a life of jealousy,
To follow still the changes of the moon
With fresh suspicions? No; to be once in doubt
Is once to be resolv'd.[41] Exchange me for a goat
When I shall turn the business of my soul
To such exsufflicate[42] and blown surmises,
Matching thy inference. 'Tis not to make me jealous
To say my wife is fair, feeds well, loves company,
Is free of speech, sings, plays, and dances well.
Where virtue is, these are more virtuous.
Nor from mine own weak merits will I draw
The smallest fear or doubt of her revolt;[43]
For she had eyes and chose me. No, Iago.
I'll see before I doubt; when I doubt, prove;
And, on the proof, there is no more but this:
Away at once with love or jealousy!

IAGO.   I am glad of this; for now I shall have reason
To show the love and duty that I bear you
With franker spirit. Therefore (as I am bound)[44]
Receive it from me—I speak not yet of proof.
Look to your wife. Observe her well with Cassio.
Wear your eye thus, not jealous nor secure.[45]
I would not have your free and noble nature
Out of self-bounty[46] be abus'd. Look to't!

---

[39] Makes a mockery of.   [40] Unlimited.   [41] To find out the truth at once.
[42] Blown up, inflated.   [43] Unfaithfulness.   [44] I.e., as it is my duty.   [45] Overconfident.
[46] Inherent goodness.

I know our country disposition well;
In Venice they do let God see the pranks
They dare not show their husbands. Their best conscience
Is not to leave undone, but keep unknown.

OTHELLO.   Dost thou say so?

IAGO.   She did deceive her father, marrying you:
And when she seem'd to shake and fear your looks,
She lov'd them most.

OTHELLO.   And so she did.

IAGO.   Why, go to, then.
She that so young could give out such a seeming,
To seel [47] her father's eyes up close as oak,—
He thought 'twas witchcraft—but I am much to blame.
I humbly do beseech you of your pardon
For too much loving you.

OTHELLO.   I am bound to thee for ever.

IAGO.   I see, this hath a little dash'd your spirits.

OTHELLO.   Not a jot, not a jot.

IAGO.   I' faith, I fear it has.
I hope you will consider what is spoke
Comes from my love. But I do see you're mov'd.
I am to pray you not to strain my speech
To grosser issues[48] nor to larger reach[49]
Than to suspicion.

OTHELLO.   I will not.

IAGO.   Should you do so, my lord,
My speech should fall into such vile success[50]
As my thoughts aim not at. Cassio's my trusty friend—
My lord, I see you're mov'd.

OTHELLO.   No, not much mov'd.
I do not think but Desdemona's honest.[51]

IAGO.   Long live she so! and long live you to think so!

OTHELLO.   And, yet, how nature erring from itself,—

IAGO.   Ay, there's the point: as (to be bold with you)
Not to affect[52] many proposed matches
Of her own clime, complexion, and degree,
Whereto, we see, in all things nature tends—
Foh! one may smell, in such a will, most rank,[53]
Foul disproportion, thoughts unnatural.
But pardon me; I do not in position[54]
Distinctly speak of her, though I may fear
Her will, recoiling[55] to her better judgment,
May fall [56] to match you with her country forms[57]
And happily[58] repent.

---

[47] Blind.   [48] Coarser conclusions.   [49] To a greater extent.   [50] Consequences.
[51] Applied to a woman, the word usually means, as here, "chaste."   [52] Favor.
[53] Lustful.   [54] Out of definite proof.   [55] Readjusting itself.   [56] Begin.
[57] Her native types.   [58] By chance.

OTHELLO.   Farewell, farewell.
  If more thou dost perceive, let me know more.
  Set on thy wife to observe. Leave me, Iago.
IAGO. My lord, I take my leave.

                                                 [Going]

OTHELLO. Why did I marry? This honest creature, doubtless,
  Sees and knows more, much more, than he unfolds.
IAGO. [*Returning*] My lord, I would I might entreat your honor
  To scan this thing no further; leave it to time.
  Though it be fit that Cassio have his place
  (For sure he fills it up with great ability),
  Yet if you please to hold him off awhile,
  You shall by that perceive him and his means.
  Note if your lady strain his entertainment[59]
  With any strong or vehement importunity;
  Much will be seen in that. In the mean time,
  Let me be thought too busy in my fears,
  As worthy cause I have to fear I am,
  And hold her free,[60] I do beseech your honor.
OTHELLO. Fear not my government.[61]
IAGO. I once more take my leave.

                                           [Exit IAGO*]*

OTHELLO. This fellow's of exceeding honesty,
  And knows all qualities,[62] with a learned spirit,
  Of human dealing. If I do prove her haggard,[63]
  Though that her jesses[64] were my dear heartstrings,
  I'd whistle her off and let her down the wind,[65]
  To prey at fortune. Haply, for I am black,
  And have not those soft parts of conversation[66]
  That chamberers[67] have, or for I am declin'd
  Into the vale of years (yet that's not much)—
  She's gone, I am abus'd, and my relief
  Must be to loathe her. O curse of marriage!
  That we can call these delicate creatures ours,
  And not their appetites. I had rather be a toad,
  And live upon the vapor of a dungeon,
  Than keep a corner in the thing I love
  For others' uses. Yet, 'tis the plague of great ones;
  Prerogativ'd [68] are they less than the base.
  'Tis destiny unshunnable, like death:
  Even then this forked plague[69] is fated to us
  When we do quicken.[70]
               Look, where she comes!

---

[59] Press his reinstatement.   [60] Guiltless.   [61] Self-control.   [62] Types of humans.
[63] Wild (literally, a "wild hawk").   [64] Straps by which hawks were held.
[65] Release her forever, as with a hawk.   [66] Social graces.   [67] Gallants at court.
[68] Privileged.   [69] Horns of the cuckold. It is an old belief that a cuckold grows horns.
[70] Become alive.

If she be false, O then heaven mocks itself.
I'll not believe't.
[*Enter* DESDEMONA *and* EMILIA]
DESDEMONA. How now, my dear Othello?
    Your dinner and the generous[71] islanders
    By you invited do attend your presence.
OTHELLO. I am to blame.
DESDEMONA.   Why is your speech so faint?
    Are you not well?
OTHELLO. I have a pain upon my forehead here.
DESDEMONA. Faith, that's with watching;[72] 'twill away again.
    Let me but bind your head; within this hour
    It will be well.
OTHELLO.   Your napkin[73] is too little.
[*He puts the handkerchief from him, and it drops*]
    Let it alone. Come, I'll go in with you.
DESDEMONA. I am very sorry that you are not well.
                        [*Exeunt* OTHELLO *and* DESDEMONA]
EMILIA. I am glad I have found this napkin.
    This was her first remembrance from the Moor.
    My wayward husband hath a hundred times
    Woo'd me to steal it, but she so loves the token
    (For he conjur'd her[74] she should ever keep it)
    That she reserves it evermore about her
    To kiss and talk to. I'll have the work ta'en out,[75]
    And give't Iago.
    What he will do with it heaven knows, not I.
    I nothing know, but for his fantasy—[76]
    [*Enter* IAGO]
IAGO. How now! what do you here alone?
EMILIA. Do not you chide. I have a thing for you.
IAGO. A thing for me? It is a common thing—
EMILIA. Ha?
IAGO. To have a foolish wife.
EMILIA. O, is that all? What will you give me now
    For that same handkerchief?
IAGO.   What handkerchief?
EMILIA. What handkerchief?
    Why, that the Moor first gave to Desdemona;
    That which so often you did bid me steal.
IAGO. Hast stol'n it from her?
EMILIA. No, faith. She let it drop by negligence,
    And, to th' advantage,[77] I, being here, took't up.
    Look, here it is.
IAGO.   A good wench! give it me.

---

[71] Noble.   [72] Lack of sleep.   [73] Handkerchief.   [74] Made her swear.
[75] Pattern copied.   [76] Whim.   [77] Making use of the opportunity.

EMILIA.   What will you do with't, that you have been so earnest
   To have me filch it?
IAGO.   Why, what's that to you?
   [*Snatches it*]
EMILIA.   If it be not for some purpose of import,
   Give me't again. Poor lady, she'll run mad
   When she shall lack it.
IAGO.   Be not acknown on't.[78] I have use for it.
   Go, leave me.

                                          [*Exit* EMILIA]

   I will in Cassio's lodging lose this napkin,
   And let him find it. Trifles light as air
   Are to the jealous confirmations strong
   As proofs of holy writ; this may do something.
   The Moor already changes with my poison.
   Dangerous conceits are in their natures poisons,
   Which at the first are scarce found to distaste,[79]
   But, with a little act[80] upon the blood,
   Burn like the mines of sulphur. I did say so.
   Look, where he comes [81]
   [*Enter* OTHELLO]
                         Not poppy, nor mandragora,
   Nor all the drowsy syrups of the world,
   Shall ever medicine thee to that sweet sleep
   Which thou ow'dst[82] yesterday.
OTHELLO.   Ha! ha! false to me?
IAGO.   Why, how now, general? No more of that.
OTHELLO.   Avaunt! be gone! Thou hast set me on the rack.
   I swear 'tis better to be much abus'd
   Than but to know't a little.
IAGO.   How now, my lord?
OTHELLO.   What sense had I of her stol'n hours of lust?
   I saw't not, thought it not, it harm'd not me.
   I slept the next night well, was free and merry;
   I found not Cassio's kisses on her lips.
   He that is robb'd, not wanting[83] what is stol'n,
   Let him not know't and he's not robb'd at all.
IAGO.   I am sorry to hear this.
OTHELLO.   I had been happy if the general camp,
   Pioneers[84] and all, had tasted her sweet body,
   So I had nothing known. O, now for ever
   Farewell the tranquil mind! farewell content!
   Farewell the plumed troops and the big wars
   That make ambition virtue! O, farewell!
   Farewell the neighing steed, and the shrill trump,

---

[78] Don't admit you know anything about it.   [79] Unpleasant.   [80] Action.
[81] Look, here's proof. Iago sees the agitated Othello approaching.   [82] Possessed.
[83] Missing.   [84] Pioneers, engineers. Then the lowest type of soldier.

The spirit-stirring drum, th' ear-piercing fife,
The royal banner, and all quality,[85]
Pride, pomp, and circumstance[86] of glorious war!
And, O ye mortal engines,[87] whose rude throats
Th' immortal Jove's great clamor counterfeit,[88]
Farewell! Othello's occupation's gone!

IAGO. Is't possible, my lord?

OTHELLO. Villain, be sure thou prove my love a whore,
Be sure of it! Give me the ocular proof;
Or by the worth of man's eternal soul,
Thou hadst been better have been born a dog
Than answer my wak'd wrath.

IAGO.   Is't come to this?

OTHELLO. Make me to see't; or, at the least, so prove it
That the probation[89] bear no hinge nor loop
To hang a doubt on, or woe upon thy life!

IAGO. My noble lord,—

OTHELLO. If thou dost slander her and torture me,
Never pray more. Abandon all remorse;[90]
On horror's head horrors accumulate;
Do deeds to make heaven weep, all earth amaz'd;
For nothing canst thou to damnation add
Greater than that.

IAGO.   O grace! O heaven defend me!
Are you a man? Have you a soul or sense?
God be wi' you! Take mine office. O wretched fool!
That liv'st to make thine honesty a vice.
O monstrous world! Take note, take note, O world,
To be direct and honest is not safe.
I thank you for this profit,[91] and from hence
I'll love no friend, sith[92] love breeds such offence.

OTHELLO. Nay, stay. Thou shouldst be honest.

IAGO. I should be wise, for honesty's a fool,
And loses that it works for.

OTHELLO.   By the world,
I think my wife be honest and think she is not;
I think that thou art just and think thou are not.
I'll have some proof. Her name, that was as fresh
As Dian's[93] visage, is now begrim'd and black
As mine own face. If there be cords or knives,
Poison or fire or suffocating streams,
I'll not endure it. Would I were satisfied!

IAGO. I see, sir, you are eaten up with passion.
I do repent me that I put it to you.[94]
You would be satisfied?

[85] Military hierarchy.   [86] Ceremony.   [87] Deadly cannon.
[88] Imitate thunder, i.e., Jove's thunderbolts.   [89] Proof.   [90] Pity.   [91] Profitable lesson.
[92] Since.   [93] Diana, goddess of chastity.   [94] Confided in you.

OTHELLO.   Would? Nay, I will!

IAGO.   And may; but how? How satisfied, my lord?
    Would you, the supervisor,[95] grossly gape on,
    Behold her topp'd?

OTHELLO.   Death and damnation! O!

IAGO.   It were a tedious difficulty, I think,
    To bring them to that prospect.[96] Damn them, then,
    If ever mortal eyes do see them bolster[97]
    More than their own. What then? how then?
    What shall I say? Where's satisfaction?
    It is impossible you should see this,
    Were they as prime[98] as goats, as hot as monkeys,
    As salt as wolves in pride,[99] and fools as gross
    As ignorance made drunk. But yet, I say,
    If imputation,[100] and strong circumstances,
    Which lead directly to the door of truth,
    Will give you satisfaction, you may have't.

OTHELLO.   Give me a living[101] reason she's disloyal.

IAGO.   I do not like the office;
    But sith I am enter'd in this cause so far
    (Prick'd [102] to't by foolish honesty and love),
    I will go on. I lay with Cassio lately;
    And, being troubled with a raging tooth,
    I could not sleep.
    There are a kind of men so loose of soul
    That in their sleeps will mutter their affairs.
    One of this kind is Cassio.
    In sleep I heard him say, 'Sweet Desdemona,
    Let us be wary, let us hide our loves!'
    And then, sir, would he gripe[103] and wring my hand,
    Cry out 'Sweet creature!' and then kiss me hard,
    As if he pluck'd up kisses by the roots
    That grew upon my lips; then laid his leg
    Over my thigh, and sigh'd, and kiss'd; and then
    Cried, 'Cursed fate, that gave thee to the Moor!'

OTHELLO.   O monstrous! monstrous!

IAGO.   Nay, this was but his dream.

OTHELLO.   But this denoted a foregone conclusion.[104]

IAGO.   'Tis a shrewd doubt,[105] though it be but a dream;
    And this may help to thicken other proofs
    That do demonstrate thinly.

OTHELLO.   I'll tear her all to pieces!

IAGO.   Nay, but be wise. Yet we see nothing done;
    She may be honest yet. Tell me but this:

---

[95] Looker-on.   [96] Situation (before an observer).
[97] In bed together, i.e., on the same bolster.   [98] Lecherous.   [99] In heat.   [100] Probability
[101] Tangible.   [102] Urged, spurred.   [103] Grip.   [104] An earlier experience.
[105] It provides good evidence for suspicion.

Have you not sometimes seen a handkerchief
Spotted with strawberries[106] in your wife's hand?
OTHELLO.   I gave her such a one. 'Twas my first gift.
IAGO.   I know not that; but such a handkerchief
(I am sure it was your wife's) did I to-day
See Cassio wipe his beard with.
OTHELLO.   If't be that,—
IAGO.   If it be that, or any that was hers,
It speaks against her with the other proofs.
OTHELLO.   O that the slave[107] had forty thousand lives!
One is too poor, too weak, for my revenge.
Now do I see 'tis true. Look here, Iago;
All my fond love thus do I blow to heaven.
'Tis gone.
Arise, black vengeance, from thy hollow[108] cell!
Yield up, O love, thy crown and hearted [109] throne
To tyrannous hate. Swell, bosom, with thy fraught,[110]
For 'tis of aspics' [111] tongues!
IAGO.   Pray, be content.[112]
OTHELLO.   O blood! Iago, blood!
IAGO.   Patience, I say. Your mind, perhaps, may change.
OTHELLO.   Never Iago. Like to the Pontic sea,[113]
Whose icy current and compulsive course
Ne'er feels retiring ebb, but keeps due on
To the Propontic and the Hellespont,
Even so my bloody thoughts, with violent pace,
Shall ne'er look back, ne'er ebb to humble love,
Till that a capable[114] and wide revenge
Swallow them up.
[*He kneels*]
                    Now, by yond marble[115] heaven,
In the due reverence of a sacred vow
I here engage[116] my words.
IAGO.   Do not rise yet.
[*Kneels*]
Witness, you ever-burning lights above!
You elements that clip us round about! [117]
Witness that here Iago doth give up
The execution of his wit, hands, heart,
To wrong'd Othello's service! Let him command,
And to obey shall be in me remorse,[118]
What bloody work soever.
[*They rise*]

---

[106] Embroidered with strawberry patterns.   [107] Cassio.   [108] Underground.
[109] In my heart.   [110] Freight, load.   [111] Asp, a small poisonous snake.   [112] Calm.
[113] Black Sea, the current of which was always supposed to run only in one direction to the Propontic (Sea of Marmora) and the Hellespont (Dardanelles).
[114] Comprehensive.   [115] Firm.   [116] Pledge.   [117] Surround us.   [118] Obligation.

OTHELLO.   I greet thy love,
  Not with vain thanks, but with acceptance bounteous,
  And will upon the instant put thee to't.[119]
  Within these three days let me hear thee say
  That Cassio's not alive.
IAGO. My friend is dead; 'tis done as you request.
  But let her live.
OTHELLO. Damn her, lewd minx! O, damn her!
  Come, go with me apart. I will withdraw
  To furnish me with some swift means of death
  For the fair devil. Now art thou my lieutenant.
IAGO. I am your own for ever.

                                                    [*Exeunt*]

SCENE FOURTH: *Before the Citadel.*

[*Enter* DESDEMONA, EMILIA, *and the* CLOWN]

DESDEMONA. Do you know, sirrah, where Lieutenant Cassio lies?
CLOWN. I dare not say he lies anywhere.
DESDEMONA. Why, man?
CLOWN. He is a soldier, and for one to say a soldier lies is stabbing.
DESDEMONA. Go to! Where lodges he?
CLOWN. To tell you where he lodges is to tell you where I lie.
DESDEMONA. Can anything be made of this?
CLOWN. I know not where he lodges, and for me to devise a lodging, and say he
  lies here or he lies there, were to lie in mine own throat.
DESDEMONA. Can you inquire him out, and be edified by report? [120]
CLOWN. I will catechize the world for him; that is, make questions, and by
  them answer.
DESDEMONA. Seek him. Bid him come hither; tell him I have moved my lord in
  his behalf, and hope all will be well.
CLOWN. To do this is within the compass of man's wit, and therefore I will
  attempt the doing it.

                                                    [*Exit* CLOWN]

DESDEMONA. Where should I lose that handkerchief, Emilia?
EMILIA. I know not, madam.
DESDEMONA. Believe me, I had rather have lost my purse
  Full of cruzadoes;[121] and but my noble Moor
  Is true of mind, and made of no such baseness
  As jealous creatures are, it were enough
  To put him to ill thinking.
EMILIA.   Is he not jealous?
DESDEMONA. Who, he? I think the sun where he was born
  Drew all such humors from him.
EMILIA.   Look where he comes!

---

[119] To the test.   [120] Benefit by the information thus obtained.   [121] Portuguese gold coins.

DESDEMONA. I will not leave him now till Cassio
  Be call'd to him.
  [*Enter* OTHELLO]
              How is't with you, my lord?
OTHELLO. Well, my good lady. [*Aside*] O hardness to dissemble!—
  How do you, Desdemona?
DESDEMONA.   Well, my good lord.
OTHELLO. Give me your hand. This hand is moist,[122] my lady.
DESDEMONA. It yet has felt no age nor known no sorrow.
OTHELLO. This argues fruitfulness and liberal heart:
  Hot, hot, and moist. This hand of yours requires
  A sequester[123] from liberty, fasting and prayer,
  Much castigation, exercise devout;
  For here's a young and sweating devil here
  That commonly rebels. 'Tis a good hand,
  A frank one.
DESDEMONA. You may, indeed, say so,
  For 'twas that hand that gave away my heart.
OTHELLO. A liberal hand! The hearts of old gave hands,
  But our new heraldry is hands not hearts.[124]
DESDEMONA. I cannot speak of this. Come now, your promise.
OTHELLO. What promise, chuck? [125]
DESDEMONA. I have sent to bid Cassio come speak with you.
OTHELLO. I have a salt and sorry rheum[126] offends me.
  Lend me thy handkerchief.
DESDEMONA.   Here, my lord.
OTHELLO. That which I gave you.
DESDEMONA.   I have it not about me.
OTHELLO. Not?
DESDEMONA. No, 'faith, my lord.
OTHELLO.   That is a fault.
  That handkerchief
  Did an Egyptian[127] to my mother give.
  She was a charmer[128] and could almost read
  The thoughts of people. She told her, while she kept it,
  'Twould make her amiable[129] and subdue my father
  Entirely to her love, but if she lost it
  Or made a gift of it, my father's eye
  Should hold her loathly, and his spirits should hunt
  After new fancies. She dying gave it me;
  And bid me, when my fate would have me wive,
  To give it her. I did so,—and take heed on't;
  Make it a darling like your precious eye.
  To lose or give't away were such perdition
  As nothing else could match.

---

[122] In folk-belief indicative of a lecherous nature.   [123] Separation.
[124] In the old days, marriage meant loyal love, now it has become a mere act.   [125] Dear.
[126] Distressing cold.   [127] Gipsy.   [128] Sorcerer.   [129] Desirable.

DESDEMONA. Is't possible?

OTHELLO. 'Tis true. There's magic in the web of it.
A sibyl,[130] that had number'd in the world
The sun to course two hundred compasses,[131]
In her prophetic fury[132] sew'd the work.
The worms were hallow'd that did breed the silk,
And it was dy'd in mummy[133] which the skilful
Conserv'd[134] of maidens' hearts.

DESDEMONA. I' faith? is't true?

OTHELLO. Most veritable; therefore look to't well.

DESDEMONA. Then would to God that I had never seen it!

OTHELLO. Ha? wherefore?

DESDEMONA. Why do you speak so startingly and rash?

OTHELLO. Is't lost? is't gone? Speak! Is't out o' the way?

DESDEMONA. Heaven bless us!

OTHELLO. Say you?

DESDEMONA. It is not lost: but what an if it were?

OTHELLO. How!

DESDEMONA. I say, it is not lost.

OTHELLO. Fetch't, let me see't.

DESDEMONA. Why, so I can, sir, but I will not now.
This is a trick to put me from my suit.
Pray you, let Cassio be receiv'd again.

OTHELLO. Fetch me that handkerchief. My mind misgives.

DESDEMONA. Come, come;
You'll never meet a more sufficient man.

OTHELLO. The handkerchief!

DESDEMONA. I pray, talk me of Cassio.

OTHELLO. The handkerchief!

DESDEMONA. A man that all his time
Hath founded his good fortunes on your love,
Shar'd dangers with you,—

OTHELLO. The handkerchief!

DESDEMONA. I' faith, you are to blame.

OTHELLO. Zounds!

[*Exit* OTHELLO]

EMILIA. Is not this man jealous?

DESDEMONA. I ne'er saw this before.
Sure, there's some wonder in this handkerchief.
I am most unhappy in the loss of it.

EMILIA. 'Tis not a year or two shows us a man.[135]
They are all but stomachs, and we all but food.
They eat us hungerly, and when they are full
They belch us. Look you! Cassio and my husband.

[*Enter* IAGO *and* CASSIO]

[130] Prophetess.   [131] Revolutions, i.e., was two hundred years old.   [132] Inspiration.
[133] Concoction prepared from mummies.   [134] Made.
[135] It doesn't take long to find out what men are like.

IAGO.   There is no other way; 'tis she must do't.
> And, lo, the happiness! [136] Go and importune her.

DESDEMONA.   How now, good Cassio? what's the news with you?

CASSIO.   Madam, my former suit. I do beseech you
> That by your virtuous[137] means I may again
> Exist, and be a member of his love
> Whom I with all the office[138] of my heart
> Entirely honor. I would not be delay'd.
> If my offence be of such mortal kind
> That nor my service past, nor present sorrows,
> Nor purpos'd merit in futurity,[139]
> Can ransom me into his love again,
> But[140] to know so must be my benefit.
> So shall I clothe me in a forc'd content,
> And shut myself up in some other course
> To fortune's alms.

DESDEMONA.   Alas, thrice-gentle Cassio,
> My advocation is not now in tune.
> My lord is not my lord; nor should I know him,
> Were he in favor[141] as in humor alter'd.
> So help me every spirit sanctified,
> As I have spoken for you all my best
> And stood within the blank[142] of his displeasure
> For my free speech. You must awhile be patient.
> What I can do I will, and more I will
> Than for myself I dare. Let that suffice you.

IAGO.   Is my lord angry?

EMILIA.   He went hence but now,
> And certainly in strange unquietness.

IAGO.   Can he be angry? I have seen the cannon,
> When it hath blown his ranks into the air,
> And, like the devil, from his very arm
> Puff'd his own brother,—and can he be angry?
> Something of moment then. I will go meet him;
> There's matter in't indeed, if he be angry.

DESDEMONA.   I prithee, do so.

> [*Exit* IAGO]

>   Something, sure, of state,
> Either from Venice, or some unhatch'd practice[143]
> Made demonstrable here in Cyprus to him,
> Hath puddled his clear spirit; and in such cases
> Men's natures wrangle with inferior things,
> Though great ones are their object. 'Tis even so;
> For let our finger ache, and it endues[144]
> Our other healthful members ev'n to that sense

---

[136] What good luck!, i.e., here is Desdemona.   [137] Effective.   [138] Duty.
[139] My good resolutions for the future.   [140] Merely.   [141] Face.
[142] Range, literally the bull's eye.   [143] Plot brewing.   [144] Brings.

Of pain. Nay, we must think men are not gods,
Nor of them look for such observancy[145]
As fits the bridal.[146] Beshrew me much,[147] Emilia,
I was (unhandsome warrior[148] as I am)
Arraigning his unkindness with my soul;
But now I find I had suborn'd the witness,
And he's indicted falsely.

EMILIA.   Pray heaven it be state-matters, as you think,
And no conception,[149] nor no jealous toy
Concerning you.

DESDEMONA.   Alas the day! I never gave him cause.

EMILIA.   But jealous souls will not be answer'd so.
They are not ever jealous for the cause,
But jealous for they are jealous. 'Tis a monster
Begot upon itself, born on itself.

DESDEMONA.   Heaven keep that monster from Othello's mind!

EMILIA.   Lady, amen.

DESDEMONA.   I will go seek him. Cassio, walk hereabout.
If I do find him fit, I'll move your suit
And seek to effect it to my uttermost.

CASSIO.   I humbly thank your ladyship.

> [*Exeunt* DESDEMONA *and* EMILIA]

[*Enter* BIANCA]

BIANCA.   'Save you,[150] friend Cassio!

CASSIO.   What make you from home? [151]
How is it with you, my most fair Bianca?
I' faith, sweet love, I was coming to your house.

BIANCA.   And I was going to your lodging, Cassio.
What! keep a week away? seven days and nights?
Eight score eight hours? and lovers' absent hours,
More tedious than the dial eight score times?
O weary reckoning!

CASSIO.   Pardon me, Bianca,
I have this while with leaden thoughts been press'd,
But I shall, in a more continuate[152] time,
Strike off this score of absence. Sweet Bianca,
[*giving her* DESDEMONA's *handkerchief*]
Take me this work out.[153]

BIANCA.   O Cassio! whence came this?
This is some token from a newer friend;
To the felt absence now I feel a cause;
Is't come to this? Well, well.

CASSIO.   Go to, woman!
Throw your vile guesses in the devil's teeth,

---

[145] Close attention.   [146] Honeymoon.
[147] Imprecation, literally "curse me" but closer to our "indeed" in meaning.
[148] Poor soldier.   [149] Wrong ideas.   [150] May God preserve (or save) you!
[151] What are you doing away from home?   [152] Uninterrupted.   [153] Copy this pattern.

From whence you have them. You are jealous now
That this is from some mistress, some remembrance.
No, by my faith, Bianca.

BIANCA.   Why, whose is it?

CASSIO. I know not, sweet. I found it in my chamber.
I like the work well. Ere it be demanded
(As like enough it will), I'd have it copied.
Take it and do't; and leave me for this time.

BIANCA. Leave you? wherefore?

CASSIO. I do attend here on[154] the general,
And think it no addition[155] nor my wish
To have him see me woman'd.

BIANCA.   Why, I pray you?

CASSIO. Not that I love you not.

BIANCA.   But that you do not love me.
I pray you, bring me on the way a little
And say if I shall see you soon at night.

CASSIO. 'Tis but a little way that I can bring you,
For I attend here; but I'll see you soon.

BIANCA. 'Tis very good. I must be circumstanc'd.[156]

[*Exeunt*]

Act Fourth

SCENE FIRST: *Before the Citadel.*

[*Enter* OTHELLO *and* IAGO]

IAGO. Will you think so?

OTHELLO.   Think so, Iago!

IAGO.   What!
To kiss in private?

OTHELLO.   An unauthoriz'd kiss.

IAGO. Or to be naked with her friend abed
An hour or more, not meaning any harm?

OTHELLO. Naked abed, Iago, and not mean harm?
It is hypocrisy against the devil.[1]
They that mean virtuously, and yet do so,
The devil their virtue tempts,[2] and they tempt heaven.

IAGO. So[3] they do nothing, 'tis a venial slip.
But if I give my wife a handkerchief,—

OTHELLO. What then?

IAGO. Why, then, 'tis hers, my lord; and, being hers,
She may, I think, bestow't on any man.

---

[154] Wait upon.   [155] Honor.   [156] Accept the inevitable.
[1] To deceive the devil.   [2] Their virtue tempts the devil to make them sin.   [3] So long as.

OTHELLO.   She is protectress of her honor too.
   May she give that?
IAGO.   Her honor is an essence that's not seen.
   They have it very oft that have it not;[4]
   But for the handkerchief,—
OTHELLO.   By heaven, I would most gladly have forgot it.
   Thou said'st (O it comes o'er my memory
   As doth the raven o'er the infected house,[5]
   Boding to all) he had my handkerchief.
IAGO.   Ay, what of that?
OTHELLO.   That's not so good now.
IAGO.   What
   If I had said I had seen him do you wrong?
   Or heard him say (as knaves be such abroad,
   Who having, by their own importunate suit
   Or voluntary dotage[6] of some mistress,
   Convinced or supplied [7] them, cannot choose
   But they must blab)—
OTHELLO.   Hath he said anything?
IAGO.   He hath, my lord; but be you well assur'd,
   No more than he'll unswear.
OTHELLO.   What hath he said?
IAGO.   Faith, that he did—I know not what he did.
OTHELLO.   What? what?
IAGO.   Lie—
OTHELLO.   With her?
IAGO.   With her, on her—what you will.
OTHELLO.   Lie with her! lie on her! We say, lie on her, when they belie her. Lie with her? Zounds, that's fulsome! [8] Handkerchief!—confessions!—handkerchief! To confess, and be hanged for his labor. First, to be hanged, and then to confess: I tremble at it. Nature would not invest herself in such shadowing passion without some instruction.[9] It is not words that shake me thus. Pish! Noses, ears, and lips. Is't possible?—Confess!—Handkerchief!—O devil!
   [*Falls in a trance*]
IAGO.   Work on,
   My medicine, work! Thus credulous fools are caught;
   And many worthy and chaste dames even thus,
   All guiltless, meet reproach. What, ho! my lord!
   My lord, I say! Othello!
   [*Enter* CASSIO]
                   How now, Cassio!
CASSIO.   What's the matter?
IAGO.   My lord is fallen into an epilepsy.

---

[4] People often receive respect (honor) who are really not honorable.
[5] As a bird of prey hovers over a house in which death is shortly expected.
[6] Infatuation.   [7] Persuaded them or satisfied.   [8] Disgusting.
[9] Nature would not have granted me such overwhelming passion unless to teach me (of the truth of the charges).

This is his second fit; he had one yesterday.

CASSIO.   Rub him about the temples.

IAGO.   No, forbear.
The lethargy[10] must have his[11] quiet course.
If not he foams at mouth, and by and by
Breaks out to savage madness. Look! he stirs.
Do you withdraw yourself a little while,
He will recover straight. When he is gone,
I would on great occasion speak with you.

[Exit CASSIO]

How is it, general? Have you not hurt your head? [12]

OTHELLO.   Dost thou mock me?

IAGO.   I mock you! no, by heaven.
Would you would bear your fortunes like a man!

OTHELLO.   A horned man's a monster and a beast.

IAGO.   There's many a beast then, in a populous city,
And many a civil [13] monster.

OTHELLO.   Did he confess?

IAGO.   Good sir, be a man.
Think every bearded fellow that's but yok'd
May draw with you.[14] There's millions now alive
That nightly lie in those unproper[15] beds
Which they dare swear peculiar.[16] Your case is better.
O, 'tis the spite of hell, the fiend's arch-mock,
To lip[17] a wanton in a secure[18] couch,
And to suppose her chaste. No, let me know;
And knowing what I am, I know what she shall be.[19]

OTHELLO.   O, thou art wise, 'tis certain.

IAGO.   Stand you awhile apart;
Confine yourself but in a patient list.[20]
Whilst you were here o'erwhelmed with your grief
(A passion most unsuiting such a man),
Cassio came hither. I shifted him away,
And laid good 'scuse upon your ecstasy;[21]
Bade him anon return and here speak with me,
The which he promis'd. Do but encave[22] yourself,
And mark the fleers, the gibes, and notable[23] scorns
That dwell in every region of his face;
For I will make him tell the tale anew,
Where, how, how oft, how long ago, and when
He has, and is again to cope[24] your wife.
I say, but mark his gesture. Marry, patience;

---

[10] Fit.   [11] Its.

[12] A pun, the second allusion being to cuckoldry and its attendant headache from the horns.

[13] Respectable and urban.   [14] Draw the same carriage with you, i.e., be in the same boat.

[15] Not their own.   [16] Theirs alone.   [17] Kiss.   [18] Supposedly safe.

[19] What to call her.   [20] Within the bounds of patience.   [21] Used your fit as an excuse.

[22] Hide.   [23] Conspicuous.   [24] Meet.

Or I shall say you're all in all in spleen,[25]
And nothing of a man.

OTHELLO.   Dost thou hear, Iago?
I will be found most cunning in my patience,
But—dost thou hear?—most bloody.

IAGO.   That's not amiss;
But yet keep time[26] in all. Will you withdraw?

[OTHELLO *goes apart*]

Now will I question Cassio of Bianca,
A housewife[27] that by selling her desires
Buys herself bread and clothes. It is a creature
That dotes on Cassio (as 'tis the strumpet's plague
To beguile many and be beguil'd by one).
He, when he hears of her, cannot refrain
From the excess of laughter. Here he comes.
[*Enter* CASSIO]
As he shall smile, Othello shall go mad;
And his unbookish[28] jealousy must construe
Poor Cassio's smiles, gestures, and light behavior
Quite in the wrong. [*Aloud*] How do you now, lieutenant?

CASSIO. The worser that you give me the addition[29]
Whose want even kills me.

IAGO. Ply Desdemona well, and you are sure on't.
[*Speaking lower*] Now, if this suit lay in Bianca's power,
How quickly should you speed! [30]

CASSIO.   Alas! poor caitiff! [31]

OTHELLO. Look how he laughs already!

IAGO. I never knew a woman love man so.

CASSIO. Alas! poor rogue! I think, i' faith, she loves me.

OTHELLO. Now he denies it faintly, and laughs it out.

IAGO. Do you hear, Cassio?

OTHELLO.   Now he importunes him
To tell it o'er. Go to! well said, well said.

IAGO. She gives it out that you shall marry her.
Do you intend it?

CASSIO. Ha, ha, ha!

OTHELLO. Do you triumph, Roman? do you triumph? [32]

CASSIO. I marry her! what? a customer? [33] I prithee, bear some charity to my
wit; do not think it so unwholesome.[34] Ha, ha, ha!

OTHELLO. So, so, so, so. Laugh that wins! [35]

IAGO. Faith, the cry goes you shall marry her.

CASSIO. Prithee, say true.

IAGO. I am a very villain else.

OTHELLO. Have you scored [36] me? Well!

---

[25] In anger.   [26] Proceed in a measured manner.   [27] Hussy.
[28] Uncalculated, passionate.   [29] Title.   [30] Succeed.
[31] Wretch, used here in affectionate superiority.
[32] The allusion here is to the famous Roman triumphal processions after great victories.
[33] Prostitute.   [34] Weak.   [35] Let him laugh who wins.   [36] Branded.

CASSIO. This is the monkey's own giving out. She is persuaded I will marry her, out of her own love and flattery,[37] not out of my promise.

OTHELLO. Iago beckons me. Now he begins the story.

CASSIO. She was here even now; she haunts me in every place. I was t'other day talking on the sea bank with certain Venetians, and thither comes the bauble,[38] and falls me thus about my neck—

OTHELLO. Crying, 'O dear Cassio!' as it were. His gesture imports it.

CASSIO. So hangs and lolls and weeps upon me; so hales and pulls me. Ha, ha, ha!

OTHELLO. Now he tells how she plucked him to my chamber. O, I see that nose of yours, but not that dog I shall throw it to.

CASSIO. Well, I must leave her company.

IAGO. Before me! look where she comes!

CASSIO. 'Tis such another fitchew! [39] marry, a perfumed one!

[*Enter* BIANCA]

What do you mean by this haunting of me?

BIANCA. Let the devil and his dam[40] haunt you! What did you mean by that same handkerchief you gave me even now? I was a fine fool to take it. I must take out the work? A likely piece of work, that you should find it in your chamber and not know who left it there! This is some minx's token, and I must take out the work! There, give it your hobbyhorse,[41] wheresoever you had it. I'll take out no work on't.

CASSIO. How now, my sweet Bianca? how now? how now?

OTHELLO. By heaven, that should be my handkerchief!

BIANCA. An[42] you'll come to supper to-night, you may. An you will not, come when you are next prepared for.

[*Exit* BIANCA]

IAGO. After her! after her!

CASSIO. Faith, I must. She'll rail i' the street else.

IAGO. Will you sup there?

CASSIO. Faith, I intend so.

IAGO. Well, I may chance to see you, for I would very fain speak with you.

CASSIO. Prithee, come; will you?

IAGO. Go to! Say no more.

[*Exit* CASSIO]

OTHELLO. [*Advancing*] How shall I murder him, Iago?

IAGO. Did you perceive how he laughed at his vice?

OTHELLO. O Iago!

IAGO. And did you see the handkerchief?

OTHELLO. Was that mine?

IAGO. Yours, by this hand. And to see how he prizes the foolish woman your wife! She gave it him, and he hath given it his whore.

OTHELLO. I would have him nine years a-killing. A fine woman! a fair woman! a sweet woman!

IAGO. Nay, you must forget that.

OTHELLO. Ay, let her rot and perish, and be damned to-night, for she shall not live. No, my heart is turned to stone. I strike it, and it hurts my hand. O,

---

[37] Self-love.   [38] Plaything.   [39] Such a polecat (a lecherous animal).
[40] Dame, mother.   [41] Harlot.   [42] If.

the world has not a sweeter creature. She might lie by an emperor's side and command him tasks.

IAGO. Nay, that's not your way.[43]

OTHELLO. Hang her! I do but say what she is. So delicate with her needle! An admirable musician! O, she will sing the savageness out of a bear. Of so high and plenteous wit and invention!

IAGO. She's the worse for all this.

OTHELLO. O, a thousand, a thousand times. And then, of so gentle a condition! [44]

IAGO. Ay, too gentle.

OTHELLO. Nay, that's certain. But yet the pity of it, Iago! O, Iago, the pity of it, Iago!

IAGO. If you be so fond over her iniquity, give her patent[45] to offend; for, if it touches not you, it comes near nobody.

OTHELLO. I will chop her into messes.[46] Cuckold me—

IAGO. O, 'tis foul in her.

OTHELLO. With mine officer!

IAGO. That's fouler.

OTHELLO. Get me some poison, Iago, this night. I'll not expostulate with her, lest her body and beauty unprovide[47] my mind again. This night, Iago.

IAGO. Do it not with poison. Strangle her in her bed, even the bed she hath contaminated.

OTHELLO. Good, good. The justice of it pleases. Very good.

IAGO. And for Cassio, let me be his undertaker.
You shall hear more by midnight.

OTHELLO. Excellent good.
    [*A trumpet*]
                              What trumpet is that same?

IAGO. Something from Venice, sure. 'Tis Lodovico,
Come from the duke; and see, your wife is with him.
    [*Enter* LODOVICO, DESDEMONA, *and* ATTENDANTS]

LODOVICO. God save you, worthy general!

OTHELLO.   With all my heart, sir.

LODOVICO. The duke and senators of Venice greet you.
    [*Gives him a letter*]

OTHELLO. I kiss the instrument of their pleasures.
    [*Opens the letter and reads*]

DESDEMONA. And what's the news, good cousin Lodovico?

IAGO. I am very glad to see you, signior.
Welcome to Cyprus.

LODOVICO. I thank you. How does Lieutenant Cassio?

IAGO. Lives, sir.

DESDEMONA. Cousin, there's fall'n between him and my lord
An unkind breach, but you shall make all well.

OTHELLO. Are you sure of that?

DESDEMONA. My lord?

---

[43] The proper way (to think).   [44] Of such good family.   [45] Permission.
[46] Little pieces.   [47] Weaken.

OTHELLO. [*Reads*] 'This fail you not to do, as you will'—[48]
LODOVICO. He did not call. He's busy in the paper.
    Is there division 'twixt thy lord and Cassio?
DESDEMONA. A most unhappy one. I would do much
    T'atone[49] them for the love I bear to Cassio.
OTHELLO. Fire and brimstone!
DESDEMONA.   My lord?
OTHELLO.   Are you wise?
DESDEMONA. What! is he angry?
LODOVICO.   May be the letter mov'd him;
    For, as I think, they do command him home,
    Deputing Cassio in his government.
DESDEMONA. By my troth, I am glad on't.
OTHELLO.   Indeed?
DESDEMONA.   My lord?
OTHELLO. I am glad to see you mad.
DESDEMONA.   How, sweet Othello?
OTHELLO. Devil!
    [*Strikes her*]
DESDEMONA.   I have not deserved this.
LODOVICO. My lord, this would not be believ'd in Venice,
    Though I should swear I saw't. 'Tis very much.[50]
    Make her amends, she weeps.
OTHELLO.   O devil, devil!
    If that the earth could teem with women's tears,
    Each drop she falls would prove a crocodile.
    Out of my sight!
DESDEMONA. [*Going*] I will not stay to offend you.
LODOVICO. Truly, an obedient lady!
    I do beseech your lordship, call her back.
OTHELLO. Mistress!
DESDEMONA.   My lord?
OTHELLO.   What would you with her, sir?
LODOVICO. Who, I, my lord?
OTHELLO. Ay, you did wish that I would make her turn.
    Sir, she can turn, and turn, and yet go on,
    And turn again. And she can weep, sir, weep;
    And she's obedient, as you say, obedient,
    Very obedient.—Proceed you in your tears.—
    Concerning this, sir,—O well painted [51] passion!—
    I am commanded here—Get you away;
    I'll send for you anon.—Sir, I obey the mandate,
    And will return to Venice.—Hence! avaunt!

                              [*Exit* DESDEMONA]

    Cassio shall have my place. And, sir, to-night,
    I do entreat that we may sup together.

[48] Formal close to a letter giving orders to a subordinate.   [49] Reconcile.
[50] This is going too far.   [51] Feigned.

You are welcome, sir, to Cyprus.—Goats and monkeys!

[*Exit*]

LODOVICO. Is this the noble Moor whom our full senate
　　Call all-in-all sufficient? Is this the nature
　　Whom passion could not shake, whose solid virtue
　　The shot of accident nor dart of chance
　　Could neither graze nor pierce?
IAGO.　　　　　　　　　　　He is much chang'd.
LODOVICO. Are his wits safe?　is he not light on brain?
IAGO. He's that he is. I may not breathe my censure.
　　What he might[52] be (if what he might he is not)
　　I would to heaven he were!
LODOVICO.　　　　　　　What! strike his wife!
IAGO. Faith, that was not so well; yet would I knew
　　That stroke would prove the worst!
LODOVICO.　　　　　　　　　Is it his use? [53]
　　Or did the letters work upon his blood,
　　And new-create this fault?
IAGO.　　　　　　　　　Alas, alas!
　　It is not honesty in me to speak
　　What I have seen and known. You shall observe him,
　　And his own courses[54] will denote him so
　　That I may save my speech. Do but go after
　　And mark how he continues.
LODOVICO. I am sorry that I am deceiv'd in him.

[*Exeunt*]

SCENE SECOND: *A room in the Citadel.*

[*Enter* OTHELLO *and* EMILIA]
OTHELLO. You have seen nothing, then?
EMILIA. Nor ever heard, nor ever did suspect.
OTHELLO. Yes, you have seen Cassio and she together.
EMILIA. But then I saw no harm, and then I heard
　　Each syllable that breath made up between 'em.
OTHELLO. What! did they never whisper?
EMILIA.　　　　　　　　　Never, my lord.
OTHELLO. Nor send you out o' the way?
EMILIA.　　　　　　　　　Never.
OTHELLO. To fetch her fan, her gloves, her mask, nor nothing?
EMILIA. Never, my lord.
OTHELLO. That's strange.
EMILIA. I durst, my lord, to wager she is honest,
　　Lay down my soul at stake. If you think other,[55]
　　Remove your thought. It doth abuse your bosom.
　　If any wretch have put this in your head,

---

[52] Ought to.　[53] Customary behavior.　[54] Behavior.　[55] Otherwise.

Let heaven requite it with the serpent's curse! [56]
For if she be not honest, chaste, and true,
There's no man happy; the purest of their wives
Is foul as slander.

OTHELLO.   Bid her come hither. Go.

[*Exit* EMILIA]

She says enough; yet she's a simple bawd [57]
That cannot say as much. This is a subtle whore,
A closet[58] lock and key of villainous secrets;
And yet she'll kneel and pray. I have seen her do't.
[*Enter* DESDEMONA *and* EMILIA]

DESDEMONA. My lord, what is your will?

OTHELLO.   Pray, chuck, come hither.

DESDEMONA. What is your pleasure?

OTHELLO.   Let me see your eyes;
Look in my face.

DESDEMONA.   What horrible fancy's this?

OTHELLO. [*To* EMILIA] Some of your function,[59] mistress.
Leave procreants alone and shut the door;
Cough or cry 'hem' if anybody come.
Your mystery,[60] your mystery. Nay, dispatch.[61]

[*Exit* EMILIA]

DESDEMONA. Upon my knees, what does your speech import?
I understand a fury in your words
But not the words.

OTHELLO. Why, what are thou?

DESDEMONA.   Your wife, my lord; your true
And loyal wife.

OTHELLO.   Come, swear it, damn thyself;
Lest, being like one of heaven, the devils themselves
Should fear to seize thee. Therefore be double damn'd.
Swear thou art honest.

DESDEMONA.   Heaven doth truly know it.

OTHELLO. Heaven truly knows that thou art false as hell.

DESDEMONA. To whom, my lord? with whom? how am I false?

OTHELLO. Ah! Desdemon! Away, away, away!

DESDEMONA. Alas, the heavy day! Why do you weep?
Am I the motive of these tears, my lord?
If haply you my father do suspect
An instrument of this your calling back,
Lay not your blame on me. If you have lost him,
Why, I have lost him too.

OTHELLO.   Had it pleas'd heaven
To try me with affliction, had they rain'd
All kinds of sores and shames on my bare head,

---

[56] The curse laid on the serpent by God in the Garden of Eden.
[57] Here, bawdy house keeper.   [58] Small box for keeping valuables.
[59] Carry out your job (as bawd).   [60] Trade.   [61] Be quick.

Steep'd me in poverty to the very lips,
Given to captivity me and my utmost hopes,
I should have found in some part of my soul
A drop of patience. But, alas!, to make me
A fixed figure for the time of scorn
To point his slow unmoving fingers at! [62]
Yet could I bear that too. Well! very well!
But there, where I have garner'd up my heart,[63]
Where either I must live or bear no life;
The fountain from the which my current runs
Or else dries up: to be discarded thence,
Or keep it as a cistern for foul toads
To knot and gender[64] in! Turn thy complexion there,[65]
Patience, thou young and rose-lipp'd cherubin.
I here look grim as hell!

DESDEMONA.   I hope my noble lord esteems me honest.

OTHELLO.   O, ay. As summer flies are in the shambles,
That quicken even with blowing.[66]
O thou black weed, why art so lovely fair?
Thou smell'st so sweet that the sense aches at thee.
Would thou hadst ne'er been born!

DESDEMONA.   Alas, what ignorant sin have I committed?

OTHELLO.   Was this fair paper, this most goodly book,
Made to write 'whore' on? What committed?
Committed! O thou public commoner! [67]
I should make very forges of my cheeks,
That would to cinders burn up modesty,
Did I but speak thy deeds. What committed?
Heaven stops the nose at it and the moon winks,[68]
The bawdy wind that kisses all it meets
Is hush'd within the hollow mine of earth,[69]
And will not hear't. What committed?
Impudent strumpet!

DESDEMONA.   By heaven, you do me wrong.

OTHELLO.   Are not you a strumpet?

DESDEMONA.   No, as I am a Christian.
If to preserve this vessel for my lord
From any other foul unlawful touch
Be not to be a strumpet, I am none.

OTHELLO.   What! not a whore?

DESDEMONA.   No, as I shall be sav'd.

OTHELLO.   Is't possible?

DESDEMONA.   O heaven, forgiveness! [70]

---

[62] A clock image. The fingers are equivalent to the hands which seem not to move.
[63] Stored up my love as the harvest.   [64] Engender.   [65] Blush.
[66] Become pregnant again as soon as they have laid their eggs.   [67] Harlot.
[68] Closes its eyes.   [69] The Elizabethans believed that the winds were kept in caves underground.   [70] Give me power to forgive him for this thought.

OTHELLO.   I cry you mercy,[71] then.
I took you for that cunning whore of Venice
That married with Othello. You, mistress,
That have the office opposite to Saint Peter,
And keep the gate of hell!
[*Enter* EMILIA]
                          You, you, ay, you!
We have done our course. There's money for your pains.
I pray you, turn the key[72] and keep our counsel.[73]

                                                    [*Exit*]

EMILIA. Alas! what does this gentleman conceive? [74]
How do you, madame? how do you, my good lady?
DESDEMONA. Faith, half asleep.
EMILIA. Good madam, what's the matter with my lord?
DESDEMONA. With who?
EMILIA.   Why, with my lord, madam.
DESDEMONA. Who is thy lord?
EMILIA.   He that is yours, sweet lady.
DESDEMONA. I have none; do not talk to me, Emilia;
I cannot weep, nor answer have I none,
But what should go by water.[75] Prithee, to-night
Lay on my bed our wedding sheets. Remember;
And call thy husband hither.
EMILIA.   Here is a change indeed!

                                                    [*Exit*]

DESDEMONA. 'Tis meet I should be us'd so, very meet.
How have I been behav'd, that he might stick
The small'st opinion[76] on my greatest abuse?
[*Enter* IAGO *and* EMILIA]
IAGO. What is your pleasure, madam? How is't with you?
DESDEMONA. I cannot tell. Those that do teach young babes
Do it with gentle means and easy tasks.
He might have chid me so, for, in good faith,
I am a child [77] to chiding.
IAGO. What is the matter, lady?
EMILIA. Alas! Iago, my lord hath so bewhor'd her,
Thrown such despite and heavy terms upon her,
As true hearts cannot bear.
DESDEMONA. Am I that name, Iago?
IAGO.   What name, fair lady?
DESDEMONA. Such as she says my lord did say I was.
EMILIA. He call'd her whore. A beggar in his drink
Could not have laid such terms upon his callet.[78]
IAGO. Why did he so?
DESDEMONA. I do not know. I am sure I am none such.
IAGO. Do not weep, do not weep. Alas the day!

[71] I ask your pardon (ironical).   [72] Open the door.   [73] Secret.   [74] Imagine.
[75] Be expressed by tears.   [76] The least censure.   [77] React as a child.   [78] Whore.

EMILIA.   Has she forsook so many noble matches,
　　　Her father, and her country, and her friends,
　　　To be call'd whore? Would it not make one weep?
DESDEMONA.   It is my wretched fortune.
IAGO.   Beshrew him for't!
　　　How comes this trick[79] upon him?
DESDEMONA.   Nay, heaven doth know.
EMILIA.   I will be hang'd if some eternal villain,
　　　Some busy and insinuating rogue,
　　　Some cogging,[80] cozening[81] slave, to get some office
　　　Have not devis'd this slander. I'll be hang'd else.
IAGO.   Fie! there is no such man. It is impossible.
DESDEMONA.   If any such there be, heaven pardon him!
EMILIA.   A halter pardon him, and hell gnaw his bones!
　　　Why should he call her whore? who keeps her company?
　　　What place? what time? what form? what likelihood?
　　　The Moor's abus'd by some outrageous knave,
　　　Some base notorious knave, some scurvy fellow.
　　　O heaven! that such companions[82] thou'dst unfold,[83]
　　　And put in every honest hand a whip
　　　To lash the rascal naked through the world,
　　　Even from the east to the west!
IAGO.   Speak within doors.[84]
EMILIA.   O, fie upon him! Some such squire[85] he was
　　　That turn'd your wit the seamy side without,
　　　And made you to suspect me with the Moor.
IAGO.   You are a fool. Go to!
DESDEMONA.   O good Iago,
　　　What shall I do to win my lord again?
　　　Good friend, go to him; for, by this light of heaven,
　　　I know not how I lost him. Here I kneel.
　　　If e'er my will did trespass 'gainst his love,
　　　Either in discourse of thought or actual deed,
　　　Or that mine eyes, mine ears, or any sense
　　　Delighted them in any other form;
　　　Or that I do not yet, and ever did,
　　　And ever will (though he do shake me off
　　　To beggarly divorcement) love him dearly,
　　　Comfort forswear[86] me! Unkindness may do much;
　　　And his unkindness may defeat[87] my life,
　　　But never taint my love. I cannot say 'whore.'
　　　It does abhor me[88] now I speak the word;
　　　To do the act that might th' addition earn
　　　Not the world's mass of vanity[89] could make me.
IAGO.   I pray you be content. 'Tis but his humor.

---

[79] Whim.   [80] Deceiving.   [81] Cheating.   [82] Rascals.   [83] Expose.   [84] Quietly.
[85] Fellow.   [86] Forsake.   [87] Destroy.   [88] I feel abhorrence—with a pun on *whore*.
[89] Vain wealth.

The business of the state does him offence
And he does chide with you.

DESDEMONA. If 'twere no other,—

[*Trumpets within*]

IAGO.   'Tis but so, I warr'nt you.
Hark how these instruments summon you to supper,
And the great messengers of Venice stay.[90]
Go in, and weep not. All things shall be well.

[*Exeunt women*]

[*Enter* RODERIGO]

How now, Roderigo?

RODERIGO. I do not find that thou deal'st justly with me.

IAGO. What in the contrary? [91]

RODERIGO. Every day thou daffest me[92] with some device, Iago; and rather, as it seems to me, thou keepest from me all conveniency,[93] than suppliest me with the least advantage[94] of hope. I will indeed no longer endure it, nor am I yet persuaded to put up[95] in peace what already I have foolishly suffered.

IAGO. Will you hear me, Roderigo?

RODERIGO. Faith, I have heard too much, for your words and performance are no kin together.

IAGO. You charge me most unjustly.

RODERIGO. With nought but truth. I have wasted myself out of my means. The jewels you have had from me to deliver to Desdemona would half have corrupted a votarist.[96] You have told me she has received them, and returned me expectations and comforts of sudden respect[97] and acquaintance, but I find none.

IAGO. Well, go to! Very well.

RODERIGO. Very well? go to? I cannot go to, man; nor 'tis not very well. By this hand, I say 'tis very scurvy, and begin to find myself fopped [98] in it.

IAGO. Very well.

RODERIGO. I tell you 'tis not very well. I will make myself known to Desdemona. If she will return me my jewels, I will give over my suit and repent my unlawful solicitation. If not, assure yourself I will seek satisfaction of you.

IAGO. You have said now? [99]

RODERIGO. Ay, and said nothing but what I protest intendment of doing.

IAGO. Why, now I see there's mettle in thee, and even from this instant do build on thee a better opinion than ever before. Give me thy hand, Roderigo. Thou hast taken against me a most just exception; but yet, I protest, I have dealt most directly in thy affair.

RODERIGO. It hath not appeared.

IAGO. I grant indeed it hath not appeared, and your suspicion is not without wit and judgment. But, Roderigo, if thou hast that within thee indeed, which I have greater reason to believe now than ever (I mean purpose, cour-

---

[90] Are waiting.   [91] What have you to back up that remark?   [92] Put me off.
[93] Opportunity.   [94] Increase.   [95] Bear.   [96] Nun.   [97] Speedy notice.   [98] Cheated.
[99] Have you finished talking?

age, and valor), this night show it. If thou the next night following enjoyest not Desdemona, take me from this world with treachery and devise engines for[100] my life.

RODERIGO.   Well, what is it? is it within reason and compass?

IAGO.   Sir, there is especial commission come from Venice to depute Cassio in Othello's place.

RODERIGO.   Is that true? Why, then Othello and Desdemona return again to Venice.

IAGO.   O, no! he goes into Mauritania, and takes away with him the fair Desdemona, unless his abode be lingered here by some accident; wherein none can be so determinate[101] as the removing of Cassio.

RODERIGO.   How do you mean, removing of him?

IAGO.   Why, by making him uncapable of Othello's place. Knocking out his brains.

RODERIGO.   And that you would have me to do!

IAGO.   Ay; if you dare do yourself a profit and right. He sups to-night with a harlotry, and thither will I go to him. He knows not yet of his honorable fortune. If you will watch his going thence (which I will fashion to fall out between twelve and one), you may take him at your pleasure. I will be near to second your attempt, and he shall fall between us. Come, stand not amazed as it, but go along with me. I will show you such a necessity in his death that you shall think yourself bound to put it on him. It is now high supper-time, and the night grows to waste.[102] About it.

RODERIGO.   I will hear further reason for this.

IAGO.   And you shall be satisfied.

[*Exeunt*]

SCENE THIRD: *State bedroom in the Citadel.*

[*Enter* OTHELLO, LODOVICO, DESDEMONA, EMILIA, *and* ATTENDANTS]

LODOVICO.   I do beseech you, sir, trouble yourself no further.

OTHELLO.   O pardon me;[103] 'twill do me good to walk.

LODOVICO.   Madam, good night. I humbly thank your ladyship.

DESDEMONA.   Your honor is most welcome.

OTHELLO.   Will you walk, sir?—

O! Desdemona.

DESDEMONA.   My lord?

OTHELLO.   Get you to bed o' the instant. I will be returned forthwith. Dispatch your attendant there. Look it be done.

DESDEMONA.   I will, my lord.

[*Exit* OTHELLO, *with* LODOVICO *and* ATTENDANTS]

EMILIA.   How goes it now? He looks gentler than he did.

DESDEMONA.   He says he will return incontinent.

He hath commanded me to go to bed,

And bade me to dismiss you.

EMILIA.   Dismiss me!

---

[100] Schemes against.   [101] Decisive.   [102] Is wasting away.   [103] Not at all.

DESDEMONA. It was his bidding. Therefore, good Emilia,
Give me my nightly wearing, and adieu.
We must not now displease him.

EMILIA. I would you had never seen him.

DESDEMONA. So would not I. My love doth so approve him,
That even his stubbornness, his checks and frowns,—
Prithee, unpin me,—have grace and favor in them.

EMILIA. I have laid those sheets you bade me on the bed.

DESDEMONA. All's one.[104] Good faith! how foolish are our minds!
If I do die before thee, prithee, shroud me
In one of those same sheets.

EMILIA.   Come, come, you talk!

DESDEMONA. My mother had a maid call'd Barbary:
She was in love, and he she lov'd prov'd mad [105]
And did forsake her. She had a song of 'willow';
An old thing 'twas, but it express'd her fortune,[106]
And she died singing it. That song to-night
Will not go from my mind. I have much to do
But to[107] go hang my head all at one side,
And sing it like poor Barbary. Prithee, dispatch.

EMILIA. Shall I go fetch your night-gown?

DESDEMONA.   No, unpin me here.
This Lodovico is a proper man.

EMILIA. A very handsome man.

DESDEMONA. He speaks well.

EMILIA. I know a lady in Venice would have walked barefoot to Palestine for
a touch of his nether lip.

DESDEMONA   [*Sings*]
      The poor soul sat sighing by a sycamore tree,—
        Sing all a green willow.
      Her hand on her bosom, her head on her knee,—
        Sing willow, willow, willow.
      The fresh streams ran by her, and murmur'd her moans.
        Sing willow, &c.
      Her salt tears fell from her, and soften'd the stones.
        Sing willow, &c.
Lay by these.—
      Willow, willow.
Prithee, hie thee;[108] he'll come anon.
      Sing all a green willow must be my garland.
      Let nobody blame him, his scorn I approve,—
Nay, that's not next. Hark! who is it that knocks?

EMILIA. It is the wind.

DESDEMONA.
      I call'd my love false love; but what said he then?
        Sing willow, &c.
      If I court mo women, you'll couch with mo men.

---

[104] Good.   [105] Untrue, inconstant.   [106] Fate.   [107] Not to.   [108] Hurry.

Now get thee gone. Good night. Mine eyes do itch;
Does that bode weeping?

EMILIA.   'Tis neither here nor there.

DESDEMONA.   I have heard it said so. O these men, these men!
Dost thou in conscience think (tell me, Emilia)
That there be women do abuse their husbands
In such gross kind? [109]

EMILIA.   There be some such, no question.

DESDEMONA.   Wouldst thou do such a deed for all the world?

EMILIA.   Why, would not you?

DESDEMONA.   No, by this heavenly light!

EMILIA.   Nor I neither by this heavenly light. I might do't as well i' th' dark.

DESDEMONA.   Wouldst thou do such a deed for all the world?

EMILIA.   The world is a huge thing. It is a great price for a small vice.

DESDEMONA.   Good troth, I think thou wouldst not.

EMILIA.   By my troth, I think I should, and undo't when I had done it. Marry,
I would not do such a thing for a joint-ring,[110] nor for measures of lawn,[111]
nor for gowns, petticoats, nor caps, nor any petty exhibition.[112] But for the
whole world? Ud's[113] pity! who would not make her husband a cuckold to
make him a monarch? I should venture purgatory for't.

DESDEMONA.   Beshrew me, if I would do such a wrong
For the whole world.

EMILIA.   Why, the wrong is but a wrong i' the world; and having the world
for your labor, 'tis a wrong in your own world, and you might quickly make
it right.

DESDEMONA.   I do not think there is any such woman.

EMILIA.   Yes, a dozen; and as many to the vantage,[114] as would store[115] the
world they played for.
But I do think it is their husbands' faults
If wives do fall. Say that they slack their duties,
And pour our treasures into foreign laps,
Or else break out in peevish[116] jealousies,
Throwing[117] restraint upon us; or say they strike us,
Or scant our former having[118] in despite;[119]
Why, we have galls,[120] and though we have some grace,
Yet have we some revenge. Let husbands know
Their wives have sense like them. They see and smell,
And have their palates both for sweet and sour,
As husbands have. What is it that they do
When they change us for others? Is it sport?
I think it is. And doth affection[121] breed it?
I think it doth. Is't frailty that thus errs?
It is so too. And have not we affections,
Desires for sport, and frailty as men have?

[109] In such a vulgar way.   [110] A ring made up of two interlocking parts.
[111] Lengths of fine linen.   [112] Small amount of money.   [113] God's.
[114] And as many more too.   [115] Fill up.   [116] Silly.   [117] Putting.
[118] Cut down our regular allowance.   [119] Out of spite.   [120] We can resent things too.
[121] Inclination.

Then, let them use us well; else let them know,
The ills we do, their ills instruct us so.
DESDEMONA.   Good night, good night! God me such usage[122] send,
Not to pick bad from bad, but by bad mend!

[Exeunt]

Act Fifth

SCENE FIRST: A street near BIANCA's lodging.

[*Enter* IAGO *and* RODERIGO]
IAGO.   Here, stand behind this bulk.[1] Straight[2] will he come.
Wear thy good rapier bare, and put it home.
Quick, quick. Fear nothing; I'll be at thy elbow.
It makes us, or it mars us. Think of that,
And fix most firm thy resolution.
RODERIGO.   Be near at hand. I may miscarry in't.
IAGO.   Here, at thy hand. Be bold, and take thy stand.

[Retires]

RODERIGO.   I have no great devotion to the deed;
And yet he has given me satisfying reasons.
'Tis but a man gone. Forth, my sword! he dies.
IAGO.   I have rubb'd this young quat[3] almost to the sense,[4]
And he grows angry. Now, whether he kill Cassio,
Or Cassio him, or each do kill the other,
Every way makes my gain. Live Roderigo,[5]
He calls me to a restitution large
Of gold and jewels that I bobb'd[6] from him,
As gifts to Desdemona.
It must not be. If Cassio do remain,
He has a daily beauty in his life
That makes me ugly; and, besides, the Moor
May unfold[7] me to him. There stand I in peril.
No, he must die. Be it so! I hear him coming.
[*Enter* CASSIO]
RODERIGO.   I know his gait; 'tis he. Villain, thou diest!
[*Makes a pass at* CASSIO]
CASSIO.   That thrust had been my enemy indeed
But that my coat is better than thou think'st.[8]
I will make proof of thine.
[*Draws, and wounds* RODERIGO]
RODERIGO.   O! I am slain!
[IAGO *from behind wounds* CASSIO *in the leg, and exit*]
CASSIO.   I am maim'd for ever! Light, ho! murder! murder!
[*Falls*]
[*Enter* OTHELLO]

---

[122] Habits.   [1] Projecting part of a building.   [2] Immediately.   [3] Pimple.
[4] To the quick.   [5] If Roderigo lives.   [6] Swindled.   [7] Expose.
[8] He wears a coat of mail under his jacket.

OTHELLO.   The voice of Cassio. Iago keeps his word.

RODERIGO.   O villain that I am!

OTHELLO.   Hark! 'Tis even so.

CASSIO.   O, help, ho! light! a surgeon!

OTHELLO.   'Tis he. O brave Iago, honest and just,
That hast such noble sense of thy friend's wrong!
Thou teachest me. Minion,[9] your dear lies dead,
And your fate hies apace.[10] Strumpet, I come!
Forth of my heart those charms, thine eyes, are blotted.
Thy bed, lust-stain'd, shall with lust's blood be spotted.

                                                    [*Exit* OTHELLO]

[*Enter* LODOVICO *and* GRATIANO]

CASSIO.   What ho! no watch? [11] no passage? [12] murder! murder!

GRATIANO.   'Tis some mischance. The cry is very direful.

CASSIO.   O, help!

LODOVICO.   Hark!

RODERIGO.   O wretched villain!

LODOVICO.   Two or three groan. It is a heavy[13] night;
These may be counterfeits. Let's think't unsafe
To come in to the cry without more help.

RODERIGO.   Nobody come? then shall I bleed to death.

LODOVICO.   Hark!

[*Enter* IAGO, *with a light*]

GRATIANO.   Here's one comes in his shirt, with light and weapons.

IAGO.   Who's there? Whose noise is this that cries on[14] murder?

LODOVICO.   We do not know.

IAGO.   Did not you hear a cry?

CASSIO.   Here, here! For heaven's sake, help me.

IAGO.   What's the matter?

GRATIANO.   This is Othello's ancient, as I take it.

LODOVICO.   The same indeed. A very valiant fellow.

IAGO.   What are you here that cry so grievously?

CASSIO.   Iago? O, I am spoil'd, undone by villains!
Give me some help.

IAGO.   O my lieutenant! what villains have done this?

CASSIO.   I think that one of them is hereabout,
And cannot make away.

IAGO.   O treacherous villains!
[*To* LODOVICO *and* GRATIANO] What are you there? Come in, and give some
help.

RODERIGO.   O help me here!

CASSIO.   That's one of them.

IAGO.   O murderous slave! O villain!
[*Stabs* RODERIGO]

RODERIGO.   O damn'd Iago! O inhuman dog!

IAGO.   Kill men i' the dark! Where be those bloody thieves?

---

[9] Hussy.   [10] Is coming on fast.   [11] City watch (police).   [12] Passers-by.   [13] Dark.
[14] Cries out.

How silent is this town! Ho! murder! murder!
What may you be? are you of good or evil?

LODOVICO.   As you shall prove us, praise[15] us.

IAGO.   Signior Lodovico?

LODOVICO.   He, sir.

IAGO.   I cry you mercy. Here's Cassio hurt by villains.

GRATIANO.   Cassio?

IAGO.   How is it, brother?

CASSIO.   My leg is cut in two.

IAGO.   Marry, heaven forbid!
Light, gentlemen. I'll bind it with my shirt.

[*Enter* BIANCA]

BIANCA.   What is the matter, ho? who is't that cried?

IAGO.   Who is't that cried!

BIANCA.   O my dear Cassio! O my sweet Cassio!
Cassio! Cassio!

IAGO.   O notable strumpet! Cassio, may you suspect
Who they should be that thus have mangled you?

CASSIO.   No.

GRATIANO.   I am sorry to find you thus. I have been to seek you.

IAGO.   Lend me a garter. So. O for a chair,
To bear him easily hence!

BIANCA.   Alas! he faints! O Cassio, Cassio, Cassio!

IAGO.   Gentlemen all, I do suspect this trash
To bear a part in this.
Patience awhile, good Cassio. Come, come.
Lend me a light. Know we this face, or no?
Alas! my friend and my dear countryman,
Roderigo? no: yes, sure. O heaven! Roderigo.

GRATIANO.   What? of Venice?

IAGO.   Even he, sir. Did you know him?

GRATIANO.   Know him? ay.

IAGO.   Signior Gratiano? I cry you gentle pardon.
These bloody accidents must excuse my manners,
That so neglected you.

GRATIANO.   I am glad to see you.

IAGO.   How do you, Cassio? O, a chair, a chair!

GRATIANO.   Roderigo!

[*A chair brought in*]

IAGO.   He. 'Tis he.—O! that's well said; the chair.
Some good man bear him carefully from hence.
I'll fetch the general's surgeon. [*To* BIANCA] For you, mistress,
Save you your labor. He that lies slain here, Cassio,
Was my dear friend. What malice was betwixt you?

CASSIO.   None in the world; nor do I know the man.

IAGO.   [*To* BIANCA] What! look you pale? O, bear him out o' the air.

[CASSIO *borne off*]

---

[15] Appraise.

Stay you, good gentlemen. Look you pale, mistress?—
Do you perceive the gastness[16] of her eye?—
Nay, if you stare, we shall hear more anon.—
Behold her well; I pray you, look upon her.
Do you see, gentlemen? nay, guiltiness
Will speak though tongues were out of use.
[*Enter* EMILIA]

EMILIA. 'Las! what's the matter? what's the matter, husband?

IAGO. Cassio has here been set on in the dark
By Roderigo and fellows that are 'scap'd.
He's almost slain, and Roderigo dead.

EMILIA. Alas, good gentleman! alas, good Cassio!

IAGO. This is the fruit of whoring. Pray, Emilia,
Go know of Cassio where he supp'd to-night.—
What! do you shake at that?

BIANCA. He supp'd at my house, but I therefore shake not.

IAGO. O, did he so? I charge you, go with me.

EMILIA. Fie, fie upon thee, strumpet!

BIANCA. I am no strumpet, but of life as honest
As you that thus abuse me.

EMILIA.   As I! foh! fie upon thee!

IAGO. Kind gentlemen, let's go see poor Cassio dress'd.
Come, mistress, you must tell's another tale.
Emilia, run you to the citadel,
And tell my lord and lady what has happ'd.
Will you go on afore? [*Aside*] This is the night
That either makes me or fordoes[17] me quite.

[*Exeunt*]

SCENE SECOND: *State bedroom in the Citadel.*

[*Enter* OTHELLO *with a light, and* DESDEMONA *in her bed*]
OTHELLO. It is the cause,[18] it is the cause, my soul.
Let me not name it to you, you chaste stars!
It is the cause. Yet I'll not shed her blood,
Nor scar that whiter skin of hers than snow,
And smooth as monumental alabaster.[19]
Yet she must die, else she'll betray more men.
Put out the light,[20] and then put out the light.[21]
If I quench thee, thou flaming minister,
I can again thy former light restore,
Should I repent me; but once put out thy light,

---

[16] Ghastliness.   [17] Destroys.
[18] Othello conceives of himself as acting from and for the highest principles and not out of any petty personal motives. He is serving a higher cause than the personal.
[19] A white translucent stone much used for elaborate funeral effigies and monuments.
[20] At this point, Othello puts out the flaming torches by the bed.   [21] Of Desdemona's life.

Thou cunning'st pattern of excelling nature,
I know not where is that Promethean heat[22]
That can thy light relume.[23] When I have pluck'd thy rose,
I cannot give it vital growth again.
It needs must wither. I'll smell it on the tree.
[*He kisses her*]
O balmy breath, that doth almost persuade
Justice to break her sword! One more, one more.
Be thus when thou art dead, and I will kill thee
And love thee after. Once more, and this the last!
So sweet was ne'er so fatal.[24] I must weep,
But they are cruel tears. This sorrow's heavenly,
It strikes where it doth love. She wakes.

DESDEMONA.   Who's there? Othello?

OTHELLO.   Ay, Desdemona.

DESDEMONA.   Will you come to bed, my lord?

OTHELLO.   Have you pray'd to-night, Desdemon?

DESDEMONA.   Ay, my lord.

OTHELLO.   If you bethink yourself of any crime
Unreconcil'd as yet to heaven and grace,[25]
Solicit for it straight.

DESDEMONA.   Alas, my lord, what may you mean by that?

OTHELLO.   Well, do it, and be brief. I will walk by.[26]
I would not kill thy unprepared spirit.
No (heaven forfend!), I would not kill thy soul.

DESDEMONA.   Talk you of killing?

OTHELLO.   Ay, I do.

DESDEMONA.   Then heaven
Have mercy on me!

OTHELLO.   Amen! with all my heart.

DESDEMONA.   If you say so, I hope you will not kill me.

OTHELLO.   Humh!

DESDEMONA.   And yet I fear you; for you are fatal then
When your eyes roll so. Why I should fear I know not,
Since guiltiness I know not; but yet I feel I fear.

OTHELLO.   Think on thy sins.

DESDEMONA.   They are loves I bear to you.

OTHELLO.   Ay, and for that thou diest.

DESDEMONA.   That death's unnatural that kills for loving.
Alas, why gnaw you so your nether lip?
Some bloody passion shakes your very frame.
These are portents, but yet, I hope, I hope,
They do not point on me.

OTHELLO.   Peace, and be still!

DESDEMONA.   I will so. What's the matter?

---

[22] The divine fire of life. Prometheus, in Greek mythology, stole fire from heaven for the use of mortals.   [23] Relight.   [24] Nothing as sweet as you was ever so deadly.
[25] God's grace or mercy.   [26] Aside.

OTHELLO. That handkerchief which I so lov'd and gave thee
    Thou gav'st to Cassio.

DESDEMONA.   No, by my life and soul!
    Send for the man and ask him.

OTHELLO.   Sweet soul, take heed,
    Take heed of perjury. Thou'rt on thy death-bed.

DESDEMONA. Ay, but not yet to die.

OTHELLO.   Yes, presently.
    Therefore confess thee freely of thy sin;
    For to deny each article with oath
    Cannot remove nor choke the strong conception[27]
    That I do groan withal. Thou art to die.

DESDEMONA. Then Lord have mercy on me!

OTHELLO.   I say, amen.

DESDEMONA. And have you mercy too! I never did
    Offend you in my life; never lov'd Cassio
    But with such general warranty[28] of heaven
    As I might love. I never gave him token.

OTHELLO. By heaven, I saw my handkerchief in his hand.
    O perjur'd woman! thou dost stone[29] my heart,
    And mak'st me call what I intend to do
    A murder, which I thought a sacrifice.
    I saw the handkerchief.

DESDEMONA.   He found it then.
    I never gave it him. Send for him hither;
    Let him confess a truth.

OTHELLO.   He has confess'd.

DESDEMONA. What, my lord?

OTHELLO. That he hath us'd thee.

DESDEMONA.   How? unlawfully?

OTHELLO. Ay.

DESDEMONA. He will not say so.

OTHELLO.   No; his mouth is stopp'd.
    Honest Iago hath ta'en order[30] for't.

DESDEMONA. O! my fear interprets. What! is he dead?

OTHELLO. Had all his hairs been lives, my great revenge
    Had stomach for them all.

DESDEMONA. Alas, he is betray'd and I undone!

OTHELLO. O strumpet! Weep'st thou for him to my face?

DESDEMONA. O, banish me, my lord, but kill me not!

OTHELLO. Down, strumpet!

DESDEMONA. Kill me to-morrow; let me live to-night!

OTHELLO. Nay, an you strive,—

DESDEMONA. But half an hour!

OTHELLO.   Being done, there is no pause.[31]

DESDEMONA. But while I say one prayer!

---

[27] Purpose.   [28] Permission.   [29] Make like stone.   [30] Measures.
[31] Now that it is being done, there can be no delay.

OTHELLO. It is too late.

[*He stifles her*]

EMILIA. [*Calls within*] My lord, my lord! what, ho! my lord, my lord!

OTHELLO. What noise is this? Not dead? not yet quite dead?
I that am cruel am yet merciful;
I would not have thee linger in thy pain.
So, so.

EMILIA. [*Within*] What, ho! my lord, my lord!

OTHELLO. Who's there?

EMILIA. [*Within*] O! good my lord, I'ld speak a word with you.

OTHELLO. Yes; 'tis Emilia.—By and by.—She's dead.
'Tis like she comes to speak of Cassio's death.
The noise was high. Ha! no more moving?
Still as the grave. Shall she come in? Were't good?
I think she stirs again: no. What's the best?
If she come in, she'll sure speak to my wife:
My wife! my wife! what wife? I have no wife:
O, insupportable! O heavy hour!
Methinks it should be now a huge eclipse
Of sun and moon, and that the affrighted globe
Should yawn at alteration.[32]

EMILIA. [*Within*] I do beseech you
That I may speak with you, O good my lord.

OTHELLO. I had forgot thee. O, come in, Emilia!—
Soft,[33] by and by.—Let me the curtains[34] draw.—
Where art thou?
[*Unlocks the door*]
[*Enter* EMILIA]
What's the matter with thee now?

EMILIA. O! my good lord, yonder's foul murders done.

OTHELLO. What! now?

EMILIA. But[35] now, my lord.

OTHELLO. It is the very error[36] of the moon.
She comes more near the earth than she was wont,
And makes men mad.

EMILIA. Cassio, my lord, has kill'd a young Venetian
Call'd Roderigo.

OTHELLO. Roderigo kill'd!
And Cassio kill'd!

EMILIA. No, Cassio is not kill'd.

OTHELLO. Not Cassio kill'd! then murder's out of tune,
And sweet revenge grows harsh.

DESDEMONA. O falsely, falsely murder'd.

EMILIA. O Lord! what cry is that?

OTHELLO. That? what?

---

[32] Gape at this horrible change.   [33] Wait.
[34] Of the bed. Elizabethan beds were surrounded by curtains.   [35] Just.
[36] Wandering from her proper movement.

EMILIA.   Out and alas! it is my lady's voice.
  Help! Help, ho! help! O lady, speak again!
  Sweet Desdemona! O sweet mistress, speak!
DESDEMONA.   A guiltless death I die.
EMILIA.   O! who has done this deed?
DESDEMONA.   Nobody. I myself. Farewell!
  Commend me to my kind lord. O farewell!
  [*She dies*]
OTHELLO.   Why, how should she be murder'd?
EMILIA.   Alas, who knows?
OTHELLO.   You heard her say herself it was not I.
EMILIA.   She said so. I must needs report a truth.
OTHELLO.   She's like a liar gone to burning hell.
  'Twas I that kill'd her.
EMILIA.   O the more angel she,
  And you the blacker devil.
OTHELLO.   She turn'd to folly,[37] and she was a whore.
EMILIA.   Thou dost belie her, and thou art a devil.
OTHELLO.   She was false as water.
EMILIA.   Thou art rash as fire to say
  That she was false. O she was heavenly true.
OTHELLO.   Cassio did top her. Ask thy husband else.
  O I were damn'd beneath all depth in hell
  But that I did proceed upon just grounds
  To this extremity. Thy husband knew it all.
EMILIA.   My husband?
OTHELLO.   Thy husband.
EMILIA.   That she was false to wedlock?
OTHELLO.   Ay, with Cassio. Nay, had she been true,
  If heaven would make me such another world
  Of one entire and perfect chrysolite,[38]
  I'd not have sold her for it.
EMILIA.   My husband?
OTHELLO.   Ay, 'twas he that told me first.
  An honest man he is, and hates the slime
  That sticks on filthy deeds.
EMILIA.   My husband?
OTHELLO.   What needs this iterance,[39] woman? I say thy husband.
EMILIA.   O mistress! villainy hath made mocks with[40] love.
  My husband say that she was false?
OTHELLO.   He, woman.
  I say, thy husband; dost understand the word?
  My friend, thy husband, honest, honest Iago.
EMILIA.   If he say so, may his pernicious soul
  Rot half a grain a day! He lies to the heart.
  She was too fond of her most filthy bargain.

---

[37] Lechery.   [38] A precious green stone.   [39] Repetition.   [40] Made a fool of.

OTHELLO. Ha!

EMILIA. Do thy worst.

This deed of thine is no more worthy heaven

Than thou wast worthy her.

OTHELLO.   Peace! you were best.[41]

EMILIA. Thou hast not half the power to do me harm

As I have to be hurt. O gull! O dolt!

As ignorant as dirt! Thou hast done a deed,—

I care not for thy sword. I'll make thee known,

Though I lost twenty lives. Help! help, ho! help!

The Moor has kill'd my mistress! Murder! murder!

[*Enter* MONTANO, GRATIANO, IAGO, *and others*]

MONTANO. What is the matter? How now, general?

EMILIA. O, are you come, Iago? You have done well,

That men must lay their murders on your neck.

GRATIANO. What is the matter?

EMILIA. Disprove this villain if thou be'st a man:

He says thou told'st him that his wife was false.

I know thou didst not. Thou'rt not such a villain.

Speak, for my heart is full.

IAGO. I told him what I thought, and told no more

Than what he found himself was apt[42] and true.

EMILIA. But did you ever tell him she was false?

IAGO. I did.

EMILIA. You told a lie, an odious damned lie;

Upon my soul, a lie, a wicked lie.

She false with Cassio! Did you say with Cassio?

IAGO. With Cassio, mistress. Go to, charm[43] your tongue.

EMILIA. I will not charm my tongue; I am bound to speak.

My mistress here lies murder'd in her bed.

ALL. O heavens forfend!

EMILIA. And your reports have set the murder on.

OTHELLO. Nay, stare not, masters. It is true indeed.

GRATIANO. 'Tis a strange truth.

MONTANO. O monstrous act!

EMILIA.   Villainy! villainy! villainy!

I think upon't, I think, I smell't. O villainy!

I thought so then.[44] I'll kill myself for grief.

O villainy, villainy!

IAGO. What! are you mad? I charge you, get you home.

EMILIA. Good gentlemen, let me have leave to speak.

'Tis proper I obey him, but not now.

Perchance, Iago, I will ne'er go home.

OTHELLO. Oh! Oh! Oh!

[OTHELLO *falls on the bed*]

---

[41] It would be best for you to be quiet.   [42] Likely.   [43] Put a spell of silence on.

[44] See above IV, ii, or III, iii.

EMILIA.   Nay, lay thee down and roar,
For thou hast kill'd the sweetest innocent
That e'er did lift up eye.

OTHELLO.   O! she was foul.
I scarce did know you, uncle. There lies your niece,
Whose breath, indeed, these hands have newly stopp'd.
I know this act shows[45] terrible and grim.

GRATIANO.   Poor Desdemon, I am glad thy father's dead.
Thy match was mortal to him,[46] and pure grief
Shore his old thread a-twain.[47] Did he live now,
This sight would make him do a desperate turn,[48]
Yea, curse his better angel from his side,
And fall to reprobation.[49]

OTHELLO.   'Tis pitiful; but yet Iago knows
That she with Cassio hath the act of shame
A thousand times committed. Cassio confess'd it;
And she did gratify his amorous works
With the recognizance[50] and pledge of love
Which I first gave her. I saw it in his hand.
It was a handkerchief, an antique token
My father gave my mother.

EMILIA.   O God! O heavenly God!

IAGO.   Zounds! hold your peace.

EMILIA.   'Twill out, 'twill out! I hold my peace, sir? No!
No, I will speak as liberal as the north.[51]
Let heaven and men and devils, let them all,
All, all, cry shame against me, yet I'll speak.

IAGO.   Be wise, and get you home.

EMILIA.   I will not.

[IAGO *threatens* EMILIA]

GRATIANO.   Fie!
Your sword upon a woman?

EMILIA.   O thou dull Moor! that handkerchief thou speak'st of
I found by fortune[52] and did give my husband,
For often with a solemn earnestness
(More than, indeed, belong'd to such a trifle)
He begg'd of me to steal it.

IAGO.   Villainous whore!

EMILIA.   She give it Cassio? No, alas! I found it,
And I did give't my husband.

IAGO.   Filth, thou liest!

EMILIA.   By heaven, I do not. I do not, gentlemen.
O murderous coxcomb! what should such a fool
Do with so good a wife?

---

[45] Looks.   [46] Killed him.   [47] Cut his life in two.   [48] Deed.
[49] Damnation. Gratiano suggests Brabantio would have committed suicide at this news.
[50] Token.   [51] As freely as the north wind.   [52] Chance.

OTHELLO.   Are there no stones[53] in heaven
But what serves for the thunder? Precious villain!
[*The* MOOR *runs at* IAGO. IAGO *kills his wife*]
GRATIANO.   The woman falls. Sure, he has kill'd his wife.

[Exit IAGO]

EMILIA.   Ay, ay. O lay me by my mistress' side.
GRATIANO.   He's gone, but his wife's kill'd.
MONTANO.   'Tis a notorious villain. [*To* GRATIANO] Take you this weapon,
Which I have here recover'd from the Moor.
Come, guard the door without. Let him not pass,
But kill him rather. I'll after that same villain,
For 'tis a damned slave.

[Exeunt MONTANO and GRATIANO]

OTHELLO.   I am not valiant neither,
But every puny whipster[54] gets my sword .
But why should honor outlive honesty?
Let it go all.
EMILIA.   What did thy song bode, lady?
Hark, canst thou hear me? I will play the swan,
And die in music.[55]

[Sings]

Willow, willow, willow.

Moor, she was chaste. She lov'd thee, cruel Moor.
So come my soul to bliss as I speak true.
So speaking as I think, I die, I die.
[*She dies*]
OTHELLO.   I have another weapon in this chamber.
It is a sword of Spain, the ice brook's temper.[56]
O here it is.—Uncle, I must come forth.
GRATIANO.   [*Within*] If thou attempt it, it will cost thee dear.
Thou hast no weapon, and perforce must suffer.
OTHELLO.   Look in upon me then, and speak to me,
Or, naked [57] as I am, I will assault thee.
[*Enter* GRATIANO]
GRATIANO.   What is the matter?
OTHELLO.   Behold! I have a weapon.
A better never did itself sustain
Upon a soldier's thigh. I have seen the day
That with this little arm and this good sword
I have made my way through more impediments
Than twenty times your stop.[58] But O vain boast!
Who can control his fate? 'Tis not so now.
Be not afraid, though you do see me weapon'd.
Here is my journey's end, here is my butt[59]

---

[53] Thunderbolts, i.e., cannot one strike Iago?   [54] Whippersnapper.
[55] Die like a swan, singing at my death.   [56] Spanish sword, tempered in icy water.
[57] Unarmed.   [58] The impediment you offer.   [59] Goal.

And very sea-mark[60] of my utmost sail.
Do you go back dismay'd? 'Tis a lost fear.
Man but a rush[61] against Othello's breast,
And he retires. Where should Othello go?—
Now, how dost thou look now? O ill-starr'd [62] wench!
Pale as thy smock! When we shall meet at compt,[63]
This look of thine will hurl my soul from heaven,
And fiends will snatch at it. Cold, cold, my girl,
Even like thy chastity.
O cursed, cursed slave! Whip me, ye devils,
From the possession of this heavenly sight!
Blow me about in winds! roast me in sulphur!
Wash me in steep-down[64] gulfs of liquid fire!
O Desdemona! Desdemona! dead!
O! O! O!

[*Enter* LODOVICO, MONTANO, IAGO *as a prisoner, and* OFFICERS, CASSIO *in a chair*]

LODOVICO.   Where is this rash and most unfortunate man?

OTHELLO.   That's he that was Othello. Here I am.

LODOVICO.   Where is that viper? bring the villain forth.

OTHELLO.   I look down towards his feet,[65] but that's a fable.
If that thou be'st a devil,[66] I cannot kill thee.

[*Wounds* IAGO]

LODOVICO.   Wring his sword from him.

IAGO.   I bleed,[67] sir, but not kill'd.

OTHELLO.   I am not sorry neither. I'd have thee live,
For in my sense 'tis happiness to die.

LODOVICO.   O thou Othello that wert once so good,
Fall'n in the practice[68] of a damned slave,
What shall be said to thee?

OTHELLO.   Why, anything:
An honorable murderer, if you will;
For nought did I in hate, but all in honor.

LODOVICO.   This wretch hath part confess'd his villainy.
Did you and he consent in Cassio's death?

OTHELLO.   Ay.

CASSIO.   Dear general, I did never give you cause.

OTHELLO.   I do believe it, and I ask you pardon.
Will you, I pray, demand that demi-devil
Why he hath thus ensnar'd my soul and body.

IAGO.   Demand me nothing. What you know, you know:
From this time forth I never will speak word.

LODOVICO.   What! not to pray?

GRATIANO.   Torments will ope your lips.

OTHELLO.   Well, thou dost best.

---

[60] Limit.   [61] Attack with only a reed.   [62] Ill-fated.
[63] The Last Day, the Day of Judgment.   [64] Sheer.   [65] I.e., to see if he has cloven hoofs.
[66] I.e., invulnerable to weapons.   [67] I.e., I'm human.   [68] Victim of the plot.

LODOVICO. Sir, you shall understand what hath befall'n,
Which, as I think, you know not. Here is a letter
Found in the pocket of the slain Roderigo,
And here another. The one of them imports[69]
The death of Cassio to be undertook
By Roderigo.

OTHELLO. O villain!

CASSIO.   Most heathenish and most gross!

LODOVICO. Now here's another discontented paper,[70]
Found in his pocket too; and this, it seems,
Roderigo meant t' have sent this damned villain,
But that, belike, Iago in the interim
Came in and satisfied him.

OTHELLO.   O the pernicious caitiff!
How came you, Cassio, by that handkerchief
That was my wife's?

CASSIO.   I found it in my chamber;
And he himself confess'd it even now
That there he dropp'd it for a special purpose
Which wrought to[71] his desire.

OTHELLO.   O fool! fool! fool!

CASSIO. There is besides in Roderigo's letter
How he upbraids Iago that he made him
Brave[72] me upon the watch, whereon it came
That I was cast:[73] and even but now he spake
(After long seeming dead): Iago hurt him,
Iago set him on.

LODOVICO. You must forsake this room and go with us.
Your power and your command is taken off,
And Cassio rules in Cyprus. For this slave,
If there be any cunning cruelty
That can torment him much and hold him long,[74]
It shall be his. You shall close prisoner rest,
Till that the nature of your fault be known
To the Venetian state. Come, bring him away.

OTHELLO. Soft you! [75] A word or two before you go.
I have done the state some service, and they know't;
No more of that. I pray you, in your letters,
When you shall these unlucky deeds relate,
Speak of them as they are. Nothing extenuate,
Nor set down aught in malice. Then must you speak
Of one that lov'd not wisely but too well;
Of one not easily jealous, but, being wrought,[76]
Perplex'd [77] in the extreme; of one whose hand
(Like the base Indian) threw a pearl away
Richer than all his tribe; of one whose subdu'd eyes,

---

[69] Concerns.   [70] Expressing discontent.   [71] Fitted in with.   [72] Defy.   [73] Dismissed
[74] In dying.   [75] Wait!   [76] Worked upon.   [77] Distraught.

Albeit unused to the melting mood,[78]
Drops tears as fast as the Arabian trees
Their medicinal gum. Set you down this;
And say besides, that in Aleppo once,
Where a malignant and a turban'd Turk
Beat a Venetian and traduc'd the state,
I took by the throat the circumcised dog,
And smote him thus.
[*He stabs himself*]

LODOVICO. O bloody period! [79]

GRATIANO.   All that's spoke is marr'd.[80]

OTHELLO. I kiss'd thee ere I kill'd thee. No way but this,
Killing myself to die upon a kiss.
[*He dies*]

CASSIO. This did I fear, but thought he had no weapon;
For he was great of heart.

LODOVICO. [*To* IAGO] O Spartan[81] dog,
More fell [82] than anguish, hunger, or the sea,
Look on the tragic loading of this bed!
This is thy work. The object poisons sight;
Let it be hid. Gratiano, keep the house,
And seize upon the fortunes of the Moor,
For they succeed to you. To you, lord governor,
Remains the centure[83] of this hellish villain,
The time, the place, the torture. O, enforce it! [84]
Myself will straight aboard, and to the state
This heavy act with heavy heart relate.

                                        [*Exeunt omnes*]

---

[78] Crying.   [79] End.   [80] Spoiled.   [81] Fierce (like a Spartan).   [82] Cruel.
[83] Sentencing.   [84] Make it hard.

The Misanthrope

Molière

Molière

The first actor to play the role of Alceste, protagonist of *The Misanthrope*, was the man who created the role: Molière himself. His wife played the role of Célimène. It is not necessary to identify Molière with Alceste to think that in some sense Alceste's passionate outbursts against the insincerity, the self-interest, the treachery he sees everywhere about him reflect Molière's own feelings. In 1666, the year *The Misanthrope* was first produced, Molière had reason to be dissatisfied with the way of the world, despite his success in the theatre: his play *Tartuffe* had been banned as a result of the pressures exerted by a secret organization of religious zealots; his wife, Armande, was unfaithful to him; he had been deceived by his friend Racine, the great writer of tragedies. But if something of all this is indirectly echoed in Alceste's bitterness, it is wholly characteristic of Molière that he should laugh at the extravagance of Alceste's demand for a world of perfect sincerity and uprightness. That utopian vision must have seemed remote indeed from the world in which Molière had struggled to achieve his eminence.

Jean-Baptiste Poquelin was born in Paris in 1622. His father was a prosperous businessman, an upholsterer and decorator, so successful that he did work by appointment to the king and held the post of *valet de chambre du Roi*. The boy was sent to the Collège de Clermont, an aristocratic Jesuit school, where he received excellent training in the humanities, and he may also have studied law. At the age of 21, however, young Poquelin suddenly tossed over his background and his prospects to become an actor. It was a dramatic gesture: in respectable circles in seventeenth-century France the theatre was looked upon as a moral plague—all actors, for example, were automatically excommunicated from the Church. Jean-Baptiste Poquelin's decision was heavily influenced by a red-headed actress, Madeleine Béjart, one of a family of actors with whom the young man (who soon took the name Molière) was to be intimately involved for the rest of his life.

Molière and his new associates formed an acting troupe, and for over a year they performed in Paris. They failed badly. Molière was sent to prison for debt. His father bailed him out, but if he had hoped for his son's reformation he was disappointed. Molière, the red-headed Madeleine, and the rest of the Béjart family headed for the provinces. For the next thirteen years they wandered from town to village to provincial city, setting up in barns, innyards—wherever they could make accommodation to produce their plays. Almost nothing is known directly of Molière's life during those years, but when finally, in 1658, the troupe returned to Paris, now under the protection of the king's brother, Molière was writing plays for the company, directing its productions, and playing leading roles. The first major success came in November 1659 with the production of his *Les Précieuses ridicules* which set all Paris abuzz. From this time until his death in 1673 Molière's success as a dramatist was never in question. He was a favorite of Louis XIV, the Court, the public—if not of the Catholic Church. His company, which was allowed to call itself *La Troupe du Roi*, is the direct ancestor of the present Comédie Française.

When he was 40, Molière married Armande Béjart, who was declared to be Madeleine's younger sister, although gossip said she was in fact Madeleine's daughter. Madeleine had long been Molière's mistress. The situation was defiantly scandalous.

Professional success was accompanied by trouble of many kinds. Enemies sought to undermine Molière's position with the king. Rival players and playwrights tried various means to cut him down. Armande was unfaithful. His health was wretched—he suffered particularly from a persistent cough. But through it all Molière continued to write and produce comedy after superb comedy—many critics think the most brilliant galaxy of comedies ever written.

His last play, written in 1673, was *Le Malade imaginaire* (*The Imaginary Invalid*), a very funny satire on the pompous fakery of doctors, at whose hands Molière had suffered for years. At the fourth performance of the play, in which he played the role of the imaginary invalid himself, Molière was seized by a violent fit of coughing. He managed to finish the performance before he collapsed. A blood vessel had broken, and a few hours after being carried from the stage on which he had lived most of his life, Molière died.

The Misanthrope is one of the most brilliantly enigmatic plays in the history of the drama. As with *Hamlet*, no two readers, critics, or actors can be found who agree on its essential meaning. Even in the Comédie Francaise, with its strongly conservative tradition going back to Molière himself, each new Alceste inevitably brings his own (or his director's) conception of the role to the stage and thus in effect brings a new meaning to the play—or, more accurately, brings a new meaning out of the play. For *The Misanthrope* is an amazingly "open" work; sound justification for the most diverse readings can be found in the language of the play itself.

The major issue, which so many critics have debated, can be simply put. Whose side are we to take in the major confrontation of the play: that of Alceste or that of Philinte? M. Michaut (*Les Luttes de Molière*) has an admirable summary of the enormous critical literature which can be divided roughly, he says, into three principal schools. First (the largest group) are those who think Molière intended Alceste to be the sympathetic character of the play, a model to be admired and followed—an intemperate model, perhaps, but noble compared with the temporizing man of the world, Philinte. Second is a smaller group (including Michaut himself) which takes exactly the opposite position: Philinte, the urbane and reasonable gentleman, is the model, as opposed to the outrageous malcontent, Alceste. Philinte is the *honnête homme* who often speaks for Molière. A third group, plumping for the *juste-milieu*, holds that neither Alceste nor Philinte is a model, but that one must put together the best qualities of each, avoiding their respective extremes.

Major impetus to the critical division came in the eighteenth century when Jean-Jacques Rousseau (*Lettre à Mr. d'Alembert*) wrote a diatribe against the theatre in general and *The Misanthrope* in particular, a play he called "vicious" and "immoral." In his view, Molière commits the unforgivable sin of making Alceste an embodiment of virtue in the corrupt world of the aristocracy in seventeenth-century Paris and then ridiculing him in favor of the immoral Philinte. A hundred critics have responded to this analysis, their characterization of the play depending upon their balancing of the issues and the deployment of their sympathies. For Goethe, who thinks of Alceste as a pure and noble spirit doing battle against a corrupt society, *The Misanthrope* is a tragedy. For Voltaire it is a satire, wiser and finer than any of Horace or Boileau. For M. René Bray in our time, it is pure comedy in which taking sides is absurd.

There is no harm in all this disagreement. It is folly to think that there is only one "real" interpretation of so richly ambiguous a play as *The Misanthrope,* although unquestionably some interpretations are more real than others. The themes Molière deals with are perennially engaging: the Roman satirists debated them in their poems, Thomas More and Raphael Hythloday met head-on over them in More's *Utopia,* they are argued on college campuses and in political forums throughout our country today. Molière's great play makes imaginatively available to us issues that we all encounter. We know the Alcestes, the Philintes, the Célimènes of the world; but it is a condition of life that each generation— each individual—must respond to them as he finds best.

Richard Wilbur's translation conveys brilliantly the formal, controlled, epigrammatic quality of Molière's verse. The play has found the translation it deserves.

The Misanthrope

Molière

TRANSLATED BY RICHARD WILBUR

CHARACTERS

ALCESTE, *in love with Célimène*
PHILINTE, *Alceste's friend*
ORONTE, *in love with Célimène*
CELIMENE, *Alceste's beloved*
ELIANTE, *Célimène's cousin*
ARSINOE, *a friend of Célimène's*

ACASTE ⎱ *marquesses*
CLITANDRE ⎰
BASQUE, *Célimène's servant*
A GUARD *of the Marshalsea*
DUBOIS, *Alceste's valet*

The scene throughout is in Célimène's house at Paris.

Act One

SCENE ONE: PHILINTE, ALCESTE

PHILINTE
Now, what's got into you?
ALCESTE [*Seated*]
                              Kindly leave me alone.
PHILINTE
Come, come, what is it? This lugubrious tone . . .
ALCESTE
Leave me, I said; you spoil my solitude.
PHILINTE
Oh, listen to me, now, and don't be rude.
ALCESTE
I choose to be rude, Sir, and to be hard of hearing.

PHILINTE
   These ugly moods of yours are not endearing;
   Friends though we are, I really must insist . . .
ALCESTE [*Abruptly rising*]
   Friends? Friends, you say? Well, cross me off your list.
   I've been your friend till now, as you well know;
   But after what I saw a moment ago
   I tell you flatly that our ways must part.
   I wish no place in a dishonest heart.
PHILINTE
   Why, what have I done, Alceste? Is this quite just?
ALCESTE
   My God, you ought to die of self-disgust.
   I call your conduct inexcusable, Sir,
   And every man of honor will concur.
   I see you almost hug a man to death,
   Exclaim for joy until you're out of breath,
   And supplement these loving demonstrations
   With endless offers, vows, and protestations;
   Then when I ask you "Who was that?", I find
   That you can barely bring his name to mind!
   Once the man's back is turned, you cease to love him,
   And speak with absolute indifference of him!
   By God, I say it's base and scandalous
   To falsify the heart's affections thus;
   If I caught myself behaving in such a way,
   I'd hang myself for shame, without delay.
PHILINTE
   It hardly seems a hanging matter to me;
   I hope that you will take it graciously
   If I extend myself a slight reprieve,
   And live a little longer, by your leave.
ALCESTE
   How dare you joke about a crime so grave?
PHILINTE
   What crime? How else are people to behave?
ALCESTE
   I'd have them be sincere, and never part
   With any word that isn't from the heart.
PHILINTE
   When someone greets us with a show of pleasure,
   It's but polite to give him equal measure,
   Return his love the best that we know how,
   And trade him offer for offer, vow for vow.
ALCESTE
   No, no, this formula you'd have me follow,
   However fashionable, is false and hollow,
   And I despise the frenzied operations

Of all these barterers of protestations,
These lavishers of meaningless embraces,
These utterers of obliging commonplaces,
Who court and flatter everyone on earth
And praise the fool no less than the man of worth.
Should you rejoice that someone fondles you,
Offers his love and service, swears to be true,
And fills your ears with praises of your name,
When to the first damned fop he'll say the same?
No, no: no self-respecting heart would dream
Of prizing so promiscuous an esteem;
However high the praise, there's nothing worse
Than sharing honors with the universe.
Esteem is founded on comparison:
To honor all men is to honor none.
Since you embrace this indiscriminate vice,
Your friendship comes at far too cheap a price;
I spurn the easy tribute of a heart
Which will not set the worthy man apart:
I choose, Sir, to be chosen; and in fine,
The friend of mankind is no friend of mine.

PHILINTE

But in polite society, custom decrees
That we show certain outward courtesies. . . .

ALCESTE

Ah, no! we should condemn with all our force
Such false and artificial intercourse.
Let men behave like men; let them display
Their inmost hearts in everything they say;
Let the heart speak, and let our sentiments
Not mask themselves in silly compliments.

PHILINTE

In certain cases it would be uncouth
And most absurd to speak the naked truth;
With all respect for your exalted notions,
It's often best to veil one's true emotions.
Wouldn't the social fabric come undone
If we were wholly frank with everyone?
Suppose you met with someone you couldn't bear;
Would you inform him of it then and there?

ALCESTE

Yes.

PHILINTE

Then you'd tell old Emilie it's pathetic
The way she daubs her features with cosmetic
And plays the gay coquette at sixty-four?

ALCESTE

I would.

PHILINTE

          And you'd call Dorilas a bore,
And tell him every ear at court is lame
From hearing him brag about his noble name?

ALCESTE

   Precisely.

PHILINTE

          Ah, you're joking.

ALCESTE

                        Au contraire:
In this regard there's none I'd choose to spare.
All are corrupt; there's nothing to be seen
In court or town but aggravates my spleen.
I fall into deep gloom and melancholy
When I survey the scene of human folly,
Finding on every hand base flattery,
Injustice, fraud, self-interest, treachery. . . .
Ah, it's too much; mankind has grown so base,
I mean to break with the whole human race.

PHILINTE

This philosophic rage is a bit extreme;
You've no idea how comical you seem;
Indeed, we're like those brothers in the play
Called *School for Husbands*,[1] one of whom was prey . .

ALCESTE

Enough, now! None of your stupid similes.

PHILINTE

Then let's have no more tirades, if you please.
The world won't change, whatever you say or do;
And since plain speaking means so much to you,
I'll tell you plainly that by being frank
You've earned the reputation of a crank,
And that you're thought ridiculous when you rage
And rant against the manners of the age.

ALCESTE

So much the better; just what I wish to hear.
No news could be more grateful to my ear.
All men are so detestable in my eyes,
I should be sorry if they thought me wise.

PHILINTE

Your hatred's very sweeping, is it not?

ALCESTE

Quite right: I hate the whole degraded lot.

PHILINTE

Must all poor human creatures be embraced,
Without distinction, by your vast distaste?
Even in these bad times, there are surely a few . . .

[1] A play by Molière.

ALCESTE

No, I include all men in one dim view:
Some men I hate for being rogues; the others
I hate because they treat the rogues like brothers,
And, lacking a virtuous scorn for what is vile,
Receive the villain with a complaisant smile.
Notice how tolerant people choose to be
Toward that bold rascal who's at law with me.
His social polish can't conceal his nature;
One sees at once that he's a treacherous creature;
No one could possibly be taken in
By those soft speeches and that sugary grin.
The whole world knows the shady means by which
The low-brow's grown so powerful and rich,
And risen to a rank so bright and high
That virtue can but blush, and merit sigh.
Whenever his name comes up in conversation,
None will defend his wretched reputation;
Call him knave, liar, scoundrel, and all the rest,
Each head will nod, and no one will protest.
And yet his smirk is seen in every house,
He's greeted everywhere with smiles and bows,
And when there's any honor that can be got
By pulling strings, he'll get it, like as not.
My God! It chills my heart to see the ways
Men come to terms with evil nowadays;
Sometimes, I swear, I'm moved to flee and find
Some desert land unfouled by humankind.

PHILINTE

Come, let's forget the follies of the times
And pardon mankind for its petty crimes;
Let's have an end of rantings and of railings,
And show some leniency toward human failings.
This world requires a pliant rectitude;
Too stern a virtue makes one stiff and rude;
Good sense views all extremes with detestation,
And bids us to be noble in moderation.
The rigid virtues of the ancient days
Are not for us; they jar with all our ways
And ask of us too lofty a perfection.
Wise men accept their times without objection,
And there's no greater folly, if you ask me,
Than trying to reform society.
Like you, I see each day a hundred and one
Unhandsome deeds that might be better done,
But still, for all the faults that meet my view,
I'm never known to storm and rave like you.
I take men as they are, or let them be,

And teach my soul to bear their frailty;
And whether in court or town, whatever the scene,
My phlegm's as philosophic as your spleen.[2]

ALCESTE

This phlegm which you so eloquently commend,
Does nothing ever rile it up, my friend?
Suppose some man you trust should treacherously
Conspire to rob you of your property,
And do his best to wreck your reputation?
Wouldn't you feel a certain indignation?

PHILINTE

Why, no. These faults of which you so complain
Are part of human nature, I maintain,
And it's no more a matter for disgust
That men are knavish, selfish and unjust,
Than that the vulture dines upon the dead,
And wolves are furious, and apes ill-bred.

ALCESTE

Shall I see myself betrayed, robbed, torn to bits,
And not . . . Oh, let's be still and rest our wits.
Enough of reasoning, now. I've had my fill.

PHILINTE

Indeed, you would do well, Sir, to be still.
Rage less at your opponent, and give some thought
To how you'll win this lawsuit that he's brought.

ALCESTE

I assure you I'll do nothing of the sort.

PHILINTE

Then who will plead your case before the court?

ALCESTE

Reason and right and justice will plead for me.

PHILINTE

Oh, Lord. What judges do you plan to see? [3]

ALCESTE

Why, none. The justice of my cause is clear.

PHILINTE

Of course, man; but there's politics to fear. . . .

ALCESTE

No, I refuse to lift a hand. That's flat.
I'm either right, or wrong.

PHILINTE

                                        Don't count on that.

ALCESTE

No, I'll do nothing.

---

[2] A reference to opposing "humours" in the old physiology. A preponderance of phlegm produced an apathetic temperament; a preponderance of bile a splenetic temperament.
[3] It was customary to try to influence judges before a trial.

PHILINTE
Your enemy's influence
Is great you know . . .
ALCESTE
That makes no difference.
PHILINTE
It will; you'll see.
ALCESTE
Must honor bow to guile?
If so, I shall be proud to lose the trial.
PHILINTE
Oh, really . . .
ALCESTE
I'll discover by this case
Whether or not men are sufficiently base
And impudent and villainous and perverse
To do me wrong before the universe.
PHILINTE
What a man!
ALCESTE
Oh, I could wish, whatever the cost,
Just for the beauty of it, that my trial were lost.
PHILINTE
If people heard you talking so, Alceste,
They'd split their sides. Your name would be a jest.
ALCESTE
So much the worse for jesters.
PHILINTE
May I enquire
Whether this rectitude you so admire,
And these hard virtues you're enamored of
Are qualities of the lady whom you love?
It much surprises me that you, who seem
To view mankind with furious disesteem,
Have yet found something to enchant your eyes
Amidst a species which you so despise.
And what is more amazing, I'm afraid,
Is the most curious choice your heart has made.
The honest Eliante is fond of you,
Arsinoé, the prude, admires you too;
And yet your spirit's been perversely led
To choose the flighty Célimène instead,
Whose brittle malice and coquettish ways
So typify the manners of our days.
How is it that the traits you most abhor
Are bearable in this lady you adore?
Are you so blind with love that you can't find them?
Or do you contrive, in her case, not to mind them?

ALCESTE

My love for that young widow's not the kind
That can't perceive defects; no, I'm not blind.
I see her faults, despite my ardent love,
And all I see I fervently reprove.
And yet I'm weak; for all her falsity,
That woman knows the art of pleasing me,
And though I never cease complaining of her,
I swear I cannot manage not to love her.
Her charm outweighs her faults; I can but aim
To cleanse her spirit in my love's pure flame.

PHILINTE

That's no small task; I wish you all success.
You think then that she loves you?

ALCESTE

                                        Heavens, yes!
I wouldn't love her did she not love me.

PHILINTE

Well, if her taste for you is plain to see,
Why do these rivals cause you such despair?

ALCESTE

True love, Sir, is possessive, and cannot bear
To share with all the world. I'm here today
To tell her she must send that mob away.

PHILINTE

If I were you, and had your choice to make,
Eliante, her cousin, would be the one I'd take;
That honest heart, which cares for you alone,
Would harmonize far better with your own.

ALCESTE

True, true: each day my reason tells me so;
But reason doesn't rule in love, you know.

PHILINTE

I fear some bitter sorrow is in store;
This love . . .

SCENE TWO: ORONTE, ALCESTE, PHILINTE

ORONTE [*To* ALCESTE]

                The servants told me at the door
That Eliante and Célimène were out,
But when I heard, dear Sir, that you were about,
I came to say, without exaggeration,
That I hold you in the vastest admiration,
And that it's always been my dearest desire
To be the friend of one I so admire.
I hope to see my love of merit requited,

And you and I in friendship's bond united.
I'm sure you won't refuse—if I may be frank—
A friend of my devotedness—and rank.
[*During this speech of* ORONTE'S, ALCESTE *is abstracted, and seems unaware
that he is being spoken to. He only breaks off his reverie when* ORONTE *says*]
It was for you, if you please, that my words were intended.

ALCESTE

For me, Sir?

ORONTE

     Yes, for you. You're not offended?

ALCESTE

By no means. But this much surprises me. . . .
The honor comes most unexpectedly. . . .

ORONTE

My high regard should not astonish you;
The whole world feels the same. It is your due.

ALCESTE

Sir . . .

ORONTE

    Why, in all the State there isn't one
Can match your merits; they shine, Sir, like the sun.

ALCESTE

Sir . . .

ORONTE

    You are higher in my estimation
Than all that's most illustrious in the nation.

ALCESTE

Sir . . .

ORONTE

    If I lie, may heaven strike me dead!
To show you that I mean what I have said,
Permit me, Sir, to embrace you most sincerely,
And swear that I will prize our friendship dearly.
Give me your hand. And now, Sir, if you choose,
We'll make our vows.

ALCESTE

     Sir . . .

ORONTE

       What! You refuse?

ALCESTE

Sir, it's a very great honor you extend:
But friendship is a sacred thing, my friend;
It would be profanation to bestow
The name of friend on one you hardly know.
All parts are better played when well-rehearsed;
Let's put off friendship, and get acquainted first.
We may discover it would be unwise
To try to make our natures harmonize.

ORONTE

By heaven! You're sagacious to the core;
This speech has made me admire you even more.
Let time, then, bring us closer day by day;
Meanwhile, I shall be yours in every way.
If, for example, there should be anything
You wish at court, I'll mention it to the King.
I have his ear, of course; it's quite well known
That I am much in favor with the throne.
In short, I am your servant. And now, dear friend,
Since you have such fine judgment, I intend
To please you, if I can, with a small sonnet
I wrote not long ago. Please comment on it,
And tell me whether I ought to publish it.

ALCESTE

You must excuse me, Sir; I'm hardly fit
To judge such matters.

ORONTE

                           Why not?

ALCESTE

                                        I am, I fear,
Inclined to be unfashionably sincere.

ORONTE

Just what I ask; I'd take no satisfaction
In anything but your sincere reaction.
I beg you not to dream of being kind.

ALCESTE

Since you desire it, Sir, I'll speak my mind.

ORONTE

Sonnet. It's a sonnet. . . . *Hope* . . . The poem's addressed
To a lady who wakened hopes within my breast.
Hope . . . this is not the pompous sort of thing,
Just modest little verses, with a tender ring.

ALCESTE

Well, we shall see.

ORONTE

                      Hope . . . I'm anxious to hear
Whether the style seems properly smooth and clear,
And whether the choice of words is good or bad.

ALCESTE

We'll see, we'll see.

ORONTE

                         Perhaps I ought to add
That it took me only a quarter-hour to write it.

ALCESTE

The time's irrelevant, Sir: kindly recite it.

ORONTE [*Reading*]

                    Hope comforts us awhile, t'is true,

> Lulling our cares with careless laughter,
>   And yet such joy is full of rue,
> My Phyllis, if nothing follows after.

PHILINTE
I'm charmed by this already; the style's delightful.

ALCESTE [*Sotto voce to* PHILINTE]
How can you say that? Why, the thing is frightful.

ORONTE

> Your fair face smiled on me awhile,
>   But was it kindness so to enchant me?
> 'Twould have been fairer not to smile,
>   If hope was all you meant to grant me.

PHILINTE
What a clever thought! How handsomely you phrase it!

ALCESTE [*Sotto voce to* PHILINTE]
You know the thing is trash. How dare you praise it?

ORONTE

> If it's to be my passion's fate
> Thus everlastingly to wait,
> Then death will come to set me free:
> For death is fairer than the fair;
> Phyllis, to hope is to despair
> When one must hope eternally.

PHILINTE
The close is exquisite—full of feeling and grace.

ALCESTE [*Sotto voce, aside*]
Oh, blast the close; you'd better close your face
Before you send your lying soul to hell.

PHILINTE
I can't remember a poem I've liked so well.

ALCESTE [*Sotto voce, aside*]
Good Lord!

ORONTE [*To* PHILINTE]
      I fear you're flattering me a bit.

PHILINTE
Oh, no!

ALCESTE [*Sotto voce, aside*]
      What else d'you call it, you hypocrite?

ORONTE [*To* ALCESTE]
But you, Sir, keep your promise now: don't shrink
From telling me sincerely what you think.

ALCESTE
Sir, these are delicate matters; we all desire
To be told that we've the true poetic fire.
But once, to one whose name I shall not mention,
I said, regarding some verse of his invention,
That gentlemen should rigorously control
That itch to write which often afflicts the soul;

That one should curb the heady inclination
To publicize one's little avocation;
And that in showing off one's works of art
One often plays a very clownish part.

ORONTE

Are you suggesting in a devious way
That I ought not . . .

ALCESTE

                       Oh, that I do not say.
Further, I told him that no fault is worse
Than that of writing frigid, lifeless verse,
And that the merest whisper of such a shame
Suffices to destroy a man's good name.

ORONTE

D'you mean to say my sonnet's dull and trite?

ALCESTE

I don't say that. But I went on to cite
Numerous cases of once-respected men
Who came to grief by taking up the pen.

ORONTE

And am I like them? Do I write so poorly?

ALCESTE

I don't say that. But I told this person, "Surely
You're under no necessity to compose;
Why you should wish to publish, heaven knows.
There's no excuse for printing tedious rot
Unless one writes for bread, as you do not.
Resist temptation, then, I beg of you;
Conceal your pastimes from the public view;
And don't give up, on any provocation,
Your present high and courtly reputation,
To purchase at a greedy printer's shop
The name of silly author and scribbling fop."
These were the points I tried to make him see.

ORONTE

I sense that they are also aimed at me;
But now—about my sonnet—I'd like to be told . . .

ALCESTE

Frankly, that sonnet should be pigeonholed.
You've chosen the worst models to imitate.
The style's unnatural. Let me illustrate:

Followed by, *'Twould have been fairer not to smile!*
For example, *Your fair face smiled on me awhile,*
Or this: *such joy is full of rue;*
Or this: *For death is fairer than the fair;*
Or, *Phyllis, to hope is to despair*
    When one must hope eternally!

This artificial style, that's all the fashion,
Has neither taste, nor honesty, nor passion;
It's nothing but a sort of wordy play,
And nature never spoke in such a way.
What, in this shallow age, is not debased?
Our fathers, though less refined, had better taste;
I'd barter all that men admire today
For one old love-song I shall try to say:

> If the King had given me for my own
> Paris, his citadel,
> And I for that must leave alone
> Her whom I love so well,
> I'd say then to the Crown,
> Take back your glittering town;
> My darling is more fair, I swear,
> My darling is more fair.

The rhyme's not rich, the style is rough and old,
But don't you see that it's the purest gold
Beside the tinsel nonsense now preferred,
And that there's passion in its every word?

> If the King had given me for my own
> Paris, his citadel,
> And I for that must leave alone
> Her whom I love so well,
> I'd say then to the Crown,
> Take back your glittering town;
> My darling is more fair, I swear,
> My darling is more fair.

There speaks a loving heart. [*To* PHILINTE] You're laughing, eh?
Laugh on, my precious wit. Whatever you say,
I hold that song's worth all the bibelots
That people hail today with ah's and oh's.

ORONTE
And I maintain my sonnet's very good.

ALCESTE
It's not at all surprising that you should.
You have your reasons; permit me to have mine
For thinking that you cannot write a line.

ORONTE
Others have praised my sonnet to the skies.

ALCESTE
I lack their art of telling pleasant lies.

ORONTE
You seem to think you've got no end of wit.

ALCESTE
> To praise your verse, I'd need still more of it.

ORONTE
> I'm not in need of your approval, Sir.

ALCESTE
> That's good; you couldn't have it if you were.

ORONTE
> Come now, I'll lend you the subject of my sonnet;
> I'd like to see you try to improve upon it.

ALCESTE
> I might, by chance, write something just as shoddy;
> But then I wouldn't show it to everybody.

ORONTE
> You're most opinionated and conceited.

ALCESTE
> Go find your flatterers, and be better treated.

ORONTE
> Look here, my little fellow, pray watch your tone.

ALCESTE
> My great big fellow, you'd better watch your own.

PHILINTE [*Stepping between them*]
> Oh, please, please, gentlemen! This will never do.

ORONTE
> The fault is mine, and I leave the field to you.
> I am your servant, Sir, in every way.

ALCESTE
> And I, Sir, am your most abject valet.

SCENE THREE: PHILINTE, ALCESTE

PHILINTE
> Well, as you see, sincerity in excess
> Can get you into a very pretty mess;
> Oronte was hungry for appreciation. . . .

ALCESTE
> Don't speak to me.

PHILINTE
> What?

ALCESTE
> No more conversation.

PHILINTE
> Really, now . . .

ALCESTE
> Leave me alone.

PHILINTE
> If I . . .

ALCESTE

Out of my sight!

PHILINTE
But what . . .

ALCESTE
I won't listen.

PHILINTE
But . . .

ALCESTE
Silence!

PHILINTE
Now, is it polite . . .

ALCESTE
By heaven, I've had enough. Don't follow me.

PHILINTE
Ah, you're just joking. I'll keep you company.

Act Two

SCENE ONE: ALCESTE, CELIMENE

ALCESTE
Shall I speak plainly, Madam? I confess
Your conduct gives me infinite distress,
And my resentment's grown too hot to smother.
Soon, I foresee, we'll break with one another.
If I said otherwise, I should deceive you;
Sooner or later, I shall be forced to leave you,
And if I swore that we shall never part,
I should misread the omens of my heart.

CELIMENE
You kindly saw me home, it would appear,
So as to pour invectives in my ear.

ALCESTE
I've no desire to quarrel. But I deplore
Your inability to shut the door
On all these suitors who beset you so.
There's what annoys me, if you care to know.

CELIMENE
Is it my fault that all these men pursue me?
Am I to blame if they're attracted to me?
And when they gently beg an audience,
Ought I to take a stick and drive them hence?

ALCESTE
Madam, there's no necessity for a stick;

A less responsive heart would do the trick.
Of your attractiveness I don't complain;
But those your charms attract, you then detain
By a most melting and receptive manner,
And so enlist their hearts beneath your banner.
It's the agreeable hopes which you excite
That keep these lovers round you day and night;
Were they less liberally smiled upon,
That sighing troop would very soon be gone.
But tell me, Madam, why it is that lately
This man Clitandre interests you so greatly?
Because of what high merits do you deem
Him worthy of the honor of your esteem?
Is it that your admiring glances linger
On the splendidly long nail of his little finger?
Or do you share the general deep respect
For the blond wig he chooses to affect?
Are you in love with his embroidered hose?
Do you adore his ribbons and his bows?
Or is it that this paragon bewitches
Your tasteful eye with his vast German breeches?
Perhaps his giggle, or his falsetto voice,
Makes him the latest gallant of your choice? [4]

CELIMENE
You're much mistaken to resent him so.
Why I put up with him you surely know:
My lawsuit's very shortly to be tried,
And I must have his influence on my side.

ALCESTE
Then lose your lawsuit, Madam, or let it drop;
Don't torture me by humoring such a fop.

CELIMENE
You're jealous of the whole world, Sir.

ALCESTE
                                 That's true,
Since the whole world is well-received by you.

CELIMENE
That my good nature is so unconfined
Should serve to pacify your jealous mind;
Were I to smile on one, and scorn the rest,
Then you might have some cause to be distressed.

ALCESTE
Well, if I mustn't be jealous, tell me, then,
Just how I'm better treated than other men.

CELIMENE
You know you have my love. Will that not do?

---

[4] Molière frequently ridicules the fashionable fops of the day.

ALCESTE

What proof have I that what you say is true?

CELIMENE

I would expect, Sir, that my having said it
Might give the statement a sufficient credit.

ALCESTE

But how can I be sure that you don't tell
The selfsame thing to other men as well?

CELIMENE

What a gallant speech! How flattering to me!
What a sweet creature you make me out to be!
Well then, to save you from the pangs of doubt,
All that I've said I hereby cancel out;
Now, none but yourself shall make a monkey of you:
Are you content?

ALCESTE

     Why, why am I doomed to love you?
I swear that I shall bless the blissful hour
When this poor heart's no longer in your power!
I make no secret of it: I've done my best
To exorcise this passion from my breast;
But thus far all in vain; it will not go;
It's for my sins that I must love you so.

CELIMENE

Your love for me is matchless, Sir; that's clear.

ALCESTE

Indeed, in all the world it has no peer;
Words can't describe the nature of my passion,
And no man ever loved in such a fashion.

CELIMENE

Yes, it's a brand-new fashion, I agree:
You show your love by castigating me,
And all your speeches are enraged and rude.
I've never been so furiously wooed.

ALCESTE

Yet you could calm that fury, if you chose.
Come, shall we bring our quarrels to a close?
Let's speak with open hearts, then, and begin . . .

SCENE TWO: CELIMENE, ALCESTE, BASQUE

CELIMENE

What is it?

BASQUE

    Acaste is here.

CELIMENE

      Well, send him in.

SCENE THREE: CELIMENE, ALCESTE

ALCESTE

What! Shall we never be alone at all?
You're always ready to receive a call,
And you can't bear, for ten ticks of the clock,
Not to keep open house for all who knock.

CELIMENE

I couldn't refuse him: he'd be most put out.

ALCESTE

Surely that's not worth worrying about.

CELIMENE

Acaste would never forgive me if he guessed
That I consider him a dreadful pest.

ALCESTE

If he's a pest, why bother with him then?

CELIMENE

Heavens! One can't antagonize such men;
Why, they're the chartered gossips of the court,
And have a say in things of every sort.
One must receive them, and be full of charm;
They're no great help, but they can do you harm,
And though your influence be ever so great,
They're hardly the best people to alienate.

ALCESTE

I see, dear lady, that you could make a case
For putting up with the whole human race;
These friendships that you calculate so nicely . . .

SCENE FOUR: ALCESTE, CELIMENE, BASQUE

BASQUE

Madam, Clitandre is here as well.

ALCESTE

                     Precisely.

CELIMENE

Where are you going?

ALCESTE

              Elsewhere.

CELIMENE

                   Stay.

ALCESTE

                        No, no.

CELIMENE

Stay, Sir.

ALCESTE

      I can't.

CELIMENE
                    I wish it.
ALCESTE
                        No, I must go.
I beg you, Madam, not to press the matter;
You know I have no taste for idle chatter.
CELIMENE
Stay: I command you.
ALCESTE
                    No, I cannot stay.
CELIMENE
Very well; you have my leave to go away.

SCENE FIVE: ELIANTE, PHILINTE, ACASTE, CLITANDRE,
            ALCESTE, CELIMENE, BASQUE

ELIANTE [*To* CELIMENE]
The Marquesses have kindly come to call.
Were they announced?
CELIMENE
                    Yes. Basque, bring chairs for all.
                [BASQUE *provides the chairs, and exits*]
[*To* ALCESTE]
You haven't gone?
ALCESTE
                    No; and I shan't depart
Till you decide who's foremost in your heart.
CELIMENE
Oh, hush.
ALCESTE
            It's time to choose; take them, or me.
CELIMENE
You're mad.
ALCESTE
                I'm not, as you shall shortly see.
CELIMENE
Oh?
ALCESTE
        You'll decide.
CELIMENE
                        You're joking now, dear friend.
ALCESTE
No, no; you'll choose; my patience is at an end.
CLITANDRE
Madam, I come from court, where poor Cléonte
Behaved like a perfect fool, as is his wont.

Has he no friend to counsel him, I wonder,
And teach him less unerringly to blunder?

CELIMENE

It's true, the man's a most accomplished dunce;
His gauche behavior strikes the eye at once;
And every time one sees him, on my word,
His manner's grown a trifle more absurd.

ACASTE

Speaking of dunces, I've just now conversed
With old Damon, who's one of the very worst;
I stood a lifetime in the broiling sun
Before his dreary monologue was done.

CELIMENE

Oh, he's a wondrous talker, and has the power
To tell you nothing hour after hour:
If, by mistake, he ever came to the point,
The shock would put his jawbone out of joint.

ELIANTE [*To* PHILINTE]

The conversation takes its usual turn,
And all our dear friends' ears will shortly burn.

CLITANDRE

Timante's a character, Madam.

CELIMENE

                              Isn't he, though?
A man of mystery from top to toe,
Who moves about in a romantic mist
On secret missions which do not exist.
His talk is full of eyebrows and grimaces;
How tired one gets of his momentous faces;
He's always whispering something confidential
Which turns out to be quite inconsequential;
Nothing's too slight for him to mystify;
He even whispers when he says "good-by."

ACASTE

Tell us about Géralde.

CELIMENE

                        That tiresome ass.
He mixes only with the titled class,
And fawns on dukes and princes, and is bored
With anyone who's not at least a lord.
The man's obsessed with rank, and his discourses
Are all of hounds and carriages and horses;
He uses Christian names with all the great,
And the word Milord, with him, is out of date.

CLITANDRE

He's very taken with Bélise, I hear.

CELIMENE

She is the dreariest company, poor dear.

Whenever she comes to call, I grope about
To find some topic which will draw her out,
But, owing to her dry and faint replies,
The conversation wilts, and droops, and dies.
In vain one hopes to animate her face
By mentioning the ultimate commonplace;
But sun or shower, even hail or frost
Are matters she can instantly exhaust.
Meanwhile her visit, painful though it is,
Drags on and on through mute eternities,
And though you ask the time, and yawn, and yawn,
She sits there like a stone and won't be gone.

ACASTE

Now for Adraste.

CELIMENE

                Oh, that conceited elf
Has a gigantic passion for himself;
He rails against the court, and cannot bear it
That none will recognize his hidden merit;
All honors given to others give offense
To his imaginary excellence.

CLITANDRE

What about young Cléon? His house, they say,
Is full of the best society, night and day.

CELIMENE

His cook has made him popular, not he:
It's Cléon's table that people come to see.

ELIANTE

He gives a splendid dinner, you must admit.

CELIMENE

But must he serve himself along with it?
For my taste, he's a most insipid dish
Whose presence sours the wine and spoils the fish.

PHILINTE

Damis, his uncle, is admired no end.
What's your opinion, Madam?

CELIMENE

                   Why, he's my friend.

PHILINTE

He seems a decent fellow, and rather clever.

CELIMENE

He works too hard at cleverness, however.
I hate to see him sweat and struggle so
To fill his conversation with bon mots.
Since he's decided to become a wit
His taste's so pure that nothing pleases it;
He scolds at all the latest books and plays,
Thinking that wit must never stoop to praise,

That finding fault's a sign of intellect,
That all appreciation is abject,
And that by damning everything in sight
One shows oneself in a distinguished light.
He's scornful even of our conversations:
Their trivial nature sorely tries his patience;
He folds his arms, and stands above the battle,
And listens sadly to our childish prattle.

ACASTE

Wonderful, Madam! You've hit him off precisely.

CLITANDRE

No one can sketch a character so nicely.

ALCESTE

How bravely, Sirs, you cut and thrust at all.
These absent fools, till one by one they fall:
But let one come in sight, and you'll at once
Embrace the man you lately called a dunce,
Telling him in a tone sincere and fervent
How proud you are to be his humble servant.

CLITANDRE

Why pick on us? Madame's been speaking, Sir,
And you should quarrel, if you must, with her.

ALCESTE

No, no, by God, the fault is yours, because
You lead her on with laughter and applause,
And make her think that she's the more delightful
The more her talk is scandalous and spiteful.
Oh, she would stoop to malice far, far less
If no such claque approved her cleverness.
It's flatterers like you whose foolish praise
Nourishes all the vices of these days.

PHILINTE

But why protest when someone ridicules
Those you'd condemn, yourself, as knaves or fools?

CELIMENE

Why, Sir? Because he loves to make a fuss.
You don't expect him to agree with us,
When there's an opportunity to express
His heaven-sent spirit of contrariness?
What other people think, he can't abide;
Whatever they say, he's on the other side;
He lives in deadly terror of agreeing;
'Twould make him seem an ordinary being.
Indeed, he's so in love with contradiction,
He'll turn against his most profound conviction
And with a furious eloquence deplore it,
If only someone else is speaking for it.

ALCESTE

Go on, dear lady, mock me as you please;
You have your audience in ecstasies.

PHILINTE

But what she says is true: you have a way
Of bridling at whatever people say;
Whether they praise or blame, your angry spirit
Is equally unsatisfied to hear it.

ALCESTE

Men, Sir, are always wrong, and that's the reason
That righteous anger's never out of season;
All that I hear in all their conversation
Is flattering praise or reckless condemnation.

CELIMENE

But . . .

ALCESTE

   No, no, Madam, I am forced to state
That you have pleasures which I deprecate,
And that these others, here, are much to blame
For nourishing the faults which are your shame.

CLITANDRE

I shan't defend myself, Sir; but I vow
I'd thought this lady faultless until now.

ACASTE

I see her charms and graces, which are many;
But as for faults, I've never noticed any.

ALCESTE

I see them, Sir; and rather than ignore them,
I strenuously criticize her for them.
The more one loves, the more one should object
To every blemish, every least defect.
Were I this lady, I would soon get rid
Of lovers who approved of all I did,
And by their slack indulgence and applause
Endorsed my follies and excused my flaws.

CELIMENE

If all hearts beat according to your measure,
The dawn of love would be the end of pleasure;
And love would find its perfect consummation
In ecstasies of rage and reprobation.

ELIANTE

Love, as a rule, affects men otherwise,
And lovers rarely love to criticize.
They see their lady as a charming blur,
And find all things commendable in her.
If she has any blemish, fault, or shame,
They will redeem it by a pleasing name.

The pale-faced lady's lily-white, perforce;
The swarthy one's a sweet brunette, of course;
The spindly lady has a slender grace;
The fat one has a most majestic pace;
The plain one, with her dress in disarray,
They classify as *beauté négligée;*
The hulking one's a goddess in their eyes,
The dwarf, a concentrate of Paradise;
The haughty lady has a noble mind;
The mean one's witty, and the dull one's kind;
The chatterbox has liveliness and verve,
The mute one has a virtuous reserve.
So lovers manage, in their passion's cause,
To love their ladies even for their flaws.[5]

ALCESTE
But I still say . . .

CELIMENE
                    I think it would be nice.
To stroll around the gallery once or twice.
What! You're not going, Sirs?

CLITANDRE AND ACASTE
                              No, Madam, no.

ALCESTE
You seem to be in terror lest they go.
Do what you will, Sirs; leave, or linger on,
But I shan't go till after you are gone.

ACASTE
I'm free to linger, unless I should perceive
Madame is tired, and wishes me to leave.

CLITANDRE
And as for me, I needn't go today
Until the hour of the King's *coucher.*

CELIMENE [*To* ALCESTE]
You're joking, surely?

ALCESTE
                      Not in the least; we'll see
Whether you'd rather part with them, or me.

SCENE SIX: ALCESTE, CELIMENE, ELIANTE, ACASTE,
PHILINTE, CLITANDRE, BASQUE

BASQUE [*To* ALCESTE]
Sir, there's a fellow here who bids me state
That he must see you, and that it can't wait.

---

[5] A paraphrase of a passage from Lucretius, *De Rerum Natura,* Book IV. Molière is said to
have translated Lucretius' poem as a student.

ALCESTE
Tell him that I have no such pressing affairs.
BASQUE
It's a long tailcoat that this fellow wears,
With gold all over.
CELIMENE [*To* ALCESTE]
You'd best go down and see.
Or—have him enter.

SCENE SEVEN: ALCESTE, CELIMENE, ELIANTE, ACASTE, PHILINTE,
CLITANDRE, A GUARD *of the Marshalsea*

ALCESTE [*Confronting the* GUARD]
Well, what do you want with me?
Come in, Sir.
GUARD
I've a word, Sir, for your ear.
ALCESTE
Speak it aloud, Sir; I shall strive to hear.
GUARD
The Marshals have instructed me to say
You must report to them without delay.
ALCESTE
Who? Me, Sir?
GUARD
Yes, Sir; you.
ALCESTE
But what do they want?
PHILINTE [*To* ALCESTE]
To scotch your silly quarrel with Oronte.
CELIMENE [*To* PHILINTE]
What quarrel?
PHILINTE
Oronte and he have fallen out
Over some verse he spoke his mind about;
The Marshals wish to arbitrate the matter.[6]
ALCESTE
Never shall I equivocate or flatter!
PHILINTE
You'd best obey their summons; come, let's go.
ALCESTE
How can they mend our quarrel, I'd like to know?
Am I to make a cowardly retraction,
And praise those jingles to his satisfaction?

[6] The Marshalls were charged with preventing duels, which, though against the law, were frequent.

I'll not recant; I've judged that sonnet rightly.
It's bad.
PHILINTE
                    But you might say so more politely. . . .
ALCESTE
I'll not back down; his verses make me sick.
PHILINTE
If only you could be more politic!
But come, let's go.
ALCESTE
                              I'll go, but I won't unsay
A single word.
PHILINTE
                    Well, let's be on our way.
ALCESTE
Till I am ordered by my lord the King
To praise that poem, I shall say the thing
Is scandalous, by God, and that the poet
Ought to be hanged for having the nerve to show it.
[*To* CLITANDRE *and* ACASTE, *who are laughing*]
By heaven, Sirs, I really didn't know
That I was being humorous.
CELIMENE
                              Go, Sir, go;
Settle your business.
ALCESTE
                    I shall, and when I'm through,
I shall return to settle things with you.

Act Three

SCENE ONE: CLITANDRE, ACASTE

CLITANDRE
Dear Marquess, how contented you appear;
All things delight you, nothing mars your cheer.
Can you, in perfect honesty, declare
That you've a right to be so debonair?
ACASTE
By Jove, when I survey myself, I find
No cause whatever for distress of mind.
I'm young and rich; I can in modesty
Lay claim to an exalted pedigree;
And owing to my name and my condition

I shall not want for honors and position.
Then as to courage, that most precious trait,
I seem to have it, as was proved of late
Upon the field of honor, where my bearing,
They say, was very cool and rather daring.
I've wit, of course; and taste in such perfection
That I can judge without the least reflection,
And at the theater, which is my delight,
Can make or break a play on opening night,
And lead the crowd in hisses or bravos,
And generally be known as one who knows.
I'm clever, handsome, gracefully polite;
My waist is small, my teeth are strong and white;
As for my dress, the world's astonished eyes
Assure me that I bear away the prize.
I find myself in favor everywhere,
Honored by men, and worshiped by the fair;
And since these things are so, it seems to me
I'm justified in my complacency.

CLITANDRE

Well, if so many ladies hold you dear,
Why do you press a hopeless courtship here?

ACASTE

Hopeless, you say? I'm not the sort of fool
That likes his ladies difficult and cool.
Men who are awkward, shy, and peasantish
May pine for heartless beauties, if they wish,
Grovel before them, bear their cruelties,
Woo them with tears and sighs and bended knees,
And hope by dogged faithfulness to gain
What their poor merits never could obtain.
For men like me, however, it makes no sense
To love on trust, and foot the whole expense.
Whatever any lady's merits be,
I think, thank God, that I'm as choice as she;
That if my heart is kind enough to burn
For her, she owes me something in return;
And that in any proper love affair
The partners must invest an equal share.

CLITANDRE

You think, then, that our hostess favors you?

ACASTE

I've reason to believe that that is true.

CLITANDRE

How did you come to such a mad conclusion?
You're blind, dear fellow. This is sheer delusion.

ACASTE

All right, then: I'm deluded and I'm blind.

CLITANDRE
Whatever put the notion in your mind?

ACASTE
Delusion.

CLITANDRE
What persuades you that you're right?

ACASTE
I'm blind.

CLITANDRE
But have you any proofs to cite?

ACASTE
I tell you I'm deluded.

CLITANDRE
Have you, then,
Received some secret pledge from Célimène?

ACASTE
Oh, no: she scorns me.

CLITANDRE
Tell me the truth, I beg.

ACASTE
She just can't bear me.

CLITANDRE
Ah, don't pull my leg.
Tell me what hope she's given you, I pray.

ACASTE
I'm hopeless, and it's you who win the day.
She hates me thoroughly, and I'm so vexed
I mean to hang myself on Tuesday next.

CLITANDRE
Dear Marquess, let us have an armistice
And make a treaty. What do you say to this?
If ever one of us can plainly prove
That Célimène encourages his love,
The other must abandon hope, and yield,
And leave him in possession of the field.

ACASTE
Now, there's a bargain that appeals to me;
With all my heart, dear Marquess, I agree.
But hush.

SCENE TWO: CELIMENE, ACASTE, CLITANDRE

CELIMENE
Still here?

CLITANDRE
T'was love that stayed our feet.

CELIMENE
  I think I heard a carriage in the street.
  Whose is it? D'you know?

SCENE THREE: CELIMENE, ACASTE, CLITANDRE, BASQUE

BASQUE
      Arsinoé is here,
  Madame.
CELIMENE
          Arsinoé, you say? Oh, dear.
BASQUE
  Eliante is entertaining her below.
CELIMENE
  What brings the creature here, I'd like to know?
ACASTE
  They say she's dreadfully prudish, but in fact
  I think her piety . . .
CELIMENE
                  It's all an act.
  At heart she's worldly, and her poor success
  In snaring men explains her prudishness.
  It breaks her heart to see the beaux and gallants
  Engrossed by other women's charms and talents,
  And so she's always in a jealous rage
  Against the faulty standards of the age.
  She lets the world believe that she's a prude
  To justify her loveless solitude,
  And strives to put a brand of moral shame
  On all the graces that she cannot claim.
  But still she'd love a lover; and Alceste
  Appears to be the one she'd love the best.
  His visits here are poison to her pride;
  She seems to think I've lured him from her side;
  And everywhere, at court or in the town,
  The spiteful, envious woman runs me down.
  In short, she's just as stupid as can be,
  Vicious and arrogant in the last degree,
  And . . .

SCENE FOUR: ARSINOE, CELIMENE, CLITANDRE, ACASTE

CELIMENE
      Ah! What happy chance has brought you here?
  I've thought about you ever so much, my dear.
ARSINOE
  I've come to tell you something you should know.

CELIMENE

How good of you to think of doing so!

[CLITANDRE *and* ACASTE *go out, laughing*]

SCENE FIVE: ARSINOE, CELIMENE

ARSINOE

It's just as well those gentlemen didn't tarry.

CELIMENE

Shall we sit down?

ARSINOE

That won't be necessary.
Madam, the flame of friendship ought to burn
Brightest in matters of the most concern,
And as there's nothing which concerns us more
Than honor, I have hastened to your door
To bring you, as your friend, some information
About the status of your reputation.
I visited, last night, some virtuous folk,
And, quite by chance, it was of you they spoke;
There was, I fear, no tendency to praise
Your light behavior and your dashing ways.
The quantity of gentlemen you see
And your by now notorious coquetry
Were both so vehemently criticized
By everyone, that I was much surprised.
Of course, I needn't tell you where I stood;
I came to your defense as best I could,
Assured them you were harmless, and declared
Your soul was absolutely unimpaired.
But there are some things, you must realize,
One can't excuse, however hard one tries,
And I was forced at last into conceding
That your behavior, Madam, is misleading,
That it makes a bad impression, giving rise
To ugly gossip and obscene surmise,
And that if you were more *overtly* good,
You wouldn't be so much misunderstood.
Not that I think you've been unchaste—no! no!
The saints preserve me from a thought so low!
But mere good conscience never did suffice:
One must avoid the outward show of vice.
Madam, you're too intelligent, I'm sure,
To think my motives anything but pure
In offering you this counsel—which I do
Out of a zealous interest in you.

CELIMENE

Madam, I haven't taken you amiss;
I'm very much obliged to you for this;
And I'll at once discharge the obligation
By telling you about *your* reputation.
You've been so friendly as to let me know
What certain people say of me, and so
I mean to follow your benign example
By offering you a somewhat similar sample.
The other day, I went to an affair
And found some most distinguished people there
Discussing piety, both false and true.
The conversation soon came round to you.
Alas! Your prudery and bustling zeal
Appeared to have a very slight appeal.
Your affectation of a grave demeanor,
Your endless talk of virtue and of honor,
The aptitude of your suspicious mind
For finding sin where there is none to find,
Your towering self-esteem, that pitying face
With which you contemplate the human race,
Your sermonizings and your sharp aspersions
On people's pure and innocent diversions—
All these were mentioned, Madam, and, in fact,
Were roundly and concertedly attacked.
"What good," they said, "are all these outward shows,
When everything belies her pious pose?
She prays incessantly; but then, they say,
She beats her maids and cheats them of their pay;
She shows her zeal in every holy place,
But still she's vain enough to paint her face;
She holds that naked statues are immoral,
But with a naked *man* she'd have no quarrel."
Of course, I said to everybody there
That they were being viciously unfair;
But still they were disposed to criticize you,
And all agreed that someone should advise you
To leave the morals of the world alone,
And worry rather more about your own.
They felt that one's self-knowledge should be great
Before one thinks of setting others straight;
That one should learn the art of living well
Before one threatens other men with hell,
And that the Church is best equipped, no doubt,
To guide our souls and root our vices out.
Madam, you're too intelligent, I'm sure,
To think my motives anything but pure

In offering you this counsel—which I do
Out of a zealous interest in you.

ARSINOE

I dared not hope for gratitude, but I
Did not expect so acid a reply;
I judge, since you've been so extremely tart,
That my good counsel pierced you to the heart.

CELIMENE

Far from it, Madam. Indeed, it seems to me
We ought to trade advice more frequently.
One's vision of oneself is so defective
That it would be an excellent corrective.
If you are willing, Madam, let's arrange
Shortly to have another frank exchange
In which we'll tell each other, *entre nous,*
What you've heard tell of me, and I of you.

ARSINOE

Oh, people never censure you, my dear;
It's me they criticize. Or so I hear.

CELIMENE

Madam, I think we either blame or praise
According to our taste and length of days.
There is a time of life for coquetry,
And there's a season, too, for prudery.
When all one's charms are gone, it is, I'm sure,
Good strategy to be devout and pure:
It makes one seem a little less forsaken.
Some day, perhaps, I'll take the road you've taken:
Time brings all things. But I have time aplenty,
And see no cause to be a prude at twenty.

ARSINOE

You give your age in such a gloating tone
That one would think I was an ancient crone;
We're not so far apart, in sober truth,
That you can mock me with a boast of youth!
Madam, you baffle me. I wish I knew
What moves you to provoke me as you do.

CELIMENE

For my part, Madam, I should like to know
Why you abuse me everywhere you go.
Is it my fault, dear lady, that your hand
Is not, alas, in very great demand?
If men admire me, if they pay me court
And daily make me offers of the sort
You'd dearly love to have them make to you,
How can I help it? What would you have me do?
If what you want is lovers, please feel free
To take as many as you can from me.

ARSINOE

    Oh, come. D'you think the world is losing sleep
    Over that flock of lovers which you keep,
    Or that we find it difficult to guess
    What price you pay for their devotedness?
    Surely you don't expect us to suppose
    Mere merit could attract so many beaux?
    It's not your virtue that they're dazzled by;
    Nor is it virtuous love for which they sigh.
    You're fooling no one, Madam; the world's not blind;
    There's many a lady heaven has designed
    To call men's noblest, tenderest feelings out,
    Who has no lovers dogging her about;
    From which it's plain that lovers nowadays
    Must be acquired in bold and shameless ways,
    And only pay one court for such reward
    As modesty and virtue can't afford.
    Then don't be quite so puffed up, if you please,
    About your tawdry little victories;
    Try, if you can, to be a shade less vain,
    And treat the world with somewhat less disdain.
    If one were envious of your amours,
    One soon could have a following like yours;
    Lovers are no great trouble to collect
    If one prefers them to one's self-respect.

CELIMENE

    Collect them then, my dear; I'd love to see
    You demonstrate that charming theory;
    Who knows, you might . . .

ARSINOE

                       Now, Madam, that will do;
    It's time to end this trying interview.
    My coach is late in coming to your door,
    Or I'd have taken leave of you before.

CELIMENE

    Oh, please don't feel that you must rush away;
    I'd be delighted, Madam, if you'd stay.
    However, lest my conversation bore you,
    Let me provide some better company for you;
    This gentleman, who comes most apropos,
    Will please you more than I could do, I know.

Scene Six: ALCESTE, CELIMENE, ARSINOE

CELIMENE

    Alceste, I have a little note to write
    Which simply must go out before tonight;

Please entertain *Madame;* I'm sure that she
Will overlook my incivility.

SCENE SEVEN: ALCESTE, ARSINOE

ARSINOE

Well, Sir, our hostess graciously contrives
For us to chat until my coach arrives;
And I shall be forever in her debt
For granting me this little tête-à-tête.
We women very rightly give our hearts
To men of noble character and parts,
And your especial merits, dear Alceste,
Have roused the deepest sympathy in my breast.
Oh, how I wish they had sufficient sense
At court, to recognize your excellence!
They wrong you greatly, Sir. How it must hurt you
Never to be rewarded for your virtue!

ALCESTE

Why, Madam, what cause have I to feel aggrieved?
What great and brilliant thing have I achieved?
What service have I rendered to the King
That I should look to him for anything?

ARSINOE

Not everyone who's honored by the State
Has done great services. A man must wait
Till time and fortune offer him the chance.
Your merit, Sir, is obvious at a glance,
And . . .

ALCESTE

                    Ah, forget my merit; I'm not neglected.
The court, I think, can hardly be expected
To mine men's souls for merit, and unearth
Our hidden virtues and our secret worth.

ARSINOE

Some virtues, though, are far too bright to hide;
Yours are acknowledged, Sir, on every side.
Indeed, I've heard you warmly praised of late
By persons of considerable weight.

ALCESTE

This fawning age has praise for everyone,
And all distinctions, Madam, are undone.
All things have equal honor nowadays,
And no one should be gratified by praise.
To be admired, one only need exist,
And every lackey's on the honors list.

ARSINOE

    I only wish, Sir, that you had your eye
    On some position at court, however high;
    You'd only have to hint at such a notion
    For me to set the proper wheels in motion;
    I've certain friendships I'd be glad to use
    To get you any office you might choose.

ALCESTE

    Madam, I fear that any such ambition
    Is wholly foreign to my disposition.
    The soul God gave me isn't of the sort
    That prospers in the weather of a court.
    It's all too obvious that I don't possess
    The virtues necessary for success.
    My one great talent is for speaking plain;
    I've never learned to flatter or to feign;
    And anyone so stupidly sincere
    Had best not seek a courtier's career.
    Outside the court, I know, one must dispense
    With honors, privilege, and influence;
    But still one gains the right, foregoing these,
    Not to be tortured by the wish to please.
    One needn't live in dread of snubs and slights,
    Nor praise the verse that every idiot writes,
    Nor humor silly Marquesses, nor bestow
    Politic sighs on Madam So-and-So.

ARSINOE

    Forget the court, then; let the matter rest.
    But I've another cause to be distressed
    About your present situation, Sir.
    It's to your love affair that I refer.
    She whom you love, and who pretends to love you,
    Is, I regret to say, unworthy of you.

ALCESTE

    Why, Madam! Can you seriously intend
    To make so grave a charge against your friend?

ARSINOE

    Alas, I must. I've stood aside too long
    And let that lady do you grievous wrong;
    But now my debt to conscience shall be paid:
    I tell you that your love has been betrayed.

ALCESTE

    I thank you, Madam; you're extremely kind.
    Such words are soothing to a lover's mind.

ARSINOE

    Yes, though she *is* my friend, I say again
    You're very much too good for Célimène.
    She's wantonly misled you from the start.

ALCESTE

You may be right; who knows another's heart?
But ask yourself if it's the part of charity
To shake my soul with doubts of her sincerity.

ARSINOE

Well, if you'd rather be a dupe than doubt her,
That's your affair. I'll say no more about her.

ALCESTE

Madam, you know that doubt and vague suspicion
Are painful to a man in my position;
It's most unkind to worry me this way
Unless you've some real proof of what you say.

ARSINOE

Sir, say no more: all doubt shall be removed,
And all that I've been saying shall be proved.
You've only to escort me home, and there
We'll look into the heart of this affair.
I've ocular evidence which will persuade you
Beyond a doubt, that Célimène's betrayed you.
Then, if you're saddened by that revelation,
Perhaps I can provide some consolation.

Act Four

Scene One: ELIANTE, PHILINTE

PHILINTE

Madam, he acted like a stubborn child;
I thought they never would be reconciled;
In vain we reasoned, threatened, and appealed;
He stood his ground and simply would not yield.
The Marshals, I feel sure, have never heard
An argument so splendidly absurd.
"No, gentlemen," said he, "I'll not retract.
His verse is bad: extremely bad, in fact.
Surely it does the man no harm to know it.
Does it disgrace him, not to be a poet?
A gentleman may be respected still,
Whether he writes a sonnet well or ill.
That I dislike his verse should not offend him;
In all that touches honor, I commend him;
He's noble, brave, and virtuous—but I fear
He can't in truth be called a sonneteer.
I'll gladly praise his wardrobe; I'll endorse
His dancing, or the way he sits a horse;

But, gentlemen, I cannot praise his rhyme.
In fact, it ought to be a capital crime
For anyone so sadly unendowed
To write a sonnet, and read the thing aloud."
At length he fell into a gentler mood
And, striking a concessive attitude,
He paid Oronte the following courtesies:
"Sir, I regret that I'm so hard to please,
And I'm profoundly sorry that your lyric
Failed to provoke me to a panegyric."
After these curious words, the two embraced,
And then the hearing was adjourned—in haste.

ELIANTE

His conduct has been very singular lately;
Still, I confess that I respect him greatly.
The honesty in which he takes such pride
Has—to my mind—its noble, heroic side.
In this false age, such candor seems outrageous;
But I could wish that it were more contagious.

PHILINTE

What most intrigues me in our friend Alceste
Is the grand passion that rages in his breast.
The sullen humors he's compounded of
Should not, I think, dispose his heart to love;
But since they do, it puzzles me still more
That he should choose your cousin to adore.

ELIANTE

It does, indeed, belie the theory
That love is born of gentle sympathy,
And that the tender passion must be based
On sweet accords of temper and of taste.

PHILINTE

Does she return his love, do you suppose?

ELIANTE

Ah, that's a difficult question, Sir. Who knows?
How can we judge the truth of her devotion?
Her heart's a stranger to its own emotion.
Sometimes it thinks it loves, when no love's there;
At other times it loves quite unaware.

PHILINTE

I rather think Alceste is in for more
Distress and sorrow than he's bargained for;
Were he of my mind, Madam, his affection
Would turn in quite a different direction,
And we would see him more responsive to
The kind regard which he receives from you.

ELIANTE

Sir, I believe in frankness, and I'm inclined,

In matters of the heart, to speak my mind.
I don't oppose his love for her; indeed,
I hope with all my heart that he'll succeed,
And were it in my power, I'd rejoice
In giving him the lady of his choice.
But if, as happens frequently enough
In love affairs, he meets with a rebuff—
If Célimène should grant some rival's suit—
I'd gladly play the role of substitute;
Nor would his tender speeches please me less
Because they'd once been made without success.

PHILINTE

Well, Madam, as for me, I don't oppose
Your hopes in this affair; and heaven knows
That in my conversations with the man
I plead your cause as often as I can.
But if those two should marry, and so remove
All chance that he will offer you his love,
Then I'll declare my own, and hope to see
Your gracious favor pass from him to me.
In short, should you be cheated of Alceste,
I'd be most happy to be second best.

ELIANTE

Philinte, you're teasing.

PHILINTE

                              Ah, Madam, never fear;
No words of mine were ever so sincere,
And I shall live in fretful expectation
Till I can make a fuller declaration.

Scene Two: ALCESTE, ELIANTE, PHILINTE

ALCESTE

Avenge me, Madam! I must have satisfaction,
Or this great wrong will drive me to distraction!

ELIANTE

Why, what's the matter? What's upset you so?

ALCESTE

Madam, I've had a mortal, mortal blow.
If Chaos repossessed the universe,
I swear I'd not be shaken any worse.
I'm ruined. . . . I can say no more. . . . My soul . . .

ELIANTE

Do try, Sir, to regain your self-control.

ALCESTE

Just heaven! Why were so much beauty and grace
Bestowed on one so vicious and so base?

ELIANTE
Once more,.Sir, tell us. . . .

ALCESTE
                          My world has gone to wrack;
I'm—I'm betrayed; she's stabbed me in the back:
Yes, Célimène (who would have thought it of her?)
Is false to me, and has another lover.

ELIANTE
Are you quite certain? Can you prove these things?

PHILINTE
Lovers are prey to wild imaginings
And jealous fancies. No doubt there's some mistake. . . .

ALCESTE
Mind your own business, Sir, for heaven's sake.
[*To* ELIANTE]
Madam, I have the proof that you demand
Here in my pocket, penned by her own hand.
Yes, all the shameful evidence one could want
Lies in this letter written to Oronte—
Oronte! whom I felt sure she couldn't love,
And hardly bothered to be jealous of.

PHILINTE
Still, in a letter, appearances may deceive;
This may not be so bad as you believe.

ALCESTE
Once more I beg you, Sir, to let me be;
Tend to your own affairs; leave mine to me.

ELIANTE
Compose yourself; this anguish that you feel . . .

ALCESTE
Is something, Madam, you alone can heal.
My outraged heart, beside itself with grief,
Appeals to you for comfort and relief.
Avenge me on your cousin, whose unjust
And faithless nature has deceived my trust;
Avenge a crime your pure soul must detest.

ELIANTE
But how, Sir?

ALCESTE
                          Madam, this heart within my breast
Is yours; pray take it; redeem my heart from her,
And so avenge me on my torturer.
Let her be punished by the fond emotion,
The ardent love, the bottomless devotion,
The faithful worship which this heart of mine
Will offer up to yours as to a shrine.

ELIANTE
You have my sympathy, Sir, in all you suffer;

Nor do I scorn the noble heart you offer;
But I suspect you'll soon be mollified,
And this desire for vengeance will subside.
When some beloved hand has done us wrong
We thirst for retribution—but not for long;
However dark the deed that she's committed,
A lovely culprit's very soon acquitted.
Nothing's so stormy as an injured lover,
And yet no storm so quickly passes over.

ALCESTE

No, Madam, no—this is no lovers' spat;
I'll not forgive her; it's gone too far for that;
My mind's made up; I'll kill myself before
I waste my hopes upon her any more.
Ah, here she is. My wrath intensifies.
I shall confront her with her tricks and lies,
And crush her utterly, and bring you then
A heart no longer slave to Célimène.

SCENE THREE: CELIMENE, ALCESTE

ALCESTE [*Aside*]

Sweet heaven, help me to control my passion.

CELIMENE

[*Aside*]

[*To* ALCESTE]

Oh, Lord. Why stand there staring in that fashion?
And what d'you mean by those dramatic sighs,
And that malignant glitter in your eyes?

ALCESTE

I mean that sins which cause the blood to freeze
Look innocent beside your treacheries;
That nothing Hell's or Heaven's wrath could do
Ever produced so bad a thing as you.

CELIMENE

Your compliments were always sweet and pretty.

ALCESTE

Madam, it's not the moment to be witty.
No, blush and hang your head; you've ample reason,
Since I've the fullest evidence of your treason.
Ah, this is what my sad heart prophesied;
Now all my anxious fears are verified;
My dark suspicion and my gloomy doubt
Divined the truth, and now the truth is out.
For all your trickery, I was not deceived;
It was my bitter stars that I believed.

But don't imagine that you'll go scot-free;
You shan't misuse me with impunity.
I know that love's irrational and blind;
I know the heart's not subject to the mind,
And can't be reasoned into beating faster;
I know each soul is free to choose its master;
Therefore had you but spoken from the heart,
Rejecting my attentions from the start,
I'd have no grievance, or at any rate
I could complain of nothing but my fate.
Ah, but so falsely to encourage me—
That was a treason and a treachery
For which you cannot suffer too severely,
And you shall pay for that behavior dearly.
Yes, now I have no pity, not a shred;
My temper's out of hand; I've lost my head;
Shocked by the knowledge of your double-dealings,
My reason can't restrain my savage feelings;
A righteous wrath deprives me of my senses,
And I won't answer for the consequences.

CELIMENE

What does this outburst mean? Will you please explain?
Have you, by any chance, gone quite insane?

ALCESTE

Yes, yes, I went insane the day I fell
A victim to your black and fatal spell,
Thinking to meet with some sincerity
Among the treacherous charms that beckoned me.

CELIMENE

Pooh. Of what treachery can you complain?

ALCESTE

How sly you are, how cleverly you feign!
But you'll not victimize me any more.
Look: here's a document you've seen before.
This evidence, which I acquired today,
Leaves you, I think, without a thing to say.

CELIMENE

Is this what sent you into such a fit?

ALCESTE

You should be blushing at the sight of it.

CELIMENE

Ought I to blush? I truly don't see why.

ALCESTE

Ah, now you're being bold as well as sly;
Since there's no signature, perhaps you'll claim . . .

CELIMENE

I wrote it, whether or not it bears my name.

ALCESTE
> And you can view with equanimity
> This proof of your disloyalty to me!

CELIMENE
> Oh, don't be so outrageous and extreme.

ALCESTE
> You take this matter lightly, it would seem.
> Was it no wrong to me, no shame to you,
> That you should send Oronte this billet-doux?

CELIMENE
> Oronte! Who said it was for him?

ALCESTE
>   Why, those
> Who brought me this example of your prose.
> But what's the difference? If you wrote the letter
> To someone else, it pleases me no better.
> My grievance and your guilt remain the same.

CELIMENE
> But need you rage, and need I blush for shame,
> If this was written to a *wòman* friend?

ALCESTE
> Ah! Most ingenious. I'm impressed no end;
> And after that incredible evasion
> Your guilt is clear. I need no more persuasion.
> How dare you try so clumsy a deception?
> D'you think I'm wholly wanting in perception?
> Come, come, let's see how brazenly you'll try
> To bolster up so palpable a lie:
> Kindly construe this ardent closing section
> As nothing more than sisterly affection!
> Here, let me read it. Tell me, if you dare to,
> That this is for a woman . . .

CELIMENE
>   I don't care to.
> What right have you to badger and berate me,
> And so highhandedly interrogate me?

ALCESTE
> Now, don't be angry; all I ask of you
> Is that you justify a phrase or two . . .

CELIMENE
> No, I shall not. I utterly refuse,
> And you may take those phrases as you choose.

ALCESTE
> Just show me how this letter could be meant
> For a woman's eyes, and I shall be content.

CELIMENE
> No, no, it's for Oronte; you're perfectly right.

I welcome his attentions with delight,
I prize his character and his intellect,
And everything is just as you suspect.
Come, do your worst now; give your rage free rein;
But kindly cease to bicker and complain.

ALCESTE [*Aside*]

Good God! Could anything be more inhuman?
Was ever a heart so mangled by a woman?
When I complain of how she has betrayed me,
She bridles, and commences to upbraid me!
She tries my tortured patience to the limit;
She won't deny her guilt; she glories in it!
And yet my heart's too faint and cowardly
To break these chains of passion, and be free,
To scorn her as it should, and rise above
This unrewarded, mad, and bitter love.

[*To* CELIMENE]

Ah, traitress, in how confident a fashion
You take advantage of my helpless passion,
And use my weakness for your faithless charms
To make me once again throw down my arms!
But do at least deny this black transgression;
Take back that mocking and perverse confession;
Defend this letter and your innocence,
And I, poor fool, will aid in your defense.
Pretend, pretend, that you are just and true,
And I shall make myself believe in you.

CELIMENE

Oh, stop it. Don't be such a jealous dunce,
Or I shall leave off loving you at once.
Just why should I *pretend*? What could impel me
To stoop so low as that? And kindly tell me
Why, if I loved another, I shouldn't merely
Inform you of it, simply and sincerely!
I've told you where you stand, and that admission
Should altogether clear me of suspicion;
After so generous a guarantee,
What right have you to harbor doubts of me?
Since women are (from natural reticence)
Reluctant to declare their sentiments,
And since the honor of our sex requires
That we conceal our amorous desires,
Ought any man for whom such laws are broken
To question what the oracle has spoken?
Should he not rather feel an obligation
To trust that most obliging declaration?
Enough, now. Your suspicions quite disgust me;

Why should I love a man who doesn't trust me?
I cannot understand why I continue,
Fool that I am, to take an interest in you.
I ought to choose a man less prone to doubt,
And give you something to be vexed about.

ALCESTE

Ah, what a poor enchanted fool I am;
These gentle words, no doubt, were all a sham;
But destiny requires me to entrust
My happiness to you, and so I must.
I'll love you to the bitter end, and see
How false and treacherous you dare to be.

CELIMENE

No, you don't really love me as you ought.

ALCESTE

I love you more than can be said or thought;
Indeed, I wish you were in such distress
That I might show my deep devotedness.
Yes, I could wish that you were wretchedly poor,
Unloved, uncherished, utterly obscure;
That fate had set you down upon the earth
Without possessions, rank, or gentle birth;
Then, by the offer of my heart, I might
Repair the great injustice of your plight;
I'd raise you from the dust, and proudly prove
The purity and vastness of my love.

CELIMENE

This is a strange benevolence indeed!
God grant that I may never be in need. . . .
Ah, here's Monsieur Dubois, in quaint disguise.

SCENE FOUR: CELIMENE, ALCESTE, DUBOIS

ALCESTE

Well, why this costume? Why those frightened eyes?
What ails you?

DUBOIS

                Well, Sir, things are most mysterious.

ALCESTE

What do you mean?

DUBOIS

                I fear they're very serious.

ALCESTE

What?

DUBOIS

           Shall I speak more loudly?

ALCESTE

> Yes; speak out.

DUBOIS

Isn't there someone here, Sir?

ALCESTE

> Speak, you lout!

Stop wasting time.

DUBOIS

> Sir, we must slip away.

ALCESTE

How's that?

DUBOIS

> We must decamp without delay.

ALCESTE

Explain yourself.

DUBOIS

> I tell you we must fly.

ALCESTE

What for?

DUBOIS

> We mustn't pause to say good-by.

ALCESTE

Now what d'you mean by all of this, you clown?

DUBOIS

I mean, Sir, that we've got to leave this town.

ALCESTE

I'll tear you limb from limb and joint from joint
If you don't come more quickly to the point.

DUBOIS

Well, Sir, today a man in a black suit,
Who wore a black and ugly scowl to boot,
Left us a document scrawled in such a hand
As even Satan couldn't understand.
It bears upon your lawsuit, I don't doubt;
But all hell's devils couldn't make it out.

ALCESTE

Well, well, go on. What then? I fail to see
How this event obliges us to flee.

DUBOIS

Well, Sir: an hour later, hardly more,
A gentleman who's often called before
Came looking for you in an anxious way.
Not finding you, he asked me to convey
(Knowing I could be trusted with the same)
The following message. . . . Now, what *was* his name?

ALCESTE

Forget his name, you idiot. What did he say?

DUBOIS

Well, it was one of your friends, Sir, anyway.
He warned you to begone, and he suggested
That if you stay, you may well be arrested.

ALCESTE

What? Nothing more specific? Think, man, think!

DUBOIS

No, Sir. He had me bring him pen and ink,
And dashed you off a letter which, I'm sure,
Will render things distinctly less obscure.

ALCESTE

Well—let me have it!

CELIMENE

What *is* this all about?

ALCESTE

God knows; but I have hopes of finding out.
How long am I to wait, you blitherer?

DUBOIS [*After a protracted search for the letter*]

I must have left it on your table, Sir.

ALCESTE

I ought to . . .

CELIMENE

No, no, keep your self-control;
Go find out what's behind his rigmarole.

ALCESTE

It seems that fate, no matter what I do,
Has sworn that I may not converse with you;
But, Madam, pray permit your faithful lover
To try once more before the day is over.

Act Five

Scene One: ALCESTE, PHILINTE

ALCESTE

No, it's too much. My mind's made up, I tell you.

PHILINTE

Why should this blow, however hard, compel you . . .

ALCESTE

No, no, don't waste your breath in argument;
Nothing you say will alter my intent;
This age is vile, and I've made up my mind
To have no further commerce with mankind.
Did not truth, honor, decency, and the laws
Oppose my enemy and approve my cause?

My claims were justified in all men's sight;
I put my trust in equity and right;
Yet, to my horror and the world's disgrace,
Justice is mocked, and I have lost my case!
A scoundrel whose dishonesty is notorious
Emerges from another lie victorious!
Honor and right condone his brazen fraud,
While rectitude and decency applaud!
Before his smirking face, the truth stands charmed,
And virtue conquered, and the law disarmed!
His crime is sanctioned by a court decree!
And not content with what he's done to me,
The dog now seeks to ruin me by stating
That I composed a book now circulating,
A book so wholly criminal and vicious
That even to speak its title is seditious!
Meanwhile Oronte, my rival, lends his credit
To the same libelous tale, and helps to spread it!
Oronte! a man of honor and of rank,
With whom I've been entirely fair and frank;
Who sought me out and forced me, willy-nilly,
To judge some verse I found extremely silly;
And who, because I properly refused
To flatter him, or see the truth abused,
Abets my enemy in a rotten slander!
There's the reward of honesty and candor!
The man will hate me to the end of time
For failing to commend his wretched rhyme!
And not this man alone, but all humanity
Do what they do from interest and vanity;
They prate of honor, truth, and righteousness,
But lie, betray, and swindle nonetheless.
Come then: man's villainy is too much to bear;
Let's leave this jungle and this jackal's lair.
Yes! treacherous and savage race of men,
You shall not look upon my face again.

PHILINTE
Oh, don't rush into exile prematurely;
Things aren't as dreadful as you make them, surely.
It's rather obvious, since you're still at large,
That people don't believe your enemy's charge.
Indeed, his tale's so patently untrue
That it may do more harm to him than you.

ALCESTE
Nothing could do that scoundrel any harm:
His frank corruption is his greatest charm,
And, far from hurting him, a further shame
Would only serve to magnify his name.

PHILINTE

> In any case, his bald prevarication
> Has done no injury to your reputation,
> And you may feel secure in that regard.
> As for your lawsuit, it should not be hard
> To have the case reopened, and contest
> This judgment . . .

ALCESTE

>   No, no, let the verdict rest.
> Whatever cruel penalty it may bring,
> I wouldn't have it changed for anything.
> It shows the times' injustice with such clarity
> That I shall pass it down to our posterity
> As a great proof and signal demonstration
> Of the black wickedness of this generation.
> It may cost twenty thousand francs; but I
> Shall pay their twenty thousand, and gain thereby
> The right to storm and rage at human evil,
> And send the race of mankind to the devil.

PHILINTE

> Listen to me. . . .

ALCESTE

>   Why? What can you possibly say?
> Don't argue, Sir; your labor's thrown away.
> Do you propose to offer lame excuses
> For men's behavior and the times' abuses?

PHILINTE

> No, all you say I'll readily concede:
> This is a low, conniving age indeed;
> Nothing but trickery prospers nowadays,
> And people ought to mend their shabby ways.
> Yes, man's a beastly creature; but must we then
> Abandon the society of men?
> Here in the world, each human frailty
> Provides occasion for philosophy,
> And that is virtue's noblest exercise;
> If honesty shone forth from all men's eyes,
> If every heart were frank and kind and just,
> What could our virtues do but gather dust
> (Since their employment is to help us bear
> The villainies of men without despair)?
> A heart well-armed with virtue can endure. . . .

ALCESTE

> Sir, you're a matchless reasoner, to be sure;
> Your words are fine and full of cogency;
> But don't waste time and eloquence on me.
> *My* reason bids me go, for my own good.
> My tongue won't lie and flatter as it should;

God knows what frankness it might next commit,
And what I'd suffer on account of it.
Pray let me wait for Célimène's return
In peace and quiet. I shall shortly learn,
By her response to what I have in view,
Whether her love for me is feigned or true.

PHILINTE

Till then, let's visit Eliante upstairs.

ALCESTE

No, I am too weighed down with somber cares.
Go to her, do; and leave me with my gloom
Here in the darkened corner of this room.

PHILINTE

Why, that's no sort of company, my friend;
I'll see if Eliante will not descend.

SCENE TWO: CELIMENE, ORONTE, ALCESTE

ORONTE

Yes, Madam, if you wish me to remain
Your true and ardent lover, you must deign
To give me some more positive assurance.
All this suspense is quite beyond endurance.
If your heart shares the sweet desires of mine,
Show me as much by some convincing sign;
And here's the sign I urgently suggest:
That you no longer tolerate Alceste,
But sacrifice him to my love, and sever
All your relations with the man forever.

CELIMENE

Why do you suddenly dislike him so?
You praised him to the skies not long ago.

ORONTE

Madam, that's not the point. I'm here to find
Which way your tender feelings are inclined.
Choose, if you please, between Alceste and me,
And I shall stay or go accordingly.

ALCESTE [*Emerging from the corner*]

Yes, Madam, choose; this gentleman's demand
Is wholly just, and I support his stand.
I too am true and ardent; I too am here
To ask you that you make your feelings clear.
No more delays, now; no equivocation;
The time has come to make your declaration.

ORONTE

Sir, I've no wish in any way to be
An obstacle to your felicity.

ALCESTE
>Sir, I've no wish to share her heart with you;
>That may sound jealous, but at least it's true.

ORONTE
>If, weighing us, she leans in your direction . . .

ALCESTE
>If she regards you with the least affection . . .

ORONTE
>I swear I'll yield her to you there and then.

ALCESTE
>I swear I'll never see her face again.

ORONTE
>Now, Madam, tell us what we've come to hear.

ALCESTE
>Madam, speak openly and have no fear.

ORONTE
>Just say which one is to remain your lover.

ALCESTE
>Just name one name, and it will all be over.

ORONTE
>What! Is it possible that you're undecided?

ALCESTE
>What! Can your feelings possibly be divided?

CELIMENE
>Enough: this inquisition's gone too far:
>How utterly unreasonable you are!
>Not that I couldn't make the choice with ease;
>My heart has no conflicting sympathies;
>I know full well which one of you I favor,
>And you'd not see me hesitate or waver.
>But how can you expect me to reveal
>So cruelly and bluntly what I feel?
>I think it altogether too unpleasant
>To choose between two men when both are present;
>One's heart has means more subtle and more kind
>Of letting its affections be divined,
>Nor need one be uncharitably plain
>To let a lover know he loves in vain.

ORONTE
>No, no, speak plainly; I for one can stand it.
>I beg you to be frank.

ALCESTE
>   And I demand it.
>The simple truth is what I wish to know,
>And there's no need for softening the blow.
>You've made an art of pleasing everyone,
>But now your days of coquetry are done:
>You have no choice now, Madam, but to choose,

For I'll know what to think if you refuse;
I'll take your silence for a clear admission
That I'm entitled to my worst suspicion.

ORONTE

I thank you for this ultimatum, Sir,
And I may say I heartily concur.

CELIMENE

Really, this foolishness is very wearing:
Must you be so unjust and overbearing?
Haven't I told you why I must demur?
Ah, here's Eliante; I'll put the case to her.

SCENE THREE: ELIANTE, PHILINTE, CELIMENE, ORONTE, ALCESTE

CELIMENE

Cousin, I'm being persecuted here
By these two persons, who, it would appear,
Will not be satisfied till I confess
Which one I love the more, and which the less,
And tell the latter to his face that he
Is henceforth banished from my company.
Tell me, has ever such a thing been done?

ELIANTE

You'd best not turn to me; I'm not the one
To back you in a matter of this kind:
I'm all for those who frankly speak their mind.

ORONTE

Madam, you'll search in vain for a defender.

ALCESTE

You're beaten, Madam, and may as well surrender.

ORONTE

Speak, speak, you must; and end this awful strain.

ALCESTE

Or don't, and your position will be plain.

ORONTE

A single word will close this painful scene.

ALCESTE

But if you're silent, I'll know what you mean.

SCENE FOUR: ARSINOE, CELIMENE, ELIANTE, ALCESTE, PHILINTE,
ACASTE, CLITANDRE, ORONTE

ACASTE [*To* CELIMENE]

Madam, with all due deference, we two
Have come to pick a little bone with you.

CLITANDRE [*To* ORONTE *and* ALCESTE]
I'm glad you're present, Sirs; as you'll soon learn,
Our business here is also your concern.

ARSINOE [*To* CELIMENE]
Madam, I visit you so soon again
Only because of these two gentlemen,
Who came to me indignant and aggrieved
About a crime too base to be believed.
Knowing your virtue, having such confidence in it,
I couldn't think you guilty for a minute,
In spite of all their telling evidence;
And, rising above our little difference,
I've hastened here in friendship's name to see
You clear yourself of this great calumny.

ACASTE
Yes, Madam, let us see with what composure
You'll manage to respond to this disclosure.
You lately sent Clitandre this tender note.

CLITANDRE
And this one, for Acaste, you also wrote.

ACASTE [*To* ORONTE *and* ALCESTE]
You'll recognize this writing, Sirs, I think;
The lady is so free with pen and ink
That you must know it all too well, I fear.
But listen: this is something you should hear.

"How absurd you are to condemn my lightheartedness in society, and to accuse me of being happiest in the company of others. Nothing could be more unjust; and if you do not come to me instantly and beg pardon for saying such a thing, I shall never forgive you as long as I live. Our big bumbling friend the Viscount . . ."

What a shame that he's not here.

"Our big bumbling friend the Viscount, whose name stands first in your complaint, is hardly a man to my taste; and ever since the day I watched him spend three-quarters of an hour spitting into a well, so as to make circles in the water, I have been unable to think highly of him. As for the little Marquess . . ."

In all modesty, gentlemen, that is I.

"As for the little Marquess, who sat squeezing my hand for such a long while yesterday, I find him in all respects the most trifling creature alive; and the only things of value about him are his cape and his sword. As for the man with the green ribbons . . ."

[*To* ALCESTE]
It's your turn now, Sir.

"As for the man with the green ribbons, he amuses me now and then with his bluntness and his bearish ill-humor; but there are many times in-

deed when I think him the greatest bore in the world. And as for the sonneteer . . ."

[*To* ORONTE]
Here's your helping.

"And as for the sonneteer, who has taken it into his head to be witty,
and insists on being an author in the teeth of opinion, I simply cannot be
bothered to listen to him, and his prose wearies me quite as much as his
poetry. Be assured that I am not always so well-entertained as you suppose;
that I long for your company, more than I dare to say, at all these enter-
tainments to which people drag me; and that the presence of those one loves
is the true and perfect seasoning to all one's pleasures."

CLITANDRE
And now for me.

"Clitandre, whom you mention, and who so pesters me with his saccha-
rine speeches, is the last man on earth for whom I could feel any affection.
He is quite mad to suppose that I love him, and so are you, to doubt that
you are loved. Do come to your senses; exchange your suppositions for his;
and visit me as often as possible, to help me bear the annoyance of his un-
welcome attentions."

It's a sweet character that these letters show,
And what to call it, Madam, you well know.
Enough. We're off to make the world acquainted
With this sublime self-portrait that you've painted.

ACASTE
Madam, I'll make you no farewell oration;
No, you're not worthy of my indignation.
Far choicer hearts than yours, as you'll discover,
Would like this little Marquess for a lover.

SCENE FIVE: CELIMENE, ELIANTE, ARSINOE, ALCESTE,
ORONTE, PHILINTE

ORONTE
So! After all those loving letters you wrote,
You turn on me like this, and cut my throat!
And your dissembling, faithless heart, I find,
Has pledged itself by turns to all mankind!
How blind I've been! But now I clearly see;
I thank you, Madam, for enlightening me.
My heart is mine once more, and I'm content;
The loss of it shall be your punishment.
[*To* ALCESTE]
Sir, she is yours; I'll seek no more to stand
Between your wishes and this lady's hand.

SCENE SIX: CELIMENE, ELIANTE, ARSINOE, ALCESTE, PHILINTE

ARSINOE [*To* CELIMENE]

Madam, I'm forced to speak. I'm far too stirred
To keep my counsel, after what I've heard.
I'm shocked and staggered by your want of morals.
It's not my way to mix in others' quarrels;
But really, when this fine and noble spirit,
This man of honor and surpassing merit,
Laid down the offering of his heart before you,
How *could* you . . .

ALCESTE

                    Madam, permit me, I implore you,
To represent myself in this debate.
Don't bother, please, to be my advocate.
My heart, in any case, could not afford
To give your services their due reward;
And if I chose, for consolation's sake,
Some other lady, t'would not be you I'd take.

ARSINOE

What makes you think you could, Sir? And how dare you
Imply that I've been trying to ensnare you?
If you can for a moment entertain
Such flattering fancies, you're extremely vain.
I'm not so interested as you suppose
In Célimène's discarded gigolos.
Get rid of that absurd illusion, do.
Women like me are not for such as you.
Stay with this creature, to whom you're so attached;
I've never seen two people better matched.

SCENE SEVEN: CELIMENE, ELIANTE, ALCESTE, PHILINTE

ALCESTE [*To* CELIMENE]

Well, I've been still throughout this exposé,
Till everyone but me has said his say.
Come, have I shown sufficient self-restraint?
And may I now . . .

CELIMENE

                    Yes, make your just complaint.
Reproach me freely, call me what you will;
You've every right to say I've used you ill.
I've wronged you, I confess it; and in my shame
I'll make no effort to escape the blame.
The anger of those others I could despise;
My guilt toward you I sadly recognize.

Your wrath is wholly justified, I fear;
I know how culpable I must appear,
I know all things bespeak my treachery,
And that, in short, you've grounds for hating me.
Do so; I give you leave.

ALCESTE

                    Ah, traitress—how,
How should I cease to love you, even now?
Though mind and will were passionately bent
On hating you, my heart would not consent.

[*To* ELIANTE *and* PHILINTE]

Be witness to my madness, both of you;
See what infatuation drives one to;
But wait; my folly's only just begun,
And I shall prove to you before I'm done
How strange the human heart is, and how far
From rational we sorry creatures are.

[*To* CELIMENE]

Woman, I'm willing to forget your shame,
And clothe your treacheries in a sweeter name;
I'll call them youthful errors, instead of crimes,
And lay the blame on these corrupting times.
My one condition is that you agree
To share my chosen fate, and fly with me
To that wild, trackless, solitary place
In which I shall forget the human race.
Only by such a course can you atone
For those atrocious letters; by that alone
Can you remove my present horror of you,
And make it possible for me to love you.

CELIMENE

What! *I* renounce the world at my young age,
And die of boredom in some hermitage?

ALCESTE

Ah, if you really loved me as you ought,
You wouldn't give the world a moment's thought;
Must you have me, and all the world beside?

CELIMENE

Alas, at twenty one is terrified
Of solitude. I fear I lack the force
And depth of soul to take so stern a course.
But if my hand in marriage will content you,
Why, there's a plan which I might well consent to,
And . . .

ALCESTE

                    No, I detest you now. I could excuse
Everything else, but since you thus refuse
To love me wholly, as a wife should do,

And see the world in me, as I in you,
Go! I reject your hand, and disenthrall
My heart from your enchantments, once for all.

Scene Eight: eliante, alceste, philinte

alceste [*To* eliante]

Madam, your virtuous beauty has no peer;
Of all this world, you only are sincere;
I've long esteemed you highly, as you know;
Permit me ever to esteem you so,
And if I do not now request your hand,
Forgive me, Madam, and try to understand.
I feel unworthy of it; I sense that fate
Does not intend me for the married state,
That I should do you wrong by offering you
My shattered heart's unhappy residue,
And that in short . . .

eliante

Your argument's well taken:
Nor need you fear that I shall feel forsaken.
Were I to offer him this hand of mine,
Your friend Philinte, I think, would not decline.

philinte

Ah, Madam, that's my heart's most cherished goal,
For which I'd gladly give my life and soul.

alceste [*To* eliante *and* philinte]

May you be true to all you now profess,
And so deserve unending happiness.
Meanwhile, betrayed and wronged in everything,
I'll flee this bitter world where vice is king,
And seek some spot unpeopled and apart
Where I'll be free to have an honest heart.

philinte

Come, Madam, let's do everything we can
To change the mind of this unhappy man.

The Way of the World

William Congreve

William Congreve

William Congreve (1670-1729) was born in Yorkshire, England, but grew up in Ireland, where his father, an army officer, was stationed. He had an excellent education at Kilkenny School (the Eton of Ireland) and at Trinity College, Dublin. It is recorded that he spent six times more money on beer and wine at Trinity than did Jonathan Swift, his senior there by three years. At the time of the Revolution, Congreve and his family returned to England. In 1691 he was admitted to the Middle Temple to undertake the practice of law; but the law not proving to his taste he turned to the drama, and with his first play, *The Old Bachelor* (1693), achieved resounding success. Congreve was born for success: Dryden praised him to the skies, Swift wrote an ode in his honor, aristocrats cultivated him, the incomparable Ann Bracegirdle, who played the feminine lead in all his plays, became his intimate friend. He followed *The Old Bachelor* with *The Double Dealer* (1694); *Love for Love* (1695), which was immensely popular; *The Mourning Bride* (1697), a tragedy; and *The Way of the World* (1700).

At the age of thirty Congreve was at the top of the literary world; but he was also somewhat disillusioned with that world, and he was afflicted with a variety of physical ailments. He retired from the stage into a life of gentlemanly, though impecunious, leisure and painful invalidism. His old friend Jonathan Swift made this entry in the *Journal to Stella* in 1710:

> I was to-day to see Mr. Congreve, who is almost blind with cataracts growing on his eyes . . . and besides he is never rid of the gout, yet he looks young and fresh, and is as cheerful as ever. He is younger by three years or more than I, and I am twenty years younger than he. He gave me a pain in the great toe, by mentioning the gout.

This was to be very much the story of Congreve's life for the next twenty years. He died in 1729. In an age of angular personalities and acrimonious relations among men of letters, Congreve was a widely beloved man.

Congreve called his greatest play *The Way of the World*, and by "world" he meant the spectacularly licentious group of people associated with the courts of the Restoration. A modern scholar describes the Restoration audience thus:

> The spectators . . . for whom the poets wrote and the actors played were the courtiers and their satellites. The noblemen in the pit and boxes, the fops and beaux and wits or would-be

wits who hung on to their society, the women of the court, depraved and licentious as the men, the courtesans with whom these women of quality moved and conversed as on equal terms, made up at least four-fifths of the entire audience. Add a sprinkling of footmen in the upper gallery, a stray country cousin or two scattered throughout the theatre, and the picture of the audience is complete (Allardyce Nicoll, *History of English Drama, 1600-1900*, Vol. I [Cambridge, 1952], p. 8).

This is the world to which Congreve showed its own ways.

From his time to ours, audiences, readers, and critics have been sharply, even violently, divided on what the proper response to that world, as depicted in the theatre, should be. Its wickedness and its wit have always been startlingly evident; but is it right, goes the perennial question, to take delight in the witty depiction of wickedness?

Several responses are possible. The most forthright is that of outraged moralists like Jeremy Collier, a contemporary of Congreve, who published *A Short View of the Immorality and Profaneness of the English Stage* (1698), and William Thackeray, the great nineteenth-century novelist, who wrote of "that miserable, rouged, tawdry, sparkling, hollow-hearted comedy of the Restoration." Charles Lamb's reaction was more subtle. In a famous essay he proposed that the characters of Restoration comedy have no connection with reality whatever and so do not engage our moral judgments:

> The Fainalls and the Mirabells . . . in their own sphere do not offend my moral sense; in fact they do not appeal to it at all. They seem engaged in their proper element. They break through no laws, or conscientious restraints. They know of none. They have got out of Christendom into the land—what shall I call it?—of cuckoldry—the Utopia of gallantry, where pleasure is a duty, and the manners perfect freedom. It is altogether a speculative scene of things, which has no reference whatever to the world that is.

Still another response is that of people who see at least some Restoration comedies as mirroring, and so exposing, the follies of libertine life. Congreve himself clearly had some such idea in view, as the epigraph from Horace's *Satires*, introducing *The Way of the World*, indicates. In the Prologue to the play Congreve warns the audience: don't expect satire in what follows, for who would dare try to correct so reformed a town as London? Here, he says, I try only to please, not to instruct; but if by chance a knave or a fool should be exposed, that would affect nobody in *this* audience: "sure, here are none of those." The elaborately ironic disavowal of satire can mean only that satire is precisely what we will get. The way of the world is not to be taken as Congreve's way.

Still, he is very subtle. Part of our joy in the play lies in watching the delicate modulations of his art as he discriminates true wit from false, gentlemen and ladies from pretenders, lovers from the perverters of love—those who affect the civilized style of life from those who authentically have it. *The Way of the World*, like a sizable proportion of our literature, is about money and sex and how they make the world go round; but over and above this it is about style in its most inclusive sense—about elegance and grace and decorum as these find (or do not find) expression in manners and become the energizing force of an entire way of life.

In matters of style Congreve's splendid lovers, Millamant and Mirabell, have absolute pitch. As they play it, the love duel (synonymous here with the love chase) is an exquisite performance. Against the shining standard of these true wits, the pretenders to wit—Witwoud and his crew—show up as comic butts. Congreve believed, like Henry Fielding after him, that the true source of the ridiculous is affectation. Of this he provides great plenty.

The plot of *The Way of the World* is conventional but complicated—it demands more than one reading. Some of the minor characters are superb, especially Lady Wishfort, whose grotesquery is almost sublime. But what one remembers, and will continue to remember, is the sparkle and thrust of the language, the lovely dance of the wit. In this respect, as in others, *The Way of the World* bears comparison with Molière's *Misanthrope*.

A Note on the Restoration Stage

From 1642 until 1660 public theatrical performances were banned in England by the regime of Oliver Cromwell. With the restoration of Charles II to the throne, however, new theatres were quickly built to satisfy public demand. These structures differed in several important respects from their Elizabethan prototypes, and, as is always the case, new physical features of the theatres made new demands upon the dramatists. The Restoration theatres were oblong in shape with facilities for nearly all the audience to sit down. They were roofed in, and they were lighted by lamps and candles. The stage was large and jutted out into the pit so that the "apron," as it was called, was surrounded on three sides by spectators. A curtain could be dropped from the proscenium arch, and considerable use was made of scenery. This last innovation was particularly important. The fluidity of Shakespeare's stage, where the platform was a kind of neutral territory, was succeeded by a highly specific sense of place; scenery, poorly lighted as it was, pinned down the locale of each scene and made for a closer approximation of realism. Poetic descriptions of place, common in Elizabethan plays, became increasingly rare.

One further change in theatrical conditions should be mentioned. During the Restoration, actresses appeared on the stage for the first time in the history of English drama and replaced the men and boys who had formerly played all feminine roles. Again playwrights were affected as the theatre moved closer to reality.

The Way of the World

William Congreve

Audire est operae pretium, procedere recte
Qui maechis non vultis—
—Metuat doti deprensa.—[1]

CHARACTERS

FAINALL, *in love with Mrs. Marwood*[2]

MIRABELL, *in love with Mrs. Millamant*

WITWOUD ⎱ *followers of*
PETULANT ⎰ *Mrs. Millamant*

SIR WILFULL WITWOUD, *half brother to Witwoud and nephew to Lady Wishfort*

WAITWELL, *servant to Mirabell*

LADY WISHFORT, *enemy to Mirabell for having falsely pretended love to her*

MRS. MILLAMANT, *a fine lady, niece to Lady Wishfort, and loves Mirabell*

MRS. MARWOOD, *friend to Mr. Fainall, and likes Mirabell*

MRS. FAINALL, *daughter to Lady Wishfort and wife to Fainall, formerly friend to Mirabell*

FOIBLE, *woman to Lady Wishfort*

MINCING, *woman to Mrs. Millamant*

DANCERS, FOOTMEN, *and* ATTENDANTS

SCENE: *London*

[1] O you that do not wish well to the proceedings of adulterers, it is worth your while to hear how they are hampered on all sides.—Caught in the act, the woman fears for her dowry. —Horace, *Satires*, II, 1, 37-38, 131.

[2] Unmarried ladies, as well as married ones, are called "Mrs."

PROLOGUE

Of those few fools who with ill stars are cursed,
Sure scribbling fools, called poets, fare the worst;
For they're a sort of fools which Fortune makes,
And after she has made 'em fools, forsakes.
With Nature's oafs 'tis quite a different case,
For Fortune favors all her idiot-race;
In her own nest the cuckoo-eggs we find,
O'er which she broods to hatch the changeling-kind.
No portion for her own she has to spare,
So much she dotes on her adopted care.

    Poets are bubbles,[3] by the town drawn in,
Suffered at first some trifling stakes to win;
But what unequal hazards do they run!
Each time they write they venture all they've won;
The squire that's buttered [4] still, is sure to be undone.
This author heretofore has found your favor,
But pleads no merit from his past behavior;
To build on that might prove a vain presumption,
Should grants to poets made admit resumption;[5]
And in Parnassus he must lose his seat,
If that be found a forfeited estate.

    He owns, with toil he wrought the following scenes,
But, if they're naught, ne'er spare him for his pains;
Damn him the more; have no commiseration
For dullness on mature deliberation.
He swears he'll not resent one hissed-off scene,
Nor, like those peevish wits, his play maintain,
Who, to assert their sense, your taste arraign.
Some plot we think he has, and some new thought;
Some humor, too, no farce—but that's a fault.
Satire, he thinks, you ought not to expect;
For so reformed a town who dares correct?
To please this time has been his sole pretense;
He'll not instruct, lest it should give offense.
Should he by chance a knave or fool expose,
That hurts none here; sure, here are none of those.
In short, our play shall (with your leave to show it)
Give you one instance of a passive poet,
Who to your judgments yields all resignation;
So save or damn after your own discretion.

---

[3] Easy marks, dupes.   [4] Flattered, egged on.   [5] Capable of being taken back.

Act I

SCENE I. *A chocolate-house.* MIRABELL *and* FAINALL [*Rising from cards*] BETTY *waiting.*

MIRABELL. You are a fortunate man, Mr. Fainall!

FAINALL. Have we done?

MIRABELL. What you please. I'll play on to entertain you.

FAINALL. No, I'll give you your revenge another time, when you are not so indifferent; you are thinking of something else now, and play too negligently. The coldness of a losing gamester lessens the pleasure of the winner. I'd no more play with a man that slighted his ill fortune than I'd make love to a woman who undervalued the loss of her reputation.

MIRABELL. You have a taste extremely delicate, and are for refining on your pleasures.

FAINALL. Prithee, why so reserved? Something has put you out of humor.

MIRABELL. Not at all. I happen to be grave to-day, and you are gay; that's all.

FAINALL. Confess, Millamant and you quarrelled last night after I left you; my fair cousin has some humors that would tempt the patience of a stoic. What, some coxcomb came in, and was well received by her, while you were by?

MIRABELL. Witwoud and Petulant; and what was worse, her aunt, your wife's mother, my evil genius; or to sum up all in her own name, my old Lady Wishfort came in.

FAINALL. Oh, there it is then! She has a lasting passion for you, and with reason.—What, then my wife was there?

MIRABELL. Yes, and Mrs. Marwood, and three or four more, whom I never saw before. Seeing me, they all put on their grave faces, whispered one another; then complained aloud of the vapors[6] and after fell into a profound silence.

FAINALL. They had a mind to be rid of you.

MIRABELL. For which reason I resolved not to stir. At last the good old lady broke through her painful taciturnity with an invective against long visits. I would not have understood her, but Millamant joining in the argument, I rose, and with a constrained smile, told her I thought nothing was so easy as to know when a visit began to be troublesome. She reddened, and I withdrew without expecting her reply.

FAINALL. You were to blame to resent what she spoke only in compliance with her aunt.

MIRABELL. She is more mistress of herself than to be under the necessity of such a resignation.

FAINALL. What! though half her fortune depends upon her marrying with my lady's approbation?

MIRABELL. I was then in such a humor that I should have been better pleased if she had been less discreet.

FAINALL. Now I remember, I wonder not they were weary of you; last night was one of their cabal nights. They have 'em three times a week, and meet by

---

[6] Boredom, the blues.

turns at one another's apartments, where they come together like the coroner's inquest, to sit upon the murdered reputations of the week. You and I are excluded, and it was once proposed that all the male sex should be excepted; but somebody moved that, to avoid scandal, there might be one man of the community, upon which motion Witwoud and Petulant were enrolled members.

MIRABELL.   And who may have been the foundress of this sect? My Lady Wishfort, I warrant, who publishes her detestation of mankind, and, full of the vigor of fifty-five, declares for a friend and ratafia;[7] and let posterity shift for itself, she'll breed no more.

FAINALL.   The discovery of your sham addresses to her, to conceal your love to her niece, has provoked this separation; had you dissembled better, things might have continued in the state of nature.

MIRABELL.   I did as much as man could, with any reasonable conscience; I proceeded to the very last act of flattery with her, and was guilty of a song in her commendation. Nay, I got a friend to put her into a lampoon and compliment her with the imputation of an affair with a young fellow, which I carried so far that I told her the malicious town took notice that she was grown fat of a sudden; and when she lay in of a dropsy, persuaded her she was reported to be in labor. The devil's in't, if an old woman is to be flattered further, unless a man should endeavor downright personally to debauch her; and that my virtue forbade me. But for the discovery of this amour I am indebted to your friend, or your wife's friend, Mrs. Marwood.

FAINALL.   What should provoke her to be your enemy, unless she has made you advances which you have slighted? Women do not easily forgive omissions of that nature.

MIRABELL.   She was always civil to me till of late. I confess I am not one of those coxcombs who are apt to interpret a woman's good manners to her prejudice, and think that she who does not refuse 'em everything, can refuse 'em nothing.

FAINALL.   You are a gallant man, Mirabell; and though you may have cruelty enough not to satisfy a lady's longing, you have too much generosity not to be tender of her honor. Yet you speak with an indifference which seems to be affected and confesses you are conscious of a negligence.

MIRABELL.   You pursue the argument with a distrust that seems to be unaffected and confesses you are conscious of a concern for which the lady is more indebted to you than is your wife.

FAINALL.   Fie, fie, friend! If you grow censorious I must leave you.—I'll look upon the gamesters in the next room.

MIRABELL.   Who are they?

FAINALL.   Petulant and Witwoud.—[*To* BETTY] Bring me some chocolate.

[*Exit* FAINALL]

MIRABELL.   Betty, what says your clock?

BETTY.   Turned of the last canonical hour,[8] sir.

MIRABELL.   How pertinently the jade answers me!—[*Looking on his watch*]—Ha? almost one o'clock!—Oh, y'are come!

---

[7] A fruit-flavored liqueur.   [8] Last hour for legal marriage in the parish church.

[*Enter a* SERVANT]

Well, is the grand affair over? You have been something tedious.

SERVANT. Sir, there's such coupling at Pancras[9] that they stand behind one another, as 'twere in a country dance. Ours was the last couple to lead up, and no hopes appearing of dispatch—besides, the parson growing hoarse, we were afraid his lungs would have failed before it came to our turn; so we drove round to Duke's Place[10] and there they were riveted in a trice.

MIRABELL. So, so! You are sure they are married?

SERVANT. Married and bedded, sir; I am witness.

MIRABELL. Have you the certificate?

SERVANT. Here it is, sir.

MIRABELL. Has the tailor brought Waitwell's clothes home, and the new liveries?

SERVANT. Yes, sir.

MIRABELL. That's well. Do you go home again, d'ye hear, and adjourn the consummation till further orders. Bid Waitwell shake his ears, and Dame Partlet[11] rustle up her feathers and meet me at one o'clock by Rosamond's Pond,[12] that I may see her before she returns to her lady; and as you tender your ears be secret.

[*Exit* SERVANT]

[*Re-enter* FAINALL]

FAINALL. Joy of your success, Mirabell; you look pleased.

MIRABELL. Aye; I have been engaged in a matter of some sort of mirth, which is not yet ripe for discovery. I am glad this is not a cabal night. I wonder, Fainall, that you, who are married and of consequence should be discreet, will suffer your wife to be of such a party.

FAINALL. Faith, I am not jealous. Besides, most who are engaged are women and relations; and for the men, they are of a kind too contemptible to give scandal.

MIRABELL. I am of another opinion. The greater the coxcomb, always the more the scandal; for a woman who is not a fool can have but one reason for associating with a man who is one.

FAINALL. Are you jealous as often as you see Witwoud entertained by Millamant?

MIRABELL. Of her understanding I am, if not of her person.

FAINALL. You do her wrong; for, to give her her due, she has wit.

MIRABELL. She has beauty enough to make any man think so; and complaisance enough not to contradict him who shall tell her so.

FAINALL. For a passionate lover, methinks you are a man somewhat too discerning in the failings of your mistress.

MIRABELL. And for a discerning man, somewhat too passionate a lover; for I like her with all her faults—nay, like her for her faults. Her follies are so natural, or so artful, that they become her; and those affectations which in another woman would be odious, serve but to make her more agreeable. I'll tell thee, Fainall, she once used me with that insolence, that in revenge I took

---

[9] St. Pancras Church. Marriages could be performed here without a license.

[10] Site of St. James's Church, famous for hasty marriages.   [11] Traditional name for the hen.

[12] In fashionable St. James's Park.

her to pieces, sifted her, and separated her failings; I studied 'em, and got 'em by rote. The catalogue was so large that I was not without hopes one day or other to hate her heartily; to which end I so used myself to think of 'em that at length, contrary to my design and expectation, they gave me every hour less and less disturbance, till in a few days it became habitual to me to remember 'em without being displeased. They are now grown as familiar to me as my own frailties, and, in all probability, in a little time longer I shall like 'em as well.

FAINALL.   Marry her, marry her! Be half as well acquainted with her charms as you are with her defects, and my life on't, you are your own man again.

MIRABELL.   Say you so?

FAINALL.   Aye, aye, I have experience: I have a wife, and so forth.

[*Enter* MESSENGER]

MESSENGER.   I have a letter for him from his brother Sir Wilfull, which I am charged to deliver into his own hands.

BETTY.   He's in the next room, friend—that way.

[*Exit* MESSENGER]

MIRABELL.   What, is the chief of that noble family in town—Sir Wilfull Witwoud?

FAINALL.   He is expected today. Do you know him?

MIRABELL.   I have seen him; he promises to be an extraordinary person. I think you have the honor to be related to him.

FAINALL.   Yes; he is half-brother to this Witwoud by a former wife, who was sister to my Lady Wishfort, my wife's mother. If you marry Millamant, you must call cousins too.

MIRABELL.   I had rather be his relation than his acquaintance.

FAINALL.   He comes to town in order to equip himself for travel.

MIRABELL.   For travel! Why, the man that I mean is above forty.[13]

FAINALL.   No matter for that; 'tis for the honor of England, that all Europe should know we have blockheads of all ages.

MIRABELL.   I wonder there is not an act of parliament to save the credit of the nation, and prohibit the exportation of fools.

FAINALL.   By no means; 'tis better as 'tis. 'Tis better to trade with a little loss, than to be quite eaten up with being overstocked.

MIRABELL.   Pray, are the follies of this knight-errant and those of the squire his brother anything related?

FAINALL.   Not at all; Witwoud grows by the knight, like a medlar grafted on a crab.[14] One will melt in your mouth, and t'other set your teeth on edge; one is all pulp, and the other all core.

MIRABELL.   So one will be rotten before he be ripe, and the other will be rotten without ever being ripe at all.

FAINALL.   Sir Wilfull is an odd mixture of bashfulness and obstinacy.—But when he's drunk, he's as loving as the monster in *The Tempest*,[15] and much after the same manner. To give t'other his due, he has something of good nature, and does not always want[16] wit.

[13] The grand tour of Europe was customarily for young men.
[14] The fruit of the medlar tree is edible only when very ripe.
[15] Caliban in Shakespeare's play, Act II, scene ii.   [16] Lack.

MIRABELL.   Not always; but as often as his memory fails him, and his common-place[17] of comparisons. He is a fool with a good memory and some few scraps of other folks' wit. He is one whose conversation can never be approved; yet it is now and then to be endured. He has indeed one good quality—he is not exceptious; for he so passionately affects the reputation of understanding raillery, that he will construe an affront into a jest, and call downright rudeness and ill language, satire and fire.

FAINALL.   If you have a mind to finish his picture, you have an opportunity to do it at full length.—Behold the original!

[*Enter* WITWOUD]

WITWOUD.   Afford me your compassion, my dears! Pity me, Fainall! Mirabell, pity me!

MIRABELL.   I do, from my soul.

FAINALL.   Why, what's the matter?

WITWOUD.   No letters for me, Betty?

BETTY.   Did not the messenger bring you one but now, sir?

WITWOUD.   Aye, but no other?

BETTY.   No, sir.

WITWOUD.   That's hard, that's very hard.—A messenger, a mule, a beast of burden! He has brought me a letter from the fool my brother, as heavy as a panegyric in a funeral sermon, or a copy of commendatory verses from one poet to another. And what's worse, 'tis as sure a forerunner of the author as an epistle dedicatory.

MIRABELL.   A fool,—and your brother, Witwoud!

WITWOUD.   Aye, aye, my half-brother. My half-brother he is, no nearer, upon honor.

MIRABELL.   Then 'tis possible he may be but half a fool.

WITWOUD.   Good, good, Mirabell, *le drôle!* Good, good; hang him, don't let's talk of him.—Fainall, how does your lady? Gad, I say anything in the world to get this fellow out of my head. I beg pardon that I should ask a man of pleasure and the town, a question at once so foreign and domestic. But I talk like an old maid at a marriage; I don't know what I say. But she's the best woman in the world.

FAINALL.   'Tis well you don't know what you say, or else your commendation would go near to make me either vain or jealous.

WITWOUD.   No man in town lives well with a wife but Fainall.—Your judgment, Mirabell?

MIRABELL.   You had better step and ask his wife if you would be credibly informed.

WITWOUD.   Mirabell?

MIRABELL.   Aye?

WITWOUD.   My dear, I ask ten thousand pardons—gad, I have forgot what I was going to say to you!

MIRABELL.   I thank you heartily, heartily.

WITWOUD.   No, but prithee, excuse me—my memory is such a memory.

---

[17] A memorandum book: a compendium of borrowed witty remarks.

MIRABELL.   Have a care of such apologies, Witwoud; for I never knew a fool but he affected to complain either of the spleen[18] or his memory.

FAINALL.   What have you done with Petulant?

WITWOUD.   He's reckoning his money—my money it was. I have no luck to-day.

FAINALL.   You may allow him to win of you at play, for you are sure to be too hard for him at repartee. Since you monopolize the wit that is between you, the fortune must be his, of course.

MIRABELL.   I don't find that Petulant confesses the superiority of wit to be your talent, Witwoud.

WITWOUD.   Come, come, you are malicious now, and would breed debates.— Petulant's my friend, and a very honest fellow, and a very pretty fellow, and has a smattering—faith and troth, a pretty deal of an odd sort of a small wit. Nay, I'll do him justice. I'm his friend, I won't wrong him.—And if he had any judgment in the world, he would not be altogether contemptible. Come, come, don't detract from the merits of my friend.

FAINALL.   You don't take your friend to be over-nicely bred?

WITWOUD.   No, no, hang him, the rogue has no manners at all, that I must own —no more breeding than a bumbaily[19] that I grant you—'tis pity, faith; the fellow has fire and life.

MIRABELL.   What, courage?

WITWOUD.   Hum, faith I don't know as to that; I can't say as to that. Yes, faith, in a controversy, he'll contradict anybody.

MIRABELL.   Though 'twere a man whom he feared, or a woman whom he loved?

WITWOUD.   Well, well, he does not always think before he speaks—we have all our failings. You're too hard upon him—you are, faith. Let me excuse him. I can defend most of his faults, except one or two. One he has, that's the truth on't; if he were my brother, I could not acquit him—that, indeed, I could wish were otherwise.

MIRABELL.   Aye, marry, what's that, Witwoud?

WITWOUD.   O pardon me!—Expose the infirmities of my friend?—No, my dear, excuse me there.

FAINALL.   What! I warrant he's unsincere, or 'tis some such trifle.

WITWOUD.   No, no, what if he be? 'Tis no matter for that; his wit will excuse that. A wit should no more be sincere than a woman constant; one argues a decay of parts,[20] as t'other of beauty.

MIRABELL.   Maybe you think him too positive?

WITWOUD.   No, no, his being positive is an incentive to argument, and keeps up conversation.

FAINALL.   Too illiterate?

WITWOUD.   That? That's his happiness; his want of learning gives him the more opportunities to show his natural parts.

MIRABELL.   He wants words?

WITWOUD.   Aye, but I like him for that, now; for his want of words gives me the pleasure very often to explain his meaning.

FAINALL.   He's impudent?

WITWOUD.   No, that's not it.

---

[18] Melancholy; ill-humor.   [19] Colloquial for bailiff.   [20] Abilities.

MIRABELL. Vain?

WITWOUD. No.

MIRABELL. What! He speaks unseasonable truth sometimes, because he has not wit enough to invent an evasion?

WITWOUD. Truths! ha! ha! ha! No, no; since you will have it—I mean, he never speaks truth at all—that's all. He will lie like a chambermaid, or a woman of quality's porter. Now, that is a fault.

[*Enter* COACHMAN]

COACHMAN. Is Master Petulant here, mistress?

BETTY. Yes.

COACHMAN. Three gentlewomen in the coach would speak with him.

FAINALL. O brave Petulant!—three!

BETTY. I'll tell him.

COACHMAN. You must bring two dishes of chocolate and a glass of cinnamon-water.

[*Exit* COACHMAN]

WITWOUD. That should be for two fasting strumpets, and a bawd troubled with wind. Now you may know what the three are.

MIRABELL. You are very free with your friend's acquaintance.

WITWOUD. Aye, aye, friendship without freedom is as dull as love without enjoyment, or wine without toasting. But to tell you a secret, these are trulls whom he allows coach-hire, and something more by the week, to call on him once a day at public places.

MIRABELL. How!

WITWOUD. You shall see he won't go to 'em, because there's no more company here to take notice of him.—Why, this is nothing to what he used to do; before he found out this way, I have known him call for himself.

FAINALL. Call for himself! What dost thou mean?

WITWOUD. Mean! Why, he would slip you out of this chocolate-house just when you had been talking to him; as soon as your back was turned—whip, he was gone!—then trip to his lodging, clap on a hood and scarf and a mask, slap into a hackney-coach, and drive hither to the door again in a trice, where he would send in for himself, that is, I mean—call for himself, wait for himself; nay, and what's more, not finding himself, sometimes leave a letter for himself.

MIRABELL. I confess this is something extraordinary.—I believe he waits for himself now, he is so long a-coming.—Oh! I ask his pardon.

[*Enter* PETULANT]

BETTY. Sir, the coach stays.

PETULANT. Well, well; I come.—'Sbud,[21] a man had as good be a professed midwife as a professed whoremaster, at this rate! To be knocked up and raised at all hours, and in all places! Pox on 'em, I won't come!—D'ye hear, tell 'em I won't come—let 'em snivel and cry their hearts out.

FAINALL. You are very cruel, Petulant.

PETULANT. All's one, let it pass. I have a humor to be cruel.

MIRABELL. I hope they are not persons of condition that you use at this rate.

---

[21] A contraction of "God's blood."

PETULANT.   Condition! condition's a dried fig if I am not in humor!—By this
hand, if they were your—a—a—your what-d'ye-call-'ems themselves, they
must wait or rub off,[22] if I want appetite.

MIRABELL.   What-d'ye-call-'ems! What are they, Witwoud?

WITWOUD.   Empresses, my dear: by your what-d'ye-call-'ems he means sultana
queens.

PETULANT.   Aye, Roxolanas.[23]

MIRABELL.   Cry you mercy.

FAINALL.   Witwoud says they are—

PETULANT.   What does he say th' are?

WITWOUD.   I? Fine ladies, I say.

PETULANT.   Pass on, Witwoud.—Hark'ee, by this light, his relations—two co-
heiresses, his cousins, and an old aunt who loves caterwauling better than a
conventicle.[24]

WITWOUD.   Ha, ha, ha! I had a mind to see how the rogue would come off.—Ha,
ha, ha! Gad, I can't be angry with him if he had said they were my mother
and my sisters.

MIRABELL.   No?

WITWOUD.   No; the rogue's wit and readiness of invention charm me. Dear
Petulant!

BETTY.   They are gone, sir, in great anger.

PETULANT.   Enough; let 'em trundle. Anger helps complexion—saves paint.

FAINALL.   This continence is all dissembled; this is in order to have something
to brag of the next time he makes court to Millamant and swear he has
abandoned the whole sex for her sake.

MIRABELL.   Have you not left off your impudent pretensions there yet? I shall
cut your throat some time or other, Petulant, about that business.

PETULANT.   Aye, aye, let that pass—there are other throats to be cut.

MIRABELL.   Meaning mine, sir?

PETULANT.   Not I—I mean nobody—I know nothing. But there are uncles
and nephews in the world—and they may be rivals—what then? All's one
for that.

MIRABELL.   How! Hark'ee, Petulant, come hither—explain, or I shall call your
interpreter.[25]

PETULANT.   Explain? I know nothing. Why, you have an uncle, have you not,
lately come to town, and lodges by my Lady Wishfort's?

MIRABELL.   True.

PETULANT.   Why, that's enough—you and he are not friends; and if he should
marry and have a child you may be disinherited, ha?

MIRABELL.   Where hast thou stumbled upon all this truth?

PETULANT.   All's one for that; why, then, say I know something.

MIRABELL.   Come, thou art an honest fellow, Petulant, and shalt make love to
my mistress; thou sha't, faith. What hast thou heard of my uncle?

PETULANT.   I? Nothing, I. If throats are to be cut, let swords clash! snug's the
word; I shrug and am silent.

[22] Slang: take off.   [23] The sultan's queen in Davenant's play *The Siege of Rhodes* (1656).
[24] A meeting of religious nonconformists, like the Puritans.
[25] Your sword; i.e., challenge you to a duel.

MIRABELL. Oh, raillery, raillery! Come, I know thou art in the women's secrets. —What, you're a cabalist; I know you stayed at Millamant's last night after I went. Was there any mention made of my uncle or me? Tell me. If thou hadst but good nature equal to thy wit, Petulant, Tony Witwoud, who is now thy competitor in fame, would show as dim by thee as a dead whiting's[26] eye by a pearl of orient; he would no more be seen by thee than Mercury is by the sun. Come, I'm sure thou wo't tell me.

PETULANT. If I do, will you grant me common sense then, for the future?

MIRABELL. Faith, I'll do what I can for thee, and I'll pray that Heaven may grant it thee in the meantime.

PETULANT. Well, hark'ee.

[MIRABELL *and* PETULANT *talk apart*]

FAINALL. [*To* WITWOUD] Petulant and you both will find Mirabell as warm a rival as a lover.

WITWOUD. Pshaw! pshaw! that she laughs at Petulant is plain. And for my part, but that it is almost a fashion to admire her, I should—hark'ee—to tell you a secret, but let it go no further—between friends, I shall never break my heart for her.

FAINALL. How!

WITWOUD. She's handsome; but she's a sort of an uncertain woman.

FAINALL. I thought you had died for her.

WITWOUD. Umh—no—

FAINALL. She has wit.

WITWOUD. 'Tis what she will hardly allow anybody else. Now, demme! I should hate that, if she were as handsome as Cleopatra. Mirabell is not so sure of her as he thinks for.

FAINALL. Why do you think so?

WITWOUD. We stayed pretty late there last night, and heard something of an uncle[27] to Mirabell, who is lately come to town—and is between him and the best part of his estate. Mirabell and he are at some distance, as my Lady Wishfort has been told; and you know she hates Mirabell worse than a Quaker hates a parrot,[28] or than a fishmonger hates a hard frost. Whether this uncle has seen Mrs. Millamant or not, I cannot say, but there were items of such a treaty being in embryo; and if it should come to life, poor Mirabell would be in some sort unfortunately fobbed,[29] i'faith.

FAINALL. 'Tis impossible Millamant should hearken to it.

WITWOUD. Faith, my dear, I can't tell; she's a woman, and a kind of humorist.[30]

MIRABELL. [*To* PETULANT] And this is the sum of what you could collect last night?

PETULANT. The quintessence. Maybe Witwoud knows more, he stayed longer. Besides, they never mind him; they say anything before him.

MIRABELL. I thought you had been the greatest favorite.

PETULANT. Aye, *tête-à-tête*, but not in public, because I make remarks.

MIRABELL. Do you?

PETULANT. Aye, aye; pox, I'm malicious, man! Now, he's soft, you know;

[26] A fish.
[27] The uncle, "Sir Rowland," is an invention of Mirabell's and will be impersonated by Waitwell.   [28] Because parrots swear.   [29] Cheated.   [30] Whimsical, unpredictable person.

they are not in awe of him—the fellow's well-bred; he's what you call a—
what-d'ye-call-'em, a fine gentleman.—But he's silly withal.

MIRABELL. I thank you. I know as much as my curiosity requires.—Fainall, are
you for the Mall? [31]

FAINALL. Aye, I'll take a turn before dinner.

WITWOUD. Aye, we'll all walk in the Park; the ladies talked of being there.

MIRABELL. I thought you were obliged to watch for your brother Sir Wilfull's
arrival.

WITWOUD. No, no; he comes to his aunt's, my Lady Wishfort. Pox on him! I
shall be troubled with him, too; what shall I do with the fool?

PETULANT. Beg him for his estate, that I may beg you afterwards, and so have
but one trouble with you both.

WITWOUD. Oh, rare Petulant! Thou art as quick as fire in a frosty morning.
Thou shalt to the Mall with us, and we'll be very severe.

PETULANT. Enough! I'm in a humor to be severe.

MIRABELL. Are you? Pray then, walk by yourselves; let not us be accessory to
your putting the ladies out of countenance with your senseless ribaldry,
which you roar out aloud as often as they pass by you; and when you have
made a handsome woman blush, then you think you have been severe.

PETULANT. What, what? Then let 'em either show their innocence by not
understanding what they hear, or else show their discretion by not hearing
what they would not be thought to understand.

MIRABELL. But hast not thou then sense enough to know that thou oughtest to
be most ashamed thyself when thou hast put another out of countenance?

PETULANT. Not I, by this hand!—I always take blushing either for a sign of
guilt or ill breeding.

MIRABELL. I confess you ought to think so. You are in the right, that you may
plead the error of your judgment in defence of your practice.
Where modesty's ill manners, 'tis but fit
That impudence and malice pass for wit.

[*Exeunt*]

Act II

Scene i. *St. James's Park.*

[*Enter* MRS. FAINALL *and* MRS. MARWOOD]

MRS. FAINALL. Aye, aye, dear Marwood, if we will be happy, we must find the
means in ourselves and among ourselves. Men are ever in extremes—either
doting or averse. While they are lovers, if they have fire and sense, their
jealousies are insupportable; and when they cease to love—(we ought to
think at least) they loathe; they look upon us with horror and distaste; they
meet us like the ghosts of what we were, and as from such, fly from us.

---

[31] A fashionable walk bordering St. James's Park.

MRS. MARWOOD. True, 'tis an unhappy circumstance of life that love should ever die before us, and that the man so often should outlive the lover. But say what you will, 'tis better to be left than never to have been loved. To pass our youth in dull indifference, to refuse the sweets of life because they once must leave us, is as preposterous as to wish to have been born old because we one day must be old. For my part, my youth may wear and waste, but it shall never rust in my possession.

MRS. FAINALL. Then it seems you dissemble an aversion to mankind only in compliance to my mother's humor?

MRS. MARWOOD. Certainly. To be free; I have no taste of those insipid dry discourses with which our sex of force must entertain themselves apart from men. We may affect endearments to each other, profess eternal friendships, and seem to dote like lovers; but 'tis not in our natures long to persevere. Love will resume his empire in our breasts, and every heart, or soon or late, receive and readmit him as its lawful tyrant.

MRS. FAINALL. Bless me, how have I been deceived? Why, you profess a libertine.

MRS. MARWOOD. You see my friendship by my freedom. Come, be as sincere; acknowledge that your sentiments agree with mine.

MRS. FAINALL. Never!

MRS. MARWOOD. You hate mankind?

MRS. FAINALL. Heartily, inveterately.

MRS. MARWOOD. Your husband?

MRS. FAINALL. Most transcendently; aye, though I say it, meritoriously.

MRS. MARWOOD. Give me your hand upon it.

MRS. FAINALL. There.

MRS. MARWOOD. I join with you; what I have said has been to try you.

MRS. FAINALL. Is it possible? Dost thou hate those vipers, men?

MRS. MARWOOD. I have done hating 'em, and am now come to despise 'em; the next thing I have to do is eternally to forget 'em.

MRS. FAINALL. There spoke the spirit of an Amazon, a Penthesilea!

MRS. MARWOOD. And yet I am thinking sometimes to carry my aversion further.

MRS. FAINALL. How?

MRS. MARWOOD. Faith, by marrying; if I could but find one that loved me very well and would be thoroughly sensible of ill usage, I think I should do myself the violence of undergoing the ceremony.

MRS. FAINALL. You would not make him a cuckold?

MRS. MARWOOD. No; but I'd make him believe I did, and that's as bad.

MRS. FAINALL. Why had not you as good do it?

MRS. MARWOOD. Oh, if he should ever discover it, he would then know the worst and be out of his pain; but I would have him ever to continue upon the rack of fear and jealousy.

MRS. FAINALL. Ingenious mischief! would thou wert married to Mirabell.

MRS. MARWOOD. Would I were!

MRS. FAINALL. You change color.

MRS. MARWOOD. Because I hate him.

MRS. FAINALL. So do I, but I can hear him named. But what reason have you to hate him in particular?

MRS. MARWOOD. I never loved him; he is, and always was, insufferably proud.

MRS. FAINALL.   By the reason you give for your aversion, one would think it dissembled; for you have laid a fault to his charge, of which his enemies must acquit him.

MRS. MARWOOD.   Oh, then it seems you are one of his favorable enemies! Methinks you look a little pale—and now you flush again.

MRS. FAINALL.   Do I? I think I am a little sick o' the sudden.

MRS. MARWOOD.   What ails you?

MRS. FAINALL.   My husband. Don't you see him? He turned short upon me unawares, and has almost overcome me.

[*Enter* FAINALL *and* MIRABELL]

MRS. MARWOOD.   Ha, ha, ha! He comes opportunely for you.

MRS. FAINALL.   For you, for he has brought Mirabell with him.

FAINALL.   [*To* MRS. FAINALL] My dear!

MRS. FAINALL.   My soul!

FAINALL.   You don't look well to-day, child.

MRS. FAINALL.   D'ye think so?

MIRABELL.   He is the only man that does, madam.

MRS. FAINALL.   The only man that would tell me so, at least, and the only man from whom I could hear it without mortification.

FAINALL.   Oh, my dear, I am satisfied of your tenderness; I know you cannot resent anything from me, especially what is an effect of my concern.

MRS. FAINALL.   Mr. Mirabell, my mother interrupted you in a pleasant relation last night; I would fain hear it out.

MIRABELL.   The persons concerned in that affair have yet a tolerable reputation. I am afraid Mr. Fainall will be censorious.

MRS. FAINALL.   He has a humor more prevailing than his curiosity, and will willingly dispense with the hearing of one scandalous story, to avoid giving an occasion to make another by being seen to walk with his wife. This way, Mr. Mirabell, and I dare promise you will oblige us both.

[*Exeunt* MRS. FAINALL *and* MIRABELL]

FAINALL.   Excellent creature! Well, sure if I should live to be rid of my wife, I should be a miserable man.

MRS. MARWOOD.   Aye?

FAINALL.   For having only that one hope, the accomplishment of it, of consequence, must put an end to all my hopes; and what a wretch is he who must survive his hopes! Nothing remains when that day comes but to sit down and weep like Alexander when he wanted other worlds to conquer.

MRS. MARWOOD.   Will you not follow 'em?

FAINALL.   Faith, I think not.

MRS. MARWOOD.   Pray, let us; I have a reason.

FAINALL.   You are not jealous?

MRS. MARWOOD.   Of whom?

FAINALL.   Of Mirabell.

MRS. MARWOOD.   If I am, is it inconsistent with my love to you that I am tender of your honor?

FAINALL.   You would intimate, then, as if [there] were a fellow-feeling between my wife and him.

MRS. MARWOOD.   I think she does not hate him to that degree she would be thought.

FAINALL.   But he, I fear, is too insensible.

MRS. MARWOOD.   It may be you are deceived.

FAINALL.   It may be so. I do not now begin to apprehend it.

MRS. MARWOOD.   What?

FAINALL.   That I have been deceived, madam, and you are false.

MRS. MARWOOD.   That I am false! What mean you?

FAINALL.   To let you know I see through all your little arts.—Come, you both love him, and both have equally dissembled your aversion. Your mutual jealousies of one another have made you clash till you have both struck fire. I have seen the warm confession reddening on your cheeks and sparkling from your eyes.

MRS. MARWOOD.   You do me wrong.

FAINALL.   I do not. 'Twas for my ease to oversee and willfully neglect the gross advances made him by my wife, that by permitting her to be engaged, I might continue unsuspected in my pleasures and take you oftener to my arms in full security. But could you think, because the nodding husband would not wake, that e'er the watchful lover slept?

MRS. MARWOOD.   And wherewithal can you reproach me?

FAINALL.   With infidelity, with loving another—with love of Mirabell.

MRS. MARWOOD.   'Tis false! I challenge you to show an instance that can confirm your groundless accusation. I hate him!

FAINALL.   And wherefore do you hate him? He is insensible, and your resentment follows his neglect. An instance!—the injuries you have done him are a proof—your interposing in his love. What cause had you to make discoveries of his pretended passion?—to undeceive the credulous aunt, and be the officious obstacle of his match with Millamant?

MRS. MARWOOD.   My obligations to my lady urged me. I had professed a friendship to her, and could not see her easy nature so abused by that dissembler.

FAINALL.   What, was it conscience then? Professed a friendship! Oh, the pious friendships of the female sex!

MRS. MARWOOD.   More tender, more sincere, and more enduring than all the vain and empty vows of men, whether professing love to us or mutual faith to one another.

FAINALL.   Ha, ha, ha! You are my wife's friend, too.

MRS. MARWOOD.   Shame and ingratitude! Do you reproach me? You, you upbraid me? Have I been false to her, through strict fidelity to you, and sacrificed my friendship to keep my love inviolate? And have you the baseness to charge me with the guilt, unmindful of the merit? To you it should be meritorious that I have been vicious; and do you reflect that guilt upon me which should lie buried in your bosom?

FAINALL.   You misinterpret my reproof. I meant but to remind you of the slight account you once could make of strictest ties when set in competition with your love to me.

MRS. MARWOOD.   'Tis false; you urged it with deliberate malice! 'Twas spoke in scorn, and I never will forgive it.

FAINALL. Your guilt, not your resentment, begets your rage. If yet you loved, you could forgive a jealousy; but you are stung to find you are discovered.

MRS. MARWOOD. It shall be all discovered.—You too shall be discovered; be sure you shall. I can but be exposed.—If I do it myself I shall prevent your baseness.

FAINALL. Why, what will you do?

MRS. MARWOOD. Disclose it to your wife; own what has passed between us.

FAINALL. Frenzy!

MRS. MARWOOD. By all my wrongs I'll do't!—I'll publish to the world the injuries you have done me, both in my fame and fortune! With both I trusted you,—you bankrupt in honor, as indigent of wealth.

FAINALL. Your fame I have preserved. Your fortune has been bestowed as the prodigality of your love would have it, in pleasures which we both have shared. Yet, had not you been false, I had ere this repaid it. 'Tis true. Had you permitted Mirabell with Millamant to have stolen their marriage, my lady had been incensed beyond all means of reconcilement; Millamant had forfeited the moiety of her fortune, which then would have descended to my wife— and wherefore did I marry but to make lawful prize of a rich widow's wealth, and squander it on love and you?

MRS. MARWOOD. Deceit and frivolous pretence!

FAINALL. Death, am I not married? What's pretence? Am I not imprisoned, fettered? Have I not a wife?—nay, a wife that was a widow, a young widow, a handsome widow; and would be again a widow, but that I have a heart of proof, and something of a constitution to bustle through the ways of wedlock and this world! Will you yet be reconciled to truth and me?

MRS. MARWOOD. Impossible. Truth and you are inconsistent—I hate you, and shall forever.

FAINALL. For loving you?

MRS. MARWOOD. I loathe the name of love after such usage; and next to the guilt with which you would asperse me, I scorn you most. Farewell!

FAINALL. Nay, we must not part thus.

MRS. MARWOOD. Let me go.

FAINALL. Come, I'm sorry.

MRS. MARWOOD. I care not—let me go—break my hands, do! I'd leave 'em to get loose.

FAINALL. I would not hurt you for the world. Have I no other hold to keep you here?

MRS. MARWOOD. Well, I have deserved it all.

FAINALL. You know I love you.

MRS. MARWOOD. Poor dissembling!—Oh, that—well, it is not yet—

FAINALL. What? What is it not? What is it not yet? It is not yet too late—

MRS. MARWOOD. No, it is not yet too late—I have that comfort.

FAINALL. It is, to love another.

MRS. MARWOOD. But not to loathe, detest, abhor mankind, myself, and the whole treacherous world.

FAINALL. Nay, this is extravagance!—Come, I ask your pardon—no tears—I was to blame, I could not love you and be easy in my doubts. Pray, forbear— I believe you; I'm convinced I've done you wrong, and any way, every way will make amends. I'll hate my wife yet more, damn her! I'll part with her, rob her of all she's worth, and we'll retire somewhere—anywhere—to another world. I'll marry thee—be pacified—'Sdeath, they come! Hide your face, your tears.—You have a mask; wear it a moment. This way, this way—be persuaded.

[*Exeunt*]

[*Enter* MIRABELL *and* MRS. FAINALL]

MRS. FAINALL.   They are here yet.

MIRABELL.   They are turning into the other walk.

MRS. FAINALL.   While I only hated my husband, I could bear to see him; but since I have despised him, he's too offensive.

MIRABELL.   Oh, you should hate with prudence.

MRS. FAINALL.   Yes, for I have loved with indiscretion.

MIRABELL.   You should have just so much disgust for your husband as may be sufficient to make you relish your lover.

MRS. FAINALL.   You have been the cause that I have loved without bounds, and would you set limits to that aversion of which you have been the òccasion? Why did you make me marry this man?

MIRABELL.   Why do we daily commit disagreeable and dangerous actions? To save that idol, reputation. If the familiarities of our loves had produced that consequence of which you were apprehensive, where could you have fixed a father's name with credit but on a husband? I knew Fainall to be a man lavish of his morals, an interested and professing friend, a false and a designing lover, yet one whose wit and outward fair behavior have gained a reputation with the town enough to make that woman stand excused who has suffered herself to be won by his addresses. A better man ought not to have been sacrificed to the occasion, a worse had not answered to the purpose. When you are weary of him, you know your remedy.

MRS. FAINALL.   I ought to stand in some degree of credit with you, Mirabell.

MIRABELL.   In justice to you, I have made you privy to my whole design, and put it in your power to ruin or advance my fortune.

MRS. FAINALL.   Whom have you instructed to represent your pretended uncle?

MIRABELL.   Waitwell, my servant.

MRS. FAINALL.   He is an humble servant[32] to Foible, my mother's woman, and may win her to your interest.

MIRABELL.   Care is taken for that—she is won and worn by this time. They were married this morning.

MRS. FAINALL.   Who?

MIRABELL.   Waitwell and Foible. I would not tempt my servant to betray me by trusting him too far. If your mother, in hopes to ruin me should consent to marry my pretended uncle, he might, like Mosca[33] in *The Fox*, stand upon terms; so I made him sure beforehand.

MRS. FAINALL.   So if my poor mother is caught in a contract,[34] you will discover the imposture betimes, and release her by producing a certificate of her gallant's former marriage.

[32] Suitor.   [33] The parasite in Ben Jonson's *Volpone, or the Fox* (1605). See Act V, scene v.
[34] A marriage contract with the pretended uncle.

MIRABELL.   Yet, upon condition that she consent to my marriage with her niece, and surrender the moiety of her fortune in her possession.

MRS. FAINALL.   She talked last night of endeavoring at a match between Millamant and your uncle.

MIRABELL.   That was by Foible's direction and my instruction, that she might seem to carry it more privately.

MRS. FAINALL.   Well, I have an opinion of your success; for I believe my lady will do anything to get a husband; and when she has this which you have provided for her, I suppose she will submit to anything to get rid of him.

MIRABELL.   Yes, I think the good lady would marry anything that resembled a man, though 'twere no more than what a butler could pinch out of a napkin.

MRS. FAINALL.   Female frailty! We must all come to it if we live to be old and feel the craving of a false appetite when the true is decayed.

MIRABELL.   An old woman's appetite is depraved like that of a girl—'tis the green sickness of a second childhood, and, like the faint offer of a latter spring, serves but to usher in the fall, and withers in an affected bloom.

MRS. FAINALL.   Here's your mistress.

[*Enter* MRS. MILLAMANT, WITWOUD, *and* MINCING]

MIRABELL.   Here she comes, i'faith, full sail, with her fan spread and her streamers out, and a shoal of fools for tenders. Ha, no, I cry her mercy!

MRS. FAINALL.   I see but one poor empty sculler, and he tows her woman after him.

MIRABELL.   [*To* MRS. MILLAMANT] You seem to be unattended, madam. You used to have the *beau monde*[35] throng after you, and a flock of gay fine perukes hovering round you.

WITWOUD.   Like moths about a candle.—I had like to have lost my comparison for want of breath.

MRS. MILLAMANT.   Oh, I have denied myself airs to-day. I have walked as fast through the crowd—

WITWOUD.   As a favorite just disgraced, and with as few followers.

MRS. MILLAMANT.   Dear Mr. Witwoud, truce with your similitudes; for I'm as sick of 'em—

WITWOUD.   As a physician of a good air.—I cannot help it, madam, though 'tis against myself.

MRS. MILLAMANT.   Yet again! Mincing, stand between me and his wit.

WITWOUD.   Do, Mrs. Mincing, like a screen before a great fire.—I confess I do blaze to-day; I am too bright.

MRS. FAINALL.   But, dear Millamant, why were you so long?

MRS. MILLAMANT.   Long! Lord, have I not made violent haste? I have asked every living thing I met for you; I have inquired after you as after a new fashion.

WITWOUD.   Madam, truce with your similitudes.—No, you met her husband, and did not ask him for her.

MRS. MILLAMANT.   By your leave, Witwoud, that were like inquiring after an old fashion, to ask a husband for his wife.

WITWOUD.   Hum, a hit! a hit! a palpable hit! I confess it.

MRS. FAINALL.   You were dressed before I came abroad.

[35] The fashionable world.

MRS. MILLAMANT. Aye, that's true.—Oh, but then I had—Mincing, what had I? Why was I so long?

MINCING. O mem, your la'ship stayed to peruse a pecquet of letters.

MRS. MILLAMANT. Oh, aye, letters—I had letters—I am persecuted with letters—I hate letters.—Nobody knows how to write letters—and yet one has 'em, one does not know why. They serve one to pin up one's hair.

WITWOUD. Is that the way? Pray, madam, do you pin up your hair with all your letters? I find I must keep copies.

MRS. MILLAMANT. Only with those in verse, Mr. Witwoud; I never pin up my hair with prose. I think I tried once, Mincing.

MINCING. O mem, I shall never forget it.

MRS. MILLAMANT. Aye, poor Mincing tift and tift[36] all the morning.

MINCING. Till I had the cremp in my fingers, I'll vow, mem; and all to no purpose. But when your la'ship pins it up with poetry, it sits so pleasant the next day as anything, and is so pure and so crips.

WITWOUD. Indeed, so "crips"?

MINCING. You're such a critic, Mr. Witwoud.

MRS. MILLAMANT. Mirabell, did you take exceptions last night? Oh, aye, and went away. Now I think on't I'm angry—No, now I think on't I'm pleased—for I believe I gave you some pain.

MIRABELL. Does that please you?

MRS. MILLAMANT. Infinitely; I love to give pain.

MIRABELL. You would affect a cruelty which is not in your nature; your true vanity is in the power of pleasing.

MRS. MILLAMANT. Oh, I ask your pardon for that—one's cruelty is one's power; and when one parts with one's cruelty, one parts with one's power; and when one has parted with that, I fancy one's old and ugly.

MIRABELL. Aye, aye, suffer your cruelty to ruin the object of your power, to destroy your lover—and then how vain, how lost a thing you'll be! Nay, 'tis true: you are no longer handsome when you've lost your lover; your beauty dies upon the instant, for beauty is the lover's gift. 'Tis he bestows your charms—your glass is all a cheat. The ugly and the old, whom the looking-glass mortifies, yet after commendation can be flattered by it and discover beauties in it; for that reflects our praises, rather than your face.

MRS. MILLAMANT. Oh, the vanity of these men! Fainall, d'ye hear him? If they did not commend us, we were not handsome! Now you must know they could not commend one, if one was not handsome. Beauty the lover's gift!—Lord, what is a lover, that it can give? Why, one makes lovers as fast as one pleases, and they live as long as one pleases, and they die as soon as one pleases: and then, if one pleases, one makes more.

WITWOUD. Very pretty. Why, you make no more of making of lovers, madam, than of making so many card-matches.

MRS. MILLAMANT. One no more owes one's beauty to a lover, than one's wit to an echo. They can but reflect what we look and say—vain empty things if we are silent or unseen, and want a being.

MIRABELL. Yet to those two vain empty things you owe two of the greatest pleasures of your life.

---

[36] Crimped the hair.

MRS. MILLAMANT. How so?

MIRABELL. To your lover you owe the pleasure of hearing yourselves praised, and to an echo the pleasure of hearing yourselves talk.

WITWOUD. But I know a lady that loves talking so incessantly, she won't give an echo fair play; she has that everlasting rotation of tongue, that an echo must wait till she dies before it can catch her last words.

MRS. MILLAMANT. Oh, fiction!—Fainall, let us leave these men.

MIRABELL. [*Aside to* MRS. FAINALL] Draw off Witwoud.

MRS. FAINALL. Immediately.—[*Aloud*] I have a word or two for Mr. Witwoud.
[*Exeunt* WITWOUD *and* MRS. FAINALL]

MIRABELL. [*To* MRS. MILLAMANT] I would beg a little private audience too.— You had the tyranny to deny me last night, though you knew I came to impart a secret to you that concerned my love.

MRS. MILLAMANT. You saw I was engaged.

MIRABELL. Unkind! You had the leisure to entertain a herd of fools—things who visit you from their excessive idleness, bestowing on your easiness that time which is the encumbrance of their lives. How can you find delight in such society? It is impossible they should admire you; they are not capable —or if they were, it should be to you as a mortification, for sure to please a fool is some degree of folly.

MRS. MILLAMANT. I please myself. Besides, sometimes to converse with fools is for my health.

MIRABELL. Your health! Is there a worse disease than the conversation of fools?

MRS. MILLAMANT. Yes, the vapors; fools are physic for it, next to asafoetida.

MIRABELL. You are not in a course of fools?

MRS. MILLAMANT. Mirabell, if you persist in this offensive freedom, you'll displease me. I think I must resolve, after all, not to have you. We shan't agree.

MIRABELL. Not in our physic, it may be.

MRS. MILLAMANT. And yet our distemper, in all likelihood, will be the same; for we shall be sick of one another. I shan't endure to be reprimanded nor instructed; 'tis so dull to act always by advice, and so tedious to be told of one's faults—I can't bear it. Well, I won't have you, Mirabell,—I'm resolved—I think—you may go.—Ha, ha, ha! What would you give that you could help loving me?

MIRABELL. I would give something that you did not know I could not help it.

MRS. MILLAMANT. Come, don't look grave, then. Well, what do you say to me?

MIRABELL. I say that a man may as soon make a friend by his wit, or a fortune by his honesty, as win a woman with plain dealing and sincerity.

MRS. MILLAMANT. Sententious Mirabell! Prithee, don't look with that violent and inflexible wise face, like Solomon at the dividing of the child [37] in an old tapestry hanging.

MIRABELL. You are merry, madam, but I would persuade you for a moment to be serious.

MRS. MILLAMANT. What, with that face? No, if you keep your countenance, 'tis impossible I should hold mine. Well, after all, there is something very moving in a lovesick face. Ha, ha, ha!—Well, I won't laugh; don't be

[37] See I Kings iii.16-28.

peevish—Heigho! now I'll be melancholy—as melancholy as a watch-light.[38]
Well, Mirabell, if ever you will win me, woo me now.—Nay, if you are so
tedious, fare you well; I see they are walking away.

MIRABELL.   Can you not find in the variety of your disposition one moment—

MRS. MILLAMANT.   To hear you tell me Foible's married, and your plot like to
speed? No.

MIRABELL.   But how came you to know it?

MRS. MILLAMANT.   Without the help of the devil, you can't imagine—unless
she should tell me herself. Which of the two it may have been I will leave
you to consider; and when you have done thinking of that, think of me.

[*Exit* MRS. MILLAMANT]

MIRABELL.   I have something more—Gone!—Think of you? To think of a
whirlwind, though 'twere in a whirlwind, were a case of more steady contemplation—a very tranquillity of mind and mansion. A fellow that lives
in a windmill, has not a more whimsical dwelling than the heart of a man
that is lodged in a woman. There is no point of the compass to which they
cannot turn, and by which they are not turned; and by one as well as another. For motion, not method, is their occupation. To know this, and yet
continue to be in love, is to be made wise from the dictates of reason, and
yet persevere to play the fool by the force of instinct.—Oh, here come my
pair of turtles![39]—What, billing so sweetly! Is not Valentine's Day over with
you yet?

[*Enter* WAITWELL *and* FOIBLE]

Sirrah Waitwell; why, sure you think you were married for your own recre-
ation, and not for my conveniency.

WAITWELL.   Your pardon, sir. With submission, we have indeed been solacing in
lawful delights; but still with an eye to business, sir. I have instructed her
as well as I could. If she can take your directions as readily as my instruc-
tions, sir, your affairs are in a prosperous way.

MIRABELL.   Give you joy, Mrs. Foible.

FOIBLE.   Oh, 'las, sir, I'm so ashamed!—I'm afraid my lady has been in a thousand inquietudes for me. But I protest, sir, I made as much haste as I could.

WAITWELL.   That she did indeed sir. It was my fault that she did not make
more.

MIRABELL.   That I believe.

FOIBLE.   But I told my lady as you instructed me, sir, that I had a prospect of
seeing Sir Rowland, your uncle; and that I would put her ladyship's picture
in my pocket to show him, which I'll be sure to say has made him so enamored of her beauty, that he burns with impatience to lie at her ladyship's
feet and worship the original.

MIRABELL.   Excellent Foible! Matrimony has made you eloquent in love.

WAITWELL.   I think she has profited, sir; I think so.

FOIBLE.   You have seen Madam Millamant, sir?

MIRABELL.   Yes.

FOIBLE.   I told her, sir, because I did not know that you might find an opportunity; she had so much company last night.

---

[38] A candle in a sick person's room.   [39] Turtledoves.

MIRABELL.   Your diligence will merit more—in the meantime—
[*Gives her money*]

FOIBLE.   O dear sir, your humble servant!

WAITWELL.   Spouse.

MIRABELL.   Stand off, sir, not a penny!—Go on and prosper, Foible. The lease shall be made good and the farm stocked if we succeed.

FOIBLE.   I don't question your generosity, sir, and you need not doubt of success. If you have no more commands, sir, I'll be gone; I'm sure my lady is at her toilet, and can't dress till I come.—Oh, dear, [*Looking out*] I'm sure that was Mrs. Marwood that went by in a mask! If she has seen me with you, I'm sure she'll tell my lady. I'll make haste home and prevent her. Your servant, sir.—B'w'y,[40] Waitwell.

[*Exit* FOIBLE]

WAITWELL.   Sir Rowland, if you please.—The jade's so pert upon her preferment she forgets herself.

MIRABELL.   Come, sir, will you endeavor to forget yourself, and transform into Sir Rowland?

WAITWELL.   Why, sir, it will be impossible I should remember myself.—Married, knighted, and attended all in one day! 'tis enough to make any man forget himself. The difficulty will be how to recover my acquaintance and familiarity with my former self, and fall from my transformation to a reformation into Waitwell. Nay, I shan't be quite the same Waitwell neither; for now I remember me, I'm married and can't be my own man again.

　　Aye, there's the grief; that's the sad change of life,
　　To lose my title, and yet keep my wife.

[*Exeunt*]

Act III

SCENE I. *A room in* LADY WISHFORT's *house.* LADY WISHFORT
at her toilet, PEG *waiting.*

LADY WISHFORT.   Merciful! no news of Foible yet?

PEG.   No, madam.

LADY WISHFORT.   I have no more patience. If I have not fretted myself till I am pale again, there's no veracity in me! Fetch me the red—the red, do you hear, sweetheart? An arrant ash-color, as I'm a person! Look you how this wench stirs! Why dost thou not fetch me a little red? Didst thou not hear me, Mopus?[41]

PEG.   The red ratafia, does your ladyship mean, or the cherry-brandy?

LADY WISHFORT.   Ratafia, fool! No, fool. Not the ratafia, fool—grant me patience!—I mean the Spanish paper,[42] idiot—complexion, darling. Paint, paint, paint!—dost thou understand that, changeling, dangling thy hands

---

[40] Contraction of "God be with you."　　[41] Mope; dullard.　　[42] Rouge.

like bobbins before thee? Why dost thou not stir, puppet? Thou wooden thing upon wires!

PEG.   Lord, madam, your ladyship is so impatient!—I cannot come at the paint, madam; Mrs. Foible has locked it up and carried the key with her.

LADY WISHFORT.   A pox take you both! Fetch me the cherry-brandy then. [*Exit* PEG] I'm as pale and as faint, I look like Mrs. Qualmsick, the curate's wife, that's always breeding.—Wench! Come, come, wench, what art thou doing? Sipping? Tasting? Save thee, dost thou not know the bottle?

[*Enter* PEG *with a bottle and china cup*]

PEG.   Madam, I was looking for a cup.

LADY WISHFORT.   A cup, save thee! and what a cup hast thou brought! Dost thou take me for a fairy, to drink out of an acorn? Why didst thou not bring thy thimble? Hast thou ne'er a brass thimble clinking in thy pocket with a bit of nutmeg?—I warrant thee. Come, fill, fill!—So—again.—[*One knocks*]—See who that is. Set down the bottle first. Here, here, under the table. What, wouldst thou go with the bottle in thy hand, like a tapster? As I'm a person, this wench has lived in an inn upon the road before she came to me, like Maritornes[43] the Asturian in *Don Quixote!*—No Foible yet?

PEG.   No, madam, Mrs. Marwood.

LADY WISHFORT.   Oh, Marwood; let her come in.—Come in, good Marwood.

[*Enter* MRS. MARWOOD]

MRS. MARWOOD.   I'm surprised to find your ladyship in dishabille at this time of day.

LADY WISHFORT.   Foible's a lost thing—has been abroad since morning, and never heard of since.

MRS. MARWOOD.   I saw her but now as I came masked through the park, in conference with Mirabell.

LADY WISHFORT.   With Mirabell! You call my blood into my face, with mentioning that traitor. She durst not have the confidence! I sent her to negotiate an affair in which, if I'm detected, I'm undone. If that wheedling villain has wrought upon Foible to detect me, I'm ruined. Oh, my dear friend, I'm a wretch of wretches if I'm detected.

MRS. MARWOOD.   O madam, you cannot suspect Mrs. Foible's integrity.

LADY WISHFORT.   Oh, he carries poison in his tongue that would corrupt integrity itself! If she has given him an opportunity, she has as good as put her integrity into his hands. Ah, dear Marwood, what's integrity to an opportunity?—Hark! I hear her! [*To* PEG] Go, you thing, and send her in.

[*Exit* PEG]

[*To* MRS. MARWOOD] Dear friend, retire into my closet, that I may examine her with more freedom.—You'll pardon me, dear friend; I can make bold with you. There are books over the chimney—Quarles and Prynne, and *The Short View of the Stage,* with Bunyan's works, to entertain you.[44]

[*Exit* MRS. MARWOOD]

[*Enter* FOIBLE]

LADY WISHFORT.   O Foible, where hast thou been? What hast thou been doing?

FOIBLE.   Madam, I have seen the party.

---

[43] *Don Quixote,* Part I, chap. xvi.   [44] All highly moral books.

LADY WISHFORT. But what hast thou done?

FOIBLE. Nay, 'tis your ladyship has done, and are to do; I have only promised.
But a man so enamored—so transported!—Well, if worshipping of pictures
be a sin—poor Sir Rowland, I say.

LADY WISHFORT. The miniature has been counted like—but hast thou not betrayed me, Foible? Hast thou not detected me to that faithless Mirabell?—
What hadst thou to do with him in the Park? Answer me; has he got nothing out of thee?

FOIBLE. [*Aside*] So the devil has been beforehand with me. What shall I say?
—[*Aloud*]—Alas, madam, could I help it if I met that confident thing?
Was I in fault? If you had heard how he used me, and all upon your ladyship's account, I'm sure you would not suspect my fidelity. Nay, if that had
been the worst, I could have borne; but he had a fling at your ladyship too,
and then I could not hold; but i'faith I gave him his own.

LADY WISHFORT. Me? What did the filthy fellow say?

FOIBLE. Oh, madam! 'tis a shame to say what he said—with his taunts and his
fleers, tossing up his nose. Humh! (says he) what, you are a hatching some
plot (says he), you are so early abroad, or catering (says he), ferreting for
some disbanded officer, I warrant.—Half-pay is but thin subsistence (says
he)—well, what pension does your lady propose? Let me see (says he); what,
she must come down pretty deep now, she's superannuated (says he) and—

LADY WISHFORT. Odds[45] my life, I'll have him—I'll have him murdered! I'll
have him poisoned! Where does he eat?—I'll marry a drawer[46] to have him
poisoned in his wine. I'll send for Robin from Locket's[47] immediately.

FOIBLE. Poison him! poisoning's too good for him. Starve him, madam, starve
him: marry Sir Rowland, and get him disinherited. Oh, you would bless
yourself to hear what he said!

LADY WISHFORT. A villain! Superannuated!

FOIBLE. Humh (says he), I hear you are laying designs against me too (says
he), and Mrs. Millamant is to marry my uncle (he does not suspect a word
of your ladyship); but (says he) I'll fit you for that, I warrant you (says he),
I'll hamper you for that (says he)—you and your old frippery[48] too (says
he); I'll handle you—

LADY WISHFORT. Audacious villain! Handle me, would he durst!—Frippery?
old frippery! Was there ever such a foul-mouthed fellow? I'll be married
to-morrow; I'll be contracted to-night.

FOIBLE. The sooner the better, madam.

LADY WISHFORT. Will Sir Rowland be here, sayest thou? When, Foible?

FOIBLE. Incontinently, madam. No new sheriff's wife expects the return of her
husband after knighthood with that impatience in which Sir Rowland burns
for the dear hour of kissing your ladyship's hand after dinner.

LADY WISHFORT. Frippery! superannuated frippery! I'll frippery the villain;
I'll reduce him to frippery and rags! a tatterdemalion! I hope to see him
hung with tatters, like a Long Lane penthouse[49] or a gibbet thief. A slander-
mouthed railer! I warrant the spendthrift prodigal's in debt as much as the

---

[45] "God's." [46] Waiter. [47] A fashionable tavern. [48] Tawdry finery.
[49] A stall dealing in old rags.

million lottery,[50] or the whole Court upon a birthday. I'll spoil his credit with his tailor. Yes, he shall have my niece with her fortune, he shall.

FOIBLE. He! I hope to see him lodge in Ludgate[51] first, and angle into Black-friars for brass farthings with an old mitten.[52]

LADY WISHFORT. Aye, dear Foible; thank thee for that, dear Foible. He has put me out of all patience. I shall never recompose my features to receive Sir Rowland with any economy of face. This wretch has fretted me that I am absolutely decayed. Look, Foible.

FOIBLE. Your ladyship has frowned a little too rashly, indeed, madam. There are some cracks discernible in the white varnish.

LADY WISHFORT. Let me see the glass.—Cracks, sayest thou?—why, I am ar-rantly flayed—I look like an old peeled wall. Thou must repair me, Foible, before Sir Rowland comes, or I shall never keep up to my picture.

FOIBLE. I warrant you, madam, a little art once made your picture like you, and now a little of the same art must make you like your picture. Your picture must sit for you, madam.

LADY WISHFORT. But art thou sure Sir Rowland will not fail to come? Or will he not fail when he does come? Will he be importunate, Foible, and push? For if he should not be importunate, I shall never break decorums—I shall die with confusion if I am forced to advance.—Oh, no, I can never ad-vance!—I shall swoon if he should expect advances. No. I hope Sir Rowland is better bred than to put a lady to the necessity of breaking her forms. I won't be too coy, neither.—I won't give him despair—but a little disdain is not amiss, a little scorn is alluring.

FOIBLE. A little scorn becomes your ladyship.

LADY WISHFORT. Yes, but tenderness becomes me best—a sort of dyingness— you see that picture has a sort of a—ha, Foible? a swimmingness in the eyes —yes, I'll look so.—My niece affects it, but she wants features. Is Sir Row-land handsome? Let my toilet be removed—I'll dress above. I'll receive Sir Rowland here.—Is he handsome? Don't answer me. I won't know; I'll be surprised. I'll be taken by surprise.

FOIBLE. By storm, madam. Sir Rowland's a brisk man.

LADY WISHFORT. Is he? Oh, then he'll importune, if he's a brisk man. I shall save decorums if Sir Rowland importunes. I have a mortal terror at the apprehension of offending against decorums. Oh, I'm glad he's a brisk man! —Let my things be removed, good Foible.

[*Exit* LADY WISHFORT]

[*Enter* MRS. FAINALL]

MRS. FAINALL. Oh, Foible, I have been in a fright lest I should come too late! That devil Marwood [53] saw you in the Park with Mirabell, and I'm afraid will discover it to my lady.

FOIBLE. Discover what, madam?

MRS. FAINALL. Nay, nay, put not on that strange face! I am privy to the whole design and know that Waitwell, to whom thou wert this morning

---

[50] A government lottery. [51] A debtor's prison in Blackfriars.
[52] Let down a mitten on a cord to beg for alms.
[53] Mrs. Marwood, who is in the adjoining closet, overhears this conversation.

married, is to personate Mirabell's uncle, and as such, winning my lady, to involve her in those difficulties from which Mirabell only must release her, by his making his conditions to have my cousin and her fortune left to her own disposal.

FOIBLE.   Oh, dear madam, I beg your pardon. It was not my confidence in your ladyship that was deficient, but I thought the former good correspondence between your ladyship and Mr. Mirabell might have hindered his communicating this secret.

MRS. FAINALL.   Dear Foible, forget that.

FOIBLE.   O dear madam, Mr. Mirabell is such a sweet, winning gentleman—but your ladyship is the pattern of generosity. Sweet lady, to be so good! Mr. Mirabell cannot choose but be grateful. I find your ladyship has his heart still. Now, madam, I can safely tell your ladyship our success; Mrs. Marwood has told my lady, but I warrant I managed myself. I turned it all for the better. I told my lady that Mr. Mirabell railed at her; I laid horrid things to his charge, I'll vow; and my lady is so incensed that she'll be contracted to Sir Rowland tonight, she says. I warrant I worked her up, that he may have her for asking for, as they say of a Welsh maidenhead.

MRS. FAINALL.   O rare Foible!

FOIBLE.   Madam, I beg your ladyship to acquaint Mr. Mirabell of his success. I would be seen as little as possible to speak to him; besides, I believe Madam Marwood watches me.—She has a month's mind,[54] but I know Mr. Mirabell can't abide her.—[*Enter* FOOTMAN] John, remove my lady's toilet.— Madam, your servant; my lady is so impatient I fear she'll come for me if I stay.

MRS. FAINALL.   I'll go with you up the back stairs lest I should meet her.

[*Exeunt*]

[*Enter* MRS. MARWOOD]

MRS. MARWOOD.   Indeed, Mrs. Engine, is it thus with you? Are you become a go-between of this importance?—Yes, I shall watch you. Why, this wench is the *passe-partout*, a very master-key to everybody's strong-box. My friend Fainall, have you carried it so swimmingly? I thought there was something in it, but it seems it's over with you. Your loathing is not from a want of appetite, then, but from a surfeit. Else you could never be so cool to fall from a principal to be an assistant,—to procure for him! A pattern of generosity, that, I confess. Well, Mr. Fainall, you have met with your match.—O man, man! Woman, woman! The devil's an ass; if I were a painter, I would draw him like an idiot, a driveller with a bib and bells. Man should have his head and horns,[55] and woman the rest of him. Poor simple fiend!—"Madam Marwood has a month's mind, but he can't abide her."—'Twere better for him you had not been his confessor in that affair, without you could have kept his counsel closer. I shall not prove another pattern of generosity; he has not obliged me to that with those excesses of himself! And now I'll have none of him.—Here comes the good lady, panting ripe, with a heart full of hope, and a head full of care, like any chemist upon the day of projection.[56]

---

[54] An eager desire for Mirabell.   [55] The horns of the cuckold.
[56] Like an alchemist on the day of transmuting base metal into gold.

[*Enter* LADY WISHFORT]

LADY WISHFORT. Oh, dear Marwood, what shall I say for this rude forgetfulness?—but my dear friend is all goodness.

MRS. MARWOOD. No apologies, dear madam; I have been very well entertained.

LADY WISHFORT. As I'm a person, I am in a very chaos to think I should so forget myself: but I have such an olio[57] of affairs, really I know not what to do.—[*Calls*] Foible!—I expect my nephew, Sir Wilfull, every moment, too.—[*Calls again*] Why, Foible!—He means to travel for improvement.

MRS. MARWOOD. Methinks Sir Wilfull should rather think of marrying than travelling, at his years. I hear he is turned of forty.

LADY WISHFORT. Oh, he's in less danger of being spoiled by his travels. I am against my nephew's marrying too young. It will be time enough when he comes back and has acquired discretion to choose for himself.

MRS. MARWOOD. Methinks Mrs. Millamant and he would make a very fit match. He may travel afterwards. 'Tis a thing very usual with young gentlemen.

LADY WISHFORT. I promise you I have thought on't—and since 'tis your judgment, I'll think on't again. I assure you I will. I value your judgment extremely. On my word, I'll propose it.

[*Enter* FOIBLE]

LADY WISHFORT. Come, come, Foible—I had forgot my nephew will be here before dinner. I must make haste.

FOIBLE. Mr. Witwoud and Mr. Petulant are come to dine with your ladyship.

LADY WISHFORT. Oh, dear, I can't appear till I'm dressed! Dear Marwood, shall I be free with you again, and beg you to entertain 'em? I'll make all imaginable haste. Dear friend, excuse me.

[*Exeunt* LADY WISHFORT *and* FOIBLE]

[*Enter* MRS. MILLAMANT *and* MINCING]

MRS. MILLAMANT. Sure never anything was so unbred as that odious man!—Marwood, your servant.

MRS. MARWOOD. You have a color; what's the matter?

MRS. MILLAMANT. That horrid fellow, Petulant, has provoked me into a flame. I have broken my fan.—Mincing, lend me yours. Is not all the powder out of my hair?

MRS. MARWOOD. No. What has he done?

MRS. MILLAMANT. Nay, he has done nothing; he has only talked—nay, he has said nothing neither, but he has contradicted everything that has been said. For my part, I thought Witwoud and he would have quarrelled.

MINCING. I vow, mem, I thought once they would have fit.

MRS. MILLAMANT. Well, 'tis a lamentable thing, I swear, that one has not the liberty of choosing one's acquaintance as one does one's clothes.

MRS. MARWOOD. If we had that liberty, we should be as weary of one set of acquaintance, though never so good, as we are of one suit, though never so fine. A fool and a doily stuff [58] would now and then find days of grace, and be worn for variety.

MRS. MILLAMANT. I could consent to wear 'em if they would wear alike; but fools never wear out—they are such *drap-de-Berry*[59] things. Without one could give 'em to one's chambermaid after a day or two!

[57] Muddle.   [58] Unfashionable material.   [59] French woolens.

MRS. MARWOOD.   'Twere better so indeed. Or what think you of the playhouse? A fine, gay, glossy fool should be given there, like a new masking habit, after the masquerade is over and we have done with the disguise. For a fool's visit is always a disguise, and never admitted by a woman of wit but to blind her affair with a lover of sense. If you would but appear barefaced now, and own Mirabell, you might as easily put off Petulant and Witwoud as your hood and scarf. And indeed, 'tis time, for the town has found it; the secret is grown too big for the pretence. 'Tis like Mrs. Primly's great belly; she may lace it down before, but it burnishes on her hips. Indeed, Millamant, you can no more conceal it than my Lady Strammel can her face—that goodly face, which, in defiance of her Rhenish-wine tea,[60] will not be comprehended [61] in a mask.

MRS. MILLAMANT.   I'll take my death, Marwood, you are more censorious than a decayed beauty or a discarded toast.—Mincing, tell the men they may come up.—My aunt is not dressing here; their folly is less provoking than your malice.

[*Exit* MINCING]

—The town has found it! what has it found? That Mirabell loves me is no more a secret than it is a secret that you discovered it to my aunt, or than the reason why you discovered it is a secret.

MRS. MARWOOD.   You are nettled.

MRS. MILLAMANT.   You're mistaken. Ridiculous!

MRS. MARWOOD.   Indeed, my dear, you'll tear another fan if you don't mitigate those violent airs.

MRS. MILLAMANT.   Oh, silly! ha, ha, ha! I could laugh immoderately. Poor Mirabell! His constancy to me has quite destroyed his complaisance for all the world beside. I swear, I never enjoined it him to be so coy. If I had the vanity to think he would obey me, I would command him to show more gallantry—'tis hardly well-bred to be so particular on one hand, and so insensible on the other. But I despair to prevail, and so let him follow his own way. Ha, ha, ha! Pardon me, dear creature, I must laugh—ha, ha, ha!— though I grant you 'tis a little barbarous—ha, ha, ha!

MRS. MARWOOD.   What pity 'tis, so much fine raillery and delivered with so significant gesture, should be so unhappily directed to miscarry.

MRS. MILLAMANT.   Ha? Dear creature, I ask your pardon. I swear, I did not mind you.

MRS. MARWOOD.   Mr. Mirabell and you both may think it a thing impossible, when I shall tell him by telling you—

MRS. MILLAMANT.   Oh dear, what? for it is the same thing if I hear it—ha, ha, ha!

MRS. MARWOOD.   That I detest him, hate him, madam.

MRS. MILLAMANT.   O, madam! why, so do I—and yet the creature loves me— ha, ha, ha! How can one forbear laughing to think of it. I am a sibyl if I am not amazed to think what he can see in me. I'll take my death, I think you are handsomer—and within a year or two as young; if you could but stay for me, I should overtake you—but that cannot be. Well, that thought makes me melancholic. Now I'll be sad.

[60] For reducing.   [61] Contained.

MRS. MARWOOD. Your merry note may be changed sooner than you think.

MRS. MILLAMANT. D'ye say so? Then I'm resolved I'll have a song to keep up my spirits.

[*Enter* MINCING]

MINCING. The gentlemen stay but to comb,[62] madam, and will wait on you.

MRS. MILLAMANT. Desire Mrs. —— that is in the next room to sing the song I would have learned yesterday.—You shall hear it, madam—not that there's any great matter in it, but 'tis agreeable to my humor.

SONG

Set by Mr. John Eccles, and sung by Mrs. Hodgson

1

Love's but the frailty of the mind,
    When 'tis not with ambition joined;
A sickly flame, which, if not fed, expires,
And feeding, wastes in self-consuming fires.

2

'Tis not to wound a wanton boy
    Or amorous youth, that gives the joy;
But 'tis the glory to have pierced a swain,
For whom inferior beauties sighed in vain.

3

Then I alone the conquest prize,
    When I insult a rival's eyes:
If there's delight in love, 'tis when I see
That heart, which others bleed for, bleed for me.

[*Enter* PETULANT *and* WITWOUD]

MRS. MILLAMANT. Is your animosity composed, gentlemen?

WITWOUD. Raillery, raillery, madam; we have no animosity—we hit off a little wit now and then, but no animosity. The falling out of wits is like the falling out of lovers. We agree in the main, like treble and bass. Ha, Petulant?

PETULANT. Aye, in the main—but when I have a humor to contradict—

WITWOUD. Aye, when he has a humor to contradict, then I contradict, too. What! I know my cue. Then we contradict one another like two battledoers;[63] for contradictions beget one another like Jews.

PETULANT. If he says black's black—if I have a humor to say 'tis blue—let that pass—all's one for that. If I have a humor to prove it, it must be granted.

WITWOUD. Not positively must—but it may—it may.

PETULANT. Yes, it positively must, upon proof positive.

WITWOUD. Aye, upon proof positive it must; but upon proof presumptive it only may.—That's a logical distinction now, madam.

MRS. MARWOOD. I perceive your debates are of importance and very learnedly handled.

---

[62] Comb their wigs.   [63] Rackets like those used in badminton.

PETULANT.   Importance is one thing, and learning's another. But a debate's a debate; that I assert.

WITWOUD.   Petulant's an enemy to learning; he relies altogether on his parts.

PETULANT.   No, I'm no enemy to learning. It hurts not me.

MRS. MARWOOD.   That's a sign indeed 'tis no enemy to you.

PETULANT.   No, no, 'tis no enemy to anybody but them that have it.

MRS. MILLAMANT.   Well, an illiterate man's my aversion. I wonder at the impudence of any illiterate man to offer to make love.

WITWOUD.   That I confess I wonder at, too.

MRS. MILLAMANT.   Ah! to marry an ignorant that can hardly read or write!

PETULANT.   Why should a man be any further from being married, though he can't read, than he is from being hanged? The ordinary's[64] paid for setting the psalm, and the parish priest for reading the ceremony. And for the rest which is to follow in both cases, a man may do it without book—so all's one for that.

MRS. MILLAMANT.   D'ye hear the creature?—Lord, here's company, I'll be gone.

[*Exeunt* MRS. MILLAMANT *and* MINCING]

[*Enter* SIR WILFULL WITWOUD *in a country riding habit, and* SERVANT *to* Lady Wishfort]

WITWOUD.   In the name of Bartlemew and his fair,[65] what have we here?

MRS. MARWOOD.   'Tis your brother, I fancy. Don't you know him?

WITWOUD.   Not I. Yes, I think it is he—I've almost forgot him; I have not seen him since the Revolution.[66]

SERVANT.   [*To* SIR WILFULL] Sir, my lady's dressing. Here's company; if you please to walk in, in the meantime.

SIR WILFULL.   Dressing! What, 'tis but morning here I warrant, with you in London; we should count it towards afternoon in our parts, down in Shropshire. Why, then belike, my aunt han't dined yet,—ha, friend?

SERVANT.   Your aunt, sir?

SIR WILFULL.   My aunt, sir! Yes, my aunt, sir, and your lady, sir; your lady is my aunt, sir.—Why, what! Dost thou not know me, friend? Why, then send somebody hither that does. How long hast thou lived with thy lady, fellow, ha?

SERVANT.   A week, sir—longer than anybody in the house, except my lady's woman.

SIR WILFULL.   Why, then belike thou dost not know thy lady, if thou seest her, ha, friend?

SERVANT.   Why, truly, sir, I cannot safely swear to her face in a morning, before she is dressed. 'Tis like I may give a shrewd guess at her by this time.

SIR WILFULL.   Well, prithee try what thou canst do; if thou canst not guess, inquire her out, dost hear, fellow? And tell her, her nephew, Sir Wilfull Witwoud, is in the house.

SERVANT.   I shall, sir.

SIR WILFULL.   Hold ye; hear me, friend; a word with you in your ear. Prithee, who are these gallants?

---

[64] Prison chaplain.

[65] The annual Bartholomew Fair in Smithfield, a favorite attraction for country people.

[66] The revolution of 1688, when James II was dethroned.

SERVANT. Really, sir, I can't tell; here come so many here, 'tis hard to know 'em all.

[*Exit* SERVANT]

SIR WILFULL. Oons,[67] this fellow knows less than a starling; I don't think a' knows his own name.

MRS. MARWOOD. Mr. Witwoud, your brother is not behindhand in forgetfulness—I fancy he has forgot you too.

WITWOUD. I hope so—the devil take him that remembers first, I say.

SIR WILFULL. Save you, gentlemen and lady!

MRS. MARWOOD. For shame, Mr. Witwoud; why don't you speak to him? And you, sir.

WITWOUD. Petulant, speak.

PETULANT. And you, sir.

SIR WILFULL. No offense, I hope. [*Salutes*[68] MRS. MARWOOD]

MRS. MARWOOD. No, sure, sir.

WITWOUD. [*Aside*] This is a vile dog, I see that already. No offence! ha, ha, ha!—To him; to him, Petulant, smoke him.[69]

PETULANT. [*Surveying him round*] It seems as if you had come a journey, sir; —hem, hem.

SIR WILFULL. Very likely, sir, that it may seem so.

PETULANT. No offence, I hope, sir.

WITWOUD. [*Aside*] Smoke the boots, the boots, Petulant, the boots! Ha, ha, ha!

SIR WILFULL. May be not, sir; thereafter, as 'tis meant, sir.

PETULANT. Sir, I presume upon the information of your boots.

SIR WILFULL. Why, 'tis like you may, sir; if you are not satisfied with the information of my boots, sir, if you will step to the stable, you may inquire further of my horse, sir.

PETULANT. Your horse, sir? your horse is an ass, sir!

SIR WILFULL. Do you speak by way of offence, sir?

MRS. MARWOOD. The gentleman's merry, that's all, sir.—[*Aside*] 'Slife, we shall have a quarrel betwixt an horse and an ass before they find one another out.—[*Aloud*] You must not take anything amiss from your friends, sir. You are among your friends here, though it may be you don't know it. If I am not mistaken, you are Sir Wilfull Witwoud.

SIR WILFULL. Right, lady; I am Sir Wilful Witwoud—so I write myself. No offence to anybody, I hope—and nephew to the Lady Wishfort of this mansion.

MRS. MARWOOD. Don't you know this gentleman, sir?

SIR WILFULL. Hum! What, sure 'tis not—yea, by'r Lady, but 'tis—'sheart, I know not whether 'tis or no—yea, but 'tis, by the Wrekin[70] Brother Anthony. What, Tony, i'faith!—what, dost thou not know me? By'r Lady, nor I thee, thou art so be-cravated, and so be-periwigged!—'Sheart, why dost not speak? art thou overjoyed?

WITWOUD. Odso, brother, is it you? Your servant, brother.

SIR WILFULL. Your servant!—why yours, sir. Your servant again—'sheart, and your friend and servant to that—and a [*puff*]—and a—flap-dragon[71] for your service, sir! and a hare's foot and a hare's scut[72] for your service, sir! and you be so cold and so courtly.

WITWOUD.   No offence, I hope, brother.

SIR WILFULL.   'Sheart, sir, but there is, and much offence!—A pox, is this your Inns o' Court[73] breeding, not to know your friends and your relations, your elders, and your betters?

WITWOUD.   Why, brother Wilfull of Salop,[74] you may be as short as a Shrewsbury-cake, if you please. But I tell you 'tis not modish to know relations in town. You think you're in the country, where great lubberly brothers slabber and kiss one another when they meet, like a call of sergeants[75]—'tis not the fashion here; 'tis not indeed, dear brother.

SIR WILFULL.   The fashion's a fool; and you're a fop, dear brother. 'Sheart, I've suspected this—by'r Lady, I conjectured you were a fop since you began to change the style of your letters, and write in a scrap of paper gilt round the edges, no bigger than a *subpoena*. I might expect this when you left off "Honored Brother," and "hoping you are in good health," and so forth— to begin with a "Rat me,[76] knight, I'm so sick of a last night's debauch— 'ods heart," and then tell a familiar tale of a cock and a bull, and a whore and a bottle, and so conclude.—You could write news before you were out of your time,[77] when you lived with honest Pumple Nose, the attorney of Furnival's Inn—you could entreat to be remembered then to your friends round the Wrekin. We could have gazettes, then, and Dawks's Letter, and the Weekly Bill,[78] till of late days.

PETULANT.   'Slife, Witwoud, were you ever an atorney's clerk? of the family of the Furnivals? Ha, ha, ha!

WITWOUD.   Aye, aye, but that was but for a while—not long, not long. Pshaw! I was not in my own power then; an orphan, and this fellow was my guardian. Aye, aye, I was glad to consent to that man to come to London. He had the disposal of me then. If I had not agreed to that, I might have been bound 'prentice to a felt-maker in Shrewsbury; this fellow would have bound me to a maker of felts.

SIR WILFULL.   'Sheart, and better than to be bound to a maker of fops—where, I suppose, you have served your time, and now you may set up for yourself.

MRS. MARWOOD.   You intend to travel, sir, as I'm informed.

SIR WILFULL.   Belike I may, madam. I may chance to sail upon the salt seas, if my mind hold.

PETULANT.   And the wind serve.

SIR WILFULL.   Serve or not serve, I shan't ask licence of you, sir; nor the weathercock your companion. I direct my discourse to the lady, sir.—'Tis like my aunt may have told you, madam—yes, I have settled my concerns, I may say now, and am minded to see foreign parts—if an' how that the peace holds, whereby, that is, taxes abate.

MRS. MARWOOD.   I thought you had designed for France at all adventures.

[72] Tail.   [73] Law societies in London.   [74] Shropshire.
[75] When sergeants-at-law are called to the bar to become barristers.
[76] Corruption of "God rot me."   [77] Of apprenticeship.
[78] A news sheet and the weekly death lists from London.

SIR WILFULL.   I can't tell that; 'tis like I may, and 'tis like I may not. I am somewhat dainty in making a resolution because when I make it I keep it. I don't stand shill I, shall I, then; if I say't, I'll do't. But I have thoughts to tarry a small matter in town to learn somewhat of your lingo first, before I cross the seas. I'd gladly have a spice of your French, as they say, whereby to hold discourse in foreign countries.

MRS. MARWOOD.   Here's an academy in town for that use.

SIR WILFULL.   There is? 'Tis like there may.

MRS. MARWOOD.   No doubt you will return very much improved.

WITWOUD.   Yes, refined, like a Dutch skipper from a whale-fishing.

[*Enter* LADY WISHFORT *and* FAINALL]

LADY WISHFORT.   Nephew, you are welcome.

SIR WILFULL.   Aunt, your servant.

FAINALL.   Sir Wilfull, your most faithful servant.

SIR WILFULL.   Cousin Fainall, give me your hand.

LADY WISHFORT.   Cousin Witwoud, your servant; Mr. Petulant, your servant. —Nephew, you are welcome again. Will you drink anything after your journey, nephew, before you eat? Dinner's almost ready.

SIR WILFULL.   I'm very well, I thank you, aunt—however, I thank you for your courteous offer. 'Sheart, I was afraid you would have been in the fashion, too, and have remembered to have forgot your relations. Here's your cousin Tony; belike, I mayn't call him brother for fear of offence.

LADY WISHFORT.   Oh, he's a rallier, nephew—my cousin's a wit. And your great wits always rally their best friends to choose.[79] When you have been abroad, nephew, you'll understand raillery better.

[FAINALL *and* MRS. MARWOOD *talk apart*]

SIR WILFULL.   When then, let him hold his tongue in the meantime, and rail when that day comes.

[*Enter* MINCING]

MINCING.   Mem, I am come to acquaint your la'ship that dinner is impatient.

SIR WILFULL.   Impatient! why, then, belike it won't stay till I pull off my boots.—Sweetheart, can you help me to a pair of slippers?—My man's with his horses, I warrant.

LADY WISHFORT.   Fie, fie, nephew! you would not pull off your boots here! Go down into the hall—dinner shall stay for you.

[*Exit* SIR WILFULL]

My nephew's a little unbred; you'll pardon him, madam.—Gentlemen, will you walk? Marwood?

MRS. MARWOOD.   I'll follow you, madam—before Sir Wilfull is ready.

[*Manent* MRS. MARWOOD *and* FAINALL]

FAINALL.   Why then, Foible's a bawd, an arrant, rank, match-making bawd. And I, it seems, am a husband, a rank husband; and my wife a very errant, rank wife—all in the way of the world. 'Sdeath, to be an anticipated cuckold, a cuckold in embryo! Sure, I was born with budding antlers, like a young satyr or a citizen's child. 'Sdeath! to be outwitted, to be out-jilted—out-matrimony'd!—If I had kept my speed like a stag, 'twere somewhat—but

---

[79] Probably means: as a matter of choice.

to crawl after with my horns like a snail, and be outstripped by my wife—
'tis scurvy wedlock.

MRS. MARWOOD.   Then shake it off. You have often wished for an opportunity
to part, and now you have it. But first prevent their plot—the half of Millamant's fortune is too considerable to be parted with to a foe, to Mirabell.

FAINALL.   Damn him! that had been mine, had you not made that fond discovery.[80]—That had been forfeited, had they been married. My wife had
added lustre to my horns by that increase of fortune; I could have worn
'em tipped with gold, though my forehead had been furnished like a deputy-
lieutenant's hall.[81]

MRS. MARWOOD.   They may prove a cap of maintenance[82] to you still, if you
can away[83] with your wife. And she's no worse than when you had her—I
dare swear she had given up her game before she was married.

FAINALL.   Hum! that may be. She might throw up her cards, but I'll be hanged
if she did not put pam[84] in her pocket.

MRS. MARWOOD.   You married her to keep you; and if you can contrive to have
her keep you better than you expected, why should you not keep her longer
than you intended?

FAINALL.   The means, the means?

MRS. MARWOOD.   Discover to my lady your wife's conduct; threaten to part
with her! My lady loves her, and will come to any composition to save her
reputation. Take the opportunity of breaking it just upon the discovery of
this imposture. My lady will be enraged beyond bounds, and sacrifice niece,
and fortune, and all, at that conjuncture. And let me alone to keep her
warm; if she should flag in her part, I will not fail to prompt her.

FAINALL.   Faith, this has an appearance.

MRS. MARWOOD.   I'm sorry I hinted to my lady to endeavor a match between
Millamant and Sir Wilfull; that may be an obstacle.

FAINALL.   Oh, for that matter, leave me to manage him. I'll disable him for
that; he will drink like a Dane. After dinner I'll set his hand in.

MRS. MARWOOD.   Well, how do you stand affected towards your lady?

FAINALL.   Why, faith, I'm thinking of it.—Let me see—I am married already,
so that's over. My wife has played the jade with me—well, that's over, too.
I never loved her, or if I had, why, that would have been over, too, by this
time. Jealous[85] of her I cannot be, for I am certain; so there's an end of
jealousy. Weary of her I am, and shall be—no, there's no end of that—no,
no, that were too much to hope. Thus far concerning my repose; now for
my reputation. As to my own, I married not for it, so that's out of the
question; and as to my part in my wife's—why, she had parted with hers
before; so bringing none to me, she can take none from me. 'Tis against all
rule of play that I should lose to one who has not wherewithal to stake.

MRS. MARWOOD.   Besides, you forgot marriage is honorable.

FAINALL.   Hum, faith, and that's well thought on. Marriage is honorable, as

[80] Foolish disclosure; i.e., that Mirabell and Millamant were plotting to get married.
[81] I.e., with many sets of antlers.
[82] A term from heraldry: the horns may still prove profitable.   [83] Endure.
[84] The highest trump in loo, a popular card game.   [85] Suspicious.

you say; and if so, wherefore should cuckoldom be a discredit, being derived from so honorable a root?

MRS. MARWOOD. Nay, I know not; if the root be honorable, why not the branches?

FAINALL. So, so; why, this point's clear.—Well, how do we proceed?

MRS. MARWOOD. I will contrive a letter which shall be delivered to my lady at the time when that rascal who is to act Sir Rowland is with her. It shall come as from an unknown hand—for the less I appear to know of the truth, the better I can play the incendiary. Besides, I would not have Foible provoked if I could help it—because you know she knows some passages—nay, I expect all will come out. But let the mine be sprung first, and then I care not if I am discovered.

FAINALL. If the worst come to the worst, I'll turn my wife to grass. I have already a deed of settlement of the best part of her estate, which I wheedled out of her, and that you shall partake at least.

MRS. MARWOOD. I hope you are convinced that I hate Mirabell. Now you'll be no more jealous?

FAINALL. Jealous! No, by this kiss. Let husbands be jealous, but let the lover still believe; or, if he doubt, let it be only to endear his pleasure, and prepare the joy that follows when he proves his mistress true. But let husbands' doubts convert to endless jealousy; or, if they have belief, let it corrupt to superstition and blind credulity. I am single, and will herd no more with 'em. True, I wear the badge, but I'll disown the order. And since I take my leave of 'em, I care not if I leave 'em a common motto to their common crest:

All husbands must or pain or shame endure;
The wise too jealous are, fools too secure.

[*Exeunt*]

Act IV

SCENE I. [*Scene continues*].

[*Enter* LADY WISHFORT *and* FOIBLE]

LADY WISHFORT. Is Sir Rowland coming, sayest thou Foible? And are things in order?

FOIBLE. Yes, madam, I have put wax lights in the sconces, and placed the footmen in a row in the hall, in their best liveries, with the coachman and postilion to fill up the equipage.

LADY WISHFORT. Have you pulvilled [86] the coachman and postilion, that they may not stink of the stable when Sir Rowland comes by?

FOIBLE. Yes, madam.

LADY WISHFORT. And are the dancers and the music ready, that he may be entertained in all points with correspondence to his passion?

FOIBLE. All is ready, madam.

LADY WISHFORT. And—well—how do I look, Foible?

FOIBLE. Most killing well, madam.

LADY WISHFORT. Well, and how shall I receive him? in what figure shall I give his heart the first impression? There is a great deal in the first impression. Shall I sit?—no, I won't sit—I'll walk—aye, I'll walk from the door upon his entrance, and then turn full upon him—no, that will be too sudden. I'll lie,—aye, I'll lie down—I'll receive him in my little dressing-room; there's a couch—yes, yes, I'll give the first impression on a couch. I won't lie neither, but loll and lean upon one elbow with one foot a little dangling off, jogging in a thoughtful way—yes—and then as soon as he appears, start, aye, start and be surprised, and rise to meet him in a pretty disorder—yes. Oh, nothing is more alluring than a levee from a couch, in some confusion; it shows the foot to advantage, and furnishes with blushes and recomposing airs beyond comparison. Hark! there's a coach.

FOIBLE. 'Tis he, madam.

LADY WISHFORT. Oh, dear, has my nephew made his addresses to Millamant? I ordered him.

FOIBLE. Sir Wilfull is set to in drinking, madam, in the parlor.

LADY WISHFORT. Odds my life, I'll send him to her. Call her down, Foible; bring her hither. I'll send him as I go. When they are together, then come to me, Foible, that I may not be too long alone with Sir Rowland.

[*Exit* LADY WISHFORT]

[*Enter* MRS. MILLAMANT *and* MRS. FAINALL]

FOIBLE. Madam, I stayed here to tell your ladyship that Mr. Mirabell has waited this half-hour for an opportunity to talk with you—though my lady's orders were to leave you and Sir Wilfull together. Shall I tell Mr. Mirabell that you are at leisure?

MRS. MILLAMANT. No. What would the dear man have? I am thoughtful, and would amuse myself. Bid him come another time. [*Repeating, and walking about*]

> There never yet was woman made
> Nor shall, but to be cursed.[87]

That's hard!

MRS. FAINALL. You are very fond of Sir John Suckling to-day, Millamant, and the poets.

MRS. MILLAMANT. He? Aye, and filthy verses—so I am.

FOIBLE. Sir Wilfull is coming, madam. Shall I send Mr. Mirabell away?

MRS. MILLAMANT. Aye, if you please, Foible, send him away, or send him

---

[86] Sprinkled with a scented powder.   [87] From a poem of Sir John Suckling.

hither—just as you will, dear Foible. I think I'll see him—shall I? Aye, let the wretch come.

> [*Exit* FOIBLE]
> [*Repeating*]

> Thyrsis, a youth of the inspired train.[88]

Dear Fainall, entertain Sir Wilfull—thou hast philosophy to undergo a fool. Thou art married and hast patience. I would confer with my own thoughts.

MRS. FAINALL.   I am obliged to you that you would make me your proxy in this affair, but I have business of my own.

[*Enter* SIR WILFULL]

O Sir Wilfull, you are come at the critical instant. There's your mistress up to the ears in love and contemplation; pursue your point now or never.

SIR WILFULL.   Yes; my aunt will have it so. I would gladly have been encouraged with a bottle or two, because I'm somewhat wary at first before I am acquainted. [*This while* MILLAMANT *walks about repeating to herself*]—But I hope, after a time, I shall break my mind—that is, upon further acquaintance. So for the present, cousin, I'll take my leave. If so be you'll be so kind to make my excuse, I'll return to my company—

MRS. FAINALL.   Oh, fie, Sir Wilfull! What! You must not be daunted.

SIR WILFULL.   Daunted! No, that's not it; it is not so much for that—for if it so be that I set on't, I'll do't. But only for the present, 'tis sufficient till further acquaintance, that's all—your servant.

MRS. FAINALL.   Nay, I'll swear you shall never lose so favorable an opportunity if I can help it. I'll leave you together, and lock the door.

> [*Exit*]

SIR WILFULL.   Nay, nay, cousin—I have forgot my gloves!—What d'ye do?— 'Sheart, a' has locked the door indeed, I think. Nay, Cousin Fainall, open the door! Pshaw, what a vixen trick is this?—Nay, now a' has seen me too.— Cousin, I made bold to pass through as it were—I think this door's enchanted!

MRS. MILLAMANT.   [*Repeating*]

> I prithee spare me, gentle boy,
> Press me no more for that slight toy.[89]

SIR WILFULL.   Anan?[90] Cousin, your servant.

MRS. MILLAMANT.

> —That foolish trifle of a heart.—

Sir Wilfull!

SIR WILFULL.   Yes—your servant. No offence, I hope, cousin.

MRS. MILLAMANT.   [*Repeating*]

> I swear it will not do its part,
> Though thou dost thine, employ'st thy power and art.

---

[88] From a poem of Edmund Waller.   [89] From Suckling.   [90] What's that?

Natural, easy Suckling!

SIR WILFULL.   Anan? Suckling? No such suckling neither, cousin, nor stripling; I thank heaven, I'm no minor.

MRS. MILLAMANT.   Ah, rustic, ruder than Gothic!

SIR WILFULL.   Well, well, I shall understand your lingo one of these days, cousin; in the meanwhile I must answer in plain English.

MRS. MILLAMANT.   Have you any business with me, Sir Wilfull?

SIR WILFULL.   Not at present, cousin.—Yes, I made bold to see, to come and know if that how you were disposed to fetch a walk this evening; if so be that I might not be troublesome, I would have sought a walk with you.

MRS. MILLAMANT.   A walk! what then?

SIR WILFULL.   Nay, nothing—only for the walk's sake, that's all.

MRS. MILLAMANT.   I nauseate walking; 'tis a country diversion. I loathe the country and everything that relates to it.

SIR WILFULL.   Indeed! ha! Look ye, look ye—you do? Nay, 'tis like you may— here are choice of pastimes here in town, as plays and the like; that must be confessed, indeed.

MRS. MILLAMANT.   *Ah, l'étourdie!* [91] I hate the town too.

SIR WILFULL.   Dear heart, that's much—ha! that you should hate 'em both! Ha! 'tis like you may; there are some can't relish the town, and others can't away with the country—'tis like you may be one of those, cousin.

MRS. MILLAMANT.   Ha, ha, ha! yes, 'tis like I may. You have nothing further to say to me?

SIR WILFULL.   Not at present, cousin. 'Tis like when I have an opportunity to be more private, I may break my mind in some measure—I conjecture you partly guess—however, that's as time shall try—but spare to speak and spare to speed, as they say.

MRS. MILLAMANT.   If it is of no great importance, Sir Wilfull, you will oblige me to leave me; I have just now a little business—

SIR WILFULL.   Enough, enough, cousin; yes, yes, all a case.—When you're disposed, when you're disposed. Now's as well as another time, and another time as well as now. All's one for that—Yes, yes, if your concerns call you, there's no haste; it will keep cold, as they say. Cousin, your servant.—I think this door's locked.

MRS. MILLAMANT.   You may go this way, sir.

SIR WILFULL.   Your servant; then with your leave I'll return to my company.

MRS. MILLAMANT.   Aye, aye; ha, ha, ha!

Like Phœbus sung the no less amorous boy.[92]

[*Exit*]

[*Enter* MIRABELL]

MIRABELL.   "Like Daphne she, as lovely and as coy." Do you lock yourself up from me to make my search more curious, or is this pretty artifice contrived to signify that here the chase must end, and my pursuit be crowned? For you can fly no further.

[91] The dolt!   [92] From Waller. Mirabell caps the quotation in the following line.

MRS. MILLAMANT. Vanity! No—I'll fly and be followed to the last moment. Though I am upon the very verge of matrimony, I expect you should solicit me as much as if I were wavering at the grate of a monastery, with one foot over the threshold. I'll be solicited to the very last—nay, and afterwards.

MIRABELL. What, after the last?

MRS. MILLAMANT. Oh, I should think I was poor and had nothing to bestow, if I were reduced to an inglorious ease and freed from the agreeable fatigues of solicitation.

MIRABELL. But do not know that when favors are conferred upon instant[93] and tedious solicitation, that they diminish in their value, and that both the giver loses the grace, and the receiver lessens his pleasure?

MRS. MILLAMANT. It may be in things of common application; but never, sure, in love. Oh, I hate a lover that can dare to think he draws a moment's air, independent of the bounty of his mistress. There is not so impudent a thing in nature as the saucy look of an assured man, confident of success. The pedantic arrogance of a very husband has not so pragmatical[94] an air. Ah! I'll never marry unless I am first made sure of my will and pleasure.

MIRABELL. Would you have 'em both before marriage? or will you be contented with the first now, and stay for the other till after grace?

MRS. MILLAMANT. Ah! don't be impertinent.—My dear liberty, shall I leave thee? my faithful solitude, my darling contemplation, must I bid you then adieu? Ay-h adieu—my morning thoughts, agreeable wakings, indolent slumbers, all ye *douceurs*, ye *sommeils du matin*,[95] *adieu*.—I can't do't, 'tis more than impossible.—Positively, Mirabell, I'll lie abed in a morning as long as I please.

MIRABELL. Then I'll get up in a morning as early as I please.

MRS. MILLAMANT. Ah? Idle creature, get up when you will—and d'ye hear, I won't be called names after I'm married; positively, I won't be called names.

MIRABELL. Names!

MRS. MILLAMANT. Aye, as wife, spouse, my dear, joy, jewel, love, sweetheart, and the rest of that nauseous cant, in which men and their wives are so fulsomely familiar—I shall never bear that. Good Mirabell, don't let us be familiar or fond, nor kiss before folks, like my Lady Fadler and Sir Francis; nor go to Hyde Park together the first Sunday in a new chariot, to provoke eyes and whispers, and then never be seen there together again, as if we were proud of one another the first week, and ashamed of one another ever after. Let us never visit together, nor go to a play together; but let us be very strange and well-bred. Let us be as strange as if we had been married a great while, and as well-bred as if we were not married at all.

MIRABELL. Have you any more conditions to offer? Hitherto your demands are pretty reasonable.

MRS. MILLAMANT. Trifles—as liberty to pay and receive visits to and from whom I please; to write and receive letters, without interrogatories or wry faces on your part; to wear what I please, and choose conversation with regard only to my own taste; to have no obligation upon me to converse with wits that I don't like, because they are your acquaintance; or to be intimate with

---

[93] Urgent.   [94] Officious.   [95] Sweetnesses, morning naps.

fools, because they may be your relations. Come to dinner when I please; dine in my dressing-room when I'm out of humor, without giving a reason. To have my closet[96] inviolate; to be sole empress of my tea-table, which you must never presume to approach without first asking leave. And lastly, wherever I am, you shall always knock at the door before you come in. These articles subscribed, if I continue to endure you a little longer, I may by degrees dwindle into a wife.

MIRABELL. Your bill of fare is something advanced in this latter account. Well, have I liberty to offer conditions—that when you are dwindled into a wife, I may not be beyond measure enlarged into a husband?

MRS. MILLAMANT. You have free leave. Propose your utmost; speak and spare not.

MIRABELL. I thank you.—*Imprimis*[97] then, I covenant that your acquaintance be general; that you admit no sworn confidante or intimate of your own sex —no she-friend to screen her affairs under your countenance, and tempt you to make trial of a mutual secrecy. No decoy-duck to wheedle you a fop-scrambling to the play in a mask,[98] then bring you home in a pretended fright, when you think you shall be found out, and rail at me for missing the play and disappointing the frolic which you had, to pick me up and prove my constancy.

MRS. MILLAMANT. Detestable *imprimis!* I go to the play in a mask!

MIRABELL. *Item*, I article that you continue to like your own face as long as I shall; and while it passes current with me, that you endeavor not to new-coin it. To which end, together with all vizards for the day, I prohibit all masks for the night, made of oiled-skins and I know not what—hog's bones, hare's gall, pig-water, and the marrow of a roasted cat. In short, I forbid all commerce with the gentlewoman in what-d'ye-call-it. Court. *Item,* I shut my doors against all bawds with baskets, and pennyworths of muslin, china, fans, atlases,[99] etc.—*Item,* when you shall be breeding—

MRS. MILLAMANT. Ah! name it not.

MIRABELL. Which may be presumed, with a blessing on our endeavors—

MRS. MILLAMANT. Odious endeavors!

MIRABELL. I denounce against all strait lacing, squeezing for a shape, till you mould my boy's head like a sugar-loaf, and instead of a man-child, make me father to a crooked billet. Lastly, to the dominion of the tea-table I submit —but with proviso, that you exceed not in your province, but restrain yourself to native and simple tea-table drinks, as tea, chocolate, and coffee; as likewise to genuine and authorized tea-table talk—such as mending of fashions, spoiling reputations, railing at absent friends, and so forth—but that on no account you encroach upon the men's prerogative, and presume to drink healths, or toast fellows; for prevention of which I banish all foreign forces, all auxiliaries to the tea-table, as orange-brandy, all aniseed, cinnamon, citron, and Barbadoes waters, together with ratafia, and the most noble spirit of clary,[100] but for cowslip wine, poppy water, and all dormitives, those I allow. These provisos admitted, in other things I may prove a tractable and complying husband.

[96] Boudoir.　　[97] In the first place.　　[98] Wheedle you to the theatre to scramble for a fop.
[99] Satins.　　[100] All notably intoxicating drinks.

MRS. MILLAMENT. O horrid provisos! filthy strong-waters! I toast fellows! odious men! I hate your odious provisos.

MIRABELL. Then we're agreed. Shall I kiss your hand upon the contract? And here comes one to be a witness to the sealing of the deed.

[*Enter* MRS. FAINALL]

MRS. MILLAMANT. Fainall, what shall I do? Shall I have him? I think I must have him.

MRS. FAINALL. Aye, aye, take him, take him; what should you do?

MRS. MILLAMANT. Well then—I'll take my death, I'm in a horrid fright.—Fainall, I shall never say it—well—I think—I'll endure you.

MRS. FINALL. Fie! fie! Have him, have him, and tell him so in plain terms; for I am sure you have a mind to him.

MRS. MILLAMANT. Are you? I think I have—and the horrid man looks as if he thought so too. Well, you ridiculous thing you, I'll have you—I won't be kissed, nor I won't be thanked—here, kiss my hand though.—So, hold your tongue now; don't say a word.

MRS. FAINALL. Mirabell, there's a necessity for your obedience; you have neither time to talk nor stay. My mother is coming, and in my conscience if she should see you, would fall into fits, and maybe not recover time enough to return to Sir Rowland, who, as Foible tells me, is in a fair way to succeed. Therefore spare your ecstasies for another occasion, and slip down the back-stairs, where Foible waits to consult you.

MRS. MILLAMANT. Aye, go, go. In the meantime I suppose you have said something to please me.

MIRABELL. I am all obedience.

[*Exit* MIRABELL]

MRS. FAINALL. Yonder, Sir Wilfull's drunk, and so noisy that my mother has been forced to leave Sir Rowland to appease him; but he answers her only with singing and drinking. What they may have done by this time I know not, but Petulant and he were upon quarrelling as I came by.

MRS. MILLAMANT. Well, if Mirabell should not make a good husband, I am a lost thing, for I find I love him violently.

MRS. FAINALL. So it seems, for you mind not what's said to you.—If you doubt him, you had best take up with Sir Wilfull.

MRS. MILLAMANT. How can you name that superannuated lubber? Foh!

[*Enter* WITWOUD *from drinking*]

MRS. FAINALL. So! Is the fray made up, that you have left 'em?

WITWOUD. Left 'em? I could stay no longer. I have laughed like ten christ'nings—I am tipsy with laughing. If I had stayed any longer I should have burst—I must have been let out and pieced in the sides like an unfixed camlet.[101]—Yes, yes, the fray is composed; my lady came in like a *nolle prosequi*,[102] and stopped their proceedings.

MRS. MILLAMANT. What was the dispute?

WITWOUD. That's the jest; there was no dispute. They could neither of 'em speak for rage, and so fell a sputtering at one another like two roasting apples.

[*Enter* PETULANT, *drunk*]

---

[101] Unstiffened material.   [102] Legal term: unwilling to prosecute.

Now, Petulant, all's over, all's well. Gad, my head begins to whim it about— Why dost thou not speak? Thou art both as drunk and mute as a fish.

PETULANT.   Look you, Mrs. Millamant—if you can love me, dear nymph, say it—and that's the conclusion. Pass on, or pass off—that's all.

WITWOUD.   Thou hast uttered volumes, folios, in less than *decimo sexto*,[103] *my dear Lacedemonian.*[104] Sirrah Petulant, thou art an epitomizer of words.

PETULANT.   Witwoud—you are an annihilator of sense.

WITWOUD.   Thou art a retailer of phrases, and dost deal in remnants of remnants, like a maker of pincushions—thou art in truth (metaphorically speaking) a speaker of shorthand.

PETULANT.   Thou art (without a figure) just one-half of an ass, and Baldwin[105] yonder, thy half-brother, is the rest.—A Gemini[106] of asses split would make just four of you.

WITWOUD.   Thou dost bite, my dear mustard seed; kiss me for that.

PETULANT.   Stand off!—I'll kiss no more males—I have kissed your twin yonder in a humor of reconciliation, till he [*hiccup*] rises upon my stomach like a radish.

MRS. MILLAMANT.   Eh! filthy creature! What was the quarrel?

PETULANT.   There was no quarrel—there might have been a quarrel.

WITWOUD.   If there had been words enow between 'em to have expressed provocation, they had gone together by the ears like a pair of castanets.

PETULANT.   You were the quarrel.

MRS. MILLAMANT.   Me!

PETULANT.   If I have a humor to quarrel, I can make less matters conclude premises.—If you are not handsome, what then, if I have a humor to prove it? If I shall have my reward, say so; if not, fight for your face the next time yourself. I'll go sleep.

WITWOUD.   Do; wrap thyself up like a wood-louse, and dream revenge—and hear me; if thou canst learn to write by tomorrow morning, pen me a challenge.—I'll carry it for thee.

PETULANT.   Carry your mistress's monkey a spider!—Go, flea dogs, and read romances!—I'll go to bed to my maid.

[*Exit* PETULANT]

MRS. FAINALL.   He's horridly drunk. How came you all in this pickle?

WITWOUD.   A plot, a plot, to get rid of the knight—your husband's advice, but he sneaked off.

[*Enter* LADY WISHFORT, *and* SIR WILFULL, *drunk*]

LADY WISHFORT.   Out upon't, out upon't! At years of discretion, and comport yourself at this rantipole[107] rate!

SIR WILFULL.   No offence, aunt.

LADY WISHFORT.   Offence! as I'm a person, I'm ashamed of you. Foh! how you stink of wine! D'ye think my niece will ever endure such a borachio! you're an absolute borachio.[108]

SIR WILFULL.   Borachio?

---

[103] Sixteenmo: a tiny book.   [104] Spartan. Like inhabitants of Maine, Spartans were noted for being spare of speech.   [105] The ass in *Reynard the Fox.*   [106] Twins.   [107] Boisterous.
[108] Spanish for drunkard.

LADY WISHFORT. At a time when you should commence an amour and put your best foot foremost—

SIR WILFULL. 'Sheart, an you grutch[109] me your liquor, make a bill—give me more drink, and take my purse—

[*Sings*]

> Prithee fill me the glass,
>   Till it laugh in my face,
> With ale that is potent and mellow;
>   He that whines for a lass,
>   Is an ignorant ass,
> For a bumper has not its fellow.

But if you would have me marry my cousin—say the word, and I'll do't. Wilfull will do't; that's the word. Wilfull will do't; that's my crest. My motto I have forgot.

LADY WISHFORT. [*To* MRS. MILLAMANT] My nephew's a little overtaken, cousin, but 'tis with drinking your health. O' my word, you are obliged to him.

SIR WILFULL. *In vino veritas,*[110] aunt.—If I drunk your health to-day, cousin, I am a borachio. But if you have a mind to be married, say the word, and send for the piper; Wilfull will do't. If not, dust it away, and let's have t'other round.—Tony?—Odds heart, where's Tony?—Tony's an honest fellow; but he spits after a bumper, and that's a fault.

[*Sings*]

> We'll drink, and we'll never ha' done, boys,
>   Put the glass then around with the sun, boys,
> Let Apollo's example invite us;
>   For he's drunk every night,
>   And that makes him so bright,
> That he's able next morning to light us.

The sun's a good pimple,[111] an honest soaker; he has a cellar at your Antipodes. If I travel, aunt, I touch at your Antipodes.—Your Antipodes are a good, rascally sort of topsy-turvy fellow: if I had a bumper, I'd stand upon my head and drink a health to 'em.—A match or no match, cousin with the hard name—Aunt, Wilfull will do't. If she has her maidenhead, let her look to't; if she has not, let her keep her own counsel in the meantime, and cry out at the nine months' end.

MRS. MILLAMANT. Your pardon, madam, I can stay no longer—Sir Wilfull grows very powerful. Eh! how he smells! I shall be overcome, if I stay. Come, cousin.

[*Exeunt* MRS. MILLAMANT *and* MRS. FAINALL]

LADY WISHFORT. Smells! He would poison a tallow-chandler and his family! Beastly creature, I know not what to do with him! Travel, quotha! Aye,

---

[109] Grudge.   [110] In wine there is truth.   [111] A good fellow.

travel, travel—get thee gone; get thee gone; get thee but far enough, to the
Saracens, or the Tartars, or the Turks—for thou art not fit to live in a
Christian commonwealth, thou beastly pagan!

SIR WILFULL.   Turks? No; no Turks, aunt. Your Turks are infidels, and believe
not in the grape. Your Mahometan, your Mussulman, is a dry stinkard—no
offence, aunt. My map says that your Turk is not so honest a man as your
Christian. I cannot find by the map that your Mufti[112] is orthodox—whereby
it is a plain case that orthodox is a hard word, aunt, and [*hiccup*]—Greek
for claret.—

[*Sings*]

To drink is a Christian diversion,
Unknown to the Turk or the Persian:
    Let Mahometan fools
    Live by heathenish rules,
And be damned over tea-cups and coffee.
    But let British lads sing,
    Crown a health to the king,
And a fig for your sultan and sophy! [113]

Ah, Tony!

[*Enter* FOIBLE, *and whispers to* LADY WISHFORT]

LADY WISHFORT.   [*Aside to* FOIBLE] Sir Rowland impatient? Good lack! what
shall I do with this beastly tumbril?—[*Aloud*] Go lie down and sleep, you
sot!—or, as I'm a person, I'll have you bastinadoed with broomsticks.—Call
up the wenches.

[*Exit* FOIBLE]

SIR WILFULL.   Ahey! wenches; where are the wenches?

LADY WISHFORT.   Dear Cousin Witwoud, get him away, and you will bind me to
you inviolably. I have an affair of moment that invades me with some
precipitation. You will oblige me to all futurity.

WITWOUD.   Come, knight.—Pox on him, I don't know what to say to him.—
Will you go to a cock-match?

SIR WILFULL.   With a wench, Tony? Is she a shakebag, sirrah? Let me bite your
cheek for that.

WITWOUD.   Horrible! he has a breath like a bagpipe—Aye, aye; come, will you
march, my Salopian? [114]

SIR WILFULL.   Lead on, little Tony—I'll follow thee, my Anthony, my Tantony.
Sirrah, thou shalt be my Tantony, and I'll be thy pig.[115]

[*Sings*]

And a fig for your sultan and sophy.

[*Exit singing with* WITWOUD]

LADY WISHFORT.   This will never do. It will never make a match—at least before
he has been abroad.

---

[112] A Mohammedan priest.   [113] A Mohammedan ruler.   [114] Native of Shropshire.
[115] A pig is commonly found in the legends and iconography of St. Anthony.

[*Enter* WAITWELL, *disguised as* SIR ROWLAND]

LADY WISHFORT.   Dear Sir Rowland, I am confounded with confusion at the retrospection of my own rudeness! I have more pardons to ask than the pope distributes in the year of jubilee. But I hope, where there is likely to be so near an alliance, we may unbend the severity of decorum and dispense with a little ceremony.

WAITWELL.   My impatience, madam, is the effect of my transport; and till I have the possession of your adorable person, I am tantalized on the rack; and do but hang, madam, on the tenter of expectation.

LADY WISHFORT.   You have excess of gallantry, Sir Rowland, and press things to a conclusion with a most prevailing vehemence.—But a day or two for decency of marriage—

WAITWELL.   For decency of funeral, madam! The delay will break my heart—or, if that should fail, I shall be poisoned. My nephew will get an inkling of my designs, and poison me; and I would willingly starve him before I die—I would gladly go out of the world with that satisfaction.—That would be some comfort to me, if I could but live so long as to be revenged on that unnatural viper!

LADY WISHFORT.   Is he so unnatural, say you? Truly, I would contribute much, both to the saving of your life and the accomplishment of your revenge— not that I respect myself, though he has been a perfidious wretch to me.

WAITWELL.   Perfidious to you!

LADY WISHFORT.   O Sir Rowland, the hours that he has died away at my feet, the tears that he has shed, the oaths that he has sworn, the palpitations that he has left, the trances and the tremblings, the ardors and the ecstasies, the kneelings and the risings, the heart-heavings and the handgrippings, the pangs and the pathetic regards of his protesting eyes! Oh, no memory can register!

WAITWELL.   What, my rival! Is the rebel my rival?—a' dies!

LADY WISHFORT.   No, don't kill him at once, Sir Rowland; starve him gradually, inch by inch.

WAITWELL.   I'll do't. In three weeks he shall be barefoot; in a month out at knees with begging an alms. He shall starve upward and upward, till he has nothing living but his head, and then go out in a stink like a candle's end upon a save-all.[116]

LADY WISHFORT.   Well, Sir Rowland, you have the way—you are no novice in the labyrinth of love; you have the clue.[117] But as I am a person, Sir Rowland, you must not attribute my yielding to any sinister appetite, or indigestion of widowhood; nor impute my complacency to any lethargy of continence. I hope you do not think me prone to any iteration of nuptials—

WAITWELL.   Far be it from me—

LADY WISHFORT.   If you do, I protest I must recede—or think that I have made a prostitution of decorums; but in the vehemence of compassion, and to save the life of a person of so much importance—

WAITWELL.   I esteem it so—

LADY WISHFORT.   Or else you wrong my condescension.

[116] A device for holding candle ends so that they will burn.
[117] Like Theseus, who followed Ariadne's clue out of the labyrinth.

WAITWELL. I do not, I do not—

LADY WISHFORT. Indeed you do.

WAITWELL. I do not, fair shrine of virtue!

LADY WISHFORT. If you think the least scruple of carnality was an ingredient,—

WAITWELL. Dear madam, no. You are all camphire and frankincense, all chastity and odor.

LADY WISHFORT. Or that—

[*Enter* FOIBLE]

FOIBLE. Madam, the dancers are ready; and there's one with a letter, who must deliver it into your own hands.

LADY WISHFORT. Sir Rowland, will you give me leave? Think favorably, judge candidly, and conclude you have found a person who would suffer racks in honor's cause, dear Sir Rowland, and will wait on you incessantly.

[*Exit* LADY WISHFORT]

WAITWELL. Fie, fie!—What a slavery have I undergone! Spouse, hast thou any cordial? I want spirits.

FOIBLE. What a washy rogue art thou, to pant thus for a quarter of an hour's lying and swearing to a fine lady!

WAITWELL. Oh, she is the antidote to desire! Spouse, thou wilt fare the worse for't—I shall have no appetite to iteration of nuptials this eight-and-forty hours. By this hand I'd rather be a chairman in the dog-days than act Sir Rowland till this time to-morrow!

[*Enter* LADY WISHFORT, *with a letter*]

LADY WISHFORT. Call in the dancers.—Sir Rowland, we'll sit, if you please, and see the entertainment. [*A dance*] Now, with your permission, Sir Rowland, I will peruse my letter. I would open it in your presence, because I would not make you uneasy. If it should make you uneasy. I would burn it. Speak, if it does—but you may see the superscription is like a woman's hand.

FOIBLE. [*Aside to* WAITWELL] By heaven! Mrs. Marwood's, I know it. My heart aches—get it from her.

WAITWELL. A woman's hand? No, madam, that's no woman's hand; I see that already. That's somebody whose throat must be cut.

LADY WISHFORT. Nay, Sir Rowland, since you give me a proof of your passion by your jealousy, I promise you I'll make a return by a frank communication. You shall see it—we'll open it together—look you here.—[*Reads*]—"Madam, though unknown to you"—Look you there, 'tis from nobody that I know— "I have that honor for your character, that I think myself obliged to let you know you are abused. He who pretends to be Sir Rowland, is a cheat and a rascal."—Oh, heavens! what's this?

FOIBLE. [*Aside*] Unfortunate, all's ruined!

WAITWELL. How, how! Let me see, let me see!—[*Reads*] "A rascal, and disguised and suborned for that imposture,"—O villainy! O villainy!—"by the contrivance of—"

LADY WISHFORT. I shall faint! I shall die!—Oh!

FOIBLE. [*Aside to* WAITWELL] Say 'tis your nephew's hand—quickly, his plot, —swear, swear it!

WAITWELL. Here's a villain! Madam, don't you perceive it? Don't you see it?

LADY WISHFORT. Too well, too well! I have seen too much.

WAITWELL. I told you at first I knew the hand.—A woman's hand! The rascal writes a sort of a large hand—your Roman hand.—I saw there was a throat to be cut presently. If he were my son, as he is my nephew, I'd pistol him!

FOIBLE. O treachery!—But are you sure, Sir Rowland, it is his writing?

WAITWELL. Sure? Am I here? Do I live? Do I love this pearl of India? I have twenty letters in my pocket from him in the same character.

LADY WISHFORT. How!

FOIBLE. Oh, what luck it is, Sir Rowland, that you were present at this juncture! This was the business that brought Mr. Mirabell disguised to Madam Millamant this afternoon. I thought something was contriving when he stole by me and would have hid his face.

LADY WISHFORT. How, how!—I heard the villain was in the house, indeed; and now I remember, my niece went away abruptly when Sir Wilfull was to have made his addresses.

FOIBLE. Then, then, madam, Mr. Mirabell waited for her in her chamber; but I would not tell your ladyship to discompose you when you were to receive Sir Rowland.

WAITWELL. Enough; his date is short.

FOIBLE. No, good Sir Rowland, don't incur the law.

WAITWELL. Law! I care not for law. I can but die and 'tis in a good cause. My lady shall be satisfied of my truth and innocence, though it cost me my life.

LADY WISHFORT. No, dear Sir Rowland, don't fight. If you should be killed, I must never show my face; or hanged—oh, consider my reputation, Sir Rowland!—No, you shan't fight.—I'll go in and examine my niece; I'll make her confess. I conjure you, Sir Rowland, by all your love, not to fight.

WAITWELL. I am charmed, madam; I obey. But some proof you must let me give you; I'll go for a black box which contains the writings of my whole estate, and deliver that into your hands.

LADY WISHFORT. Aye, dear Sir Rowland, that will be some comfort. Bring the black box.

WAITWELL. And may I presume to bring a contract to be signed this night? May I hope so far?

LADY WISHFORT. Bring what you will, but come alive, pray, come alive! Oh, this is a happy discovery!

WAITWELL. Dead or alive I'll come—and married we will be in spite of treachery; aye, and get an heir that shall defeat the last remaining glimpse of hope in my abandoned nephew. Come, my buxom widow:

> Ere long you shall substantial proofs receive,
> That I'm an errant knight—

FOIBLE.   [*Aside*] Or arrant knave.

                                                    [*Exeunt*]

Act V

SCENE I. [*Scene continues*].

[*Enter* LADY WISHFORT *and* FOIBLE]

LADY WISHFORT.   Out of my house! Out of my house, thou viper, thou serpent, that I have fostered! thou bosom traitress, that I raised from nothing!— Begone, begone, begone, go! go!—That I took from washing of old gauze and weaving of dead hair,[118] with a bleak blue nose over a chafing-dish of starved embers, and dining behind a traverse rag, in a shop no bigger than a bird-cage!—Go, go! Starve again! Do, do!

FOIBLE.   Dear madam, I'll beg pardon on my knees.

LADY WISHFORT.   Away! out, out!—Go, set up for yourself again!—Do, drive a trade, do, with your three-pennyworth of small ware, flaunting upon a packthread under a brandy-seller's bulk,[119] or against a dead wall by a ballad-monger! Go, hang out an old Frisoneer gorget,[120] with a yard of yellow colbertine[121] again, do! An old gnawed mask, two rows of pins, and a child's fiddle; a glass necklace with the beads broken, and a quilted night-cap with one ear! Go, go, drive a trade!—These were your commodities, you treacherous trull! this was the merchandise you dealt in when I took you into my house, placed you next myself, and made you governante of my whole family! You have forgot this, have you, now you have feathered your nest?

FOIBLE.   No, no, dear madam. Do but hear me; have but a moment's patience. I'll confess all. Mr. Mirabell seduced me. I am not the first he has wheedled with his dissembling tongue; your ladyship's own wisdom has been deluded by him—then how should I, a poor ignorant, defend myself? O madam, if you knew but what he promised me, and how he assured me your ladyship should come to no damage!—Or else the wealth of the Indies should not have bribed me to conspire against so good, so sweet, so kind a lady as you have been to me.

LADY WISHFORT.   No damage! What, to betray me, and marry me to a cast serving-man! to make me a receptacle, an hospital for a decayed pimp! No damage! O thou frontless[122] impudence, more than a big-bellied actress!

FOIBLE.   Pray, do but hear me, madam! He could not marry your ladyship, madam.—No, indeed; his marriage was to have been void in law, for he was married to me first, to secure your ladyship. He could not have bedded your ladyship; for if he had consummated with your ladyship, he must have run the risk of the law, and been put upon his clergy.[123]—Yes, indeed, I inquired of the law in that case before I would meddle or make.

LADY WISHFORT.   What, then I have been your property, have I? I have been convenient to you, it seems!—while you were catering for Mirabell, I have been broker for you! What, have you made a passive bawd of me?—This exceeds all precedent! I am brought to fine uses, to become a botcher of second-hand marriages between Abigails and Andrews.[124] I'll couple you!

---

[118] I.e., making wigs.   [119] Stall.   [120] A woolen kerchief worn over the bosom.
[121] Cheap lace.   [122] Shameless.   [123] Forced to plead benefit of clergy; i.e., prove that he could read.   [124] Generic names for servants.

Yes, I'll baste you together, you and your Philander.[125] I'll Duke's-place[126] you, as I'm a person! Your turtle is in custody already: you shall coo in the same cage if there be a constable or warrant in the parish.

[*Exit* LADY WISHFORT]

FOIBLE. Oh, that ever I was born! Oh, that I was ever married!—A bride!— aye, I shall be a Bridewell-bride[127]—Oh!

[*Enter* MRS. FAINALL]

MRS. FAINALL. Poor Foible, what's the matter?

FOIBLE. O madam, my lady's gone for a constable! I shall be had to a justice and put to Bridewell to beat hemp. Poor Waitwell's gone to prison already.

MRS. FAINALL. Have a good heart, Foible; Mirabell's gone to give security for him. This is all Marwood's and my husband's doing.

FOIBLE. Yes, yes; I know it, madam. She was in my lady's closet, and overheard all that you said to me before dinner. She sent the letter to my lady, and that missing effect, Mr. Fainall laid this plot to arrest Waitwell when he pretended to go for the papers, and in the meantime Mrs. Marwood declared all to my lady.

MRS. FAINALL. Was there no mention made of me in the letter? My mother does not suspect my being in the confederacy? I fancy Marwood has not told her, though she has told my husband.

FOIBLE. Yes, madam, but my lady did not see that part; we stifled the letter before she read so far. Has that mischievous devil told Mr. Fainall of your ladyship, then?

MRS. FAINALL. Aye, all's out, my affair with Mirabell—everything discovered. This is the last day of our living together, that's my comfort.·

FOIBLE. Indeed, madam; and so 'tis a comfort if you knew all—he has been even with your ladyship, which I could have told you long enough since, but I love to keep peace and quietness by my goodwill. I had rather bring friends together than set 'em at distance. But Mrs. Marwood and he are nearer related than ever their parents thought for.

MRS. FAINALL. Sayest thou so, Foible? Canst thou prove this?

FOIBLE. I can take my oath of it, madam; so can Mrs. Mincing. We have had many a fair word from Madam Marwood, to conceal something that passed in our chamber one evening when you were at Hyde Park, and we were thought to have gone a-walking, but we went up unawares—though we were sworn to secrecy, too; Madam Marwood took a book and swore us upon it, but it was but a book of poems. So long as it was not a Bible oath, we may break it with a safe conscience.

MRS. FAINALL. This discovery is the most opportune thing I could wish.— Now, Mincing!

[*Enter* MINCING]

MINCING. My lady would speak with Mrs. Foible, mem. Mr. Mirabell is with her; he has set your spouse at liberty, Mrs. Foible, and would have you hide yourself in my lady's closet till my old lady's anger is abated. Oh, my old lady is in a perilous passion at something Mr. Fainall has said; he swears, and

---

[125] Lover.   [126] Site of St. James's Church (as in Act I).
[127] A prison-bride.

my old lady cries. There's a fearful hurricane, I vow. He says, mem, how that he'll have my lady's fortune made over to him, or he'll be divorced.

MRS. FAINALL. Does your lady or Mirabell know that?

MINCING. Yes, mem; they have sent me to see if Sir Wilfull be sober, and to bring him to them. My lady is resolved to have him, I think, rather than lose such a vast sum as six thousand pound.—Oh, come, Mrs. Foible, I hear my old lady.

MRS. FAINALL. Foible, you must tell Mincing that she must prepare to vouch when I call her.

FOIBLE. Yes, yes, madam.

MINCING. Oh, yes! mem, I'll vouch anything for your ladyship's service, be what it will.

[*Exeunt* MINCING *and* FOIBLE]

[*Enter* LADY WISHFORT *and* MRS. MARWOOD]

LADY WISHFORT. Oh, my dear friend, how can I enumerate the benefits that I have received from your goodness! To you I owe the timely discovery of the false vows of Mirabell; to you I owe the detection of the imposter Sir Rowland. And now you are become an intercessor with my son-in-law, to save the honor of my house and compound for the frailties of my daughter. Well, friend, you are enough to reconcile me to the bad world, or else I would retire to deserts and solitudes, and feed harmless sheep by groves and purling streams. Dear Marwood, let us leave the world, and retire by ourselves and be shepherdesses.

MRS. MARWOOD. Let us first dispatch the affair in hand, madam. We shall have leisure to think of retirement afterwards. Here is one who is concerned in the treaty.

LADY WISHFORT. Oh, daughter, daughter! is it possible thou shouldst be my child, bone of my bone, and flesh of my flesh, and, as I may say, another me, and yet transgress the most minute particle of severe virtue? Is it possible you should lean aside to iniquity, who have been cast in the direct mould of virtue? I have not only been a mould but a pattern for you and a model for you, after you were brought into the world.

MRS. FAINALL. I don't understand your ladyship.

LADY WISHFORT. Not understand? Why, have you not been naught?[128] have you not been sophisticated? Not understand! here I am ruined to compound for your caprices and your cuckoldoms. I must pawn my plate and my jewels, and ruin my niece, and all little enough—

MRS. FAINALL. I am wronged and abused, and so are you. 'Tis a false accusation—as false as hell, as false as your friend there, aye, or your friend's friend, my false husband!

MRS. MARWOOD. My friend, Mrs. Fainall! Your husband my friend? What do you mean?

MRS. FAINALL. I know what I mean, madam, and so do you; and so shall the world at a time convenient.

MRS. MARWOOD. I am sorry to see you so passionate, madam. More temper would look more like innocence. But I have done. I am sorry my zeal to

----

[128] Naughty.

serve your ladyship and family should admit of misconstruction, or make me liable to affronts. You will pardon me, madam, if I meddle no more with an affair in which I am not personally concerned.

LADY WISHFORT. O dear friend, I am so ashamed that you should meet with such returns!—[*To* MRS. FAINALL] You ought to ask pardon on your knees, ungrateful creature; she deserves more from you than all your life can accomplish.—[*To* MRS. MARWOOD] Oh, don't leave me destitute in this perplexity! No, stick to me, my good genius.

MRS. FAINALL. I tell you, madam, you're abused.—Stick to you! aye, like a leech, to suck your best blood—she'll drop off when she's full. Madam, you shan't pawn a bodkin, nor part with a brass counter, in composition for me. I defy 'em all. Let 'em prove their aspersions; I know my own innocence, and dare stand a trial.

[*Exit* MRS. FAINALL]

LADY WISHFORT. Why, if she should be innocent, if she should be wronged after all, ha? I don't know what to think—and I promise you her education has been unexceptionable—I may say it; for I chiefly made it my own care to initiate her very infancy in the rudiments of virtue, and to impress upon her tender years a young odium and aversion to the very sight of men. Aye, friend, she would ha' shrieked if she had but seen a man, till she was in her teens. As I am a person, 'tis true—she was never suffered to play with a male child, though but in coats; nay, her very babies[129] were of the feminine gender. Oh, she never looked a man in the face but her own father, or the chaplain, and him we made a shift to put upon her for a woman, by the help of his long garments and his sleek face, till she was going in her fifteen.

MRS. MARWOOD. 'Twas much she should be deceived so long.

LADY WISHFORT. I warrant you, or she would never have borne to have been catechized by him; and have heard his long lectures against singing and dancing, and such debaucheries; and going to filthy plays, and profane music-meetings, where the lewd trebles squeak nothing but bawdy, and the basses roar blasphemy. Oh, she would have swooned at the sight or name of an obscene play-book!—and can I think, after all this, that my daughter can be naught? What, a whore? and thought it excommunication to set her foot within the door of a playhouse! O dear friend, I can't believe it. No, no! As she says, let him prove it—let him prove it.

MRS. MARWOOD. Prove it, madam? What, and have your name prostituted in a public court—yours and your daughter's reputation worried at the bar by a pack of bawling lawyers? To be ushered in with an "O yez" [130] of scandal, and have your case opened by an old fumbling lecher in a quoif [131] like a man-midwife; to bring your daughter's infamy to light; to be a theme for legal punsters and quibblers by the statute; and become a jest against a rule of court, where there is no precedent for a jest in any record—not even in Domesday Book; to discompose the gravity of the bench, and provoke naughty interrogatories in more naughty law Latin; while the good judge, tickled with the proceeding, simpers under a grey beard, and figes[132] off and

---

[129] Dolls.   [130] The traditional call of "Hear ye," demanding silence in court.
[131] Lawyer's white cap.   [132] Fidgets.

on his cushion as if he had swallowed cantharides,[133] or sat upon cow-itch.

LADY WISHFORT.   Oh, 'tis very hard!

MRS. MARWOOD.   And then to have my young revellers of the Temple[134] take notes, like 'prentices at a conventicle, and after, talk it all over again in commons, or before drawers in an eating-house.

LADY WISHFORT.   Worse and worse!

MRS. MARWOOD.   Nay, this is nothing; if it would end here, 'twere well. But it must after this be consigned by the shorthand writers to the public press; and from thence be transferred to the hands, nay, into the throats and lungs of hawkers, with voices more licentious than the loud flounder-man's, or the woman that cries grey peas. And this you must hear till you are stunned— nay, you must hear nothing else for some days.

LADY WISHFORT.   Oh, 'tis insupportable! No, no, dear friend, make it up, make it up; aye, aye, I'll compound. I'll give up all, myself and my all, my niece and her all—anything, everything for composition.

MRS. MARWOOD.   Nay, madam, I advise nothing; I only lay before you, as a friend, the inconveniences which perhaps you have overseen. Here comes Mr. Fainall. If he will be satisfied to huddle up all in silence, I shall be glad. You must think I would rather congratulate than condole with you.

LADY WISHFORT.   Aye, aye, I do not doubt it, dear Marwood; no, no, I do not doubt it.

[*Enter* FAINALL]

FAINALL.   Well, madam, I have suffered myself to be overcome by the importunity of this lady, your friend; and am content you shall enjoy your own proper estate during life, on condition you oblige yourself never to marry, under such penalty as I think convenient.

LADY WISHFORT.   Never to marry!

FAINALL.   No more Sir Rowlands; the next imposture may not be so timely detected.

MRS. MARWOOD.   That condition, I dare answer, my lady will consent to without difficulty; she has already but too much experienced the perfidiousness of men.—Besides, madam, when we retire to our pastoral solitude we shall bid adieu to all other thoughts.

LADY WISHFORT.   Aye, that's true; but in case of necessity, as of health, or some such emergency—

FAINALL.   Oh, if you are prescribed marriage, you shall be considered; I only will reserve to myself the power to choose for you. If your physic be wholesome, it matters not who is your apothecary. Next, my wife shall settle on me the remainder of her fortune not made over already, and for her maintenance depend entirely on my discretion.

LADY WISHFORT.   This is most inhumanly savage, exceeding the barbarity of a Muscovite husband.

FAINALL.   I learned it from his Czarish majesty's[135] retinue, in a winter evening's conference over brandy and pepper, amongst other secrets of matrimony and policy as they are at present practised in the northern hemisphere. But this must be agreed unto, and that positively. Lastly, I will be endowed, in right of my wife, with that six thousand pounds which is the moiety of Mrs.

---

[133] An aphrodisiac.   [134] Law students.   [135] Peter the Great visited England in 1698.

Millamant's fortune in your possession, and which she has forfeited (as will appear by the last will and testament of your deceased husband, Sir Jonathan Wishfort) by her disobedience in contracting herself against your consent or knowledge and by refusing the offered match with Sir Wilfull Witwoud, which you, like a careful aunt, had provided for her.

LADY WISHFORT.   My nephew was *non compos*,[136] and could not make his addresses.

FAINALL.   I come to make demands—I'll hear no objections.

LADY WISHFORT.   You will grant me time to consider?

FAINALL.   Yes, while the instrument is drawing, to which you must get your hand till more sufficient deeds can be perfected, which I will take care shall be done with all possible speed. In the meanwhile I will go for the said instrument, and till my return you may balance this matter in your own discretion.

[*Exit* FAINALL]

LADY WISHFORT.   This insolence is beyond all precedent, all parallel. Must I be subject to this merciless villain?

MRS. MARWOOD.   'Tis severe indeed, madam, that you should smart for your daughter's wantonness.

LADY WISHFORT.   'Twas against my consent that she married this barbarian, but she would have him, though her year[137] was not out.—Ah! her first husband, my son Languish, would not have carried it thus! Well, that was my choice, this is hers: she is matched now with a witness.—I shall be mad!—Dear friend, is there no comfort for me? must I live to be confiscated at this rebelrate? [138]—Here come two more of my Egyptian plagues too.

[*Enter* MRS. MILLAMANT *and* SIR WILFULL WITWOUD]

SIR WILFULL.   Aunt, your servant.

LADY WISHFORT.   Out, caterpillar! Call not me aunt! I know thee not!

SIR WILFULL.   I confess I have been a little in disguise,[139] as they say.—'Sheart! and I'm sorry for't. What would you have? I hope I committed no offence, aunt—and if I did I am willing to make satisfaction; and what can a man say fairer? If I have broke anything, I'll pay for't, an it cost a pound. And so let that content for what's past, and make no more words. For what's to come, to pleasure you I'm willing to marry my cousin; so pray let's all be friends. She and I are agreed upon the matter before a witness.

LADY WISHFORT.   How's this, dear niece? Have I any comfort? Can this be true?

MRS. MILLAMANT.   I am content to be a sacrifice to your repose, madam; and to convince you that I had no hand in the plot, as you were misinformed, I have laid my commands on Mirabell to come in person and be a witness that I give my hand to this flower of knighthood; and for the contract that passed between Mirabell and me, I have obliged him to make a resignation of it in your ladyship's presence. He is without, and waits your leave for admittance.

LADY WISHFORT.   Well, I'll swear I am something revived at this testimony of your obedience, but I cannot admit that traitor—I fear I cannot fortify myself to support his appearance. He is as terrible to me as a gorgon,[140] if I see him I fear I shall turn to stone, petrify incessantly.

[136] Not in his right mind.   [137] Of mourning.
[138] At the rate the property of rebels is confiscated.   [139] Drunk.
[140] Whose head turned beholders to stone.

MRS. MILLAMANT.   If you disoblige him, he may resent your refusal and insist
upon the contract still. Then 'tis the last time he will be offensive to you.

LADY WISHFORT.   Are you sure it will be the last time?—If I were sure of that
—shall I never see him again?

MRS. MILLAMANT.   Sir Wilfull, you and he are to travel together, are you not?

SIR WILFULL.   'Sheart, the gentleman's a civil gentleman, aunt; let him come in.
Why, we are sworn brothers and fellow-travellers.—We are to be Pylades
and Orestes,[141] he and I. He is to be my interpreter in foreign parts. He has
been overseas once already, and with proviso that I marry my cousin, will
cross 'em once again only to bear me company.—'Sheart, I'll call him in. An
I set on't once, he shall come in; and see who'll hinder him.

[*Exit* SIR WILFULL]

MRS. MARWOOD.   This is precious fooling, if it would pass; but I'll know the
bottom of it.

LADY WISHFORT.   O dear Marwood, you are not going?

MRS. MARWOOD.   Not far, madam; I'll return immediately.

[*Exit* MRS. MARWOOD]

[*Re-enter* SIR WILFULL *and* MIRABELL]

SIR WILFULL.   Look up, man, I'll stand by you. 'Sbud, an she do frown, she
can't kill you; besides—harkee, she dare not frown desperately, because her
face is none of her own. 'Sheart, an she should, her forehead would wrinkle
like the coat of a cream-cheese; but mum for that, fellow-traveller.

MIRABELL.   If a deep sense of the many injuries I have offered to so good a lady,
with a sincere remorse and a hearty contrition, can but obtain the least
glance of compassion, I am too happy. Ah, madam, there was a time!—but
let it be forgotten—I confess I have deservedly forfeited the high place I
once held, of sighing at your feet. Nay, kill me not by turning from me in
disdain. I come not to plead for favor—nay, not for pardon; I am a suppliant
only for your pity. I am going where I never shall behold you more—

SIR WILFULL.   How, fellow-traveller! you shall go by yourself then.

MIRABELL.   Let me be pitied first, and afterwards forgotten. I ask no more.

SIR WILFULL.   By'r Lady, a very reasonable request, and will cost you nothing,
aunt! Come, come, forgive and forget, aunt. Why, you must, an you are a
Christian.

MIRABELL.   Consider, madam, in reality you could not receive much prejudice. It
was an innocent device; though I confess it had a face of guiltiness, it was at
most an artifice which love contrived—and errors which love produces have
ever been accounted venial. At least think it is punishment enough that I
have lost what in my heart I hold most dear, that to your cruel indignation
I have offered up this beauty, and with her my peace and quiet—nay, all
my hopes of future comfort.

SIR WILFULL.   An he does not move me, would I may never be o' the quorum! [142]
An it were not as good a deed as to drink, to give her to him again, I would
I might never take shipping!—Aunt, if you don't forgive quickly, I shall
melt, I can tell you that. My contract went no farther than a little mouth
glue, and that's hardly dry—one doleful sigh more from my fellow-traveller,
and 'tis dissolved.

[141] Famous friends from Greek legend.   [142] Be a justice of the peace.

LADY WISHFORT. Well, nephew, upon your account—Ah, he has a false insinuating tongue!—Well, sir, I will stifle my just resentment at my nephew's request. I will endeavor what I can to forget, but on proviso that you resign the contract with my niece immediately.

MIRABELL. It is in writing, and with papers of concern; but I have sent my servant for it, and will deliver it to you with all acknowledgments for your transcendent goodness.

LADY WISHFORT. [*Aside*] Oh, he has witchcraft in his eyes and tongue! When I did not see him, I could have bribed a villain to his assassination; but his appearance rakes the embers which have so long lain smothered in my breast. [*Enter* FAINALL *and* MRS. MARWOOD]

FAINALL. Your date of deliberation, madam, is expired. Here is the instrument; are you prepared to sign?

LADY WISHFORT. If I were prepared, I am not impowered. My niece exerts a lawful claim, having matched herself by my direction to Sir Wilfull.

FAINALL. That sham is too gross to pass on me—though 'tis imposed on you, madam.

MRS. MILLAMANT. Sir, I have given my consent.

MIRABELL. And, sir, I have resigned my pretensions.

SIR WILFULL. And, sir, I assert my right and will maintain it in defiance of you, sir, and of your instrument. 'Sheart, an you talk of an instrument, sir, I have an old fox[143] by my thigh shall hack your instrument of ram vellum[144] to shreds, sir! It shall not be sufficient for a mittimus[145] or a tailor's measure. Therefore withdraw your instrument, sir, or by'r Lady, I shall draw mine.

LADY WISHFORT. Hold, nephew, hold!

MRS. MILLAMANT. Good Sir Wilfull, respite your valor!

FAINALL. Indeed! Are you provided of a guard, with your single beef-eater[146] there? But I'm prepared for you, and insist upon my first proposal. You shall submit your own estate to my management, and absolutely make over my wife's to my sole use, as pursuant to the purport and tenor of this other covenant.—[*To* MRS. MILLAMANT] I suppose, madam, your consent is not requisite in this case; nor, Mr. Mirabell, your resignation; nor, Sir Wilfull, your right.—You may draw your fox if you please, sir, and make a bear-garden flourish somewhere else, for here it will not avail. This, my Lady Wishfort, must be subscribed, or your darling daughter's turned adrift, like a leaky hulk, to sink or swim, as she and the current of this lewd town can agree.

LADY WISHFORT. Is there no means, no remedy to stop my ruin? Ungrateful wretch! dost thou not owe thy being, thy subsistence, to my daughter's fortune?

FAINALL. I'll answer you when I have the rest of it in my possession.

MIRABELL. But that you would not accept of a remedy from my hands—I own I have not deserved you should owe any obligation to me; or else perhaps I could advise—

LADY WISHFORT. Oh, what?—what? To save me and my child from ruin, from

---

[143] Sword.
[144] Legal documents were written on sheepskin.
[145] Writ of commitment to prison.
[146] A guard of the Tower of London.

want, I'll forgive all that's past; nay, I'll consent to anything to come, to be delivered from this tyranny.

MIRABELL.   Aye, madam, but that is too late; my reward is intercepted. You have disposed of her who only could have made me a compensation for all my services. But be it as it may, I am resolved I'll serve you! You shall not be wronged in this savage manner.

LADY WISHFORT.   How! Dear Mr. Mirabell, can you be so generous at last? But it is not possible. Harkee, I'll break my nephew's match; you shall have my niece yet, and all her fortune, if you can but save me from this imminent danger.

MIRABELL.   Will you? I'll take you at your word. I ask no more. I must have leave for two criminals to appear.

LADY WISHFORT.   Aye, aye; anybody, anybody!

MIRABELL.   Foible is one, and a penitent.

[*Enter* MRS. FAINALL, FOIBLE, *and* MINCING]

MRS. MARWOOD.   [*Aside*] Oh, my shame! [*To* FAINALL] These corrupt things are brought hither to expose me.

[MIRABELL *and* LADY WISHFORT *go to* MRS. FAINALL *and* FOIBLE]

FAINALL.   If it must all come out, why let 'em know it; 'tis but the way of the world. That shall not urge me to relinquish or abate one tittle of my terms; no, I will insist the more.

FOIBLE.   Yes, indeed, madam, I'll take my Bible oath of it.

MINCING.   And so will I, mem.

LADY WISHFORT.   O Marwood, Marwood, art thou false? My friend deceive me? Hast thou been a wicked accomplice with that profligate man?

MRS. MARWOOD.   Have you so much ingratitude and injustice to give credit against your friend to the aspersions of two such mercenary trulls?

MINCING.   Mercenary, mem? I scorn your words. 'Tis true we found you and Mr. Fainall in the blue garret; by the same token, you swore us to secrecy upon Messalina's poems.[147] Mercenary? No, if we would have been mercenary, we should have held our tongues; you would have bribed us sufficiently.

FAINALL.   Go, you are an insignificant thing!—Well, what are you the better for this? Is this Mr. Mirabell's expedient? I'll be put off no longer.—You, thing that was a wife, shall smart for this! I will not leave thee wherewithal to hide thy shame; your body shall be naked as your reputation.

MRS. FAINALL.   I despise you and defy your malice! You have aspersed me wrongfully—I have proved your falsehood! Go, you and your treacherous —I will not name it, but, starve together. Perish!

FAINALL.   Not while you are worth a groat, indeed, my dear. Madam, I'll be fooled no longer.

LADY WISHFORT.   Ah, Mr. Mirabell, this is small comfort, the detection of this affair.

MIRABELL.   Oh, in good time. Your leave for the other offender and penitent to appear, madam.

[*Enter* WAITWELL *with a box of writings*]

LADY WISHFORT.   O Sir Rowland!—Well, rascal!

---

[147] Probably Mincing's mispronunciation of "Miscellany." Messalina was a notoriously lewd Roman empress.

WAITWELL. What your ladyship pleases. I have brought the black box at last, madam.

MIRABELL. Give it me. Madam, you remember your promise?

LADY WISHFORT. Aye, dear sir.

MIRABELL. Where are the gentlemen?

WAITWELL. At hand, sir, rubbing their eyes—just risen from sleep.

FAINALL. 'Sdeath, what's this to me? I'll not wait your private concerns.

[*Enter* PETULANT *and* WITWOUD]

PETULANT. How now! What's the matter? Whose hand's out?

WITWOUD. Heyday! What, are you all got together like players at the end of the last act?

MIRABELL. You may remember, gentlemen, I once requested your hands as witnesses to a certain parchment.

WITWOUD. Aye, I do; my hand I remember—Petulant set his mark.

MIRABELL. You wrong him. His name is fairly written, as shall appear.—[*Undoing the box*] You do not remember, gentlemen, anything of what that parchment contained?

WITWOUD. No.

PETULANT. Not I; I writ, I read nothing.

MIRABELL. Very well, now you shall know.—Madam, your promise.

LADY WISHFORT. Aye, aye, sir, upon my honor.

MIRABELL. Mr. Fainall, it is now time that you should know that your lady, while she was at her own disposal, and before you had by your insinuations wheedled her out of a pretended settlement of the greatest part of her fortune—

FAINALL. Sir! pretended!

MIRABELL. Yes, sir. I say that this lady while a widow, having, it seems, received some cautions respecting your inconstancy and tyranny of temper, which from her own partial opinion and fondness of you she could never have suspected—she did, I say, by the wholesome advice of friends and of sages learned in the laws of this land, deliver this same as her act and deed to me in trust, and to the uses within mentioned. You may read if you please—[*Holding out the parchment*] though perhaps what is written on the back may serve your occasions.

FAINALL. Very likely, sir. What's here?—Damnation! [*Reads*] "A deed of conveyance of the whole estate real of Arabella Languish, widow, in trust to Edward Mirabell."—Confusion!

MIRABELL. Even so, sir; 'tis the way of the world, sir,—of the widows of the world. I suppose this deed may bear an elder date than what you have obtained from your lady?

FAINALL. Perfidious fiend! then thus I'll be revenged. [*Offers to run at* MRS. FAINALL]

SIR WILFULL. Hold, sir! Now you may make your bear-garden flourish somewhere else, sir.

FAINALL. Mirabell, you shall hear of this, sir, be sure you shall.—Let me pass, oaf!

[*Exit* FAINALL]

MRS. FAINALL.   Madam, you seem to stifle your resentment; you had better give it vent.

MRS. MARWOOD.   Yes, it shall have vent—and to your confusion, or I'll perish in the attempt.

[Exit MRS. MARWOOD]

LADY WISHFORT.   O daughter, daughter! 'Tis plain thou hast inherited thy mother's prudence.

MRS. FAINALL.   Thank Mr. Mirabell, a cautious friend, to whose advice all is owing.

LADY WISHFORT.   Well, Mr. Mirabell, you have kept your promise—and I must perform mine. First, I pardon, for your sake, Sir Rowland there, and Foible. The next thing is to break the matter to my nephew—and how to do that—

MIRABELL.   For that, madam, give yourself no trouble; let me have your consent. Sir Wilfull is my friend. He has had compassion upon lovers, and generously engaged a volunteer in this action for our service, and now designs to prosecute his travels.

SIR WILFULL.   'Sheart, aunt, I have no mind to marry. My cousin's a fine lady, and the gentleman loves her, and she loves him, and they deserve one another. My resolution is to see foreign parts—I have set on't—and when I'm set on't I must do't. And if these two gentlemen would travel too, I think they may be spared.

PETULANT.   For my part, I say little—I think things are best off or on.

WITWOUD.   'Ygad, I understand nothing of the matter; I'm in a maze yet, like a dog in a dancing-school.

LADY WISHFORT.   Well, sir, take her, and with her all the joy I can give you.

MRS. MILLAMANT.   Why does not the man take me? Would you have me give myself to you over again?

MIRABELL.   Aye, and over and over again; [*Kisses her hand*] I would have you as often as possibly I can. Well, Heaven grant I love you not too well; that's all my fear.

SIR WILFULL.   'Sheart, you'll have time enough to toy after you're married; or if you will toy now, let us have a dance in the meantime, that we who are not lovers may have some other employment besides looking on.

MIRABELL.   With all my heart, dear Sir Wilfull. What shall we do for music?

FOIBLE.   Oh, sir, some that were provided for Sir Rowland's entertainment are yet within call. [*A dance*]

LADY WISHFORT.   As I am a person, I can hold out no longer. I have wasted my spirits so to-day already, that I am ready to sink under the fatigue, and I cannot but have some fears upon me yet, that my son Fainall will pursue some desperate course.

MIRABELL.   Madam, disquiet not yourself on that account; to my knowledge his circumstances are such he must of force comply. For my part, I will contribute all that in me lies to a reunion; in the meantime, madam—[*To* MRS. FAINALL] let me before these witnesses restore to you this deed of trust. It may be a means, well-managed, to make you live easily together.

> From hence let those be warned who mean to wed,
> Lest mutual falsehood stain the bridal bed;

For each deceiver to his cost may find
That marriage-frauds too oft are paid in kind.

[*Exeunt omnes*]

EPILOGUE

After our epilogue this crowd dismisses,
I'm thinking how this play'll be pulled to pieces;
But pray consider, ere you doom its fall,
How hard a thing 'twould be to please you all.
There are some critics so with spleen diseased,
They scarcely come inclining to be pleased;
And sure he must have more than mortal skill,
Who pleases anyone against his will.
Then all bad poets, we are sure, are foes,
And how their number's swelled the town well knows;
In shoals I've marked 'em judging in the pit;
Though they're on no pretense for judgment fit,
But that they have been damned for want of wit.
Since then, they by their own offenses taught,
Set up for spies on plays, and finding fault.
Others there are whose malice we'd prevent;
Such who watch plays with scurrilous intent
To mark out who by characters are meant;
And though no perfect likeness they can trace,
Yet each pretends to know the copied face.
These with false glosses feed their own ill nature,
And turn to libel what was meant a satire.
May such malicious fops this fortune find,
To think themselves alone the fools designed,
If any are so arrogantly vain,
To think they singly can support a scene,
And furnish fool enough to entertain.
For well the learn'd and the judicious know
That satire scorns to stoop so meanly low
As any one abstracted [148] fop to show.
For, as when painters form a matchless face,
They from each fair one catch some different grace,
And shining features in one portrait blend,
To which no single beauty must pretend,
So poets oft do in one piece expose
Whole *belles-assemblées*[149] of coquettes and beaux.

---

[148] Singled out.   [149] Fashionable gatherings.

Miss Julie

August Strindberg

August Strindberg

Although Strindberg wrote plays of various sorts, historical, realistic, symbolic, and so forth, it is his naturalistic plays which are best known to the world outside his native Sweden. Among these latter, *The Father* and *Miss Julie* are the most famous. *Miss Julie* has been selected here because of the two it is the better constructed and the less melodramatic. It also reveals in clearer fashion the tendency of naturalism to pass beyond itself and move into the realm of the symbolic and expressionistic. In fact, in his later years, Strindberg himself repudiated naturalism and wrote important symbolic plays. His own dramatic evolution sums up in a remarkable way the evolution of drama in the first half of our century.

Miss Julie is naturalistic in its fidelity to everyday life and speech, in its outspoken frankness (with references to menstruation, privies, religious hypocrisy, all more shocking eighty-five years ago than now), in its sense of inevitability. Yet at the same time it has symbolic overtones and thematic interweavings. Strindberg recognized this last quality himself when he wrote in his celebrated introduction to the play: "My dialogue wanders here and there, gathers material in the first scenes which is later picked up, repeated, reworked, developed, and expanded like the theme in a piece of music."

Because of its intrinsic power and its position in dramatic history as a typical naturalistic play, and because it is an important forerunner of modern expressionist drama, *Miss Julie* is well worth knowing and studying. It is one of the great plays of the modern stage.

Its author, August Strindberg, was one of the most unhappy and self-tormented of men. A contemporary of Ibsen's, he lacked the latter's sanity and balance. But together with his Scandinavian fellow playwright, he ushered in the period of modern drama, breaking once and for all, among significant dramatists, the outworn conventions of nineteenth-century drama. He was born in 1849 to a more-or-less successful merchant and a former servant girl who had been his father's mistress before she became his wife. Strindberg was brought up in a harsh and demanding household in which there was a social chasm between his parents and intense sibling rivalry among his many brothers and sisters. All these tensions were aggravated by the death of his mother when he was thirteen and the subsequent acquisition of a stepmother who had been the housekeeper of the family.

After a succession of jobs and some study at Upsala University, he turned to writing. He had attempted to become an actor, an experience which stood him in good stead in his dramatic writing. After only minor success as a playwright, he tried to make a living as a journalist and librarian.

His first success was a novel, *The Red Room,* published in 1879. It was followed by further successes. Although he is primarily known to the world as a dramatist—and a most prolific one—he is also notable as a novelist, poet, essayist, autobiographer, and scholar, albeit an eccentric one. *The Father* appeared in 1887, and *Miss Julie* in the next year.

Strindberg was singularly unhappy in his relations with women largely because of his impossible demands, bizarre conduct, and psychotic personality. His first marriage broke up in 1891, and the two subsequent ones were no more successful. In his later years, he went through periods of madness or near madness but always recovered sufficiently to be able to remain at large. In these periods of acute paranoia, he wrote remarkable self-defensive autobiographical fragments, imposed unconscionably on friends, quarreled with almost everyone, and even tried to prove fantastic chemical theories. Although he continued to write for the press, he spent his last years in Stockholm more or less as a recluse. He died in 1912.

Throughout his adult life Strindberg was obsessed by all kinds of manias, especially hatred of women. With Schopenhauer, he is the greatest misogynist of Western civilization. He tended' both to humiliate and idealize his women. Still, although this attitude toward women colored everything he wrote, he always managed to retain some objectivity. In *Miss Julie,* for instance, his initial purpose was to portray his central character as a monster, but in the play as it is written there is pity for her.

Miss Julie is a well-constructed play centered around one episode that moves steadily and firmly to its climax and close. Through the conversations of the two leading characters the audience learns enough about their backgrounds to understand their behavior and the dilemmas that Miss Julie faces and that lead inevitably to the play's tragic denouement. Strindberg himself was torn between God and man, between aristocrat and peasant, between love and hate for women; these conflicts appear in this play transformed into an objectivity which is of the essence of great drama.

Miss Julie is essentially a simple story. A decadent, bored, and unhappy young aristocratic woman seeks a new thrill in a liaison with a smooth, vulgar, but virile servant. D. H. Lawrence's *Lady Chatterley's Lover* is based on a similar kind of love affair between a highborn lady and a humble man. But in the novel, which lacks many of the overtones of *Miss Julie,* the lover regenerates the bored and decadent lady. Lawrence had hopes in, and illusions about, the poor and about the sex act which Strindberg certainly did not share. His servant, Jean, is even more despicable than his aristocratic Miss Julie.

Miss Julie's situation, which is gradually revealed, demands a violent solution. In order to preserve her honor as an aristocrat and her dignity as a woman, there is no other way for her. Jean's background of poverty and struggle makes the audience sympathetic toward him at the beginning, but as the play progresses the sympathies shift to the woman who earlier had been despised and away from the servant whose base, vulgar, and even cruel nature becomes clearer. Christine, the cook, the only other character in the play, is essentially a minor figure who contrasts with Julie and at the same time promotes the action. She is a petty, pietistic, hypocritical soul.

The dialogue is free and outspoken and has the fits and starts of real-life conversations. In it the audience sees the duel between the two lovers and gains insight into their natures. The dialogue's frankness shocked the Victorian sensitivities of the late nineteenth century, and after the first performance of the play in Copenhagen, it was banned for a while in Denmark.

The play is full of symbols, and the dreams related are characteristic of both the lovers. The events that are emphasized have symbolic and foreshadowing functions. The Count, father of Miss Julie, who never appears on the stage, broods over the play and suggests law, retribution, and divine order. The time of the play—Midsummer Eve—and the songs and dances of the peasants all present a backdrop of paganism to the lust of the protagonists. The violent end of the play is continually foreshadowed, and the symbols culminate in the brutal decapitation of a pet bird of Miss Julie's.

There has been some debate as to whether *Miss Julie* is a true tragedy. Certainly from a Sophoclean or Shakespearean point of view, this play cannot be considered a tragedy because it does not create the necessary terror. Nor is the heroine of sufficient stature to engage totally the audience's sympathies although there may be some feeling of pity for her. In short, no one can identify closely enough with Miss Julie's dilemma. Yet in the broader sense of the term "tragedy," the play may be said to be a tragedy of a naturalistic type with a sense of necessity, of futility, of waste. The tight organization of *Miss Julie* contributes to its great power by the creation of a unity of mood and a sense of inexorable destiny marching on.

Miss Julie

August Strindberg

TRANSLATED BY E. M. SPRINCHORN

CHARACTERS

MISS JULIE, *twenty-five years old*
JEAN, *valet, thirty years old*

CHRISTINE, *the cook, thirty-five years old*

The action of the play takes place in the kitchen of the Count's manor house on Midsummer Eve in Sweden in the 1880's.

The scene is a large kitchen. The walls and ceiling are covered with draperies and hangings. The rear wall runs obliquely upstage from the left. On this wall to the left are two shelves with pots and pans of copper, iron, and pewter. The shelves are decorated with goffered paper. A little to the right can be seen three-fourths of a deep arched doorway with two glass doors, and through them can be seen a fountain with a statue of Cupid, lilac bushes in bloom, and the tops of some Lombardy poplars. From the left of the stage the corner of a large, Dutch-tile kitchen stove protrudes with part of the hood showing. Projecting from the right side of the stage is one end of the servants' dining table of white pine, with a few chairs around it. The stove is decorated with branches of birch leaves; the floor is strewn with juniper twigs. On the end of the table is a large Japanese spice jar filled with lilacs. An icebox, a sink, a wash basin. Over the door a big, old-fashioned bell; and to the left of the door the gaping mouth of a speaking tube.

CHRISTINE is standing at the stove, frying something. She is wearing a light-colored cotton dress and an apron. JEAN enters, dressed in livery and carrying a pair of high-top boots with spurs. He sets them where they are clearly visible.

JEAN. Tonight she's wild again. Miss Julie's absolutely wild!
CHRISTINE. You took your time getting back!
JEAN. I took the Count down to the station, and on my way back as I passed the barn I went in for a dance. And there was Miss Julie leading the dance

---

with the game warden. But then she noticed me. And she came right up and chose me for the ladies' waltz. And she's been dancing ever since like—like I don't know what. She's absolutely wild!

CHRISTINE. That's nothing new. But she's been worse than ever during the last two weeks, ever since her engagement was broken off.

JEAN. Yes, I never did hear all there was to that. He was a good man, too, even if he wasn't rich. Well, that's a woman for you.

[*He sits down at the end of the table*]

But, tell me, isn't it strange that a young girl like her—all right, young woman—prefers to stay home here with the servants rather than go with her father to visit her relatives?

CHRISTINE. I suppose she's ashamed to face them after that fiasco with her young man.

JEAN. No doubt. He wouldn't take any nonsense from her. Do you know what happened, Christine? I do. I saw the whole thing, even though I didn't let on.

CHRISTINE. Don't tell me you were there?

JEAN. Well, I was. They were in the barnyard one evening—and she was training him, as she called it. Do you know what she was doing? She was making him jump over her riding whip—training him like a dog. He jumped over twice, and she whipped him both times. But the third time, he grabbed the whip from her, broke it in a thousand pieces—and walked off.

CHRISTINE. So that's what happened. Well, what do you know.

JEAN. Yes, that put an end to that affair.—Now have you got something good for me, Christine?

CHRISTINE. [*Serving him from the frying pan*] Just a little bit of kidney. I cut it especially for you.

JEAN. [*Smelling it*] Wonderful! My special *délice!* [*Feeling the plate*] Hey, you didn't warm the plate!

CHRISTINE. You're more fussy than the Count himself when you set your mind to it. [*She rumples his hair gently*]

JEAN. [*Irritated*] Cut it out! Don't muss up my hair. You know I don't like that!

CHRISTINE. Oh, now don't get mad. Can I help it if I like you?

[JEAN *eats.* CHRISTINE *gets out a bottle of beer*]

JEAN. Beer on Midsummer Eve! No thank you! I've got something much better than that. [*He opens a drawer in the table and takes out a bottle of red wine with a gold seal*] Do you see that? Gold Seal. Now give me a glass.— No, a wine glass of course. I'm drinking it straight.

CHRISTINE. [*Goes back to the stove and puts on a small saucepan*] Lord help the woman who gets you for a husband. You're an old fussbudget!

JEAN. Talk, talk! You'd consider yourself lucky if you got yourself a man as good as me. It hasn't done you any harm to have people think I'm your fiancé. [*He tastes the wine*] Very good. Excellent. But warmed just a little too little. [*Warming the glass in his hands*] We bought this in Dijon. Four francs a liter, unbottled—and the tax on top of that. . . . What on earth are you cooking? It smells awful!

CHRISTINE. Some damn mess that Miss Julie wants for her dog.

JEAN. You should watch your language, Christine. . . . Why do you have to stand in front of the stove on a holiday, cooking for that mutt? Is it sick?

CHRISTINE.   Oh, she's sick, all right! She sneaked out to the gatekeeper's mongrel and—got herself in a fix. And Miss Julie, you know, can't stand anything like that.

JEAN.   She's too stuck-up in some ways and not proud enough in others. Just like her mother. The Countess felt right at home in the kitchen or down in the barn with the cows, but when she went driving, *one* horse wasn't enough for her; she had to have a pair. Her sleeves were always dirty, but her buttons had the royal crown on them. As for Miss Julie, she doesn't seem to care how she looks and acts. I mean, she's not really refined. Just now, down at the barn, she grabbed the game warden away from Anna and asked him to dance. You wouldn't see anybody in our class doing a thing like that. But that's what happens when the gentry try to act like the common people— they become common! . . . But she *is* beautiful! Magnificent! Ah, those shoulders—those——and so forth, and so forth!

CHRISTINE.   Oh, don't exaggerate. Clara tells me all about her, and Clara dresses her.

JEAN.   Clara, pooh! You women are always jealous of each other. *I've* been out riding with her. . . . And how she can dance!

CHRISTINE.   Listen, Jean, you *are* going to dance with me, aren't you, when I am finished here?

JEAN.   Certainly! Of course I am.

CHRISTINE.   Promise?

JEAN.   Promise! Listen if I say I'm going to do a thing, I do it. . . . Christine, I thank you for a delicious meal. [*He shoves the cork back into the bottle*] [MISS JULIE *appears in the doorway, talking to someone outside*]

MISS JULIE.   I'll be right back. Don't wait for me.

   [JEAN *slips the bottle into the table drawer quickly and rises respectfully.*

MISS JULIE *comes in and crosses over to* CHRISTINE, *who is at the mirror*]

MISS JULIE.   Did you get it ready?

   [CHRISTINE *signals that* JEAN *is present*]

JEAN.   [*Polite and charming*] Are you ladies sharing secrets?

MISS JULIE.   [*Flipping her handkerchief in his face*] Don't be nosey!

JEAN.   Oh, that smells good! Violets.

MISS JULIE.   [*Flirting with him*] Don't be impudent! And don't tell me you're an expert on perfumes, too. I know you're an expert dancer.—No, don't look! Go away!

JEAN.   [*Inquisitive, but deferential*] What are you cooking? A witch's brew for Midsummer Eve? Something that reveals what the stars have in store for you, so you can see the face of your future husband?

MISS JULIE.   [*Curtly*] You'd have to have good eyes to see that. [*To* CHRISTINE] Pour it into a small bottle, and seal it tight. . . . Jean, come and dance a schottische with me.

JEAN.   [*Hesitating*] I hope you don't think I'm being rude, but I've already promised this dance to Christine.

MISS JULIE.   She can always find someone else. Isn't that so, Christine? You don't mind if I borrow Jean for a minute, do you?

CHRISTINE.   It isn't up to me. If Miss Julie is gracious enough to invite you, it isn't right for you to say no, Jean. You go on, and thank her for the honor.

JEAN.   Frankly, Miss Julie, I don't want to hurt your feelings, but I wonder if it is wise—I mean for you to dance twice in a row with the same partner. Especially since the people around here are so quick to spread gossip.

MISS JULIE.   [*Bridling*] What do you mean? What kind of gossip? What are you trying to say?

JEAN.   [*Retreating*] If you insist on misunderstanding me, I'll have to speak more plainly. It just doesn't look right for you to prefer one of your servants to the others who are hoping for the same unusual honor.

MISS JULIE.   Prefer! What an idea! I'm really surprised. I, the mistress of the house, am good enough to come to their dance, and when I feel like dancing, I want to dance with someone who knows how to lead. After all I don't want to look ridiculous.

JEAN.   As you wish. I am at your orders.

MISS JULIE.   [*Gently*] Don't take it as an order. Tonight we're all just happy people at a party. There's no question of rank. Now give me your arm.— Don't worry, Christine. I won't run off with your boy friend.

[JEAN *gives her his arm and leads her out*]

PANTOMIME SCENE. *This should be played as if the actress were actually alone. She turns her back on the audience when she feels like it; she does not look out into the auditorium; she does not hurry as if she were afraid the audience would grow impatient.*

CHRISTINE *alone. In the distance the sound of the violins playing the schottische.* CHRISTINE, *humming in time with the music, cleans up after* JEAN, *washes the dishes, dries them, and puts them away in a cupboard. Then she takes off her apron, takes a little mirror from one of the table drawers, and leans it against the jar of lilacs on the table. She lights a tallow candle, heats a curling iron, and curls the bangs on her forehead. Then she goes to the doorway and stands listening to the music. She comes back to the table and finds the handkerchief that* MISS JULIE *left behind. She smells it, spreads it out, and then, as if lost in thought, stretches it, smooths it out, folds it in four, and so on.*

[JEAN *enters alone*]

JEAN.   I told you she was wild! You should have seen the way she was dancing. They were peeking at her from behind the doors and laughing at her. Can you figure her out, Christine?

CHRISTINE.   You might know it's her monthlies, Jean. She always acts peculiar then. . . . Well, are you going to dance with me?

JEAN.   You're not mad at me because I broke my promise?

CHRISTINE.   Of course not. Not for a little thing like that, you know that. And I know my place.

JEAN.   [*Grabs her around the waist*] You're a sensible girl, Christine. You're going to make somebody a good wife——

[MISS JULIE, *coming in, sees them together. She is unpleasantly surprised*]

MISS JULIE.   [*With forced gaiety*] Well, aren't you the gallant beau—running away from your partner!

JEAN.   On the contrary, Miss Julie. As you can see, I've hurried back to the partner I deserted.

MISS JULIE. [*Changing tack*] You know, you're the best dancer I've met.—
But why are you wearing livery on a holiday. Take it off at once.
JEAN. I'd have to ask you to leave for a minute. My black coat is hanging
right here—[*He moves to the right and points*]
MISS JULIE. You're not embarrassed because I'm here, are you? Just to change
your coat? Go in your room and come right back again. Or else you can
stay here and I'll turn my back.
JEAN. If you'll excuse me, Miss Julie. [*He goes off to the right. His arm can
be seen as he changes his coat*]
MISS JULIE. [*To* CHRISTINE] Tell me something, Christine. Is Jean your fiancé?
He seems so intimate with you.
CHRISTINE. Fiancé? I suppose so. At least that's what we say.
MISS JULIE. What do you mean?
CHRISTINE. Well, Miss Julie, you have had fiancés yourself, and you know—
MISS JULIE. But we were properly engaged—!
CHRISTINE. I know, but did anything come of it?
[JEAN *comes back, wearing a cutaway coat and derby*]
MISS JULIE. *Très gentil, monsieur Jean! Très gentil!*
JEAN. *Vous voulez plaisanter, madame.*
MISS JULIE. *Et vous voulez parler français!* [1] Where did you learn to speak
French?
JEAN. In Switzerland. I was *sommelier* in one of the biggest hotels in Lucerne.
MISS JULIE. But you look quite the gentleman in that coat! *Charmant!* [*She
sits down at the table*]
JEAN. Flatterer!
MISS JULIE. [*Stiffening*] Who said I was flattering you?
JEAN. My natural modesty would not allow me to presume that you were pay-
ing sincere compliments to someone like me, and therefore I assumed that
you were exaggerating, or, in other words, flattering me.
MISS JULIE. Where on earth did you learn to talk like that? Do you go to the
theater often?
JEAN. And other places. I get around.
MISS JULIE. But weren't you born in this district?
JEAN. My father worked as a farm hand on the county attorney's estate, next
door to yours. I used to see you when you were little. But of course you
didn't notice me.
MISS JULIE. Did you really?
JEAN. Yes. I remember one time in particular—. But I can't tell you about
that!
MISS JULIE. Of course you can. Oh, come on, tell me. Just this once—for me.
JEAN. No. No, I really couldn't. Not now. Some other time maybe.
MISS JULIE. Some other time? That means never. What's the harm in telling me
now?
JEAN. There's no harm. I just don't feel like it.—Look at her. [*He nods at
CHRISTINE, who has fallen asleep in a chair by the stove*]

[1] MISS JULIE. Very elegant, Mr. Jean! Very elegant.
JEAN: You wish to joke, my lady.
MISS JULIE: And you wish to speak French!

MISS JULIE. Won't she make somebody a pretty wife! I'll bet she snores, too.

JEAN. No, she doesn't. But she talks in her sleep.

MISS JULIE. [*Cynically*] Now how would you know she talks in her sleep?

JEAN . [*Coolly*] I've heard her. . . .

[*Pause. They look at each other*]

MISS JULIE. Why don't you sit down?

JEAN. I wouldn't take the liberty in your presence.

MISS JULIE. But if I were to order you—?

JEAN. I'd obey.

MISS JULIE. Well then, sit down.—Wait a minute. Could you get me something to drink first?

JEAN. I don't know what there is in the icebox. Only beer, I suppose.

MISS JULIE. *Only* beer?! I have simple tastes. I prefer beer to wine.

[JEAN *takes a bottle of beer from the icebox and opens it. He looks in the cupboard for a glass and a saucer, and serves her*]

JEAN. At your service.

MISS JULIE. Thank you. Don't you want to drink, too?

JEAN. I'm not much of a beer-drinker, but if it's your wish—

MISS JULIE. My wish! I should think a gentleman would want to keep his lady company.

JEAN. That's a point well taken! [*He opens another bottle and takes a glass*]

MISS JULIE. Now drink a toast to me! [JEAN *hesitates*] You're not shy, are you? A big, strong man like you? [*Playfully,* JEAN *kneels and raises his glass in mock gallantry*]

JEAN. To my lady's health!

MISS JULIE. Bravo! Now if you would kiss my shoe, you will have hit it off perfectly. [JEAN *hesitates, then boldly grasps her foot and touches it lightly with his lips*] Superb! You should have been an actor.

JEAN. [*Rising*] This has got to stop, Miss Julie! Someone might come and see us.

MISS JULIE. What difference would that make?

JEAN. People would talk, that's what! If you knew how their tongues were wagging out there just a few minutes ago, you wouldn't—

MISS JULIE. What sort of things did they say? Tell me. Sit down and tell me.

JEAN. [*Sitting down*] I don't want to hurt your feelings, but they used expressions that—that hinted at certain—you know what I mean. After all, you're not a child. And when they see a woman drinking, alone with a man —and a servant at that—in the middle of the night—well . . .

MISS JULIE. Well what?! Besides, we're not alone. Christine is here.

JEAN. Yes, asleep!

MISS JULIE. I'll wake her up then. [*She goes over to* CHRISTINE] Christine! Are you asleep? [CHRISTINE *babbles in her sleep*] Christine!—How sound she sleeps!

CHRISTINE. [*Talking in her sleep*] Count's boots are brushed . . . put on the coffee . . . right away, right away, right . . . mm—mm . . . pooffff . . .

[MISS JULIE *grabs* CHRISTINE'S *nose*]

MISS JULIE. Wake up, will you!

JEAN. [*Sternly*] Let her alone!

MISS JULIE. [*Sharply*] What!

JEAN. She's been standing over the stove all day. She's worn out when evening comes. Anyone asleep is entitled to some respect.

MISS JULIE. [*Changing tack*] That's a very kind thought. It does you credit. Thank you. [*She offers* JEAN *her hand*] Now come on out and pick some lilacs for me.

[*During the following,* CHRISTINE *wakes up and, drunk with sleep, shuffles off to the right to go to bed*]

JEAN. With you, Miss Julie?

MISS JULIE. Yes, with me.

JEAN. That's no good. Absolutely not.

MISS JULIE. I don't know what you're thinking. Maybe you're letting your imagination run away with you.

JEAN. I'm not. The other people are.

MISS JULIE. In what way? Imagining that I'm—*verliebt* in a servant? [2]

JEAN. I'm not conceited, but it's been known to happen. And to these people nothing's sacred.

MISS JULIE. Why, I believe you're an aristocrat!

JEAN. Yes, I am.

MISS JULIE. I'm climbing down—

JEAN. Don't climb down, Miss Julie! Take my advice. No one will ever believe that you climbed down deliberately. They'll say that you fell.

MISS JULIE. I think more highly of these people than you do. Let's see who's right! Come on! [*She looks him over, challenging him*]

JEAN. You know, you're very strange.

MISS JULIE. Perhaps. But then so are you. . . . Besides, everything is strange. Life, people, everything. It's all scum, drifting and drifting on the water until it sinks—sinks. There's a dream I have every now and then. It's coming back to me now. I'm sitting on top of a pillar that I've climbed up somehow and I don't know how to get back down. When I look down I get dizzy. I have to get down but I don't have the courage to jump. I can't hold on much longer and I want to fall; but I don't fall. I know I won't have any peace until I get down; no rest until I get down, down on the ground. And if I ever got down on the ground, I'd want to go farther down, right down into the earth. . . . Have you ever felt anything like that?

JEAN. Never! I used to dream that I'm lying under a tall tree in a dark woods. I want to get up, up to the very top, to look out over the bright landscape with the sun shining on it, to rob the bird's nest up there with the golden eggs in it. I climb and I climb, but the trunk is so thick, and so smooth, and it's such a long way to that first branch. But I know that if I could just reach that first branch, I'd go right to the top as if on a ladder. I've never reached it yet, but some day I will—even if only in my dreams.

MISS JULIE. Here I am talking about dreams with you. Come out with me. Only into the park a way. [*She offers him her arm, and they start to go*]

JEAN. Let's sleep on nine midsummer flowers, Miss Julie, and then our dreams will come true!

[2] . . . in love with a servant?

[MISS JULIE *and* JEAN *suddenly turn around in the doorway.* JEAN *is holding his hand over one eye*]

MISS JULIE.   You've caught something in your eye. Let me see.

JEAN.   It's nothing. Just a bit of dust. It'll go away.

MISS JULIE.   The sleeve of my dress must have grazed your eye. Sit down and I'll help you. [*She takes him by the arm and sits him down. She takes his head and leans it back. With the corner of her handkerchief she tries to get out the bit of dust*] Now sit still, absolutely still. [*She slaps his hand*] Do as you're told. Why, I believe you're trembling—a big, strong man like you. [*She feels his biceps*] With such big arms!

JEAN.   [*Warningly*] Miss Julie!

MISS JULIE.   Yes, *monsieur Jean?*

JEAN.   *Attention! Je ne suis qu'un homme!* [3]

MISS JULIE.   Sit still, I tell you! . . . There now! It's out. Kiss my hand and thank me!

JEAN.   [*Rising to his feet*] Listen to me, Miss Julie!—Christine has gone to bed!—Listen to me, I tell you!

MISS JULIE.   Kiss my hand first!

JEAN.   Listen to me!

MISS JULIE.   Kiss my hand first!

JEAN.   All right. But you'll have no one to blame but yourself.

MISS JULIE.   For what?

JEAN.   For what! Are you twenty-five years old and still a child? Don't you know it's dangerous to play with fire?

MISS JULIE.   Not for me. I'm insured!

JEAN.   [*Boldly*] Oh, no you're not! And even if you are, there's inflammable stuff next door.

MISS JULIE.   Meaning you?

JEAN.   Yes. Not just because it's me, but because I'm a young man—

MISS JULIE.   And irresistibly handsome? What incredible conceit! A Don Juan, maybe! Or a Joseph! Yes, bless my soul, that's it: you're a Joseph!

JEAN.   You think so?!

MISS JULIE.   I'm almost afraid so! [JEAN *boldly steps up to her, grabs her around the waist, kisses her. She slaps his face*] None of that!

JEAN.   Are you still playing games or are you serious?

MISS JULIE.   I'm serious.

JEAN.   Then you must have been serious just a moment ago, too! You take your games too seriously and that's dangerous. Well, I'm tired of your games, and if you'll excuse me, I'll return to my work. The Count will be wanting his boots on time, and it's long past midnight.

MISS JULIE.   Put those boots down.

JEAN.   No! This is my job. It's what I'm here for. But I never undertook to be a playmate for you. That's something I could never be. I consider myself too good for that.

MISS JULIE.   You are proud.

JEAN.   In some ways. Not in others.

[3] Be careful! I'm only a man.

MISS JULIE.   Have you ever been in love?

JEAN.   We don't use that word around here. But I've been interested in a lot of girls, if that's what you mean. . . . I even got sick once because I couldn't have the one I wanted—really sick, like the princes in the *Arabian Nights*—who couldn't eat or drink for love.

MISS JULIE.   Who was the girl? [JEAN *does not reply*] Who was she?

JEAN.   You can't make me tell you that.

MISS JULIE.   Even if I ask you as an equal—ask you—as˘ a friend? . . . Who was she?

JEAN.   You.

MISS JULIE.   [*Sitting down*] How—amusing. . . .

JEAN.   Yes, maybe so. Ridiculous. . . . That's why I didn't want to tell you about it before. But now I'll tell you the whole story. . . . Have you any idea what the world looks like from below? Of course you haven't. No more than a hawk or eagle has. You hardly ever see their backs because they're always soaring above us. I lived with seven brothers and sisters—and a pig —out on the waste land where there wasn't even a tree growing. But from my window I could see the wall of the Count's garden with the apple trees sticking up over it. That was the Garden of Eden for me, and there were many angry angels with flaming swords standing guard over it. But in spite of them, I and the other boys found a way to the Tree of Life. . . . I'll bet you despise me.

MISS JULIE.   All boys steal apples.

JEAN.   That's what you say now. But you still despise me. Never mind. One day I went with my mother into this paradise to weed the onion beds. Next to the vegetable garden stood a Turkish pavilion,[4] shaded by jasmine and hung all over with honeysuckle. I couldn't imagine what it was used for. I only knew I had never seen such a beautiful building. People went in, and came out again. And one day the door was left open. I sneaked in. The walls were covered with portraits of kings and emperors, and the windows had red curtains with tassels on them.—You do know what kind of place I'm talking about, don't you? . . . I—[*He breaks off a lilac and holds it under* MISS JULIE's *nose*] I had never been inside a castle, never seen anything besides the church. But this was more beautiful. And no matter what I tried to think about, my thoughts always came back—to that little pavilion. And little by little there arose in me a desire to experience just for once the whole pleasure of . . . *Enfin*,[5] I sneaked in, looked about, and marveled. Then I heard someone coming! There was only one way out—for the upper-class people. But for me there was one more—a lower one. And I had no other choice but to take it. [MISS JULIE, *who has taken the lilac from* JEAN, *lets it fall to the table*] Then I began to run like mad, plunging through the raspberry bushes, ploughing through the strawberry patches, and came up on the rose terrace. And there I caught sight of a pink dress and a pair of white stockings. That was you. I crawled under a pile of weeds, under—well, you can imagine what it was like—under thistles that pricked me and wet dirt that stank to high heaven. And all the while I could see you walking among

---

[4] A privy.   [5] Finally.

the roses. I said to myself, "If it's true that a thief can enter heaven and be with the angels, isn't it strange that a poor man's child here on God's green earth can't enter the Count's park and play with the Count's daughter."

MISS JULIE.   [*Sentimentally*] Do you think all poor children have felt that way?

JEAN.   [*Hesitatingly at first, then with mounting conviction*] If all poor ch—? Yes—yes, naturally. Of course!

MISS JULIE.   It must be terrible to be poor.

JEAN.   [*With exaggerated pain and poignancy*] Oh, Miss Julie! You don't know! A dog can lie on the sofa with its mistress; a horse can have its nose stroked by the hand of a countess; but a servant—! [*Changing his tone*] Of course, now and then you meet somebody with guts enough to work his way up in the world, but how often?—Anyway, you know what I did afterwards? I threw myself into the millstream with all my clothes on. Got fished out and spanked. But the following Sunday, when Pa and everybody else in the house went to visit Grandma, I arranged things so I'd be left behind. Then I washed myself all over with soap and warm water, put on my best clothes, and went off to church—just to see you there once more. I saw you, and then I went home determined to die. But I wanted to die beautifully and comfortably, without pain. I remembered that it was fatal to sleep under an alder bush. And we had a big one that had just blossomed out. I stripped it of every leaf and blossom it had and made a bed of them in a bin of oats. Have you ever noticed how smooth oats are? As smooth to the touch as human skin. . . . So I pulled the lid of the bin shut and closed my eyes—fell asleep. And when they woke me I was really very sick. But I didn't die, as you can see.—— What was I trying to prove? I don't know. There was no hope of winning you. But you were a symbol of the absolute hopelessness of my ever getting out of the circle I was born in.

MISS JULIE.   You know, you have a real gift for telling stories. Did you go to school?

JEAN.   A little. But I've read a lot of novels and gone to the theater. And I've also listened to educated people talk. That's how I've learned the most.

MISS JULIE.   You mean to tell me you stand around listening to what we're saying!

JEAN.   Certainly! And I've heard an awful lot, I can tell you—sitting on the coachman's seat or rowing the boat. One time I heard you and a girl friend talking——

MISS JULIE.   Really? . . . And just what did you hear?

JEAN.   Well, now, I don't know if I could repeat it. I can tell you I was a little amazed. I couldn't imagine where you had learned such words. Maybe at bottom there isn't such a big difference as you might think, between people and people.

MISS JULIE.   How vulgar! At least people in my class don't behave like you when we're engaged.

JEAN.   [*Looking her in the eye*] Are you sure?—Come on now, it's no use playing the innocent with me.

MISS JULIE.   He was a beast. The man I offered my love was a beast.

JEAN.   That's what you all say—afterwards.

MISS JULIE.   All?

JEAN. I'd say so, since I've heard the same expression used several time before in similar circumstances.

MISS JULIE. What kind of circumstances?

JEAN. The kind we're talking about. I remember the last time I—

MISS JULIE. [*Rising*] That's enough! I don't want to hear any more.

JEAN. How strange! Neither did she! . . . Well, now if you'll excuse me, I'll go to bed.

MISS JULIE. [*Softly*] Go to bed on Midsummer Eve? [6]

JEAN. That's right. Dancing with that crowd up there really doesn't amuse me.

MISS JULIE. Jean, get the key to the boathouse and row me out on the lake. I want to see the sun come up.

JEAN. Do you think that's wise?

MISS JULIE. You sound as if you were worried about your reputation.

JEAN. Why not? I don't particularly care to be made ridiculous, or to be kicked out without a recommendation just when I'm trying to establish myself. Besides, I have a certain obligation to Christine.

MISS JULIE. Oh, I see. It's Christine now.

JEAN. Yes, but I'm thinking of you, too. Take my advice, Miss Julie, and go up to your room.

MISS JULIE. When did you start giving me orders?

JEAN. Just this once. For your own sake! Please! It's very late. You're so tired, you're drunk. You don't know what you're doing. Go to bed, Miss Julie.—— Besides, if my ears aren't deceiving me, they're coming this way, looking for me. If they find us here together, you're done for!

[THE CHORUS *is heard coming nearer, singing*]

> Two ladies came from out the clover,
> Tri-di-ri-di-ralla, tri-di-ri-di-ra.
> And one of them was green all over,
> Tri-di-ri-di-ralla-la.
> They told us they had gold aplenty,
> Tri-di-ri-di-ralla, tri-di-ri-di-ra.
> But neither of them owned a penny.
> Tri-di-ri-di-ralla-la.
> This wreath for you I may be plaiting,
> Tri-di-ri-di-ralla, tri-di-ri-di-ra.
> But it's for another I am waiting,
> Tri-di-ri-ralla-la!

MISS JULIE. I know these people. I love them just as they love me. Let them come. You'll find out.

JEAN. No, Miss Julie, they don't love you! They take the food you give them, but they spit on it as soon as your back is turned. Believe me! Just listen to them. Listen to what they're singing.——No, you'd better not listen.

MISS JULIE. [*Listening*] What are they singing?

JEAN. A dirty song—about you and me!

[6] A festive occasion, especially in northern lands. It is a festival ultimately of pagan origin which still retains some of its original license.

MISS JULIE. How disgusting! Oh, what cowardly, sneaking—

JEAN. That's what the mob always is—cowards! You can't fight them; you can only run away.

MISS JULIE. Run away? Where? There's no way out of here. And we can't go in to Christine.

JEAN. What about my room? What do you say? The rules don't count in a situation like this. You can trust me. I'm your friend, remember? Your true, devoted, and respectful friend.

MISS JULIE. But suppose—suppose they looked for you there?

JEAN. I'll bolt the door. If they try to break it down, I'll shoot. Come, Miss Julie! [*On his knees*] Please, Miss Julie!

MISS JULIE. [*Meaningfully*] You promise me that you—?

JEAN. I swear to you!

[MISS JULIE *goes out quickly to the right.* JEAN *follows her impetuously*]

[THE BALLET. *The country people enter in festive costumes, with flowers in their hats. The fiddler is in the lead. A keg of small beer and a little keg of liquor, decorated with greenery, are set up on the table. Glasses are brought out. They all drink, after which they form a circle and sing and dance the round dance, "Two ladies came from out the clover." At the end of the dance they all leave singing*]

[MISS JULIE *comes in alone; looks at the devastated kitchen; clasps her hands together; then takes out a powder puff and powders her face.* JEAN *enters. He is in high spirits*]

JEAN. You see! You heard them, didn't you? You've got to admit it's impossible to stay here.

MISS JULIE. No, I don't. But even if I did, what could we do?

JEAN. Go away, travel, get away from here!

MISS JULIE. Travel? Yes—but where?

JEAN. Switzerland, the Italian lakes. You've never been there?

MISS JULIE. No. Is it beautiful?

JEAN. Eternal summer, oranges, laurel trees, ah . . . !

MISS JULIE. But what are we going to do there?

JEAN. I'll set up a hotel—a first-class hotel with a first-class clientele.

MISS JULIE. Hotel?

JEAN. I tell you that's the life! Always new faces, new languages. Not a minute to think about yourself or worry about your nerves. No looking for something to do. The work keeps you busy. Day and night the bells ring, the trains whistle, the busses come and go. And all the while the money comes rolling in. I tell you it's the life!

MISS JULIE. Yes, that's the life. But what about me?

JEAN. The mistress of the whole place, the star of the establishment! With your looks—and your personality—it can't fail. It's perfect! You'll sit in the office like a queen, setting your slaves in motion by pressing an electric button. The guests will file before your throne and timidly lay their treasures on your table. You can't imagine how people tremble when you shove a bill in their face! I'll salt the bills and you'll sugar them with your prettiest smile. Come on, let's get away from here—[*He takes a timetable from his pocket*] —right away—the next train! We'll be in Malmo at 6:30; Hamburg 8:40 in the morning; Frankfurt to Basle in one day; and to Como[7] by way of the Gotthard tunnel in—let me see—three days! Three days!

MISS JULIE.   You make it sound so wonderful. But, Jean, you have to give me strength. Tell me you love me. Come and put your arms around me.

JEAN.   [*Hesitates*] I want to . . . but I don't dare. Not any more, not in this house. I do love you—without a shadow of a doubt. How can you doubt that, Miss Julie?

MISS JULIE.   [*Shyly, very becomingly*] You don't have to be formal with me, Jean. You can call me Julie. There aren't any barriers between us now. Call me Julie.

JEAN.   [*Agonized*] I can't! There are still barriers between us, Miss Julie, as long as we stay in this house! There's the past, there's the Count. I've never met anyone I feel so much respect for. I've only got to see his gloves lying on a table and I shrivel up. I only have to hear that bell ring and I shy like a frightened horse. I only have to look at his boots standing there so stiff and proud and I feel my spine bending. [*He kicks the boots*] Superstitions, prejudices that they've drilled into us since we were children! But they can be forgotten just as easily! Just we get to another country where they have a republic! They'll crawl on their hands and knees when they see my uniform. On their hands and knees, I tell you! But not me! Oh, no. I'm not made for crawling. I've got guts, backbone. And once I grab that first branch, you just watch me climb. I may be a valet now, but next year I'll be owning property; in ten years, I'll be living off my investments. Then I'll go to Rumania, get myself some decorations, and maybe—notice I only say maybe —end up as a count!

MISS JULIE.   How wonderful, wonderful.

JEAN.   Listen, in Rumania you can buy titles. You'll be a countess after all. *My* countess.

MISS JULIE.   But I'm not interested in that. I'm leaving all that behind. Tell me you love me, Jean, or else—or else what difference does it make what I am?

JEAN.   I'll tell you a thousand times—but later! Not now. And not here. Above all, let's keep our feelings out of this or we'll make a mess of everything. We have to look at this thing calmly and coolly, like sensible people. [*He takes out a cigar, clips the end, and lights it*] Now you sit there and I'll sit here, and we'll talk as if nothing had happened.

MISS JULIE.   [*In anguish*] My God, what are you? Don't you have any feelings?

JEAN.   Feelings? Nobody's got more feelings than I have. But I've learned how to control them.

MISS JULIE.   A few minutes ago you were kissing my shoe—and now—!

JEAN.   [*Harshly*] That was a few minutes ago. We've got other things to think about now!

MISS JULIE.   Don't speak to me like that, Jean!

JEAN.   I'm just trying to be sensible. We've been stupid once; let's not be stupid again. Your father might be back at any moment, and we've got to decide our future before then.—Now what do you think about my plans? Do you approve or don't you?

[7] In northern Italy.

MISS JULIE.   I don't see anything wrong with them. Except one thing. For a big
undertaking like that, you'd need a lot of capital. Have you got it?

JEAN.   [*Chewing on his cigar*] Have I got it? Of course I have. I've got my
knowledge of the business, my vast experience, my familiarity with languages. That's capital that counts for something, let me tell you.

MISS JULIE.   You can't even buy the railway tickets with it.

JEAN.   That's true. That's why I need a backer—someone to put up the money.

MISS JULIE.   Where can you find him on a moment's notice?

JEAN.   You'll find him—if you want to be my partner.

MISS JULIE.   I can't. And I don't have a penny to my name.

[*Pause*]

JEAN.   Then you can forget the whole thing.

MISS JULIE.   Forget—?

JEAN.   And things will stay just the way they are.

MISS JULIE.   Do you think I'm going to live under the same roof with you, as
your mistress? Do you think I'm going to have people sneering at me behind
my back? How do you think I'll ever be able to look my father in the face
after this? No, no! Take me away from here, Jean—the shame, the humiliation. . . . What have I done? Oh, my God, my God! What have I done?
[*She bursts into tears*]

JEAN.   Now don't start singing that tune. It won't work. What have you done
that's so awful? You're not the first.

MISS JULIE.   [*Crying hysterically*] Now you despise me!—I'm falling, I'm
falling!

JEAN.   Fall down to me, and I'll lift you up again!

MISS JULIE.   What awful hold did you have over me? What drove me to you?
The weak to the strong? The falling to the rising! Or maybe it was love?
Love? This? You don't know what love is!

JEAN.   Want to bet? Did you think I was a virgin?

MISS JULIE.   You're vulgar! The things you say, the things you think!

JEAN.   That's the way I was brought up and that's the way I am! Now don't
get hysterical and don't play the fine lady with me. We're eating off the
same platter now. . . . That's better. Come over here and be a good girl and
I'll treat you to something special. [*He opens the table drawer and takes out
the wine bottle. He pours the wine into two used glasses*]

MISS JULIE.   Where did you get that wine?

JEAN.   From the wine cellar.

MISS JULIE.   My father's burgundy!

JEAN.   Should be good enough for his son-in-law.

MISS JULIE.   I was drinking beer and you—!

JEAN.   That shows that I have better taste than you.

MISS JULIE.   Thief!

JEAN.   You going to squeal on me?

MISS JULIE.   Oh, God! Partner in crime with a petty house thief! I must have
been drunk; I must have been walking in my sleep. Midsummer Night!
Night of innocent games—

JEAN.   Yes, very innocent!

MISS JULIE. [*Pacing up and down*] Is there anyone here on earth as miserable as I am?

JEAN. Why be miserable? After such a conquest! Think of poor Christine in there. Don't you think she's got any feelings?

MISS JULIE. I thought so a while ago, but I don't now. A servant's a servant—

JEAN. And a whore's a whore!

MISS JULIE. [*Falls to her knees and clasps her hands together*] Oh, God in heaven, put an end to my worthless life! Lift me out of this awful filth I'm sinking in! Save me! Save me!

JEAN. I feel sorry for you, I have to admit it. When I was lying in the onion beds, looking up at you on the rose terrace, I—I'm telling you the truth now —I had the same dirty thoughts that all boys have.

MISS JULIE. And you said you wanted to die for me!

JEAN. In the oat bin? That was only a story.

MISS JULIE. A lie, you mean.

JEAN. [*Beginning to get sleepy*] Practically. I think I read it in a paper about a chimney sweep who curled up in a wood-bin with some lilacs because they were going to arrest him for nonsupport of his child.

MISS JULIE. Now I see you for what you are.

JEAN. What did you expect me to do? It's always the fancy talk that gets the women.

MISS JULIE. You dog!

JEAN. You bitch!

MISS JULIE. Well, now you've seen the eagle's back—

JEAN. Wasn't exactly its back—!

MISS JULIE. I was going to be your first branch—!

JEAN. A rotten branch—

MISS JULIE. I was going to be the window dressing for your hotel—!

JEAN. And I the hotel—!

MISS JULIE. Sitting at the desk, attracting your customers, padding your bills—!

JEAN. I could manage that myself—!

MISS JULIE. How can a human soul be so dirty and filthy?

JEAN. Then why don't you clean it up?

MISS JULIE. You lackey! You shoeshine boy! Stand up when I talk to you!

JEAN. You lackey lover! You bootblack's tramp! Shut your mouth and get out of here! Who do you think you are telling me I'm coarse? I've never seen anybody in my class behave as crudely as you did tonight. Have you ever seen any of the girls around here grab at a man like you did? Do you think any of the girls of my class would throw themselves at a man like that? I've never seen the like of it except in animals and prostitutes!

MISS JULIE. [*Crushed*] That's right! Hit me! Walk all over me! It's all I deserve. I'm rotten. But help me! Help me to get out of this—if there is any way out for me!

JEAN. [*Less harsh*] I'd be doing myself an injustice if I didn't admit that part of the credit for this seduction belongs to me. But do you think a person in my position would have dared to look twice at you if you hadn't asked for it? I'm still amazed—

MISS JULIE.   And still proud.

JEAN.   Why not? But I've got to confess the victory was a little too easy to give me any real thrill.

MISS JULIE.   Go on, hit me more!

JEAN.   [*Standing up*] No. . . . I'm sorry for what I said. I never hit a person who's down, especially a woman. I can't deny that, in one way, it was good to find out that what I saw glittering up above was only fool's gold, to have seen that the eagle's back was as gray as its belly, that the smooth cheek was just powder, and that there could be dirt under the manicured nails, that the handkerchief was soiled even though it smelled of perfume. But, in another way, it hurt me to find that everything I was striving for wasn't very high above me after all, wasn't even real. It hurts me to see you sink far lower than your own cook. Hurts, like seeing the last flowers cut to pieces by the autumn rains and turned to muck.

MISS JULIE.   You talk as if you already stood high above me.

JEAN.   Well, don't I? Don't forget I could make you a countess but you can never make me a count.

MISS JULIE.   But I have a father for a count. You can never have that!

JEAN.   True. But I might father my own counts—that is, if—

MISS JULIE.   You're a thief! I'm not!

JEAN.   There are worse things than being a thief. A lot worse. And besides, when I take a position in a house, I consider myself a member of the family —in a way, like a child in the house. It's no crime for a child to steal a few ripe cherries when they're falling off the trees, is it? [*He begins to feel passionate again*] Miss Julie, you're a beautiful woman, much too good for the likes of me. You got carried away by your emotions and now you want to cover up your mistake by telling yourself that you love me. You don't love me. You might possibly have been attracted by my looks—in which case your kind of love is no better than mine. But I could never be satisfied to be just an animal for you, and I could never make you love me.

MISS JULIE.   Are you so sure of that?

JEAN.   You mean there's a chance? I could love you, there's no doubt about that. You're beautiful, you're refined—[*He goes up to her and takes her hand*]—educated, lovable when you want to be, and once you set a man's heart on fire, I'll bet it burns forever. [*He puts his arm around her waist*] You're like hot wine with strong spices. One of your kisses is enough to— [*He attempts to lead her out, but she rather reluctantly breaks away from him*]

MISS JULIE.   Let me go. You don't get me that way.

JEAN.   Then how? Not by petting you and not with pretty words, not by planning for the future, not by saving you from humiliation! Then how, tell me how?

MISS JULIE.   How? How? I don't know how! I don't know at all!—I hate you like I hate rats, but I can't get away from you.

JEAN.   Then come away *with* me!

MISS JULIE.   [*Pulling herself together*] Away? Yes, we'll go away!——But I'm so tired. Pour me a glass of wine, will you? [JEAN *pours the wine.* MISS

JULIE *looks at her watch*] Let's talk first. We still have a little time. [*She empties the glass of wine and holds it out for more*]

JEAN. Don't overdo it. You'll get drunk.

MISS JULIE. What difference does it make?

JEAN. What difference? It looks cheap.——What did you want to say to me?

MISS JULIE. We're going to run away together, right? But we'll talk first—that is, I'll talk. So far you've done all the talking. You've told me your life, now I'll tell you mine. That way we'll know each other through and through before we become traveling companions.

JEAN. Wait a minute. Excuse me, but are you sure you won't regret this afterwards, when you've surrendered your secrets?

MISS JULIE. I thought you were my friend.

JEAN. I am—sometimes. But don't count on me.

MISS JULIE. You don't mean that. Anyway, everybody knows my secrets.—My mother's parents were very ordinary people, just commoners. She was brought up, according to the theories of her time, to believe in equality, the independence of women, and all that. And she had a strong aversion to marriage. When my father proposed to her, she swore she would never become his wife. . . . But she did anyway. I was born—against my mother's wishes, as far as I can make out. My mother decided to bring me up as a nature child. And on top of that I had to learn everything a boy learns, so I could be living proof that women were just as good as men. I had to wear boy's clothes, learn to handle horses—but not to milk the cows. I was made to groom the horses and handle them, and go out hunting—and even had to try and learn farming! And on the estate all the men were set to doing the work of women, and the women to doing men's work—with the result that the whole place threatened to fall to pieces, and we became the local laughing-stock. Finally my father must have come out of his trance. He rebelled, and everything was changed according to his wishes. Then my mother got sick. I don't know what kind of sickness it was, but she often had convulsions, and she would hide herself in the attic or in the garden, and sometimes she would stay out all night. Then there occurred that big fire you've heard about. The house, the stables, the cowsheds, all burned down—and under very peculiar circumstances that led one to suspect arson. You see, the accident occurred the day after the insurance expired, and the premiums on the new policy, which my father had sent in, were delayed through the messenger's carelessness, and didn't arrive on time. [*She refills her glass and drinks*]

JEAN. You've had enough.

MISS JULIE. Who cares!——We were left without a penny to our name. We had to sleep in the carriages. My father didn't know where to turn for money to rebuild the house. Then Mother suggested to him that he might try to borrow money from an old friend of hers, who owned a brick factory, not far from here. Father takes out a loan, but there's no interest charged, which surprises him. So the place was rebuilt. [*She drinks some more*] Do you know who set fire to the place?

JEAN. Your honorable mother!

MISS JULIE.   Do you know who the brick manufacturer was?

JEAN.   Your mother's lover?

MISS JULIE.   Do you know whose money it was?

JEAN.   Let me think a minute. . . . No, I give up.

MISS JULIE.   It was my mother's!

JEAN.   The Count's, you mean. Or was there a marriage settlement?

MISS JULIE.   There wasn't a settlement. My mother had a little money of her own which she didn't want under my father's control, so she invested it with her—friend.

JEAN.   Who grabbed it!

MISS JULIE.   Precisely. He appropriated it. Well, my father finds out what happened. But he can't go to court, can't pay his wife's lover, can't prove that it's his wife's money. That was how my mother got her revenge because he had taken control of the house. He was on the verge of shooting himself. There was even a rumor that he tried and failed. But he took a new lease on life and he forced my mother to pay for her mistakes. Can you imagine what those five years were like for me? I felt sorry for my father, but I took my mother's side because I didn't know the whole story. She had taught me to distrust and hate all men—you've heard how she hated men—and I swore to her that I'd never be slave to any man.

JEAN.   But you got engaged to the attorney.

MISS JULIE.   Only to make him slave to me.

JEAN.   But he didn't want any of that?

MISS JULIE.   Oh, he wanted to well enough, but I didn't give him the chance. I got bored with him.

JEAN.   Yes, so I noticed—in the barnyard.

MISS JULIE.   What did you notice?

JEAN.   I saw what I saw. *He* broke off the engagement.

MISS JULIE.   That's a lie! It was I who broke it off. Did he tell you that? He's beneath contempt!

JEAN.   Come on now, he isn't as bad as that. So you hate men, Miss Julie?

MISS JULIE.   Yes, I do. . . . Most of the time. But sometimes, when I can't help myself—oh. . . . [*She shudders in disgust*]

JEAN.   Then you hate me, too?

MISS JULIE.   You have no idea how much! I'd like to see you killed like an animal—

JEAN.   Like a mad dog, without a moment's hesitation, right?

MISS JULIE.   Right!

JEAN.   But we don't have anything to shoot him with—and no dog! What are we going to do?

MISS JULIE.   Go away from here.

JEAN.   To torture ourselves to death?

MISS JULIE.   No. To enjoy ourselves for a day or two, or a week, for as long as we can—and then—to die—

JEAN.   Die? How stupid! I've got a better idea: start a hotel!

MISS JULIE.   [*Continuing without hearing* JEAN]—on the shores of Lake Como, where the sun is always shining, where the laurels bloom at Christmas, and the golden oranges glow on the trees.

JEAN. Lake Como is a stinking hole, and the only oranges I saw there were on the fruit stands. But it's a good tourist spot with a lot of villas and cottages that are rented out to lovers. Now there's a profitable business. You know why? They rent the villa for the whole season, but they leave after three weeks.

MISS JULIE. [*Innocently*] Why after only three weeks?

JEAN. Because they can't stand each other any longer. Why else? But they still have to pay the rent. Then you rent it out again to another couple, and so on. There's no shortage of love—even if it doesn't last very long.

MISS JULIE. Then you don't want to die with me?

JEAN. I don't want to die at all! I enjoy life too much. And moreover, I consider taking your own life a sin against the Providence that gave us life.

MISS JULIE. You believe in God? You?

JEAN. Yes, certainly I do! I go to church every other Sunday.—Honestly, I've had enough of this talk. I'm going to bed.

MISS JULIE. Really? You think you're going to get off that easy? Don't you know that a man owes something to the woman he's dishonored?

JEAN. [*Takes out his purse and throws a silver coin on the table*] There you are. I don't want to owe anybody anything.

MISS JULIE. [*Ignoring the insult*] Do you know what the law says—?

JEAN. Aren't you lucky the law says nothing about the women who seduce men!

MISS JULIE. What else can we do but go away from here, get married, and get divorced?

JEAN. Suppose I refuse to enter into this *mésalliance?* [8]

MISS JULIE. *Mésalliance?*

JEAN. For me! I've got better ancestors than you. I don't have any female arsonist in my family.

MISS JULIE. How can you know?

JEAN. You can't prove the opposite because we don't have any family records —except in the police courts. But I've read the whole history of your family in that book on the drawing-room table. Do you know who the founder of your family line was? A miller—who let his wife sleep with the king one night during the Danish war. I don't have any ancestors like that. I don't have any ancestors at all! But I can become an ancestor myself.

MISS JULIE. This is what I get for baring my heart and soul to someone too low to understand, for sacrificing the honor of my family—

JEAN. Dishonor!—I warned you, remember? Drinking makes one talk, and talking's bad.

MISS JULIE. Oh, how sorry I am! . . . If only it had never happened! . . . If only you at least loved me!

JEAN. For the last time—What do you expect of me? Do you want me to cry? Jump over your whip? Kiss you? Do you want me to lure you to Lake Como for three weeks and then—? What am I supposed to do? What do you want? I've had more than I can take. This is what I get for involving myself with women. . . . Miss Julie, I can see that you're unhappy; I know that you're

---

[8] Misalliance.

suffering; but I simply cannot understand you. My people don't behave like this. We don't hate each other. We make love for the fun of it, when we can get any time off from our work. But we don't have time for it all day and all night like you do. If you ask me, you're sick, Miss Julie. I'm sure that's it, Miss Julie.

MISS JULIE.   You can be understanding, Jean. You're talking to me like a human being now.

JEAN.   Well, be human yourself. You spit on me but you don't let me wipe it off—on you!

MISS JULIE.   Help me, Jean. Help me. Tell me what I should do, that's all—which way to go.

JEAN.   For Christ's sake, if only I knew myself!

MISS JULIE.   I've been crazy—I've been out of my mind—but does that mean there's no way out for me?

JEAN.   Stay here as if nothing had happened. Nobody knows anything.

MISS JULIE.   Impossible! Everybody who works here knows. Christine knows.

JEAN.   They don't know a thing. And anyhow they'd never believe it.

MISS JULIE.   [*Slowly, significantly*] But . . . it might happen again.

JEAN.   That's true!

MISS JULIE.   And there might be consequences.

JEAN.   [*Stunned*] Consequences!! What on earth have I been thinking of! You're right! There's only one thing to do: get away from here! Immediately! I can't go with you—that would give the whole game away. You'll have to go by yourself. Somewhere—I don't care where!

MISS JULIE.   By myself? Where?—Oh, no, Jean, I can't. I can't!

JEAN.   You've got to! Before the Count comes back. You know as well as I do what will happen if you stay here. After one mistake, you figure you might as well go on, since the damage is already done. Then you get more and more careless until—finally you're exposed. I tell you, you've got to get out of the country. Afterwards you can write to the Count and tell him everything—leaving me out, of course. He'd never be able to guess it was me. Anyway, I don't think he'd exactly like to find that out.

MISS JULIE.   I'll go—if you'll come with me!

JEAN.   Lady, are you out of your mind!? "Miss Julie elopes with her footman." The day after tomorrow it would be in all the papers. The Count would never live it down.

MISS JULIE.   I can't go away. I can't stay. Help me. I'm so tired, so awfully tired. . . . Tell me what to do. Order me. Start me going. I can't think any more, can't move any more. . . .

JEAN.   Now do you realize how weak you all are? What gives you the right to go strutting around with your noses in the air as if you owned the world? All right, I'll give you your orders. Go up and get dressed. Get some traveling money. And come back down here.

MISS JULIE.   [*Almost in a whisper*] Come up with me!

JEAN.   To your room? . . . You're going crazy again! [*He hesitates a moment*] No! No! Go! Right now! [*He takes her hand and leads her out*]

MISS JULIE.   [*As she is leaving*] Don't be so harsh, Jean.

JEAN.   Orders always sound harsh. You've never had to take them.

[JEAN, *left alone, heaves a sigh of relief and sits down at the table. He takes out a notebook and a pencil and begins to calculate, counting aloud now and then. The pantomime continues until* CHRISTINE *enters, dressed for church, and carrying* JEAN's *white tie and shirt front in her hand*]

CHRISTINE.   Lord in Heaven, what a mess! What on earth have you been doing?

JEAN.   It was Miss Julie. She dragged the whole crowd in here. You must have been sleeping awfully sound if you didn't hear anything.

CHRISTINE.   I slept like a log.

JEAN.   You already dressed for church?

CHRISTINE.   Yes, indeed. Don't you remember you promised to go to Communion with me today?

JEAN.   Oh, yes, of course. I remember. I see you've brought my things. All right. Come on, put it on me. [*He sits down, and* CHRISTINE *starts to put the white tie and shirt front on him. Pause*]

JEAN.   [*Yawning*] What's the lesson for today?

CHRISTINE.   The beheading of John the Baptist, I suppose.

JEAN.   My God, that will go on forever.—Hey, you're choking me! . . . Oh, I'm so sleepy, so sleepy.

CHRISTINE.   What were you doing up all night? You look green in the face.

JEAN.   I've been sitting here talking with Miss Julie.

CHRISTINE.   That girl! She doesn't know how to behave herself!

[*Pause*]

JEAN.   Tell me something, Christine. . . .

CHRISTINE.   Well, what?

JEAN.   Isn't it strange when you think about it? Her, I mean.

CHRISTINE.   What's so strange?

JEAN.   Everything!

[*Pause.* CHRISTINE *looks at the half-empty glasses on the table*]

CHRISTINE.   Have you been drinking with her?

JEAN.   Yes!

CHRISTINE.   Shame on you!—Look me in the eyes! You haven't . . . ?

JEAN.   Yes!

CHRISTINE.   Is it possible? Is it really possible?

JEAN.   [*After a moment's consideration*] Yes. It is.

CHRISTINE.   Oh, how disgusting! I could never have believed anything like this would happen! No. No. This is too much!

JEAN.   Don't tell me you're jealous of her?

CHRISTINE.   No, not of her. If it had been Clara—or Sophie—I would have scratched your eyes out! But her—? That's different. I don't know why. . . . But it's still disgusting!

JEAN.   Then you're mad at her?

CHRISTINE.   No. Mad at you. You were mean and cruel to do a thing like that, very mean. The poor girl! . . . But let me tell you, I'm not going to stay in this house a moment longer, not when I can't have any respect for my employers.

JEAN.   Why do you want to respect them?

CHRISTINE.   Don't try to be smart. You don't want to work for people who behave immorally, do you? Well, do you? If you ask me, you'd be lowering yourself by doing that.

JEAN.   Oh, I don't know. I think it's rather comforting to find out that they're not one bit better than we are.

CHRISTINE.   Well, I don't. If they're not any better, there's no point in us trying to be like them.—And think of the Count. Think of all the sorrows he's been through in his time. No, sir, I won't stay in this house any longer. . . . Imagine! You, of all people! If it had been the attorney fellow; if it had been somebody respectable—

JEAN.   Now just a minute—!

CHRISTINE.   Oh, you're all right in your own way. But there's a big difference between one class and another. You can't deny that.——No, this is something I can never get over. She was so proud, and so sarcastic about men, you'd never believe she'd go and throw herself at one. And at someone like you! And *she* was going to have Diana shot, because the poor thing ran after the gatekeeper's mongrel!—Well, I tell you, I've had enough! I'm not going to stay here any longer. On the twenty-fourth of October, I'm leaving.

JEAN.   Then what'll you do?

CHRISTINE.   Well, since you brought it up, it's about time that you got yourself a decent place, if we're going to get married.

JEAN.   Why should I go looking for another place? I could never get a place like this if I'm married.

CHRISTINE.   Well, of course not! But you could get a job as a doorkeeper, or maybe try to get a government job as a caretaker somewhere. The government don't pay much, but they pay regular. And there's a pension for the wife and children.

JEAN.   [*Wryly*] Fine, fine! But I'm not the kind of fellow who thinks about dying for his wife and children this early in the game. I hate to say it, but I've got slightly bigger plans than that.

CHRISTINE.   Plans! Hah! What about your obligations? You'd better start giving them a little thought!

JEAN.   Don't start nagging me about obligations! I know what I have to do without you telling me. [*He hears a sound upstairs*] Anyhow, we'll have plenty of chance to talk about this later. You just go and get yourself ready, and we'll be off to church.

CHRISTINE.   Who is that walking around up there?

JEAN.   I don't know. Clara, I suppose. Who else?

CHRISTINE.   [*Starting to leave*] It can't be the Count, can it? Could he have come back without anybody hearing him?

JEAN.   [*Frightened*] The Count? No, it can't be. He would have rung.

CHRISTINE.   [*Leaving*] God help us! I've never heard of the like of this.

[*The sun has now risen and strikes the tops of the trees in the park. The light shifts gradually until it is shining very obliquely through the windows. JEAN goes to the door and signals. MISS JULIE enters, dressed for travel, and carrying a small bird cage, covered with a towel. She sets the cage down on a chair*]

MISS JULIE.   I'm ready now.

JEAN.   Shh! Christine's awake.

MISS JULIE.   [*She is extremely tense and nervous during the following*] Did she suspect anything?

JEAN.   She doesn't know a thing.——My God, what happened to you?

MISS JULIE.   What do you mean? Do I look so strange?

JEAN.   You're white as a ghost, and you've—excuse me—but you've got dirt on your face.

MISS JULIE.   Let me wash it off. [*She goes over to the wash basin and washes her face and hands*] There! Do you have a towel? . . . Oh, look the sun's coming up!

JEAN.   That breaks the magic spell!

MISS JULIE.   Yes, we were spellbound last night, weren't we? Midsummer madness . . . Jean, listen to me! Come with me. I've got the money!

JEAN.   [*Suspiciously*] Enough?

MISS JULIE.   Enough for a start. Come with me, Jean. I can't travel alone today. Midsummer Day on a stifling hot train, packed in with crowds of people, all staring at me—stopping at every station when I want to be flying. I can't Jean, I can't! . . . And everything will remind me of the past. Midsummer Day when I was a child and the church was decorated with leaves—birch leaves and lilacs . . . the table spread for dinner with friends and relatives . . . and after dinner, dancing in the park, with flowers and games. Oh, no matter how far you travel, the memories tag right along in the baggage car . . . and the regrets and the remorse.

JEAN.   All right, I'll go with you! But it's got to be now—before it's too late! This very instant!

MISS JULIE.   Hurry and get dressed! [*She picks up the bird cage*]

JEAN.   But no baggage! It would give us away.

MISS JULIE.   Nothing. Only what we can take to our seats.

JEAN.   [*As he gets his hat*] What in the devil have you got there? What is that?

MISS JULIE.   It's only my canary. I can't leave it behind.

JEAN.   A canary! My God, do you expect us to carry a bird cage around with us? You're crazy. Put that cage down!

MISS JULIE.   It's the only thing I'm taking with me from my home—the only living thing who loves me since Diana was unfaithful to me! Don't be cruel, Jean. Let me take it with me.

JEAN.   I told you to put that cage down!——And don't talk so loud. Christine can hear us.

MISS JULIE.   No, I won't leave it with a stranger. I won't. I'd rather have you kill it.

JEAN.   Let me have the little pest, and I'll wring its neck.

MISS JULIE.   Yes, but don't hurt it. Don't——. No, I can't do it!

JEAN.   Don't worry, I can. Give it here.

[MISS JULIE *takes the bird out of the cage and kisses it*]

MISS JULIE.   Oh, my little Serena, must you die and leave your mistress?

JEAN.   You don't have to make a scene of it. It's a question of your whole life and future. You're wasting time! [JEAN *grabs the canary from her, carries it to the chopping block, and picks up a meat cleaver.* MISS JULIE *turns away*] You should have learned how to kill chickens instead of shooting revolvers—[*He brings the cleaver down*]—then a drop of blood wouldn't make you faint.

MISS JULIE. [*Screaming*] Kill me too! Kill me! You can kill an innocent creature without turning a hair—then kill me. Oh, how I hate you! I loathe you! There's blood between us. I curse the moment I first laid eyes on you! I curse the moment I was conceived in my mother's womb.

JEAN. What good does your cursing do? Let's get out of here!

MISS JULIE. [*Approaches the chopping block as if drawn to it against her will*] No, I don't want to go yet. I can't.—I have to see.—Shh! I hear a carriage coming! [*She listens but keeps her eyes fastened on the chopping block and cleaver*] You don't think I can stand the sight of blood, do you? You think I'm so weak! Oh, I'd love to see your blood and your brains on that chopping block. I'd love to see the whole of your sex swimming in a sea of blood just like that. I think I could drink out of your skull. I'd like to bathe my feet in your ribs! I could eat your heart roasted whole!——You think I'm weak! You think I loved you because my womb hungered for your seed. You think I want to carry your brood under my heart and nourish it with my blood! Bear your child and take your name!—Come to think of it, what is your name anyway? I've never heard your last name. You probably don't even have one. I'd be Mrs. Doorkeeper or Madame Floorsweeper. You dog with my name on your collar—you lackey with my initials on your buttons! Do you think I'm going to share you with my cook and fight over you with my maid?! Ohhh!—You think I'm a coward who wants to run away. No, I'm going to stay. Come hell or high water, I don't care! My father comes home—finds his bureau broken into—his money gone. Then he rings—on that bell—two rings for the valet. And then he sends for the sheriff—and I tell him everything. Everything! Oh, it'll be wonderful to have it all over . . . If only it will be over. . . . He'll have a stroke and die. Then there'll be an end to all of us. There'll be peace . . . and quiet . . . forever. . . . His coat of arms will be broken on the coffin; the Count's line dies out. But the valet's line will continue in an orphanage, win triumphs in the gutter, and end in jail! [9]

[CHRISTINE *enters, dressed for church and with a hymn-book in her hand.* MISS JULIE *rushes over to her and throws herself into her arms as if seeking protection*]

MISS JULIE. Help me, Christine! Help me against this man!

CHRISTINE. [*Cold and unmoved*] This is a fine way to behave on a holy day! [*She sees the chopping block*] Just look at the mess you've made there! How do you explain that? And what's all this shouting and screaming about?

MISS JULIE. Christine, you're a woman, you're my friend! I warn you, watch out for this—this monster!

JEAN. [*Ill at ease and a little embarrassed*] If you ladies are going to talk, I think I'll go and shave. [*He slips out to the right*]

MISS JULIE. You've got to understand, Christine! You've got to listen to me!

---

[9] Most editions of *Miss Julie* have a speech by Jean at this point: "Now there speaks the royal blood! Brava, Miss Julie. Only you mustn't let the cat out of the bag about the miller and his wife." Strindberg wanted this speech expunged as not in keeping with Jean's character [Professor Sprinchorn's note].

CHRISTINE.   No, I don't. I don't understand this kind of shenanigans at all. Where do you think you're going dressed like that? And Jean with his hat on?—Well?—Well?

MISS JULIE.   Listen to me, Christine! If you'll just listen to me, I'll tell you everything.

CHRISTINE.   I don't want to know anything.

MISS JULIE.   You've got to listen to me—!

CHRISTINE.   What about? About your stupid behavior with Jean? I tell you that doesn't bother me at all, because it's none of my business. But if you have any silly idea about talking him into skipping out with you, I'll soon put a stop to that.

MISS JULIE.   [*Extremely tense*] Christine, please don't get upset. Listen to me. I can't stay here, and Jean can't stay here. So you see, we have to go away.

CHRISTINE.   Hm, hm, hm.

MISS JULIE.   [*Suddenly brightening up*] Wait! I've got an idea! Why couldn't all three of us go away together?—out of the country—to Switzerland—and start a hotel. I've got the money, you see. Jean and I would be responsible for the whole affair—and Christine, you could run the kitchen, I thought. Doesn't that sound wonderful! Say yes! Say you'll come, Christine, then everything will be settled. Say you will! Please! [*She throws her arms around* CHRISTINE *and pats her*]

CHRISTINE.   [*Remaining aloof and unmoved*] Hm. Hm.

MISS JULIE.   [*Presto tempo*] You've never been traveling, Christine. You have to get out and see the world. You can't imagine how wonderful it is to travel by train—constantly new faces—new countries. We'll go to Hamburg, and stop over to look at the zoo—you'll love that. And we'll go to the theater and the opera. And then when we get to Munich, we'll go to the museums, Christine. They have Rubenses and Raphaels there—those great painters, you know. Of course you've heard about Munich where King Ludwig lived— you know, the king who went mad. And then we can go and see his castles —they're built just like the ones you read about in fairy tales. And from there it's just a short trip to Switzerland—with the Alps. Think of the Alps, Christine, covered with snow in the middle of summer. And oranges grow there, and laurel trees that are green the whole year round.—[JEAN *can be seen in the wings at the right, sharpening his straight razor on a strap held between his teeth and his left hand. He listens to* MISS JULIE *with a satisfied expression on his face, now and then nodding approvingly.* MISS JULIE *continues tempo prestissimo*]—And that's where we'll get a hotel. I'll sit at the desk while Jean stands at the door and receives the guests, goes out shopping, writes the letters. What a life that will be! The train whistle blowing, then the bus arriving, then a bell ringing upstairs, then the bell in the restaurant rings—and I'll be making out the bills—and I know just how much to salt them—you can't imagine how timid tourists are when you shove a bill in their face!—And you, Christine, you'll run the whole kitchen —there'll be no standing at the stove for you—of course not. If you're going to talk to the people, you'll have to dress neatly and elegantly. And with your looks—I'm not trying to flatter you, Christine—you'll run off with some man one fine day—a rich Englishman, that's who it'll be, they're so easy to—[*slowing down*]—to catch.—Then we'll all be rich.—We'll build a villa on Lake Como.—Maybe it does rain there sometimes, but— [*more and more lifelessly*]—the sun has to shine sometimes, too—even if it looks cloudy.—And—then . . . Or else we can always travel some more— and come back . . . [*pause*]—here . . . or somewhere else. . . .

CHRISTINE. Do you really believe a word of that yourself, Miss Julie?

MISS JULIE. [*Completely beaten*] Do I believe a word of it myself?

CHRISTINE. Do you?

MISS JULIE. [*Exhausted*] I don't know. I don't believe anything any more. [*She sinks down on the bench and lays her head between her arms on the table*] Nothing. Nothing at all.

CHRISTINE. [*Turns to the right and faces* JEAN] So! You were planning to run away, were you?

JEAN. [*Nonplused, lays his razor down on the table*] We weren't exactly going to run away! Don't exaggerate. You heard Miss Julie's plans. Even if she's tired now after being up all night, her plans are perfectly practical.

CHRISTINE. Well, just listen to you! Did you really think you could get me to cook for that little—

JEAN. [*Sharply*] You keep a respectful tongue in your mouth when you talk to your mistress! Understand?

CHRISTINE. Mistress!

JEAN. Yes, mistress!

CHRISTINE. Well of all the—! I don't have to listen—

JEAN. Yes, you do! You need to listen more and talk less. Miss Julie is your mistress. Don't forget that! And if you're going to despise her for what she did, you ought to despise yourself for the same reason.

CHRISTINE. I've always held myself high enough to—

JEAN. High enough to make you look down on others!

CHRISTINE. —enough to keep from lowering myself beneath my position. No one can say that the Count's cook has ever had anything to do with the stable groom or the swineherd. No one can say that!

JEAN. Yes, aren't you lucky you got involved with a decent man!

CHRISTINE. What kind of a decent man is it who sells the oats from the Count's stables?

JEAN. Listen to who's talking! You get a commission on the groceries and take bribes from the butcher!

CHRISTINE. How can you say a thing like that!

JEAN. And you tell me you can't respect your employers any more! You! You!

CHRISTINE. Are you going to church or aren't you? I should think you'd need a good sermon after your exploits.

JEAN. No, I'm not going to church! You can go alone and confess your own sins.

CHRISTINE. Yes, I'll do just that. And I'll come back with enough forgiveness to cover yours, too. Our Redeemer suffered and died on the cross for all our sins, and if we come to Him in faith and with a penitent heart, He will take all our sins upon Himself.

JEAN. Grocery sins included?

MISS JULIE. Do you really believe that, Christine?

CHRISTINE. With all my heart, as sure as I'm standing here. It was the faith I was born into, and I've held on to it since I was a little girl, Miss Julie. Where sin aboundeth, there grace aboundeth also.

MISS JULIE. If I had your faith, Christine, if only—

CHRISTINE. But you see, that's something you can't have without God's special grace. And it is not granted to everyone to receive it.

MISS JULIE. Then who receives it?

CHRISTINE. That's the secret of the workings of grace, Miss Julie, and God is no respecter of persons. With him the last shall be the first—

MISS JULIE. In that case, he does have respect for the last, doesn't he?

CHRISTINE. [*Continuing*] —and it is easier for a camel to go through the eye of a needle than for a rich man to enter the kingdom of God. That's how things are, Miss Julie. I'm going to leave now—alone. And on my way out I'm going to tell the stable boy not to let any horses out, in case anyone has any ideas about leaving before the Count comes home. Goodbye. [*She leaves*]

JEAN. She's a devil in skirts!—And all because of a canary!

MISS JULIE. [*Listlessly*] Never mind the canary. . . . Do you see any way out of this, any end to it?

JEAN. [*After thinking for a moment*] No.

MISS JULIE. What would you do if you were in my place?

JEAN. In your place? Let me think. . . . An aristocrat, a woman, and— fallen. . . . I don't know.——Or maybe I do.

MISS JULIE. [*Picks up the razor and makes a gesture with it*] Like this?

JEAN. Yes. But *I* wouldn't do it, you understand. That's the difference between us.

MISS JULIE. Because you're a man and I'm a woman? What difference does that make?

JEAN. Just the difference that there is—between a man and a woman.

MISS JULIE. [*Holding the razor in her hand*] I want to! But I can't do it. My father couldn't do it either, that time he should have done it.

JEAN. No, he was right not to do it. He had to get his revenge first.

MISS JULIE. And now my mother is getting her revenge again through me.

JEAN. Haven't you ever loved your father, Miss Julie?

MISS JULIE. Yes, enormously. But I must have hated him too. I must have hated him without knowing it. It was he who brought me up to despise my own sex, to be half woman and half man. Who's to blame for what has happened? My father, my mother, myself? Myself? I don't have a self that's my own. I don't have a single thought I didn't get from my father, not an emotion I didn't get from my mother. And that last idea—about all people being equal—I got that from him, my betrothed. That's why I say he's beneath contempt. How can it be my own fault? Put the blame on Jesus, like Christine does? I'm too proud to do that—and too intelligent, thanks to what my father taught me. . . . A rich man can't get into heaven? That's a lie. But at least Christine, who's got money in the savings bank, won't get in. . . . Who's to blame? What difference does it make who's to blame? I'm still the one who has to bear the guilt, suffer the consequences—

JEAN. Yes, but—

[*The bell rings sharply twice.* MISS JULIE *jumps up.* JEAN *changes his coat*]

JEAN.   The Count's back! What if Christine—? [*He goes to the speaking tube, taps on it, and listens*]

MISS JULIE.   Has he looked in his bureau yet?

JEAN.   This is Jean, sir! [*Listens. The audience cannot hear what the* COUNT *says*] Yes, sir! [*Listens*] Yes, sir! Yes, as soon as I can. [*Listens*] Yes, at once, sir! [*Listens*] Very good, sir! In half an hour.

MISS JULIE.   [*Trembling with anxiety*] What did he say? For God's sake, what did he say?

JEAN.   He ordered his boots and his coffee in half an hour.

MISS JULIE.   Half an hour then! . . . Oh, I'm so tired. I can't bring myself to do anything. Can't repent, can't run away, can't stay, can't live . . . can't die. Help me, Jean. Command me, and I'll obey like a dog. Do me this last favor. Save my honor, save his name. You know what I ought to do but can't force myself to do. Let me use your will power. You command me and I'll obey.

JEAN.   I don't know—I can't either, not now. I don't know why. It's as if this coat made me—. I can't give you orders in this. And now, after the Count has spoken to me, I—I can't really explain it—but—I've got the backbone of a damned lackey! If the Count came down here now and ordered me to cut my throat, I'd do it on the spot.

MISS JULIE.   Pretend that you're him, and that I'm you. You were such a good actor just a while ago, when you were kneeling before me. You were the aristocrat then. Or else—have you ever been to the theater and seen a hypnotist? [JEAN *nods*] He says to his subject, "Take this broom!" and he takes it. He says, "Now sweep!" and he sweeps.

JEAN.   But the person has to be asleep!

MISS JULIE.   [*Ecstatic*] I'm already asleep. The whole room has turned to smoke. You seem like an iron stove, a stove that looks like a man in black with a high hat. Your eyes are glowing like coals when the fire dies out. Your face is a white smudge, like ashes. [*The sun is now shining in on the floor and falls on* JEAN] It's so good and warm— [*She rubs her hands together as if warming them at a fire*] —and so bright—and so peaceful.

JEAN.   [*Takes the razor and puts it in her hand*] There's the broom. Go now, when the sun is up—out into the barn—and— [*He whispers in her ear*]

MISS JULIE.   [*Waking up*] Thanks! I'm going to get my rest. But tell me one thing. Tell me that the first can also receive the gift of grace. Tell me that, even if you don't believe it.

JEAN.   The first? I can't tell you that.——But wait a moment, Miss Julie. I know what I can tell you. You're no longer among the first. You're among —the last.

MISS JULIE.   That's true! I'm among the very last. I am the last!—Oh! Now I can't go! Tell me just once more, tell me to go!

JEAN.   Now I can't either. I can't!

MISS JULIE.   And the first shall be the last. . . .

JEAN.   Don't think—don't think! You're taking all my strength away. You're making me a coward. . . . What! I thought I saw the bell move. No. . . . Let me stuff some paper in it.—Afraid of a bell! But it isn't just a bell. There's somebody behind it. A hand that makes it move. And there's something that makes the hand move.——Stop your ears, that's it, stop your ears! But it only rings louder. Rings louder and louder until you answer it. And then it's too late. Then the sheriff comes—and then—[*There are two sharp rings on the bell.* JEAN *gives a start, then straightens himself up*] It's horrible! But there's no other way for it to end.—Go! [MISS JULIE *walks resolutely out through the door*]

THE END

Hedda Gabler

Henrik Ibsen

Henrik Ibsen

No play in modern times has attracted more great actresses to its leading role than has *Hedda Gabler*. Eleonora Duse, Mrs. Patrick Campbell, Nazimova, Eve Le Gallienne, Joan Greenwood, Claire Bloom—the list reads like a roll call of the great of the last seventy years. The reason is clear: the challenge inherent in the role is enormous. The bewildering complexity of Hedda's character demands the most sensitive reading of her part; even a momentary lapse of insight or of skill can make Hedda out to be a monster—or even ridiculous. But as the dangers in the role are great, so, proportionally, are the rewards. It is only in the most taxing roles that a great actress can give full scope to her powers.

Ibsen wrote *Hedda Gabler* when he was over sixty, still in self-imposed exile from his native Norway. His life had not been a happy one. He was born in Skien in 1828, spent a childhood miserably burdened with poverty, and drudged for years as an apothecary's assistant before he became associated with the theatre. His early dramas were anything but popular, and after a series of frustrating experiences Ibsen determined, with considerable bitterness, to leave Norway (1863). Most of the work which brought him fame (and over which boiled international controversy of incredible proportions) he wrote in Germany and Italy. One after another his fiercely realistic plays on social issues scandalized the intellectual world. *A Doll's House* (1879), *Ghosts* (1881), *An Enemy of the People* (1882)—each in its turn provoked bitter attacks by conservative critics who damned the plays on moral grounds. But in the face of almost unparalleled abuse, Ibsen continued to produce his dramatizations of the plight of the individual in conflict with society. His work was taken up by the "little theatres" of Paris, Berlin, and London, and by individual champions like Bernard Shaw and William Archer; and gradually the enthusiasm of a small group of the intelligentsia for his dramas spread to a wider audience. Before his death in 1906, Ibsen received world-wide acclaim as the founder of a new and vital form of drama. Today he is generally recognized as the most influential playwright of modern times.

The world of Ibsen's plays is a world dominated by the scientific thought of the nineteenth century with its emphasis on massive natural and social forces over which the individual has little or no control. But although Ibsen insistently shows the influence of such forces on the lives of his characters, he is not a narrow determinist; his characters are shaped by their heredity and their environment, but he emphasizes constantly the crucial significance of the individual's moral responsibility. In this play, Hedda is an "emancipated" woman; but in her attempt to free herself from conventions that she despises (and to which, in a sense, she is a slave), she has removed herself from all ties of moral responsibility. Hedda is not the passive tool of social forces. In her irresponsible cultivation of individualism for its own sake, she has rejected humanity; and this is the source of her evil. Ibsen has here transcended the limitations of the play that deals with social problems and has given universal significance to the actions of his characters.

Like most of Ibsen's plays, *Hedda Gabler* is very carefully constructed. The author picks up the lives of his characters as they are approaching a climactic situation and by means of skillfully handled dialogue weaves in, unobtrusively, sufficient background information so that the audience is fully aware of the tensions that have led to the climax. The action of the play is severely limited as to time and place; and, as in the Greek drama, all violent action takes place off stage and is reported. Except for one or two improbabilities (it seems unlikely, for example, that Mrs. Elvsted would be carrying around the notes from which Lövborg's book was written), the play has a beautifully articulated structure.

So completely does the character of Hedda, with all its complexity and ambiguity, dominate the play that the other characters are thrown somewhat in the background. There are subtle touches in the drawing of Tesman and Judge Brack, but they come really to life only in their relationship to Hedda. The dialogue throughout is deceptively naturalistic, flat; but each act ends on a note of extreme emotional tension. To see a great actress in the scene at the end of Act III when Hedda burns Lövborg's manuscript is to experience one of the most intense moments of the modern drama.

Hedda Gabler

Henrik Ibsen

TRANSLATED FROM THE NORWEGIAN BY
EDMUND GOSSE AND WILLIAM ARCHER

CHARACTERS

GEORGE TESMAN
HEDDA TESMAN, *his wife*
MISS JULIANA TESMAN, *his aunt*
MRS. ELVSTED

JUDGE BRACK
EILERT LÖVBORG
BERTA, *servant at the Tesmans'*

The scene of the action is Tesman's villa, in the west end of Christiania.

Act One

A spacious, handsome and tastefully furnished drawing-room, decorated in dark colors. In the back, a wide doorway with curtains drawn back, leading into a smaller room decorated in the same style as the drawing-room. In the right-hand wall of the front room, a folding door leading out to the hall. In the opposite wall, on the left, a glass door, also with curtains drawn back. Through the panes can be seen part of a veranda outside, and trees covered with autumn foliage. An oval table, with a cover on it, and surrounded by chairs, stands well forward. In front, by the wall on the right, a wide stove of dark porcelain, a high-backed arm-chair, a cushioned foot-rest, and two footstools. A settee, with a small round table in front of it, fills the upper right-hand corner. In front, on the left, a little way from the wall, a sofa. Further back than the glass door, a piano. On either side of the doorway at the back a whatnot with terra-cotta and majolica ornaments.—Against the back wall of the inner room a sofa, with a table, and one or two chairs. Over the sofa hangs the portrait of a handsome elderly man in a General's uniform. Over the table a hanging lamp, with an *opal glass shade.—A number of bouquets are arranged about the drawing-room, in vases and glasses. Others lie upon the tables. The floors in both rooms are covered with thick carpets.—Morning light. The sun shines in through the glass door.*

MISS JULIANA TESMAN, *with her bonnet on and carrying a parasol, comes in from the hall, followed by* BERTA, *who carries a bouquet wrapped in paper.* MISS TESMAN *is a comely and pleasant-looking lady of about sixty-five. She is nicely but simply dressed in a gray walking-costume.* BERTA *is a middle-aged woman of plain and rather countrified appearance.*

MISS TESMAN. [*Stops close to the door, listens, and says softly*] Upon my word, I don't believe they are stirring yet!

BERTA. [*Also softly*] I told you so, Miss. Remember how late the steamboat got in last night. And then, when they got home!—good Lord, what a lot the young mistress had to unpack before she could get to bed.

MISS TESMAN. Well, well—let them have their sleep out. But let us see that they get a good breath of the fresh morning air when they do appear. [*She goes to the glass door and throws it open*]

BERTA. [*Beside the table, at a loss what to do with the bouquet in her hand*] I declare there isn't a bit of room left. I think I'll put it down here, Miss. [*She places it on the piano*]

MISS TESMAN. So you've got a new mistress now, my dear Berta. Heaven knows it was a wrench to me to part with you.

BERTA. [*On the point of weeping*] And do you think it wasn't hard for me, too, Miss? After all the blessed years I've been with you and Miss Rina.

MISS TESMAN. We must make the best of it, Berta. There was nothing else to be done. George can't do without you, you see—he absolutely can't. He has had you to look after him ever since he was a little boy.

BERTA. Ah, but, Miss Julia, I can't help thinking of Miss Rina lying helpless at home there, poor thing. And with only that new girl, too! She'll never learn to take proper care of an invalid.

MISS TESMAN. Oh, I shall manage to train her. And, of course, you know I shall take most of it upon myself. You needn't be uneasy about my poor sister, my dear Berta.

BERTA. Well, but there's another thing, Miss. I'm so mortally afraid I shan't be able to suit the young mistress.

MISS TESMAN. Oh, well—just at first there may be one or two things——

BERTA. Most like she'll be terrible grand in her ways.

MISS TESMAN. Well, you can't wonder at that—General Gabler's daughter! Think of the sort of life she was accustomed to in her father's time. Don't you remember how we used to see her riding down the road along with the General? In that long black habit—and with feathers in her hat?

BERTA. Yes, indeed—I remember well enough!—But, good Lord, I should never have dreamt in those days that she and Master George would make a match of it.

MISS TESMAN. Nor I.—But by the by, Berta—while I think of it: in future you mustn't say Master George. You must say Dr. Tesman.

BERTA. Yes, the young mistress spoke of that, too—last night—the moment they set foot in the house. Is it true then, Miss?

MISS TESMAN. Yes, indeed it is. Only think, Berta—some foreign university has made him a doctor—while he has been abroad, you understand. I hadn't heard a word about it, until he told me himself upon the pier.

BERTA. Well, well, he's clever enough for anything, he is. But I didn't think he'd have gone in for doctoring people, too.

MISS TESMAN. No, no, it's not that sort of doctor he is. [*Nods significantly*] But let me tell you, we may have to call him something still grander before long.

BERTA. You don't say so! What can that be, Miss?

MISS TESMAN. [*Smiling*] H'm—wouldn't you like to know! [*With emotion*] Ah, dear, dear—if my poor brother could only look up from his grave now, and see what his little boy has grown into! [*Looks around*] But bless me, Berta—why have you done this? Taken the chintz covers off all the furniture?

BERTA. The mistress told me to. She can't abide covers on the chairs, she says.

MISS TESMAN. Are they going to make this their everyday sitting-room then?

BERTA. Yes, that's what I understood—from the mistress. Master George—the doctor—he said nothing.

[GEORGE TESMAN *comes from the right into the inner room, humming to himself, and carrying an unstrapped empty portmanteau. He is a middle-sized, young-looking man of thirty-three, rather stout, with a round, open, cheerful face, fair hair and beard. He wears spectacles, and is somewhat carelessly dressed in comfortable indoor clothes*]

MISS TESMAN. Good morning, good morning, George.

TESMAN. [*In the doorway between the rooms*] Aunt Julia! Dear Aunt Julia! [*Goes up to her and shakes hands warmly*] Come all this way—so early! Eh?

MISS TESMAN. Why, of course I had to come and see how you were getting on.

TESMAN. In spite of your having had no proper night's rest?

MISS TESMAN. Oh, that makes no difference to me.

TESMAN. Well, I suppose you got home all right from the pier? Eh?

MISS TESMAN. Yes, quite safely, thank goodness. Judge Brack was good enough to see me right to my door.

TESMAN. We were so sorry we couldn't give you a seat in the carriage. But you saw what a pile of boxes Hedda had to bring with her.

MISS TESMAN. Yes, she had certainly plenty of boxes.

BERTA. [*To* TESMAN] Shall I go in and see if there's anything I can do for the mistress?

TESMAN. No thank you, Berta—you needn't. She said she would ring if she wanted anything.

BERTA. [*Going towards the right*] Very well.

TESMAN. But look here—take this portmanteau with you.

BERTA. [*Taking it*] I'll put it in the attic.

[*She goes out by the hall door*]

TESMAN. Fancy, Auntie—I had the whole of that portmanteau chock full of copies of documents. You wouldn't believe how much I have picked up from all the archives I have been examining—curious old details that no one has had any idea of——

MISS TESMAN. Yes, you don't seem to have wasted your time on your wedding trip, George.

TESMAN. No, that I haven't. But do take off your bonnet, Auntie. Look here! Let me untie the strings—eh?

MISS TESMAN. [*While he does so*] Well, well—this is just as if you were still at home with us.

TESMAN. [*With the bonnet in his hand, looks at it from all sides*] Why, what a gorgeous bonnet you've been investing in!

MISS TESMAN. I bought it on Hedda's account.

TESMAN. On Hedda's account? Eh?

MISS TESMAN. Yes, so that Hedda needn't be ashamed of me if we happened to go out together.

TESMAN. [*Patting her cheek*] You always think of everything, Aunt Julia. [*Lays the bonnet on a chair beside the table*] And now, look here—suppose we sit comfortably on the sofa and have a little chat, till Hedda comes.
[*They seat themselves. She places her parasol in the corner of the sofa*]

MISS TESMAN. [*Takes both his hands and looks at him*] What a delight it is to have you again, as large as life, before my very eyes, George! My George— my poor brother's own boy!

TESMAN. And it's a delight for me, too, to see you again, Aunt Julia! You, who have been father and mother in one to me.

MISS TESMAN. Oh yes, I know you will always keep a place in your heart for your old aunts.

TESMAN. And what about Aunt Rina? No improvement—eh?

MISS TESMAN. Oh no—we can scarcely look for any improvement in her case, poor thing. There she lies, helpless, as she has lain for all these years. But heaven grant I may not lose her yet awhile. For if I did, I don't know what I should make of my life, George—especially now that I haven't you to look after any more.

TESMAN. [*Patting her back*] There, there, there——!

MISS TESMAN. [*Suddenly changing her tone*] And to think that here are you a married man, George!—And that you should be the one to carry off Hedda Gabler—the beautiful Hedda Gabler! Only think of it—she, that was so beset with admirers!

TESMAN. [*Hums a little and smiles complacently*] Yes, I fancy I have several good friends about town who would like to stand in my shoes—eh?

MISS TESMAN. And then this fine long wedding-tour you have had! More than five—nearly six months——

TESMAN. Well, for me it has been a sort of tour of research as well. I have had to do so much grubbing among old records—and to read no end of books too, Auntie.

MISS TESMAN. Oh yes, I suppose so. [*More confidentially, and lowering her voice a little*] But listen now, George,—have you nothing—nothing special to tell me?

TESMAN. As to our journey?

MISS TESMAN. Yes.

TESMAN. No, I don't know of anything except what I have told you in my letters. I had a doctor's degree conferred on me—but that I told you yesterday.

MISS TESMAN. Yes, yes, you did. But what I mean is—haven't you any—any—expectations——?

TESMAN. Expectations?

MISS TESMAN. Why you know, George—I'm your old auntie!

TESMAN. Why, of course I have expectations.

MISS TESMAN. Ah!

TESMAN. I have every expectation of being a professor one of these days.

MISS TESMAN. Oh yes, a professor——

TESMAN. Indeed, I may say I am certain of it. But my dear Auntie—you know all about that already!

MISS TESMAN. [*Laughing to herself*] Yes, of course I do. You are quite right there. [*Changing the subject*] But we were talking about your journey. It must have cost a great deal of money, George?

TESMAN. Well, you see—my handsome traveling-scholarship went a good way.

MISS TESMAN. But I can't understand how you can have made it go far enough for two.

TESMAN. No, that's not so easy to understand—eh?

MISS TESMAN. And especially traveling with a lady—they tell me that makes it ever so much more expensive.

TESMAN. Yes, of course—it makes it a little more expensive. But Hedda had to have this trip, Auntie! She really had to. Nothing else would have done.

MISS TESMAN. No, no, I suppose not. A wedding-tour seems to be quite indispensable nowadays.—But tell me now—have you gone thoroughly over the house yet?

TESMAN. Yes, you may be sure I have. I have been afoot ever since daylight.

MISS TESMAN. And what do you think of it all?

TESMAN. I'm delighted! Quite delighted! Only I can't think what we are to do with the two empty rooms between this inner parlor and Hedda's bedroom.

MISS TESMAN. [*Laughing*] Oh my dear George, I daresay you may find some use for them—in the course of time.

TESMAN. Why of course you are quite right, Aunt Julia! You mean as my library increases—eh?

MISS TESMAN. Yes, quite so, my dear boy. It was your library I was thinking of.

TESMAN. I am specially pleased on Hedda's account. Often and often, before we were engaged, she said that she would never care to live anywhere but in Secretary Falk's villa.

MISS TESMAN. Yes, it was lucky that this very house should come into the market, just after you had started.

TESMAN. Yes, Aunt Julia, the luck was on our side, wasn't it—eh?

MISS TESMAN. But the expense, my dear George! You will find it very expensive, all this.

TESMAN. [*Looks at her, a little cast down*] Yes, I suppose I shall, Aunt!

MISS TESMAN. Oh, frightfully!

TESMAN. How much do you think? In round numbers?—Eh?

MISS TESMAN. Oh, I can't even guess until all the accounts come in.

TESMAN. Well, fortunately, Judge Brack has secured the most favorable terms for me,—so he said in a letter to Hedda.

MISS TESMAN. Yes, don't be uneasy, my dear boy.—Besides, I have given security for the furniture and all the carpets.

TESMAN. Security? You? My dear Aunt Julia—what sort of security could you give?

MISS TESMAN. I have given a mortgage on our annuity.

TESMAN. [*Jumps up*] What! On your—and Aunt Rina's annuity!

MISS TESMAN. Yes, I knew of no other plan, you see.

TESMAN. [*Placing himself before her*] Have you gone out of your senses, Auntie! Your annuity—it's all that you and Aunt Rina have to live upon.

MISS TESMAN. Well, well—don't get so excited about it. It's only a matter of form you know—Judge Brack assured me of that. It was he that was kind enough to arrange the whole affair for me. A mere matter of form, he said.

TESMAN. Yes, that may be all very well. But nevertheless——

MISS TESMAN. You will have your own salary to depend upon now. And, good heavens, even if we did have to pay up a little——! To eke things out a bit at the start——! Why, it would be nothing but a pleasure to us.

TESMAN. Oh Auntie—will you never be tired of making sacrifices for me!

MISS TESMAN. [*Rises and lays her hands on his shoulders*] Have I any other happiness in this world except to smooth your way for you, my dear boy? You, who have had neither father nor mother to depend on. And now we have reached the goal, George! Things have looked black enough for us, sometimes; but, thank heaven, now you have nothing to fear.

TESMAN. Yes, it is really marvelous how everything has turned out for the best.

MISS TESMAN. And the people who opposed you—who wanted to bar the way for you—now you have them at your feet. They have fallen, George. Your most dangerous rival—his fall was the worst.—And now he has to lie on the bed he has made for himself—poor misguided creature.

TESMAN. Have you heard anything of Eilert? Since I went away, I mean.

MISS TESMAN. Only that he is said to have published a new book.

TESMAN. What! Eilert Lövborg! Recently—eh?

MISS TESMAN. Yes, so they say. Heaven knows whether it can be worth anything! Ah, when your new book appears—that will be another story, George! What is it to be about?

TESMAN. It will deal with the domestic industries of Brabant during the Middle Ages.

MISS TESMAN. Fancy—to be able to write on such a subject as that!

TESMAN. However, it may be some time before the book is ready. I have all these collections to arrange first, you see.

MISS TESMAN. Yes, collecting and arranging—no one can beat you at that. There you are my poor brother's own son.

TESMAN. I am looking forward eagerly to setting to work at it; especially now that I have my own delightful home to work in.

MISS TESMAN. And, most of all, now that you have got the wife of your heart, my dear George.

TESMAN. [*Embracing her*] Oh yes, yes, Aunt Julia. Hedda—she is the best part of it all! [*Looks towards the doorway*] I believe I hear her coming—eh? [HEDDA *enters from the left through the inner room. She is a woman of nine-and-twenty. Her face and figure show refinement and distinction. Her complexion is pale and opaque. Her steel-gray eyes express a cold, unruffled repose. Her hair is of an agreeable medium brown, but not particularly abundant. She is dressed in a tasteful, somewhat loose-fitting morning gown*]

MISS TESMAN. [*Going to meet* HEDDA] Good morning, my dear Hedda! Good morning, and a hearty welcome!

HEDDA. [*Holds out her hand*] Good morning, dear Miss Tesman! So early a call! That is kind of you.

MISS TESMAN. [*With some embarrassment*] Well—has the bride slept well in her new home?

HEDDA. Oh yes, thanks. Passably.

TESMAN. [*Laughing*] Passably! Come, that's good, Hedda! You were sleeping like a stone when I got up.

HEDDA. Fortunately. Of course one has always to accustom one's self to new surroundings, Miss Tesman—little by little. [*Looking towards the left*] Oh—there the servant has gone and opened the veranda door, and let in a whole flood of sunshine.

MISS TESMAN. [*Going towards the door*] Well, then we will shut it.

HEDDA. No, no, not that! Tesman, please draw the curtains. That will give a softer light.

TESMAN. [*At the door*] All right—all right.—There now, Hedda, now you have both shade and fresh air.

HEDDA. Yes, fresh air we certainly must have, with all these stacks of flowers——. But—won't you sit down, Miss Tesman?

MISS TESMAN. No, thank you. Now that I have seen that everything is all right here—thank heaven!—I must be getting home again. My sister is lying longing for me, poor thing.

TESMAN. Give her my very best love, Auntie; and say I shall look in and see her later in the day.

MISS TESMAN. Yes, yes, I'll be sure to tell her. But by the by, George—[*Feeling in her dress pocket*]—I had almost forgotten—I have something for you here.

TESMAN. What is it, Auntie? Eh?

MISS TESMAN. [*Produces a flat parcel wrapped in newspaper and hands it to him*] Look here, my dear boy.

TESMAN. [*Opening the parcel*] Well, I declare!—Have you really saved them for me, Aunt Julia! Hedda! isn't this touching—eh?

HEDDA. [*Beside the whatnot on the right*] Well, what is it?

TESMAN. My old morning-shoes! My slippers.

HEDDA. Indeed. I remember you often spoke of them while we were abroad.

TESMAN. Yes, I missed them terribly. [*Goes up to her*] Now you shall see them, Hedda!

HEDDA. [*Going towards the stove*] Thanks, I really don't care about it.

TESMAN. [*Following her*] Only think—ill as she was, Aunt Rina embroidered these for me. Oh you can't think how many associations cling to them.

HEDDA. [*At the table*] Scarcely for me.

MISS TESMAN. Of course not for Hedda, George.

TESMAN. Well, but now that she belongs to the family, I thought—

HEDDA. [*Interrupting*] We shall never get on with this servant, Tesman.

MISS TESMAN. Not get on with Berta?

TESMAN. Why, dear, what puts that in your head? Eh?

HEDDA. [*Pointing*] Look there! She has left her old bonnet lying about on a chair.

TESMAN. [*In consternation, drops the slippers on the floor*] Why, Hedda——

HEDDA. Just fancy, if any one should come in and see it!

TESMAN. But Hedda—that's Aunt Julia's bonnet.

HEDDA. Is it!

MISS TESMAN. [*Taking up the bonnet*] Yes, indeed it's mine. And, what's more, it's not old, Madam Hedda.

HEDDA. I really did not look closely at it, Miss Tesman.

MISS TESMAN. [*Trying on the bonnet*] Let me tell you it's the first time I have worn it—the very first time.

TESMAN. And a very nice bonnet it is too—quite a beauty!

MISS TESMAN. Oh, it's no such great thing, George. [*Looks around her*] My parasol——? Ah, here. [*Takes it*] For this is mine too—[*mutters*]—not Berta's.

TESMAN. A new bonnet and a new parasol! Only think, Hedda!

HEDDA. Very handsome indeed.

TESMAN. Yes, isn't it? Eh? But Auntie, take a good look at Hedda before you go! See how handsome she is!

MISS TESMAN. Oh, my dear boy, there's nothing new in that. Hedda was always lovely.

[*She nods and goes towards the right*]

TESMAN. [*Following*] Yes, but have you noticed what splendid condition she is in? How she has filled out on the journey?

HEDDA. [*Crossing the room*] Oh, do be quiet——!

MISS TESMAN. [*Who has stopped and turned*] Filled out?

TESMAN. Of course you don't notice it so much now that she has that dress on. But I, who can see——

HEDDA. [*At the glass door, impatiently*] Oh, you can't see anything.

TESMAN. It must be the mountain air in the Tyrol——

HEDDA. [*Curtly, interrupting*] I am exactly as I was when I started.

TESMAN. So you insist; but I'm quite certain you are not. Don't you agree with me, Auntie?

MISS TESMAN. [*Who has been gazing at her with folded hands*] Hedda is lovely —lovely—lovely. [*Goes up to her, takes her head between both hands, draws it downwards, and kisses her hair*] God bless and preserve Hedda Tesman— for George's sake.

HEDDA. [*Gently freeing herself*] Oh—! Let me go.

MISS TESMAN. [*In quiet emotion*] I shall not let a day pass without coming to see you.

TESMAN. No you won't, will you, Auntie? Eh?

MISS TESMAN. Good-bye—good-bye!

[*She goes out by the hall door.* TESMAN *accompanies her. The door remains half open.* TESMAN *can be heard repeating his message to* AUNT RINA *and his thanks for the slippers. In the meantime,* HEDDA *walks about the room, raising her arms and clenching her hands as if in desperation. Then she flings back the curtains from the glass door, and stands there looking out. Presently* TESMAN *returns and closes the door behind him*]

TESMAN. [*Picks up the slippers from the floor*] What are you looking at, Hedda?

HEDDA. [*Once more calm and mistress of herself*] I am only looking at the leaves. They are so yellow—so withered.

TESMAN. [*Wraps up the slippers and lays them on the table*] Well you see, we are well into September now.

HEDDA. [*Again restless*] Yes, to think of it!—Already in—in September.

TESMAN. Don't you think Aunt Julia's manner was strange, dear? Almost solemn? Can you imagine what was the matter with her? Eh?

HEDDA. I scarcely know her, you see. Is she not often like that?

TESMAN. No, not as she was to-day.

HEDDA. [*Leaving the glass door*] Do you think she was annoyed about the bonnet?

TESMAN. Oh, scarcely at all. Perhaps a little, just at the moment——

HEDDA. But what an idea, to pitch her bonnet about in the drawing-room! No one does that sort of thing.

TESMAN. Well you may be sure Aunt Julia won't do it again.

HEDDA. In any case, I shall manage to make my peace with her.

TESMAN. Yes, my dear, good Hedda, if you only would.

HEDDA. When you call this afternoon, you might invite her to spend the evening here.

TESMAN. Yes, that I will. And there's one thing more you could do that would delight her heart.

HEDDA. What is it?

TESMAN. If you could only prevail on yourself to say *du*[1] to her. For my sake, Hedda? Eh?

HEDDA. No, no, Tesman—you really mustn't ask that of me. I have told you so already. I shall try to call her "Aunt"; and you must be satisfied with that.

TESMAN. Well, well. Only I think now that you belong to the family, you——

HEDDA. H'm—I can't in the least see why——

[*She goes up towards the middle doorway*]

TESMAN. [*After a pause*] Is there anything the matter with you, Hedda? Eh?

HEDDA. I'm only looking at my old piano. It doesn't go at all well with all the other things.

TESMAN. The first time I draw my salary, we'll see about exchanging it.

HEDDA. No, no—no exchanging. I don't want to part with it. Suppose we put it there in the inner room, and then get another here in its place. When it's convenient, I mean.

TESMAN. [*A little taken aback*] Yes—of course we could do that.

[1] The familiar form of the pronoun, used only between persons who are on a footing of intimacy; hence its significance here and later.

HEDDA. [*Takes up the bouquet from the piano*] These flowers were not here last night when we arrived.

TESMAN. Aunt Julia must have brought them for you.

HEDDA. [*Examining the bouquet*] A visiting-card. [*Takes it out and reads*] "Shall return later in the day." Can you guess whose card it is?

TESMAN. No. Whose? Eh?

HEDDA. The name is "Mrs. Elvsted."

TESMAN. Is it really? Sheriff Elvsted's wife? Miss Rysing that was.

HEDDA. Exactly. The girl with the irritating hair, that she was always showing off. An old flame of yours I've been told.

TESMAN. [*Laughing*] Oh, that didn't last long; and it was before I knew you, Hedda. But fancy her being in town!

HEDDA. It's odd that she should call upon us. I have scarcely seen her since we left school.

TESMAN. I haven't seen her either for—heaven knows how long. I wonder how she can endure to live in such an out-of-the-way hole—eh?

HEDDA. [*After a moment's thought, says suddenly*] Tell me, Tesman—isn't it somewhere near there that he—that—Eilert Lövborg is living?

TESMAN. Yes, he is somewhere in that part of the country.

[BERTA *enters by the hall door*]

BERTA. That lady, ma'am, that brought some flowers a little while ago, is here again. [*Pointing*] The flowers you have in your hand, ma'am.

HEDDA. Ah, is she? Well, please show her in.

[BERTA *opens the door for* MRS. ELVSTED, *and goes out herself.* MRS. ELVSTED *is a woman of fragile figure, with pretty, soft features. Her eyes are light blue, large, round, and somewhat prominent, with a startled, inquiring expression. Her hair is remarkably light, almost flaxen, and unusually abundant and wavy. She is a couple of years younger than* HEDDA. *She wears a dark visiting dress, tasteful, but not quite in the latest fashion*]

HEDDA. [*Receives her warmly*] How do you do, my dear Mrs. Elvsted? It's delightful to see you again.

MRS. ELVSTED. [*Nervously, struggling for self-control*] Yes, it's a very long time since we met.

TESMAN. [*Gives her his hand*] And we too—eh?

HEDDA. Thanks for your lovely flowers——

MRS. ELVSTED. Oh, not at all—— I would have come straight here yesterday afternoon; but I heard that you were away——

TESMAN. Have you just come to town? Eh?

MRS. ELVSTED. I arrived yesterday, about midday. Oh, I was quite in despair when I heard that you were not at home.

HEDDA. In despair! How so?

TESMAN. Why, my dear Mrs. Rysing—I mean Mrs. Elvsted——

HEDDA. I hope that you are not in any trouble?

MRS. ELVSTED. Yes, I am. And I don't know another living creature here that I can turn to.

HEDDA. [*Laying the bouquet on the table*] Come—let us sit here on the sofa——

MRS. ELVSTED. Oh, I am too restless to sit down.

HEDDA. Oh no, you're not. Come here.

[*She draws* MRS. ELVSTED *down upon the sofa and sits at her side*]

TESMAN. Well? what is it, Mrs. Elvsted——?

HEDDA. Has anything particular happened to you at home?

MRS. ELVSTED. Yes—and no. Oh—I am so anxious you should not misunder-stand me——

HEDDA. Then your best plan is to tell us the whole story, Mrs. Elvsted.

TESMAN. I suppose that's what you have come for—eh?

MRS. ELVSTED. Yes, yes—of course it is. Well then, I must tell you—if you don't already know—that Eilert Lövborg is in town, too.

HEDDA. Lövborg——!

TESMAN. What! Has Eilert Lövborg come back? Fancy that, Hedda!

HEDDA. Well, well—I hear it.

MRS. ELVSTED. He has been here a week already. Just fancy—a whole week! In this terrible town, alone! With so many temptations on all sides.

HEDDA. But, my dear Mrs. Elvsted—how does he concern you so much?

MRS. ELVSTED. [*Looks at her with a startled air, and says rapidly*] He was the children's tutor.

HEDDA. Your children's?

MRS. ELVSTED. My husband's. I have none.

HEDDA. Your step-children's, then?

MRS. ELVSTED. Yes.

TESMAN. [*Somewhat hesitatingly*] Then was he—I don't know how to express it—was he—regular enough in his habits to be fit for the post? Eh?

MRS. ELVSTED. For the last two years his conduct has been irreproachable.

TESMAN. Has it indeed? Fancy that, Hedda!

HEDDA. I hear it.

MRS. ELVSTED. Perfectly irreproachable, I assure you! In every respect. But all the same—now that I know he is here—in this great town—and with a large sum of money in his hands—I can't help being in mortal fear for him.

TESMAN. Why did he not remain where he was? With you and your husband? Eh?

MRS. ELVSTED. After his book was published he was too restless and unsettled to remain with us.

TESMAN. Yes, by the by, Aunt Julia told me he had published a new book.

MRS. ELVSTED. Yes, a big book, dealing with the march of civilization—in broad outline, as it were. It came out about a fortnight ago. And since it has sold so well, and been so much read—and made such a sensation——

TESMAN. Has it indeed? It must be something he has had lying by since his better days.

MRS. ELVSTED. Long ago, you mean?

TESMAN. Yes.

MRS. ELVSTED. No, he has written it all since he has been with us—within the last year.

TESMAN. Isn't that good news, Hedda? Think of that.

MRS. ELVSTED. Ah yes, if only it would last!

HEDDA. Have you seen him here in town?

MRS. ELVSTED. No, not yet. I have had the greatest difficulty in finding out his address. But this morning I discovered it at last.

HEDDA. [*Looks searchingly at her*] Do you know, it seems to me a little odd of your husband—h'm——

MRS. ELVSTED. [*Starting nervously*] Of my husband! What?

HEDDA. That he should send you to town on such an errand—that he does not come himself and look after his friend.

MRS. ELVSTED. Oh no, no—my husband has no time. And besides, I—I had some shopping to do.

HEDDA. [*With a slight smile*] Ah, that is a different matter.

MRS. ELVSTED. [*Rising quickly and uneasily*] And now I beg and implore you, Mr. Tesman—receive Eilert Lövborg kindly if he comes to you! And that he is sure to do. You see you were such great friends in the old days. And then you are interested in the same studies—the same branch of science—so far as I can understand.

TESMAN. We used to be, at any rate.

MRS. ELVSTED. That is why I beg so earnestly that you—you too—will keep a sharp eye upon him. Oh, you will promise me that, Mr. Tesman—won't you?

TESMAN. With the greatest of pleasure, Mrs. Rysing——

HEDDA. Elvsted.

TESMAN. I assure you I shall do all I possibly can for Eilert. You may rely upon me.

MRS. ELVSTED. Oh, how very, very kind of you! [*Presses his hands*] Thanks, thanks, thanks! [*Frightened*] You see, my husband is so very fond of him!

HEDDA. [*Rising*] You ought to write to him, Tesman. Perhaps he may not care to come to you of his own accord.

TESMAN. Well, perhaps it would be the right thing to do, Hedda? Eh?

HEDDA. And the sooner the better. Why not at once?

MRS. ELVSTED. [*Imploringly*] Oh, if you only would!

TESMAN. I'll write this moment. Have you his address, Mrs.—Mrs. Elvsted.

MRS. ELVSTED. Yes. [*Takes a slip of paper from her pocket, and hands it to him*] Here it is.

TESMAN. Good, good. Then I'll go in—— [*Looks about him*] By the by—my slippers? Oh, here.

[*Takes the packet, and is about to go*]

HEDDA. Be sure you write him a cordial, friendly letter. And a good long one too.

TESMAN. Yes, I will.

MRS. ELVSTED. But please, please don't say a word to show that I have suggested it.

TESMAN. No, how could you think I would? Eh?

[*He goes out to the right, through the inner room*]

HEDDA. [*Goes up to* MRS. ELVSTED, *smiles and says in a low voice*] There! We have killed two birds with one stone.

MRS. ELVSTED. What do you mean?

HEDDA. Could you not see that I wanted him to go?

MRS. ELVSTED. Yes, to write the letter——

HEDDA.   And that I might speak to you alone.

MRS. ELVSTED.   [*Confused*] About the same thing?

HEDDA.   Precisely.

MRS. ELVSTED.   [*Apprehensively*] But there is nothing more, Mrs. Tesman! Absolutely nothing!

HEDDA.   Oh yes, but there is. There is a great deal more—I can see that. Sit here—and we'll have a cosy, confidential chat.

[*She forces* MRS. ELVSTED *to sit in the easy-chair beside the stove, and seats herself on one of the footstools*]

MRS. ELVSTED.   [*Anxiously, looking at her watch*] But, my dear Mrs. Tesman —I was really on the point of going.

HEDDA.   Oh, you can't be in such a hurry.—Well? Now tell me something about your life at home.

MRS. ELVSTED.   Oh, that is just what I care least to speak about.

HEDDA.   But to me, dear——? Why, weren't we schoolfellows?

MRS. ELVSTED.   Yes, but you were in the class above me. Oh, how dreadfully afraid of you I was then!

HEDDA.   Afraid of me?

MRS. ELVSTED.   Yes, dreadfully. For when we met on the stairs you used always to pull my hair.

HEDDA.   Did I, really?

MRS. ELVSTED.   Yes, and once you said you would burn it off my head.

HEDDA.   Oh, that was all nonsense, of course.

MRS. ELVSTED.   Yes, but I was so silly in those days.—And since then, too—we have drifted so far—far apart from each other. Our circles have been so entirely different.

HEDDA.   Well then, we must try to drift together again. Now listen! At school we said *du*[2] to each other; and we called each other by our Christian names——

MRS. ELVSTED.   No, I am sure you must be mistaken.

HEDDA.   No, not at all! I can remember quite distinctly. So now we are going to renew our old friendship. [*Draws the footstool closer to* MRS. ELVSTED] There now! [*Kisses her cheek*] You must say *du* to me and call me Hedda.

MRS. ELVSTED.   [*Presses and pats her hands*] Oh, how good and kind you are! I am not used to such kindness.

HEDDA.   There, there, there! And I shall say *du* to you, as in the old days, and call you my dear Thora.

MRS. ELVSTED.   My name is Thea.

HEDDA.   Why, of course! I meant Thea. [*Looks at her compassionately*] So you are not accustomed to goodness and kindness, Thea? Not in your own home?

MRS. ELVSTED.   Oh, if I only had a home! But I haven't any; I have never had a home.

HEDDA.   [*Looks at her for a moment*] I almost suspected as much.

MRS. ELVSTED.   [*Gazing helplessly before her*] Yes—yes—yes.

HEDDA.   I don't quite remember—was it not as housekeeper that you first went to Mr. Elvsted's?

[2] See note, p. 294.

MRS. ELVSTED. I really went as governess. But his wife—his late wife—was an invalid,—and rarely left her room. So I had to look after the housekeeping as well.

HEDDA. And then—at last—you became mistress of the house.

MRS. ELVSTED. [*Sadly*] Yes, I did.

HEDDA. Let me see—about how long ago was that?

MRS. ELVSTED. My marriage?

HEDDA. Yes.

MRS. ELVSTED. Five years ago.

HEDDA. To be sure; it must be that.

MRS. ELVSTED. Oh those five years——! Or at all events the last two or three of them! Oh, if you[3] could only imagine——

HEDDA. [*Giving her a little slap on the hand*] De? Fie, Thea!

MRS. ELVSTED. Yes, yes, I will try—— Well, if—you could only imagine and understand——

HEDDA. [*Lightly*] Eilert Lövborg has been in your neighborhood about three years, hasn't he?

MRS. ELVSTED. [*Looks at her doubtfully*] Eilert Lövborg? Yes—he has.

HEDDA. Had you known him before, in town here?

MRS. ELVSTED. Scarcely at all. I mean—I knew him by name of course.

HEDDA. But you saw a good deal of him in the country?

MRS. ELVSTED. Yes, he came to us every day. You see, he gave the children lessons; for in the long run I couldn't manage it all myself.

HEDDA. No, that's clear.—And your husband——? I suppose he is often away from home?

MRS. ELVSTED. Yes. Being sheriff, you know, he has to travel about a good deal in his district.

HEDDA. [*Leaning against the arm of the chair*] Thea—my poor, sweet Thea—now you must tell me everything—exactly as it stands.

MRS. ELVSTED. Well then, you must question me.

HEDDA. What sort of a man is your husband, Thea? I mean—you know—in everyday life. Is he kind to you?

MRS. ELVSTED. [*Evasively*] I am sure he means well in everything.

HEDDA. I should think he must be altogether too old for you. There is at least twenty years' difference between you, is there not?

MRS. ELVSTED. [*Irritably*] Yes, that is true, too. Everything about him is repellent to me! We have not a thought in common. We have no single point of sympathy—he and I.

HEDDA. But is he not fond of you all the same? In his own way?

MRS. ELVSTED. Oh I really don't know. I think he regards me simply as a useful property. And then it doesn't cost much to keep me. I am not expensive.

HEDDA. That is stupid of you.

MRS. ELVSTED. [*Shakes her head*] It cannot be otherwise—not with him. I don't think he really cares for any one but himself—and perhaps a little for the children.

HEDDA. And for Eilert Lövborg, Thea.

---

[3] Instead of *du*, Mrs. Elvsted uses *De*, the formal pronoun. After being rebuked, she says *du*.

MRS. ELVSTED. [*Looking at her*] For Eilert Lövborg? What puts that into your head?

HEDDA. Well, my dear—I should say, when he sends you after him all the way to town—— [*Smiling almost imperceptibly*] And besides, you said so yourself, to Tesman.

MRS. ELVSTED. [*With a little nervous twitch*] Did I? Yes, I suppose I did. [*Vehemently, but not loudly*] No—I may just as well make a clean breast of it at once! For it must all come out in any case.

HEDDA. Why, my dear Thea——?

MRS. ELVSTED. Well, to make a long story short: My husband did not know that I was coming.

HEDDA. What! Your husband didn't know it!

MRS. ELVSTED. No, of course not. For that matter, he was away from home himself—he was traveling. Oh, I could bear it no longer, Hedda! I couldn't indeed—so utterly alone as I should have been in future.

HEDDA. Well? And then?

MRS. ELVSTED. So I put together some of my things—what I needed most—as quietly as possible. And then I left the house.

HEDDA. Without a word?

MRS. ELVSTED. Yes—and took the train straight to town.

HEDDA. Why, my dear, good Thea—to think of you daring to do it!

MRS. ELVSTED. [*Rises and moves about the room*] What else could I possibly do?

HEDDA. But what do you think your husband will say when you go home again?

MRS. ELVSTED. [*At the table, looks at her*] Back to him?

HEDDA. Of course.

MRS. ELVSTED. I shall never go back to him again.

HEDDA. [*Rising and going towards her*] Then you have left your home—for good and all?

MRS. ELVSTED. Yes. There was nothing else to be done.

HEDDA. But then—to take flight so openly.

MRS. ELVSTED. Oh, it's impossible to keep things of that sort secret.

HEDDA. But what do you think people will say of you, Thea?

MRS. ELVSTED. They may say what they like, for aught I care. [*Seats herself wearily and sadly on the sofa*] I have done nothing but what I had to do.

HEDDA. [*After a short silence*] And what are your plans now? What do you think of doing?

MRS. ELVSTED. I don't know yet. I only know this, that I must live here, where Eilert Lövborg is—if I am to live at all.

HEDDA. [*Takes a chair from the table, seats herself beside her, and strokes her hands*] My dear Thea—how did this—this friendship—between you and Eilert Lövborg come about?

MRS. ELVSTED. Oh it grew up gradually. I gained a sort of influence over him.

HEDDA. Indeed?

MRS. ELVSTED. He gave up his old habits. Not because I asked him to, for I never dared do that. But of course he saw how repulsive they were to me; and so he dropped them.

HEDDA. [*Concealing an involuntary smile of scorn*] Then you have reclaimed him—as the saying goes—my little Thea.

MRS. ELVSTED. So he says himself, at any rate. And he, on his side, has made a real human being of me—taught me to think, and to understand so many things.

HEDDA. Did he give you lessons too, then?

MRS. ELVSTED. No, not exactly lessons. But he talked to me—talked about such an infinity of things. And then came the lovely, happy time when I began to share in his work—when he allowed me to help him!

HEDDA. Oh he did, did he?

MRS. ELVSTED. Yes! He never wrote anything without my assistance.

HEDDA. You were two good comrades, in fact?

MRS. ELVSTED. [*Eagerly*] Comrades! Yes, fancy, Hedda—that is the very word he used!—Oh, I ought to feel perfectly happy; and yet I cannot; for I don't know how long it will last.

HEDDA. Are you no surer of him than that?

MRS. ELVSTED. [*Gloomily*] A woman's shadow stands between Eilert Lövborg and me.

HEDDA. [*Looks at her anxiously*] Who can that be?

MRS. ELVSTED. I don't know. Some one he knew in his—in his past. Some one he has never been able wholly to forget.

HEDDA. What has he told you—about this?

MRS. ELVSTED. He has only once—quite vaguely—alluded to it.

HEDDA. Well! And what did he say?

MRS. ELVSTED. He said that when they parted, she threatened to shoot him with a pistol.

HEDDA. [*With cold composure*] Oh, nonsense! No one does that sort of thing here.

MRS. ELVSTED. No. And that is why I think it must have been that red-haired singing-woman whom he once——

HEDDA. Yes, very likely.

MRS. ELVSTED. For I remember they used to say of her that she carried loaded firearms.

HEDDA. Oh—then of course it must have been she.

MRS. ELVSTED. [*Wringing her hands*] And now just fancy, Hedda—I hear that this singing-woman—that she is in town again! Oh, I don't know what to do——

HEDDA. [*Glancing towards the inner room*] Hush! Here comes Tesman. [*Rises and whispers*] Thea—all this must remain between you and me.

MRS. ELVSTED. [*Springing up*] Oh yes—yes! For heaven's sake——!

[GEORGE TESMAN, *with a letter in his hand, comes from the right through the inner room*]

TESMAN. There now—the epistle is finished.

HEDDA. That's right. And now Mrs. Elvsted is just going. Wait a moment— I'll go with you to the garden gate.

TESMAN. Do you think Berta could post the letter, Hedda dear?

HEDDA. [*Takes it*] I will tell her to.

[BERTA *enters from the hall*]

BERTA. Judge Brack wishes to know if Mrs. Tesman will receive him.

HEDDA. Yes, ask Judge Brack to come in. And look here—put this letter in the post.

BERTA. [*Taking the letter*] Yes, ma'am.

[*She opens the door for* JUDGE BRACK *and goes out herself.* BRACK *is a man of forty-five; thick-set, but well-built and elastic in his movements. His face is roundish with an aristocratic profile. His hair is short, still almost black, and carefully dressed. His eyes are lively and sparkling. His eyebrows thick. His moustaches are also thick, with short-cut ends. He wears a well-cut walking-suit, a little too youthful for his age. He uses an eyeglass, which he now and then lets drop*]

JUDGE BRACK. [*With his hat in his hand, bowing*] May one venture to call so early in the day?

HEDDA. Of course one may.

TESMAN. [*Presses his hand*] You are welcome at any time. [*Introducing him*] Judge Brack—Miss Rysing——

HEDDA. Oh——!

BRACK. [*Bowing*] Ah—delighted——

HEDDA. [*Looks at him and laughs*] It's nice to have a look at you by daylight, Judge!

BRACK. Do you find me—altered?

HEDDA. A little younger, I think.

BRACK. Thank you so much.

TESMAN. But what do you think of Hedda—eh? Doesn't she look flourishing? She has actually——

HEDDA. Oh, do leave me alone. You haven't thanked Judge Brack for all the trouble he has taken——

BRACK. Oh, nonsense—it was a pleasure to me——

HEDDA. Yes, you are a friend indeed. But here stands Thea all impatience to be off—so *au revoir*, Judge. I shall be back again presently.

[*Mutual salutations.* MRS. ELVSTED *and* HEDDA *go out by the hall door*]

BRACK. Well,—is your wife tolerably satisfied——

TESMAN. Yes, we can't thank you sufficiently. Of course she talks of a little rearrangement here and there; and one or two things are still wanting. We shall have to buy some additional trifles.

BRACK. Indeed!

TESMAN. But we won't trouble you about these things. Hedda says she herself will look after what is wanting.—Shan't we sit down? Eh?

BRACK. Thanks, for a moment. [*Seats himself beside the table*] There is something I wanted to speak to you about, my dear Tesman.

TESMAN. Indeed? Ah, I understand! [*Seating himself*] I suppose it's the serious part of the frolic that is coming now. Eh?

BRACK. Oh, the money question is not so very pressing; though, for that matter, I wish we had gone a little more economically to work.

TESMAN. But that would never have done, you know! Think of Hedda, my dear fellow! You, who know her so well——. I couldn't possibly ask her to put up with a shabby style of living!

BRACK. No, no—that is just the difficulty.

TESMAN.   And then—fortunately—it can't be long before I receive my appointment.[4]

BRACK.   Well, you see—such things are often apt to hang fire for a time.

TESMAN.   Have you heard anything definite? Eh?

BRACK.   Nothing exactly definite—— [*Interrupting himself*] But by the by—I have one piece of news for you.

TESMAN.   Well?

BRACK.   Your old friend, Eilert Lövborg, has returned to town.

TESMAN.   I know that already.

BRACK.   Indeed! How did you learn it?

TESMAN.   From that lady who went out with Hedda.

BRACK.   Really? What was her name? I didn't quite catch it.

TESMAN.   Mrs. Elvsted.

BRACK.   Aha—Sheriff Elvsted's wife? Of course—he has been living up in their regions.

TESMAN.   And fancy—I'm delighted to hear that he is quite a reformed character!

BRACK.   So they say.

TESMAN.   And then he has published a new book—eh?

BRACK.   Yes, indeed he has.

TESMAN.   And I hear it has made some sensation!

BRACK.   Quite an unusual sensation.

TESMAN.   Fancy—isn't that good news! A man of such extraordinary talents——. I felt so grieved to think that he had gone irretrievably to ruin.

BRACK.   That was what everybody thought.

TESMAN.   But I cannot imagine what he will take to now! How in the world will he be able to make his living? Eh?

[*During the last words,* HEDDA *has entered by the hall door*]

HEDDA.   [*To* BRACK, *laughing with a touch of scorn*] Tesman is for ever worrying about how people are to make their living.

TESMAN.   Well you see, dear—we were talking about poor Eilert Lövborg.

HEDDA.   [*Glancing at him rapidly*] Oh, indeed? [*Seats herself in the arm-chair beside the stove and asks indifferently*] What is the matter with him?

TESMAN.   Well—no doubt he has run through all his property long ago; and he can scarcely write a new book every year—eh? So I really can't see what is to become of him.

BRACK.   Perhaps I can give you some information on that point.

TESMAN.   Indeed!

BRACK.   You must remember that his relations have a good deal of influence.

TESMAN.   Oh, his relations, unfortunately, have entirely washed their hands of him.

BRACK.   At one time they called him the hope of the family.

TESMAN.   At one time, yes! But he has put an end to all that.

HEDDA.   Who knows? [*With a slight smile*] I hear they have reclaimed him up at Sheriff Elvsted's——

BRACK.   And then this book that he has published——

[4] As professor.

TESMAN. Well, well, I hope to goodness they may find something for him to do. I have just written to him. I asked him to come and see us this evening, Hedda dear.

BRACK. But my dear fellow, you are booked for my bachelors' party this evening. You promised on the pier last night.

HEDDA. Had you forgotten, Tesman?

TESMAN. Yes, I had utterly forgotten.

BRACK. But it doesn't matter, for you may be sure he won't come.

TESMAN. What makes you think that? Eh?

BRACK. [*With a little hesitation, rising and resting his hands on the back of his chair*] My dear Tesman—and you too, Mrs. Tesman—I think I ought not to keep you in the dark about something that—that——

TESMAN. That concerns Eilert——?

BRACK. Both you and him.

TESMAN. Well, my dear Judge, out with it.

BRACK. You must be prepared to find your appointment deferred longer than you desired or expected.

TESMAN. [*Jumping up uneasily*] Is there some hitch about it? Eh?

BRACK. The nomination may perhaps be made conditional on the result of a competition——

TESMAN. Competition! Think of that, Hedda!

HEDDA. [*Leans further back in the chair*] Aha—aha!

TESMAN. But who can my competitor be? Surely not——?

BRACK. Yes, precisely—Eilert Lövborg.

TESMAN. [*Clasping his hands*] No, no—it's quite inconceivable! Quite impossible! Eh?

BRACK. H'm—that is what it may come to, all the same.

TESMAN. Well but, Judge Brack—it would show the most incredible lack of consideration for me. [*Gesticulates with his arms*] For—just think—I'm a married man! We have married on the strength of these prospects, Hedda and I; and run deep into debt; and borrowed money from Aunt Julia too. Good heavens, they had as good as promised me the appointment. Eh?

BRACK. Well, well, well—no doubt you will get it in the end; only after a contest.

HEDDA. [*Immovable in her arm-chair*] Fancy, Tesman, there will be a sort of sporting interest in that.

TESMAN. Why, my dearest Hedda, how can you be so indifferent about it?

HEDDA. [*As before*] I am not at all indifferent. I am most eager to see who wins.

BRACK. In any case, Mrs. Tesman, it is best that you should know how matters stand. I mean—before you set about the little purchases I hear you are threatening.

HEDDA. This can make no difference.

BRACK. Indeed! Then I have no more to say. Good-bye! [*To* TESMAN] I shall look in on my way back from my afternoon walk, and take you home with me.

TESMAN. Oh yes, yes—your news has quite upset me.

HEDDA. [*Reclining, holds out her hand*] Good-bye, Judge; and be sure you call in the afternoon.

BRACK. Many thanks. Good-bye, good-bye!

TESMAN. [*Accompanying him to the door*] Good-bye, my dear Judge! You must really excuse me——

[JUDGE BRACK *goes out by the hall door*]

TESMAN. [*Crosses the room*] Oh Hedda—one should never rush into adventures. Eh?

HEDDA. [*Looks at him, smiling*] Do you do that?

TESMAN. Yes, dear—there is no denying—it was adventurous to go and marry and set up house upon mere expectations.

HEDDA. Perhaps you are right there.

TESMAN. Well—at all events, we have our delightful home, Hedda! Fancy, the home we both dreamed of—the home we were in love with, I may almost say. Eh?

HEDDA. [*Rising slowly and wearily*] It was part of our compact that we were to go into society—to keep open house.

TESMAN. Yes, if you only knew how I had been looking forward to it! Fancy—to see you as hostess—in a select circle! Eh? Well, well, well—for the present we shall have to get on without society, Hedda—only to invite Aunt Julia now and then.—Oh, I intended you to lead such an utterly different life, dear——!

HEDDA. Of course I cannot have my man in livery just yet.

TESMAN. Oh no, unfortunately. It would be out of the question for us to keep a footman, you know.

HEDDA. And the saddle-horse I was to have had——

TESMAN. [*Aghast*] The saddle-horse!

HEDDA. ——I suppose I must not think of that now.

TESMAN. Good heavens, no!—that's as clear as daylight.

HEDDA. [*Goes up the room*] Well, I shall have one thing at least to kill time with in the meanwhile.

TESMAN. [*Beaming*] Oh thank heaven for that! What is it, Hedda? Eh?

HEDDA. [*In the middle doorway, looks at him with covert scorn*] My pistols, George.

TESMAN. [*In alarm*] Your pistols!

HEDDA. [*With cold eyes*] General Gabler's pistols.

[*She goes out through the inner room, to the left*]

TESMAN. [*Rushes up to the middle doorway and calls after her*] No, for heaven's sake, Hedda darling—don't touch those dangerous things! For my sake, Hedda! Eh?

Act Two

The room at the TESMANS' *as in the first act, except that the piano has been removed, and an elegant little writing-table with book-shelves put in its place. A smaller table stands near the sofa on the left. Most of the bouquets have been taken away.* MRS. ELVSTED'S *bouquet is upon the large table in front.—It is afternoon.* HEDDA, *dressed to receive callers, is alone in the room. She stands by the open glass door, loading a revolver. The fellow to it lies in an open pistol-case on the writing-table.*

HEDDA.   [*Looks down the garden, and calls*] So you are here again, Judge!
BRACK.   [*Is heard calling from a distance*] As you see, Mrs. Tesman!
HEDDA.   [*Raises the pistol and points*] Now I'll shoot you, Judge Brack!
BRACK.   [*Calling unseen*] No, no, no! Don't stand aiming at me!
HEDDA.   This is what comes of sneaking in by the back way. [*She fires*]
BRACK.   [*Nearer*] Are you out of your senses!——
HEDDA.   Dear me—did I happen to hit you?
BRACK.   [*Still outside*] I wish you would let these pranks alone!
HEDDA.   Come in then, Judge.
        [JUDGE BRACK, *dressed as though for a men's party, enters by the glass door. He carries a light overcoat over his arm*]
BRACK.   What the deuce—haven't you tired of that sport, yet? What are you shooting at?
HEDDA.   Oh, I am only firing in the air.
BRACK.   [*Gently takes the pistol out of her hand*] Allow me, Madam! [*Looks at it*] Ah—I know this pistol well! [*Looks around*] Where is the case? Ah, here it is. [*Lays the pistol in it, and shuts it*] Now we won't play at that game any more to-day.
HEDDA.   Then what in heaven's name would you have me do with myself?
BRACK.   Have you had no visitors?
HEDDA.   [*Closing the glass door*] Not one. I suppose all our set are still out of town.
BRACK.   And is Tesman not at home either?
HEDDA.   [*At the writing-table, putting the pistol-case in a drawer which she shuts*] No. He rushed off to his aunt's directly after lunch; he didn't expect you so early.
BRACK.   H'm—how stupid of me not to have thought of that!
HEDDA.   [*Turning her head to look at him*] Why stupid?
BRACK.   Because if I had thought of it I should have come a little—earlier.
HEDDA.   [*Crossing the room*] Then you would have found no one to receive you; for I have been in my room changing my dress ever since lunch.
BRACK.   And is there no sort of little chink that we could hold a parley through?
HEDDA.   You have forgotten to arrange one.
BRACK.   That was another piece of stupidity.
HEDDA.   Well, we must just settle down here—and wait. Tesman is not likely to be back for some time yet.
BRACK.   Never mind; I shall not be impatient.

[HEDDA *seats herself in the corner of the sofa.* BRACK *lays his overcoat over the back of the nearest chair, and sits down, but keeps his hat in his hand. A short silence. They look at each other.*]

HEDDA. Well?

BRACK. [*In the same tone*] Well?

HEDDA. I spoke first.

BRACK. [*Bending a little forward*] Come, let us have a cosy little chat, Mrs. Hedda.

HEDDA. [*Leaning further back in the sofa*] Does it not seem like a whole eternity since our last talk? Of course I don't count those few words yesterday evening and this morning.

BRACK. You mean since our last confidential talk? Our last *tête-à-tête?*

HEDDA. Well, yes—since you put it so.

BRACK. Not a day has passed but I have wished that you were home again.

HEDDA. And I have done nothing but wish the same thing.

BRACK. You? Really, Mrs. Hedda? And I thought you had been enjoying your tour so much!

HEDDA. Oh, yes, you may be sure of that!

BRACK. But Tesman's letters spoke of nothing but happiness.

HEDDA. Oh, Tesman! You see, he thinks nothing so delightful as grubbing in libraries and making copies of old parchments, or whatever you call them.

BRACK. [*With a spice of malice*] Well, that is his vocation in life—or part of it at any rate.

HEDDA. Yes, of course; and no doubt when it's your vocation——. But *I!* Oh, my dear Mr. Brack, how mortally bored I have been.

BRACK. [*Sympathetically*] Do you really say so? In downright earnest?

HEDDA. Yes, you can surely understand it——! To go for six whole months without meeting a soul that knew anything of our circle, or could talk about the things we are interested in.

BRACK. Yes, yes—I, too, should feel that a deprivation.

HEDDA. And then, what I found most intolerable of all—

BRACK. Well?

HEDDA. ——was being everlastingly in the company of—one and the same person——

BRACK. [*With a nod of assent*] Morning, noon, and night, yes—at all possible times and seasons.

HEDDA. I said "everlastingly."

BRACK. Just so. But I should have thought, with our excellent Tesman, one could——

HEDDA. Tesman is—a specialist, my dear Judge.

BRACK. Undeniably.

HEDDA. And specialists are not at all amusing to travel with. Not in the long run at any rate.

BRACK. Not even—the specialist one happens to love?

HEDDA. Faugh—don't use that sickening word!

BRACK. [*Taken aback*] What do you say, Mrs. Hedda?

HEDDA. [*Half laughingly, half irritated*] You should just try it! To hear of nothing but the history of civilization morning, noon, and night——

BRACK. Everlastingly.

HEDDA. Yes, yes, yes! And then all this about the domestic industry of the Middle Ages——! That's the most disgusting part of it!

BRACK. [*Looks searchingly at her*] But tell me—in that case, how am I to understand your——? H'm——

HEDDA. My accepting George Tesman, you mean?

BRACK. Well, let us put it so.

HEDDA. Good heavens, do you see anything so wonderful in that?

BRACK. Yes and no—Mrs. Hedda.

HEDDA. I had positively danced myself tired, my dear Judge. My day was done—— [*With a slight shudder*] Oh, no—I won't say that; nor think it, either!

BRACK. You have assuredly no reason to.

HEDDA. Oh, reasons—— [*Watching him closely*] And George Tesman—after all, you must admit that he is correctness itself.

BRACK. His correctness and respectability are beyond all question.

HEDDA. And I don't see anything absolutely ridiculous about him.—Do you?

BRACK. Ridiculous? N—no—I shouldn't exactly say so——

HEDDA. Well—and his powers of research, at all events, are untiring.—I see no reason why he should not one day come to the front, after all.

BRACK. [*Looks at her hesitatingly*] I thought that you, like every one else, expected him to attain the highest distinction.

HEDDA. [*With an expression of fatigue*] Yes, so I did—And then, since he was bent, at all hazards, on being allowed to provide for me—I really don't know why I should not have accepted his offer?

BRACK. No—if you look at it in that light——

HEDDA. It was more than my other adorers were prepared to do for me, my dear Judge.

BRACK. [*Laughing*] Well, I can't answer for all the rest; but as for myself, you know quite well that I have always entertained a—a certain respect for the marriage tie—for marriage as an institution, Mrs. Hedda.

HEDDA. [*Jestingly*] Oh, I assure you I have never cherished any hopes with respect to you.

BRACK. All I require is a pleasant and intimate interior, where I can make myself useful in every way, and am free to come and go as—as a trusted friend——

HEDDA. Of the master of the house, do you mean?

BRACK. [*Bowing*] Frankly—of the mistress first of all; but, of course, of the master, too, in the second place. Such a triangular friendship—if I may call it so—is really a great convenience for all parties, let me tell you.

HEDDA. Yes, I have many a time longed for some one to make a third on our travels. Oh—those railway-carriage *tête-à-têtes*——!

BRACK. Fortunately your wedding journey is over now.

HEDDA. [*Shaking her head*] Not by a long—long way. I have only arrived at a station on the line.

BRACK. Well, then the passengers jump out and move about a little, Mrs. Hedda.

HEDDA. I never jump out.

BRACK.   Really?

HEDDA.   No—because there is always some one standing by to——

BRACK.   [*Laughing*] To look at your legs, do you mean?

HEDDA.   Precisely.

BRACK.   Well, but, dear me——

HEDDA.   [*With a gesture of repulsion*] I won't have it. I would rather keep my seat where I happen to be—and continue the *tête-à-tête*.

BRACK.   But suppose a third person were to jump in and join the couple.

HEDDA.   Ah—that is quite another matter!

BRACK.   A trusted, sympathetic friend——

HEDDA.   ——with a fund of conversation on all sorts of lively topics——

BRACK.   ——and not the least bit of a specialist!

HEDDA.   [*With an audible sigh*] Yes, that would be a relief, indeed.

BRACK.   [*Hears the front door open, and glances in that direction*] The triangle is completed.

HEDDA.   [*Half aloud*] And on goes the train.

[GEORGE TESMAN, *in a gray walking-suit, with a soft felt hat, enters from the hall. He has a number of unbound books under his arm and in his pockets*]

TESMAN.   [*Goes up to the table beside the corner settee*] Ouf—what a load for a warm day—all these books. [*Lays them on the table*] I'm positively perspiring, Hedda. Hallo—are you there already, my dear Judge? Eh? Berta didn't tell me.

BRACK.   [*Rising*] I came in through the garden.

HEDDA.   What books have you got there?

TESMAN.   [*Stands looking them through*] Some new books on my special subjects—quite indispensable to me.

HEDDA.   Your special subjects?

BRACK.   Yes, books on his special subjects, Mrs. Tesman.

[BRACK *and* HEDDA *exchange a confidential smile*]

HEDDA.   Do you need still more books on your special subjects?

TESMAN.   Yes, my dear Hedda, one can never have too many of them. Of course, one must keep up with all that is written and published.

HEDDA.   Yes, I suppose one must.

TESMAN.   [*Searching among his books*] And look here—I have got hold of Eilert Lövborg's new book, too. [*Offering it to her*] Perhaps you would like to glance through it, Hedda? Eh?

HEDDA.   No, thank you. Or rather—afterwards perhaps.

TESMAN.   I looked into it a little on the way home.

BRACK.   Well, what do you think of it—as a specialist?

TESMAN.   I think it shows quite remarkable soundness of judgment. He never wrote like that before. [*Putting the books together*] Now I shall take all these into my study. I'm longing to cut the leaves——! And then I must change my clothes. [*To* BRACK] I suppose we needn't start just yet? Eh?

BRACK.   Oh, dear, no—there is not the slightest hurry.

TESMAN.   Well, then, I will take my time. [*Is going with his books, but stops in the doorway and turns*] By the by, Hedda—Aunt Julia is not coming this evening.

HEDDA. Not coming? Is it that affair of the bonnet that keeps her away?

TESMAN. Oh, not at all. How could you think such a thing of Aunt Julia? Just fancy——! The fact is, Aunt Rina is very ill.

HEDDA. She always is.

TESMAN. Yes, but to-day she is much worse than usual, poor dear.

HEDDA. Oh, then it's only natural that her sister should remain with her. I must bear my disappointment.

TESMAN. And you can't imagine, dear, how delighted Aunt Julia seemed to be —because you had come home looking so flourishing!

HEDDA. [*Half aloud, rising*] Oh, those everlasting Aunts!

TESMAN. What?

HEDDA. [*Going to the glass door*] Nothing.

TESMAN. Oh, all right.

[*He goes through the inner room, out to the right*]

BRACK. What bonnet were you talking about?

HEDDA. Oh, it was a little episode with Miss Tesman this morning. She had laid down her bonnet on the chair there—[*Looks at him and smiles*]—and I pretended to think it was the servant's.

BRACK. [*Shaking his head*] Now, my dear Mrs. Hedda, how could you do such a thing? To that excellent old lady, too!

HEDDA. [*Nervously crossing the room*] Well, you see—these impulses come over me all of a sudden; and I cannot resist them. [*Throws herself down in the easy-chair by the stove*] Oh, I don't know how to explain it.

BRACK. [*Behind the easy-chair*] You are not really happy—that is at the bottom of it.

HEDDA. [*Looking straight before her*] I know of no reason why I should be— happy. Perhaps you can give me one?

BRACK. Well—amongst other things, because you have got exactly the home you had set your heart on.

HEDDA. [*Looks up at him and laughs*] Do you, too, believe in that legend?

BRACK. Is there nothing in it, then?

HEDDA. Oh, yes, there is something in it.

BRACK. Well?

HEDDA. There is this in it, that I made use of Tesman to see me home from evening parties last summer——

BRACK. I, unfortunately, had to go quite a different way.

HEDDA. That's true. I know you were going a different way last summer.

BRACK. [*Laughing*] Oh fie, Mrs. Hedda! Well, then—you and Tesman——?

HEDDA. Well, we happened to pass here one evening; Tesman, poor fellow, was writhing in the agony of having to find conversation; so I took pity on the learned man——

BRACK. [*Smiles doubtfully*] You took pity? H'm——

HEDDA. Yes, I really did. And so—to help him out of his torment—I happened to say, in pure thoughtlessness, that I should like to live in this villa.

BRACK. No more than that?

HEDDA. Not that evening.

BRACK. But afterwards?

HEDDA. Yes, my thoughtlessness had consequences, my dear Judge.

BRACK. Unfortunately that too often happens, Mrs. Hedda.

HEDDA. Thanks! So you see it was this enthusiasm for Secretary Falk's villa that first constituted a bond of sympathy between George Tesman and me. From that came our engagement and our marriage, and our wedding journey, and all the rest of it. Well, well, my dear judge—as you make your bed so you must lie, I could almost say.

BRACK. This is exquisite! And you really cared not a rap about it all the time?

HEDDA. No, heaven knows I didn't.

BRACK. But now? Now that we have made it so homelike for you?

HEDDA. Ugh—the rooms all seem to smell of lavender and dried rose-leaves.—But perhaps it's Aunt Julia that has brought that scent with her.

BRACK. [*Laughing*] No, I think it must be a legacy from the late Mrs. Secretary Falk.

HEDDA. Yes, there is an odor of mortality about it. It reminds me of a bouquet—the day after the ball. [*Clasps her hands behind her head, leans back in her chair and looks at him*] Oh, my dear Judge—you cannot imagine how horribly I shall bore myself here.

BRACK. Why should not you, too, find some sort of vocation in life, Mrs. Hedda?

HEDDA. A vocation—that should attract me?

BRACK. If possible, of course.

HEDDA. Heaven knows what sort of a vocation that could be. I often wonder whether—— [*Breaking off*] But that would never do, either.

BRACK. Who can tell? Let me hear what it is.

HEDDA. Whether I might not get Tesman to go into politics, I mean.

BRACK. [*Laughing*] Tesman? No, really now, political life is not the thing for him—not at all in his line.

HEDDA. No, I daresay not.—But if I could get him into it all the same?

BRACK. Why—what satisfaction could you find in that? If he is not fitted for that sort of thing, why should you want to drive him into it?

HEDDA. Because I am bored, I tell you! [*After a pause*] So you think it quite out of the question that Tesman should ever get into the ministry?

BRACK. H'm—you see, my dear Mrs. Hedda—to get into the ministry, he would have to be a tolerably rich man.

HEDDA. [*Rising impatiently*] Yes, there we have it! It is this genteel poverty I have managed to drop into——! [*Crosses the room*] That is what makes life so pitiable! So utterly ludicrous!—For that's what it is.

BRACK. Now *I* should say the fault lay elsewhere.

HEDDA. Where, then?

BRACK. You have never gone through any really stimulating experience.

HEDDA. Anything serious, you mean?

BRACK. Yes, you may call it so. But now you may perhaps have one in store.

HEDDA. [*Tossing her head*] Oh, you're thinking of the annoyances about this wretched professorship! But that must be Tesman's own affair. I assure you I shall not waste a thought upon it.

BRACK. No, no, I daresay not. But suppose now that what people call—in elegant language—a solemn responsibility were to come upon you? [*Smiling*] A new responsibility, Mrs. Hedda?

HEDDA. [*Angrily*] Be quiet! Nothing of that sort will ever happen!

BRACK. [*Warily*] We will speak of this again a year hence—at the very outside.

HEDDA. [*Curtly*] I have no turn for anything of the sort, Judge Brack. No responsibilities for me!

BRACK. Are you so unlike the generality of women as to have no turn for duties which——?

HEDDA. [*Beside the glass door*] Oh, be quiet, I tell you!—I often think there is only one thing in the world I have any turn for.

BRACK. [*Drawing near to her*] And what is that, if I may ask?

HEDDA. [*Stands looking out*] Boring myself to death. Now you know it. [*Turns, looks towards the inner room, and laughs*] Yes, as I thought! Here comes the Professor.

BRACK. [*Softly, in a tone of warning*] Come, come, come, Mrs. Hedda!

[GEORGE TESMAN, *dressed for the party, with his gloves and hat in his hand, enters from the right through the inner room*]

TESMAN. Hedda, has no message come from Eilert Lövborg? Eh?

HEDDA. No.

TESMAN. Then you'll see he'll be here presently.

BRACK. Do you really think he will come?

TESMAN. Yes, I am almost sure of it. For what you were telling us this morning must have been a mere floating rumor.

BRACK. You think so?

TESMAN. At any rate, Aunt Julia said she did not believe for a moment that he would ever stand in my way again. Fancy that!

BRACK. Well, then, that's all right.

TESMAN. [*Placing his hat and gloves on a chair on the right*] Yes, but you must really let me wait for him as long as possible.

BRACK. We have plenty of time yet. None of my guests will arrive before seven or half-past.

TESMAN. Then meanwhile we can keep Hedda company, and see what happens. Eh?

HEDDA. [*Placing* BRACK's *hat and overcoat upon the corner settee*] And at the worst Mr. Lövborg can remain here with me.

BRACK. [*Offering to take his things*] Oh, allow me, Mrs. Tesman!—What do you mean by "at the worst"?

HEDDA. If he won't go with you and Tesman.

TESMAN. [*Looks dubiously at her*] But, Hedda, dear—do you think it would quite do for him to remain with you? Eh? Remember, Aunt Julia can't come.

HEDDA. No, but Mrs. Elvsted is coming. We three can have a cup of tea together.

TESMAN. Oh, yes, that will be all right.

BRACK. [*Smiling*] And that would perhaps be the safest plan for him.

HEDDA. Why so?

BRACK. Well, you know, Mrs. Tesman, how you used to gird at my little bachelor parties. You declared they were adapted only for men of the strictest principles.

HEDDA. But no doubt Mr. Lövborg's principles are strict enough now. A converted sinner——

[BERTA *appears at the hall door*]

BERTA. There's a gentleman asking if you are at home, ma'am——

HEDDA. Well, show him in.

TESMAN. [*Softly*] I'm sure it is he! Fancy that!

[EILERT LÖVBORG *enters from the hall. He is slim and lean; of the same age as* TESMAN, *but looks older and somewhat worn-out. His hair and beard are of a blackish brown, his face long and pale, but with patches of color on the cheekbones. He is dressed in a well-cut black visiting suit, quite new. He has dark gloves and a silk hat. He stops near the door, and makes a rapid bow, seeming somewhat embarrassed*]

TESMAN. [*Goes up to him and shakes him warmly by the hand*] Well, my dear Eilert—so at last we meet again!

EILERT LÖVBORG. [*Speaks in a subdued voice*] Thanks for your letter, Tesman. [*Approaching* HEDDA] Will you, too, shake hands with me, Mrs. Tesman?

HEDDA. [*Taking his hand*] I am glad to see you, Mr. Lövborg. [*With a motion of her hand*] I don't know whether you two gentlemen——?

LÖVBORG. [*Bowing slightly*] Judge Brack, I think.

BRACK. [*Doing likewise*] Oh, yes,—in the old days——

TESMAN. [*To* LÖVBORG, *with his hands on his shoulders*] And now you must make yourself entirely at home, Eilert! Mustn't he, Hedda?—For I hear you are going to settle in town again? Eh?

LÖVBORG. Yes, I am.

TESMAN. Quite right, quite right. Let me tell you, I have got hold of your new book; but I haven't had time to read it yet.

LÖVBORG. You may spare yourself the trouble.

TESMAN. Why so?

LÖVBORG. Because there is very little in it.

TESMAN. Just fancy—how can you say so?

BRACK. But it has been very much praised, I hear.

LÖVBORG. That was what I wanted; so I put nothing into the book but what every one would agree with.

BRACK. Very wise of you.

TESMAN. Well, but, my dear Eilert——!

LÖVBORG. For now I mean to win myself a position again—to make a fresh start.

TESMAN. [*A little embarrassed*] Ah, that is what you wish to do? Eh?

LÖVBORG. [*Smiling, lays down his hat, and draws a packet, wrapped in paper, from his coat pocket*] But when this one appears, George Tesman, you will have to read it. For this is the real book—the book I have put my true self into.

TESMAN. Indeed? And what is it?

LÖVBORG. It is the continuation.

TESMAN. The continuation? Of what?

LÖVBORG. Of the book.

TESMAN. Of the new book?

LÖVBORG. Of course.

TESMAN. Why, my dear Eilert—does it not come down to our own days?

LÖVBORG. Yes, it does; and this one deals with the future.

TESMAN. With the future! But, good heavens, we know nothing of the future!

LÖVBORG. No; but there is a thing or two to be said about it all the same. [*Opens the packet*] Look here——

TESMAN. Why, that's not your handwriting.

LÖVBORG. I dictated it. [*Turning over the pages*] It falls into two sections. The first deals with the civilizing forces of the future. And here is the second—[*Running through the pages towards the end*]—forecasting the probable line of development.

TESMAN. How odd now! I should never have thought of writing anything of that sort.

HEDDA. [*At the glass door, drumming on the pane*] H'm—— I daresay not.

LÖVBORG. [*Replacing the manuscript in its paper and laying the packet on the table*] I brought it, thinking I might read you a little of it this evening.

TESMAN. That was very good of you, Eilert. But this evening——? [*Looking at* BRACK] I don't quite see how we can manage it——

LÖVBORG. Well, then, some other time. There is no hurry.

BRACK. I must tell you, Mr. Lövborg—there is a little gathering at my house this evening—mainly in honor of Tesman, you know——

LÖVBORG. [*Looking for his hat*] Oh—then I won't detain you——

BRACK. No, but listen—will you not do me the favor of joining us?

LÖVBORG. [*Curtly and decidedly*] No, I can't—thank you very much.

BRACK. Oh, nonsense—do! We shall be quite a select little circle. And I assure you we shall have a "lively time," as Mrs. Hed—as Mrs. Tesman says.

LÖVBORG. I have no doubt of it. But nevertheless——

BRACK. And then you might bring your manuscript with you, and read it to Tesman at my house. I could give you a room to yourselves.

TESMAN. Yes, think of that, Eilert,—why shouldn't you? Eh?

HEDDA. [*Interposing*] But, Tesman, if Mr. Lövborg would really rather not! I am sure Mr. Lövborg is much more inclined to remain here and have supper with me.

LÖVBORG. [*Looking at her*] With you, Mrs. Tesman?

HEDDA. And with Mrs. Elvsted.

LÖVBORG. Ah—— [*Lightly*] I saw her for a moment this morning.

HEDDA. Did you? Well, she is coming this evening. So you see you are almost bound to remain, Mr. Lövborg, or she will have no one to see her home.

LÖVBORG. That's true. Many thanks, Mrs. Tesman—in that case I will remain.

HEDDA. Then I have one or two orders to give the servant——

  [*She goes to the hall door and rings.* BERTA *enters.* HEDDA *talks to her in a whisper, and points towards the inner room.* BERTA *nods and goes out again*]

TESMAN. [*At the same time, to* LÖVBORG] Tell me, Eilert—is it this new subject—the future—that you are going to lecture about?

LÖVBORG. Yes.

TESMAN. They told me at the bookseller's that you are going to deliver a course of lectures this autumn.

LÖVBORG. That is my intention. I hope you won't take it ill, Tesman.

TESMAN. Oh no, not in the least! But——?

LÖVBORG. I can quite understand that it must be disagreeable to you.

TESMAN. [*Cast down*] Oh, I can't expect you, out of consideration for me, to——

LÖVBORG. But I shall wait till you have received your appointment.

TESMAN. Will you wait? Yes, but—yes, but—are you not going to compete with me? Eh?

LÖVBORG. No; it is only the moral victory I care for.

TESMAN. Why, bless me—then Aunt Julia was right after all! Oh, yes—I knew it! Hedda! Just fancy—Eilert Lövborg is not going to stand in our way!

HEDDA. [*Curtly*] Our way? Pray leave me out of the question.

[*She goes up towards the inner room, where* BERTA *is placing a tray with decanters and glasses on the table.* HEDDA *nods approval, and comes forward again.* BERTA *goes out*]

TESMAN. [*At the same time*] And you, Judge Brack—what do you say to this? Eh?

BRACK. Well, I say that a moral victory—h'm—may be all very fine——

TESMAN. Yes, certainly. But all the same——

HEDDA. [*Looking at* TESMAN *with a cold smile*] You stand there looking as if you were thunderstruck——

TESMAN. Yes—so I am—I almost think——

BRACK. Don't you see, Mrs. Tesman, a thunderstorm has just passed over?

HEDDA. [*Pointing towards the inner room*] Will you not take a glass of cold punch, gentlemen?

BRACK. [*Looking at his watch*] A stirrup-cup? Yes, it wouldn't come amiss.

TESMAN. A capital idea, Hedda! Just the thing! Now that the weight has been taken off my mind——

HEDDA. Will you not join them, Mr. Lövborg?

LÖVBORG. [*With a gesture of refusal*] No, thank you. Nothing for me.

BRACK. Why bless me—cold punch is surely not poison.

LÖVBORG. Perhaps not for every one.

HEDDA. I will keep Mr. Lövborg company in the meantime.

TESMAN. Yes, yes, Hedda dear, do.

[*He and* BRACK *go into the inner room, seat themselves, drink punch, smoke cigarettes, and carry on a lively conversation during what follows.* EILERT LÖV-BORG *remains standing beside the stove.* HEDDA *goes to the writing-table.*]

HEDDA. [*Raising her voice a little*] Do you care to look at some photographs, Mr. Lövborg? You know Tesman and I made a tour in the Tyrol on our way home?

[*She takes up an album, and places it on the table beside the sofa, in the further corner of which she seats herself.* EILERT LÖVBORG *approaches, stops, and looks at her. Then he takes a chair and seats himself to her left, with his back towards the inner room*]

HEDDA. [*Opening the album*] Do you see this range of mountains, Mr. Lövborg? It's the Ortler group. Tesman has written the name underneath. Here it is: "The Ortler group near Meran."

LÖVBORG. [*Who has never taken his eyes off her, says softly and slowly*] Hedda—Gabler!

HEDDA. [*Glancing hastily at him*] Ah! Hush!

LÖVBORG. [*Repeats softly*] Hedda Gabler!

HEDDA. [*Looking at the album*] That was my name in the old days—when we two knew each other.

LÖVBORG. And I must teach myself never to say Hedda Gabler again—never, as long as I live.

HEDDA. [*Still turning over the pages*] Yes, you must. And I think you ought to practise in time. The sooner the better, I should say.

LÖVBORG. [*In a tone of indignation*] Hedda Gabler married? And married to—George Tesman!

HEDDA. Yes—so the world goes.

LÖVBORG. Oh, Hedda, Hedda—how could you[5] throw yourself away!

HEDDA. [*Looks sharply at him*] What? I can't allow this!

LÖVBORG. What do you mean?

[TESMAN *comes into the room and goes towards the sofa*]

HEDDA. [*Hears him coming and says in an indifferent tone*] And this is a view from the Val d'Ampezzo, Mr. Lövborg. Just look at these peaks! [*Looks affectionately up at* TESMAN] What's the name of these curious peaks, dear?

TESMAN. Let me see. Oh, those are the Dolomites.

HEDDA. Yes, that's it!—Those are the Dolomites, Mr. Lövborg.

TESMAN. Hedda, dear,—I only wanted to ask whether I shouldn't bring you a little punch after all? For yourself, at any rate—eh?

HEDDA. Yes, do, please; and perhaps a few biscuits.

TESMAN. No cigarettes?

HEDDA. No.

TESMAN. Very well.

[*He goes into the inner room and out to the right.* BRACK *sits in the inner room, and keeps an eye from time to time on* HEDDA *and* LÖVBORG]

LÖVBORG. [*Softly, as before*] Answer me, Hedda—how could you go and do this?

HEDDA. [*Apparently absorbed in the album*] If you continue to say *du* to me I won't talk to you.

LÖVBORG. May I not say *du* even when we are alone?

HEDDA. No. You may think it; but you mustn't say it.

LÖVBORG. Ah, I understand. It is an offence against George Tesman, whom you[6] love.

HEDDA. [*Glances at him and smiles*] Love? What an idea!

LÖVBORG. You don't love him then!

HEDDA. But I won't hear of any sort of unfaithfulness! Remember that.

LÖVBORG. Hedda—answer me one thing——

HEDDA. Hush!

[TESMAN *enters with a small tray from the inner room*]

TESMAN. Here you are! Isn't this tempting?

[*He puts the tray on the table*]

---

[5] Lövborg uses the familiar *du*.   [6] From here on Lövborg uses the formal *De*.

HEDDA. Why do you bring it yourself?

TESMAN. [*Filling the glasses*] Because I think it's such fun to wait upon you, Hedda.

HEDDA. But you have poured out two glasses. Mr. Lövborg said he wouldn't have any——

TESMAN. No, but Mrs. Elvsted will soon be here, won't she?

HEDDA. Yes, by the by—Mrs. Elvsted——

TESMAN. Had you forgotten her? Eh?

HEDDA. We were so absorbed in these photographs. [*Shows him a picture*] Do you remember this little village?

TESMAN. Oh, it's that one just below the Brenner Pass. It was there we passed the night——

HEDDA. ——and met that lively party of tourists.

TESMAN. Yes, that was the place. Fancy—if we could only have had you with us, Eilert! Eh?

[*He returns to the inner room and sits beside* BRACK]

LÖVBORG. Answer me this one thing, Hedda——

HEDDA. Well?

LÖVBORG. Was there no love in your friendship for me, either? Not a spark—not a tinge of love in it?

HEDDA. I wonder if there was? To me it seems as though we were two good comrades—two thoroughly intimate friends. [*Smilingly*] You especially were frankness itself.

LÖVBORG. It was you that made me so.

HEDDA. As I look back upon it all, I think there was really something beautiful, something fascinating—something daring—in—in that secret intimacy—that comradeship which no living creature so much as dreamed of.

LÖVBORG. Yes, yes, Hedda! Was there not?—When I used to come to your father's in the afternoon—and the General sat over at the window reading his papers—with his back towards us——

HEDDA. And we two on the corner sofa——

LÖVBORG. Always with the same illustrated paper before us——

HEDDA. For want of an album, yes.

LÖVBORG. Yes, Hedda, and when I made my confessions to you—told you about myself, things that at that time no one else knew! There I would sit and tell you of my escapades—my days and nights of devilment. Oh, Hedda—what was the power in you that forced me to confess these things?

HEDDA. Do you think it was any power in me?

LÖVBORG. How else can I explain it? And all those—those roundabout questions you used to put to me——

HEDDA. Which you understood so particularly well——

LÖVBORG. How could you sit and question me like that? Question me quite frankly——

HEDDA. In roundabout terms, please observe.

LÖVBORG. Yes, but frankly nevertheless. Cross-question me about—all that sort of thing?

HEDDA. And how could you answer, Mr. Lövborg?

LÖVBORG. Yes, that is just what I can't understand—in looking back upon it.

But tell me now, Hedda—was there not love at the bottom of our friendship? On your side, did you not feel as though you might purge my stains away—If I made you my confessor? Was it not so?

HEDDA.   No, not quite.

LÖVBORG.   What was your motive, then?

HEDDA.   Do you think it quite incomprehensible that a young girl—when it can be done—without any one knowing——

LÖVBORG.   Well?

HEDDA.   ——should be glad to have a peep, now and then, into a world which——

LÖVBORG.   Which——?

HEDDA.   ——which she is forbidden to know anything about?

LÖVBORG.   So that was it?

HEDDA.   Partly. Partly—I almost think.

LÖVBORG.   Comradeship in the thirst for life. But why should not that, at any rate, have continued?

HEDDA.   The fault was yours.

LÖVBORG.   It was you that broke with me.

HEDDA.   Yes, when our friendship threatened to develop into something more serious. Shame upon you, Eilert Lövborg! How could you think of wronging your—your frank comrade?

LÖVBORG.   [*Clenching his hands*] Oh, why did you not carry out your threat? Why did you not shoot me down?

HEDDA.   Because I have such a dread of scandal.

LÖVBORG.   Yes, Hedda, you are a coward at heart.

HEDDA.   A terrible coward. [*Changing her tone*] But it was a lucky thing for you. And now you have found ample consolation at the Elvsteds'.

LÖVBORG.   I know what Thea has confided to you.

HEDDA.   And perhaps you have confided to her something about us?

LÖVBORG.   Not a word. She is too stupid to understand anything of that sort.

HEDDA.   Stupid?

LÖVBORG.   She is stupid about matters of that sort.

HEDDA.   And I am cowardly. [*Bends over towards him, without looking him in the face, and says more softly:*] But now I will confide something to you.

LÖVBORG.   [*Eagerly*] Well?

HEDDA.   The fact that I dared not shoot you down——

LÖVBORG.   Yes!

HEDDA.   ——that was not my most arrant cowardice—that evening.

LÖVBORG.   [*Looks at her a moment, understands, and whispers passionately*] Oh, Hedda! Hedda Gabler! Now I begin to see a hidden reason beneath our comradeship! You[7] and I——! After all, then, it was your craving for life——

HEDDA.   [*Softly, with a sharp glance*] Take care! Believe nothing of the sort! [*Twilight has begun to fall. The hall door is opened from without by* BERTA]

HEDDA.   [*Closes the album with a bang and calls smilingly:*] Ah, at last! My darling Thea,—come along!

---

[7] *Du* once more. Hedda uses *De* consistently.

[MRS. ELVSTED *enters from the hall. She is in evening dress. The door is closed behind her*]

HEDDA. [*On the sofa, stretches out her arms towards her*] My sweet Thea—you can't think how I have been longing for you!

[MRS. ELVSTED, *in passing, exchanges slight salutations with the gentlemen in the inner room, then goes up to the table and gives* HEDDA *her hand.* EILERT LÖVBORG *has risen. He and* MRS. ELVSTED *greet each other with a silent nod*]

MRS. ELVSTED. Ought I to go in and talk to your husband for a moment?

HEDDA. Oh, not at all. Leave those two alone. They will soon be going.

MRS. ELVSTED. Are they going out?

HEDDA. Yes, to a supper-party.

MRS. ELVSTED. [*Quickly, to* LÖVBORG] Not you?

LÖVBORG. No.

HEDDA. Mr. Lövborg remains with us.

MRS. ELVSTED. [*Takes a chair and is about to seat herself at his side*] Oh, how nice it is here!

HEDDA. No, thank you, my little Thea! Not there! You'll be good enough to come over here to me. I will sit between you.

MRS. ELVSTED. Yes, just as you please.

[*She goes round the table and seats herself on the sofa on* HEDDA'S *right.* LÖVBORG *re-seats himself on his chair*]

LÖVBORG. [*After a short pause, to* HEDDA] Is not she lovely to look at?

HEDDA. [*Lightly stroking her hair*] Only to look at?

LÖVBORG. Yes. For we two—she and I—we are two real comrades. We have absolute faith in each other; so we can sit and talk with perfect frankness——

HEDDA. Not round about, Mr. Lövborg?

LÖVBORG. Well——

MRS. ELVSTED. [*Softly clinging close to* HEDDA] Oh, how happy I am, Hedda! For, only think, he says I have inspired him, too.

HEDDA. [*Looks at her with a smile*] Ah! Does say that, dear?

LÖVBORG. And then she is so brave, Mrs. Tesman!

MRS. ELVSTED. Good heavens—am I brave?

LÖVBORG. Exceedingly—where your comrade is concerned.

HEDDA. Ah, yes—courage! If one only had that!

LÖVBORG. What then? What do you mean?

HEDDA. Then life would perhaps be livable, after all. [*With a sudden change of tone*] But now, my dearest Thea, you really must have a glass of cold punch.

MRS. ELVSTED. No, thanks—I never take anything of that kind.

HEDDA. Well, then, you, Mr. Lövborg.

LÖVBORG. Nor I, thank you.

MRS. ELVSTED. No, he doesn't, either.

HEDDA. [*Looks fixedly at him*] But if I say you shall?

LÖVBORG. It would be no use.

HEDDA. [*Laughing*] Then I, poor creature, have no sort of power over you?

LÖVBORG. Not in that respect.

HEDDA. But seriously, I think you ought to—for your own sake.

MRS. ELVSTED. Why, Hedda——!

LÖVBORG. How so?

HEDDA.   Or rather on account of other people.

LÖVBORG.   Indeed?

HEDDA.   Otherwise people might be apt to suspect that—in your heart of hearts —you did not feel quite secure—quite confident in yourself.

MRS. ELVSTED.   [*Softly*] Oh, please, Hedda——!

LÖVBORG.   People may suspect what they like—for the present.

MRS. ELVSTED.   [*Joyfully*] Yes, let them!

HEDDA.   I saw it plainly in Judge Brack's face a moment ago.

LÖVBORG.   What did you see?

HEDDA.   His contemptuous smile, when you dared not go with them into the inner room.

LÖVBORG.   Dared not? Of course I preferred to stop here and talk to you.

MRS. ELVSTED.   What could be more natural, Hedda?

HEDDA.   But the Judge could not guess that. And I saw, too, the way he smiled and glanced at Tesman when you dared not accept his invitation to this wretched little supper-party of his.

LÖVBORG.   Dared not! Do you say I dared not?

HEDDA.   *I* don't say so. But that was how Judge Brack understood it.

LÖVBORG.   Well, let him.

HEDDA.   Then you are not going with them?

LÖVBORG.   I will stay here with you and Thea.

MRS. ELVSTED.   Yes, Hedda—how can you doubt that?

HEDDA.   [*Smiles and nods approvingly to* LÖVBORG] Firm as a rock! Faithful to your principles, now and forever! Ah, that is how a man should be! [*Turns to* MRS. ELVSTED *and caresses her*] Well, now, what did I tell you, when you came to us this morning in such a state of distraction——

LÖVBORG.   [*Surprised*] Distraction!

MRS. ELVSTED.   [*Terrified*] Hedda—oh, Hedda——!

HEDDA.   You can see for yourself! You haven't the slightest reason to be in such mortal terror—— [*Interrupting herself*] There! Now we can all three enjoy ourselves!

LÖVBORG.   [*Who has given a start*] Ah—what is all this, Mrs. Tesman?

MRS. ELVSTED.   Oh, my God, Hedda! What are you saying? What are you doing?

HEDDA.   Don't get excited! That horrid Judge Brack is sitting watching you.

LÖVBORG.   So she was in mortal terror! On my account!

MRS. ELVSTED.   [*Softly and piteously*] Oh, Hedda—now you have ruined everything!

LÖVBORG.   [*Looks fixedly at her for a moment. His face is distorted*] So that was my comrade's frank confidence in me?

MRS. ELVSTED.   [*Imploringly*] Oh, my dearest friend—only let me tell you——

LÖVBORG.   [*Takes one of the glasses of punch, raises it to his lips, and says in a low, husky voice*] Your health, Thea!
[*He empties the glass, puts it down, and takes the second*]

MRS. ELVSTED.   [*Softly*] Oh, Hedda, Hedda—how could you do this?

HEDDA.   *I* do it? I? Are you crazy?

LÖVBORG.   Here's to your health, too, Mrs. Tesman. Thanks for the truth. Hurrah for the truth!

[*He empties the glass and is about to re-fill it*]

HEDDA. [*Lays her hand on his arm*] Come, come—no more for the present. Remember you are going out to supper.

MRS. ELVSTED. No, no, no!

HEDDA. Hush! They are sitting watching you.

LÖVBORG. [*Putting down the glass*] Now, Thea—tell me the truth——

MRS. ELVSTED. Yes.

LÖVBORG. Did your husband know that you had come after me?

MRS. ELVSTED. [*Wringing her hands*] Oh, Hedda—do you hear what he is asking?

LÖVBORG. Was it arranged between you and him that you were to come to town and look after me? Perhaps it was the Sheriff himself that urged you to come? Aha, my dear—no doubt he wanted my help in his office. Or was it at the card-table that he missed me?

MRS. ELVSTED. [*Softly, in agony*] Oh, Lövborg, Lövborg——!

LÖVBORG. [*Seizes a glass and is on the point of filling it*] Here's a glass for the old Sheriff, too!

HEDDA. [*Preventing him*] No more just now. Remember, you have to read your manuscript to Tesman.

LÖVBORG. [*Calmly, putting down the glass*] It was stupid of me all this, Thea —to take it in this way, I mean. Don't be angry with me, my dear, dear comrade. You shall see—both you and the others—that if I was fallen once —now I have risen again! Thanks to you, Thea.

MRS. ELVSTED. [*Radiant with joy*] Oh, heaven be praised——!

[BRACK *has in the meantime looked at his watch. He and* TESMAN *rise and come into the drawing room*]

BRACK. [*Takes his hat and overcoat*] Well, Mrs. Tesman, our time has come.

HEDDA. I suppose it has.

LÖVBORG. [*Rising*] Mine too, Judge Brack.

MRS. ELVSTED. [*Softly and imploringly*] Oh, Lövborg, don't do it!

HEDDA. [*Pinching her arm*] They can hear you!

MRS. ELVSTED. [*With a suppressed shriek*] Ow!

LÖVBORG. [*To* BRACK] You were good enough to invite me.

BRACK. Well, are you coming after all?

LÖVBORG. Yes, many thanks.

BRACK. I'm delighted——

LÖVBORG. [*To* TESMAN, *putting the parcel of MS. in his pocket*] I should like to show you one or two things before I send it to the printers.

TESMAN. Fancy—that will be delightful. But, Hedda dear, how is Mrs. Elvsted to get home? Eh?

HEDDA. Oh, that can be managed somehow.

LÖVBORG. [*Looking towards the ladies*] Mrs. Elvsted? Of course, I'll come again and fetch her. [*Approaching*] At ten or thereabouts, Mrs. Tesman? Will that do?

HEDDA. Certainly. That will do capitally.

TESMAN. Well, then, that's all right. But you must not expect me so early, Hedda.

HEDDA.   Oh, you may stop as long—as long as ever you please.

MRS. ELVSTED.   [*Trying to conceal her anxiety*] Well, then, Mr. Lövborg—I shall remain here until you come.

LÖVBORG.   [*With his hat in his hand*] Pray do, Mrs. Elvsted.

BRACK.   And now off goes the excursion train, gentlemen! I hope we shall have a lively time, as a certain fair lady puts it.

HEDDA.   Ah, if only the fair lady could be present unseen——!

BRACK.   Why unseen?

HEDDA.   In order to hear a little of your liveliness at first hand, Judge Brack.

BRACK.   [*Laughing*] I should not advise the fair lady to try it.

TESMAN.   [*Also laughing*] Come, you're a nice one, Hedda! Fancy that!

BRACK.   Well, good-bye, good-bye, ladies.

LÖVBORG.   [*Bowing*] About ten o'clock, then.

[BRACK, LÖVBORG, *and* TESMAN *go out by the hall door. At the same time,* BERTA *enters from the inner room with a lighted lamp, which she places on the drawing-room table; she goes out by the way she came*]

MRS. ELVSTED.   [*Who has risen and is wandering restlessly about the room*] Hedda—Hedda—what will come of all this?

HEDDA.   At ten o'clock—he will be here. I can see him already—with vine-leaves[8] in his hair—flushed and fearless——

MRS. ELVSTED.   Oh, I hope he may.

HEDDA.   And then, you see—then he will have regained control over himself. Then he will be a free man for all his days.

MRS. ELVSTED.   Oh, God!—If he would only come as you see him now!

HEDDA.   He will come as I see him—so, and not otherwise! [*Rises and approaches* THEA] You may doubt him as long as you please; *I* believe in him. And now we will try——

MRS. ELVSTED.   You have some hidden motive in this, Hedda!

HEDDA.   Yes, I have. I want for once in my life to have power to mould a human destiny.

MRS. ELVSTED.   Have you not the power?

HEDDA.   I have not—and have never had it.

MRS. ELVSTED.   Not your husband's?

HEDDA.   Do you think that is worth the trouble? Oh, if you could only understand how poor I am. And fate has made you so rich! [*Clasps her passionately in her arms*] I think I must burn your hair off, after all.

MRS. ELVSTED.   Let me go! Let me go! I am afraid of you, Hedda!

BERTA.   [*In the middle doorway*] Tea is laid in the dining-room, ma'am.

HEDDA.   Very well. We are coming.

MRS. ELVSTED.   No, no, no! I would rather go home alone! At once!

HEDDA.   Nonsense! First you shall have a cup of tea, you little stupid. And then —at ten o'clock—Eilert Lövborg will be here—with vine-leaves in his hair. [*She drags* MRS. ELVSTED *almost by force towards the middle doorway*]

---

[8]   Bacchus (Greek god of wine) wore vine-leaves in his hair. For Hedda, the vine-leaves symbolize triumphantly courageous unconventionality.

Act Three

The room at the TESMANS'. *The curtains are drawn over the middle doorway, and also over the glass door. The lamp, half turned down, and with a shade over it, is burning on the table. In the stove, the door of which stands open, there has been a fire, which is now nearly burnt out.* MRS. ELVSTED, *wrapped in a large shawl, and with her feet upon a foot-rest, sits close to the stove, sunk back in the armchair.* HEDDA, *fully dressed, lies sleeping upon the sofa, with a sofa-blanket over her.*

MRS. ELVSTED. [*After a pause, suddenly sits up in her chair, and listens eagerly. Then she sinks back again wearily, moaning to herself*] Not yet!—Oh, God —oh, God—not yet!

[BERTA *slips cautiously in by the hall door. She has a letter in her hand*]

MRS. ELVSTED. [*Turns and whispers eagerly*] Well—has anyone come?

BERTA. [*Softly*] Yes, a girl has just brought this letter.

MRS. ELVSTED. [*Quickly, holding out her hand*] A letter! Give it to me!

BERTA. No, it's for Dr. Tesman, ma'am.

MRS. ELVSTED. Oh, indeed.

BERTA. It was Miss Tesman's servant that brought it. I'll lay it here on the table.

MRS. ELVSTED. Yes, do.

BERTA. [*Laying down the letter*] I think I had better put out the lamp. It's smoking.

MRS. ELVSTED. Yes, put it out. It must soon be daylight now.

BERTA. [*Putting out the lamp*] It is daylight already, ma'am.

MRS. ELVSTED. Yes, broad day! And no one come back yet——!

BERTA. Lord bless you, ma'am—I guessed how it would be.

MRS. ELVSTED. You guessed?

BERTA. Yes, when I saw that a certain person had come back to town—and that he went off with them. For we've heard enough about that gentleman before now.

MRS. ELVSTED. Don't speak so loud. You will waken Mrs. Tesman.

BERTA. [*Looks towards the sofa and sighs*] No, no—let her sleep, poor thing. Shan't I put some wood on the fire?

MRS. ELVSTED. Thanks, not for me.

BERTA. Oh, very well.

[*She goes softly out by the hall door*]

HEDDA. [*Is awakened by the shutting of the door, and looks up*] What's that——?

MRS. ELVSTED. It was only the servant——

HEDDA. [*Looking about her*] Oh, we're here——! Yes, now I remember. [*Sits erect upon the sofa, stretches herself, and rubs her eyes*] What o'clock is it, Thea?

MRS. ELVSTED. [*Looks at her watch*] It's past seven.

HEDDA. When did Tesman come home?

MRS. ELVSTED. He has not come.

HEDDA. Not come home yet?

MRS. ELVSTED. [*Rising*] No one has come.

HEDDA. Think of our watching and waiting here till four in the morning——

MRS. ELVSTED. [*Wringing her hands*] And how I watched and waited for him!

HEDDA. [*Yawns, and says with her hand before her mouth*] Well, well—we might have spared ourselves the trouble.

MRS. ELVSTED. Did you get a little sleep?

HEDDA. Oh, yes; I believe I have slept pretty well. Have you not?

MRS. ELVSTED. Not for a moment. I couldn't, Hedda!—not to save my life.

HEDDA. [*Rises and goes towards her*] There, there, there! There's nothing to be so alarmed about. I understand quite well what has happened.

MRS. ELVSTED. Well, what do you think? Won't you tell me?

HEDDA. Why, of course, it has been a very late affair at Judge Brack's——

MRS. ELVSTED. Yes, yes—that is clear enough. But all the same——

HEDDA. And then, you see, Tesman hasn't cared to come home and ring us up in the middle of the night. [*Laughing*] Perhaps he wasn't inclined to show himself either—immediately after a jollification.

MRS. ELVSTED. But in that case—where can he have gone?

HEDDA. Of course, he has gone to his aunts' and slept there. They have his old room ready for him.

MRS. ELVSTED. No, he can't be with them; for a letter has just come for him from Miss Tesman. There it lies.

HEDDA. Indeed? [*Looks at the address*] Why, yes, it's addressed in Aunt Julia's own hand. Well, then, he has remained at Judge Brack's. And as for Eilert Lövborg—he is sitting, with vine-leaves in his hair, reading his manuscript.

MRS. ELVSTED. Oh, Hedda, you are just saying things you don't believe a bit.

HEDDA. You really are a little blockhead, Thea.

MRS. ELVSTED. Oh, yes, I suppose I am.

HEDDA. And how mortally tired you look.

MRS. ELVSTED. Yes, I am mortally tired.

HEDDA. Well, then, you must do as I tell you. You must go into my room and lie down for a little while.

MRS. ELVSTED. Oh, no, no—I shouldn't be able to sleep.

HEDDA. I am sure you would.

MRS. ELVSTED. Well, but your husband is certain to come soon now; and then I want to know at once——

HEDDA. I shall take care to let you know when he comes.

MRS. ELVSTED. Do you promise me, Hedda?

HEDDA. Yes, rely upon me. Just you go in and have a sleep in the meantime.

MRS. ELVSTED. Thanks; then I'll try to.

[*She goes off through the inner room.* HEDDA *goes up to the glass door and draws back the curtains. The broad daylight streams into the room. Then she takes a little hand-glass from the writing-table, looks at herself in it and arranges her hair. Next she goes to the hall door and presses the bell-button.* BERTA *presently appears at the hall door*]

BERTA. Did you want anything ma'am?

HEDDA. Yes; you must put some more wood in the stove. I am shivering.

BERTA. Bless me—I'll make up the fire at once. [*She rakes the embers together and lays a piece of wood upon them; then stops and listens*] That was a ring at the front door, ma'am.

HEDDA. Then go to the door. I will look after the fire.

BERTA. It'll soon burn up.

[*She goes out by the hall door.* HEDDA *kneels on the foot-rest and lays some more pieces of wood in the stove. After a short pause,* GEORGE TESMAN *enters from the hall. He looks tired and rather serious. He steals on tip-toe towards the middle doorway and is about to slip through the curtains*]

HEDDA. [*At the stove, without looking up*] Good morning.

TESMAN. [*Turns*] Hedda! [*Approaching her*] Good heavens—are you up so early? Eh?

HEDDA. Yes, I am up very early this morning.

TESMAN. And I never doubted you were still sound asleep! Fancy that, Hedda!

HEDDA. Don't speak so loud. Mrs. Elvsted is resting in my room.

TESMAN. Has Mrs. Elvsted been here all night?

HEDDA. Yes, since no one came to fetch her.

TESMAN. Ah, to be sure.

HEDDA. [*Closes the door of the stove and rises*] Well, did you enjoy yourselves at Judge Brack's?

TESMAN. Have you been anxious about me? Eh?

HEDDA. No, I should never think of being anxious. But I asked if you had enjoyed yourself.

TESMAN. Oh, yes,—for once in a way. Especially the beginning of the evening; for then Eilert read me part of his book. We arrived more than an hour too early—fancy that! And Brack had all sorts of arrangements to make—so Eilert read to me.

HEDDA. [*Seating herself by the table on the right*] Well? Tell me, then——

TESMAN. [*Sitting on a footstool near the stove*] Oh, Hedda, you can't conceive what a book that is going to be! I believe it is one of the most remarkable things that have ever been written. Fancy that!

HEDDA. Yes, yes; I don't care about that—

TESMAN. I must make a confession to you, Hedda. When he had finished reading—a horrid feeling came over me.

HEDDA. A horrid feeling?

TESMAN. I felt jealous of Eilert for having had it in him to write such a book. Only think, Hedda!

HEDDA. Yes, yes, I am thinking!

TESMAN. And then how pitiful to think that he—with all his gifts—should be irreclaimable, after all.

HEDDA. I suppose you mean that he has more courage than the rest?

TESMAN. No, not at all—I mean that he is incapable of taking his pleasures in moderation.

HEDDA. And what came of it all—in the end?

TESMAN. Well, to tell the truth, I think it might best be described as an orgy, Hedda.

HEDDA. Had he vine-leaves in his hair?

TESMAN. Vine-leaves? No, I saw nothing of the sort. But he made a long,

rambling speech in honor of the woman who had inspired him in his work—
that was the phrase he used.

HEDDA.   Did he name her?

TESMAN.   No, he didn't; but I can't help thinking he meant Mrs. Elvsted. You
may be sure he did.

HEDDA.   Well—where did you part from him?

TESMAN.   On the way to town. We broke up—the last of us at any rate—all
together; and Brack came with us to get a breath of fresh air. And then,
you see, we agreed to take Eilert home; for he had had far more than was
good for him.

HEDDA.   I daresay.

TESMAN.   But now comes the strange part of it, Hedda; or, I should rather say,
the melancholy part of it. I declare I am almost ashamed—on Eilert's account
—to tell you——

HEDDA.   Oh, go on——!

TESMAN.   Well, as we were getting near town, you see, I happened to drop a
little behind the others. Only for a minute or two—fancy that!

HEDDA.   Yes, yes, yes, but——?

TESMAN.   And then, as I hurried after them—what do you think I found by
the wayside? Eh?

HEDDA.   Oh, how should I know!

TESMAN.   You mustn't speak of it to a soul, Hedda! Do you hear! Promise me,
for Eilert's sake. [*Draws a parcel, wrapped in paper, from his coat pocket*]
Fancy, dear—I found this.

HEDDA.   Is not that the parcel he had with him yesterday?

TESMAN.   Yes, it is the whole of his precious, irreplaceable manuscript! And he
had gone and lost it, and knew nothing about it. Only fancy, Hedda! So
deplorably——

HEDDA.   But why did you not give him back the parcel at once?

TESMAN.   I didn't dare to—in the state he was then in——

HEDDA.   Did you not tell any of the others that you had found it?

TESMAN.   Oh, far from it! You can surely understand that, for Eilert's sake, I
wouldn't do that.

HEDDA.   So no one knows that Eilert Lövborg's manuscript is in your possession?

TESMAN.   No. And no one must know it.

HEDDA.   Then what did you say to him afterwards?

TESMAN.   I didn't talk to him again at all; for when we got in among the
streets, he and two or three of the others gave us the slip and disappeared.
Fancy that!

HEDDA.   Indeed! They must have taken him home then.

TESMAN.   Yes, so it would appear. And Brack, too, left us.

HEDDA.   And what have you been doing with yourself since?

TESMAN.   Well, I and some of the others went home with one of the party, a
jolly fellow, and took our morning coffee with him; or perhaps I should
rather call it our night coffee—eh? But now, when I have rested a little, and
given Eilert, poor fellow, time to have his sleep out, I must take this back to
him.

HEDDA. [*Holds out her hand for the packet*] No—don't give it to him! Not in such a hurry, I mean. Let me read it first.

TESMAN. No, my dearest Hedda, I mustn't, I really mustn't.

HEDDA. You must not?

TESMAN. No—for you can imagine what a state of despair he will be in when he wakens and misses the manuscript. He has no copy of it, you must know! He told me so.

HEDDA. [*Looking searchingly at him*] Can such a thing not be reproduced? Written over again?

TESMAN. No, I don't think that would be possible. For the inspiration, you see——

HEDDA. Yes, yes—I suppose it depends on that—— [*Lightly*] But, by the by— here is a letter for you.

TESMAN. Fancy——!

HEDDA. [*Handing it to him*] It came early this morning.

TESMAN. It's from Aunt Julia! What can it be? [*He lays the packet on the other footstool, opens the letter, runs his eye through it, and jumps up*] Oh, Hedda—she says that poor Aunt Rina is dying!

HEDDA. Well, we were prepared for that.

TESMAN. And that if I want to see her again, I must make haste. I'll run in to them at once.

HEDDA. [*Suppressing a smile*] Will you run?

TESMAN. Oh, my dearest Hedda—if you could only make up your mind to come with me! Just think!

HEDDA. [*Rises and says wearily, repelling the idea*] No, no, don't ask me. I will not look upon sickness and death. I loathe all sorts of ugliness.

TESMAN. Well, well, then——! [*Bustling around*] My hat——? My overcoat ——? Oh, in the hall——. I do hope I mayn't come too late, Hedda! Eh?

HEDDA. Oh, if you run——

[BERTA *appears at the hall door*]

BERTA. Judge Brack is at the door, and wishes to know if he may come in.

TESMAN. At this time! No, I can't possibly see him.

HEDDA. But I can. [*To* BERTA] Ask Judge Brack to come in.

[BERTA *goes out*]

HEDDA. [*Quickly, whispering*] The parcel, Tesman!

[*She snatches it up from the stool*]

TESMAN. Yes, give it to me!

HEDDA. No, no, I will keep it till you come back.

[*She goes to the writing-table and places it in the bookcase.* TESMAN *stands in a flurry of haste, and cannot get his gloves on.* JUDGE BRACK *enters from the hall*]

HEDDA. [*Nodding to him*] You are an early bird, I must say.

BRACK. Yes, don't you think so? [*To* TESMAN] Are you on the move, too?

TESMAN. Yes, I must rush off to my aunts'. Fancy—the invalid one is lying at death's door, poor creature.

BRACK. Dear me, is she indeed? Then on no account let me detain you. At such a critical moment——

TESMAN.   Yes, I must really rush—— Good-bye, Good-bye!

[*He hastens out by the hall door*]

HEDDA.   [*Approaching*] You seem to have made a particularly lively night of it at your rooms, Judge Brack.

BRACK.   I assure you I have not had my clothes off, Mrs. Hedda.

HEDDA.   Not you, either?

BRACK.   No, as you may see. But what has Tesman been telling you of the night's adventures?

HEDDA.   Oh, some tiresome story. Only that they went and had coffee somewhere or other.

BRACK.   I have heard about that coffee-party already. Eilert Lövborg was not with them, I fancy?

HEDDA.   No, they had taken him home before that.

BRACK.   Tesman too?

HEDDA.   No, but some of the others, he said.

BRACK.   [*Smiling*] George Tesman is really an ingenuous creature, Mrs. Hedda.

HEDDA.   Yes, heaven knows he is. Then is there something behind all this?

BRACK.   Yes, perhaps there may be.

HEDDA.   Well then, sit down, my dear Judge, and tell your story in comfort.

[*She seats herself to the left of the table.* BRACK *sits near her, at the long side of the table*]

HEDDA.   Now then?

BRACK.   I had special reasons for keeping track of my guests—or rather of some of my guests—last night.

HEDDA.   Of Eilert Lövborg among the rest, perhaps?

BRACK.   Frankly—yes.

HEDDA.   Now you make me really curious——

BRACK.   Do you know where he and one or two of the others finished the night, Mrs. Hedda?

HEDDA.   If it is not quite unmentionable, tell me.

BRACK.   Oh no, it's not at all unmentionable. Well, they put in an appearance at a particularly animated *soirée*.

HEDDA.   Of the lively kind?

BRACK.   Of the very liveliest——

HEDDA.   Tell me more of this, Judge Brack——

BRACK.   Lövborg, as well as the others, had been invited in advance. I knew all about it. But he had declined the invitation; for now, as you know, he has become a new man.

HEDDA.   Up at the Elvsteds', yes. But he went after all, then?

BRACK.   Well, you see, Mrs. Hedda—unhappily the spirit moved him at my rooms last evening——

HEDDA.   Yes, I hear he found inspiration.

BRACK.   Pretty violent inspiration. Well, I fancy that altered his purpose; for we menfolk are unfortunately not always so firm in our principles as we ought to be.

HEDDA.   Oh, I am sure you are an exception, Judge Brack. But as to Lövborg——?

BRACK. To make a long story short—he landed at last in Mademoiselle Diana's rooms.

HEDDA. Mademoiselle Diana's?

BRACK. It was Mademoiselle Diana that was giving the *soirée*, to a select circle of her admirers and her lady friends.

HEDDA. Is she a red-haired woman?

BRACK. Precisely.

HEDDA. A sort of a—singer?

BRACK. Oh yes—in her leisure moments. And moreover a mighty huntress—of men—Mrs. Hedda. You have no doubt heard of her. Eilert Lövborg was one of her most enthusiastic protectors—in the days of his glory.

HEDDA. And how did all this end?

BRACK. Far from amicably, it appears. After a most tender meeting, they seem to have come to blows——

HEDDA. Lövborg and she?

BRACK. Yes. He accused her or her friends of having robbed him. He declared that his pocket-book had disappeared—and other things as well. In short, he seems to have made a furious disturbance.

HEDDA. And what came of it all?

BRACK. It came to a general scrimmage, in which the ladies as well as the gentlemen took part. Fortunately the police at last appeared on the scene.

HEDDA. The police too?

BRACK. Yes. I fancy it will prove a costly frolic for Eilert Lövborg, crazy being that he is.

HEDDA. How so?

BRACK. He seems to have made a violent resistance—to have hit one of the constables on the head and torn the coat off his back. So they had to march him off to the police-station with the rest.

HEDDA. How have you learnt all this?

BRACK. From the police themselves.

HEDDA. [*Gazing straight before her*] So that is what happened. Then he had no vine-leaves in his hair.

BRACK. Vine-leaves, Mrs. Hedda?

HEDDA. [*Changing her tone*] But tell me now, Judge—what is your real reason for tracking out Eilert Lövborg's movements so carefully?

BRACK. In the first place, it could not be entirely indifferent to me if it should appear in the police-court that he came straight from my house.

HEDDA. Will the matter come into court then?

BRACK. Of course. However, I should scarcely have troubled so much about that. But I thought that, as a friend of the family, it was my duty to supply you and Tesman with a full account of his nocturnal exploits.

HEDDA. Why so, Judge Brack?

BRACK. Why, because I have a shrewd suspicion that he intends to use you as a sort of blind.

HEDDA. Oh, how can you think such a thing!

BRACK. Good heavens, Mrs. Hedda—we have eyes in our head. Mark my words! This Mrs. Elvsted will be in no hurry to leave town again.

HEDDA.   Well, even if there should be anything between them, I suppose there are plenty of other places where they could meet.

BRACK.   Not a single home. Henceforth, as before, every respectable house will be closed against Eilert Lövborg.

HEDDA.   And so ought mine to be, you mean?

BRACK.   Yes. I confess it would be more than painful to me if this personage were to be made free of your house. How superfluous, how intrusive, he would be, if he were to force his way into——

HEDDA.   ——into the triangle?

BRACK.   Precisely. It would simply mean that I should find myself homeless.

HEDDA.   [*Looks at him with a smile*] So you want to be the one cock in the basket[9]—that is your aim.

BRACK.   [*Nods slowly and lowers his voice*] Yes, that is my aim. And for that I will fight—with every weapon I can command.

HEDDA.   [*Her smile vanishing*] I see you are a dangerous person—when it comes to the point.

BRACK.   Do you think so?

HEDDA.   I am beginning to think so. And I am exceedingly glad to think—that you have no sort of hold over me.

BRACK.   [*Laughing equivocally*] Well, well, Mrs. Hedda—perhaps you are right there. If I had, who knows what I might be capable of?

HEDDA.   Come, come now, Judge Brack! That sounds almost like a threat.

BRACK.   [*Rising*] Oh, not at all! The triangle, you know, ought, if possible, to be spontaneously constructed.

HEDDA.   There I agree with you.

BRACK.   Well, now I have said all I had to say; and I had better be getting back to town. Good-bye, Mrs. Hedda. [*He goes towards the glass door*]

HEDDA.   [*Rising*] Are you going through the garden?

BRACK.   Yes, it's a short cut for me.

HEDDA.   And then it is a back way, too.

BRACK.   Quite so. I have no objection to back ways. They may be piquant enough at times.

HEDDA.   When there is shooting practice going on, you mean?

BRACK.   [*In the doorway, laughing to her*] Oh, people don't shoot their tame poultry, I fancy.

HEDDA.   [*Also laughing*] Oh, no, when there is only one cock in the basket——
    [*They exchange laughing nods of farewell. He goes. She closes the door behind him.* HEDDA, *who has become quite serious, stands for a moment looking out. Presently she goes and peeps through the curtain over the middle doorway. Then she goes to the writing-table, takes* LÖVBORG'S *packet out of the bookcase, and is on the point of looking through its contents.* BERTA *is heard speaking loudly in the hall.* HEDDA *turns and listens. Then she hastily locks up the packet in the drawer, and lays the key on the inkstand.* EILERT LÖVBORG, *with his greatcoat on and his hat in his hand, tears open the hall door. He looks somewhat confused and irritated*]

---

[9] A proverbial saying in Norway.

LÖVBORG. [*Looking towards the hall*] And I tell you I must and will come in! There!

[*He closes the door, turns, sees* HEDDA, *at once regains his self-control, and bows*]

HEDDA. [*At the writing-table*] Well, Mr. Lövborg, this is rather a late hour to call for Thea.

LÖVBORG. You mean rather an early hour to call on you. Pray pardon me.

HEDDA. How do you know that she is still here?

LÖVBORG. They told me at her lodgings that she had been out all night.

HEDDA. [*Going to the oval table*] Did you notice anything about the people of the house when they said that?

LÖVBORG. [*Looks inquiringly at her*] Notice anything about them?

HEDDA. I mean, did they seem to think it odd?

LÖVBORG. [*Suddenly understanding*] Oh yes, of course! I am dragging her down with me! However, I didn't notice anything.—I suppose Tesman is not up yet?

HEDDA. No—I think not——

LÖVBORG. When did he come home?

HEDDA. Very late.

LÖVBORG. Did he tell you anything?

HEDDA. Yes, I gathered that you had had an exceedingly jolly evening at Judge Brack's.

LÖVBORG. Nothing more?

HEDDA. I don't think so. However, I was so dreadfully sleepy——

[MRS. ELVSTED *enters through the curtains of the middle doorway*]

MRS. ELVSTED. [*Going towards him*] Ah, Lövborg! At last——!

LÖVBORG. Yes, at last. And too late!

MRS. ELVSTED. [*Looks anxiously at him*] What is too late?

LÖVBORG. Everything is too late now. It is all over with me.

MRS. ELVSTED. Oh no, no—don't say that!

LÖVBORG. You will say the same when you hear——

MRS. ELVSTED. I won't hear anything!

HEDDA. Perhaps you would prefer to talk to her alone? If so, I will leave you.

LÖVBORG. No, stay—you too. I beg you to stay.

MRS. ELVSTED. Yes, but I won't hear anything, I tell you.

LÖVBORG. It is not last night's adventures that I want to talk about.

MRS. ELVSTED. What is it then——?

LÖVBORG. I want to say that now our ways must part.

MRS. ELVSTED. Part!

HEDDA. [*Involuntarily*] I knew it!

LÖVBORG. You can be of no more service to me, Thea.

MRS. ELVSTED. How can you stand there and say that! No more service to you! Am I not to help you now, as before? Are we not to go on working together?

LÖVBORG. Henceforward I shall do no work.

MRS. ELVSTED. [*Despairingly*] Then what am I to do with my life?

LÖVBORG. You must try to live your life as if you had never known me.

MRS. ELVSTED. But you know I cannot do that!

LÖVBORG. Try if you cannot, Thea. You must go home again——

MRS. ELVSTED. [*In vehement protest*] Never in this world! Where you are, there will I be also! I will not let myself be driven away like this! I will remain here! I will be with you when the book appears.

HEDDA. [*Half aloud, in suspense*] Ah yes—the book!

LÖVBORG. [*Looks at her*] My book and Thea's; for that is what it is.

MRS. ELVSTED. Yes, I feel that it is. And that is why I have a right to be with you when it appears! I will see with my own eyes how respect and honor pour in upon you afresh. And the happiness—the happiness—oh, I must share it with you!

LÖVBORG. Thea—our book will never appear.

HEDDA. Ah!

MRS. ELVSTED. Never appear!

LÖVBORG. Can never appear.

MRS. ELVSTED. [*In agonized foreboding*] Lövborg—what have you done with the manuscript?

HEDDA. [*Looks anxiously at him*] Yes, the manuscript——?

MRS. ELVSTED. Where is it?

LÖVBORG. Oh Thea—don't ask me about it!

MRS. ELVSTED. Yes, yes, I will know. I demand to be told at once.

LÖVBORG. The manuscript——. Well then—I have torn the manuscript into a thousand pieces.

MRS. ELVSTED. [*Shrieks*] Oh no, no——!

HEDDA. [*Involuntarily*] But that's not——

LÖVBORG. [*Looks at her*] Not true, you think?

HEDDA. [*Collecting herself*] Oh well, of course—since you say so. But it sounded so improbable——

LÖVBORG. It is true, all the same.

MRS. ELVSTED. [*Wringing her hands*] Oh God—oh God, Hedda—torn his own work to pieces!

LÖVBORG. I have torn my own life to pieces. So why should I not tear my life-work too——?

MRS. ELVSTED. And you did this last night?

LÖVBORG. Yes, I tell you! Tore it into a thousand pieces—and scattered them on the fjord—far out. There, there is cool sea-water at any rate—let them drift upon it—drift with the current and the wind. And then presently they will sink—deeper and deeper—as I shall, Thea.

MRS. ELVSTED. Do you know, Lövborg, that what you have done with the book —I shall think of it to my dying day as though you had killed a little child.

LÖVBORG. Yes, you are right. It is a sort of child-murder.

MRS. ELVSTED. How could you, then——! Did not the child belong to me too?

HEDDA. [*Almost inaudibly*] Ah, the child——

MRS. ELVSTED. [*Breathing heavily*] It is all over then. Well, well, now I will go, Hedda.

HEDDA. But you are not going away from town?

MRS. ELVSTED. Oh, I don't know what I shall do. I see nothing but darkness before me. [*She goes out by the hall door*]

HEDDA. [*Stands waiting for a moment*] So you are not going to see her home, Mr. Lövborg?

LÖVBORG. I? Through the streets? Would you have people see her walking with me?

HEDDA. Of course I don't know what else may have happened last night. But is it so utterly irretrievable?

LÖVBORG. It will not end with last night—I know that perfectly well. And the thing is that now I have no taste for that sort of life either. I won't begin it anew. She has broken my courage and my power of braving life out.

HEDDA. [*Looking straight before her*] So that pretty little fool has had her fingers in a man's destiny. [*Looks at him*] But all the same, how could you treat her so heartlessly?

LÖVBORG. Oh, don't say that it was heartless!

HEDDA. To go and destroy what has filled her whole soul for months and years! You do not call that heartless!

LÖVBORG. To you I can tell the truth, Hedda.

HEDDA. The truth?

LÖVBORG. First promise me—give me your word—that what I now confide to you Thea shall never know.

HEDDA. I give you my word.

LÖVBORG. Good. Then let me tell you that what I said just now was untrue.

HEDDA. About the manuscript?

LÖVBORG. Yes. I have not torn it to pieces—nor thrown it into the fjord.

HEDDA. No, no——. But—where is it then?

LÖVBORG. I have destroyed it none the less—utterly destroyed it, Hedda!

HEDDA. I don't understand.

LÖVBORG. Thea said that what I had done seemed to her like a child-murder.

HEDDA. Yes, so she said.

LÖVBORG. But to kill his child—that is not the worst thing a father can do to it.

HEDDA. Not the worst?

LÖVBORG. No. I wanted to spare Thea from hearing the worst.

HEDDA. Then what is the worst?

LÖVBORG. Suppose now, Hedda, that a man—in the small hours of the morning—came home to his child's mother after a night of riot and debauchery, and said: "Listen—I have been here and there—in this place and in that. And I have taken our child with me—to this place and to that. And I have lost the child—utterly lost it. The devil knows into what hands it may have fallen—who may have had their clutches on it."

HEDDA. Well—but when all is said and done, you know—this was only a book——

LÖVBORG. Thea's pure soul was in that book.

HEDDA. Yes, so I understand.

LÖVBORG. And you can understand, too, that for her and me together no future is possible.

HEDDA. What path do you mean to take then?

LÖVBORG. None. I will only try to make an end of it all—the sooner the better.

HEDDA. [*A step nearer him*] Eilert Lövborg—listen to me.—Will you not try to—to do it beautifully?

LÖVBORG. Beautifully? [*Smiling*] With vine-leaves in my hair, as you used to dream in the old days——?

HEDDA.   No, no. I have lost my faith in the vine-leaves. But beautifully never-theless! For once in a way!—Good-bye! You must go now—and do not come here any more.

LÖVBORG.   Good-bye, Mrs. Tesman. And give George Tesman my love. [*He is on the point of going*]

HEDDA.   No, wait! I must give you a memento to take with you.

[*She goes to the writing-table and opens the drawer and the pistol-case; then returns to* LÖVBORG *with one of the pistols*]

LÖVBORG.   [*Looks at her*] This? Is this the memento?

HEDDA.   [*Nodding slowly*] Do you recognize it? It was aimed at you once.

LÖVBORG.   You should have used it then.

HEDDA.   Take it—and do you use it now.

LÖVBORG.   [*Puts the pistol in his breast pocket*] Thanks!

HEDDA.   And beautifully, Eilert Lövborg. Promise me that!

LÖVBORG.   Good-bye, Hedda Gabler.

[*He goes out by the hall door.* HEDDA *listens for a moment at the door. Then she goes up to the writing-table, takes out the packet of manuscript, peeps under the cover, draws a few of the sheets half out, and looks at them. Next she goes over and seats herself in the arm-chair beside the stove, with the packet in her lap. Presently she opens the stove door, and then the packet*]

HEDDA.   [*Throws one of the quires into the fire and whispers to herself*] Now I am burning your child, Thea!—Burning it, curly-locks! [*Throwing one or two more quires into the stove*] Your child and Eilert Lövborg's. [*Throws the rest in*] I am burning—I am burning your child.

Act Four

The same rooms at the TESMANS'. *It is evening. The drawing-room is in darkness. The back room is lighted by the hanging lamp over the table. The curtains over the glass door are drawn close.* HEDDA, *dressed in black, walks to and fro in the dark room. Then she goes into the back room and disappears for a moment to the left. She is heard to strike a few chords on the piano. Presently she comes in sight again, and returns to the drawing-room.* BERTA *enters from the right, through the inner room, with a lighted lamp, which she places on the table in front of the corner settee in the drawing-room. Her eyes are red with weeping, and she has black ribbons in her cap. She goes quietly and circumspectly out to the right.* HEDDA *goes up to the glass door, lifts the curtain a little aside, and looks out into the darkness. Shortly afterwards,* MISS TESMAN, *in mourning, with a bonnet and veil on, comes in from the hall.* HEDDA *goes towards her and holds out her hand.*

MISS TESMAN.   Yes, Hedda, here I am, in mourning and forlorn; for now my poor sister has at last found peace.

HEDDA.   I have heard the news already, as you see. Tesman sent me a card.

MISS TESMAN. Yes, he promised me he would. But nevertheless I thought that to Hedda—here in the house of life—I ought myself to bring the tidings of death.

HEDDA. That was very kind of you.

MISS TESMAN. Ah, Rina ought not to have left us just now. This is not the time for Hedda's house to be a house of mourning.

HEDDA. [*Changing the subject*] She died quite peacefully, did she not, Miss Tesman?

MISS TESMAN. Oh, her end was so calm, so beautiful. And then she had the unspeakable happiness of seeing George once more—and bidding him good-bye.—Has he not come home yet?

HEDDA. No. He wrote that he might be detained. But won't you sit down?

MISS TESMAN. No thank you, my dear, dear Hedda. I should like to, but I have so much to do. I must prepare my dear one for her rest as well as I can. She shall go to her grave looking her best.

HEDDA. Can I not help you in any way?

MISS TESMAN. Oh, you must not think of it! Hedda Tesman must have no hand in such mournful work. Nor let her thoughts dwell on it either—not at this time.

HEDDA. One is not always mistress of one's thoughts—

MISS TESMAN. [*Continuing*] Ah yes, it is the way of the world. At home we shall be sewing a shroud; and here there will soon be sewing too, I suppose—but of another sort, thank God!

[GEORGE TESMAN *enters by the hall door*]

HEDDA. Ah, you have come at last!

TESMAN. You here, Aunt Julia? With Hedda? Fancy that!

MISS TESMAN. I was just going, my dear boy. Well, have you done all you promised?

TESMAN. No; I'm really afraid I have forgotten half of it. I must come to you again to-morrow. To-day my brain is all in a whirl. I can't keep my thoughts together.

MISS TESMAN. Why, my dear George, you mustn't take it in this way.

TESMAN. Mustn't——? How do you mean?

MISS TESMAN. Even in your sorrow you must rejoice, as I do—rejoice that she is at rest.

TESMAN. Oh yes, yes—you are thinking of Aunt Rina.

HEDDA. You will feel lonely now, Miss Tesman.

MISS TESMAN. Just at first, yes. But that will not last very long, I hope. I dare-say I shall soon find an occupant for poor Rina's little room.

TESMAN. Indeed? Who do you think will take it? Eh?

MISS TESMAN. Oh, there's always some poor invalid or other in want of nursing, unfortunately.

HEDDA. Would you really take such a burden upon you again?

MISS TESMAN. A burden! Heaven forgive you, child—it has been no burden to me.

HEDDA. But suppose you had a total stranger on your hands——

MISS TESMAN. Oh, one soon makes friends with sick folk; and it's such an ab-solute necessity for me to have some one to live for. Well, heaven be praised, there may soon be something in *this* house, too, to keep an old aunt busy.

·HEDDA.   Oh, don't trouble about anything here.

TESMAN.   Yes, just fancy what a nice time we three might have together, if——?

HEDDA.   If——?

TESMAN.   [*Uneasily*] Oh, nothing. It will all come right. Let us hope so—eh?

MISS TESMAN.   Well, well, I daresay you two want to talk to each other. [*Smiling*] And perhaps Hedda may have something to tell you too, George. Goodbye! I must go home to Rina. [*Turning at the door*] How strange it is to think that now Rina is with me and with my poor brother as well!

TESMAN.   Yes, fancy that, Aunt Julia! Eh?

[MISS TESMAN *goes out by the hall door*]

HEDDA.   [*Follows* TESMAN *coldly and searchingly with her eyes*] I almost believe your Aunt Rina's death affects you more than it does your Aunt Julia.

TESMAN.   Oh, it's not that alone. It's Eilert I am so terribly uneasy about.

HEDDA.   [*Quickly*] Is there anything new about him?

TESMAN.   I looked in at his rooms this afternoon, intending to tell him the manuscript was in safe keeping.

HEDDA.   Well, did you not find him?

TESMAN.   No. He wasn't at home. But afterwards I met Mrs. Elvsted, and she told me that he had been here early this morning.

HEDDA.   Yes, directly after you had gone.

TESMAN.   And he said that he had torn his manuscript to pieces—eh?

HEDDA.   Yes, so he declared.

TESMAN.   Why, good heavens, he must have been completely out of his mind! And I suppose you thought it best not to give it back to him, Hedda?

HEDDA.   No, he did not get it.

TESMAN.   But of course you told him that we had it?

HEDDA.   No. [*Quickly*] Did you tell Mrs. Elvsted?

TESMAN.   No; I thought I had better not. But you ought to have told him. Fancy, if, in desperation, he should go and do himself some injury! Let me have the manuscript, Hedda! I will take it to him at once. Where is it?

HEDDA.   [*Cold and immovable, leaning on the arm-chair*] I have not got it.

TESMAN.   Have not got it? What in the world do you mean?

HEDDA.   I have burnt it—every line of it.

TESMAN.   [*With a violent movement of terror*] Burnt! Burnt Eilert's manuscript!

HEDDA.   Don't scream so. The servant might hear you.

TESMAN.   Burnt! Why, good God——! No, no, no! It's impossible!

HEDDA.   It is so, nevertheless.

TESMAN.   Do you know what you have done, Hedda? It's unlawful appropriation of lost property. Fancy that! Just ask Judge Brack, and he'll tell you what it is.

HEDDA.   I advise you not to speak of it—either to Judge Brack, or to anyone else.

TESMAN.   But how could you do anything so unheard-of? What put it into your head? What possessed you? Answer me that—eh?

HEDDA.   [*Suppressing an almost imperceptible smile*] I did it for your sake, George.

TESMAN.   For my sake!

HEDDA.   This morning, when you told me about what he had read to you——

TESMAN.   Yes, yes—what then?

HEDDA.   You acknowledged that you envied him his work.

TESMAN.   Oh, of course I didn't mean that literally.

HEDDA.   No matter—I could not bear the idea that anyone should throw you into the shade.

TESMAN.   [*In an outburst of mingled doubt and joy*] Hedda! Oh, is this true? But—but—I never knew you show your love like that before. Fancy that!

HEDDA.   Well, I may as well tell you that—just at this time—— [*Impatiently, breaking off*] No, no; you can ask Aunt Julia. She will tell you, fast enough.

TESMAN.   Oh, I almost think I understand you, Hedda! [*Clasps his hands together*] Great heavens! do you really mean it? Eh?

HEDDA.   Don't shout so. The servant might hear.

TESMAN.   [*Laughing in irrepressible glee*] The servant! Why, how absurd you are, Hedda. It's only my old Berta! Why, I'll tell Berta myself.

HEDDA.   [*Clenching her hands together in desperation*] Oh, it is killing me,—it is killing me, all this!

TESMAN.   What is, Hedda? Eh?

HEDDA.   [*Coldly, controlling herself*] All this—absurdity—George.

TESMAN.   Absurdity! Do you see anything absurd in my being overjoyed at the news! But after all—perhaps I had better not say anything to Berta.

HEDDA.   Oh——why not that too?

TESMAN.   No, no, not yet! But I must certainly tell Aunt Julia. And then that you have begun to call me George too! Fancy that! Oh, Aunt Julia will be so happy—so happy!

HEDDA.   When she hears that I have burnt Eilert Lövborg's manuscript—for your sake?

TESMAN.   No, by the by—that affair of the manuscript—of course nobody must know about that. But that you love me so much, Hedda—Aunt Julia must really share my joy in that! I wonder, now, whether this sort of thing is usual in young wives? Eh?

HEDDA.   I think you had better ask Aunt Julia that question too.

TESMAN.   I will indeed, some time or other. [*Looks uneasy and downcast again*] And yet the manuscript—the manuscript! Good God! It is terrible to think what will become of poor Eilert now.

[MRS. ELVSTED, *dressed as in the first act, with hat and cloak, enters by the hall door*]

MRS. ELVSTED.   [*Greets them hurriedly, and says in evident agitation*] Oh, dear Hedda, forgive my coming again.

HEDDA.   What is the matter with you, Thea?

TESMAN.   Something about Eilert Lövborg again—eh?

MRS. ELVSTED.   Yes! I am dreadfully afraid some misfortune has happened to him.

HEDDA.   [*Seizes her arm*] Ah,—do you think so?

TESMAN.   Why, good Lord—what makes you think that, Mrs. Elvsted?

MRS. ELVSTED.   I heard them talking of him at my boarding-house—just as I came in. Oh, the most incredible rumors are afloat about him to-day.

TESMAN.   Yes, fancy, so I heard too! And I can bear witness that he went straight home to bed last night. Fancy that!

HEDDA.   Well, what did they say at the boarding-house?

MRS. ELVSTED.   Oh, I couldn't make out anything clearly. Either they knew nothing definite, or else——. They stopped talking when they saw me; and I did not dare to ask.

TESMAN.   [*Moving about uneasily*] We must hope—we must hope that you misunderstood them, Mrs. Elvsted.

MRS. ELVSTED.   No, no; I am sure it was of him they were talking. And I heard something about the hospital or——

TESMAN.   The hospital?

HEDDA.   No—surely that cannot be!

MRS. ELVSTED.   Oh, I was in such mortal terror! I went to his lodgings and asked for him there.

HEDDA.   You could make up your mind to that, Thea!

MRS. ELVSTED.   What else could I do? I really could bear the suspense no longer.

TESMAN.   But you didn't find him either—eh?

MRS. ELVSTED.   No. And the people knew nothing about him. He hadn't been home since yesterday afternoon, they said.

TESMAN.   Yesterday! Fancy, how could they say that?

MRS. ELVSTED.   Oh, I am sure something terrible must have happened to him.

TESMAN.   Hedda dear—how would it be if I were to go and make inquiries——?

HEDDA.   No, no—don't you mix yourself up in this affair.

[JUDGE BRACK, *with his hat in his hand, enters by the hall door, which* BERTA *opens, and closes behind him. He looks grave and bows in silence*]

TESMAN.   Oh, is that you, my dear Judge? Eh?

BRACK.   Yes. It was imperative I should see you this evening.

TESMAN.   I can see you have heard the news about Aunt Rina?

BRACK.   Yes, that among other things.

TESMAN.   Isn't it sad—eh?

BRACK.   Well, my dear Tesman, that depends on how you look at it.

TESMAN.   [*Looks doubtfully at him*] Has anything else happened?

BRACK.   Yes.

HEDDA.   [*In suspense*] Anything sad, Judge Brack?

BRACK.   That, too, depends on how you look at it, Mrs. Tesman.

MRS. ELVSTED.   [*Unable to restrain her anxiety*] Oh! it is something about Eilert Lövborg!

BRACK.   [*With a glance at her*] What makes you think that, Madam? Perhaps you have already heard something——?

MRS. ELVSTED.   [*In confusion*] No, nothing at all, but——

TESMAN.   Oh, for heaven's sake, tell us!

BRACK.   [*Shrugging his shoulders*] Well, I regret to say Eilert Lövborg has been taken to the hospital. He is lying at the point of death.

MRS. ELVSTED.   [*Shrieks*] Oh God! oh God——!

TESMAN.   To the hospital! And at the point of death!

HEDDA. [*Involuntarily*] So soon then——

MRS. ELVSTED. [*Wailing*] And we parted in anger, Hedda!

HEDDA. [*Whispers*] Thea—Thea—be careful!

MRS. ELVSTED. [*Not heeding her*] I must go to him! I must see him alive!

BRACK. It is useless, Madam. No one will be admitted.

MRS. ELVSTED. Oh, at least tell me what has happened to him? What is it?

TESMAN. You don't mean to say that he has himself—— Eh?

HEDDA. Yes, I am sure he has.

TESMAN. Hedda, how can you——?

BRACK. [*Keeping his eyes fixed upon her*] Unfortunately you have guessed quite correctly, Mrs. Tesman.

MRS. ELVSTED. Oh, how horrible!

TESMAN. Himself, then! Fancy that!

HEDDA. Shot himself!

BRACK. Rightly guessed again, Mrs. Tesman.

MRS. ELVSTED. [*With an effort at self-control*] When did it happen, Mr. Brack?

BRACK. This afternoon—between three and four.

TESMAN. But, good Lord, where did he do it? Eh?

BRACK. [*With some hesitation*] Where? Well—I suppose at his lodgings.

MRS. ELVSTED. No, that cannot be; for I was there between six and seven.

BRACK. Well then, somewhere else. I don't know exactly. I only know that he was found——. He had shot himself—in the breast.

MRS. ELVSTED. Oh, how terrible! That he should die like that!

HEDDA. [*To* BRACK] Was it in the breast?

BRACK. Yes—as I told you.

HEDDA. Not in the temple?

BRACK. In the breast, Mrs. Tesman.

HEDDA. Well, well—the breast is a good place, too.

BRACK. How do you mean, Mrs. Tesman?

HEDDA. [*Evasively*] Oh, nothing—nothing.

TESMAN. And the wound is dangerous, you say—eh?

BRACK. Absolutely mortal. The end has probably come by this time.

MRS. ELVSTED. Yes, yes, I feel it. The end! The end! Oh, Hedda——!

TESMAN. But tell me, how have you learnt all this?

BRACK. [*Curtly*] Through one of the police. A man I had some business with.

HEDDA. [*In a clear voice*] At last a deed worth doing!

TESMAN. [*Terrified*] Good heavens, Hedda! what are you saying?

HEDDA. I say there is beauty in this.

BRACK. H'm, Mrs. Tesman——

TESMAN. Beauty! Fancy that!

MRS. ELVSTED. Oh, Hedda, how can you talk of beauty in such an act!

HEDDA. Eilert Lövborg has himself made up his account with life. He has had the courage to do—the one right thing.

MRS. ELVSTED. No, you must never think that was how it happened! It must have been in delirium that he did it.

TESMAN. In despair!

HEDDA. That he did not. I am certain of that.

MRS. ELVSTED. Yes, yes! In delirium! Just as when he tore up our manuscript.

BRACK. [*Starting*] The manuscript? Has he torn that up?

MRS. ELVSTED. Yes, last night.

TESMAN. [*Whispers softly*] Oh, Hedda, we shall never get over this.

BRACK. H'm, very extraordinary.

TESMAN. [*Moving about the room*] To think of Eilert going out of the world in this way! And not leaving behind him the book that would have immortalized his name——

MRS. ELVSTED. Oh, if only it could be put together again!

TESMAN. Yes, if it only could! I don't know what I would not give——

MRS. ELVSTED. Perhaps it can, Mr. Tesman.

TESMAN. What do you mean?

MRS. ELVSTED. [*Searches in the pocket of her dress*] Look here. I have kept all the loose notes he used to dictate from.

HEDDA. [*A step forward*] Ah——!

TESMAN. You have kept them, Mrs. Elvsted! Eh?

MRS. ELVSTED. Yes, I have them here. I put them in my pocket when I left home. Here they still are——

TESMAN. Oh, do let me see them!

MRS. ELVSTED. [*Hands him a bundle of papers*] But they are in such disorder—all mixed up.

TESMAN. Fancy, if we could make something out of them, after all! Perhaps if we two put our heads together——

MRS. ELVSTED. Oh yes, at least let us try——

TESMAN. We will manage it! We must! I will dedicate my life to this task.

HEDDA. You, George? Your life?

TESMAN. Yes, or rather all the time I can spare. My own collections must wait in the meantime. Hedda—you understand, eh? I owe this to Eilert's memory.

HEDDA. Perhaps.

TESMAN. And so, my dear Mrs. Elvsted, we will give our whole minds to it. There is no use in brooding over what can't be undone—eh? We must try to control our grief as much as possible, and——

MRS. ELVSTED. Yes, yes, Mr. Tesman, I will do the best I can.

TESMAN. Well then, come here. I can't rest until we have looked through the notes. Where shall we sit? Here? No, in there, in the back room. Excuse me, my dear Judge. Come with me, Mrs. Elvsted.

MRS. ELVSTED. Oh, if only it were possible!

[TESMAN *and* MRS. ELVSTED *go into the back room. She takes off her hat and cloak. They both sit at the table under the hanging lamp, and are soon deep in an eager examination of the papers.* HEDDA *crosses to the stove and sits in the arm-chair. Presently* BRACK *goes up to her*]

HEDDA. [*In a low voice*] Oh, what a sense of freedom it gives one, this act of Eilert Lövborg's.

BRACK. Freedom, Mrs. Hedda? Well, of course, it is a release for him——

HEDDA. I mean for me. It gives me a sense of freedom to know that a deed of deliberate courage is still possible in this world,—a deed of spontaneous beauty.

BRACK. [*Smiling*] H'm—my dear Mrs. Hedda——

HEDDA. Oh, I know what you are going to say. For you are a kind of specialist, too, like—you know!

BRACK. [*Looking hard at her*] Eilert Lövborg was more to you than perhaps you are willing to admit to yourself. Am I wrong?

HEDDA. I don't answer such questions. I only know that Eilert Lövborg has had the courage to live his life after his own fashion. And then—the last great act, with its beauty! Ah! that he should have the will and the strength to turn away from the banquet of life—so early.

BRACK. I am sorry, Mrs. Hedda,—but I fear I must dispel an amiable illusion.

HEDDA. Illusion?

BRACK. Which could not have lasted long in any case.

HEDDA. What do you mean?

BRACK. Eilert Lövborg did not shoot himself—voluntarily.

HEDDA. Not voluntarily!

BRACK. No. The thing did not happen exactly as I told it.

HEDDA. [*In suspense*] Have you concealed something? What is it?

BRACK. For poor Mrs. Elvsted's sake I idealized the facts a little.

HEDDA. What are the facts?

BRACK. First, that he is already dead.

HEDDA. At the hospital?

BRACK. Yes—without regaining consciousness.

HEDDA. What more have you concealed?

BRACK. This—the event did not happen at his lodgings.

HEDDA. Oh, that can make no difference.

BRACK. Perhaps it may. For I must tell you—Eilert Lövborg was found shot in —in Mademoiselle Diana's boudoir.

HEDDA. [*Makes a motion as if to rise, but sinks back again*] That is impossible, Judge Brack! He cannot have been there again to-day.

BRACK. He was there this afternoon. He went there, he said, to demand the return of something which they had taken from him. Talked wildly about a lost child——

HEDDA. Ah—so that was why——

BRACK. I thought probably he meant his manuscript; but now I hear he destroyed that himself. So I suppose it must have been his pocketbook.

HEDDA. Yes, no doubt. And there—there he was found?

BRACK. Yes, there. With a pistol in his breast-pocket, discharged. The ball had lodged in a vital part.

HEDDA. In the breast—yes.

BRACK. No—in the bowels.

HEDDA. [*Looks up at him with an expression of loathing*] That, too! Oh, what curse is it that makes everything I touch turn ludicrous and mean?

BRACK. There is one point more, Mrs. Hedda—another disagreeable feature in the affair.

HEDDA. And what is that?

BRACK. The pistol he carried——

HEDDA. [*Breathless*] Well? What of it?

BRACK. He must have stolen it.

HEDDA.   [*Leaps up*] Stolen it! That is not true! He did not steal it!

BRACK.   No other explanation is possible. He must have stolen it——Hush!

[TESMAN *and* MRS. ELVSTED *have risen from the table in the back room, and come into the drawing-room*]

TESMAN.   [*With the papers in both his hands*] Hedda, dear, it is almost impossible to see under that lamp. Think of that!

HEDDA.   Yes, I am thinking.

TESMAN.   Would you mind our sitting at your writing-table—eh?

HEDDA.   If you like. [*Quickly*] No, wait! Let me clear it first!

TESMAN.   Oh, you needn't trouble, Hedda. There is plenty of room.

HEDDA.   No, no, let me clear it, I say! I will take these things in and put them on the piano. There!

[*She has drawn out an object, covered with sheet music, from under the bookcase, places several other pieces of music upon it, and carries the whole into the inner room, to the left.* TESMAN *lays the scraps of paper on the writing-table, and moves the lamp there from the corner table. He and* MRS. ELVSTED *sit down and proceed with their work.* HEDDA *returns*]

HEDDA.   [*Behind* MRS. ELVSTED'S *chair, gently ruffling her hair*] Well, my sweet Thea,—how goes it with Eilert Lövborg's monument?

MRS. ELVSTED.   [*Looks dispiritedly up at her*] Oh, it will be terribly hard to put in order.

TESMAN.   We must manage it. I am determined. And arranging other people's papers is just the work for me.

[HEDDA *goes over to the stove, and seats herself on one of the footstools.* BRACK *stands over her, leaning on the arm-chair*]

HEDDA.   [*Whispers*] What did you say about the pistol?

BRACK.   [*Softly*] That he must have stolen it.

HEDDA.   Why stolen it?

BRACK.   Because every other explanation ought to be impossible, Mrs. Hedda.

HEDDA.   Indeed?

BRACK.   [*Glances at her*] Of course, Eilert Lövborg was here this morning. Was he not?

HEDDA.   Yes.

BRACK.   Were you alone with him?

HEDDA.   Part of the time.

BRACK.   Did you not leave the room whilst he was here?

HEDDA.   No.

BRACK.   Try to recollect. Were you not out of the room a moment?

HEDDA.   Yes, perhaps just a moment—out in the hall.

BRACK.   And where was your pistol-case during that time?

HEDDA.   I had it locked up in——

BRACK.   Well, Mrs. Hedda?

HEDDA.   The case stood there on the writing-table.

BRACK.   Have you looked since, to see whether both the pistols are there?

HEDDA.   No.

BRACK.   Well, you need not. I saw the pistol found in Lövborg's pocket, and I knew it at once as the one I had seen yesterday—and before, too.

HEDDA.   Have you it with you?

BRACK. No, the police have it.

HEDDA. What will the police do with it?

BRACK. Search till they find the owner.

HEDDA. Do you think they will succeed?

BRACK. [*Bends over her and whispers*] No, Hedda Gabler—not so long as I say nothing.

HEDDA. [*Looks frightened at him*] And if you do not say nothing,—what then?

BRACK. [*Shrugs his shoulders*] There is always the possibility that the pistol was stolen.

HEDDA. [*Firmly*] Death rather than that.

BRACK. [*Smiling*] People say such things—but they don't do them.

HEDDA. [*Without replying*] And supposing the pistol was not stolen, and the owner is discovered? What then?

BRACK. Well, Hedda—then comes the scandàl.

HEDDA. The scandal!

BRACK. Yes, the scandal—of which you are so mortally afraid. You will, of course, be brought before the court—both you and Mademoiselle Diana. She will have to explain how the thing happened—whether it was an accidental shot or murder. Did the pistol go off as he was trying to take it out of his pocket, to threaten her with? Or did she tear the pistol out of his hand, shoot him, and push it back into his pocket? That would be quite like her; for she is an able-bodied young person, this same Mademoiselle Diana.

HÉDDA. But *I* have nothing to do with all this repulsive business.

BRACK. No. But you will have to answer the question: Why did you give Eilert Lövborg the pistol? And what conclusions will people draw from the fact that you did give it to him?

HEDDA. [*Lets her head sink*] That is true. I did not think of that.

BRACK. Well, fortunately, there is no danger, so long as I say nothing.

HEDDA. [*Looks up at him*] So I am in your power, Judge Brack. You have me at your beck and call, from this time forward.

BRACK. [*Whispers softly*] Dearest Hedda—believe me—I shall not abuse my advantage.

HEDDA. I am in your power none the less. Subject to your will and your demands. A slave, a slave then! [*Rises impetuously*] No, I cannot endure the thought of that! Never!

BRACK. [*Looks half-mockingly at her*] People generally get used to the inevitable.

HEDDA. [*Returns his look*] Yes, perhaps. [*She crosses to the writing-table. Suppressing an involuntary smile, she imitates* TESMAN'S *intonations*] Well? Are you getting on, George? Eh?

TESMAN. Heaven knows, dear. In any case it will be the work of months.

HEDDA. [*As before*] Fancy that! [*Passes her hands softly through* MRS. ELVSTED's *hair*] Doesn't it seem strange to you, Thea? Here are you sitting with Tesman—just as you used to sit with Eilert Lövborg?

MRS. ELVSTED. Ah, if I could only inspire your husband in the same way!

HEDDA. Oh, that will come, too—in time.

TESMAN. Yes, do you know, Hedda—I really think I begin to feel something of the sort. But won't you go and sit with Brack again?

HEDDA.   Is there nothing I can do to help you two?

TESMAN.   No, nothing in the world. [*Turning his head*] I trust to you to keep Hedda company, my dear Brack.

BRACK.   [*With a glance at* HEDDA] With the very greatest of pleasure.

HEDDA.   Thanks. But I am tired this evening. I will go in and lie down a little on the sofa.

TESMAN.   Yes, do, dear—eh?

[HEDDA *goes into the back room and draws the curtains. A short pause. Suddenly she is heard playing a wild dance on the piano*]

MRS. ELVSTED.   [*Starts from her chair*] Oh—what is that?

TESMAN.   [*Runs to the doorway*] Why, my dearest Hedda—don't play dance-music to-night! Just think of Aunt Rina! And of Eilert, too!

HEDDA.   [*Puts her head out between the curtains*] And of Aunt Julia. And of all the rest of them.—After this, I will be quiet. [*Closes the curtains again*]

TESMAN.   [*At the writing-table*] It's not good for her to see us at this distressing work. I'll tell you what, Mrs. Elvsted,—you shall take the empty room at Aunt Julia's, and then I will come over in the evenings, and we can sit and work there—eh?

HEDDA.   [*In the inner room*] I hear what you are saying, Tesman. But how am *I* to get through the evenings out here?

TESMAN.   [*Turning over the papers*] Oh, I daresay Judge Brack will be so kind as to look in now and then, even though I am out.

BRACK.   [*In the arm-chair, calls out gaily*] Every blessed evening, with all the pleasure in life, Mrs. Tesman! We shall get on capitally together, we two!

HEDDA.   [*Speaking loud and clear*] Yes, don't you flatter yourself we will, Judge Brack? Now that you are the one cock in the basket——

[*A shot is heard within.* TESMAN, MRS. ELVSTED, *and* BRACK *leap to their feet*]

TESMAN.   Oh, now she is playing with those pistols again.

[*He throws back the curtains and runs in, followed by* MRS. ELVSTED. HEDDA *lies stretched on the sofa, lifeless. Confusion and cries.* BERTA *enters in alarm from the right*]

TESMAN.   [*Shrieks to* BRACK] Shot herself! Shot herself in the temple! Fancy that!

BRACK.   [*Half-fainting in the arm-chair*] Good God!—people don't do such things.

Arms and the Man

George Bernard Shaw

George Bernard Shaw

In 1957—exactly 101 years after his birth—four plays by George Bernard Shaw were running in New York—to say nothing of *My Fair Lady,* which had been adapted from still a fifth play. There could hardly be more convincing testimony to the vitality of his work. Some critics, it is true, welcomed the influx of Shaw plays with comic condescension, saying that Shaw was as out-of-date as a late-Victorian velvet waistcoat. But G. K. Chesterton, writing of Shaw's work nearly 50 years earlier, had neatly disposed of that bit of critical snobbery: "To be up-to-date," said Chesterton, "is a paltry ambition except in an almanac. . . ."

Shaw (who would have loved the posthumous success almost as much as the controversy) was an Irishman, born in 1856 in Dublin to a respectable family that was rapidly going to seed: an "upstart" son in a "downstart" family, he described himself. In his few years of formal education he learned nothing, he claimed; he educated himself. At the age of 20 he left a clerk's job in Dublin to follow his mother to London, where she had set herself up as a music teacher. For the next eight or nine years he continued to educate himself in political science, economics, literature, music, and whatever else came into his ken. His passion for knowledge was omnivorous, his energy immense, his talent staggering.

During those early years in London, Shaw heard Henry George lecture, he read Karl Marx, and he became a Socialist—one of the most influential Socialists of his time. He and his close friends Sidney and Beatrice Webb were for a great many years the guiding force of the Fabian Society, a group of intellectuals whose purpose, Shaw once wrote, was "to make it as easy and matter-of-course for the ordinary respectable Englishman to be a Socialist as to be a Liberal or a Conservative." It is a measure of their success that everyone has forgotten how well they succeeded. Shaw's role in the Socialist movement was less that of original thinker than that of propagandist. A shy and stammering young man, he trained himself to be a superb public speaker; with his flashing wit and his splendid presence—every hair of his red beard bristling with vitality—he was a formidable figure on street corners and lecture platforms.

Shaw made his first literary success writing criticism of art, music, and drama for newspapers and magazines. W. H. Auden has said that he was probably the best music critic who ever lived. His entrance into the field of drama, however, was anything but propitious. His first two plays, *Widowers' Houses* (1892) and *Mrs. Warren's Profession* (1893) were dramatic exposés of the way the wealthy classes batten on profits from slum property and prostitution. This was rich fare for a timid Victorian society. *Widowers' Houses* had two performances in a private club; *Mrs. Warren's Profession* was banned by the government censor. (When the latter play was performed in New York in 1905, the whole company was arrested.)

Arms and the Man (1894) was Shaw's first dramatic success. "No one who was alive at the time and interested in such matters will ever forget the first acting" of that play, says Chesterton. Shaw's was a new voice in the land; and in play after play he proceeded to shock, delight, irritate, and enlighten his contemporaries. This was the way he conceived his role; for half a century he lived it strenuously. The American playwright Elmer Rice has recorded what happened to him when, shortly before World War I, he came upon a volume of Shaw's plays—his *Plays, Pleasant and Unpleasant:* "The effect was cataclysmic. Doors and windows opened, bells rang, lights went on and horizons broadened." For countless people Shaw's iconoclasm, his attachment to what seemed the realities of life rather than the illusions by which nearly all men lived, had a liberating effect. His plays conquered the world; and when movies were made of *Major Barbara, Pygmalion, Caesar and Cleopatra, St. Joan,* they only enhanced the already established reputation. In the years between the wars, Shaw was the best-known man of letters in the world: no event was complete, as Eric Bentley said, until Bernard Shaw had commented on it. But it is part of Shaw's pathos that he outlived his time. He continued to comment—an embarrassing voice from another age, peppery, outrageous as always—until the end. He died in 1950 at his home in Ayot St. Lawrence at the age of 94.

Arms and the Man has a deceptively simple surface. On one level it ridicules romantic notions of military glory, and that level alone was enough to offend the Prince of Wales, a good many other Englishmen, and nearly all Bulgarians. But Shaw is after more subtle game. Consider the questions that arise if one juxtaposes the play's title with the last line spoken in the work. "Arms and the man" is a translation of the opening words of Virgil's epic poem, the *Aeneid: arma virumque cano* . . . words that arouse in our minds all that is associated with the truly heroic man. The last line of the play is Sergius' admiring praise of Bluntschli, "What a man!" followed by his puzzled query, "Is he a man?" The quotation from Virgil forces us to think of Sergius' question in a large context: we ask ourselves, "What is a man?"

Shaw gives us one version of heroic man in Sergius, the dashing officer who leads his cavalry in a death-defying charge against machine guns. This is the man Raina idolizes at the beginning of the play. But in the midst of her raptures over Sergius' sublime courage, Bluntschli comes through the window, shattering illusions with every word. Bluntschli is like Shakespeare's Falstaff: instead of weapons, the one carries chocolate, the other sack; and both test our ideas of the heroic. Bluntschli is an antihero, a true professional soldier for whom Sergius' kind of heroism is comical nonsense. At the end Sergius has to admit that compared with Bluntschli he is nothing but an innocent child. Is Bluntschli then the true man of the play? Perhaps, but if so, manhood has come to a dreary pass. Raina's furious accusation, "You have a low shopkeeping mind," turns out to be good characterization. The only man in Bulgaria Bluntschli really admires is the butler Nicola, who pimps for his fiancée Louka so that he can get her custom when he sets up his own shop. Bluntschli praises this kind of "practicality" in such extravagant terms as to pull himself down to Nicola's level.

Perhaps the real "man" of the play is Louka, the servant girl with a soul above her station. Louka is eminently practical, certainly, but she despises Nicola's "cold-blooded wisdom," and she has the spirit and the pride to bring the swaggering Sergius to heel. In any event, she is an early sketch of those vital women, bearing the Life Force within them, who people Shaw's later plays. Robert Louis Stevenson's remark is famous: "I say, Archer, my God, what women!"

Arms and the Man

George Bernard Shaw

Act I

Night: A lady's bedchamber in Bulgaria, in a small town near the Dragoman Pass, late in November in the year 1885. Through an open window with a little balcony a peak of the Balkans, wonderfully white and beautiful in the starlit snow, seems quite close at hand, though it is really miles away. The interior of the room is not like anything to be seen in the west of Europe. It is half rich Bulgarian, half cheap Viennese. Above the head of the bed, which stands against a little wall cutting off the left hand corner of the room, is a painted wooden shrine, blue and gold, with an ivory image of Christ, and a light hanging before it in a pierced metal ball suspended by three chains. The principal seat, placed towards the other side of the room and opposite the window, is a Turkish ottoman. The counterpane and hangings of the bed, the window curtains, the little carpet, and all the ornamental textile fabrics in the room are oriental and gorgeous; the paper on the walls is occidental and paltry. The washstand, against the wall on the side nearest the ottoman and window, consists of an enamelled iron basin with a pail beneath it in a painted metal frame, and a single towel on the rail at the side. The dressing table, between the bed and the window, is a common pine table, covered with a cloth of many colours, with an expensive toilet mirror on it. The door is on the side nearest the bed; and there is a chest of drawers between. This chest of drawers is also covered by a variegated native cloth; and on it there is a pile of paper-backed novels, a box of chocolate creams, and a miniature easel with a large photograph of an extremely handsome officer, whose lofty bearing and magnetic glance can be felt even from the portrait. The room is lighted by a candle on the chest of drawers, and another on the dressing table with a box of matches beside it.

The window is hinged doorwise and stands wide open. Outside, a pair of wooden shutters, opening outwards, also stand open. On the balcony a young lady, intensely conscious of the romantic beauty of the night, and of the fact that her own youth and beauty are part of it, is gazing at the snowy Balkans. She is in her nightgown, well covered by a long mantle of furs, worth, on a moderate estimate, about three times the furniture of the room.

Reprinted by permission of The Society of Authors, on behalf of the Bernard Shaw Estate.

Her reverie is interrupted by her mother, CATHERINE PETKOFF, *a woman over forty, imperiously energetic, with magnificent black hair and eyes, who might be a very splendid specimen of the wife of a mountain farmer, but is determined to be a Viennese lady, and to that end wears a fashionable tea gown on all occasions.*

CATHERINE. [*Entering hastily, full of good news*] Raina! [*She pronounces it Rah-eena, with the stress on the ee*] Raina! [*She goes to the bed, expecting to find* RAINA *there*] Why, where—? [RAINA *looks into the room*] Heavens child! are you out in the night air instead of in your bed? Youll catch your death. Louka told me you were asleep.

RAINA. [*Dreamily*] I sent her away. I wanted to be alone. The stars are so beautiful! What is the matter?

CATHERINE. Such news! There has been a battle.

RAINA. [*Her eyes dilating*] Ah! [*She comes eagerly to* CATHERINE]

CATHERINE. A great battle at Slivnitza! [1] A victory! And it was won by Sergius.

RAINA. [*With a cry of delight*] Ah! [*They embrace rapturously*] Oh, mother! [*Then, with sudden anxiety*] Is father safe?

CATHERINE. Of course! he sends me the news. Sergius is the hero of the hour, the idol of the regiment.

RAINA. Tell me, tell me. How was it? [*Ecstatically*] Oh, mother! mother! mother! [*She pulls her mother down on the ottoman; and they kiss one another frantically*]

CATHERINE. [*With surging enthusiasm*] You cant guess how splendid it is. A cavalry charge! think of that! He defied our Russian commanders—acted without orders—led a charge on his own responsibility—headed it himself— was the first man to sweep through their guns. Cant you see it, Raina: our gallant splendid Bulgarians with their swords and eyes flashing, thundering down like an avalanche and scattering the wretched Serbs and their dandified Austrian officers like chaff. And you! you kept Sergius waiting a year before you would be betrothed to him. Oh, if you have a drop of Bulgarian blood in your veins, you will worship him when he comes back.

RAINA. What will he care for my poor little worship after the acclamations of a whole army of heroes? But no matter: I am so happy! so proud! [*She rises and walks about excitedly*] It proves that all our ideas were real after all.

CATHERINE. [*Indignantly*] Our ideas real! What do you mean?

RAINA. Our ideas of what Sergius would do. Our patriotism. Our heroic ideals. I sometimes used to doubt whether they were anything but dreams. Oh, what faithless little creatures girls are! When I buckled on Sergius's sword he looked so noble: it was treason to think of disillusion or humiliation or failure. And yet—and yet—[*She sits down again suddenly*] Promise me youll never tell him.

CATHERINE. Dont ask me for promises until I know what I'm promising.

RAINA. Well, it came into my head just as he was holding me in his arms and looking into my eyes, that perhaps we only had our heroic ideas because we are so fond of reading Byron and Pushkin, and because we were so delighted

---

[1] A village in western Bulgaria, where the Bulgarians defeated the Serbs in 1885.

with the opera that season at Bucharest. Real life is so seldom like that! indeed never, as far as I knew it then. [*Remorsefully*] Only think, mother: I doubted him: I wondered whether all his heroic qualities and his soldiership might not prove mere imagination when he went into a real battle. I had an uneasy fear that he might cut a poor figure there beside all those clever officers from the Tsar's court.

CATHERINE. A poor figure! Shame on you! The Serbs have Austrian officers who are just as clever as the Russians; but we have beaten them in every battle for all that.

RAINA. [*Laughing and snuggling against her mother*] Yes: I was only a prosaic little coward. Oh, to think that it was all true! that Sergius is just as splendid and noble as he looks! that the world is really a glorious world for women who can see its glory and men who can act its romance! What happiness! what unspeakable fulfilment!

[*They are interrupted by the entry of* LOUKA, *a handsome proud girl in a pretty Bulgarian peasant's dress with double apron, so defiant that her servility to* RAINA *is almost insolent. She is afraid of* CATHERINE, *but even with her goes as far as she dares*]

LOUKA. If you please, madam, all the windows are to be closed and the shutters made fast. They say there may be shooting in the streets. [RAINA *and* CATHERINE *rise together, alarmed*] The Serbs are being chased right back through the pass, and they say they may run into the town. Our cavalry will be after them; and our people will be ready for them, you may be sure, now theyre running away. [*She goes out on the balcony, and pulls the outside shutters to; then steps back into the room*]

CATHERINE. [*Businesslike, housekeeping instincts aroused*] I must see that everything is made safe downstairs.

RAINA. I wish our people were not so cruel. What glory is there in killing wretched fugitives?

CATHERINE. Cruel! Do you suppose they would hesitate to kill you—or worse?

RAINA. [*To* LOUKA] Leave the shutters so that I can just close them if I hear any noise.

CATHERINE. [*Authoritatively, turning on her way to the door*] Oh no, dear: you must keep them fastened. You would be sure to drop off to sleep and leave them open. Make them fast, Louka.

LOUKA. Yes, madam. [*She fastens them*]

RAINA. Dont be anxious about me. The moment I hear a shot, I shall blow out the candles and roll myself up in bed with my ears well covered.

CATHERINE. Quite the wisest thing you can do, my love. Good night.

RAINA. Good night. [*Her emotion comes back for a moment*] Wish me joy. [*They kiss*] This is the happiest night of my life—if only there are no fugitives.

CATHERINE. Go to bed, dear; and dont think of them.

[*She goes out*]

LOUKA. [*Secretly to* RAINA] If you would like the shutters open, just give them a push like this [*She pushes them: they open: she pulls them to again*] One of them ought to be bolted at the bottom; but the bolt's gone.

RAINA. [*With dignity, reproving her*] Thanks, Louka; but we must do what we are told. [LOUKA *makes a grimace*] Good night.
LOUKA. [*Carelessly*] Good night.

[*She goes out, swaggering*]

[RAINA, *left alone, takes off her fur cloak and throws it on the ottoman. Then she goes to the chest of drawers, and adores the portrait there with feelings that are beyond all expression. She does not kiss it or press it to her breast, or shew it any mark of bodily affection; but she takes it in her hands and elevates it, like a priestess*]

RAINA. [*Looking up at the picture*] Oh, I shall never be unworthy of you any more, my soul's hero: never, never, never. [*She replaces it reverently. Then she selects a novel from the little pile of books. She turns over the leaves dreamily; finds her page; turns the book inside out at it; and, with a happy sigh, gets into bed and prepares to read herself to sleep. But before abandoning herself to fiction, she raises her eyes once more, thinking of the blessed reality, and murmurs*] My hero! my hero!

[*A distant shot breaks the quiet of the night. She starts, listening; and two more shots, much nearer, follow, startling her so that she scrambles out of bed, and hastily blows out the candle on the chest of drawers. Then, putting her fingers in her ears, she runs to the dressing table, blows out the light there, and hurries back to bed in the dark, nothing being visible but the glimmer of the light in the pierced ball before the image, and the starlight seen through the slits at the top of the shutters. The firing breaks out again: there is a startling fusillade quite close at hand. Whilst it is still echoing, the shutters disappear, pulled open from without; and for an instant the rectangle of snowy starlight flashes out with the figure of a man silhouetted in black upon it. The shutters close immediately; and the room is dark again. But the silence is now broken by the sound of panting. Then there is a scratch; and the flame of a match is seen in the middle of the room*]

RAINA. [*Crouching on the bed*] Who's there? [*The match is out instantly*] Who's there? Who is that?
A MAN'S VOICE. [*In the darkness, subduedly, but threateningly*] Sh—sh! Dont call out; or youll be shot. Be good; and no harm will happen to you. [*She is heard leaving her bed, and making for the door*] Take care: it's no use trying to run away.
RAINA. But who—
THE VOICE. [*Warning*] Remember: if you raise your voice my revolver will go off. [*Commandingly*] Strike a light and let me see you. Do you hear. [*Another moment of silence and darkness as she retreats to the chest of drawers. Then she lights a candle; and the mystery is at an end. He is a man about 35, in a deplorable plight, bespattered with mud and blood and snow, his belt and the strap of his revolver case keeping together the torn ruins of the blue tunic of a Serbian artillery officer. All that the candlelight and his unwashed unkempt condition make it possible to discern is that he is of middling stature and undistinguished appearance, with strong neck and shoulders, roundish obstinate looking head covered with short crisp bronze curls, clear quick eyes and good brows and mouth, hopelessly prosaic nose*

like that of a strong minded baby, trim soldierlike carriage and energetic manner, and with all his wits about him in spite of his desperate predicament: even with a sense of the humor of it, without, however, the least intention of trifling with it or throwing away a chance. Reckoning up what he can guess about RAINA: *her age, her social position, her character, and the extent to which she is frightened, he continues, more politely but still most determinedly*] Excuse my disturbing you; but you recognize my uniform? Serb! If I'm caught I shall be killed. [*Menacingly*] Do you understand that?

RAINA.   Yes.

THE MAN.   Well, I dont intend to get killed if I can help it. [*Still more formidably*] Do you understand that? [*He locks the door quickly but quietly*]

RAINA.   [*Disdainfully*] I suppose not. [*She draws herself up superbly, and looks him straight in the face, adding, with cutting emphasis*] Some soldiers, I know, are afraid to die.

THE MAN.   [*With grim goodhumor*] All of them, dear lady, all of them, believe me. It is our duty to live as long as we can. Now, if you raise an alarm—

RAINA.   [*Cutting him short*] You will shoot me. How do you know that *I* am afraid to die?

THE MAN.   [*Cunningly*] Ah; but suppose I dont shoot you, what will happen then? A lot of your cavalry will burst into this pretty room of yours and slaughter me here like a pig; for I'll fight like a demon: they shant get me into the street to amuse themselves with: I know what they are. Are you prepared to receive that sort of company in your present undress? [RAINA, *suddenly conscious of her nightgown, instinctively shrinks and gathers it more closely about her neck. He watches her and adds pitilessly*] Hardly presentable, eh? [*She turns to the ottoman. He raises his pistol instantly, and cries*] Stop! [*She stops*] Where are you going?

RAINA.   [*With dignified patience*] Only to get my cloak.

THE MAN.   [*Passing swiftly to the ottoman and snatching the cloak*] A good idea! I'll keep the cloak; and you'll take care that nobody comes in and sees you without it. This is a better weapon than the revolver: eh? [*He throws the pistol down on the ottoman*]

RAINA.   [*Revolted*] It is not the weapon of a gentleman!

THE MAN.   It's good enough for a man with only you to stand between him and death. [*As they look at one another for a moment,* RAINA *hardly able to believe that even a Serbian officer can be so cynically and selfishly unchivalrous, they are startled by a sharp fusillade in the street. The chill of imminent death hushes* THE MAN's *voice as he adds*] Do you hear? If you are going to bring those blackguards in on me you shall receive them as you are.

[*Clamor and disturbance. The pursuers in the street batter at the house door, shouting*] Open the door! Open the door! Wake up, will you! [*A man servant's voice calls to them angrily from within*] This is Major Petkoff's house: you cant come in here. [*But a renewal of the clamor, and a torrent of blows on the door, end with his letting a chain down with a clank, followed by a rush of heavy footsteps and a din of triumphant yells, dominated at last by the voice of* CATHERINE, *indignantly addressing an officer with*] What does this mean, sir? Do you know where you are? [*The noise subsides suddenly*]

LOUKA. [*Outside, knocking at the bedroom door*] My lady! my lady! get up
quick and open the door. If you dont they will break it down.

[*The fugitive throws up his head with the gesture of a man who sees that it
is all over with him, and drops the manner he has been assuming to intimidate*
RAINA]

THE MAN. [*Sincerely and kindly*] No use, dear: I'm done for. [*Flinging the
cloak to her*] Quick! wrap yourself up: they're coming.

RAINA. Oh, thank you. [*She wraps herself up with intense relief*]

THE MAN. [*Between his teeth*] Dont mention it.

RAINA. [*Anxiously*] What will you do?

THE MAN. [*Grimly*] The first man in will find out. Keep out of the way; and
dont look. It wont last long; but it will not be nice. [*He draws his sabre and
faces the door, waiting*]

RAINA. [*Impulsively*] I'll help you. I'll save you.

THE MAN. You cant.

RAINA. I can. I'll hide you. [*She drags him towards the window*]. Here! behind
the curtains.

THE MAN. [*Yielding to her*] Theres just half a chance, if you keep your head.

RAINA. [*Drawing the curtain before him*] S-sh! [*She makes for the ottoman*]

THE MAN. [*Putting out his head*] Remember—

RAINA. [*Running back to him*] Yes?

THE MAN. —nine soldiers out of ten are born fools.

RAINA. Oh! [*She draws the curtain angrily before him*]

THE MAN. [*Looking out at the other side*] If they find me, I promise you a
fight: a devil of a fight.

[*She stamps at him. He disappears hastily. She takes off her cloak, and throws
it across the foot of the bed. Then, with a sleepy, disturbed air, she opens the
door.* LOUKA *enters excitedly*]

LOUKA. One of those beasts of Serbs has been seen climbing up the waterpipe
to your balcony. Our men want to search for him; and they are so wild and
drunk and furious. [*She makes for the other side of the room to get as far
from the door as possible*] My lady says you are to dress at once and to—
[*She sees the revolver lying on the ottoman, and stops, petrified*]

RAINA. [*As if annoyed at being disturbed*] They shall not search here. Why
have they been let in?

CATHERINE. [*Coming in hastily*] Raina, darling, are you safe? Have you seen
anyone or heard anything?

RAINA. I heard the shooting. Surely the soldiers will not dare come in here?

CATHERINE. I have found a Russian officer, thank Heaven: he knows Sergius.
[*Speaking through the door to someone outside*] Sir: will you come in now.
My daughter will receive you.

[*A young Russian officer, in Bulgarian uniform, enters, sword in hand*]

OFFICER. [*With soft feline politeness and stiff military carriage*] Good evening, gracious lady. I am sorry to intrude; but there is a Serb hiding on the
balcony. Will you and the gracious lady your mother please to withdraw
whilst we search?

RAINA. [*Petulantly*] Nonsense, sir: you can see that there is no one on the
balcony. [*She throws the shutters wide open and stands with her back to

the curtain where the man is hidden, pointing to the moonlit balcony. A couple of shots are fired right under the window; and a bullet shatters the glass opposite RAINA, *who winks and gasps, but stands her ground; whilst* CATHERINE *screams, and the officer, with a cry of* Take care! *rushes to the balcony*]

THE OFFICER. [*On the balcony, shouting savagely down to the street*] Cease firing there, you fools: do you hear? Cease firing, damn you! [*He glares down for a moment; then turns to* RAINA, *trying to resume his polite manner*] Could anyone have got in without your knowledge? Were you asleep?

RAINA. No: I have not been to bed.

THE OFFICER. [*Impatiently, coming back into the room*] Your neighbors have their heads so full of runaway Serbs that they see them everywhere. [*Politely*] Gracious lady: a thousand pardons. Good night. [*Military bow, which* RAINA *returns coldly. Another to* CATHERINE, *who follows him out*]

[RAINA *closes the shutters. She turns and sees* LOUKA, *who has been watching the scene curiously*]

RAINA. Dont leave my mother, Louka, until the soldiers go away.

[LOUKA *glances at* RAINA, *at the ottoman, at the curtain; then purses her lips secretively, laughs insolently, and goes out.* RAINA, *highly offended by this demonstration, follows her to the door, and shuts it behind her with a slam, locking it violently.* THE MAN *immediately steps out from behind the curtain, sheathing his sabre. Then, dismissing the danger from his mind in a businesslike way, he comes affably to* RAINA]

THE MAN. A narrow shave; but a miss is as good as a mile. Dear young lady: your servant to the death. I wish for your sake I had joined the Bulgarian army instead of the other one. I am not a native Serb.

RAINA. [*Haughtily*] No: you are one of the Austrians who set the Serbs on to rob us of our national liberty, and who officer their army for them. We hate them!

THE MAN. Austrian! not I. Dont hate me, dear young lady. I am a Swiss, fighting merely as a professional soldier. I joined the Serbs because they came first on the road from Switzerland. Be generous: youve beaten us hollow.

RAINA. Have I not been generous?

THE MAN. Noble! Heroic! But I'm not saved yet. This particular rush will soon pass through; but the pursuit will go on all night by fits and starts. I must take my chance to get off in a quiet interval. [*Pleasantly*] You dont mind my waiting just a minute or two, do you?

RAINA. [*Putting on her most genteel society manner*] Oh, not at all. Wont you sit down?

THE MAN. Thanks. [*He sits on the foot of the bed*]

[RAINA *walks with studied elegance to the ottoman and sits down. Unfortunately she sits on the pistol, and jumps up with a shriek.* THE MAN, *all nerves, shies like a frightened horse to the other side of the room*]

THE MAN. [*Irritably*] Dont frighten me like that. What is it?

RAINA. Your revolver! It was staring that officer in the face all the time. What an escape!

THE MAN. [*Vexed at being unnecessarily terrified*] Oh, is that all?

RAINA.   [*Staring at him rather superciliously as she conceives a poorer and poorer opinion of him, and feels proportionately more and more at her ease*] I am sorry I frightened you. [*She takes up the pistol and hands it to him*] Pray take it to protect yourself against me.

THE MAN.   [*Grinning wearily at the sarcasm as he takes the pistol*] No use, dear young lady: there's nothing in it. It's not loaded. [*He makes a grimace at it, and drops it despairingly into his revolver case*]

RAINA.   Load it by all means.

THE MAN.   I've no ammunition. What use are cartridges in battle? I always carry chocolate instead; and I finished the last cake of that hours ago.

RAINA.   [*Outraged in her most cherished ideals of manhood*] Chocolate! Do you stuff your pockets with sweets—like a schoolboy—even in the field?

THE MAN.   [*Grinning*] Yes: isnt it contemptible? [*Hungrily*] I wish I had some now.

RAINA.   Allow me. [*She sails away scornfully to the chest of drawers, and returns with the box of confectionery in her hand*] I am sorry I have eaten them all except these. [*She offers him the box*]

THE MAN.   [*Ravenously*] Youre an angel! [*He gobbles the contents*] Creams! Delicious! [*He looks anxiously to see whether there are any more. There are none: he can only scrape the box with his fingers and suck them. When that nourishment is exhausted he accepts the inevitable with pathetic goodhumor, and says, with grateful emotion*] Bless you, dear lady! You can always tell an old soldier by the inside of his holsters and cartridge boxes. The young ones carry pistols and cartridges: the old ones, grub. Thank you. [*He hands back the box. She snatches it contemptuously from him and throws it away. He shies again, as if she had meant to strike him*] Ugh! Dont do things so suddenly, gracious lady. It's mean to revenge yourself because I frightened you just now.

RAINA.   [*Loftily*] Frighten me! Do you know, sir, that though I am only a woman, I think I am at heart as brave as you.

THE MAN.   I should think so. You havnt been under fire for three days as I have. I can stand two days without shewing it much; but no man can stand three days: I'm as nervous as a mouse. [*He sits down on the ottoman, and takes his head in his hands*] Would you like to see me cry?

RAINA.   [*Alarmed*] No.

THE MAN.   If you would, all you have to do is to scold me just as if I were a little boy and you my nurse. If I were in camp now, theyd play all sorts of tricks on me.

RAINA.   [*A little moved*] I'm sorry. I wont scold you. [*Touched by the sympathy in her tone, he raises his head and looks gratefully at her: she immediately draws back and says stiffly*] You must excuse me: our soldiers are not like that. [*She moves away from the ottoman*]

THE MAN.   Oh yes they are. There are only two sorts of soldiers: old ones and young ones. I've served fourteen years: half of your fellows never smelt powder before. Why, how is it that youve just beaten us? Sheer ignorance of the art of war, nothing else. [*Indignantly*] I never saw anything so unprofessional.

RAINA. [*Ironically*] Oh! was it unprofessional to beat you?

THE MAN. Well, come! is it professional to throw a regiment of cavalry on a battery of machine guns, with the dead certainty that if the guns go off not a horse or man will ever get within fifty yards of the fire? I couldn't believe my eyes when I saw it.

RAINA. [*Eagerly turning to him, as all her enthusiasm and her dreams of glory rush back on her*] Did you see the great cavalry charge? Oh, tell me about it. Describe it to me.

THE MAN. You never saw a cavalry charge, did you?

RAINA. How could I?

THE MAN. Ah, perhaps not. No: of course not! Well, it's a funny sight. It's like slinging a handful of peas against a window pane: first one comes; then two or three close behind him; and then all the rest in a lump.

RAINA. [*Her eyes dilating as she raises her clasped hands ecstatically*] Yes, first One! the bravest of the brave!

THE MAN. [*Prosaically*] Hm! you should see the poor devil pulling at his horse.

RAINA. Why should he pull at his horse?

THE MAN. [*Impatient of so stupid a question*] It's running away with him, of course: do you suppose the fellow wants to get there before the others and be killed? Then they all come. You can tell the young ones by their wildness and their slashing. The old ones come bunched up under the number one guard: they know that theyre mere projectiles, and that it's no use trying to fight. The wounds are mostly broken knees, from the horses cannoning together.

RAINA. Ugh! But I dont believe the first man is a coward. I know he is a hero!

THE MAN. [*Goodhumoredly*] Thats what youd have said if youd seen the first man in the charge today.

RAINA. [*Breathless, forgiving him everything*] Ah, I knew it! Tell me. Tell me about him.

THE MAN. He did it like an operatic tenor. A regular handsome fellow, with flashing eyes and lovely moustache, shouting his war-cry and charging like Don Quixote at the windmills. We did laugh.

RAINA. You dared to laugh!

THE MAN. Yes; but when the sergeant ran up as white as a sheet, and told us theyd sent us the wrong ammunition, and that we couldnt fire a round for the next ten minutes, we laughed at the other side of our mouths. I never felt so sick in my life; though Ive been in one or two very tight places. And I hadnt even a revolver cartridge: only chocolate. We'd no bayonets: nothing. Of course, they just cut us to bits. And there was Don Quixote flourishing like a drum major, thinking he'd done the cleverest thing ever known, whereas he ought to be courtmartialled for it. Of all the fools ever let loose on a field of battle, that man must be the very maddest. He and his regiment simply committed suicide; only the pistol missed fire: thats all.

RAINA. [*Deeply wounded, but steadfastly loyal to her ideals*] Indeed! Would you know him again if you saw him?

THE MAN. Shall I ever forget him!

[*She again goes to the chest of drawers. He watches her with a vague hope that she may have something more for him to eat. She takes the portrait from its stand and brings it to him*]

RAINA. That is a photograph of the gentleman—the patriot and hero—to whom I am betrothed.

THE MAN. [*Recognizing it with a shock*] I'm really very sorry. [*Looking at her*] Was it fair to lead me on? [*He looks at the portrait again*] Yes: thats Don Quixote: not a doubt of it. [*He stifles a laugh*]

RAINA. [*Quickly*] Why do you laugh?

THE MAN. [*Apologetic, but still greatly tickled*] I didnt laugh, I assure you. At least I didnt mean to. But when I think of him charging the windmills and imagining he was doing the finest thing—[*He chokes with suppressed laughter*]

RAINA. [*Sternly*] Give me back the portrait, sir.

THE MAN. [*With sincere remorse*] Of course. Certainly. I'm really very sorry. [*He hands her the picture. She deliberately kisses it and looks him straight in the face before returning to the chest of drawers to replace it. He follows her, apologizing*] Perhaps I'm quite wrong, you know: no doubt I am. Most likely he had got wind of the cartridge business somehow, and knew it was a safe job.

RAINA. That is to say, he was a pretender and a coward! You did not dare say that before.

THE MAN. [*With a comic gesture of despair*] It's no use, dear lady: I cant make you see it from the professional point of view. [*As he turns away to get back to the ottoman, a couple of distant shots threaten renewed trouble*]

RAINA. [*Sternly, as she sees him listening to the shots*] So much the better for you!

THE MAN. [*Turning*] How?

RAINA. You are my enemy; and you are at my mercy. What would I do if I were a professional soldier?

THE MAN. Ah, true, dear young lady: youre always right. I know how good youve been to me: to my last hour I shall remember those three chocolate creams. It was unsoldierly; but it was angelic.

RAINA. [*Coldly*] Thank you. And now I will do a soldierly thing. You cannot stay here after what you have just said about my future husband; but I will go out on the balcony and see whether it is safe for you to climb down into the street. [*She turns to the window*]

THE MAN. [*Changing countenance*] Down that waterpipe! Stop! Wait! I cant! I darent! The very thought of it makes me giddy. I came up it fast enough with death behind me. But to face it now in cold blood—! [*He sinks on the ottoman*] It's no use: I give up: I'm beaten. Give the alarm. [*He drops his head on his hands in the deepest dejection*]

RAINA. [*Disarmed by pity*] Come: don't be disheartened. [*She stoops over him almost maternally: he shakes his head*] Oh, you are a very poor soldier: a chocolate cream soldier! Come, cheer up! it takes less courage to climb down than to face capture: remember that.

THE MAN. [*Dreamily, lulled by her voice*] No: capture only means death; and death is sleep: oh, sleep, sleep, sleep, undisturbed sleep! Climbing down the pipe means doing something—exerting myself—thinking! Death ten times over first.

RAINA.   [*Softly and wonderingly, catching the rhythm of his weariness*] Are you as sleepy as that?

THE MAN.   Ive not had two hours undisturbed sleep since I joined. I havnt closed my eyes for forty-eight hours.

RAINA.   [*At her wit's end*] But what am I to do with you?

THE MAN.   [*Staggering up, roused by her desperation*] Of course. I must do something. [*He shakes himself; pulls himself together; and speaks with rallied vigor and courage*] You see, sleep or no sleep, hunger or no hunger, tired or not tired, you can always do a thing when you know it must be done. Well, that pipe must be got down: [*He hits himself on the chest*] do you hear that, you chocolate cream soldier? [*He turns to the window*]

RAINA.   [*Anxiously*] But if you fall?

THE MAN.   I shall sleep as if the stones were a feather bed. Goodbye. [*He makes boldly for the window; and his hand is on the shutter when there is a terrible burst of firing in the street beneath*]

RAINA.   [*Rushing to him*] Stop! [*She seizes him recklessly, and pulls him quite round*] Theyll kill you.

THE MAN.   [*Coolly, but attentively*] Never mind: this sort of thing is all in my day's work. I'm bound to take my chance. [*Decisively*] Now do what I tell you. Put out the candle; so that they shant see the light when I open the shutters. And keep away from the window, whatever you do. If they see me theyre sure to have a shot at me.

RAINA.   [*Clinging to him*] Theyre sure to see you: it's bright moonlight. I'll save you. Oh, how can you be so indifferent! You want me to save you, dont you?

THE MAN.   I really dont want to be troublesome. [*She shakes him in her impatience*] I am not indifferent, dear young lady, I assure you. But how is it to be done?

RAINA.   Come away from the window. [*She takes him firmly back to the middle of the room. The moment she releases him he turns mechanically towards the window again. She seizes him and turns him back, exclaiming*] Please! [*He becomes motionless, like a hypnotized rabbit, his fatigue gaining fast on him. She releases him, and addresses him patronizingly*] Now listen. You must trust to our hospitality. You do not yet know in whose house you are. I am a Petkoff.

THE MAN.   A pet what?

RAINA.   [*Rather indignantly*] I mean that I belong to the family of the Petkoffs, the richest and best known in our country.

THE MAN.   Oh yes, of course. I beg your pardon. The Petkoffs, to be sure. How stupid of me!

RAINA.   You know you never heard of them until this moment. How can you stoop to pretend!

THE MAN.   Forgive me: I'm too tired to think; and the change of subject was too much for me. Dont scold me.

RAINA.   I forgot. It might make you cry. [*He nods, quite seriously. She pouts and then resumes her patronizing tone*] I must tell you that my father holds the highest command of any Bulgarian in our army. He is [*Proudly*] a Major.

THE MAN. [*Pretending to be deeply impressed*] A Major! Bless me! Think of that!

RAINA. You shewed great ignorance in thinking that it was necessary to climb up to the balcony because ours is the only private house that has two rows of windows. There is a flight of stairs inside to get up and down by.

THE MAN. Stairs! How grand! You live in great luxury indeed, dear young lady.

RAINA. Do you know what a library is?

THE MAN. A library? A roomful of books?

RAINA. Yes. We have one, the only one in Bulgaria.[2]

THE MAN. Actually a real library! I should like to see that.

RAINA. [*Affectedly*] I tell you these things to shew you that you are not in the house of ignorant country folk who would kill you the moment they saw your Serbian uniform, but among civilized people. We go to Bucharest every year for the opera season; and I have spent a whole month in Vienna.

THE MAN. I saw that, dear young lady. I saw at once that you knew the world.

RAINA. Have you ever seen the opera of Ernani?[3]

THE MAN. Is that the one with the devil in it in red velvet, and a soldiers' chorus?

RAINA. [*Contemptuously*] No!

THE MAN. [*Stifling a heavy sigh of weariness*] Then I dont know it.

RAINA. I thought you might have remembered the great scene where Ernani, flying from his foes just as you are tonight, takes refuge in the castle of his bitterest enemy, an old Castilian noble. The noble refuses to give him up. His guest is sacred to him.

THE MAN. [*Quickly, waking up a little*] Have your people got that notion?

RAINA. [*With dignity*] My mother and I can understand that notion, as you call it. And if instead of threatening me with your pistol as you did you had simply thrown yourself as a fugitive on our hospitality, you would have been as safe as in your father's house.

THE MAN. Quite sure?

RAINA. [*Turning her back on him in disgust*] Oh, it is useless to try to make you understand.

THE MAN. Dont be angry: you see how awkward it would be for me if there was any mistake. My father is a very hospitable man: he keeps six hotels; but I couldnt trust him as far as that. What about your father?

RAINA. He is away at Slivnitza fighting for his country. I answer for your safety. There is my hand in pledge of it. Will that reassure you? [*She offers him her hand*]

THE MAN. [*Looking dubiously at his own hand*] Better not touch my hand, dear young lady. I must have a wash first.

[2] Bulgarian patriots rioted in protest against performances of *Arms and the Man* in their country. The play was banned in Vienna at the turn of the century because of Shaw's treatment of the Balkan question. These responses, of course, delighted Shaw.

[3] An opera by Verdi based on Victor Hugo's tragic drama *Hernani*.

RAINA. [*Touched*] That is very nice of you. I see that you are a gentleman.

THE MAN. [*Puzzled*] Eh?

RAINA. You must not think I am surprised. Bulgarians of really good standing —peᵣple in our position—wash their hands nearly every day. So you see I can appreciate your delicacy. You may take my hand. [*She offers it again*]

THE MAN. [*Kissing it with his hands behind his back*] Thanks, gracious young lady: I feel safe at last. And now would you mind breaking the news to your mother? I had better not stay here secretly longer than is necessary.

RAINA. If you will be so good as to keep perfectly still whilst I am away.

THE MAN. Certainly. [*He sits down on the ottoman*]

[RAINA *goes to the bed and wraps herself in the fur cloak. His eyes close. She goes to the door. Turning for a last look at him, she sees that he is dropping off to sleep*]

RAINA. [*At the door*] You are not going asleep, are you? [*He murmurs inarticulately: she runs to him and shakes him*] Do you hear? Wake up: you are falling asleep.

THE MAN. Eh? Falling aslee—? Oh no: not the least in the world: I was only thinking. It's all right: I'm wide awake.

RAINA. [*Severely*] Will you please stand up while I am away. [*He rises reluctantly*] All the time, mind.

THE MAN. [*Standing unsteadily*] Certainly. Certainly: you may depend on me.

[RAINA *looks doubtfully at him. He smiles weakly. She goes reluctantly, turning again at the door, and almost catching him in the act of yawning. She goes out*]

THE MAN. [*Drowsily*] Sleep, sleep, sleep, sleep, slee—[*The words trail off into a murmur. He wakes again with a shock on the point of falling*] Where am I? Thats what I want to know: where am I? Must keep awake. Nothing keeps me awake except danger: remember that: [*Intently*] danger, danger, danger, dan—[*Trailing off again: another shock*] Wheres danger? Mus' find it. [*He starts off vaguely round the room in search of it*] What am I looking for? Sleep—danger—dont know. [*He stumbles against the bed*] Ah yes: now I know. All right now. I'm to go to bed, but not to sleep. Be sure not to sleep, because of danger. Not to lie down either, only sit down. [*He sits on the bed. A blissful expression comes into his face*] Ah! [*With a happy sigh he sinks back at full length; lifts his boots into the bed with a final effort; and falls fast asleep instantly*]

[CATHERINE *comes in, followed by* RAINA]

RAINA. [*Looking at the ottoman*] He's gone! I left him here.

CATHERINE. Here! Then he must have climbed down from the—

RAINA. [*Seeing him*] Oh! [*She points*]

CATHERINE. [*Scandalized*] Well! [*She strides to the bed*, RAINA *following until she is opposite her on the other side*] He's fast asleep. The brute!

RAINA. [*Anxiously*] Sh!

CATHERINE. [*Shaking him*] Sir! [*Shaking him again, harder*] Sir!! [*Vehemently, shaking very hard*] Sir!!!

RAINA. [*Catching her arm*] Dont, mamma; the poor darling is worn out. Let him sleep.

CATHERINE. [*Letting him go, and turning amazed to* RAINA] The poor darling!
Raina!!! [*She looks sternly at her daughter*]
[*The man sleeps profoundly*]

Act II

The sixth of March, 1886. In the garden of MAJOR PETKOFF'S *house. It is a
fine spring morning: the garden looks fresh and pretty. Beyond the paling the
tops of a couple of minarets can be seen, shewing that there is a valley there,
with the little town in it. A few miles further the Balkan mountains rise and
shut in the landscape. Looking towards them from within the garden, the side
of the house is seen on the left, with a garden door reached by a little flight of
steps. On the right the stable yard, with its gateway, encroaches on the garden.
There are fruit bushes along the paling and house, covered with washing spread
out to dry. A path runs by the house, and rises by two steps at the corner, where
it turns out of sight. In the middle, a small table, with two bent wood chairs at
it, is laid for breakfast with Turkish coffee pot, cups, rolls, etc.; but the cups
have been used and the bread broken. There is a wooden garden seat against the
wall on the right.*

*LOUKA, smoking a cigaret, is standing between the table and the house, turn-
ing her back with angry disdain on a man servant who is lecturing her. He is a
middle-aged man of cool temperament and low but clear and keen intelligence,
with the complacency of the servant who values himself on his rank in servi-
tude, and the imperturbability of the accurate calculator who has no illusions.
He wears a white Bulgarian costume: jacket with embroidered border, sash, wide
knickerbockers, and decorated gaiters. His head is shaved up to the crown, giving him a high Japanese forehead. His name is* NICOLA.

NICOLA. Be warned in time, Louka: mend your manners. I know the mistress.
She is so grand that she never dreams that any servant could dare be disre-
spectful to her; but if she once suspects that you are defying her, out you go.

LOUKA. I do defy her. I will defy her. What do I care for her?

NICOLA. If you quarrel with the family, I never can marry you. It's the same
as if you quarrelled with me!

LOUKA. You take her part against me, do you?

NICOLA. [*Sedately*] I shall always be dependent on the good will of the family.
When I leave their service and start a shop in Sofia, their custom will be
half my capital: their bad word would ruin me.

LOUKA. You have no spirit. I should like to catch them saying a word against
me!

NICOLA. [*Pityingly*] I should have expected more sense from you, Louka. But
youre young: youre young!

LOUKA. Yes; and you like me the better for it, dont you? But I know some
family secrets they wouldnt care to have told, young as I am. Let them
quarrel with me if they dare!

NICOLA. [*With compassionate superiority*] Do you know what they would do if they heard you talk like that?

LOUKA. What could they do?

NICOLA. Discharge you for untruthfulness. Who would believe any stories you told after that? Who would give you another situation? Who in this house would dare be seen speaking to you ever again? How long would your father be left on his little farm? [*She impatiently throws away the end of her cigaret, and stamps on it*] Child: you dont know the power such high people have over the like of you and me when we try to rise out of our poverty against them. [*He goes close to her and lowers his voice*] Look at me, ten years in their service. Do you think I know no secrets? I know things about the mistress that she wouldnt have the master know for a thousand levas. I know things about him that she wouldnt let him hear the last of for six months if I blabbed them to her. I know things about Raina that would break off her match with Sergius if—

LOUKA. [*Turning on him quickly*] How do you know? I never told you!

NICOLA. [*Opening his eyes cunningly*] So thats your little secret, is it? I thought it might be something like that. Well, you take my advice and be respectful; and make the mistress feel that no matter what you know or dont know, she can depend on you to hold your tongue and serve the family faithfully. Thats what they like; and thats how youll make most out of them.

LOUKA. [*With searching scorn*] You have the soul of a servant, Nicola.

NICOLA. [*Complacently*] Yes: thats the secret of success in service.

[*A loud knocking with a whip handle on a wooden door is heard from the stable yard*]

MALE VOICE OUTSIDE. Hollo! Hollo there! Nicola!

LOUKA. Master! back from the war!

NICOLA. [*Quickly*] My word for it, Louka, the war's over. Off with you and get some fresh coffee. [*He runs out into the stable yard*]

LOUKA. [*As she collects the coffee pot and cups on the tray, and carries it into the house*] Youll never put the soul of a servant into me.

[MAJOR PETKOFF *comes from the stable yard, followed by* NICOLA. *He is a cheerful, excitable, insignificant, unpolished man of about 50, naturally unambitious except as to his income and his importance in local society, but just now greatly pleased with the military rank which the war has thrust on him as a man of consequence in his town. The fever of plucky patriotism which the Serbian attack roused in all the Bulgarians has pulled him through the war; but he is obviously glad to be home again*]

PETKOFF. [*Pointing to the table with his whip*] Breakfast out here, eh?

NICOLA. Yes, sir. The mistress and Miss Raina have just gone in.

PETKOFF. [*Sitting down and taking a roll*] Go in and say Ive come; and get me some fresh coffee.

NICOLA. It's coming, sir. [*He goes to the house door.* LOUKA, *with fresh coffee, a clean cup, and a brandy bottle on her tray, meets him*] Have you told the mistress?

LOUKA. Yes: she's coming.

[NICOLA *goes into the house.* LOUKA *brings the coffee to the table*]

PETKOFF. Well: the Serbs havnt run away with you, have they?

LOUKA. No, sir.

PETKOFF. Thats right. Have you brought me some cognac?

LOUKA. [*Putting the bottle on the table*] Here, sir.

PETKOFF. Thats right. [*He pours some into his coffee*]

[CATHERINE, *who, having at this early hour made only a very perfunctory toilet, wears a Bulgarian apron over a once brilliant but now half worn-out dressing gown, and a colored handkerchief tied over her thick black hair, comes from the house with Turkish slippers on her bare feet, looking astonishingly handsome and stately under all the circumstances.* LOUKA *goes into the house*]

CATHERINE. My dear Paul: what a surprise for us! [*She stoops over the back of his chair to kiss him*] Have they brought you fresh coffee?

PETKOFF. Yes: Louka's been looking after me. The war's over. The treaty was signed three days ago at Bucharest; and the decree for our army to demobilize was issued yesterday.

CATHERINE. [*Springing erect, with flashing eyes*] Paul: have you let the Austrians force you to make peace?

PETKOFF. [*Submissively*] My dear: they didnt consult me. What could *I* do? [*She sits down and turns away from him*] But of course we saw to it that the treaty was an honorable one. It declares peace—

CATHERINE. [*Outraged*] Peace!

PETKOFF. [*Appeasing her*]—but not friendly relations: remember that. They wanted to put that in; but I insisted on its being struck out. What more could I do?

CATHERINE. You could have annexed Serbia and made Prince Alexander Emperor of the Balkans. Thats what I would have done.

PETKOFF. I dont doubt it in the least, my dear. But I should have had to subdue the whole Austrian Empire first; and that would have kept me too long away from you. I missed you greatly.

CATHERINE. [*Relenting*] Ah! [*She stretches her hand affectionately across the table to squeeze his*]

PETKOFF. And how have you been, my dear?

CATHERINE. Oh, my usual sore throats: thats all.

PETKOFF. [*With conviction*] That comes from washing your neck every day. Ive often told you so.

CATHERINE. Nonsense, Paul!

PETKOFF. [*Over his coffee and cigaret*] I dont believe in going too far with these modern customs. All this washing cant be good for the health: it's not natural. There was an Englishman at Philippopolis who used to wet himself all over with cold water every morning when he got up. Disgusting! It all comes from the English: their climate makes them so dirty that they have to be perpetually washing themselves. Look at my father! he never had a bath in his life; and he lived to be ninety-eight, the healthiest man in Bulgaria. I dont mind a good wash once a week to keep up my position; but once a day is carrying the thing to a ridiculous extreme.

CATHERINE. You are a barbarian at heart still, Paul. I hope you behaved yourself before all those Russian officers.

PETKOFF. I did my best. I took care to let them know that we have a library.

CATHERINE. Ah; but you didnt tell them that we have an electric bell in it? I have had one put up.

PETKOFF. Whats an electric bell?

CATHERINE. You touch a button; something tinkles in the kitchen; and then Nicola comes up.

PETKOFF. Why not shout for him?

CATHERINE. Civilized people never shout for their servants. Ive learnt that while you were away.

PETKOFF. Well, I'll tell you something Ive learnt too. Civilized people dont hang out their washing to dry where visitors can see it; so youd better have all that [*Indicating the clothes on the bushes*] put somewhere else.

CATHERINE. Oh, thats absurd, Paul: I dont believe really refined people notice such things.

SERGIUS. [*Knocking at the stable gates*] Gate, Nicola!

PETKOFF. Theres Sergius. [*Shouting*] Hollo, Nicola!

CATHERINE. Oh, dont shout, Paul: it really isnt nice.

PETKOFF. Bosh! [*He shouts louder than before*] Nicola!

NICOLA. [*Appearing at the house door*] Yes, sir.

PETKOFF. Are you deaf? Dont you hear Major Saranoff knocking? Bring him round this way. [*He pronounces the name with the stress on the second syllable:* SARAHNOFF]

NICOLA. Yes, Major. [*He goes into the stable yard*]

PETKOFF. You must talk to him, my dear, until Raina takes him off our hands. He bores my life out about our not promoting him. Over my head, if you please.

CATHERINE. He certainly ought to be promoted when he marries Raina. Besides, the country should insist on having at least one native general.

PETKOFF. Yes; so that he could throw away whole brigades instead of regiments. It's no use, my dear: he hasnt the slightest chance of promotion until we're quite sure that the peace will be a lasting one.

NICOLA. [*At the gate, announcing*] Major Sergius Saranoff! [*He goes into the house and returns presently with a third chair, which he places at the table. He then withdraws*]

[MAJOR SERGIUS SARANOFF, *the original of the portrait in* RAINA'S *room, is a tall romantically handsome man, with the physical hardihood, the high spirit, and the susceptible imagination of an untamed mountaineer chieftain. But his remarkable personal distinction is of a characteristically civilized type. The ridges of his eyebrows, curving with an interrogative twist round the projections at the outer corners; his jealously observant eye; his nose, thin, keen, and apprehensive in spite of the pugnacious high bridge and large nostril; his assertive chin would not be out of place in a Parisian salon, shewing that the clever imaginative barbarian has an acute critical faculty which has been thrown into intense activity by the arrival of western civilization in the Balkans. The result is precisely what the advent of nineteenth century thought first produced in England: to wit, Byronism. By his brooding on the perpetual failure, not only of others, but of himself, to live up to his ideals; by his consequent cynical scorn for humanity; by his jejune credulity as to the absolute validity of his concepts and the unworthiness of the world in disregarding them; by his wincings and*] *mockeries under the sting of the petty disillusions which every hour spent among men brings to his sensitive observation, he has acquired the half tragic, half ironic air, the mysterious moodiness, the suggestion of a strange and terrible history that has left nothing but undying remorse, by which Childe Harold fascinated the grandmothers of his English contemporaries.[4] It is clear that here or nowhere is* RAINA's *ideal hero.* CATHERINE *is hardly less enthusiastic about him than her daughter, and much less reserved in shewing her enthusiasm. As he enters from the stable gate, she rises effusively to greet him.* PETKOFF *is distinctly less disposed to make a fuss about him*]

PETKOFF.   Here already, Sergius! Glad to see you.

CATHERINE.   My dear Sergius! [*She holds out both her hands*]

SERGIUS.   [*Kissing them with scrupulous gallantry*] My dear mother, if I may call you so.

PETKOFF.   [*Drily*] Mother-in-law, Sergius: mother-in-law! Sit down; and have some coffee.

SERGIUS.   Thank you: none for me. [*He gets away from the table with a certain distaste for* PETKOFF's *enjoyment of it, and posts himself with conscious dignity against the rail of the steps leading to the house*]

CATHERINE.   You look superb. The campaign has improved you, Sergius. Everybody here is mad about you. We were all wild with enthusiasm about that magnificent cavalry charge.

SERGIUS.   [*With grave irony*] Madam: it was the cradle and the grave of my military reputation.

CATHERINE.   How so?

SERGIUS.   I won the battle the wrong way when our worthy Russian generals were losing it the right way. In short, I upset their plans, and wounded their self-esteem. Two Cossack colonels had their regiments routed on the most correct principles of scientific warfare. Two major-generals got killed strictly according to military etiquette. The two colonels are now major-generals; and I am still a simple major.

CATHERINE.   You shall not remain so, Sergius. The women are on your side; and they will see that justice is done you.

SERGIUS.   It is too late. I have only waited for the peace to send in my resignation.

PETKOFF.   [*Dropping his cup in his amazement*] Your resignation!

CATHERINE.   Oh, you must withdraw it!

SERGIUS.   [*With resolute measured emphasis, folding his arms*] I never withdraw.

PETKOFF.   [*Vexed*] Now who could have supposed you were going to do such a thing?

SERGIUS.   [*With fire*] Everyone that knew me. But enough of myself and my affairs. How is Raina; and where is Raina?

RAINA.   [*Suddenly coming round the corner of the house and standing at the top of the steps in the path*] Raina is here.

[*She makes a charming picture as they turn to look at her. She wears an underdress of pale green silk, draped with an overdress of thin ecru canvas embroidered with gold. She is crowned with a dainty eastern cap of gold tinsel.*

---

[4] See Byron's romantic poem *Childe Harold's Pilgrimage* (1812).

SERGIUS *goes impulsively to meet her. Posing regally, she presents her hand: he drops chivalrously on one knee and kisses it*]

PETKOFF. [*Aside to* CATHERINE, *beaming with parental pride*] Pretty, isn't it? She always appears at the right moment.

CATHERINE. [*Impatiently*] Yes; she listens for it. It is an abominable habit.

[SERGIUS *leads* RAINA *forward with splendid gallantry. When they arrive at the table, she turns to him with a bend of the head: he bows; and thus they separate, he coming to his place and she going behind her father's chair*]

RAINA. [*Stooping and kissing her father*] Dear father! Welcome home!

PETKOFF. [*Patting her cheek*] My little pet girl. [*He kisses her. She goes to the chair left by* NICOLA *for* SERGIUS, *and sits down*]

CATHERINE. And so youre no longer a soldier, Sergius.

SERGIUS. I am no longer a soldier. Soldiering, my dear madam, is the coward's art of attacking mercilessly when you are strong, and keeping out of harm's way when you are weak. That is the whole secret of successful fighting. Get your enemy at a disadvantage; and never, on any account, fight him on equal terms.

PETKOFF. They wouldnt let us make a fair stand-up fight of it. However, I suppose soldiering has to be a trade like any other trade.

SERGIUS. Precisely. But I have no ambition to shine as a tradesman; so I have taken the advice of that bagman[5] of a captain that settled the exchange of prisoners with us at Pirot, and given it up.

PETKOFF. What! that Swiss fellow? Sergius: I've often thought of that exchange since. He over-reached us about those horses.

SERGIUS. Of course he over-reached us. His father was a hotel and livery stable keeper; and he owed his first step to his knowledge of horse-dealing. [*With mock enthusiasm*] Ah, he was a soldier: every inch a soldier! If only I had bought the horses for my regiment instead of foolishily leading it into danger, I should have been a field-marshal now!

CATHERINE. A Swiss? What was he doing in the Serbian army?

PETKOFF. A volunteer, of course: keen on picking up his profession. [*Chuckling*] We shouldnt have been able to begin fighting if these foreigners hadnt shewn us how to do it: we knew nothing about it; and neither did the Serbs. Egad, there'd have been no war without them!

RAINA. Are there many Swiss officers in the Serbian Army?

PETKOFF. No. All Austrians, just as our officers were all Russians. This was the only Swiss I came across. I'll never trust a Swiss again. He humbugged us into giving him fifty ablebodied men for two hundred worn out chargers. They werent even eatable!

SERGIUS. We were two children in the hands of that consummate soldier, Major: simply two innocent little children.

RAINA. What was he like?

CATHERINE. Oh, Raina, what a silly question!

SERGIUS. He was like a commercial traveller in uniform. Bourgeois to his boots!

PETKOFF. [*Grinning*] Sergius: tell Catherine that queer story his friend told us about how he escaped after Slivnitza. You remember. About his being hid by two women.

---

[5] A commercial traveller.

SERGIUS. [*With bitter irony*] Oh yes: quite a romance! He was serving in the very battery I so unprofessionally charged. Being a thorough soldier, he ran away like the rest of them, with our cavalry at his heels. To escape their sabres he climbed a waterpipe and made his way into the bedroom of a young Bulgarian lady. The young lady was enchanted by his persuasive commercial traveller's manners. She very modestly entertained him for an hour or so, and then called in her mother lest her conduct should appear unmaidenly. The old lady was equally fascinated; and the fugitive was sent on his way in the morning, disguised in an old coat belonging to the master of the house, who was away at the war.

RAINA. [*Rising with marked stateliness*] Your life in the camp has made you coarse, Sergius. I did not think you would have repeated such a story before me. [*She turns away coldly*]

CATHERINE. [*Also rising*] She is right, Sergius. If such women exist, we should be spared the knowledge of them.

PETKOFF. Pooh! nonsense! what does it matter?

SERGIUS. [*Ashamed*] No, Petkoff: I was wrong. [*To* RAINA, *with earnest humility*] I beg your pardon. I have behaved abominably. Forgive me, Raina. [*She bows reservedly*] And you too, madam. [CATHERINE *bows graciously and sits down. He proceeds solemnly, again addressing* RAINA] The glimpses I have had of the seamy side of life during the last few months have made me cynical; but I should not have brought my cynicism here: least of all into your presence, Raina. I—[*Here, turning to the others, he is evidently going to begin a long speech when the* MAJOR *interrupts him*]

PETKOFF. Stuff and nonsense, Sergius! Thats quite enough fuss about nothing: a soldier's daughter should be able to stand up without flinching to a little strong conversation. [*He rises*] Come: it's time for us to get to business. We have to make up our minds how those three regiments are to get back to Philippopolis: theres no forage for them on the Sofia route. [*He goes towards the house*] Come along. [SERGIUS *is about to follow him when* CATHERINE *rises and intervenes*]

CATHERINE. Oh, Paul, cant you spare Sergius for a few moments? Raina has hardly seen him yet. Perhaps I can help you to settle about the regiments.

SERGIUS. [*Protesting*] My dear madam, impossible: you—

CATHERINE. [*Stopping him playfully*] You stay here, my dear Sergius: theres no hurry. I have a word or two to say to Paul. [SERGIUS *instantly bows and steps back*] Now, dear [*Taking* PETKOFF'S *arm*]: come and see the electric bell.

PETKOFF. Oh, very well, very well.

[*They go into the house together affectionately.* SERGIUS, *left alone with* RAINA, *looks anxiously at her, fearing that she is still offended. She smiles, and stretches out her arms to him*]

SERGIUS. [*Hastening to her*] Am I forgiven?

RAINA. [*Placing her hands on his shoulders as she looks up at him with admiration and worship*] My hero! My king!

SERGIUS. My queen! [*He kisses her on the forehead*]

RAINA. How I have envied you, Sergius! You have been out in the world, on the field of battle, able to prove yourself there worthy of any woman in the

world; whilst I have had to sit at home inactive—dreaming—useless—doing
nothing that could give me the right to call myself worthy of any man.

SERGIUS. Dearest: all my deeds have been yours. You inspired me. I have gone
through the war like a knight in a tournament with his lady looking down
at him!

RAINA. And you have never been absent from my thoughts for a moment.
[*Very solemnly*] Sergius: I think we two have found the higher love. When
I think of you, I feel that I could never do a base deed, or think an ignoble
thought.

SERGIUS. My lady and my saint! [*He clasps her reverently*]

RAINA. [*Returning his embrace*] My lord and my—

SERGIUS. Sh—sh! Let me be the worshipper, dear. You little know how unworthy even the best man is of a girl's pure passion!

RAINA. I trust you. I love you. You will never disappoint me, Sergius. [LOUKA
is heard singing within the house. They quickly release each other] I cant
pretend to talk indifferently before her: my heart is too full. [LOUKA *comes
from the house with her tray. She goes to the table, and begins to clear it,
with her back turned to them*] I will get my hat; and then we can go out
until lunch time. Wouldnt you like that?

SERGIUS. Be quick. If you are away five minutes, it will seem five hours. [RAINA
*runs to the top of the steps, and turns there to exchange looks with him and
wave him a kiss with both hands. He looks after her with emotion for a moment; then turns slowly away, his face radiant with the loftiest exaltation.
The movement shifts his field of vision, into the corner of which there now
comes the tail of* LOUKA's *double apron. His attention is arrested at once. He
takes a stealthy look at her, and begins to twirl his moustache mischievously,
with his left hand akimbo on his hip. Finally, striking the ground with his
heels in something of a cavalry swagger, he strolls over to the other side of
the table, opposite her, and says*] Louka: do you know what the higher love
is?

LOUKA. [*Astonished*] No, sir.

SERGIUS. Very fatiguing thing to keep up for any length of time, Louka. One
feels the need of some relief after it.

LOUKA. [*Innocently*] Perhaps you would like some coffee, sir? [*She stretches
her hand across the table for the coffee pot*]

SERGIUS. [*Taking her hand*] Thank you, Louka.

LOUKA. [*Pretending to pull*] Oh, sir, you know I didnt mean that. I'm surprised at you!

SERGIUS. [*Coming clear of the table and drawing her with him*] I am surprised
at myself, Louka. What would Sergius, the hero of Slivnitza, say if he saw
me now? What would Sergius, the apostle of the higher love, say if he saw
me now? What would the half dozen Sergiuses who keep popping in and
out of this handsome figure of mine say if they caught us here? [*Letting go
her hand and slipping his arm dexterously round her waist*] Do you consider
my figure handsome, Louka?

LOUKA. Let me go, sir. I shall be disgraced. [*She struggles: he holds her inex-
orably*] Oh, will you let go?

SERGIUS. [*Looking straight into her eyes*] No.

LOUKA.   Then stand back where we cant be seen. Have you no common sense?

SERGIUS.   Ah! thats reasonable. [*He takes her into the stable yard gateway, where they are hidden from the house*]

LOUKA.   [*Plaintively*] I may have been seen from the windows: Miss Raina is sure to be spying about after you.

SERGIUS.   [*Stung: letting her go*] Take care, Louka. I may be worthless enough to betray the higher love; but do not you insult it.

LOUKA.   [*Demurely*] Not for the world, sir, I'm sure. May I go on with my work, please, now?

SERGIUS.   [*Again putting his arm round her*] You are a provoking little witch, Louka. If you were in love with me, would you spy out of windows on me?

LOUKA.   Well, you see, sir, since you say you are half a dozen different gentlemen all at once, I should have a great deal to look after.

SERGIUS.   [*Charmed*] Witty as well as pretty. [*He tries to kiss her*]

LOUKA.   [*Avoiding him*] No: I dont want your kisses. Gentlefolk are all alike: you making love to me behind Miss Raina's back; and she doing the same behind yours.

SERGIUS.   [*Recoiling a step*] Louka!

LOUKA.   It shews how little you really care.

SERGIUS.   [*Dropping his familiarity, and speaking with freezing politeness*] If our conversation is to continue, Louka, you will please remember that a gentleman does not discuss the conduct of the lady he is engaged to with her maid.

LOUKA.   It's so hard to know what a gentleman considers right. I thought from your trying to kiss me that you had given up being so particular.

SERGIUS.   [*Turning from her and striking his forehead as he comes back into the garden from the gateway*] Devil! devil!

LOUKA.   Ha! ha! I expect one of the six of you is very like me, sir; though I am only Miss Raina's maid. [*She goes back to her work at the table, taking no further notice of him*]

SERGIUS.   [*Speaking to himself*] Which of the six is the real man? thats the question that torments me. One of them is a hero, another a buffoon, another a humbug, another perhaps a bit of a blackguard. [*He pauses, and looks furtively at* LOUKA *as he adds, with deep bitterness*] And one, at least, is a coward: jealous, like all cowards. [*He goes to the table*] Louka.

LOUKA.   Yes?

SERGIUS.   Who is my rival?

LOUKA.   You shall never get that out of me, for love or money.

SERGIUS.   Why?

LOUKA.   Never mind why. Besides, you would tell that I told you; and I should lose my place.

SERGIUS.   [*Holding out his right hand in affirmation*] No! on the honor of a— [*He checks himself; and his hand drops, nerveless, as he concludes sardonically*]—of a man capable of behaving as I have been behaving for the last five minutes. Who is he?

LOUKA.   I dont know. I never saw him. I only heard his voice through the door of her room.

SERGIUS.   Damnation! How dare you?

LOUKA. [*Retreating*] Oh, I mean no harm: youve no ·right to take up my words like that. The mistress knows all about it. And I tell you that if that gentleman ever comes here again, Miss Raina will marry him, whether he likes it or not. I know the difference between the sort of manner you and she put on before one another and the real manner.

[SERGIUS *shivers as if she had stabbed him. Then, setting his face like iron, he strides grimly to her, and grips her above the elbows with both hands*]

SERGIUS. Now listen you to me.

LOUKA. [*Wincing*] Not so tight: youre hurting me.

SERGIUS. That doesnt matter. You have stained my honor by making me a party to your eavesdropping. And you have betrayed your mistress.

LOUKA. [*Writhing*] Please—

SERGIUS. That shews that you are an abominable little clod of common clay, with the soul of a servant. [*He lets her go as if she were an unclean thing, and turns away, dusting his hands of her, to the bench by the wall, where he sits down with averted head, meditating gloomily*]

LOUKA. [*Whimpering angrily with her hands up her sleeves, feeling her bruised arms*] You know how to hurt with your tongue as well as with your hands. But I dont care, now Ive found out that whatever clay I'm made of, youre made of the same. As for her, she's a liar; and her fine airs are a cheat; and I'm worth six of her. [*She shakes the pain off hardily; tosses her head; and sets to work to put the things on the tray*]

[*He looks doubtfully at her. She finishes packing the tray, and laps the cloth over the edges, so as to carry all out together. As she stoops to lift it, he rises*]

SERGIUS. Louka! [*She stops and looks defiantly at him*] A gentleman has no right to hurt a woman under any circumstances. [*With profound humility, uncovering his head*] I beg your pardon.

LOUKA. That sort of apology may satisfy a lady. Of what use is it to a servant?

SERGIUS. [*Rudely crossed in his chivalry, throws it off with a bitter laugh, and says slightingly*] Oh! you wish to be paid for the hurt! [*He puts on his shako, and takes some money from his pocket*]

LOUKA. [*Her eyes filling with tears in spite of herself*] No: I want my hurt made well.

SERGIUS. [*Sobered by her tone*] How?

[*She rolls up her left sleeve; clasps her arm with the thumb and fingers of her right hand; and looks down at the bruise. Then she raises her head and looks straight at him. Finally, with a superb gesture, she presents her arm to be kissed. Amazed, he looks at her; at the arm; at her again; hesitates; and then, with shuddering intensity, exclaims* Never! *and gets away as far as possible from her*]

[*Her arm drops. Without a word, and with unaffected dignity, she takes her tray, and is approaching the house when* RAINA *returns, wearing a hat and jacket in the height of the Vienna fashion of the previous year, 1885.* LOUKA *makes way proudly for her, and then goes into the house*]

RAINA. I'm ready. Whats the matter? [*Gaily*] Have you been flirting with Louka?

SERGIUS. [*Hastily*] No, no. How can you think such a thing?

RAINA. [*Ashamed of herself*] Forgive me, dear: it was only a jest. I am so happy today.

[*He goes quickly to her, and kisses her hand remorsefully.* CATHERINE *comes out and calls to them from the top of the steps*]

CATHERINE. [*Coming down to them*] I am sorry to disturb you, children; but Paul is distracted over those three regiments. He doesnt know how to send them to Philippopolis; and he objects to every suggestion of mine. You must go and help him, Sergius. He is in the library.

RAINA. [*Disappointed*] But we are just going out for a walk.

SERGIUS. I shall not be long. Wait for me just five minutes. [*He runs up the steps to the door*]

RAINA. [*Following him to the foot of the steps and looking up at him with timid coquetry*] I shall go round and wait in full view of the library windows. Be sure you draw father's attention to me. If you are a moment longer than five minutes, I shall go in and fetch you, regiments or no regiments.

SERGIUS. [*Laughing*] Very well. [*He goes in*]

[RAINA *watches him until he is out of her sight. Then, with a perceptible relaxation of manner, she begins to pace up and down the garden in a brown study*]

CATHERINE. Imagine their meeting that Swiss and hearing the whole story! The very first thing your father asked for was the old coat we sent him off in. A nice mess you have got us into!

RAINA. [*Gazing thoughtfully at the gravel as she walks*] The little beast!

CATHERINE. Little beast! What little beast?

RAINA. To go and tell! Oh, if I had him here, I'd cram him with chocolate creams til he couldnt ever speak again!

CATHERINE. Dont talk such stuff. Tell me the truth, Raina. How long was he in your room before you came to me?

RAINA. [*Whisking round and recommencing her march in the opposite direction*] Oh, I forget.

CATHERINE. You cannot forget! Did he really climb up after the soldiers were gone; or was he there when that officer searched the room?

RAINA. No. Yes: I think he must have been there then.

CATHERINE. You think! Oh, Raina! Raina! Will anything ever make you straightforward? If Sergius finds out, it will be all over between you.

RAINA. [*With cool impertinence*] Oh, I know Sergius is your pet. I sometimes wish you could marry him instead of me. You would just suit him. You would pet him, and spoil him, and mother him to perfection.

CATHERINE. [*Opening her eyes very widely indeed*] Well, upon my word!

RAINA. [*Capriciously: half to herself*] I always feel a longing to do or say something dreadful to him—to shock his propriety—to scandalize the five senses out of him. [*To* CATHERINE, *perversely*] I dont care whether he finds out about the chocolate cream soldier or not. I half hope he may. [*She again turns and strolls flippantly away up the path to the corner of the house*]

CATHERINE. And what should I be able to say to your father, pray?

RAINA. [*Over her shoulder, from the top of the two steps*] Oh, poor father! As if he could help himself! [*She turns the corner and passes out of sight*]

CATHERINE. [*Looking after her, her fingers itching*] Oh, if you were only ten years younger! [LOUKA *comes from the house with a salver, which she carries hanging down by her side*] Well?

LOUKA. Theres a gentleman just called, madam. A Serbian officer.

CATHERINE. [*Flaming*] A Serb! And how dare he—[*Checking herself bitterly*] Oh, I forgot. We are at peace now. I suppose we shall have them calling every day to pay their compliments. Well: if he is an officer why dont you tell your master? He is in the library with Major Saranoff. Why do you come to me?

LOUKA. But he asks for you, madam. And I dont think he knows who you are: he said the lady of the house. He gave me this little ticket for you. [*She takes a card out of her bosom; puts it on the salver; and offers it to* CATHERINE]

CATHERINE. [*Reading*] "Captain Bluntschli"? Thats a German name.

LOUKA. Swiss, madam, I think.

CATHERINE. [*With a bound that makes* LOUKA *jump back*] Swiss! What is he like?

LOUKA. [*Timidly*] He has a big carpet bag, madam.

CATHERINE. Oh Heavens! he's come to return the coat. Send him away: say we're not at home: ask him to leave his address and I'll write to him. Oh stop: that will never do. Wait! [*She throws herself into a chair to think it out.* LOUKA *waits*] The master and Major Saranoff are busy in the library, arnt they?

LOUKA. Yes, madam.

CATHERINE. [*Decisively*] Bring the gentleman out here at once. [*Peremptorily*] And be very polite to him. Dont delay. Here [*Impatiently snatching the salver from her*]: leave that here; and go straight back to him.

LOUKA. Yes, madam. [*Going*]

CATHERINE. Louka!

LOUKA. [*Stopping*] Yes, madam.

CATHERINE. Is the library door shut?

LOUKA. I think so, madam.

CATHERINE. If not, shut it as you pass through.

LOUKA. Yes, madam. [*Going*]

CATHERINE. Stop. [LOUKA *stops*] He will have to go that way. [*Indicating the gate of the stable yard*] Tell Nicola to bring his bag here after him. Dont forget.

LOUKA. [*Surprised*] His bag?

CATHERINE. Yes: here: as soon as possible. [*Vehemently*] Be quick! [LOUKA *runs into the house.* CATHERINE *snatches her apron off and throws it behind a bush. She then takes up the salver and uses it as a mirror, with the result that the handkerchief tied round her head follows the apron. A touch to her hair and a shake to her dressing gown make her presentable*] Oh, how? how? how can a man be such a fool! Such a moment to select! [LOUKA *appears at the door of the house, announcing* CAPTAIN BLUNTSCHLI. *She stands aside at the top of the steps to let him pass before she goes in again. He is the man of the midnight adventure in* RAINA'S *room, clean, well brushed, smartly uniformed, and out of trouble, but still unmistakably the same man. The moment* LOUKA'S *back is turned,* CATHERINE *swoops on him with impetuous, urgent, coaxing appeal*] Captain Bluntschli: I am very glad to see you; but you must leave this house at once. [*He raises his eyebrows*] My husband has just returned with my future son-in-law; and they know nothing. If they did, the consequences would be terrible. You are a foreigner: you do not feel our national animosities as we do. We still hate the Serbs: the effect of the peace on my husband has been to make him feel like a lion baulked of his prey. If he discovers our secret, he will never forgive me; and my daughter's life will hardly be safe. Will you, like the chivalrous gentleman and soldier you are, leave at once before he finds you here?

BLUNTSCHLI. [*Disappointed, but philosophical*] At once, gracious lady. I only came to thank you and return the coat you lent me. If you will allow me to take it out of my bag and leave it with your servant as I pass out, I need detain you no further. [*He turns to go into the house*]

CATHERINE. [*Catching him by the sleeve*] Oh, you must not think of going back that way. [*Coaxing him across to the stable gates*] This is the shortest way out. Many thanks. So glad to have been of service to you. Good-bye.

BLUNTSCHLI. But my bag?

CATHERINE. It shall be sent on. You will leave me your address.

BLUNTSCHLI. True. Allow me. [*He takes out his cardcase, and stops to write his address, keeping* CATHERINE *in an agony of impatience. As he hands her the card,* PETKOFF, *hatless, rushes from the house in a fluster of hospitality, followed by* SERGIUS]

PETKOFF. [*As he hurries down the steps*] My dear Captain Bluntschli—

CATHERINE. Oh Heavens! [*She sinks on the seat against the wall*]

PETKOFF. [*Too preoccupied to notice her as he shakes* BLUNTSCHLI'S *hand heartily*] Those stupid people of mine thought I was out here, instead of in the—haw!—library [*He cannot mention the library without betraying how proud he is of it*] I saw you through the window. I was wondering why you didnt come in. Saranoff is with me: you remember him, dont you?

SERGIUS. [*Saluting humorously, and then offering his hand with great charm of manner*] Welcome, our friend the enemy!

PETKOFF. No longer the enemy, happily. [*Rather anxiously*] I hope youve called as a friend, and not about horses or prisoners.

CATHERINE. Oh, quite as a friend, Paul. I was just asking Captain Bluntschli to stay to lunch; but he declares he must go at once.

SERGIUS. [*Sardonically*] Impossible, Bluntschli. We want you here badly. We have to send on three cavalry regiments to Philippopolis; and we dont in the least know how to do it.

BLUNTSCHLI. [*Suddenly attentive and businesslike*] Philippopolis? The forage is the trouble, I suppose.

PETKOFF. [*Eagerly*] Yes: thats it. [*To* SERGIUS] He sees the whole thing at once.

BLUNTSCHLI. I think I can shew you how to manage that.

SERGIUS. Invaluable man! Come along! [*Towering over* BLUNTSCHLI, *he puts his hand on his shoulder and takes him to the steps,* PETKOFF *following*]

[RAINA *comes from the house as* BLUNTCHLI *puts his foot on the first step*]

RAINA. Oh! The chocolate cream soldier!

[BLUNTSCHLI *stands rigid.* SERGIUS, *amazed, looks at* RAINA, *then at* PETKOFF, *who looks back at him and then at his wife*]

CATHERINE. [*With commanding presence of mind*] My dear Raina, dont you see that we have a guest here? Captain Bluntschli: one of our new Serbian friends.

[RAINA *bows:* BLUNTSCHLI *bows*]

RAINA. How silly of me! [*She comes down into the centre of the group, between* BLUNTSCHLI *and* PETKOFF] I made a beautiful ornament this morning for the ice pudding; and that stupid Nicola has just put down a pile of plates on it and spoilt it. [*To* BLUNTSCHLI, *winningly*] I hope you didnt think that you were the chocolate cream soldier, Captain Bluntschli.

BLUNTSCHLI. [*Laughing*] I assure you I did. [*Stealing a whimsical glance at her*] Your explanation was a relief.

PETKOFF. [*Suspiciously, to* RAINA] And since when, pray, have you taken to cooking?

CATHERINE. Oh, whilst you were away. It is her latest fancy.

PETKOFF. [*Testily*] And has Nicola taken to drinking? He used to be careful enough. First he shews Captain Bluntschli out here when he knew quite well I was in the library; and then he goes downstairs and breaks Raina's chocolate soldier. He must—[NICOLA *appears at the top of the steps with the bag. He descends; places it respectfully before* BLUNTSCHLI; *and waits for further orders. General amazement.* NICOLA, *unconscious of the effect he is producing, looks perfectly satisfied with himself. When* PETKOFF *recovers his power of speech, he breaks out at him with*] Are you mad, Nicola?

NICOLA. [*Taken aback*] Sir?

PETKOFF. What have you brought that for?

NICOLA. My lady's orders, major. Louka told me that—

CATHERINE. [*Interrupting him*] My orders! Why should I order you to bring Captain Bluntschli's luggage out here? What are you thinking of, Nicola?

NICOLA. [*After a moment's bewilderment, picking up the bag as he addresses* BLUNTSCHLI *with the very perfection of servile discretion*] I beg your pardon, captain, I am sure. [*To* CATHERINE] My fault, madam: I hope youll overlook it. [*He bows, and is going to the steps with the bag, when* PETKOFF *addresses him angrily*]

PETKOFF. Youd better go and slam that bag, too, down on Miss Raina's ice pudding! [*This is too much for* NICOLA. *The bag drops from his hand almost on his master's toes, eliciting a roar of*] Begone, you butter-fingered donkey.

NICOLA. [*Snatching up the bag, and escaping into the house*] Yes, Major.

CATHERINE. Oh, never mind. Paul: dont be angry.

PETKOFF. [*Blustering*] Scoundrel! He's got out of hand while I was away. I'll teach him. Infernal blackguard! The sack next Saturday! I'll clear out the whole establishment—

[*He is stifled by the caresses of his wife and daughter, who hang round his neck, petting him*]

CATHERINE. ⎱ [*Together*] ⎰ Now, now, now, it mustnt be angry. He meant
RAINA. ⎰   ⎱ Wow, wow, wow: not on your first day at home.

⎰ no harm. Be good to please me, dear. Sh-sh-sh-sh!
⎱ I'll make another ice pudding. Tch-ch-ch!

PETKOFF. [*Yielding*] Oh well, never mind. Come, Bluntschli: lets have no more nonsense about going away. You know very well youre not going back to Switzerland yet. Until you do go back youll stay with us.

RAINA. Oh, do, Captain Bluntschli.

PETKOFF. [*To* CATHERINE] Now, Catherine: it's of you he's afraid. Press him: and he'll stay.

CATHERINE. Of course I shall be only too delighted if [*Appealingly*] Captain Bluntschli really wishes to stay. He knows my wishes.

BLUNTSCHLI. [*In his driest military manner*] I am at madam's orders.

SERGIUS. [*Cordially*] That settles it!

PETKOFF. [*Heartily*] Of course!

RAINA. You see you must stay.

BLUNTSCHLI. [*Smiling*] Well, if I must, I must.

[*Gesture of despair from* CATHERINE]

Act III

In the library after lunch. It is not much of a library. Its literary equipment consists of a single fixed shelf stocked with old paper covered novels, broken backed, coffee stained, torn and thumbed; and a couple of little hanging shelves with a few gift books on them: the rest of the wall space being occupied by trophies of war and the chase. But it is a most comfortable sitting room. A row of three large windows shews a mountain panorama, just now seen in one of its friendliest aspects in the mellowing afternoon light. In the corner next the right hand window a square earthenware stove, a perfect tower of glistening pottery, rises nearly to the ceiling and guarantees plenty of warmth. The ottoman is like that in RAINA's *room, and similarly placed; and the window seats are luxurious with decorated cushions. There is one object, however, hopelessly out of keeping with its surroundings. This is a small kitchen table, much the worse for wear, fitted as a writing table with an old canister full of pens, an eggcup filled with ink, and a deplorable scrap of heavily used pink blotting paper.*

At the side of this table, which stands to the left of anyone facing the window, BLUTSCHLI *is hard at work with a couple of maps before him, writing orders. At the head of it sits* SERGIUS, *who is supposed to be also at work, but is actually gnawing the feather of a pen, and contemplating* BLUNTSCHLI's *quick, sure, businesslike progress with a mixture of envious irritation at his own incapacity and awestruck wonder at an ability which seems to him almost miraculous, though its prosaic character forbids him to esteem it. The* MAJOR *is comfortably established on the ottoman, with a newspaper in his hand and the tube of his hookah within easy reach.* CATHERINE *sits at the stove, with her back to them, embroidering.* RAINA, *reclining on the divan, is gazing in a daydream out at the Balkan landscape, with a neglected novel in her lap.*

The door is on the same side as the stove, farther from the window. The button of the electric bell is at the opposite side, behind BLUNTSCHLI.

PETKOFF. [*Looking up from his paper to watch how they are getting on at the table*] Are you sure I cant help in any way, Bluntschli?

BLUNTSCHLI. [*Without interrupting his writing or looking up*] Quite sure, thank you. Saranoff and I will manage it.

SERGIUS. [*Grimly*] Yes: we'll manage it. He finds out what to do; draws up the orders; and I sign em. Division of labor! [BLUNTSCHLI *passes him a paper*]. Another one? Thank you. [*He plants the paper squarely before him; sets his chair carefully parallel to it; and signs with his cheek on his elbow and his protruded tongue following the movements of his pen*] This hand is more accustomed to the sword than to the pen.

PETKOFF. It's very good of you, Bluntschli: it is indeed, to let yourself be put upon in this way. Now are you quite sure I can do nothing?

CATHERINE. [*In a low warning tone*] You can stop interrupting, Paul.

PETKOFF. [*Starting and looking round at her*] Eh? Oh! Quite right. [*He takes his newspaper up again, but presently lets it drop*] Ah, you havnt been campaigning, Catherine: you dont know how pleasant it is for us to sit here, after a good lunch, with nothing to do but enjoy ourselves. Theres only one thing I want to make me thoroughly comfortable.

CATHERINE. What is that?

PETKOFF. My old coat. I'm not at home in this one: I feel as if I were on parade.

CATHERINE. My dear Paul, how absurd you are about that old coat! It must be hanging in the blue closet where you left it.

PETKOFF. My dear Catherine, I tell you Ive looked there. Am I to believe my own eyes or not? [CATHERINE *rises and crosses the room to press the button of the electric bell*] What are you shewing off that bell for? [*She looks at him majestically, and silently resumes her chair and her needlework*] My dear: if you think the obstinacy of your sex can make a coat out of two old dressing gowns of Raina's, your waterproof, and my mackintosh, youre mistaken. Thats exactly what the blue closet contains at present.

[NICOLA *presents himself*]

CATHERINE. Nicola: go to the blue closet and bring your master's old coat here: the braided one he wears in the house.

NICOLA. Yes, madame.

[*He goes out*]

PETKOFF. Catherine.

CATHERINE. Yes, Paul.

PETKOFF. I bet you any piece of jewellery you like to order from Sofia against a week's housekeeping money that the coat isnt there.

CATHERINE. Done, Paul!

PETKOFF. [*Excited by the prospect of a gamble*] Come: heres an opportunity for some sport. Wholl bet on it? Bluntschli: I'll give you six to one.

BLUNTSCHLI. [*Imperturbably*] It would be robbing you, Major. Madame is sure to be right. [*Without looking up, he passes another batch of papers to* SERGIUS]

SERGIUS. [*Also excited*] Bravo, Switzerland! Major: I bet my best charger against an Arab mare for Raina that Nicola finds the coat in the blue closet.

PETKOFF. [*Eagerly*] Your best char—

CATHERINE. [*Hastily interrupting him*] Dont be foolish, Paul. An Arabian mare will cost you 50,000 levas.

RAINA. [*Suddenly coming out of her picturesque revery*] Really, mother, if you are going to take the jewellery, I don't see why you should grudge me my Arab.

[NICOLA *comes back with the coat, and brings it to* PETKOFF, *who can hardly believe his eyes*]

CATHERINE.   Where was it, Nicola?

NICOLA.   Hanging in the blue closet, madame.

PETKOFF.   Well, I am d—

CATHERINE.   [*Stopping him*] Paul!

PETKOFF.   I could have sworn it wasnt there. Age is beginning to tell on me. I'm getting hallucinations. [*To* NICOLA] Here: help me to change. Excuse me, Bluntschli. [*He begins changing coats,* NICOLA *acting as valet*] Remember: I didnt take that bet of yours, Sergius. Youd better give Raina that Arab steed yourself, since youve roused her expectations. Eh, Raina? [*He looks round at her; but she is again rapt in the landscape. With a little gush of parental affection and pride, he points her out to them, and says*] She's dreaming, as usual.

SERGIUS.   Assuredly she shall not be the loser.

PETKOFF.   So much the better for her. *I* shant come off so cheaply, I expect. [*The change is now complete.* NICOLA *goes out with the discarded coat*] Ah, now I feel at home at last.

[*He sits down and takes his newspaper with a grunt of relief*]

BLUNTSCHLI.   [*To* SERGIUS, *handing a paper*] Thats the last order.

PETKOFF.   [*Jumping up*] What! Finished?

BLUNTSCHLI.   Finished.

PETKOFF.   [*With childlike envy*] Havnt you anything for me to sign?

BLUNTSCHLI.   Not necessary. His signature will do.

PETKOFF.   [*Inflating his chest and thumping it*] Ah well, I think weve done a thundering good day's work. Can I do anything more?

BLUNTSCHLI.   You had better both see the fellows that are to take these. [SERGIUS *rises*] Pack them off at once; and shew them that Ive marked on the orders the time they should hand them in by. Tell them that if they stop to drink or tell stories—if theyre five minutes late, theyll have the skin taken off their backs.

SERGIUS.   [*Stiffening indignantly*] I'll say so. [*He strides to the door*] And if one of them is man enough to spit in my face for insulting him, I'll buy his discharge and give him a pension. [*He goes out*]

BLUNTSCHLI.   [*Confidentially*] Just see that he talks to them properly, Major, will you?

PETKOFF.   [*Officiously*] Quite right, Bluntschli, quite right. I'll see to it. [*He goes to the door importantly, but hesitates on the threshold*] By the bye, Catherine, you may as well come too. Theyll be far more frightened of you than of me.

CATHERINE.   [*Putting down her embroidery*] I daresay I had better. You would only splutter at them. [*She goes out,* PETKOFF *holding the door for her and following her*]

BLUNTSCHLI.   What an army! They make cannons out of cherry trees; and the officers send for their wives to keep discipline! [*He begins to fold and docket the papers*]

[RAINA, *who has risen from the divan, marches slowly down the room with her hands clasped behind her, and looks mischievously at him*]

RAINA.   You look ever so much nicer than when we last met. [*He looks up, surprised*] What have you done to yourself?

BLUNTSCHLI.   Washed; brushed; good night's sleep and breakfast. Thats all.

RAINA.   Did you get back safely that morning?

BLUNTSCHLI.   Quite, thanks.

RAINA.   Were they angry with you for running away from Sergius' charge?

BLUNTSCHLI.   [*Grinning*] No: they were glad; because theyd all just run away themselves.

RAINA.   [*Going to the table, and leaning over it towards him*] It must have made a lovely story for them: all that about me and my room.

BLUNTSCHLI.   Capital story. But I only told it to one of them: a particular friend.

RAINA.   On whose discretion you could absolutely rely?

BLUNTSCHLI.   Absolutely.

RAINA.   Hm! He told it all to my father and Sergius the day you exchanged the prisoners. [*She turns away and strolls carelessly across to the other side of the room*]

BLUNTSCHLI.   [*Deeply concerned, and half incredulous*] No! You dont mean that, do you?

RAINA.   [*Turning, with sudden earnestness*] I do indeed. But they dont know that it was in this house you took refuge. If Sergius knew, he would challenge you and kill you in a duel.

BLUNTSCHLI.   Bless me! then dont tell him.

RAINA.   Please be serious, Captain Bluntschli. Can you not realize what it is to me to deceive him? I want to be quite perfect with Sergius: no meanness, no smallness, no deceit. My relation to him is the one really beautiful and noble part of my life. I hope you can understand that.

BLUNTSCHLI.   [*Sceptically*] You mean that you wouldnt like him to find out that the story about the ice pudding was a—a—a—You know.

RAINA.   [*Wincing*] Ah, don't talk of it in that flippant way. I lied: I know it. But I did it to save your life. He would have killed you. That was the second time I ever uttered a falsehood. [BLUNTSCHLI *rises quickly and looks doubtfully and somewhat severely at her*] Do you remember the first time?

BLUNTSCHLI.   I! No. Was I present?

RAINA.   Yes; and I told the officer who was searching for you that you were not present.

BLUNTSCHLI.   True. I should have remembered it.

RAINA.   [*Greatly encouraged*] Ah, it is natural that you should forget it first. It cost you nothing: it cost me a lie! A lie!

[*She sits down on the ottoman, looking straight before her with her hands clasped around her knee.* BLUNTSCHLI, *quite touched, goes to the ottoman with a particularly reassuring and considerate air, and sits down beside her*]

BLUNTSCHLI.   My dear young lady, dont let this worry you. Remember: I'm a soldier. Now what are the two things that happen to a soldier so often that he comes to think nothing of them? One is hearing people tell lies [RAINA *recoils*]: the other is getting his life saved in all sorts of ways by all sorts of people.

RAINA. [*Rising in indignant protest*] And so he becomes a creature incapable of faith and of gratitude.

BLUNTSCHLI. [*Making a wry face*] Do you like gratitude? I dont. If pity is akin to love, gratitude is akin to the other thing.

RAINA. Gratitude! [*Turning on him*] If you are incapable of gratitude you are incapable of any noble sentiment. Even animals are grateful. Oh, I see now exactly what you think of me! You were not surprised to hear me lie. To you it was something I probably did every day! every hour! That is how men think of women. [*She paces the room tragically*]

BLUNTSCHLI. [*Dubiously*] Theres reason in everything. You said youd told only two lies in your whole life. Dear young lady: isnt that rather a short allowance? I'm quite a straightforward man myself; but it wouldnt last me a whole morning.

RAINA. [*Staring haughtily at him*] Do you know, sir, that you are insulting me?

BLUNTSCHLI. I cant help it. When you strike that noble attitude and speak in that thrilling voice, I admire you; but I find it impossible to believe a single word you say.

RAINA. [*Superbly*] Captain Bluntschli!

BLUNTSCHLI. [*Unmoved*] Yes?

RAINA. [*Standing over him, as if she could not believe her senses*] Do you mean what you said just now? Do you know what you said just now?

BLUNTSCHLI. I do.

RAINA. [*Gasping*] I! I!!! [*She points to herself incredulously, meaning "I, Raina Petkoff, tell lies!" He meets her gaze unflinchingly. She suddenly sits down beside him, and adds, with a complete change of manner from the heroic to a babyish familiarity*] How did you find me out?

BLUNTSCHLI. [*Promptly*] Instinct, dear young lady. Instinct, and experience of the world.

RAINA. [*Wonderingly*] Do you know, you are the first man I ever met who did not take me seriously?

BLUNTSCHLI. You mean, dont you, that I am the first man that has ever taken you quite seriously?

RAINA. Yes: I suppose I do mean that. [*Cosily, quite at her ease with him*] How strange it is to be talked to in such a way! You know, Ive always gone on like that.

BLUNTSCHLI. You mean the——?

RAINA. I mean the noble attitude and the thrilling voice. [*They laugh together*] I did it when I was a tiny child to my nurse. She believed in it. I do it before my parents. They believe in it. I do it before Sergius. He believes in it.

BLUNTSCHLI. Yes: he's a little in that line himself, isnt he?

RAINA. [*Startled*] Oh! Do you think so?

BLUNTSCHLI. You know him better than I do.

RAINA. I wonder—I wonder is he? If I thought that—! [*Discouraged*] Ah, well; what does it matter? I suppose, now youve found me out, you despise me.

BLUNTSCHLI. [*Warmly, rising*] No, my dear young lady, no, no, no a thousand times. It's part of your youth: part of your charm. I'm like all the rest of them: the nurse, your parents, Sergius: I'm your infatuated admirer.

RAINA. [*Pleased*] Really?

BLUNTSCHLI. [*Slapping his breast smartly with his hand, German fashion*] Hand aufs Herz! Really and truly.

RAINA. [*Very happy*] But what did you think of me for giving you my portrait?

BLUNTSCHLI. [*Astonished*] Your portrait! You never gave me your portrait.

RAINA. [*Quickly*] Do you mean to say you never got it?

BLUNTSCHLI. No. [*He sits down beside her, with renewed interest, and says, with some complacency*] When did you send it to me?

RAINA. [*Indignantly*] I did not send it to you. [*She turns her head away, and adds, reluctantly*] It was in the pocket of that coat.

BLUNTSCHLI. [*Pursing his lips and rounding his eyes*] Oh-o-oh! I never found it. It must be there still.

RAINA. [*Springing up*] There still! for my father to find the first time he puts his hand in his pocket! Oh, how could you be so stupid?

BLUNTSCHLI. [*Rising also*] It doesnt matter: I suppose it's only a photograph: how can he tell who it was intended for? Tell him he put it there himself.

RAINA. [*Bitterly*] Yes: that is so clever! isnt it? [*Distractedly*] Oh! what shall I do?

BLUNTSCHLI. Ah, I see. You wrote something on it. That was rash.

RAINA. [*Vexed almost to tears*] Oh, to have done such a thing for you, who care no more—except to laugh at me—oh! Are you sure nobody has touched it?

BLUNTSCHLI. Well, I cant be quite sure. You see, I couldnt carry it about with me all the time: one cant take much luggage on active service.

RAINA. What did you do with it?

BLUNTSCHLI. When I got through to Pirot I had to put it in safe keeping somehow. I thought of the railway cloak room; but thats the surest place to get looted in modern warfare. So I pawned it.

RAINA. Pawned it!!!

BLUNTSCHLI. I know it doesnt sound nice: but it was much the safest plan. I redeemed it the day before yesterday. Heaven only knows whether the pawnbroker cleared out the pockets or not.

RAINA. [*Furious: throwing the words right into his face*] You have a low shopkeeping mind. You think of things that would never come into a gentleman's head.

BLUNTSCHLI. [*Phlegmatically*] Thats the Swiss national character, dear lady. [*He returns to the table*]

RAINA. Oh, I wish I had never met you. [*She flounces away, and sits at the window fuming*]

[*LOUKA comes in with a heap of letters and telegrams on her salver, and crosses, with her bold free gait, to the table. Her left sleeve is looped up to the shoulder with a brooch, shewing her naked arm, with a broad gilt bracelet covering the bruise*]

LOUKA. [*To* BLUNTSCHLI] For you. [*She empties the salver with a fling on to the table*] The messenger is waiting. [*She is determined not to be civil to an enemy, even if she must bring him his letters*]

BLUNTSCHLI. [*To* RAINA] Will you excuse me: the last postal delivery that reached me was three weeks ago. These are the subsequent accumulations. Four telegrams: a week old. [*He opens one*] Oho! Bad news!

RAINA. [*Rising and advancing a little remorsefully*] Bad news?

BLUNTSCHLI. My father's dead. [*He looks at the telegram with his lips pursed, musing on the unexpected change in his arrangements.* LOUKA *crosses herself hastily*]

RAINA. Oh, how very sad!

BLUNTSCHLI. Yes. I shall have to start for home in an hour. He has left a lot of big hotels behind him to be looked after. [*He takes up a fat letter in a long blue envelope*] Here's a whacking letter from the family solicitor. [*He puts out the enclosures and glances over them*] Great Heavens! Seventy! Two hundred! [*In a crescendo of dismay*] Four hundred! Four thousand!! Nine thousand six hundred!!! What on earth am I to do with them all?

RAINA. [*Timidly*] Nine thousand hotels?

BLUNTSCHLI. Hotels! nonsense. If you only knew! Oh, it's too ridiculous! Excuse me: I must give my fellow orders about starting. [*He leaves the room hastily, with the documents in his hand*]

LOUKA. [*Knowing instinctively that she can annoy* RAINA *by disparaging* BLUNTSCHLI] He has not much heart, that Swiss. He has not a word of grief for his poor father.

RAINA. [*Bitterly*] Grief! A man who has been doing nothing but killing people for years! What does he care? What does any soldier care? [*She goes to the door, restraining her tears with difficulty*]

LOUKA. Major Saranoff has been fighting too; and he has plenty of heart left. [RAINA, *at the door, draws herself up haughtily and goes out*] Aha! I thought you wouldnt get much feeling out of your soldier. [*She is following* RAINA *when* NICOLA *enters with an armful of logs for the stove*]

NICOLA. [*Grinning amorously at her*] Ive been trying all the afternoon to get a minute alone with you, my girl. [*His countenance changes as he notices her arm*] Why, what fashion is that of wearing your sleeve, child?

LOUKA. [*Proudly*] My own fashion.

NICOLA. Indeed! If the mistress catches you, she'll talk to you. [*He puts the logs down, and seats himself comfortably on the ottoman*]

LOUKA. Is that any reason why you should take it on yourself to talk to me?

NICOLA. Come! dont be so contrary with me. Ive some good news for you. [*She sits down beside him. He takes out some paper money.* LOUKA, *with an eager gleam in her eyes, tries to snatch it; but he shifts it quickly to his left hand, out of her reach*] See! a twenty leva bill! Sergius gave me that, out of pure swagger. A fool and his money are soon parted. Theres ten levas more. The Swiss gave me that for backing up the mistress' and Raina's lies about him. He's no fool, he isnt. You should have heard old Catherine down-stairs as polite as you please to me, telling me not to mind the Major being a little impatient; for they knew what a good servant I was—after making a fool and a liar of me before them all! The twenty will go to our savings;

and you shall have the ten to spend if youll only talk to me so as to remind
me I'm a human being. I get tired of being a servant occasionally.

LOUKA.   Yes. sell your manhood for 30 levas, and buy me for 10! [*Rising
scornfully*] Keep your money. You were born to be a servant. I was not.
When you set up your shop you will only be everybody's servant instead of
somebody's servant. [*She goes moodily to the table and seats herself regally
in* SERGIUS' *chair*]

NICOLA.   [*Picking up his logs, and going to the stove*] Ah, wait til you see. We
shall have our evenings to ourselves; and I shall be master in my own house,
I promise you. [*He throws the logs down and kneels at the stove*]

LOUKA.   You shall never be master in mine.

NICOLA.   [*Turning, still on his knees, and squatting down rather forlornly on
his calves, daunted by her implacable disdain*] You have a great ambition
in you, Louka. Remember: if any luck comes to you, it was I that made a
woman of you.

LOUKA.   You!

NICOLA.   [*Scrambling up and going to her*] Yes, me. Who was it made you give
up wearing a couple of pounds of false black hair on your head and reddening your lips and cheeks like any other Bulgarian girl! I did. Who taught
you to trim your nails, and keep your hands clean, and be dainty about yourself, like a fine Russian lady! Me: do you hear that? me! [*She tosses her head
defiantly; and he turns away, adding more coolly*] Ive often thought that if
Raina were out of the way, and you just a little less of a fool and Sergius
just a little more of one, you might come to be one of my grandest customers, instead of only being my wife and costing me money.

LOUKA.   I believe you would rather be my servant than my husband. You would
make more out of me. Oh, I know that soul of yours.

NICOLA.   [*Going closer to her for greater emphasis*] Never you mind my soul;
but just listen to my advice. If you want to be a lady, your present be-
haviour to me wont do at all, unless when we're alone. It's too sharp and
impudent; and impudence is a sort of familiarity: it shews affection for
me. And dont you try being high and mighty with me, either. Youre like
all country girls: you think it's genteel to treat a servant the way I treat a
stableboy. Thats only your ignorance; and dont you forget it. And dont be
so ready to defy everybody. Act as if you expected to have your own way,
not as if you expected to be ordered about. The way to get on as a lady is
the same as the way to get on as a servant: youve got to know your place:
thats the secret of it. And you may depend on me to know my place if you
get promoted. Think over it, my girl. I'll stand by you: one servant should
always stand by another.

LOUKA.   [*Rising impatiently*] Oh, I must behave in my own way. You take all
the courage out of me with your cold-blooded wisdom. Go and put those
logs in the fire: thats the sort of thing you understand.

[*Before* NICOLA *can retort,* SERGIUS *comes in. He checks himself a moment
on seeing* LOUKA; *then goes to the stove*]

SERGIUS.   [*To* NICOLA] I am not in the way of your work, I hope.

NICOLA.   [*In a smooth, elderly manner*] Oh no, sir: thank you kindly. I was
only speaking to this foolish girl about her habit of running up here to the

library whenever she gets a chance, to look at the books. Thats the worst of her education, sir: it gives her habits above her station. [*To* LOUKA] Make that table tidy, Louka, for the Major.

[*He goes out sedately*]

[LOUKA, *without looking at* SERGIUS, *pretends to arrange the papers on the table. He crosses slowly to her, and studies the arrangement of her sleeve reflectively*]

SERGIUS. Let me see: is there a mark there? [*He turns up the bracelet and sees the bruise made by his grasp. She stands motionless, not looking at him: fascinated, but on her guard*] Ffff! Does it hurt?

LOUKA. Yes.

SERGIUS. Shall I cure it?

LOUKA. [*Instantly withdrawing herself proudly, but still not looking at him*] No. You cannot cure it now.

SERGIUS. [*Masterfully*] Quite sure? [*He makes a movement as if to take her in his arms*]

LOUKA. Dont trifle with me, please. An officer should not trifle with a servant.

SERGIUS. [*Indicating the bruise with a merciless stroke of his forefinger*] That was no trifle, Louka.

LOUKA. [*Flinching; then looking at him for the first time*] Are you sorry?

SERGIUS. [*With measured emphasis, folding his arms*] I am never sorry.

LOUKA. [*Wistfully*] I wish I could believe a man could be as unlike a woman as that. I wonder are you really a brave man?

SERGIUS. [*Unaffectedly, relaxing his attitude*] Yes: I am a brave man. My heart jumped like a woman's at the first shot; but in the charge I found that I was brave. Yes: that at least is real about me.

LOUKA. Did you find in the charge that the men whose fathers are poor like mine were any less brave than the men who are rich like you?

SERGIUS. [*With bitter levity*] Not a bit. They all slashed and cursed and yelled like heroes. Psha! the courage to rage and kill is cheap. I have an English bull terrier who has as much of that sort of courage as the whole Bulgarian nation, and the whole Russian nation at its back. But he lets my groom thrash him, all the same. Thats your soldier all over! No, Louka: your poor men can cut throats; but they are afraid of their officers; they put up with insults and blows; they stand by and see one another punished like children: aye, and help to do it when they are ordered. And the officers!!! Well [*With a short harsh laugh*] I am an officer. Oh, [*Fervently*] give me the man who will defy to the death any power on earth or in heaven that sets itself up against his own will and conscience: he alone is the brave man.

LOUKA. How easy it is to talk! Men never seem to me to grow up: they all have schoolboy's ideas. You dont know what true courage is.

SERGIUS. [*Ironically*] Indeed! I am willing to be instructed.

[*He sits on the ottoman, sprawling magnificently*]

LOUKA. Look at me! How much am I allowed to have my own will? I have to get your room ready for you: to sweep and dust, to fetch and carry. How could that degrade me if it did not degrade you to have it done for you? But [*With subdued passion*] if I were Empress of Russia, above everyone in the world, then!! Ah then, though according to you I could shew no courage at all, you should see, you should see.

SERGIUS. What would you do, most noble Empress?

LOUKA. I would marry the man I loved, which no other queen in Europe has the courage to do. If I loved you, though you would be as far beneath me as I am beneath you, I would dare to be the equal of my inferior. Would you dare as much if you loved me? No: if you felt the beginnings of love for me you would not let it grow. You would not dare: you would marry a rich man's daughter because you would be afraid of what other people would say of you.

SERGIUS. [*Bounding up*] You lie: it is not so, by all the stars! If I loved you, and I were the Tsar himself, I would set you on the throne by my side. You know that I love another woman, a woman as high above you as heaven is above earth. And you are jealous of her.

LOUKA. I have no reason to be. She will never marry you now. The man I told you of has come back. She will marry the Swiss.

SERGIUS. [*Recoiling*] The Swiss!

LOUKA. A man worth ten of you. Then you can come to me; and I will refuse you. You are not good enough for me. [*She turns to the door*]

SERGIUS. [*Springing after her and catching her fiercely in his arms*] I will kill the Swiss; and afterwards I will do as I please with you.

LOUKA. [*In his arms, passive and steadfast*] The Swiss will kill you, perhaps. He has beaten you in love. He may beat you in war.

SERGIUS. [*Tormentedly*] Do you think I believe that she—she! whose worst thoughts are higher than your best ones, is capable of trifling with another man behind my back?

LOUKA. Do you think she would believe the Swiss if he told her now that I am in your arms?

SERGIUS. [*Releasing her in despair*] Damnation! Oh, damnation! Mockery! mockery everywhere! everything I think is mocked by everything I do. [*He strikes himself frantically on the breast*] Coward! liar! fool! Shall I kill myself like a man, or live and pretend to laugh at myself? [*She again turns to go*] Louka! [*She stops near the door*] Remember: you belong to me.

LOUKA. [*Turning*] What does that mean? An insult?

SERGIUS. [*Commandingly*] It means that you love me, and that I have had you here in my arms, and will perhaps have you there again. Whether that is an insult I neither know nor care: take it as you please. But [*Vehemently*] I will not be a coward and a trifler. If I choose to love you, I dare marry you, in spite of all Bulgaria. If these hands ever touch you again, they shall touch my affianced bride.

LOUKA. We shall see whether you dare keep your word. And take care. I will not wait long.

SERGIUS. [*Again folding his arms and standing motionless in the middle of the room*] Yes: we shall see. And you shall wait my pleasure.

[BLUNTSCHLI, *much preoccupied, with his papers still in his hand, enters, leaving the door open for* LOUKA *to go out. He goes across to the table, glancing at her as he passes.* SERGIUS, *without altering his resolute attitude, watches him steadily.* LOUKA *goes out, leaving the door open*]

BLUNTSCHLI. [*Absently, sitting at the table as before, and putting down his papers*] Thats a remarkable looking young woman.

SERGIUS. [*Gravely, without moving*] Captain Bluntschli.

BLUNTSCHLI. Eh?

SERGIUS. You have deceived me. You are my rival. I brook no rivals. At six o'clock I shall be in the drilling-ground on the Klissoura road, alone, on horseback, with my sabre. Do you understand?

BLUNTSCHLI. [*Staring, but sitting quite at his ease*] Oh, thank you: thats a cavalry man's proposal. I'm in the artillery; and I have the choice of weapons. If I go, I shall take a machine gun. And there shall be no mistake about the cartridges this time.

SERGIUS. [*Flushing, but with deadly coldness*] Take care, sir. It is not our custom in Bulgaria to allow invitations of that kind to be trifled with.

BLUNTSCHLI. [*Warmly*] Pooh! dont talk to me about Bulgaria. You dont know what fighting is. But have it your own way. Bring your sabre along. I'll meet you.

SERGIUS. [*Fiercely delighted to find his opponent a man of spirit*] Well said, Switzer. Shall I lend you my best horse?

BLUNTSCHLI. No: damn your horse! thank you all the same, my dear fellow. [RAINA *comes in, and hears the next sentence*] I shall fight you on foot. Horseback's too dangerous; I dont want to kill you if I can help it.

RAINA. [*Hurrying forward anxiously*] I have heard what Captain Bluntschli said, Sergius. You are going to fight. Why? [SERGIUS *turns away in silence, and goes to the stove, where he stands watching her as she continues, to* BLUNTSCHLI] What about?

BLUNTSCHLI. I dont know: he hasnt told me. Better not interfere, dear young lady. No harm will be done: Ive often acted as sword instructor. He wont be able to touch me; and I'll not hurt him. It will save explanations. In the morning I shall be off home; and youll never see me or hear of me again. You and he will then make it up and live happily ever after.

RAINA. [*Turning away deeply hurt, almost with a sob in her voice*] I never said I wanted to see you again.

SERGIUS. [*Striding forward*] Ha! That is a confession.

RAINA. [*Haughtily*] What do you mean?

SERGIUS. You love that man!

RAINA. [*Scandalized*] Sergius!

SERGIUS. You allow him to make love to you behind my back, just as you treat me as your affianced husband behind his. Bluntschli: you knew our relations; and you deceived me. It is for that that I call you to account, not for having received favors *I* never enjoyed.

BLUNTSCHLI. [*Jumping up indignantly*] Stuff! Rubbish! I have received no favors. Why, the young lady doesnt even know whether I'm married or not.

RAINA. [*Forgetting herself*] Oh! [*Collapsing on the ottoman*] Are you?

SERGIUS. You see the young lady's concern, Captain Bluntschli. Denial is useless. You have enjoyed the privilege of being received in her own room, late at night—

BLUNTSCHLI. [*Interrupting him pepperily*] Yes, you blockhead! she received me with a pistol at her head. Your cavalry were at my heels. I'd have blown out her brains if she'd uttered a cry.

SERGIUS. [*Taken aback*] Bluntschli! Raina: is this true?

RAINA. [*Rising in wrathful majesty*] Oh, how dare you, how dare you?

BLUNTSCHLI. Apologize, man: apologize. [*He resumes his seat at the table*]

SERGIUS. [*With the old measured emphasis, folding his arms*] I never apologize!

RAINA. [*Passionately*] This is the doing of that friend of yours, Captain Bluntschli. It is he who is spreading this horrible story about me. [*She walks about excitedly*]

BLUNTSCHLI. No: he's dead. Burnt alive.

RAINA. [*Stopping, shocked*] Burnt alive!

BLUNTSCHLI. Shot in the hip in a woodyard. Couldnt drag himself out. Your fellows' shells set the timber on fire and burnt him, with half a dozen other poor devils in the same predicament.

RAINA. How horrible!

SERGIUS. And how ridiculous! Oh, war! war! the dream of patriots and heroes! A fraud, Bluntschli. A hollow sham, like love.

RAINA. [*Outraged*] Like love! You say that before me!

BLUNTSCHLI. Come, Saranoff: that matter is explained.

SERGIUS. A hollow sham, I say. Would you have come back here if nothing had passed between you except at the muzzle of your pistol? Raina is mistaken about your friend who was burnt. He was not my informant.

RAINA. Who then? [*Suddenly guessing the truth*] Ah, Louka! my maid! my servant! You were with her this morning all that time after—after—Oh, what sort of god is this I have been worshipping! [*He meets her gaze with sardonic enjoyment of her disenchantment. Angered all the more, she goes closer to him, and says, in a lower, intenser tone*] Do you know that I looked out of the window as I went upstairs, to have another sight of my hero; and I saw something I did not understand then. I know now that you were making love to her.

SERGIUS. [*With grim humor*] You saw that?

RAINA. Only too well. [*She turns away, and throws herself on the divan under the centre window, quite overcome*]

SERGIUS. [*Cynically*] Raina: our romance is shattered. Life's a farce.

BLUNTSCHLI. [*To* RAINA, *whimsically*] You see: he's found himself out now.

SERGIUS. [*Going to him*] Bluntschli: I have allowed you to call me a blockhead. You may now call me a coward as well. I refuse to fight you. Do you know why?

BLUNTSCHLI. No; but it doesnt matter. I didnt ask the reason when you cried on; and I dont ask the reason now that you cry off. I'm a professional soldier! I fight when I have to, and am very glad to get out of it when I havnt to. Youre only an amateur: you think fighting's an amusement.

SERGIUS. [*Sitting down at the table, nose to nose with him*] You shall hear the reason all the same, my professional. The reason is that it takes two men—real men—men of heart, blood and honor—to make a genuine combat. I could no more fight with you than I could make love to an ugly woman. Youve no magnetism: youre not a man: youre a machine.

BLUNTSCHLI. [*Apologetically*] Quite true, quite true. I always was that sort of chap. I'm very sorry.

SERGIUS. Psha!

BLUNTSCHLI. But now that youve found that life isnt a farce, but something quite sensible and serious, what further obstacle is there to your happiness?

RAINA. [*Rising*] You are very solicitous about my happiness and his. Do you forget his new love—Louka? It is not you that he must fight now, but his rival, Nicola.

SERGIUS. Rival!! [*Bounding half across the room*]

RAINA. Dont you know that theyre engaged?

SERGIUS. Nicola! Are fresh abysses opening? Nicola!

RAINA. [*Sarcastically*] A shocking sacrifice, isnt it? Such beauty! such intellect! such modesty! wasted on a middle-aged servant man. Really, Sergius, you cannot stand by and allow such a thing. It would be unworthy of your chivalry.

SERGIUS. [*Losing all self-control*] Viper! Viper! [*He rushes to and fro, raging*]

BLUNTSCHLI. Look here, Saranoff: youre getting the worst of this.

RAINA. [*Getting angrier*] Do you realize what he has done, Captain Bluntschli? He has set this girl as a spy on us; and her reward is that he makes love to her.

SERGIUS. False! Monstrous!

RAINA. Monstrous! [*Confronting him*] Do you deny that she told you about Captain Bluntschli being in my room?

SERGIUS. No; but—

RAINA. [*Interrupting*] Do you deny that you were making love to her when she told you?

SERGIUS. No; but I tell you—

RAINA. [*Cutting him short contemptuously*] It is unnecessary to tell us anything more. That is quite enough for us. [*She turns away from him and sweeps majestically back to the window*]

BLUNTSCHLI. [*Quietly, as* SERGIUS, *in an agony of mortification, sinks on the ottoman, clutching his averted head between his fists*] I told you you were getting the worst of it, Saranoff.

SERGIUS. Tiger cat!

RAINA. [*Running excitedly to* BLUNTSCHLI] You hear this man calling me names, Captain Bluntschli?

BLUNTSCHLI. What else can he do, dear lady? He must defend himself somehow. Come [*Very persuasively*] dont quarrel. What good does it do?

[RAINA, *with a gasp, sits down on the ottoman, and after a vain effort to look vexedly at* BLUNTSCHLI, *falls a victim to her sense of humor, and actually leans back babyishly against the writhing shoulder of* SERGIUS]

SERGIUS. Engaged to Nicola! Ha! ha! Ah well, Bluntschli, you are right to take this huge imposture of a world coolly.

RAINA. [*Quaintly to* BLUNTSCHLI, *with an intuitive guess at his state of mind*] I daresay you think us a couple of grown-up babies, dont you?

SERGIUS. [*Grinning savagely*] He does: he does. Swiss civilization nursetending Bulgarian barbarism, eh?

BLUNTSCHLI. [*Blushing*] Not at all, I assure you. I'm only very glad to get you two quieted. There! there! let's be pleasant and talk it over in a friendly way. Where is this other young lady?

RAINA. Listening at the door, probably.

SERGIUS. [*Shivering as if a bullet had struck him, and speaking with quiet but deep indignation*] I will prove that that, at least, is a calumny. [*He goes with dignity to the door and opens it. A yell of fury bursts from him as he looks out. He darts into the passage, and returns dragging in* LOUKA, *whom he flings violently against the table, exclaiming*] Judge her, Bluntschli. You, the cool impartial man: judge the eavesdropper.

[LOUKA *stands her ground, proud and silent*]

BLUNTSCHLI. [*Shaking his head*] I mustnt judge her. I once listened myself outside a tent when there was a mutiny brewing. It's all a question of the degree of provocation. My life was at stake.

LOUKA. My love was at stake. I am not ashamed.

RAINA. [*Contemptuously*] Your love! Your curiosity, you mean.

LOUKA. [*Facing her and returning her contempt with interest*] My love, stronger than anything you can feel, even for your chocolate cream soldier.

SERGIUS. [*With quick suspicion, to* LOUKA] What does that mean?

LOUKA. [*Fiercely*] I mean—

SERGIUS. [*Interrupting her slightingly*] Oh, I remember: the ice pudding. A paltry taunt, girl!

[MAJOR PETKOFF *enters, in his shirtsleeves*]

PETKOFF. Excuse my shirtsleeves, gentlemen. Raina: somebody has been wearing that coat of mine: I'll swear it. Somebody with a differently shaped back. It's all burst open at the sleeve. Your mother is mending it. I wish she'd make haste: I shall catch cold. [*He looks more attentively at them*] Is anything the matter?

RAINA. No. [*She sits down at the stove, with a tranquil air*]

SERGIUS. Oh no. [*He sits down at the end of the table, as at first*]

BLUNTSCHLI. [*Who is already seated*] Nothing. Nothing.

PETKOFF. [*Sitting down on the ottoman in his old place*] Thats all right. [*He notices* LOUKA] Anything the matter, Louka?

LOUKA. No, sir.

PETKOFF. [*Genially*] Thats all right. [*He sneezes*] Go and ask your mistress for my coat, like a good girl, will you?

[NICOLA *enters with the coat.* LOUKA *makes a pretence of having business in the room by taking the little table with the hookah away to the wall near the windows*]

RAINA. [*Rising quickly as she sees the coat on* NICOLA'S *arm*] Here it is papa. Give it to me Nicola; and do you put some more wood on the fire. [*She takes the coat, and brings it to the* MAJOR, *who stands up to put it on.* NICOLA *attends to the fire*]

PETKOFF. [*To* RAINA, *teasing her affectionately*] Aha! Going to be very good to poor old papa just for one day after his return from the wars, eh?

RAINA. [*With solemn reproach*] Ah, how can you say that to me, father?

PETKOFF. Well, well, only a joke, little one. Come: give me a kiss. [*She kisses him*] Now give me the coat.

RAINA. No: I am going to put it on for you. Turn your back. [*He turns his back and feels behind him with his arms for the sleeves. She dexterously takes the photograph from the pocket and throws it on the table before* BLUNTSCHLI, *who covers it with a sheet of paper under the very nose of* SERGIUS, *who looks on amazed, with his suspicions roused in the highest degree. She then helps* PETKOFF *on with his coat*] There, dear! Now are you comfortable?

PETKOFF.   Quite, little love. Thanks [*He sits down; and* RAINA *returns to her seat near the stove*] Oh, by the bye, Ive found something funny. Whats the meaning of this? [*He puts his hand into the picked pocket*] Eh? Hallo! [*He tries the other pocket*]. Well, I could have sworn—! [*Much puzzled, he tries the breast pocket*] I wonder—[*Trying the original pocket*] Where can it—? [*He rises, exclaiming*] Your mother's taken it!

RAINA.   [*Very red*] Taken what?

PETKOFF.   Your photograph, with the inscription: "Raina, to her Chocolate Cream Soldier: a Souvenir." Now you know theres something more in this than meets the eye; and I'm going to find it out. [*Shouting*] Nicola!

NICOLA.   [*Coming to him*] Sir!

PETKOFF.   Did you spoil any pastry of Miss Raina's this morning?

NICOLA.   You heard Miss Raina say that I did, sir.

PETKOFF.   I know that, you idiot. Was it true?

NICOLA.   I am sure Miss Raina is incapable of saying anything that is not true, sir.

PETKOFF.   Are you? Then I'm not. [*Turning to the others*] Come: do you think I dont see it all? [*He goes to* SERGIUS, *and slaps him on the shoulder*] Sergius: youre the chocolate cream soldier, arnt you?

SERGIUS.   [*Starting up*] I! A chocolate cream soldier! Certainly not.

PETKOFF.   Not! [*He looks at them. They are all very serious and very conscious*] Do you mean to tell me that Raina sends things like that to other men?

SERGIUS.   [*Enigmatically*] The world is not such an innocent place as we used to think, Petkoff.

BLUNTSCHLI.   [*Rising*] It's all right, Major. I'm the chocolate cream soldier. [PETKOFF *and* SERGIUS *are equally astonished*] The gracious young lady saved my life by giving me chocolate creams when I was starving: shall I ever forget their flavour! My late friend Stolz told you the story of Pirot. I was the fugitive.

PETKOFF.   You! [*He gasps*] Sergius: do you remember how those two women went on this morning when we mentioned it? [SERGIUS *smiles cynically.* PETKOFF *confronts* RAINA *severely*] Youre a nice young woman, arnt you?

RAINA.   [*Bitterly*] Major Saranoff has changed his mind. And when I wrote that on the photograph, I did not know that Captain Bluntschli was married.

BLUNTSCHLI.   [*Startled into vehement protest*] I'm not married.

RAINA.   [*With deep reproach*] You said you were.

BLUNTSCHLI.   I did not. I positively did not. I never was married in my life.

PETKOFF.   [*Exasperated*] Raina: will you kindly inform me, if I am not asking too much, which of these gentlemen you are engaged to?

RAINA.   To neither of them. This young lady [*Introducing* LOUKA, *who faces them all proudly*] is the object of Major Saranoff's affections at present.

PETKOFF. Louka! Are you mad, Sergius? Why, this girl's engaged to Nicola.

NICOLA. I beg your pardon, sir. There is a mistake. Louka is not engaged to me.

PETKOFF. Not engaged to you, you scoundrel! Why, you had twenty-five levas from me on the day of your bethrothal; and she had that gilt bracelet from Miss Raina.

NICOLA. [*With cool unction*] We gave it out so, sir. But it was only to give Louka protection. She had a soul above her station; and I have been no more than her confidential servant. I intend, as you know, sir, to set up a shop later on in Sofia; and I look forward to her custom and recommendation should she marry into the nobility. [*He goes out with impressive discretion, leaving them all staring after him*]

PETKOFF. [*Breaking the silence*] Well, I am—hm!

SERGIUS. This is either the finest heroism or the most crawling baseness. Which is it, Bluntschli?

BLUNTSCHLI. Never mind whether it's heroism or baseness. Nicola's the ablest man Ive met in Bulgaria. I'll make him manager of a hotel if he can speak French and German.

LOUKA. [*Suddenly breaking out at* SERGIUS] I have been insulted by everyone here. You set them the example. You owe me an apology.

[SERGIUS, *like a repeating clock of which the spring has been touched, immediately begins to fold his arms*]

BLUNTSCHLI. [*Before he can speak*] It's no use. He never apologizes.

LOUKA. Not to you, his equal and his enemy. To me, his poor servant, he will not refuse to apologize.

SERGIUS. [*Approvingly*] You are right. [*He bends his knee in his grandest manner*] Forgive me.

LOUKA. I forgive you. [*She timidly gives him her hand, which he kisses*] That touch makes me your affianced wife.

SERGIUS. [*Springing up*] Ah! I forgot that.

LOUKA. [*Coldly*] You can withdraw if you like.

SERGIUS. Withdraw! Never! You belong to me. [*He puts his arm about her*]
[CATHERINE *comes in and finds* LOUKA *in* SERGIUS' *arms, with all the rest gazing at them in bewildered astonishment*]

CATHERINE. What does this mean?

[SERGIUS *releases* LOUKA]

PETKOFF. Well, my dear, it appears that Sergius is going to marry Louka instead of Raina. [*She is about to break out indignantly at him: he stops her by exclaiming testily*] Dont blame me: Ive nothing to do with it. [*He retreats to the stove*]

CATHERINE. Marry Louka! Sergius: you are bound by your word to us!

SERGIUS. [*Folding his arms*] Nothing binds me.

BLUNTSCHLI. [*Much pleased by this piece of common sense*] Saranoff: your hand. My congratulations. These heroics of yours have their practical side after all. [*To* LOUKA] Gracious young lady: the best wishes of a good Republican! [*He kisses her hand, to* RAINA's *great disgust, and returns to his seat*]

CATHERINE. Louka: you have been telling stories.

LOUKA. I have done Raina no harm.

CATHERINE. [*Haughtily*] Raina!

[RAINA, *equally indignant, almost snorts at the liberty*]

LOUKA. I have a right to call her Raina: she calls me Louka. I told Major Sara-noff she would never marry him if the Swiss gentleman came back.

BLUNTSCHLI. [*Rising, much surprised*] Hallo!

LOUKA. [*Turning to* RAINA] I thought you were fonder of him than of Sergius. You know best whether I was right.

BLUNTSCHLI. What nonsense! I assure you, my dear Major, my dear Madam, the gracious young lady simply saved my life, nothing else. She never cared two straws for me. Why, bless my heart and soul, look at the young lady and look at me. She, rich, young, beautiful, with her imagination full of fairy princes and noble natures and cavalry charges and goodness knows what! And I, a commonplace Swiss soldier who hardly knows what a decent life is after fifteen years of barracks and battles: a vagabond, a man who has spoiled all his chances in life through an incurably romantic disposition, a man—

SERGIUS. [*Starting as if a needle had pricked him and interrupting* BLUNTSCHLI *in incredulous amazement*] Excuse me, Bluntschli: what did you say had spoiled your chances in life?

BLUNTSCHLI. [*Promptly*] An incurably romantic disposition. I ran away from home twice when I was a boy. I went into the army instead of into my father's business. I climbed the balcony of this house when a man of sense would have dived into the nearest cellar. I came sneaking back here to have another look at the young lady when any other man of my age would have sent the coat back—

PETKOFF. My coat!

BLUNTSCHLI. —yes: thats the coat I mean—would have sent it back and gone quietly home. Do you suppose I am the sort of fellow a young girl falls in love with? Why, look at our ages! I'm thirty-four: I dont suppose the young lady is much over seventeen. [*This estimate produces a marked sensation, all the rest turning and staring at one another. He proceeds innocently*] All that adventure which was life or death to me, was only a schoolgirl's game to her—chocolate creams and hide and seek. Heres the proof! [*He takes the photograph from the table*] Now, I ask you, would a woman who took the affair seriously have sent me this and written on it "Raina, to her Chocolate Cream Soldier: a Souvenir"? [*He exhibits the photograph triumphantly, as if it settled the matter beyond all possibility of refutation*]

PETKOFF. Thats what I was looking for. How the deuce did it get there? [*He comes from the stove to look at it, and sits down on the ottoman*]

BLUNTSCHLI. [*To* RAINA, *complacently*] I have put everything right, I hope, gracious young lady.

RAINA. [*Going to the table to face him*] I quite agree with your account of yourself. You are a romantic idiot. [BLUNTSCHLI *is unspeakably taken aback*] Next time, I hope you will know the difference between a schoolgirl of seventeen and a woman of twenty-three.

BLUNTSCHLI. [*Stupefied*] Twenty-three!

[RAINA *snaps the photograph contemptuously from his hand; tears it up; throws the pieces in his face; and sweeps back to her former place*]

SERGIUS. [*With grim enjoyment of his rival's discomfiture*] Bluntschli: my one last belief is gone. Your sagacity is a fraud, like everything else. You have less sense than even I!

BLUNTSCHLI. [*Overwhelmed*] Twenty-three! Twenty-three!! [*He considers*] Hm! [*Swiftly making up his mind and coming to his host*] In that case, Major Petkoff, I beg to propose formally to become a suitor for your daughter's hand, in place of Major Saranoff retired.

RAINA. You dare!

BLUNTSCHLI. If you were twenty-three when you said those things to me this afternoon, I shall take them seriously.

CATHERINE. [*Loftily polite*] I doubt, sir, whether you quite realize either my daughter's position or that of Major Sergius Saranoff, whose place you propose to take. The Petkoffs and the Saranoffs are known as the richest and most important families in the country. Our position is almost historical: we can go back for twenty years.

PETKOFF. Oh, never mind that, Catherine. [*To* BLUNTSCHLI] We should be most happy, Bluntschli, if it were only a question of your position; but hang it, you know, Raina is accustomed to a very comfortable establishment. Sergius keeps twenty horses.

BLUNTSCHLI. But who wants twenty horses? We're not going to keep a circus.

CATHERINE. [*Severely*] My daughter, sir, is accustomed to a first-rate stable.

RAINA. Hush, mother: youre making me ridiculous.

BLUNTSCHLI. Oh well, if it comes to a question of an establishment, here goes! [*He darts impetuously to the table; seizes the papers in the blue envelope; and turns to Sergius*] How many horses did you say?

SERGIUS. Twenty, noble Switzer.

BLUNTSCHLI. I have two hundred horses. [*They are amazed*] How many carriages?

SERGIUS. Three.

BLUNTSCHLI. I have seventy. Twenty-four of them will hold twelve inside, besides two on the box, without counting the driver and conductor. How many tablecloths have you?

SERGIUS. How the deuce do I know?

BLUNTSCHLI. Have you four thousand?

SERGIUS. No.

BLUNTSCHLI. I have. I have nine thousand six hundred pairs of sheets and blankets, with two thousand four hundred eider-down quilts. I have ten thousand knives and forks, and the same quantity of dessert spoons. I have three hundred servants. I have six palatial establishments, besides two livery stables, a tea garden, and a private house. I have four medals for distinguished services; I have the rank of an officer and the standing of a gentleman; and I have three native languages. Shew me any man in Bulgaria that can offer as much!

PETKOFF. [*With childish awe*] Are you Emperor of Switzerland?

BLUNTSCHLI. My rank is the highest known in Switzerland: I am a free citizen.

CATHERINE. Then, Captain Bluntschli, since you are my daughter's choice—

RAINA. [*Mutinously*] He's not.

CATHERINE.　[*Ignoring her*]—I shall not stand in the way of her happiness. [PETKOFF *is about to speak*] That is Major Petkoff's feeling also.

PETKOFF.　Oh, I shall be only too glad. Two hundred horses! Whew!

SERGIUS.　What says the lady?

RAINA.　[*Pretending to sulk*] The lady says that he can keep his tablecloths and his omnibuses. I am not here to be sold to the highest bidder. [*She turns her back on him*]

BLUNTSCHLI.　I wont take that answer. I appealed to you as a fugitive, a beggar, and a starving man. You accepted me. You gave me your hand to kiss, your bed to sleep in, and your roof to shelter me.

RAINA.　I did not give them to the Emperor of Switzerland.

BLUNTSCHLI.　Thats just what I say. [*He catches her by the shoulders and turns her face-to-face with him*] Now tell us whom you did give them to.

RAINA.　[*Succumbing with a shy smile*] To my chocolate cream soldier.

BLUNTSCHLI.　[*With a boyish laugh of delight*] Thatll do. Thank you. [*He looks at his watch and suddenly becomes businesslike*] Time's up, Major. Youve managed those regiments so well that youre sure to be asked to get rid of some of the infantry of the Timok division. Send them home by way of Lom Palanka. Saranoff: dont get married until I come back: I shall be here punctually at five in the evening on Tuesday fortnight. Gracious ladies [*His heels click*] good evening. [*He makes them a military bow, and goes*]

SERGIUS.　What a man! Is he a man?

Three Sisters

Anton Chekhov

Anton Chekhov

In 1967 Sir Laurence Olivier, director of the English National Theatre, produced *Three Sisters* at the Old Vic in London. It was a stunningly brilliant performance, with Joan Plowright (Olivier's wife) as Masha and Robert Stephens as Vershinin. Next year Olivier brought the play to the United States where it was performed to great applause in several major cities. This was only the latest of many successful revivals of what is surely one of the great plays of the modern era. *Three Sisters* was first performed in 1901 by the Moscow Art Theatre under the direction of Stanislavski.

The author, Anton Chekhov, was born in Taganrog in the south of Russia in 1860. He was the son of a merchant who had risen from the serf class. His father gave him a good education which culminated at the University of Moscow, from which he graduated with a degree in medicine in 1884. Chekhov practiced little, but, stimulated in part by his family's financial need, threw his energies into journalism and literature. His first story had been published in 1880, but after 1884 a whole spate of short articles and tales, mostly of a humorous nature, began to appear, many of them written under a pseudonym. In 1886, he wrote his first play, *The Swan Song*, in one act, and in the next year, a full-length drama, *Ivanov*. At first, *Ivanov* was a failure on the stage, but within a few years it became popular. This pattern was to repeat itself during his life, for several of his plays were at first badly received and only later duly recognized.

Besides writing plays, Chekhov continued to create short stories and short novels, which appeared at intervals in collected editions. Like most Russian writers of the nineteenth century, he had trouble from the intermittent harassment of czarist censors but managed to get along. Stimulated by a treatise on the management of prisons written by a younger brother who was studying law, Chekhov made a visit in 1890 to the island of Sakhalin off the coast of Siberia to inspect the penal settlements there. His profound humanity was aroused and, on his return, he wrote a devastating book on his experiences. Even at that time, signs of tuberculosis, eventually to prove fatal, had begun to be evident.

He then threw himself into writing in his favorite forms and, during the last decade of his life, produced his greatest works and received popular acclaim. He died while on a trip to Germany in 1904.

Chekhov's most famous plays are *The Sea Gull* (1895), *Uncle Vanya* (1899), *Three Sisters* (1900), and *The Cherry Orchard* (1903). His stories are legion, and many of them approach perfection.

Although influenced by Ibsen, the father of the modern drama, Chekhov nevertheless brought a new note to literature, as all great writers do. He was moved by a deep, compassionate love of human beings that saw both their pathos and their humor. His plays seem perhaps to be somewhat plotless, but Chekhov was concerned with emphasizing the effect of action (or lack of it) on human beings, rather than the action itself. He is above all a lyric dramatist who emphasizes the changing and subtle moods of men in a quiet, objective way. His perceptions are most moving and powerful, just because they are so quietly and objectively presented. Although his writing contains social criticism, Chekhov is primarily concerned with man's striving to find dignity and meaning in the flux of existence. But Chekhov's humor as well as his tragic sense must be recognized, for he brings us laughter along with tears.

His plays, written in their minor key, are models of true form, and the serious student must study them closely to see his principles of unity. He makes much use of symbols. Some of his characters become universal types (that is, they stand for certain abstract characteristics or ideas), although they never lose their individuality. The three sisters in our play, who long for Moscow and who never get there, poignantly capture the failure of all human beings. But this steady gaze at human tragedy is redeemed and transmuted by Chekhov's humor, affection, and pity. He urges, by implication, that we cultivate humor and that we love one another. He was an artist primarily, and his "message" is always seen through the medium of his rare creations. He speaks to us as an artist, not as a preacher, but we nonetheless learn from him something of his sense of human dignity in the face of the tragedy of life.

The Russian system of personal names may be confusing to English-speaking readers. Each Russian has not only his own Christian and surname as an American would have, but also a middle name which is a patronymic. Andrey Prozorov's father was named Sergey, and therefore Andrey's full name is Andrey Sergeyevitch ("son of Sergey") Prozorov. His wife Natalya ("Natalie") was the daughter of an Ivan and hence has the middle name Ivanovna ("daughter of Ivan"). These names provide a series of variations in intimacy. The full tri-form name is used in formal discourse. Normally, however, friends address each other by their first names and patronymics together. If they feel a little more intimate or wish to express particular affection, they may use the first name alone, with or without a diminutive. Russian as a language is full of diminutives that may be used as suffixes to impart various shades of meaning, not always friendly, to words. Vanya, for instance, is an affectionate form of Ivan (Ivan + ya = Ivanya = Vanya) and Andryusha (Andrey + usha) of Andrey.

Three Sisters

Anton Chekhov

TRANSLATED BY CONSTANCE GARNETT

CHARACTERS

ANDREY SERGYEVITCH PROZOROV

NATALYA IVANOVNA, *also called* NATASHA, *his fiancée, afterwards his wife*

OLGA ⎫
MASHA ⎬ *his sisters*
IRINA ⎭

FYODOR ILYITCH KULIGIN, *a high-school teacher, husband of* MASHA

LIEUTENANT-COLONEL ALEXANDR IG-NATYEVITCH VERSHININ, *battery-commander*

BARON NIKOLAY LVOVITCH TUSEN-BACH, *lieutenant*

VASSILY VASSILYEVITCH SOLYONY, *captain*

IVAN ROMANITCH TCHEBUTYKIN, *army doctor*

ALEXEY PETROVITCH FEDOTIK, *second lieutenant*

VLADIMIR KARLOVITCH RODDEY, *second lieutenant*

FERAPONT, *an old porter from the rural board*

ANFISA, *the nurse, an old woman of eighty*

The action takes place in a provincial town.

Act One

In the house of the PROZOROVS. *A drawing-room with columns beyond which a large room is visible. Mid-day; it is bright and sunny. The table in the farther room is being laid for lunch.* OLGA, *in the dark blue uniform of a high-school teacher, is correcting exercise books, at times standing still and then walking up and down;* MASHA, *in a black dress, with her hat on her knee, is reading a book;* IRINA, *in a white dress, is standing plunged in thought.*

Three Sisters, by Anton Chekhov, translated by Constance Garnett. By permission of A. P. Watt & Son on behalf of the Estate of Constance Garnett.

OLGA. Father died just a year ago, on this very day—the fifth of May, your name-day,[1] Irina. It was very cold, snow was falling. I felt as though I should not live through it; you lay fainting as though you were dead. But now a year has passed and we can think of it calmly; you are already in a white dress, your face is radiant. [*The clock strikes twelve*] The clock was striking then too. [*A pause*] I remember the band playing and the firing at the cemetery as they carried the coffin. Though he was a general in command of a brigade, yet there weren't many people there. It was raining, though. Heavy rain and snow.

IRINA. Why recall it!

[BARON TUSENBACH, TCHEBUTYKIN *and* SOLYONY *appear near the table in the dining-room, beyond the columns*]

OLGA. It is warm to-day, we can have the windows open, but the birches are not in leaf yet. Father was given his brigade and came here with us from Moscow eleven years ago and I remember distinctly that in Moscow at this time, at the beginning of May, everything was already in flower; it was warm, and everything was bathed in sunshine. It's eleven years ago, and yet I remember it all as though we had left it yesterday. Oh, dear! I woke up this morning, I saw a blaze of sunshine. I saw the spring, and joy stirred in my heart. I had a passionate longing to be back at home again!

TCHEBUTYKIN. The devil it is!

TUSENBACH. Of course, it's nonsense.

[MASHA, *brooding over a book, softly whistles a song*]

OLGA. Don't whistle, Masha. How can you! [*A pause*] Being all day in school and then at my lessons till the evening gives me a perpetual headache and thoughts as gloomy as though I were old. And really these four years that I have been at the high-school I have felt my strength and my youth oozing away from me every day. And only one yearning grows stronger and stronger. . . .

IRINA. To go back to Moscow. To sell the house, to make an end of everything here, and off to Moscow. . . .

OLGA. Yes! To Moscow, and quickly.

[TCHEBUTYKIN *and* TUSENBACH *laugh*]

IRINA. Andrey will probably be a professor, he will not live here anyhow. The only difficulty is poor Masha.

OLGA. Masha will come and spend the whole summer in Moscow every year.

[MASHA *softly whistles a tune*]

IRINA. Please God it will all be managed. [*Looking out of window*] How fine it is to-day. I don't know why I feel so light-hearted! I remembered this morning that it was my name-day, and at once I felt joyful and thought of my childhood when mother was living. And I was thrilled by such wonderful thoughts, such thoughts!

OLGA. You are radiant to-day and looking lovelier than usual. And Masha is

---

[1] Europeans generally do not celebrate their birthdays but rather the day devoted to the memory of the saint after whom they are named. Irina was named after St. Irene, a saint of both the Russian Orthodox and Roman Catholic churches, who was martyred with two other Christians under the Emperor Diocletian (c. A.D. 300). Irina would celebrate, as a kind of birthday, that day of the year (May 5th) on which the church honors St. Irene's memory.

lovely too. Andrey would be nice-looking, but he has grown too fat and that does not suit him. And I have grown older and ever so much thinner. I suppose it's because I get so cross with the girls at school. To-day now I am free, I am at home, and my head doesn't ache, and I feel younger than yesterday. I am only twenty-eight. . . . It's all quite right, it's all from God, but it seems to me that if I were married and sitting at home all day, it would be better. [*A pause*] I should be fond of my husband.

TUSENBACH. [*To* SOLYONY] You talk such nonsense, I am tired of listening to you. [*Coming into the drawing-room*] I forgot to tell you, you will receive a visit to-day from Vershinin, the new commander of our battery.[2] [*Sits down to the piano*]

OLGA. Well, I shall be delighted.

IRINA. Is he old?

TUSENBACH. No, nothing to speak of. Forty or forty-five at the most. [*Softly plays the piano*] He seems to be a nice fellow. He is not stupid, that's certain. Only he talks a lot.

IRINA. Is he interesting?

TUSENBACH. Yes, he is all right, only he has a wife, a mother-in-law and two little girls. And it's his second wife too. He is paying calls and telling everyone that he has a wife and two little girls. He'll tell you so too. His wife seems a bit crazy, with her hair in a long plait like a girl's, always talks in a high-flown style, makes philosophical reflections and frequently attempts to commit suicide, evidently to annoy her husband. I should have left a woman like that years ago, but he puts up with her and merely complains.

SOLYONY. [*Coming into the drawing-room with* TCHEBUTYKIN] With one hand I can only lift up half a hundredweight, but with both hands I can lift up a hundredweight and a half or even a hundredweight and three-quarters. From that I conclude that two men are not only twice but three times as strong as one man, or even more. . . .

TCHEBUTYKIN. [*Reading the newspaper as he comes in*] For falling hair . . . two ounces of naphthaline in half a bottle of spirit . . . to be dissolved and used daily. . . . [*Puts it down in his note-book*] Let's make a note of it! No, I don't want it. . . . [*Scratches it out*] It doesn't matter.

IRINA. Ivan Romanitch, dear Ivan Romanitch!

TCHEBUTYKIN. What is it, my child, my joy?

IRINA. Tell me, why is it I am so happy to-day? As though I were sailing with the great blue sky above me and big white birds flying over it. Why is it? Why?

TCHEBUTYKIN. [*Kissing both her hands, tenderly*] My white bird. . . .

IRINA. When I woke up this morning, got up and washed, it suddenly seemed to me as though everything in the world was clear to me and that I knew how one ought to live. Dear Ivan Romanitch, I know all about it. A man ought to work, to toil in the sweat of his brow, whoever he may be, and all the purpose and meaning of his life, his happiness, his ecstasies lie in that

---

[2] It is obvious that the provincial town in which the action of the play takes place (and which Chekhov does not name) is a garrison town. Sergey Prozorov, father of Andrey, Olga, Masha and Irina, was, as we have been told, a brigadier-general.

alone. How delightful to be a workman who gets up before dawn and breaks stones on the road, or a shepherd, or a schoolmaster teaching children, or an engine-driver. . . . Oh, dear! to say nothing of human beings, it would be better to be an ox, better to be a humble horse and work, than a young woman who wakes at twelve o'clock, then has coffee in bed, then spends two hours dressing. . . . Oh, how awful that is! Just as one has a craving for water in hot weather I have a craving for work. And if I don't get up early and work, give me up as a friend, Ivan Romanitch.

TCHEBUTYKIN. [*Tenderly*] I'll give you up, I'll give you up. . . .

OLGA. Father trained us to get up at seven o'clock. Now Irina wakes at seven and lies in bed at least till nine thinking. And she looks so serious! [*Laughs*]

IRINA. You are used to thinking of me as a child and are surprised when I look serious. I am twenty!

TUSENBACH. The yearning for work, oh dear, how well I understand it! I have never worked in my life. I was born in cold, idle Petersburg,[3] in a family that had known nothing of work or cares of any kind. I remember, when I came home from the school of cadets, a footman used to pull off my boots. I used to be troublesome, but my mother looked at me with reverential awe, and was surprised when other people did not do the same. I was guarded from work. But I doubt if they have succeeded in guarding me completely, I doubt it! The time is at hand, an avalanche is moving down upon us, a mighty clearing storm which is coming, is already near and will soon blow the laziness, the indifference, the distaste for work, the rotten boredom out of our society. I shall work, and in another twenty-five or thirty years every one will have to work. Every one!

TCHEBUTYKIN. I am not going to work.

TUSENBACH. You don't count.

SOLYONY. In another twenty-five years you won't be here, thank God. In two or three years you will kick the bucket, or I shall lose my temper and put a bullet through your head, my angel. [*Pulls a scent-bottle out of his pocket and sprinkles his chest and hands*]

TCHEBUTYKIN. [*Laughs*] And I really have never done anything at all. I haven't done a stroke of work since I left the University, I have never read a book, I read nothing but newspapers. . . . [*Takes another newspaper out of his pocket*] Here . . . I know, for instance, from the newspapers that there was such a person as Dobrolyubov, but what he wrote, I can't say. . . . Goodness only knows. . . . [*A knock is heard on the floor from the story below*] There . . . they are calling me downstairs, someone has come for me. I'll be back directly. . . . Wait a minute . . . [*Goes out hurriedly, combing his beard*]

IRINA. He's got something up his sleeve.

TUSENBACH. Yes, he went out with a solemn face, evidently he is just going to bring you a present.

IRINA. What a nuisance!

---

[3] Modern Leningrad, built by the Russian Czar, Peter the Great (1682-1725) and originally named for him. After the Russian Revolution of 1917, the city was renamed to honor Lenin (*grad* is a Russian word meaning city and is equivalent to the German *burg*).

OLGA. Yes, it's awful. He is always doing something silly.

MASHA. By the sea-strand an oak-tree green . . . upon that oak a chain of gold . . . upon that oak a chain of gold.[4] [*Gets up, humming softly*]

OLGA. You are not very cheerful to-day, Masha.

[MASHA, *humming, puts on her hat*]

OLGA. Where are you going?

MASHA. Home.[5]

IRINA. How queer! . . .

TUSENBACH. To go away from a name-day party!

MASHA. Never mind. . . . I'll come in the evening. Good-bye, my darling. . . . [*Kisses* IRINA] Once again I wish you, be well and happy. In the old days, when father was alive, we always had thirty or forty officers here on name-days; it was noisy, but to-day there is only a man and a half, and it is as still as the desert. . . . I'll go. . . . I am blue to-day, I am feeling glum, so don't you mind what I say. [*Laughing through her tears*] We'll talk some other time, and so for now good-bye, darling, I am going. . . .

IRINA. [*Discontentedly*] Oh, how tiresome you are. . . .

OLGA. [*With tears*] I understand you, Masha.

SOLYONY. If a man philosophises, there will be philosophy or sophistry anyway, but if a woman philosophises, or two do it, then you may just snap your fingers!

MASHA. What do you mean to say by that, you terrible person?

SOLYONY. Nothing. He had not time to say "alack," before the bear was on his back.[6] [*A pause*]

MASHA. [*To* OLGA, *angrily*] Don't blubber!

[*Enter* ANFISA *and* FERAPONT *carrying a cake*]

ANFISA. This way, my good man. Come in, your boots are clean. [*To* IRINA] From the Rural Board, from Mihail Ivanitch Protopopov. . . . A cake.

IRINA. Thanks. Thank him. [*Takes the cake*]

FERAPONT. What? [7]

IRINA. [*More loudly*] Thank him from me!

OLGA. Nurse dear, give him some pie. Ferapont, go along, they will give you some pie.

FERAPONT. Eh?

ANFISA. Come along, Ferapont Spiridonitch, my good soul, come along. . . . [*Goes out with* FERAPONT]

MASHA. I don't like that Protopopov, that Mihail Potapitch or Ivanitch. He ought not to be invited.

IRINA. I did not invite him.

MASHA. That's a good thing.

[*Enter* TCHEBUTYKIN, *followed by an orderly with a silver samovar; a hum of surprise and displeasure*]

---

[4] Masha is quoting a few lines from Pushkin's poem "Ruslan and Ludmilla." They run through this play as a kind of theme. Alexander Pushkin (1799-1837) is the great Russian classic poet.   [5] Masha is the only one of the sisters married.

[6] A quotation from one of the fables of Krylov (1768-1844). Solyony repeats it again in the last act. See p. 438. He is a particularly rude person.   [7] Ferapont is somewhat deaf.

OLGA. [*Putting her hands over her face*] A samovar! How awful!
[*Goes out to the table in the dining-room*]

IRINA. My dear Ivan Romanitch, what are you thinking about!

TUSENBACH. [*Laughs*] I warned you!

MASHA. Ivan Romanitch, you really have no conscience!

TCHEBUTYKIN. My dear girls, my darlings, you are all that I have, you are the most precious treasures I have on earth. I shall soon be sixty, I am an old man, alone in the world, a useless old man. . . . There is nothing good in me, except my love for you, and if it were not for you, I should have been dead long ago. . . . [*To* IRINA] My dear, my little girl, I've known you from a baby . . . I've carried you in my arms. . . . I loved your dear mother. . . .

IRINA. But why such expensive presents?

TCHEBUTYKIN. [*Angry and tearful*] Expensive presents. . . . Get along with you! [*To the orderly*] Take the samovar in there . . . [*Mimicking*] Expensive presents . . . [*The orderly carries the samovar into the dining-room*]

ANFISA. [*Crossing the room*] My dears, a colonel is here, a stranger. . . . He has taken off his greatcoat, children, he is coming in here. Irinushka,[8] you must be nice and polite, dear . . . [*As she goes out*] And it's time for lunch already . . . mercy on us. . . .

TUSENBACH. Vershinin, I suppose.

[*Enter* VERSHININ]

TUSENBACH. Colonel Vershinin.

VERSHININ. [*To* MASHA *and* IRINA] I have the honour to introduce myself, my name is Vershinin. I am very, very glad to be in your house at last. How you have grown up! Aie-aie!

IRINA. Please sit down. We are delighted to see you.

VERSHININ. [*With animation*] How glad I am, how glad I am! But there are three of you sisters. I remember—three little girls. I don't remember your faces, but that your father, Colonel Prozorov, had three little girls I remember perfectly, and saw them with my own eyes. How time passes! Hey-ho, how it passes!

TUSENBACH. Alexandr Ignatyevitch[9] has come from Moscow.

IRINA. From Moscow? You have come from Moscow?

VERSHININ. Yes. Your father was in command of a battery there and I was an officer in the same brigade. [*To* MASHA] Your face, now, I seem to remember.

MASHA. I don't remember you.

IRINA. Olya! Olya! [10] [*Calls into the dining-room*] Olya, come!

[OLGA *comes out of the dining-room into the drawing room*]

IRINA. Colonel Vershinin is from Moscow, it appears.

VERSHININ. So you are Olga Sergeyevna,[11] the eldest. . . . And you are Marya.[12] . . . And you are Irina, the youngest. . . .

---

[8] As an old nurse of Irina's, Anfisa uses an affectionate form of the name Irina, with the diminutive, -*ushka*.   [9] Vershinin.

[10] Intimate form of Olga.

[11] Feminine form of the patronymic made up from Sergey and meaning "daughter of Sergey."   [12] A more formal form of Masha, both of which are the English name Mary.

OLGA. You come from Moscow?

VERSHININ. Yes. I studied in Moscow. I began my service there, I served there for years, and at last I have been given a battery here—I have come here as you see. I don't remember you exactly, I only remember you were three sisters. I remember your father. If I shut my eyes, I can see him as though he were living. I used to visit you in Moscow. . . .

OLGA. I thought I remembered everyone, and now all at once . . .

VERSHININ. My name is Alexandr Ignatyevitch.

IRINA. Alexandr Ignatyevitch, you have come from Moscow. . . . What a surprise!

OLGA. We are going to move there, you know.

IRINA. We are hoping to be there by the autumn. It's our native town, we were born there. . . . In Old Basmanny Street. . . . [*Both laugh with delight*]

MASHA. To see some one from our own town unexpectedly! [*Eagerly*] Now I remember! Do you remember, Olya, they used to talk of the "love-sick major"? You were a lieutenant at that time and were in love, and for some reason everyone called you "major" to tease you. . . .

VERSHININ. [*Laughs*] Yes, yes. . . . The love-sick major, that was it.

MASHA. You only had a moustache then. . . . Oh, how much older you look! [*Through tears*] how much older!

VERSHININ. Yes, when I was called the love-sick major I was young, I was in love. Now it's very different.

OLGA. But you haven't a single grey hair. You have grown older, but you are not old.

VERSHININ. I am in my forty-third year, though. Is it long since you left Moscow?

IRINA. Eleven years. But why are you crying, Masha, you queer girl? . . . [*Through her tears*] I shall cry too. . . .

MASHA. I am all right. And in which street did you live?

VERSHININ. In Old Basmanny.

OLGA. And that's where we lived too. . . .

VERSHININ. At one time I lived in Nyemetsky Street. I used to go from there to the Red Barracks. There is a gloomy-looking bridge on the way, where the water makes a noise. It makes a lonely man feel melancholy. [*A pause*] And here what a broad, splendid river! A marvellous river!

OLGA. Yes, but it is cold. It's cold here and there are gnats. . . .

VERSHININ. How can you! You've such a splendid healthy Russian climate here. Forest, river . . . and birches here too. Charming, modest birches, I love them better than any other trees. It's nice to live here. The only strange thing is that the railway station is fifteen miles away. . . . And no one knows why it is so.

SOLYONY. I know why it is. [*They all look at him*] Because if the station had been near it would not have been so far, and if it is far, it's because it is not near.

[*An awkward silence*]

TUSENBACH. He is fond of his joke, Vassily Vassilyevitch.[13]

OLGA. Now I recall you, too. I remember.

---

[13] Solyony's first name and patronymic.

VERSHININ. I knew your mother.

TCHEBUTYKIN. She was a fine woman, the Kingdom of Heaven be hers.

IRINA. Mother is buried in Moscow.

OLGA. In the Novo-Dyevitchy. . . .

MASHA. Would you believe it, I am already beginning to forget her face. So people will not remember us either . . . they will forget us.

VERSHININ. Yes. They will forget us. Such is our fate, there is no help for it. What seems to us serious, significant, very important, will one day be forgotten or will seem unimportant. [*A pause*] And it's curious that we can't possibly tell what exactly will be considered great and important, and what will seem paltry and ridiculous. Did not the discoveries of Copernicus or Columbus, let us say, seem useless and ridiculous at first, while the nonsensical writings of some wiseacre seemed true? And it may be that our present life, which we accept so readily, will in time seem queer, uncomfortable, not sensible, not clean enough, perhaps even sinful. . . .

TUSENBACH. Who knows? Perhaps our age will be called a great one and remembered with respect. Now we have no torture-chamber, no executions, no invasions, but at the same time how much unhappiness there is!

SOLYONY. [*In a high-pitched voice*] Chook, chook, chook. . . . It's bread and meat to the baron to talk about ideas.

TUSENBACH. Vassily Vassilyevitch, I ask you to let me alone. . . . [*Moves to another seat*] It gets boring, at last.

SOLONY. [*In a high-pitched voice*] Chook, chook, chook. . . .

TUSENBACH. [*To* VERSHININ] The unhappiness which one observes now— there is so much of it—does indicate, however, that society has reached a certain moral level. . . .

VERSHININ. Yes, yes, of course.

TCHEBUTYKIN. You said just now, baron, that our age will be called great; but people are small all the same. . . . [*Gets up*] Look how small I am.

[*A violin is played behind the scenes*]

MASHA. That's Andrey playing, our brother.

IRINA. He is the learned one of the family. We expect him to become a professor. Father was a military man, but his son has gone in for a learned career.

MASHA. It was father's wish.

OLGA. We have been teasing him to-day. We think he is a little in love.

IRINA. With a young lady living here. She will come in to-day most likely.

MASHA. Oh, how she dresses! It's not that her clothes are merely ugly or out of fashion, they are simply pitiful. A queer gaudy yellowish skirt with some sort of vulgar fringe and a red blouse. And her cheeks scrubbed till they shine! Andrey is not in love with her—I won't admit that, he has some taste anyway—it's simply for fun, he is teasing us, playing the fool. I heard yesterday that she is going to be married to Protopopov, the chairman of our Rural Board. And a very good thing too. . . . [*At the side door*] Andrey, come here, dear, for a minute!

[*Enter* ANDREY]

OLGA. This is my brother, Andrey Sergeyevitch.

VERSHININ. My name is Vershinin.

ANDREY. And mine is Prozorov. [*Mops his perspiring face*] You are our new battery commander?

OLGA. Only fancy, Alexandr Ignatyevitch comes from Moscow.

ANDREY. Really? Well, then, I congratulate you. My sisters will let you have no peace.

VERSHININ. I have had time to bore your sisters already.

IRINA. See what a pretty picture-frame Andrey has given me to-day! [*Shows the frame*] He made it himself.

VERSHININ. [*Looking at the frame and not knowing what to say*] Yes . . . it is a thing. . . .

IRINA. And that frame above the piano, he made that too!

[ANDREY *waves his hand in despair and moves away*]

OLGA. He is learned, and he plays the violin, and he makes all sorts of things with the fretsaw. In fact he is good all round. Andrey, don't go! That's a way he has—he always tries to make off! Come here!

[MASHA *and* IRINA *take him by the arms and, laughing, lead him back*]

MASHA. Come, come!

ANDREY. Leave me alone, please!

MASHA. How absurd he is! Alexandr Ignatyevitch used to be called the love-sick major at one time, and he was not a bit offended.

VERSHININ. Not in the least!

MASHA. And I should like to call you the love-sick violinist!

IRINA. Or the love-sick professor!

OLGA. He is in love! Andryusha is in love!

IRINA. [*Claps her hands*] Bravo, bravo! Encore! Andryusha is in love!

TCHEBUTYKIN. [*Comes up behind* ANDREY *and puts both arms round his waist*] Nature our hearts for love created [14] [*Laughs, then sits down and reads the newspaper which he takes out of his pocket*]

ANDREY. Come, that's enough, that's enough. . . . [*Mops his face*] I haven't slept all night and this morning I don't feel quite myself, as they say. I read till four o'clock and then went to bed, but it was no use. I thought of one thing and another, and then it gets light so early; the sun simply pours into my bedroom. I want while I am here during the summer to translate a book from the English. . . .

VERSHININ. You read English then?

ANDREY. Yes. Our father, the Kingdom of Heaven be his, oppressed us with education. It's absurd and silly, but it must be confessed I began to get fatter after his death, and I have grown too fat in one year, as though a weight had been taken off my body. Thanks to our father we all know English, French and German, and Irina knows Italian too. But what it cost us!

MASHA. In this town to know three languages is an unnecessary luxury! Not even a luxury, but an unnecessary encumbrance, like a sixth finger. We know a great deal that is unnecessary.

VERSHININ. What next! [*Laughs*] You know a great deal that is unnecessary!

[14] A line from a sentimental popular song of the nineties in Russia. Tchebutykin repeats it again later.

I don't think there can be a town so dull and dismal that intelligent and educated people are unnecessary in it. Let us suppose that of the hundred thousand people living in this town, which is, of course, uncultured and behind the times, there are only three of your sort. It goes without saying that you cannot conquer the mass of darkness round you; little by little, as you go on living, you will be lost in the crowd. You will have to give in to it. Life will get the better of you, but still you will not disappear without a trace. After you there may appear perhaps six like you, then twelve and so on until such as you form a majority. In two or three hundred years life on earth will be unimaginably beautiful, marvellous. Man needs such a life and, though he hasn't it yet, he must have a presentiment of it, expect it, dream of it, prepare for it; for that he must see and know more than his father and grandfather. [*Laughs*] And you complain of knowing a great deal that's unnecessary.

MASHA. [*Takes off her hat*] I'll stay to lunch.

IRINA. [*With a sigh*] All that really ought to be written down. . . .

[ANDREY *has slipped away unobserved*]

TUSENBACH. You say that after many years life on earth will be beautiful and marvellous. That's true. But in order to have any share, however far off, in it now, one must be preparing for it, one must be working. . . .

VERSHININ. [*Gets up*] Yes. What a lot of flowers you have! [*Looking round*] And delightful rooms. I envy you! I've been knocking about all my life from one wretched lodging to another, always with two chairs and a sofa and stoves which smoke. What I have been lacking all my life is just such flowers. . . . [*Rubs his hands*] But there, it's no use thinking about it!

TUSENBACH. Yes, we must work. I'll be bound you think the German[15] is getting sentimental. But on my honour I am Russian and I can't even speak German. My father belonged to the Orthodox Church. . . . [*A pause*]

VERSHININ. [*Walks about the stage*] I often think, what if one were to begin life over again, knowing what one is about! If one life, which has been already lived, were only a rough sketch so to say, and the second were the fair copy! Then, I fancy, every one of us would try before everything not to repeat himself, anyway he would create a different setting for his life; would have a house like this with plenty of light and masses of flowers. . . . I have a wife and two little girls, my wife is in delicate health and so on and so on, but if I were to begin life over again I would not marry. . . . No, no!

[*Enter* KULIGIN[16] *in the uniform of a school-master*]

KULIGIN. [*Goes up to* IRINA] Dear sister, allow me to congratulate you on your name-day and with all my heart to wish you good health and everything else that one can desire for a girl of your age. And to offer you as a gift this little book. [*Gives her a book*] The history of our high-school for fifty years, written by myself. An insignificant little book, written because I had nothing better to do, but still you can read it. Good morning, friends. [*To* VERSHININ] My name is Kuligin, teacher in the high-school here. [*To*

---

[15] Tusenbach, as his name shows, is of German origin. He is self-conscious and a little apologetic about his ancestry. Germans and Russians of German descent were often subjected to criticism by the dominant Russian majority.   [16] Masha's high-school teacher husband.

IRINA] In that book you will find a list of all who have finished their studies in our high-school during the last fifty years. *Feci quod potui, faciant meliora potentes.*[17]

[*Kisses* MASHA]

IRINA. Why, but you gave me a copy of this book at Easter.

KULIGIN. [*Laughs*] Impossible! If that's so, give it back to me, or better still, give it to the Colonel. Please accept it, Colonel. Some day when you are bored you can read it.

VERSHININ. Thank you. [*Is about to take his leave*] I am extremely glad to have made your acquaintance. . . .

OLGA. You are going? No, no!

IRINA. You must stay to lunch with us. Please do.

OLGA. Pray do!

VERSHININ. [*Bows*] I believe I have chanced on a name-day. Forgive me, I did not know and have not congratulated you. . . . [*Walks away with* OLGA *into the dining-room*]

KULIGIN. To-day, gentlemen, is Sunday, a day of rest. Let us all rest and enjoy ourselves each in accordance with our age and our position. The carpets should be taken up for the summer and put away till the winter. . . . Persian powder or naphthaline. . . . The Romans were healthy because they knew how to work and they knew how to rest, they had *mens sana in corpore sano.*[18] Their life was moulded into a certain framework. Our headmaster[19] says that the most important thing in every life is its framework. . . . What loses its framework, comes to an end—and it's the same in our everyday life. [*Puts his arm round* MASHA's *waist, laughing*] Masha loves me. My wife loves me. And the window curtains, too, ought to be put away together with the carpets. . . . To-day I feel cheerful and in the best of spirits. Masha, at four o'clock this afternoon we have to be at the headmaster's. An excursion has been arranged for the teachers and their families.

MASHA. I am not going.

KULIGIN. [*Grieved*] Dear Masha, why not?

MASHA. We'll talk about it afterwards. . . . [*Angrily*] Very well, I will go, only let me alone, please. . . . [*Walks away*]

KULIGIN. And then we shall spend the evening at the headmaster's. In spite of the delicate state of his health, that man tries before all things to be sociable. He is an excellent, noble personality. A splendid man. Yesterday, after the meeting, he said to me, "I am tired, Fyodor Ilyitch,[20] I am tired." [*Looks at the clock, then at his watch*] Your clock is seven minutes fast. "Yes," he said, "I am tired."

[*Sounds of a violin, behind the scenes*]

OLGA. Come to lunch, please. There's a pie!

KULIGIN. Ah, Olga, my dear Olga! Yesterday I was working from early morning

---

[17] "I have done what I could; the mighty may do better things." Kuligin's tendency to quote Latin phrases and tags on all occasions is indicative of his profession in the days when Latin was an inevitable subject in all non-elementary schools.

[18] "A healthy mind in a healthy body."   [19] Principal.

[20] Kuligin's Christian name and patronymic (son of Ilya).

till eleven o'clock at night and was tired out, and to-day I feel happy. [*Goes up to the table in the dining-room*] My dear. . . .

TCHEBUTYKIN. [*Puts the newspaper in his pocket and combs his beard*] Pie? Splendid!

MASHA. [*To* TCHEBUTYKIN, *sternly*] Only mind you don't drink to-day! Do you hear? It's bad for you to drink.

TCHEBUTYKIN. Oh, come, that's a thing of the past. It's two years since I got drunk. [*Impatiently*] But there, my good girl, what does it matter!

MASHA. Anyway, don't you dare to drink. Don't dare. [*Angrily, but so as not to be heard by her husband*] Again, damnation take it, I am to be bored a whole evening at the headmaster's!

TUSENBACH. I wouldn't go if I were you. . . . It's very simple.

TCHEBUTYKIN. Don't go, my love.

MASHA. Oh, yes, don't go! . . . It's a damnable life, insufferable . . . [*Goes to the dining-room*]

TCHEBUTYKIN. [*Following her*] Come, come. . . .

SOLYONY. [*Going to the dining-room*] Chook, chook, chook. . . .

TUSENBACH. Enough, Vassily Vassilyevitch! Leave off!

SOLYONY. Chook, chook, chook. . . .

KULIGIN. [*Gaily*] Your health, Colonel! I am a school-master and one of the family here, Masha's husband. . . . She is very kind, really, very kind. . . .

VERSHININ. I'll have some of this dark-coloured vodka . . . [*Drinks*] To your health! [*To* OLGA] I feel so happy with all of you!

[*No one is left in the drawing-room but* IRINA *and* TUSENBACH]

IRINA. Masha is in low spirits to-day. She was married at eighteen, when she thought him the cleverest of men. But now it's not the same. He is the kindest of men, but he is not the cleverest.

OLGA. [*Impatiently*] Andrey, do come!

ANDREY. [*Behind the scenes*] I am coming. [*Comes in and goes to the table*]

TUSENBACH. What are you thinking about?

IRINA. Nothing. I don't like that Solyony of yours, I am afraid of him. He keeps on saying such stupid things. . . .

TUSENBACH. He is a queer man. I am sorry for him and annoyed by him, but more sorry. I think he is shy. . . . When one is alone with him he is very intelligent and friendly, but in company he is rude, a bully. Don't go yet, let them sit down to the table. Let me be by you. What are you thinking of? [*A pause*] You are twenty, I am not yet thirty. How many years have we got before us, a long, long chain of days full of my love for you. . . .

IRINA. Nikolay Lvovitch, don't talk to me about love.

TUSENBACH. [*Not listening*] I have a passionate craving for life, for struggle, for work, and that craving is mingled in my soul with my love for you, Irina, and just because you are beautiful it seems to me that life too is beautiful! What are you thinking of?

IRINA. You say life is beautiful. . . . Yes, but what if it only seems so! Life for us three sisters has not been beautiful yet, we have been stifled by it as plants are choked by weeds. . . . I am shedding tears. . . . I mustn't do that. [*Hurriedly wipes her eyes and smiles*] I must work, I must work. The reason we are depressed and take such a gloomy view of life is that we know nothing of work. We come of people who despised work. . . .

[*Enter* NATALYA IVANOVA; *she is wearing a pink dress with a green sash*]

NATASHA.[21] They are sitting down to lunch already. . . . I am late. . . . [*Steals a glance at herself in the glass and sets herself to rights*] I think my hair is all right. [*Seeing* IRINA] Dear Irina Sergeyevna, I congratulate you! [*Gives her a vigorous and prolonged kiss*] You have a lot of visitors, I really feel shy. . . . Good day, Baron!

OLGA. [*Coming into the drawing-room*] Well, here is Natalya Ivanovna! How are you, my dear? [*Kisses her*]

NATASHA. Congratulations on the name-day. You have such a big party and I feel awfully shy. . . .

OLGA. Nonsense, we have only our own people. [*In an undertone, in alarm*] You've got on a green sash! My dear, that's not nice!

NATASHA. Why, is that a bad omen?

OLGA. No, it's only that it doesn't go with your dress . . . and it looks queer. . . .

NATASHA. [*In a tearful voice*] Really? But you know it's not green exactly, it's more a dead colour. [*Follows* OLGA *into the dining-room*]

[*In the dining-room they are all sitting down to lunch; there is no one in the drawing-room*]

KULIGIN. I wish you a good husband, Irina. It's time for you to think of getting married.

TCHEBUTYKIN. Natalya Ivanovna, I hope we may hear of your engagement, too.

KULIGIN. Natalya Ivanovna has got a suitor already.

MASHA. [*Strikes her plate with her fork*] Ladies and gentlemen, I want to make a speech!

KULIGIN. You deserve three bad marks for conduct.

VERSHININ. How nice this cordial is! What is it made of?

SOLONY. Beetles.

IRINA. [*In a tearful voice*] Ugh, ugh! How disgusting.

OLGA. We are going to have roast turkey and apple pie for supper. Thank God I am at home all day and shall be at home in the evening. . . . Friends, won't you come this evening?

VERSHININ. Allow me to come too.

IRINA. Please do.

NATASHA. They don't stand on ceremony.

TCHEBUTYKIN. Nature our hearts for love created! [22] [*Laughs*]

ANDREY. [*Angrily*] Do leave off, I wonder you are not tired of it!

[FEDOTIK *and* RODDEY *come in with a big basket of flowers*]

FEDOTIK. I say, they are at lunch already.

RODDEY. [*Speaking loudly, with a lisp*] At lunch? Yes, they are at lunch already. . . .

FEDOTIK. Wait a minute. [*Takes a snapshot*] One! Wait another minute. . . . [*Takes another snapshot*] Two! Now it's ready. [*They take the basket and walk into the dining-room, where they are greeted noisily*]

RODDEY. [*Loudly*] My congratulations! I wish you everything, everything!

---

[21] A more intimate form of Natalya.   [22] See p. 406, note 14.

The weather is delightful, perfectly magnificent. I've been out all the morning for a walk with the high-school boys. I teach them gymnastics.

FEDOTIK. You may move, Irina Sergeyevna, you may move. [*Taking a photograph*] You look charming to-day. [*Taking a top out of his pocket*] Here
is a top, by the way. . . . It has a wonderful note. . . .

IRINA. How lovely!

MASHA. By the sea-shore an oak-tree green. . . . Upon that oak a chain of
gold [23]. . . . [*Complainingly*] Why do I keep saying that? That phrase
has been haunting me all day. . . .

KULIGIN. Thirteen at table!

RODDEY. [*Loudly*] Surely you do not attach importance to such superstitions?
[*Laughter*]

KULIGIN. If there are thirteen at table, it means that someone present is in love.
It's not you, Ivan Romanovitch,[24] by any chance? [*Laughter*]

TCHEBUTYKIN. I am an old sinner, but why Natalya Ivanovna is overcome, I
can't imagine . . .

[*Loud laughter;* NATASHA *runs out from the dining-room into the drawing-
room followed by* ANDREY]

ANDREY. Come, don't take any notice! Wait a minute . . . stop, I entreat
you. . . .

NATASHA. I am ashamed. . . . I don't know what's the matter with me and
they make fun of me. I know it's improper for me to leave the table like this,
but I can't help it. . . . I can't . . . [*Covers her face with her hands*]

ANDREY. My dear girl, I entreat you, I implore you, don't be upset. I assure you
they are only joking, they do it in all kindness. My dear, my sweet, they are
all kind, warm-hearted people and they are fond of me and of you. Come
here to the window, here they can't see us. . . . [*Looks round*]

NATASHA. I am so unaccustomed to society! . . .

ANDREY. Oh youth, lovely, marvellous youth! My dear, my sweet, don't be so
distressed! Believe me, believe me. . . . I feel so happy, my soul is full of
love and rapture. . . . Oh, they can't see us, they can't see us! Why, why,
I love you, when I first loved you—oh, I don't know. My dear, my sweet,
pure one, be my wife! I love you, I love you . . . as I have never loved
anyone. . . . [*A kiss*]

[*Two officers come in and, seeing the pair kissing, stop in amazement*]

[*Curtain*]

Act Two

*The same scene as in the First Act but several years later. Eight o'clock in the
evening. Behind the scenes in the street there is the faintly audible sound of a
concertina. There is no light.* NATALYA IVANOVNA *enters in a dressing-gown,
carrying a candle; she comes in and stops at the door leading to* ANDREY'S *room.*

[23] See p. 402, note 4.
[24] This word (or another form of it, Romanitch) is Tchebutykin's patronymic.

NATASHA.   What are you doing, Andryusha?[25] Reading? Never mind, I only just asked. . . . [*Goes and opens another door and, peeping into it, shuts it again*] Is there a light?

ANDREY.   [*Enters with a book in his hand*] What is it, Natasha?

NATASHA.   I was looking to see whether there was a light. . . . It's Carnival,[26] the servants are not themselves; one has always to be on the lookout for fear something goes wrong. Last night at twelve o'clock I passed through the dining-room, and there was a candle left burning. I couldn't find out who had lighted it. [*Puts down the candle*] What's the time?

ANDREY.   [*Looking at his watch*] A quarter past eight.

NATASHA.   And Olga and Irina aren't in yet. They haven't come in. Still at work, poor dears! Olga is at the teachers' council and Irina at the telegraph office. . . . [*Sighs*] I was saying to your sister this morning, "Take care of yourself, Irina darling," said I. But she won't listen. A quarter past eight, you say? I am afraid our Bobik[27] is not at all well. Why is he so cold? Yesterday he was feverish and to-day he is cold all over. . . . I am so anxious!

ANDREY.   It's all right, Natasha. The boy is quite well.

NATASHA.   We had better be careful about his food, anyway. I am anxious. And I am told that the mummers are going to be here for the Carnival at nine o'clock this evening. It would be better for them not to come, Andryusha.

ANDREY.   I really don't know. They've been invited, you know.

NATASHA.   Baby woke up this morning, looked at me, and all at once he gave a smile; so he knew me. "Good morning, Bobik!" said I. "Good morning, darling!" And he laughed. Children understand; they understand very well. So I shall tell them, Andryusha, not to let the carnival party come in.

ANDREY.   [*Irresolutely*] That's for my sisters to say. It's for them to give orders.

NATASHA.   Yes, for them too; I will speak to them. They are so kind. . . . [*Is going*] I've ordered junket for supper. The doctor says you must eat nothing but junket, or you will never get thinner. [*Stops*] Bobik is cold. I am afraid his room is chilly, perhaps. We ought to put him in a different room till the warm weather comes, anyway. Irina's room, for instance, is just right for a nursery: it's dry and the sun shines there all day. I must tell her; she might share Olga's room for the time. . . . She is never at home, anyway, except for the night. . . . [*A pause*] Andryushantchik,[28] why don't you speak?

ANDREY.   Nothing. I was thinking. . . . Besides. I have nothing to say.

NATASHA.   Yes . . . what was it I meant to tell you? . . . Oh, yes; Ferapont has come from the Rural Board, and is asking for you.

ANDREY.   [*Yawns*] Send him in.

[NATASHA *goes out;* ANDREY, *bending down to the candle which she has left behind, reads. Enter* FERAPONT; *he wears an old shabby overcoat with the collar turned up, and has a scarf over his ears*]

ANDREY.   Good evening, my good man. What is it?

FERAPONT.   The Chairman has sent a book and a paper of some sort here. . . . [*Gives the book and an envelope*]

ANDREY.   Thanks. Very good. But why have you come so late? It is past eight.

---

[25] The intimate form of Andrey, made by adding the diminutive -*yusha* to the noun.

[26] The week of merrymaking before Lent, which culminates in Mardi Gras.

[27] Their baby.   [28] An even more affectionate and loving form of Andrey than Andryusha.

FERAPONT. Eh?

ANDREY. [*Louder*] I say, you have come late. It is eight o'clock.

FERAPONT. Just so. I came before it was dark, but they wouldn't let me see you. The master is busy, they told me. Well, of course, if you are busy, I am in no hurry. [*Thinking that* ANDREY *has asked him a question*] Eh?

ANDREY. Nothing. [*Examines the book*] To-morrow is Friday. We haven't a sitting,[29] but I'll come all the same . . . and do my work. It's dull at home. . . . [*A pause*] Dear old man, how strangely life changes and deceives one! To-day I was so bored and had nothing to do, so I picked up this book—old university lectures—and I laughed. . . . Good heavens! I am the secretary of the Rural Board of which Protopopov is the chairman. I am the secretary, and the most I can hope for is to become a member of the Board! Me, a member of the local Rural Board, while I dream every night I am professor of the University of Moscow—a distinguished man, of whom all Russia is proud!

FERAPONT. I can't say, sir. . . . I don't hear well. . . .

ANDREY. If you did hear well, perhaps I should not talk to you. I must talk to somebody, and my wife does not understand me. My sisters I am somehow afraid of—I'm afraid they will laugh at me and make me ashamed. . . . I don't drink, I am not fond of restaurants, but how I should enjoy sitting at Tyestov's[30] in Moscow at this moment, dear old chap!

FERAPONT. A contractor was saying at the Board the other day that there were some merchants in Moscow eating pancakes; one who ate forty, it seems, died. It was either forty or fifty, I don't remember.

ANDREY. In Moscow you sit in a huge room at a restaurant; you know no one and no one knows you, and at the same time you don't feel a stranger. . . . But here you know everyone and everyone knows you, and yet you are a stranger—a stranger. . . . A stranger, and lonely. . . .

FERAPONT. Eh? [*A pause*] And the same contractor says—maybe it's not true that there's a rope stretched right across Moscow.

ANDREY. What for?

FERAPONT. I can't say, sir. The contractor said so.

ANDREY. Nonsense. [*Reads*] Have you ever been in Moscow?

FERAPONT. [*After a pause*] No, never. It was not God's will I should. [*A pause*] Am I to go?

ANDREY. You can go. Good-bye. [FERAPONT *goes out*] Good-bye. [*Reading*] Come to-morrow morning and take some papers here. . . . Go. . . . [*A pause*] He has gone. [*A ring*] Yes, it is a business. . . .

[*Stretches and goes slowly into his own room*]

[*Behind the scenes a nurse is singing, rocking a baby to sleep. Enter* MASHA *and* VERSHININ. *While they are talking a maidservant is lighting a lamp and candles in the dining-room*]

MASHA. I don't know. [*A pause*] I don't know. Of course habit does a great deal. After father's death, for instance, it was a long time before we could get used to having no orderlies[31] in the house. But apart from habit, I think it's

---

[29] A meeting of the Rural Board for which Andrey now works. The Rural Board is a kind of township council which governs the district. [30] A well-known Moscow restaurant.

[31] As a high-ranking officer, her father would, of course, have had orderlies around.

a feeling of justice makes me say so. Perhaps it is not so in other places, but in our town the most decent, honourable, and well-bred people are all in the army.

VERSHININ. I am thirsty. I should like some tea.

MASHA. [*Glancing at the clock*] They will soon be bringing it. I was married when I was eighteen, and I was afraid of my husband because he was a teacher, and I had only just left school. In those days I thought him an awfully learned, clever, and important person. And now it is not the same, unfortunately. . . .

VERSHININ. Yes. . . . I see. . . .

MASHA. I am not speaking of my husband—I am used to him; but among civilians generally there are so many rude, ill-mannered, badly-brought-up people. Rudeness upsets and distresses me: I am unhappy when I see that a man is not refined, not gentle, not polite enough. When I have to be among the teachers, my husband's colleagues, it makes me quite miserable.

VERSHININ. Yes. . . . But, to my mind, it makes no difference whether they are civilians or military men—they are equally uninteresting, in this town anyway. It's all the same! If one listens to a man of the educated class here, civilian or military, he is worried to death by his wife, worried to death by his house, worried to death by his estate, worried to death by his horses. . . . A Russian is peculiarly given to exalted ideas, but why is it he always falls so short in life? Why?

MASHA. Why?

VERSHININ. Why is he worried to death by his children and by his wife? And why are his wife and children worried to death by him?

MASHA. You are rather depressed this evening.

VERSHININ. Perhaps. . . . I've had no dinner to-day, and had nothing to eat since the morning. My daughter is not quite well, and when my little girls are ill I am consumed by anxiety; my conscience reproaches me for having given them such a mother. Oh, if you had seen her to-day! She is a wretched creature! We began quarrelling at seven o'clock in the morning, and at nine I slammed the door and went away. [*A pause*] I never talk about it. Strange, it's only to you I complain. [*Kisses her hand*] Don't be angry with me. . . . Except for you I have no one—no one. . . . [*A pause*]

MASHA. What a noise in the stove! Before father died there was howling in the chimney. There, just like that.

VERSHININ. Are you superstitious?

MASHA. Yes.

VERSHININ. That's strange. [*Kisses her hand*] You are a splendid, wonderful woman. Splendid! Wonderful! It's dark, but I see the light in your eyes.

MASHA. [*Moves to another chair*] It's lighter here.

VERSHININ. I love you—love, love. . . . I love your eyes, your movements, I see them in my dreams. . . . Splendid, wonderful woman!

MASHA. [*Laughing softly*] When you talk to me like that, for some reason I laugh, though I am frightened. . . . Please don't do it again. . . . [*In an undertone*] You may say it, though; I don't mind. . . . [*Covers her face with her hands*] I don't mind. . . . Someone is coming. Talk of something else.

[IRINA *and* TUSENBACH *come in through the dining-room*]

TUSENBACH.   I've got a three-barrelled name. My name is Baron Tusenbach-Krone-Altschauer, but I belong to the Orthodox Church and am just as Russian as you.[32] There is very little of the German left in me—nothing, perhaps, but the patience and perseverance with which I bore you. I see you home every evening.

IRINA.   How tired I am!

TUSENBACH.   And every day I will come to the telegraph office and see you home. I'll do it for ten years, for twenty years, till you drive me away. . . . [*Seeing* MASHA *and* VERSHININ, *delightedly*] Oh, it's you! How are you?

IRINA.   Well, I am home at last. [*To* MASHA] A lady came just now to telegraph to her brother in Saratov that her son died to-day, and she could not think of the address. So she sent it without an address—simply to Saratov. She was crying. And I was rude to her for no sort of reason. Told her I had no time to waste. It was so stupid. Are the Carnival people coming to-night?

MASHA.   Yes.

IRINA.   [*Sits down in an arm-chair*] I must rest. I am tired.

TUSENBACH.   [*With a smile*] When you come from the office you seem so young, so forlorn. . . . [*A pause*]

IRINA.   I am tired. No, I don't like telegraph work, I don't like it.

MASHA.   You've grown thinner. . . . [*Whistles*] And you look younger, rather like a boy in the face.

TUSENBACH.   That's the way she does her hair.

IRINA.   I must find some other job, this does not suit me. What I so longed for, what I dreamed of is the very thing that it's lacking in. . . . It is work without poetry, without meaning. . . . [*A knock on the floor*] There's the doctor[33] knocking. . . . [*To* TUSENBACH] Do knock, dear. . . . I can't. . . . I am tired.

[TUSENBACH *knocks on the floor*]

IRINA.   He will come directly. We ought to do something about it. The doctor and our Andrey were at the Club yesterday and they lost again. I am told Andrey lost two hundred roubles.

MASHA.   [*Indifferently*] Well, it can't be helped now.

IRINA.   A fortnight ago he lost money, in December he lost money. I wish he'd make haste and lose everything, then perhaps we should go away from this town. My God, every night I dream of Moscow, it's perfect madness. [*Laughs*] We'll move there in June and there is still left February, March, April, May . . . almost half a year.

MASHA.   The only thing is Natasha must not hear of his losses.

IRINA.   I don't suppose she cares.

[TCHEBUTYKIN, *who has only just got off his bed—he has been resting after dinner—comes into the dining-room combing his beard, then sits down to the table and takes a newspaper out of his pocket*]

MASHA.   Here he is . . . has he paid his rent?

IRINA.   [*Laughs*] No. Not a kopek for eight months. Evidently he has forgotten.

---

[32] Again Tusenbach is harping on his being a genuine Russian, in spite of his name. The Orthodox Church is the Russian Orthodox church, to which the great majority of Russians belong.   [33] Tchebutykin, who lives in the Prozorov household.

MASHA. [*Laughs*] How gravely he sits. [*They all laugh; a pause*]

IRINA. Why are you so quiet, Alexandr Ignatyevitch?

VERSHININ. I don't know. I am longing for tea. I'd give half my life for a glass of tea. I have had nothing to eat since the morning.

TCHEBUTYKIN. Irina Sergeyevna!

IRINA. What is it?

TCHEBUTYKIN. Come here. *Venez ici.*[34] [IRINA *goes and sits down at the table*] I can't do without you. [IRINA *lays out the cards for patience*[35]]

VERSHININ. Well if they won't bring tea, let us discuss something.

TUSENBACH. By all means. What?

VERSHININ. What? Let us dream . . . for instance of the life that will come after us, in two or three hundred years.

TUSENBACH. Well? When we are dead, men will fly in balloons, change the fashion of their coats, will discover a sixth sense, perhaps, and develop it, but life will remain just the same, difficult, full of mysteries and happiness. In a thousand years man will sigh just the same, "Ah, how hard life is," and yet just as now he will be afraid of death and not want it.

VERSHININ. [*After a moment's thought*] Well, I don't know. . . . It seems to me that everything on earth is bound to change by degrees and is already changing before our eyes. In two or three hundred, perhaps in a thousand years—the time does not matter—a new, happy life will come. We shall have no share in that life, of course, but we are living for it, we are working, well, yes, and suffering for it, we are creating it—and that alone is the purpose of our existence, and is our happiness, if you like.

[MASHA *laughs softly*]

TUSENBACH. What is it?

MASHA. I don't know. I've been laughing all day.

VERSHININ. I was at the same school as you were, I did not go to the Military Academy; I read a great deal, but I do not know how to choose my books, and very likely I read quite the wrong things, and yet the longer I live the more I want to know. My hair is turning grey, I am almost an old man, but I know so little, oh, so little! But all the same I fancy that I do know and thoroughly grasp what is essential and matters most. And how I should like to make you see that there is no happiness for us, that there ought not be and will not be. . . . We must work and work, and happiness is the portion of our remote descendants. [*A pause*] If it is not for me, at least it is for the descendants of my descendants. . . .

[FEDOTIK *and* RODDEY *appear in the dining-room; they sit down and sing softly, playing the guitar*]

TUSENBACH. You think it's no use even dreaming of happiness! But what if I am happy?

VERSHININ. No.

TUSENBACH. [*Flinging up his hands and laughing*] It is clear we don't understand each other. Well, how am I to convince you?

[MASHA *laughs softly*]

TUSENBACH. [*Holds up a finger to her*] Laugh! [*To* VERSHININ] Not only in

---

[34] "Come here." The upper classes in Russia before the Revolution spoke a good deal of French.   [35] A card game, a form of solitaire.

two or three hundred years but in a million years life will be just the same; it does not change, it remains stationary, following its own laws which we have nothing to do with or which, anyway, we shall never find out. Migratory birds, cranes for instance, fly backwards and forwards, and whatever ideas, great or small, stray through their minds, they still go on flying just the same without knowing where or why. They fly and will continue to fly, however philosophic they may become; and it doesn't matter how philosophical they are so long as they go on flying. . . .

MASHA. But still there is a meaning?

TUSENBACH. Meaning. . . . Here it is snowing. What meaning is there in that? [*A pause*]

MASHA. I think man ought to have faith or ought to seek a faith, or else his life is empty, empty. . . . To live and not to understand why cranes fly; why children are born; why there are stars in the sky. . . . One must know what one is living for or else it is all nonsense and waste. [*A pause*]

VERSHININ. And yet one is sorry that youth is over. . . .

MASHA. Gogol [36] says: It's dull living in this world, friends!

TUSENBACH. And I say: it is difficult to argue with you, my friends, God bless you. . . .

TCHEBUTYKIN. [*Reading the newspaper*] Balzac[37] was married at Berditchev.[38] [IRINA *hums softly*]

TCHEBUTYKIN. I really must put that down in my book [*Writes*] Balzac was married at Berditchev. [*Reads the paper*]

IRINA. [*Lays out the cards for patience, dreamily*] Balzac was married at Berditchev.

TUSENBACH. The die is cast. You know, Marya Sergeyevna, I've resigned my commission.

MASHA. So I hear. And I see nothing good in that. I don't like civilians.

TUSENBACH. Never mind. . . . [*Gets up*] I am not good-looking enough for a soldier. But that does not matter, though . . . I am going to work. If only for one day in my life, to work so that I come home at night tired out and fall asleep as soon as I get into bed. . . . [*Going into the dining-room*] Workmen must sleep soundly!

FEDOTIK. [*To* IRINA] I bought these chalks for you just now as I passed the shop. . . . And this penknife. . . .

IRINA. You've got into the way of treating me as though I were little, but I am grown up, you know. . . . [*Takes the chalks and the penknife, joyfully*] How lovely!

FEDOTIK. And I bought a knife for myself . . . look . . . one blade, and another blade, a third, and this is for the ears, and here are scissors, and that's for cleaning the nails. . . .

RODDEY. [*Loudly*] Doctor, how old are you?

TCHEBUTYKIN. I? Thirty-two. [*Laughter*]

FEDOTIK. I'll show you another game of patience. . . . [*Lays out the cards*] [*The samovar is brought in;* ANFISA *is at the samovar; a little later*

---

[36] The great Russian novelist (1809-1852).

[37] The great French realistic novelist (1799-1850) who married the Polish-Russian Countess, Evelina Hanska, a few months before he died.   [38] A town in southern Russia (the Ukraine).

NATASHA *comes in and is also busy at the table;* SOLYONY *comes in, and after greeting the others sits down at the table*]

VERSHININ. What a wind there is!

MASHA. Yes, I am sick of the winter. I've forgotten what summer is like.

IRINA. It's coming out right, I see.[39] We shall go to Moscow.

FEDOTIK. No, it's not coming out. You see, the eight is over the two of spades. [*Laughs*] So that means you won't go to Moscow.

TCHEBUTYKIN. [*Reads from the newspaper*] Tsi-tsi-kar.[40] Smallpox is raging here.

ANFISA. [*Going up to* MASHA] Masha, come to tea, my dear. [*To* VERSHININ] Come, your honour . . . excuse me, sir, I have forgotten your name. . . .

MASHA. Bring it here, nurse, I am not going there.

IRINA. Nurse!

ANFISA. I am coming!

NATASHA. [*To* SOLYONY] Little babies understand very well. "Good morning, Bobik, good morning, darling," I said. He looked at me in quite a special way. You think I say that because I am a mother, but no, I assure you! He is an extraordinary child.

SOLYONY. If that child were mine, I'd fry him in a frying-pan and eat him.

[*Takes his glass,*[41] *comes into the drawing-room and sits down in a corner*]

NATASHA. [*Covers her face with her hands*] Rude, ill-bred man!

MASHA. Happy people don't notice whether it is winter or summer. I fancy if I lived in Moscow I should not mind what the weather was like. . . .

VERSHININ. The other day I was reading the diary of a French minister written in prison. The minister was condemned for the Panama affair.[42] With what enthusiasm and delight he describes the birds he sees from the prison window, which he never noticed before when he was a minister. Now that he is released, of course he notices birds no more than he did before. In the same way, you won't notice Moscow when you live in it. We have no happiness and never do have, we only long for it.

TUSENBACH. [*Takes a box from the table*] What has become of the candy?

IRINA. Solyony has eaten it.

TUSENBACH. All?

ANFISA. [*Handing tea*] There's a letter for you, sir.

VERSHININ. For me? [*Takes the letter*] From my daughter. [*Reads*] Yes, of course. . . . Excuse me, Marya Sergeyevna, I'll slip away. I won't have tea. [*Gets up in agitation*] Always these upsets. . . .

MASHA. What is it? Not a secret?

VERSHININ. [*In a low voice*] My wife has taken poison again. I must go. I'll slip off unnoticed. Horribly unpleasant it all is. [*Kisses* MASHA'S *hand*] My fine, dear, splendid woman. . . . I'll go this way without being seen. . . . [*Goes out*]

ANFISA. Where is he off to? I've just given him his tea. . . . What a man.

---

[39] Irina is looking at the cards.   [40] Tsitsihar, a town in Manchuria.

[41] Russians drink tea out of glasses.

[42] No doubt one of the many scandals connected with the French attempt (1878-1902) to construct the Panama Canal.

MASHA. [*Getting angry*] Leave off! Don't pester, you give one no peace. . . .
[*Goes with her cup to the table*] You bother me, old lady.

ANFISA. Why are you so huffy? Darling!

[ANDREY's *voice:* Anfisa!]

ANFISA. [*Mimicking*] Anfisa! he sits there. . . . [*Goes out*]

MASHA. [*By the table in the dining-room, angrily*] Let me sit down! [*Mixes
the cards on the table*] You take up all the table with your cards. Drink
your tea!

IRINA. How cross you are, Masha!

MASHA. If I'm cross, don't talk to me. Don't interfere with me.

TCHEBUTYKIN. [*Laughing*] Don't touch her, don't touch her!

MASHA. You are sixty, but you talk rot like a schoolboy.

NATASHA. [*Sighs*] Dear Masha, why make use of such expressions in conversation? With your attractive appearance I tell you straight out, you would be
simply fascinating in a well-bred social circle if it were not for the things
you say. *Je vous prie, pardonnez-moi, Marie, mais vous avez des manières un
peu grossières.*[43]

TUSENBACH. [*Suppressing a laugh*] Give me . . . give me . . . I think there
is some brandy there.

NATASHA. *Il paraît que mon Bobik déjà ne dort pas,*[44] he is awake. He is not
well to-day. I must go to him, excuse me. . . . [*Goes out*]

IRINA. Where has Alexandr Ignatyevitch gone?

MASHA. Home. Something queer with his wife again.

TUSENBACH. [*Goes up to* SOLYONY *with a decanter of brandy in his hand*]
You always sit alone, thinking, and there's no making out what you think
about. Come, let us make it up. Let us have a drink of brandy. [*They drink*]
I shall have to play the piano all night, I suppose, play all sorts of trash. . . .
Here goes!

SOLYONY. Why make it up? I haven't quarrelled with you.

TUSENBACH. You always make me feel as though something had gone wrong
between us. You are a queer character, there's no denying that.

SOLYONY. [*Declaims*] I am strange, who is not strange! Be not wroth, Aleko![45]

TUSENBACH. I don't see what Aleko has got to do with it. . . .

SOLYONY. When I am *tête-à-tête* with somebody, I am all right, just like anyone else, but in company I am depressed, ill at ease and . . . say all sorts
of idiotic things, but at the same time I am more conscientious and straightforward than many. And I can prove it. . . .

TUSENBACH. I often feel angry with you, you are always attacking me when
we are in company, and yet I somehow like you. Here goes, I am going to
drink a lot to-day. Let's drink!

SOLYONY. Let us. [*Drinks*] I have never had anything against you, Baron. But
I have the temperament of Lermontov.[46] [*In a low voice*] In fact I am

[43] "Excuse me, Masha, but you have somewhat coarse manners." Again the affectation of
using French by the pre-Revolutionary Russian upper classes (or by those hoping to be taken as
members of the upper classes).   [44] "It seems that my Bobik isn't asleep yet."

[45] A quotation from Pushkin.

[46] The Russian poet (1814-1841) of Scottish ancestry, usually considered second only to
Pushkin in literary greatness. He resembled Byron in temperament, and hence the reference
here is to the Byronic character (a mixture of pride, cynicism, irony and remorse).

rather like Lermontov to look at . . . so I am told. [*Takes out scent-bottle and sprinkles scent on his hands*]

TUSENBACH.   I have sent in my papers.[47] I've had enough of it! I have been thinking of it for five years and at last I have come up to the scratch. I am going to work.

SOLYONY.   [*Declaims*]   Be not wroth, Aleko. . . . Forget, forget thy dreams. . . .

[*While they are talking* ANDREY *comes in quietly with a book and sits down by a candle*]

TUSENBACH.   I am going to work.

TCHEBUTYKIN.   [*Coming into the drawing-room with* IRINA] And the food too was real Caucasian[48] stuff: onion soup and for the meat course *tchehartma*. . . .

SOLYONY.   *Tcheremsha* is not meat at all, it's a plant rather like our onion.

TCHEBUTYKIN.   No, my dear soul, it's not onion, but mutton roasted in a special way.

SOLYONY.   But I tell you that *tcheremsha* is an onion.

TCHEBUTYKIN.   And I tell you that *tchehartma* is mutton.

SOLYONY.   And I tell you that *tcheremsha* is an onion.

TCHEBUTYKIN.   What's the use of my arguing with you? You have never been to the Caucasus or eaten *tchehartma*.

SOLYONY.   I haven't eaten it because I can't bear it. *Tcheremsha* smells like garlic.

ANDREY.   [*Imploringly*] That's enough! Please!

TUSENBACH.   When are the Carnival party coming?

IRINA.   They promised to come at nine, so they will be here directly.

TUSENBACH.   [*Embraces* ANDREY *and sings*] "Oh my porch, oh my new porch . . ."

ANDREY.   [*Dances and sings*] "With posts of maple wood. . . ."

TCHEBUTYKIN.   [*Dances*] "And lattice work complete. . . ." [*Laughter*]

TUSENBACH.   [*Kisses* ANDREY] Hang it all, let us have a drink. Andryusha, let us drink to our everlasting friendship. I'll go to the University when you do, Andryusha.

SOLYONY.   Which? There are two universities in Moscow.

ANDREY.   There is only one university in Moscow.

SOLYONY.   I tell you there are two.

ANDREY.   There may be three for aught I care. So much the better.

SOLYONY.   There are two universities in Moscow! [*A murmur and hisses*] There are two universities in Moscow: the old one and the new one. And if you don't care to hear, if what I say irritates you, I can keep quiet. I can even go into another room. [*Goes out at one of the doors*]

TUSENBACH.   Bravo, bravo! [*Laughs*] Friends, begin, I'll sit down and play! Funny fellow that Solyony. . . . [*Sits down to the piano and plays a waltz*]

MASHA.   [*Dances a waltz alone*] The baron is drunk, the baron is drunk, the baron is drunk.

[*Enter* NATASHA]

[47] To resign from the army.
[48] In the style of the peoples of the Caucasian district of Russia.

NATASHA. [*To* TCHEBUTYKIN] Ivan Romanitch! [*Says something to* TCHE-BUTYKIN, *then goes out softly.* TCHEBUTYKIN *touches* TUSENBACH *on the shoulder and whispers something to him*]

IRINA. What is it?

TCHEBUTYKIN. It's time we were going. Good night.

TUSENBACH. Good night. It's time to be going.

IRINA. But I say . . . what about the Carnival party?

ANDREY. [*With embarrassment*] They won't be coming. You see, dear, Natasha says Bobik is not well, and so . . . In fact I know nothing about it, and don't care either.

IRINA. [*Shrugs her shoulders*] Bobik is not well!

MASHA. Well, it's not the first time we've had to lump it! If we are turned out, we must go. [*To* IRINA] It's not Bobik that is ill, but she is a bit. . . . [*Taps her forehead with her finger*] Petty, vulgar creature!

[ANDREY *goes by door on right to his own room,* TCHEBUTYKIN *following him; they are saying good-bye in the dining-room*]

FEDOTIK. What a pity! I was meaning to spend the evening, but of course if the child is ill . . . I'll bring him a toy to-morrow.

RODDEY. [*Loudly*] I had a nap to-day after dinner on purpose, I thought I would be dancing all night. . . . Why, it's only nine o'clock.

MASHA. Let us go into the street; there we can talk. We'll decide what to do.

[*Sounds of* "Good-bye! Good night!" *The good-humored laugh of* TUSEN-BACH *is heard. All go out.* ANFISA *and the maidservant clear the table and put out the light. There is the sound of the nurse singing.* ANDREY *in his hat and coat, and* TCHEBUTYKIN *come in quietly*]

TCHEBUTYKIN. I never had time to get married, because life has flashed by like lightning and because I was passionately in love with your mother, who was married.

ANDREY. One shouldn't get married. One shouldn't, because it's boring.

TCHEBUTYKIN. That's all very well, but what about loneliness? Say what you like, it's a dreadful thing to be lonely, my dear boy. . . . But no matter, though!

ANDREY. Let's make haste and go.

TCHEBUTYKIN. What's the hurry? We have plenty of time.

ANDREY. I am afraid my wife may stop me.

TCHEBUTYKIN. Oh!

ANDREY. I am not going to play to-day, I shall just sit and look on. I don't feel well. . . . What am I to do, Ivan Romanitch, I am so short of breath?

TCHEBUTYKIN. It's no use asking me! I don't remember, dear boy. . . . I don't know. . . .

ANDREY. Let us go through the kitchen.

[*They go out*]

[*A ring, then another ring; there is a sound of voices and laughter*]

IRINA. [*Enters*] What is it?

ANFISA. [*In a whisper*] The mummers, all dressed up. [*A ring*]

IRINA. Nurse, dear, say there is no one at home. They must excuse us.

[ANFISA *goes out.* IRINA *walks about the room in hesitation; she is excited. Enter* SOLYONY]

SOLYONY. [*In perplexity*] No one here. . . . Where are they all?

IRINA. They have gone home.

SOLYONY. How queer. Are you alone here?

IRINA. Yes. [*A pause*] Good night.

SOLYONY. I behaved tactlessly, without sufficient restraint just now. But you are not like other people, you are pure and lofty, you see the truth. You alone can understand me. I love you, I love you deeply, infinitely.

IRINA. Good night! You must go.

SOLYONY. I can't live without you. [*Following her*] Oh, my bliss! [*Through his tears*] Oh, happiness! Those glorious, exquisite, marvellous eyes such as I have never seen in any other woman.

IRINA. [*Coldly*] Don't, Vassily Vassilyitch!

SOLYONY. For the first time I am speaking of love to you, and I feel as though I were not on earth but on another planet. [*Rubs his forehead*] But there, it does not matter. There is no forcing kindness, of course. . . . But there must be no happy rivals. . . . There must not. . . . I swear by all that is sacred I will kill any rival. . . . O exquisite being!

[NATASHA *passes with a candle*]

NATASHA. [*Peeps in at one door, then at another and passes by the door that leads to her husband's room*] Andrey is there. Let him read. Excuse me, Vassily Vassilyitch, I did not know you were here, and I am in my dressing-gown. . . .

SOLYONY. I don't care. Good-bye!

[*Goes out*]

NATASHA. You are tired, my poor, dear little girl! [*Kisses* IRINA] You ought to go to bed earlier. . . .

IRINA. Is Bobik asleep?

NATASHA. He is asleep, but not sleeping quietly. By the way, dear, I keep meaning to speak to you, but either you are out or else I haven't the time. . . . I think Bobik's nursery is cold and damp. And your room is so nice for a baby. My sweet, my dear, you might move for a time into Olya's room!

IRINA. [*Not understanding*] Where?

[*The sound of a three-horse sledge with bells driving up to the door*]

NATASHA. You would be in the same room with Olya, and Bobik in your room. He is such a poppet. I said to him to-day, "Bobik, you are mine, you are mine!" and he looked at me with his funny little eyes. [*A ring*] That must be Olya. How late she is!

[*The maid comes up to* NATASHA *and whispers in her ear*]

NATASHA. Protopopov? What a queer fellow he is! Protopopov has come, and asks me to go out with him in his sledge. [*Laughs*] How strange men are! . . . [*A ring*] Somebody has come. I might go for a quarter of an hour. . . . [*To the maid*] Tell him I'll come directly. [*A ring*] You hear . . . it must be Olya. [*Goes out*]

[*The maid runs out;* IRINA *sits lost in thought;* KULIGIN, OLGA *and* VERSHININ *come in*]

KULIGIN. Well, this is a surprise! They said they were going to have an evening party.

VERSHININ. Strange! And when I went away half an hour ago they were expecting the Carnival people. . . .

IRINA. They have all gone.

KULIGIN. Has Masha gone too? Where has she gone? And why is Protopopov waiting below with his sledge? Whom is he waiting for?

IRINA. Don't ask questions. . . . I am tired.

KULIGIN. Oh, you little cross-patch. . . .

OLGA. The meeting is only just over. I am tired out. Our headmistress is ill and I have to take her place. Oh, my head, my head does ache; oh, my head! [*Sits down*] Andrey lost two hundred roubles yesterday at cards. . . . The whole town is talking about it. . . .

KULIGIN. Yes, I am tired out by the meeting too. [*Sits down*]

VERSHININ. My wife took it into her head to give me a fright, she nearly poisoned herself. It's all right now, and I'm glad, it's a relief. . . . So we are to go away? Very well, then, I will say good night. Fyodor Ilyitch, let us go somewhere together! I can't stay at home, I absolutely can't. . . . Come along!

KULIGIN. I am tired. I am not coming. [*Gets up*] I am tired. Has my wife gone home?

IRINA. I expect so.

KULIGIN. [*Kisses* IRINA's *hand*] Good-bye! I have all day to-morrow and next day to rest. Good night! [*Going*] I do want some tea. I was reckoning on spending the evening in pleasant company. . . . *O fallacem hominum spem!* [49] . . . Accusative of exclamation.

VERSHININ. Well, then, I must go alone. [*Goes out with* KULIGIN, *whistling*]

OLGA. My head aches, oh, how my head aches. . . . Andrey has lost at cards. . . . The whole town is talking about it. . . . I'll go and lie down. [*Is going*] To-morrow I shall be free. . . . Oh, goodness, how nice that is! To-morrow I am free, and the day after I am free. . . . My head does ache, oh, my head. . . . [*Goes out*]

IRINA. [*Alone*] They have all gone away. There is no one left.

[*A concertina plays in the street, the nurse sings*]

NATASHA. [*In a fur cap and coat crosses the dining-room, followed by the maid*] I shall be back in half an hour. I shall only go a little way. [*Goes out*]

IRINA. [*Left alone, in dejection*] Oh, to go to Moscow, to Moscow!

[*Curtain*]

Act Three

The bedroom of OLGA *and* IRINA *a year or so later. On left and right beds with screens round them. Past two o'clock in the night. Behind the scenes a bell is ringing on account of a fire in the town, which has been going on for some time. It can be seen that no one in the house has gone to bed yet. On the sofa* MASHA *is lying, dressed as usual in black. Enter* OLGA *and* ANFISA.

---

[49] "O treacherous hope of men."

ANFISA. They are sitting below, under the stairs. . . . I said to them, "Come upstairs; why, you mustn't stay there"—they only cried. "We don't know where father is," they said. "What if he is burnt!" What an idea! And the poor souls in the yard . . . they are all undressed too.

OLGA. [*Taking clothes out of the cupboard*] Take this grey dress . . . and this one . . . and the blouse too . . . and that skirt, nurse. . . . Oh, dear, what a dreadful thing! Kirsanov Street is burnt to the ground, it seems. . . . Take this . . . take this. . . . [*Throws clothes into her arms*] The Vershinins have had a fright, poor things. . . . Their house was very nearly burnt. Let them stay the night here . . . we can't let them go home. . . . Poor Fedotik has had everything burnt, he has not a thing left. . . .

ANFISA. You had better call Ferapon, Olya darling, I can't carry it all.

OLGA. [*Rings*] No one will answer the bell. [*At the door*] Come here, whoever is there! [*Through the open door can be seen a window red with fire; the fire brigade is heard passing the house*] How awful it is! And how sickening! [*Enter* FERAPONT]

OLGA. Here take these, carry them downstairs. . . . The Kolotilin young ladies are downstairs . . . give it to them . . . and give this too.

FERAPONT. Yes, miss. In 1812 Moscow was burnt too.[50] . . . Mercy on us! The French marvelled.

OLGA. You can go now.

FERAPONT. Yes, miss.

[*Goes out*]

OLGA. Nurse darling, give them everything. We don't want anything, give it all to them. . . . I am tired, I can hardly stand on my feet. . . . We mustn't let the Vershinins go home. . . . The little girls can sleep in the drawing-room, and Alexandr Ignatyevitch down below at the baron's. . . . Fedotik can go to the baron's, too, or sleep in our dining-room. . . . As ill-luck will have it, the doctor[51] is drunk, frightfully drunk, and no one can be put in his room. And Vershinin's wife can be in the drawing-room too.

ANFISA. [*Wearily*] Olya darling, don't send me away; don't send me away!

OLGA. That's nonsense, nurse. No one is sending you away.

ANFISA. [*Lays her head on* OLGA's *shoulder*] My own, my treasure, I work, I do my best. . . . I'm getting weak, everyone will say "Be off!" And where am I to go? Where? I am eighty. Eighty-one.

OLGA. Sit down, nurse darling. . . . You are tired, poor thing. . . . [*Makes her sit down*] Rest, dear good nurse. . . . How pale you are!

[*Enter* NATASHA]

NATASHA. They are saying we must form a committee at once for the assistance of those whose houses have been burnt. Well, that's a good idea. Indeed, one ought always to be ready to help the poor, it's the duty of the rich. Bobik and baby Sophie[52] are both asleep, sleeping as though nothing were happening. There are such a lot of people everywhere, wherever one goes, the house is full. There is influenza in the town now; I am so afraid the children may get it.

OLGA. [*Not listening*] In this room one does not see the fire, it's quiet here.

---

[50] A reference to the famous burning of Moscow after it fell to Napoleon in 1812.
[51] Tchebutykin.   [52] A second child.

NATASHA. Yes . . . my hair must be untidy. [*In front of the looking-glass*] They say I have grown fatter . . . but it's not true! Not a bit! Masha is asleep, she is tired out, poor dear. . . . [*To* ANFISA *coldly*] Don't dare to sit down in my presence! Get up! Go out of the room! [ANFISA *goes out; a pause*] Why you keep that old woman, I can't understand!

OLGA. [*Taken aback*] Excuse me, I don't understand either. . . .

NATASHA. She is no use here. She is a peasant; she ought to be in the country. . . . You spoil people! I like order in the house! There ought to be no useless servants in the house. [*Strokes her cheek*] You are tired, poor darling. Our headmistress is tired! When baby Sophie is a big girl and goes to the high-school, I shall be afraid of you.

OLGA. I shan't be headmistress.

NATASHA. You will be elected, Olya. That's a settled thing.

OLGA. I shall refuse. I can't. . . . It's too much for me. . . . [*Drinks water*] You were so rude to nurse just now. . . . Excuse me, I can't endure it. . . . It makes me feel faint.

NATASHA. [*Perturbed*] Forgive me, Olya; forgive me. . . . I did not mean to hurt your feelings.

[MASHA *gets up, takes her pillow, and goes out in a rage*]

OLGA. You must understand, my dear, it may be that we have been strangely brought up, but I can't endure it. . . . Such an attitude oppresses me, it makes me ill. . . . I feel simply unnerved by it. . . .

NATASHA. Forgive me; forgive me. . . . [*Kisses her*]

OLGA. The very slightest rudeness, a tactless word, upsets me. . . .

NATASHA. I often say too much, that's true, but you must admit, dear, that she might just as well be in the country.

OLGA. She has been thirty years with us.

NATASHA. But now she can't work! Either I don't understand, or you won't understand me. She is not fit for work. She does nothing but sleep or sit still.

OLGA. Well, let her sit still.

NATASHA. [*Surprised*] How, sit still? Why, she is a servant. [*Through tears*] I don't understand you, Olya. I have a nurse to look after the children as well as a wet nurse for baby, and we have a housemaid and a cook, what do we want that old woman for? What's the use of her?

[*The alarm bell rings behind the scenes*]

OLGA. This night has made me ten years older.

NATASHA. We must come to an understanding, Olya. You are at the high-school, I am at home; you are teaching while I look after the house, and if I say anything about the servants, I know what I'm talking about; I do know what I am talking about. . . . And that old thief, that old hag . . . , [*Stamps*] that old witch shall clear out of the house to-morrow! . . . I won't have people annoy me! I won't have it! [*Feeling that she has gone too far*] Really, if you don't move downstairs, we shall always be quarrelling. It's awful.

[*Enter* KULIGIN]

KULIGIN. Where is Masha? It's time to be going home. The fire is dying down, so they say. [*Stretches*] Only one part of the town has been burnt, and yet there was a wind; it seemed at first as though the whole town would be de-

stroyed. [*Sits down*] I am exhausted. Olya, my dear . . . I often think if
it had not been for Masha I should have married you. You are so good. . . .
I am tired out. [*Listens*]

OLGA. What is it?

KULIGIN. It is unfortunate the doctor should have a drinking bout just now;
he is helplessly drunk. Most unfortunate. [*Gets up*] Here he comes, I do believe. . . . Do you hear? Yes, he is coming this way. . . . [*Laughs*] What a
man he is, really. . . . I shall hide. [*Goes to the cupboard and stands in the
corner*] Isn't he a ruffian!

OLGA. He has not drunk for two years and now he has gone and done it. . . .
[*Walks away with* NATASHA *to the back of the room*]

[TCHEBUTYKIN *comes in; walking as though sober without staggering, he
walks across the room, stops, looks round; then goes up to the washing-stand
and begins to wash his hands*]

TCHEBUTYKIN. [*Morosely*] The devil take them all . . . damn them all. They
think I am a doctor, that I can treat all sorts of complaints, and I really
know nothing about it, I have forgotten all I did know, I remember nothing,
absolutely nothing. [OLGA *and* NATASHA *go out unnoticed by him*] The devil
take them. Last Wednesday treated a woman at Zasyp—she died, and it's
my fault that she died. Yes . . . I did know something twenty-five years
ago, but now I remember nothing, nothing. Perhaps I am not a man at all
but only pretend to have arms and legs and head; perhaps I don't exist at
all and only fancy that I walk about, eat and sleep. [*Weeps*] Oh, if only I
did not exist! [*Leaves off weeping, morosely*] I don't care! I don't care a
scrap! [*A pause*] Goodness knows. . . . The day before yesterday there was
a conversation at the club: they talked about Shakespeare, Voltaire. . . . I
have read nothing, nothing at all, but I looked as though I had read them.
And the others did the same as I did. The vulgarity! The meanness! And
that woman I killed on Wednesday came back to my mind . . . and it all
came back to my mind and everything seemed nasty, disgusting and all awry
in my soul. . . . I went and got drunk. . . .

[*Enter* IRINA, VERSHININ *and* TUSENBACH; TUSENBACH *is wearing a fashionable new civilian suit*[53]]

IRINA. Let us sit here. No one will come here.

VERSHININ. If it had not been for the soldiers, the whole town would have been
burnt down. Splendid fellows! [*Rubs his hands with pleasure*] They are first-
rate men! Splendid fellows!

KULIGIN. [*Going up to them*] What time is it?

TUSENBACH. It's past three. It's getting light already.

IRINA. They are all sitting in the dining-room. No one seems to think of going.
And that Solyony of yours is sitting there too. . . . [*To* TCHEBUTYKIN]
You had better go to bed, doctor.

TCHEBUTYKIN. It's all right. . . . Thank you! [*Combs his beard*]

KULIGIN. [*Laughs*] You are a bit fuddled, Ivan Romanitch! [*Slaps him on the
shoulder*] Bravo! *In vino veritas*[54] the ancients used to say.

[53] Tusenbach has carried out his intention and is now out of the army.
[54] "In wine is truth."

TUSENBACH. Everyone is asking me to get up a concert for the benefit of the families whose houses have been burnt down.

IRINA. Why, who is there? . . .

TUSENBACH. We could get it up, if we wanted to. Marya[55] Sergeyevna plays the piano splendidly, to my thinking.

KULIGIN. Yes, she plays splendidly.

IRINA. She has forgotten. She has not played for three . . . or four years.

TUSENBACH. There is absolutely no one who understands music in this town, not one soul, but I do understand and on my honour I assure you that Marya Sergeyevna plays magnificently, almost with genius.

KULIGIN. You are right, Baron. I am very fond of her; Masha, I mean. She is a good sort.

TUSENBACH. To be able to play so gloriously and to know that no one understands you!

KULIGIN. [*Sighs*] Yes. . . . But would it be suitable for her to take part in a concert? [*A pause*] I know nothing about it, my friends. Perhaps it would be all right. There is no denying that our director[56] is a fine man, indeed a very fine man, very intelligent, but he has such views. . . . Of course it is not his business, still if you like I'll speak to him about it.

[TCHEBUTYKIN *takes up a china clock and examines it*]

VERSHININ. I got dirty all over at the fire. I am a sight. [*A pause*] I heard a word dropped yesterday about our brigade being transferred ever so far away. Some say to Poland, and others to Tchita.[57]

TUSENBACH. I've heard something about it too. Well! The town will be a wilderness then.

IRINA. We shall go away too.

TCHEBUTYKIN. [*Drops the clock, which smashes*] To smithereens!

KULIGIN. [*Picking up the pieces*] To smash such a valuable thing—oh, Ivan Romanitch, Ivan Romanitch! I should give you minus zero for conduct!

IRINA. That was mother's clock.

TCHEBUTYKIN. Perhaps. . . . Well, if it was hers, it was. Perhaps I did not smash it, but it only seems as though I had. Perhaps it only seems to us that we exist, but really we are not here at all. I don't know anything—nobody knows anything. [*By the door*] What are you staring at? Natasha has got a little affair on with Protopopov, and you don't see it. . . . You sit here and see nothing, while Natasha has a little affair on with Protopopov. . . . [*Sings*] May I offer you this date? . . .

[*Goes out*]

VERSHININ. Yes. . . . [*Laughs*] How very queer it all is, really! [*A pause*] When the fire began I ran home as fast as I could. I went up and saw our house was safe and sound and out of danger, but my little girls were standing in the doorway in their nightgowns; their mother was nowhere to be seen, people were bustling about, horses and dogs were running about, and my children's faces were full of alarm, horror, entreaty, and I don't know what; it wrung my heart to see their faces. My God, I thought, what more

---

[55] Masha. [56] Kuligin's superior in the school system. [57] A city in southeastern Siberia.

have these children to go through in the long years to come! I took their hands and ran along with them, and could think of nothing else but what more they would have to go through in this world! [*A pause*] When I came to your house I found their mother here, screaming, angry.

[MASHA *comes in with the pillow and sits down on the sofa*]

VERSHININ.   And while my little girls were standing in the doorway in their nightgowns and the street was red with the fire, and there was a fearful noise, I thought that something like it used to happen years ago when the enemy would suddenly make a raid and begin plundering and burning. . . . And yet, in reality, what a difference there is between what is now and has been in the past! And when a little more time has passed—another two or three hundred years—people will look at our present manner of life with horror and derision, and everything of to-day will seem awkward and heavy, and very strange and uncomfortable. Oh, what a wonderful life that will be —what a wonderful life! [*Laughs*] Forgive me, here I am airing my theories again! Allow me to go on. I have such a desire to talk about the future. I am in the mood. [*A pause*] It's as though everyone were asleep. And so, I say, what a wonderful life it will be! Can you only imagine? . . . Here there are only three of your sort in the town now, but in generations to come there will be more and more and more; and the time will come when everything will be changed and be as you would have it; they will live in your way, and later on you too will be out of date—people will be born who will be better than you. . . . [*Laughs*] I am in such a strange state of mind to-day. I have a fiendish longing for life. . . . [*Sings*] Young and old are bound by love, and precious are its pangs. . . . [*Laughs*]

MASHA.   Tram-tam-tam!

VERSHININ.   Tam-tam!

MASHA.   Tra-ra-ra?

VERSHININ.   Tra-ta-ta! [*Laughs*]

[*Enter* FEDOTIK]

FEDOTIK.   [*Dances*] Burnt to ashes! Burnt to ashes! Everything I had in the world. [*Laughter*]

IRINA.   A queer thing to joke about. Is everything burnt?

FEDOTIK.   [*Laughs*] Everything I had in the world. Nothing is left. My guitar is burnt, and the camera and all my letters. . . . And the note-book I meant to give you—that's burnt too.

[*Enter* SOLYONY]

IRINA.   No; please go, Vassily Vassilyitch. You can't stay here.

SOLYONY.   How is it the baron can be here and I can't?

VERSHININ.   We must be going, really. How is the fire?

SOLYONY.   They say it is dying down. No, I really can't understand why the baron may be here and not I. [*Takes out a bottle of scent and sprinkles himself*]

VERSHININ.   Tram-tam-tam!

MASHA.   Tram-tam!

VERSHININ.   [*Laughs, to* SOLYONY] Let us go into the dining-room.

SOLYONY.   Very well; we'll make a note of it. I might explain my meaning fur-

ther, but fear I may provoke the geese. . . . [*Looking at* TUSENBACH]
Chook, chook, chook! . . .

[*Goes out with* VERSHININ *and* FEDOTIK]

IRINA. How that horrid Solyony has made the room smell of tobacco! . . .
[*In surprise*] The baron is asleep! Baron, Baron!

TUSENBACH. [*Waking up*] I am tired, though. . . . The brickyard. I am not
talking in my sleep. I really am going to the brickyard directly, to begin
work. . . . It's nearly settled. [*To* IRINA, *tenderly*] You are so pale and
lovely and fascinating. . . . It seems to me as though your paleness sheds
a light through the dark air. . . . You are melancholy; you are dissatisfied
with life. . . . Ah, come with me; let us go and work together!

MASHA. Nikolay Lvovitch, do go!

TUSENBACH. [*Laughing*] Are you here? I didn't see you. . . . [*Kisses* IRINA'S
hand] Good-bye, I am going. . . . I look at you now, and I remember as
though it were long ago how on your name-day you talked of the joy of
work, and were so gay and confident. . . . And what a happy life I was
dreaming of then! What has become of it? [*Kisses her hand*] There are
tears in your eyes. Go to bed, it's getting light . . . it is nearly morning.
. . . If it were granted to me to give my life for you!

MASHA. Nikolay Lvovitch, do go! Come, really. . . .

TUSENBACH. I am going.

[*Goes out*]

MASHA. [*Lying down*] Are you asleep, Fyodor?

KULIGIN. Eh?

MASHA. You had better go home.

KULIGIN. My darling Masha, my precious girl! . . .

IRINA. She is tired out. Let her rest, Fedya.[58]

KULIGIN. I'll go at once. . . . My dear, charming wife! . . . I love you, my
only one! . . .

MASHA. [*Angrily*] Amo, amas, amat; amamus, amatis, amant.[59]

KULIGIN. [*Laughs*] Yes, really she is wonderful. You have been my wife for
seven years, and it seems to me as though we were only married yesterday.
Honour bright! Yes, really you are a wonderful woman! I am content, I am
content, I am content!

MASHA. I am bored, I am bored, I am bored! . . . [*Gets up and speaks, sitting
down*] And there's something I can't get out of my head. . . . It's simply
revolting. It sticks in my head like a nail; I must speak of it. I mean about
Andrey. . . . He has mortgaged this house in the bank and his wife has
grabbed all the money, and you know the house does not belong to him
alone, but to us four! He ought to know that, if he is a decent man.

KULIGIN. Why do you want to bother about it, Masha? What is it to you?
Andryusha is in debt all round, so there it is.

MASHA. It's revolting, anyway. [*Lies down*]

---

[58] Intimate form of Fyodor (our Theodore).

[59] The Latin paradigm of the present indicative of *amo* (I love). Most students of Latin
begin by learning these forms.

KULIGIN. We are not poor. I work—I go to the high-school, and then I give private lessons. . . . I do my duty. . . . There's no nonsense about me. *Omnia mea mecum porto*,[60] as the saying is.

MASHA. I want nothing, but it's the injustice that revolts me. [*A pause*] Go, Fyodor.

KULIGIN. [*Kisses her*] You are tired, rest for half an hour, and I'll sit and wait for you. . . . Sleep. . . . [*Goes*] I am content, I am content, I am content.

[*Goes out*]

IRINA. Yes, how petty our Andrey has grown, how dull and old he has become beside that woman! At one time he was working to get a professorship, and yesterday he was boasting of having succeeded at last in becoming a member of the Rural Board. He is a member, and Protopopov is chairman. . . . The whole town is laughing and talking of it and he is the only one who sees and knows nothing.[61] . . . And here everyone has been running to the fire while he sits still in his room and takes no notice. He does nothing but play his violin. . . . [*Nervously*] Oh, it's awful, awful, awful! [*Weeps*] I can't bear it any more, I can't! I can't, I can't!

[OLGA *comes in and begins tidying up her table*]

IRINA. [*Sobs loudly*] Turn me out, turn me out, I can't bear it any more!

OLGA. [*Alarmed*] What is it? What is it, darling?

IRINA. [*Sobbing*] Where? Where has it all gone? Where is it? Oh, my God, my God! I have forgotten everything, everything . . . everything is in a tangle in my mind. . . . I don't remember the Italian for window or ceiling . . . I am forgetting everything; every day I forget something more and life is slipping away and will never come back, we shall never, never go to Moscow. . . . I see that we shan't go. . . .

OLGA. Darling, darling. . . .

IRINA. [*Restraining herself*] Oh, I am wretched. . . . I can't work, I am not going to work. I have had enough of it, enough of it! I have been a telegraph clerk and now I have a job in the town council and I hate and despise every bit of the work they give me. . . . I am nearly twenty-four, I have been working for years, my brains are drying up, I am getting thin and old and ugly and there is nothing, nothing, not the slightest satisfaction, and time is passing and one feels that one is moving away from a real, fine life, moving farther and farther away and being drawn into the depths. I am in despair and I don't know how it is I am alive and have not killed myself yet. . . .

OLGA. Don't cry, my child, don't cry. It makes me miserable.

IRINA. I am not crying, I am not crying. . . . It's over. . . . There, I am not crying now. I won't . . . I won't.

OLGA. Darling, I am speaking to you as a sister, as a friend, if you care for my advice, marry the baron!

[IRINA *weeps*]

OLGA. [*Softly*] You know you respect him, you think highly of him. . . . It's true he is ugly, but he is such a thoroughly nice man, so good. . . . One doesn't marry for love, but to do one's duty. . . . That's what I think,

---

[60] "I carry all my possessions with me." A quotation from Cicero.

[61] An allusion to the fact that Andrey is being cuckolded by Protopopov.

anyway, and I would marry without love. Whoever proposed to me I would marry him, if only he were a good man. . . . I would even marry an old man. . . .

IRINA. I kept expecting we should move to Moscow and there I should meet my real one. I've been dreaming of him, loving him. . . . But it seems that was all nonsense, nonsense. . . .

OLGA. [*Puts her arms round her sister*] My darling, lovely sister, I understand it all; when the baron left the army and came to us in a plain coat, I thought he looked so ugly that it positively made me cry. . . . He asked me, "Why are you crying?" How could I tell him! But if God brought you together I should be happy. That's a different thing, you know, quite different.

[NATASHA *with a candle in her hand walks across the stage from door on right to door on left without speaking*]

MASHA. [*Sits up*] She walks about as though it were she had set fire to the town.

OLGA. Masha, you are silly. The very silliest of the family, that's you. Please forgive me. [*A pause*]

MASHA. I want to confess my sins, dear sisters. My soul is yearning. I am going to confess to you and never again to anyone. . . . I'll tell you this minute. [*Softly*] It's my secret, but you must know everything. . . . I can't be silent. . . . [*A pause*] I am in love, I am in love. . . . I love that man. . . . You have just seen him. . . . Well, I may as well say it straight out. I love Vershinin.

OLGA. [*Going behind her screen*] Stop it. I'm not listening anyway.

MASHA. But what am I to do? [*Clutches her head*] At first I thought him queer . . . then I was sorry for him . . . then I came to love him . . . to love him with his voice, his words, his misfortunes, his two little girls. . . .

OLGA. [*Behind the screen*] I'm not listening anyway. Whatever silly things you say I shan't hear them.

MASHA. Oh, Olya, you are silly. I love him—so that's my fate. It means that that's my lot. . . . And he loves me. . . . It's all dreadful. Yes? Is it wrong? [*Takes* IRINA *by the hand and draws her to herself*] Oh, my darling. . . . How are we going to live our lives, what will become of us? . . . When one reads a novel it all seems stale and easy to understand, but when you are in love yourself you see that no one knows anything and we all have to settle things for ourselves. . . . My darling, my sister. . . . I have confessed it to you, now I'll hold my tongue. . . . I'll be like Gogol's madman[62] . . . silence . . . silence. . . .

[*Enter* ANDREY *and after him* FERAPONT]

ANDREY. [*Angrily*] What do you want? I can't make it out.

FERAPONT. [*In the doorway, impatiently*] I've told you ten times already, Andrey Sergeyevitch.

ANDREY. In the first place I am not Andrey Sergeyevitch, but your honour, to you!

FERAPONT. The firemen ask leave, your honour, to go through the garden on their way to the river. Or else they have to go round and round, an awful nuisance for them.

---

[62] A character in one of Gogol's novels.

ANDREY.   Very good. Tell them, very good. [FERAPONT *goes out*] I am sick of them. Where is Olga? [OLGA *comes from behind the screen*] I've come to ask you for the key of the cupboard, I have lost mine. You've got one, it's a little key.

[OLGA *gives him the key in silence;* IRINA *goes behind her screen; a pause*]

ANDREY.   What a tremendous fire! Now it's begun to die down. Hang it all, that Ferapont made me so cross I said something silly to him. Your honour. . . . [*A pause*] Why don't you speak, Olya? [*A pause*] It's time to drop this foolishness and sulking all about nothing. . . . You are here, Masha, and you too, Irina—very well, then, let us have things out thoroughly, once for all. What have you against me? What is it?

OLGA.   Leave off, Andryusha. Let us talk to-morrow. [*Nervously*] What an agonising night!

ANDREY.   [*Greatly confused*] Don't excite yourself. I ask you quite coolly, what have you against me? Tell me straight out.

[VERSHININ's *voice:* "Tram-tam-tam!"]

MASHA.   [*Standing up, loudly*] Tra-ta-ta! [*To* OLGA] Good night, Olya, God bless you. . . . [*Goes behind screen and kisses* IRINA] Sleep well. . . . Good night, Andrey. You'd better leave them now, they are tired out . . . you can go into things to-morrow.

[*Goes out*]

OLGA.   Yes, really, Andryusha, let us put it off till to-morrow. . . . [*Goes behind her screen*] It's time we were in bed.

ANDREY.   I'll say what I have to say and then go. Directly. . . . First, you have something against Natasha, my wife, and I've noticed that from the very day of my marriage. Natasha is a splendid woman, conscientious, straightforward and honourable—that's my opinion! I love and respect my wife, do you understand? I respect her, and I insist on other people respecting her too. I repeat, she is a conscientious, honourable woman, and all your disagreements are simply caprice, or rather the whims of old maids. Old maids never like and never have liked their sisters-in-law—that's the rule. [*A pause*] Secondly, you seem to be cross with me for not being a professor, not working at something learned. But I am in the service of the Zemstvo,[63] I am a member of the Rural Board, and I consider this service just as sacred and elevated as the service of learning. I am a member of the Rural Board and I am proud of it, if you care to know. . . . [*A pause*] Thirdly . . . there's something else I have to say. . . . I have mortgaged the house without asking your permission. . . . For that I am to blame, yes, and I ask you pardon for it. I was driven to it by my debts . . . thirty-five thousand. . . . I am not gambling now—I gave up cards long ago; but the chief thing I can say in self-defence is that you are, so to say, of the privileged sex—you get a pension . . . while I had not . . . my wages, so to speak. . . . [*A pause*]

KULIGIN.   [*At the door*] Isn't Masha here? [*Perturbed*] Where is she? It's strange. . . .

[*Goes out*]

ANDREY.   They won't listen. Natasha is an excellent, conscientious woman.

[63] The pre-Revolutionary Russian elective local district and provincial administrative assembly.

[*Paces up and down the stage in silence, then stops*] When I married her, I thought we should be happy . . . happy, all of us. . . . But, my God! [*Weeps*] Dear sisters, darling sisters, you must not believe what I say, you mustn't believe it. . . .

[Goes out]

KULIGIN.   [*At the door, uneasily*] Where is Masha? Isn't Masha here? How strange!

[Goes out]

[*The firebell rings in the street. The stage is empty*]

IRINA.   [*Behind the screen*] Olya! Who is that knocking on the floor?

OLGA.   It's the doctor, Ivan Romanitch. He is drunk.

IRINA.   What a troubled night! [*A pause*] Olya! [*Peeps out from behind the screen*] Have you heard? The brigade is going to be taken away; they are being transferred to some place very far off.

OLGA.   That's only a rumour.

IRINA.   Then we shall be alone. . . . Olya!

OLGA.   Well?

IRINA.   My dear, my darling, I respect the baron, I think highly of him, he is a fine man—I will marry him, I consent, only let us go to Moscow! I entreat you, do let us go! There's nothing in the world better than Moscow! Let us go, Olya! Let us go!

[Curtain]

Act Four

    Old garden of the PROZOROVS' *house. A long avenue of fir trees, at the end of which is a view of the river. On the farther side of the river there is a wood. On the right the verandah of the house; on the table in it are bottles and glasses; evidently they have just been drinking champagne. It is twelve o'clock in the day. People pass occasionally from the street across the garden to the river; five soldiers pass rapidly.*

    TCHEBUTYKIN, *in an affable mood, which persists throughout the act, is sitting in an easy chair in the garden, waiting to be summoned; he is wearing a military cap and has a stick.* IRINA, KULIGIN *with a decoration on his breast and with no moustache, and* TUSENBACH, *standing on the verandah, are saying good-bye to* FEDOTIK *and* RODDEY, *who are going down the steps; both officers are in marching uniform.*

TUSENBACH.   [*Kissing* FEDOTIK] You are a good fellow; we've got on so happily together. [*Kisses* RODDEY] Once more. . . . Good-bye, my dear boy. . . .

IRINA.   Till we meet again!

FEDOTIK.   No, it's good-bye for good; we shall never meet again.

KULIGIN.   Who knows! [*Wipes his eyes, smiles*] Here I am crying too.

IRINA.   We shall meet some day.

FEDOTIK. In ten years, or fifteen perhaps? But then we shall scarcely recognise each other—we shall greet each other coldly. . . . [*Takes a snapshot*] Stand still. . . . Once more, for the last time.

RODDEY. [*Embraces* TUSENBACH] We shall not see each other again. . . . [*Kisses* IRINA'S *hand*] Thank you for everything, everything. . . .

FEDOTIK. [*With vexation*] Oh, wait a little!

TUSENBACH. Please God we shall meet again. Write to us. Be sure to write to us.

RODDEY. [*Taking a long look at the garden*] Good-bye, trees! [*Shouts*] Halloo! [*A pause*] Good-bye, echo!

KULIGIN. I shouldn't wonder if you get married in Poland. . . . Your Polish wife will clasp you in her arms and call you *kochany!* [64] [*Laughs*]

FEDOTIK. [*Looking at his watch*] We have less than an hour. Of our battery only Solyony is going on the barge; we are going with the rank and file. Three divisions of the battery are going to-day and three more to-morrow— and peace and quiet will descend upon the town.

TUSENBACH. And dreadful boredom too.

RODDEY. And where is Marya Sergeyevna?

KULIGIN. Masha is in the garden.

FEDOTIK. We must say good-bye to her.

RODDEY. Good-bye. We must go, or I shall begin to cry. . . . [*Hurriedly embraces* TUSENBACH *and* KULIGIN *and kisses* IRINA'S *hand*] We've had a splendid time here.

FEDOTIK. [*To* KULIGIN] This is a little souvenir for you . . . a notebook with a pencil. . . . We'll go down here to the river. . . . [*As they go away both look back*]

RODDEY. [*Shouts*] Halloo-oo!

KULIGIN. [*Shouts*] Good-bye!

[RODDEY *and* FEDOTIK *meet* MASHA *in the background and say good-bye to her; she walks away with them*]

IRINA. They've gone. . . . [*Sits down on the bottom step of the verandah*]

TCHEBUTYKIN. They have forgotten to say good-bye to me.

IRINA. And what were you thinking about?

TCHEBUTYKIN. Why, I somehow forgot, too. But I shall see them again soon, I am setting off to-morrow. Yes . . . I have one day more. In a year I shall be on the retired list. Then I shall come here again and shall spend the rest of my life near you. . . . There is only one year now before I get my pension. [*Puts a newspaper into his pocket and takes out another*] I shall come here to you and arrange my life quite differently. . . . I shall become such a quiet . . . God-fearing . . . well-behaved person.

IRINA. Well, you do need to arrange your life differently, dear Ivan Romanitch. You certainly ought to somehow.

TCHEBUTYKIN. Yes, I feel it. [*Softly hums*] "Tarara-boom-dee-ay—Tarara-boom-dee-ay."

KULIGIN. Ivan Romanitch is incorrigible! Incorrigible!

TCHEBUTYKIN. You ought to take me in hand. Then I should reform.

IRINA. Fyodor[65] has shaved off his moustache. I can't bear to look at him.

[64] Polish word for *sweetheart*.
[65] Kuligin.

KULIGIN. Why, what's wrong?

TCHEBUTYKIN. I might tell you what your countenance looks like now, but I really can't.

KULIGIN. Well! It's the thing now, *modus vivendi.*[66] Our headmaster is clean-shaven, and now I am second to him I have taken to shaving too. Nobody likes it, but I don't care. I am content. With moustache or without moustache I am equally content. [*Sits down*]

[*In the background* ANDREY *is wheeling a baby asleep in a perambulator*]

IRINA. Ivan Romanitch, darling, I am dreadfully uneasy. You were on the boulevard yesterday, tell me what was it that happened?

TCHEBUTYKIN. What happened? Nothing. Nothing much. [*Reads the newspaper*] It doesn't matter!

KULIGIN. The story is that Solyony and the baron met yesterday on the boulevard near the theatre. . . .

TUSENBACH. Oh, stop it! Really. . . . [*With a wave of his hand walks away into the house*]

KULIGIN. Near the theatre. . . . Solyony began pestering the baron and he couldn't keep his temper and said something offensive. . . .

TCHEBUTYKIN. I don't know. It's all nonsense.

KULIGIN. A teacher at a divinity school wrote "nonsense" at the bottom of an essay and the pupil puzzled over it thinking it was a Latin word. . . . [*Laughs*] It was fearfully funny. . . . They say Solyony is in love with Irina and hates the baron. . . . That's natural, Irina is a very nice girl.

[*From the background behind the scenes,* "Aa-oo! Halloo!"]

IRINA. [*Starts*] Everything frightens me somehow to-day. [*A pause*] All my things are ready, after dinner I shall send off my luggage. The baron and I are to be married to-morrow, to-morrow we go to the brickyard and the day after that I shall be in the school. A new life is beginning. God will help me! How will it fare with me? When I passed my exam as a teacher, I felt so happy, so blissful, that I cried. . . . [*A pause*] The cart will soon be coming for my things. . . .

KULIGIN. That's all very well, but it does not seem serious. It's all nothing but ideas and very little that is serious. However, I wish you success with all my heart.

TCHEBUTYKIN. [*Moved to tenderness*] My good, delightful darling. . . . My heart of gold. . . .

KULIGIN. Well, to-day the officers will be gone and everything will go on in the old way. Whatever people may say, Masha is a true, good woman. I love her dearly and am thankful for my lot! . . . People have different lots in life. . . . There is a man called Kozyrev serving in the Excise[67] here. He was at school with me, but he was expelled from the fifth form because he could never understand *ut consecutivum.*[68] Now he is frightfully poor and ill, and when I meet him I say, "How are you, *ut consecutivum?*" "Yes," he says, "just so—*consecutivum*" . . . and then he coughs. . . . Now I have always been successful, I am fortunate, I have even got the order of Stanislav, second

---

[66] "A way of living" (or "of getting along").

[67] An official in the Tax Collection Administration.

[68] A rule of Latin grammar applying to consecutive clauses beginning with the conjunction *ut.*

class, and I am teaching others that *ut consecutivum*. Of course I am clever, cleverer than very many people, but happiness does not lie in that. . . . [*A pause*]

[*In the house the "Maiden's Prayer" is being played on the piano*]

IRINA.   To-morrow evening I shall not be hearing that "Maiden's Prayer," I shan't be meeting Protopopov.[69] . . . [*A pause*] Protopopov is sitting there in the drawing-room; he has come again to-day. . . .

KULIGIN.   The headmistress has not come yet?

IRINA.   No. They have sent for her. If only you knew how hard it is for me to live here alone, without Olya. . . . Now that she is headmistress and lives at the high-school and is busy all day long, I am alone, I am bored, I have nothing to do, and I hate the room I live in. . . . I have made up my mind, since I am not fated to be in Moscow, that so it must be. It must be destiny. There is no help for it. . . . It's all in God's hands, that's the truth. When Nikolay Lvovitch[70] made me an offer again . . . I thought it over and made up my mind. . . . He is a good man, it's wonderful really how good he is. . . . And I suddenly felt as though my soul had grown wings, my heart felt so light and again I longed for work, work. . . . Only something happened yesterday, there is some mystery hanging over me.

TCHEBUTYKIN.   Nonsense.

NATASHA.   [*At the window*] Our headmistress!

KULIGIN.   The headmistress has come. Let us go in. [*Goes into the house with* IRINA]

TCHEBUTYKIN.   [*Reads the newspaper, humming softly*] "Tarara-boom-dee-ay."

[MASHA *approaches; in the background* ANDREY *is pushing the perambulator*]

MASHA.   Here he sits, snug and settled.

TCHEBUTYKIN.   Well, what then?

MASHA.   [*Sits down*] Nothing. . . . [*A pause*] Did you love my mother?

TCHEBUTYKIN.   Very much.

MASHA.   And did she love you?

TCHEBUTYKIN.   [*After a pause*] That I don't remember.

MASHA.   Is my man here? It's just like our cook Marfa used to say about her policeman: is my man here?

TCHEBUTYKIN.   Not yet.

MASHA.   When you get happiness by snatches, by little bits, and then lose it, as I am losing it, by degrees one grows coarse and spiteful. . . . [*Points to her bosom*] I'm boiling here inside. . . . [*Looking at* ANDREY, *who is pushing the perambulator*] Here is our Andrey. . . . All our hopes are shattered. Thousands of people raised the bell, a lot of money and of labor was spent on it, and it suddenly fell and smashed. All at once, for no reason whatever. That's just how it is with Andrey. . . .

ANDREY.   When will they be quiet in the house? There is such a noise.

TCHEBUTYKIN.   Soon. [*Looks at his watch*] My watch is an old-fashioned one with a repeater. . . . [*Winds his watch, it strikes*] The first, the second, and the fifth batteries are going at one o'clock. [*A pause*] And I am going to-morrow.

[69] The lover of Natasha. Irina means that she will have moved away from the house by to-morrow.   [70] Tusenbach.

ANDREY. For good?

TCHEBUTYKIN. I don't know. Perhaps I shall come back in a year. Though goodness knows. . . . It doesn't matter one way or another.

[*There is the sound of a harp and violin being played far away in the street*]

ANDREY. The town will be empty. It's as though one put an extinguisher over it. [*A pause*] Something happened yesterday near the theatre; everyone is talking of it, and I know nothing about it.

TCHEBUTYKIN. It was nothing. Foolishness. Solyony began annoying the baron and he lost his temper and insulted him, and it came in the end to Solyony's having to challenge him. [*Looks at his watch*] It's time, I fancy. . . . It was to be at half-past twelve in the state forest that we can see from here beyond the river. . . . Piff-paff! [*Laughs*] Solyony imagines he is a Lermontov[71] and even writes verses. Joking apart, this is his third duel.

MASHA. Whose?

TCHEBUTYKIN. Solyony's.

MASHA. And the baron's?

TCHEBUTYKIN. What about the baron? [*A pause*]

MASHA. My thoughts are in a muddle. . . . Anyway, I tell you, you ought not to let them do it. He may wound the baron or even kill him.

TCHEBUTYKIN. The baron is a very good fellow, but one baron more or less in the world, what does it matter? Let them! It doesn't matter. [*Beyond the garden a shout of* "Aa-oo! Halloo!"] You can wait. That is Skvortsov, the second, shouting. He is in a boat. [*A pause*]

ANDREY. In my opinion to take part in a duel, or to be present at it even in the capacity of a doctor, is simply immoral.

TCHEBUTYKIN. That only seems so. . . . We are not real, nothing in the world is real, we don't exist, but only seem to exist. . . . Nothing matters!

MASHA. How they keep on talking, talking all day long. [*Goes*] To live in such a climate, it may snow any minute, and then all this talk on top of it. [*Stops*] I am not going indoors, I can't go in there. . . . When Vershinin comes, tell me. . . . [*Goes down the avenue*] And the birds are already flying south. . . . [*Looks up*] Swans or geese. . . . Darlings, happy things. . . .

[*Goes out*]

ANDREY. Our house will be empty. The officers are going, you are going, Irina is getting married, and I shall be left in the house alone.

TCHEBUTYKIN. What about your wife?

[*Enter* FERAPONT *with papers*]

ANDREY. A wife is a wife. She is a straightforward, upright woman, good-natured, perhaps, but for all that there is something in her which makes her no better than some petty, blind, hairy animal. Anyway she is not a human being. I speak to you as to a friend, the one man to whom I can open my soul. I love Natasha, that is so, but sometimes she seems to me wonderfully vulgar, and then I don't know what to think, I can't account for my loving her or, anyway, having loved her.

TCHEBUTYKIN. [*Gets up*] I am going away to-morrow, my boy, perhaps we

---

[71] See p. 419, note 46.

shall never meet again, so this is my advice to you. Put on your cap, you know, take your stick and walk off . . . walk off and just go, go without looking back. And the farther you go, the better. [*A pause*] But do as you like! It doesn't matter. . . .

[SOLYONY *crosses the stage in the background with two officers; seeing* TCHEBUTYKIN *he turns towards him; the officers walk on*]

SOLYONY.   Doctor, it's time! It's half-past twelve. [*Greets* ANDREY]

TCHEBUTYKIN.   Directly. I am sick of you all. [*To* ANDREY] If anyone asks for me, Andryusha, say I'll be back directly. . . . [*Sighs*] Oho-ho-ho!

SOLYONY.   He had not time to say alack before the bear was on his back.[72] [*Walks away with the doctor*] Why are you croaking, old chap?

TCHEBUTYKIN.   Come!

SOLYONY.   How do you feel?

TCHEBUTYKIN.   [*Angrily*] Like a pig in clover.

SOLYONY.   The old chap need not excite himself. I won't do anything much, I'll only shoot him like a snipe . [*Takes out scent and sprinkles his hands*] I've used a whole bottle to-day, and still they smell. My hands smell like a corpse. [*A pause*] Yes. . . . Do you remember the poem? "And, restless, seeks the stormy ocean, as though in tempest there were peace." [73] . . .

TCHEBUTYKIN.   Yes. He had not time to say alack before the bear was on his back. [*Goes out with* SOLYONY. *Shouts are heard:* "Halloo! Oo-oo!" ANDREY *and* FERAPONT *come in*]

FERAPONT.   Papers for you to sign. . . .

ANDREY.   [*Nervously*] Let me alone! Let me alone! I entreat you! [*Walks away with the perambulator*]

FERAPONT.   That's what the papers are for—to be signed. [*Retires into the background*]

[*Enter* IRINA *and* TUSENBACH *wearing a straw hat;* KULIGIN *crosses the stage shouting* "Aa-oo, Masha, aa-oo!"]

TUSENBACH.   I believe that's the only man in the town who is glad that the officers are going away.[74]

IRINA.   That's very natural. [*A pause*] Our town will be empty now.

TUSENBACH.   Dear, I'll be back directly.

IRINA.   Where are you going?

TUSENBACH.   I must go into the town, and then . . . to see my comrades off.

IRINA.   That's not true. . . . Nikolay, why are you so absent-minded to-day? [*A pause*] What happened yesterday near the theatre?

TUSENBACH.   [*With a gesture of impatience*] I'll be here in an hour and with you again. [*Kisses her hands*] My beautiful one. . . . [*Looks into her face*] For five years now I have loved you and still I can't get used to it, and you seem to me more and more lovely. What wonderful, exquisite hair! What eyes! I shall carry you off to-morrow, we will work, we will be rich, my dreams will come true. You shall be happy. There is only one thing, one thing: you don't love me!

---

[72] Solyony spouted this line earlier in the play.

[73] A quotation from Solyony's model, Lermontov. It occurs as the last lines of his poem "The Sail."

[74] A reference to Masha's amour with Vershinin.

IRINA. That's not in my power! I'll be your wife and be faithful and obedient, but there is no love, I can't help it. [*Weeps*] I've never been in love in my life! Oh, I have so dreamed of love, I've been dreaming of it for years, day and night, but my soul is like a wonderful piano of which the key has been lost. [*A pause*] You look uneasy.

TUSENBACH. I have not slept all night. There has never been anything in my life so dreadful that it could frighten me, and only that lost key frets at my heart and won't let me sleep. . . . Say something to me. . . . [*A pause*] Say something to me. . . .

IRINA. What? What am I to say to you? What?

TUSENBACH. Anything.

IRINA. There, there! [*A pause*]

TUSENBACH. What trifles, what little things suddenly *à propos* of nothing acquire importance in life! One laughs at them as before, thinks them non-sense, but still one goes on and feels that one has not the power to stop. Don't let us talk about it! I am happy. I feel as though I were seeing these pines, these maples, these birch trees for the first time in my life, and they all seem to be looking at me with curiosity and waiting. What beautiful trees, and, really, how beautiful life ought to be under them! [*A shout of* "Halloo! Aa-oo!"] I must be off; it's time. . . . See, that tree is dead, but it waves in the wind with the others. And so it seems to me that if I die I shall still have part in life, one way or another. Good-bye, my darling. . . . [*Kisses her hands*] Those papers of yours you gave me are lying under the calendar on my table.

IRINA. I am coming with you.

TUSENBACH. [*In alarm*] No, no! [*Goes off quickly, stops in the avenue*] Irina!

IRINA. What is it?

TUSENBACH. [*Not knowing what to say*] I didn't have any coffee this morn-ing. Ask them to make me some. [*Goes out quickly*]

[IRINA *stands lost in thought, then walks away into the background of the scene and sits down on the swing. Enter* ANDREY *with the perambulator, and* FERAPONT *comes into sight*]

FERAPONT. Andrey Sergeyevitch, the papers aren't mine; they are government papers. I didn't invent them.

ANDREY. Oh, where is it all gone? What has become of my past, when I was young, gay, and clever, when my dreams and thoughts were exquisite, when my present and my past were lighted up by hope? Why on the very threshold of life do we become dull, grey, uninteresting, lazy, indifferent, useless, un-happy? . . . Our town has been going on for two hundred years—there are a hundred thousand people living in it; and there is not one who is not like the rest, not one saint in the past, or the present, not one man of learning, not one artist, not one man in the least remarkable who could inspire envy or a passionate desire to imitate him. . . . They only eat, drink, sleep, and then die . . . others are born, and they also eat and drink and sleep, and not to be bored to stupefaction they vary their lives by nasty gossip, vodka, cards, litigation; and the wives deceive their husbands, and the husbands tell lies and pretend that they see and hear nothing, and an overwhelmingly vulgar influence weighs upon the children, and the divine spark is quenched in them and they become the same sort of pitiful, dead creatures, all exactly alike, as their fathers and mothers. . . . [*To* FERAPONT, *angrily*] What do you want?

FERAPONT.   Eh? There are papers to sign.

ANDREY.   You bother me!

FERAPONT.   [*Handing him the papers*] The porter from the local treasury was saying just now that there was as much as two hundred degrees of frost in Petersburg this winter.

ANDREY.   The present is hateful, but when I think of the future, it is so nice! I feel so light-hearted, so free. A light dawns in the distance, I see freedom. I see how I and my children will become free from sloth, from kvass,[75] from goose and cabbage, from sleeping after dinner, from mean, parasitic living. . . .

FERAPONT.   He says that two thousand people were frozen to death. The people were terrified. It was either in Petersburg or Moscow, I don't remember.

ANDREY.   [*In a rush of tender feeling*] My dear sisters, my wonderful sisters! [*Through tears*] Masha, my sister!

NATASHA.   [*In the window*] Who is talking so loud out there? Is that you, Andryusha? You will wake baby Sophie. *Il ne faut pas faire de bruit, la Sophie est dormée déjà. Vous êtes un ours.*[76] [*Getting angry*] If you want to talk, give the perambulator with the baby to somebody else. Ferapont, take the perambulator from the master!

FERAPONT.   Yes, ma'am. [*Takes the pram*]

ANDREY.   [*In confusion*] I am talking quietly.

NATASHA.   [*Petting her child, inside the room*] Bobik! Naughty Bobik! Little rascal!

ANDREY.   [*Looking through the papers*] Very well, I'll look through them and sign what wants signing, and then you can take them back to the Board. . . . [*Goes into the house reading the papers;* FERAPONT *pushes the pram farther into the garden*]

NATASHA.   [*Speaking indoors*] Bobik, what is mamma's name? Darling, darling! And who is this? This is auntie Olya. Say to auntie, "Good morning, Olya!"

[*Two wandering musicians, a man and a girl, enter and play a violin and a harp; from the house enter* VERSHININ *with* OLGA *and* ANFISA, *and stand for a minute listening in silence;* IRINA *comes up*]

OLGA.   Our garden is like a public passage; they walk and ride through. Nurse, give those people something.

ANFISA.   [*Gives money to the musicians*] Go away, and God bless you, my dear souls! [*The musicians bow and go away*] Poor things. People don't play if they have plenty to eat. [*To* IRINA] Good morning, Irisha![77] [*Kisses her*] Aye, aye, my little girl, I am having a time of it! Living in the high-school, in a government flat, with dear Olya—that's what the Lord has vouchsafed me in my old age! I have never lived so well in my life, sinful woman that I am. . . . It's a big flat, and I have a room to myself and a bedstead. All at

---

[75] A thin sour beer made from rye or barley.

[76] "You must not make any noise; Sophie has already gone to sleep. You are a bear." Natasha's French is not too good.   [77] Another diminutive of Irina.

the government's expense. I wake up in the night and, O Lord, Mother of God, there is no one in the world happier than I!

VERSHININ. [*Looks at his watch*] We are just going, Olga Sergeyevna. It's time to be off. [*A pause*] I wish you everything, everything. . . . Where is Marya Sergeyevna?

IRINA. She is somewhere in the garden. . . . I'll go and look for her.

VERSHININ. Please be so good. I am in a hurry.

ANFISA. I'll go and look for her too. [*Shouts*] Mashenka,[78] aa-oo!

[*Goes with* IRINA *into the farther part of the garden*] Aa-oo! Aa-oo!

VERSHININ. Everything comes to an end. Here we are parting. [*Looks at his watch*] The town has given us something like a lunch; we have been drinking champagne, the mayor made a speech. I ate and listened, but my heart was here, with you all. . . . [*Looks round the garden*] I've grown used to you. . . .

OLGA. Shall we ever see each other again?

VERSHININ. Most likely not. [*A pause*] My wife and two little girls will stay here for another two months; please, if anything happens, if they need anything . . .

OLGA. Yes, yes, of course. Set your mind at rest. [*A pause*] By to-morrow there won't be a soldier in the town—it will all turn into a memory, and of course for us it will be like beginning a new life. . . . [*A pause*] Nothing turns out as we would have it. I did not want to be a headmistress, and yet I am. It seems we are not to live in Moscow. . . .

VERSHININ. Well. . . . Thank you for everything. . . . Forgive me if anything was amiss. . . . I have talked a great deal: forgive me for that too—don't remember evil against me.

OLGA. [*Wipes her eyes*] Why doesn't Masha come?

VERSHININ. What else am I to say to you at parting? What am I to theorize about? . . . [*Laughs*] Life is hard. It seems to many of us blank and hopeless; but yet we must admit that it goes on getting clearer and easier, and it looks as though the time were not far off when it will be full of happiness. [*Looks at his watch*] It's time for me to go! In old days men were absorbed in wars, filling all their existence with marches, raids, victories, but now all that is a thing of the past, leaving behind it a great void which there is so far nothing to fill: humanity is searching for it passionately, and of course will find it. Ah, if only it could be quickly! [*A pause*] If, don't you know, industry were united with culture and culture with industry. . . . [*Looks at his watch*] But, I say, it's time for me to go. . . .

OLGA. Here she comes.

[MASHA *comes in*]

VERSHININ. I have come to say good-bye. . . .

[OLGA *moves a little away to leave them free to say good-bye*]

MASHA. [*Looking into his face*] Good-bye. . . . [*A prolonged kiss*]

OLGA. Come, come. . . .

[MASHA *sobs violently*]

VERSHININ. Write to me. . . . Don't forget me! Let me go! . . . Time is up!

[78] Another diminutive of Masha.

... Olga Sergeyevna, take her, I must ... go ... I am late. ...
[*Much moved, kisses* OLGA's *hands; then again embraces* MASHA *and quickly goes off*]

OLGA. Come, Masha! Leave off, darling.

[*Enter* KULIGIN]

KULIGIN. [*Embarrassed*] Never mind, let her cry—let her. ... My good Masha, my dear Masha! ... You are my wife, and I am happy, anyway. ... I don't complain; I don't say a word of blame. ... Here Olya is my witness. ... We'll begin the old life again, and I won't say one word, not a hint. ...

MASHA. [*Restraining her sobs*] By the sea-strand an oak-tree green. ... Upon that oak a chain of gold. ... Upon that oak a chain of gold. ... I am going mad. ... By the sea-strand ... an oak-tree green.[79] ...

OLGA. Calm yourself, Masha. ... Calm yourself. ... Give her some water.

MASHA. I am not crying now. ...

KULIGIN. She is not crying now ... she is good. ...

[*The dim sound of a far-away shot*]

MASHA. By the sea-strand an oak-tree green, upon that oak a chain of gold. ... The cat is green. ... The oak is green. ... I am mixing it up. ... [*Drinks water*] My life is a failure. ... I want nothing now. ... I shall be calm directly. ... It doesn't matter. ... What does "strand" mean? Why do these words haunt me? My thoughts are in a tangle.

[*Enter* IRINA]

OLGA. Calm yourself, Masha. Come, that's a good girl. Let us go indoors.

MASHA. [*Angrily*] I am not going in. Let me alone! [*Sobs, but at once checks herself*] I don't go into that house now and I won't.

IRINA. Let us sit together, even if we don't say anything. I am going away tomorrow, you know. ... [*A pause*]

KULIGIN. I took a false beard and moustache from a boy in the third form yesterday, just look. ... [*Puts on the beard and moustache*] I look like the German teacher. ... [*Laughs*] Don't I? Funny creatures, those boys.

MASHA. You really do look like the German teacher.

OLGA. [*Laughs*] Yes.

[MASHA *weeps*]

IRINA. There, Masha!

KULIGIN. Awfully like. ...

[*Enter* NATASHA]

NATASHA. [*To the maid*] What? Mr. Protopopov will sit with Sophie, and let Andrey Sergeyevitch wheel Bobik up and down. What a lot there is to do with children. ... [*To* IRINA] Irina, you are going away to-morrow, what a pity. Do stay just another week. [*Seeing* KULIGIN *utters a shriek; the latter laughs and takes off the beard and moustache*] Well, what next, you gave me such a fright! [*To* IRINA] I am used to you and do you suppose that I don't feel parting with you? I shall put Andrey with his violin into your room—let him saw away there!—and we will put baby Sophie in his room. Adorable, delightful baby! Isn't she a child! To-day she looked at me with such eyes and said "Mamma"!

[79] The quotation from Pushkin.

KULIGIN. A fine child, that's true.

NATASHA. So to-morrow I shall be all alone here. [*Sighs*] First of all I shall have this avenue of fir trees cut down, and then that maple. . . . It looks so ugly in the evening. . . . [*To* IRINA] My dear, that sash does not suit you at all. . . . It's in bad taste. You want something light. And then I shall have flowers, flowers planted everywhere, and there will be such a scent. . . . [*Severely*] Why is there a fork lying about on that seat? [*Going into the house, to the maid*] Why is there a fork lying about on this seat. I ask you? [*Shouts*] Hold your tongue!

KULIGIN. She is at it!

[*Behind the scenes the band plays a march; they all listen*]

OLGA. They are going.

[*Enter* TCHEBUTYKIN]

MASHA. Our people are going. Well . . . a happy journey to them! [*To her husband*] We must go home. . . . Where are my hat and cape?

KULIGIN. I took them into the house. . . . I'll get them directly. . . .

OLGA. Yes, now we can go home, it's time.

TCHEBUTYKIN. Olga Sergeyevna!

OLGA. What is it? [*A pause*] What?

TCHEBUTYKIN. Nothing. . . . I don't know how to tell you. [*Whispers in her ear*]

OLGA. [*In alarm*] It can't be!

TCHEBUTYKIN. Yes . . . such a business. . . . I am so worried and worn out, I don't want to say another word. . . . [*With vexation*] But there, it doesn't matter!

MASHA. What has happened?

OLGA. [*Puts her arms round* IRINA] This is a terrible day. . . . I don't know how to tell you, my precious. . . .

IRINA. What is it? Tell me quickly, what is it? For God's sake! [*Cries*]

TCHEBUTYKIN. The baron has just been killed in a duel.

IRINA. [*Weeping quietly*] I knew, I knew. . . .

TCHEBUTYKIN. [*In the background of the scene sits down on a garden seat*] I am worn out. . . . [*Takes a newspaper out of his pocket*] Let them cry. . . . [*Sings softly*] "Tarara-boom-dee-ay." . . . It doesn't matter.

[*The three sisters stand with their arms round one another.*]

MASHA. Oh, listen to that band! They are going away from us; one has gone altogether, gone forever. We are left alone to begin our life over again. . . . We've got to live . . . we've got to live. . . .

IRINA. [*Lays her head on* OLGA's *bosom*] A time will come when everyone will know what all this is for, why there is this misery; there will be no mysteries and, meanwhile, we have got to live . . . we have got to work, only to work! To-morrow I shall go alone; I shall teach in the school, and I will give all my life to those to whom it may be of use. Now it's autumn; soon winter will come and cover us with snow, and I will work, I will work.

OLGA. [*Embraces both her sisters*] The music is so gay, so confident, and one longs for life! O my God! Time will pass, and we shall go away for ever, and we shall be forgotten, our faces will be forgotten, our voices, and how many there were of us; but our sufferings will pass into joy for those who will live after us, happiness and peace will be established upon earth, and they will remember kindly and bless those who have lived before. Oh, dear sisters, our life is not ended yet. We shall live! The music is so gay, so joyful, and it seems as though a little more and we shall know what we are living for, why we are suffering. . . . If we only knew—if we only knew!

[*The music grows more and more subdued;* KULIGIN, *cheerful and smiling, brings the hat and cape;* ANDREY *pushes the perambulator in which* BOBIK *is sitting*]

TCHEBUTYKIN. [*Humming softly*] "Tarara-boom-de-ay!" [*Reads his paper*] It doesn't matter, it doesn't matter.

OLGA. If we only knew, if we only knew!

[*Curtain*]

The Hairy Ape

Eugene O'Neill

Eugene O'Neill

Most of Eugene O'Neill's plays are concerned with one basic theme—certainly one of the most significant themes of our confused times: man's attempt to find a place for himself in an alien universe. In his preoccupation with this problem O'Neill has constantly tried to find a mode of expression that would enable him to transcend the limitations of naturalism. In expressionism, which he employed in *The Hairy Ape, The Emperor Jones, The Great God Brown,* and other plays, he found a dramatic technique to satisfy, at least partially, his requirements. *The Hairy Ape* has been chosen because it represents so adequately this aspect of O'Neill's experimentalism, and because in so many other ways it is characteristic of his work.

The relationship between the biography of an artist and the works of art themselves is often, on the surface at least, highly tenuous; but with O'Neill the relationship is immediately striking. Actual events from his adventurous youth often turn up in the plays; but, more important, the restlessness, the struggle, the insecurity characteristic of his life are clearly mirrored in his work. He was born in New York in 1888, the son of the famous actor James O'Neill who made a great success touring the country for years in the romantic melodrama *Monte Cristo.* Eugene's education was intermittent; he left one school after another, and following a brief experience in college, started his wanderings. He shipped out to sea several times, landed "on the beach" broke and hungry, lived in a barroom, drank heavily, prospected for gold, did some acting, wrote for a newspaper—and in general led a spectacularly erratic life. An attack of tuberculosis forced him into a sanatorium in 1913; here during a six-month period of idleness he was led to examine the purpose of his existence and began to develop a serious interest in the theatre. Upon his release from the sanatorium, O'Neill enrolled during 1914-1915 in Professor George Pierce Baker's famous workshop course in the drama at Harvard and began to write plays.

In 1916, he came in contact with the group which was shortly to form the Provincetown Players, an organization concerned with raising the standards of drama in this country. The members had been influenced by the European "little theatre" movement and by the Ibsen and post-Ibsen dramatic revival, which had up to then hardly touched America. They were disgusted with a drama dominated by worn-out conventions and false values, and they looked toward a national revival of honest theatre. In their early days, O'Neill provided the group with one-act plays, in the realistic manner, based on his own sea experiences; these were produced in Provincetown, Massachusetts, and later, in Greenwich Village, New York, where the company soon permanently settled. With these plays, modern American drama came into being.

446

O'Neill moved uptown to Broadway and the commercial theatre with *Beyond the Horizon* in 1920, which was followed by *Anna Christie* in 1921 and then by *The Hairy Ape* in 1922. Throughout the twenties and until 1931, when *Mourning Becomes Electra* appeared, O'Neill experimented with various dramatic forms and techniques. *Strange Interlude*, with its use of the inner monologue, provoked the greatest curiosity during this period. In the *Electra* trilogy, there was something more solid. By following the plot and by absorbing a degree of the spirit of Aeschylus' drama of the misfortunes of Agamemnon and his family, O'Neill obtained a firmer structure and a more truly objective point of view than is usual with him. After *Electra* a notable success was the nostalgic comedy *Ah Wilderness*, produced in 1933. A "retirement" from the theatre followed, prompted by O'Neill's agonizing personal problems; and then *The Iceman Cometh* was produced in 1946 with a success rivaled only by the posthumous *Long Day's Journey into Night* (1956), O'Neill's brilliant dramatization of his tortured involvement as a young man with his family. The 1972-1973 Broadway revivals of *The Great God Brown* and *Mourning Becomes Electra* were well received, as were the 1973-1974 revivals of *The Iceman Cometh* and *A Moon for the Misbegotten*.

O'Neill died in 1953. His fame seems assured; for despite the great unevenness of his work, his creative achievement is such that he is generally recognized as the greatest of American playwrights. The award of the Nobel Prize in 1936 merely formalized the enormous esteem accorded his work all over the world.

In *The Hairy Ape*, O'Neill has tried to present the predicament of modern man who, lost in a world of machines, wants to "belong," to find a meaning to his existence. He himself has written that the play "was a symbol of man, who has lost his old harmony with nature, the harmony which he used to have as an animal and has not yet acquired in a spiritual way."

There is a certain confusion of symbolism in *The Hairy Ape*. Yank is variously the American, the worker, the animal in man, the subconscious, and the religious seeker. It is perhaps in the last category that we can find the most consistency. Under the cloak of symbolism, Yank progresses from his early complete identification with the machine and pure physical power to a state of self-questioning and doubt, brought about by his sudden meeting with Mildred. He can finally find peace, after failing to solve his dilemma by force, by radicalism, and by thought, only by dying at the hands of a beast who also will not accept him. Man cannot be at home in a technological age.

Perhaps it is valid to say that Yank is searching for God and cannot find him. He realizes that the final answer does not lie in "tree square a day and cauliflowers in de front yard—ekal rights—a woman and kids." "Dis ting's in your inside, but it ain't your belly." O'Neill is wrestling here with a great theme; and even though the play is weakened somewhat by structural defects and by occasional sentimentality, it nevertheless contributes to our understanding of man's fate. *The Hairy Ape* gets down to fundamentals and has the artistic power which may be generated when a creative artist grapples honestly with questions about man's ultimate destiny.

The Hairy Ape

Eugene O'Neill

A COMEDY OF ANCIENT AND MODERN LIFE IN EIGHT SCENES

CHARACTERS

ROBERT SMITH, "YANK"
PADDY
LONG
MILDRED DOUGLAS
HER AUNT

SECOND ENGINEER
A GUARD
A SECRETARY OF AN ORGANIZATION
STOKERS, LADIES, GENTLEMEN, ETC.

SCENES

SCENE I: *The firemen's forecastle of an ocean liner—an hour after sailing from New York.* SCENE II: *Section of promenade deck, two days out—morning.* SCENE III: *The stokehole. A few minutes later.* SCENE IV: *Same as Scene I. Half an hour later.* SCENE V: *Fifth Avenue, New York. Three weeks later.* SCENE VI: *An island near the city. The next night.* SCENE VII: *In the city. About a month later.* SCENE VIII: *In the city. Twilight of the next day.*

Scene One

The firemen's forecastle of a transatlantic liner an hour after sailing from New York for the voyage across. Tiers of narrow, steel bunks, three deep, on all sides. An entrance in rear. Benches on the floor before the bunks. The room is crowded with men, shouting, cursing, laughing, singing—a confused, inchoate uproar swelling into a sort of unity, a meaning—the bewildered, furious, baffled defiance of a beast in a cage. Nearly all the men are drunk. Many bottles are passed from hand to hand. All are dressed in dungaree pants, heavy ugly shoes. Some wear singlets, but the majority are stripped to the waist.

The treatment of this scene, or of any other scene in the play, should by no means be naturalistic. The effect sought after is a cramped space in the bowels of a ship, imprisoned by white steel. The lines of bunks, the uprights supporting them, cross each other like the steel framework of a cage. The ceiling crushes down upon the men's heads. They cannot stand upright. This accentuates the natural stooping posture which shoveling coal and the resultant over-development of back and shoulder muscles have given them. The men themselves should resemble those pictures in which the appearance of Neanderthal Man is guessed at. All are hairy-chested, with long arms of tremendous power, and low, receding brows above their small, fierce, resentful eyes. All the civilized white races are represented, but except for the slight differentiation in color of hair, skin, eyes, all these men are alike.

The curtain rises on a tumult of sound. YANK *is seated in the foreground. He seems broader, fiercer, more truculent, more powerful, more sure of himself than the rest. They respect his superior strength—the grudging respect of fear. Then, too, he represents to them a self-expression, the very last word in what they are, their most highly developed individual.*

VOICES.   Gif me trink dere, you!
    'Ave a wet!
    Salute!
    Gesundheit! [1]
    Skoal!
    Drunk as a lord, God stiffen you!
    Here's how!
    Luck!
    Pass back that bottle, damn you!
    Pourin' it down his neck!
    Ho, Froggy! [2] Where the devil have you been?
    La Touraine. [3]
    I hit him smash in yaw, py Gott!
    Jenkins—the First—he's a rotten swine—
    And the coppers nabbed him—and I run—
    I like peer better. It don't pig head gif you.
    A slut, I'm sayin'! She robbed me aslape—
    To hell with 'em all!
    You're a bloody liar!
    Say dot again! [*Commotion. Two men about to fight are pulled apart*]
    No scrappin' now!
    Tonight—
    See who's the best man!
    Bloody Dutchman!
    Tonight on the for'ard square.
    I'll bet on Dutchy.
    He packa da wallop, I tella you!

[1] German for "health," i.e., "to your health."   [2] A contemptuous word for a Frenchman.
[3] Here probably the name of a night club or of a ship. La Touraine is a district in France.

Shut up, Wop!

No fightin', maties. We're all chums, ain't we?

[*A voice starts bawling a song*]

"Beer, beer, glorious beer!

Fill yourselves right up to here."

YANK. [*For the first time seeming to take notice of the uproar about him, turns around threateningly—in a tone of contemptuous authority*] Choke off dat noise! Where d'yuh get dat beer stuff? Beer, hell! Beer's for goils—and Dutchmen. Me for somep'n wit a kick to it! Gimme a drink, one of youse guys. [*Several bottles are eagerly offered. He takes a tremendous gulp at one of them; then, keeping the bottle in his hand, glares belligerently at the owner, who hastens to acquiesce in this robbery by saying*] All righto, Yank. Keep it and have another [YANK *contemptuously turns his back on the crowd again. For a second there is an embarrassed silence. Then—*]

VOICES. We must be passing the Hook.[4]

She's beginning to roll to it.

Six days in hell—and then Southampton.

Py Yesus, I vish somepody take my first vatch for me!

Gittin' seasick, Square-head?

Drink up and forget it!

What's in your bottle?

Gin.

Dot's nigger trink.

Absinthe? It's doped. You'll go off your chump, Froggy!

Cochon! [5]

Whisky, that's the ticket!

Where's Paddy?

Going asleep.

Sing us that whisky song, Paddy. [*They all turn to an old, wizened Irishman who is dozing, very drunk, on the benches forward. His face is extremely monkey-like with all the sad, patient pathos of that animal in his small eyes*] Singa da song, Caruso[6] Pat!

He's gettin' old. The drink is too much for him.

He's too drunk.

PADDY. [*Blinking about him, starts to his feet resentfully, swaying, holding on to the edge of a bunk*] I'm never too drunk to sing. 'Tis only when I'm dead to the world I'd be wishful to sing at all. [*With a sort of sad contempt*] "Whisky Johnny," ye want? A chanty, ye want? Now that's a queer wish from the ugly like of you, God help you. But no matther.

[*He starts to sing in a thin, nasal, doleful tone*]:

> Oh, whisky is the life of man!
>   Whisky! O Johnny! [*They all join in on this*]
> Oh, whisky is the life of man!
>   Whisky for my Johnny! [*Again chorus*]

---

[4] Sandy Hook, the last view of land on leaving New York by ship.

[5] French for "pig."

[6] An allusion to the famous Italian tenor, Enrico Caruso (1873-1921).

Oh, whisky drove my old man mad!
    Whisky! O Johnny!
Oh, whisky drove my old man mad!
    Whisky for my Johnny!

YANK. [*Again turning around scornfully*] Aw hell! Nix on dat old sailing ship stuff! All dat bull's dead, see? And you're dead, too, yuh damned old Harp,[7] on'y yuh don't know it. Take it easy, see. Give us a rest. Nix on de loud noise. [*With a cynical grin*] Can't youse see I'm tryin' to t'ink?

ALL. [*Repeating the word after him as one with the same cynical amused mockery*] Think! [*The chorused word has a brazen metallic quality as if their throats were phonograph horns. It is followed by a general uproar of hard, barking laughter*]

VOICES. Don't be cracking your head wit ut, Yank.
    You gat headache, py yingo!
    One thing about it—it rhymes with drink!
    Ha, ha, ha!
    Drink, don't think!
    Drink, don't think!
    Drink, don't think! [*A whole chorus of voices has taken up this refrain, stamping on the floor, pounding on the benches with fists*]

YANK. [*Taking a gulp from his bottle—good-naturedly*] Aw right. Can de noise. I got yuh de foist time.

[*The uproar subsides. A very drunken sentimental tenor begins to sing*]:

Far away in Canada,
    Far across the sea,
There's a lass who fondly waits
    Making a home for me—

YANK. [*Fiercely contemptuous*] Shut up, yuh lousy boob! Where d'yuh get dat tripe? Home? Home, hell! I'll make a home for yuh! I'll knock yuh dead. Home! T'hell wit home! Where d'yuh get dat tripe? Dis is home, see? What d'yuh want wit home? [*Proudly*] I runned away from mine when I was a kid. On'y too glad to beat it, dat was me. Home was lickings for me, dat's all. But yuh can bet your shoit no one ain't never licked me since! Wanter try it, any of youse? Huh! I guess not. [*In a more placated but still contemptuous tone*] Goils waitin' for yuh, huh? Aw, hell! Dat's all tripe. Dey don't wait for no one. Dey'd double-cross yuh for a nickel. Dey're all tarts, get me? Treat 'em rough, dat's me. To hell wit 'em. Tarts, dat's what, de whole bunch of 'em.

LONG. [*Very drunk, jumps on a bench excitedly, gesticulating with a bottle in his hand*] Listen 'ere, Comrades! Yank 'ere is right. 'E says this 'ere stinkin' ship is our 'ome. And 'e says as 'ome is 'ell. And 'e's right! This is 'ell. We lives in 'ell, Comrades—and right enough we'll die in it. [*Raging*] And who's ter blame, I arsks yer? We ain't. We wasn't born this rotten way. All men

---

[7] A contemptuous word for an Irishman.

is born free and ekal. That's in the bleedin' Bible, maties. But what d'they care for the Bible—them lazy, bloated swine what travels first cabin? Them's the ones. They dragged us down 'til we're on'y wage slaves in the bowels of a bloody ship, sweatin', burnin' up, eatin' coal dust! Hit's them's ter blame —the damned Capitalist clarss!

[*There had been a gradual murmur of contemptuous resentment rising among the men until now he is interrupted by a storm of catcalls, hisses, boos, hard laughter*]

VOICES. Turn it off!

Shut up!

Sit down!

Closa da face!

Tamn fool! [*Etc.*]

YANK. [*Standing up and glaring at* LONG] Sit down before I knock yuh down! [LONG *makes haste to efface himself.* YANK *goes on contemptuously*] De Bible, huh? De Cap'tlist class, huh? Aw nix on dat Salvation Army-Socialist bull. Git a soapbox! Hire a hall! Come and be saved, huh? Jerk us to Jesus, huh? Aw g'wan! I've listened to lots of guys like you, see. Yuh're all wrong. Wanter know what I t'ink? Yuh ain't no good for no one. Yuh're de bunk. Yuh ain't got no noive, get me? Yuh're yellow, dat's what. Yellow, dat's you. Say! What's dem slobs in de foist cabin got to do wit us? We're better men dan dey are, ain't we? Sure! One of us guys could clean up de whole mob wit one mitt. Put one of 'em down here for one watch in de stokehole, what'd happen? Dey'd carry him off on a stretcher. Dem boids don't amount to nothin'. Dey're just baggage. Who makes dis old tub run? Ain't it us guys? Well den, we belong, don't we? We belong and dey don't. Dat's all. [*A loud chorus of approval.* YANK *goes on*] As for dis bein' hell—aw, nuts! Yuh lost your noive, dat's what. Dis is a man's job, get me? It belongs. It runs dis tub. No stiffs need apply. But yuh're a stiff, see. Yuh're yellow, dat's you.

VOICES. [*With a great hard pride in them*] Righto!

A man's job!

Talk is cheap, Long.

He never could hold up his end.

Divil take him!

Yank's right. We make it go.

Py Gott, Yank say right ting!

We don't need no one cryin' over us.

Makin' speeches.

Throw him out!

Yellow!

Chuck him overboard!

I'll break his jaw for him!

[*They crowd around* LONG *threateningly*]

YANK. [*Half good-natured again—contemptuously*] Aw, take it easy. Leave him alone. He ain't woith a punch. Drink up. Here's how, whoever owns dis. [*He takes a long swallow from his bottle. All drink with him. In a flash all is hilarious amiability again, back-slapping, loud talk, etc.*]

PADDY. [*Who has been sitting in a blinking, melancholy daze—suddenly cries out in a voice full of old sorrow*] We belong to this, you're saying? We make the ship to go, you're saying? Yerra then, that Almighty God have pity on us! [*His voice runs into the wail of a keen, he rocks back and forth on his bench. The men stare at him, startled and impressed in spite of themselves*] Oh, to be back in the fine days of my youth, ochone! [8] Oh, there was fine beautiful ships them days—clippers wid tall masts touching the sky—fine strong men in them—men that was sons of the sea as if 'twas the mother that bore them. Oh, the clean skins of them, and the clear eyes, the straight backs and full chests of them! Brave men they was, and bold men surely! We'd be sailing out, bound down round the Horn maybe. We'd be making sail in the dawn, with a fair breeze, singing a chanty song wid no care to it. And astern the land would be sinking low and dying out, but we'd give it no heed but a laugh, and never a look behind. For the day that was, was enough, for we was free men—and I'm thinking 'tis only slaves do be giving heed to the day that's gone or the day to come—until they're old like me. [*With a sort of religious exaltation*] Oh, to be scudding south again wid the power of the Trade Wind driving her on steady through the nights and the days! Full sail on her! Nights and days! Nights when the foam of the wake would be flaming wid fire, when the sky'd be blazing and winking wid stars. Or the full of the moon maybe. Then you'd see her driving through the gray night, her sails stretching aloft all silver and white, not a sound on the deck, the lot of us dreaming dreams, till you'd believe 'twas no real ship at all you was on but a ghost ship like the *Flying Dutchman*[9] they say does be roaming the seas forevermore widout touching a port. And there was the days, too. A warm sun on the clean decks. Sun warming the blood of you, and wind over the miles of shiny green ocean like strong drink to your lungs. Work —aye, hard work—but who'd mind that at all? Sure, you worked under the sky and 'twas work wid skill and daring to it. And wid the day done, in the dog watch, smoking me pipe at ease, the lookout would be raising land maybe, and we'd see the mountains of South Americy wid the red fire of the setting sun painting their white tops and the clouds floating by them! [*His tone of exaltation ceases. He goes on mournfully*] Yerra, what's the use of talking? 'Tis a dead man's whisper. [*To* YANK *resentfully*] 'Twas them days men belonged to ships, not now. 'Twas them days a ship was part of the sea, and a man was part of a ship, and the sea joined all together and made it one. [*Scornfully*] Is it one wid this you'd be, Yank—black smoke from the funnels smudging the sea, smudging the decks—the bloody engines pounding and throbbing and shaking—wid divil a sight of sun or a breath of clean air—choking our lungs wid coal dust—breaking our backs and hearts in the hell of the stokehole—feeding the bloody furnace—feeding our lives along wid the coal, I'm thinking—caged in by steel from a sight of the sky like bloody apes in the Zoo! [*With a harsh laugh*] Ho-ho, divil mend you! Is it to belong to that you're wishing? Is it a flesh and blood wheel of the engines you'd be?

YANK. [*Who has been listening with a contemptuous sneer, barks out the answer*] Sure ting! Dat's me. What about it?

[8] Irish for "alas."   [9] Famous legendary spectral ship. Subject of an opera by Wagner.

PADDY. [*As if to himself—with great sorrow*] Me time is past due. That a great wave wid sun in the heart of it may sweep me over the side sometime I'd be dreaming of the days that's gone!

YANK. Aw, yuh crazy Mick! [*He springs to his feet and advances on* PADDY *threateningly—then stops, fighting some queer struggle within himself—lets his hands fall to his sides—contemptuously*] Aw, take it easy. Yuh're aw right, at dat. Yuh're bugs, dat's all—nutty as a cuckoo. All dat tripe yuh been pullin'—Aw, dat's all right. On'y it's dead, get me? Yuh don't belong no more, see. Yuh don't get de stuff. Yuh're too old. [*Disgustedly*] But aw say, come up for air onct in a while, can't yuh? See what's happened since yuh croaked. [*He suddenly bursts forth vehemently, growing more and more excited*] Say! Sure! Sure I meant it! What de hell—Say, lemme talk! Hey! Hey, you old Harp! Hey, youse guys! Say, listen to me—wait a moment— I gotter talk, see. I belong and he don't. He's dead but I'm livin'. Listen to me! Sure I'm part of de engines! Why de hell not! Dey move, don't dey? Dey're speed, ain't dey? Dey smash trou, don't dey? Twenty-five knots a hour! Dat's goin' some! Dat's new stuff! Dat belongs! But him, he's too old. He gets dizzy. Say, listen. All dat crazy tripe about nights and days; all dat crazy tripe about stars and moons; all dat crazy tripe about suns and winds, fresh air and de rest of it—Aw hell, dat's all a dope dream! Hittin' de pipe of de past, dat's what he's doin'. He's old and don't belong no more. But me, I'm young! I'm in de pink! I move wit it! It, get me! I mean de ting dat's de guts of all dis. It ploughs trou all de tripe he's been sayin'. It blows dat up! It knocks dat dead! It slams dat offen de face of de oith! It, get me! De engines and de coal and de smoke and all de rest of it! He can't breathe and swallow coal dust, but I kin, see? Dat's fresh air for me! Dat's food for me! I'm new, get me? Hell in de stokehole? Sure! It takes a man to work in hell. Hell, sure, dat's my fav'rite climate. I eat it up! I git fat on it! It's me makes it hot! It's me makes it roar! It's me makes it move! Sure, on'y for me every- ting stops. It all goes dead, get me? De noise and smoke and all de engines movin' de woild, dey stop. Dere ain't nothin' no more! Dat's what I'm sayin'. Everyting else dat makes de woild move, somep'n makes it move. It can't move witout somep'n else, see? Den yuh get down to me. I'm at de bottom, get me! Dere ain't nothin' foither. I'm de end! I'm de start! I start somep'n and de woild moves! It—dat's me!—de new dat's moiderin' de old! I'm de ting in coal dat makes it boin; I'm steam and oil for de engines; I'm de ting in noise dat makes yuh hear it; I'm smoke and express trains and steamers and factory whistles; I'm de ting in gold dat makes it money! And I'm what makes iron into steel! Steel, dat stands for de whole ting! And I'm steel— steel—steel! I'm de muscles in steel, de punch behind it! [*As he says this he pounds with his fist against the steel bunks. All the men, roused to a pitch of frenzied self-glorification by his speech, do likewise. There is a deafening metallic roar, through which* YANK's *voice can be heard bellowing*] Slaves, hell! We run de whole woiks. All de rich guys dat tink dey're somep'n, dey ain't nothin'! Dey don't belong. But us guys, we're in de move, we're at de bottom, de whole ting is us! [PADDY *from the start of* YANK's *speech has been taking one gulp after another from his bottle, at first frightenedly, as if he were afraid to listen, then desperately, as if to drown his senses, but*

finally has achieved complete indifferent, even amused, drunkenness. YANK
sees his lips moving. He quells the uproar with a shout] Hey, youse guys,
take it easy! Wait a moment! De nutty Harp is sayin' somep'n.

PADDY. [*Is heard now—throws his head back with a mocking burst of laughter*]
Ho-ho-ho-ho-ho—

YANK. [*Drawing back his fist, with a snarl*] Aw! Look out who yuh're givin'
the bark!

PADDY. [*Begins to sing the "Miller of Dee" with enormous good nature*]

> I care for nobody, no, not I,
> And nobody cares for me.

YANK. [*Good-natured himself in a flash, interrupts* PADDY *with a slap on the
bare back like a report*] Dat's de stuff! Now yuh're gettin' wise to somep'n.
Care for nobody, dat's de dope! To hell wit 'em all! And nix on nobody else
carin'. I kin care for myself, get me! [*Eight bells sound, muffled, vibrating
through the steel walls as if some enormous brazen gong were imbedded in
the heart of the ship. All the men jump up mechanically, file through the
door silently close upon each other's heels in what is very like a prisoners'
lockstep.* YANK *slaps* PADDY *on the back*] Our watch, yuh old Harp! [*Mockingly*] Come on down in hell. Eat up de coal dust. Drink in de heat. It's it,
see! Act like yuh liked it, yuh better—or croak yuhself.

PADDY. [*With jovial defiance*] To the devil wid it! I'll not report this watch.
Let them log me and be damned. I'm no slave the like of you. I'll be sittin'
here at me ease, and drinking, and thinking, and dreaming dreams.

YANK. [*Contemptuously*] Tinkin' and dreamin', what'll that get yuh? What's
tinkin' got to do wit it? We move, don't we? Speed ain't it? Fog, dat's all
you stand for. But we drive trou dat, don't we? We split dat up and smash
trou—twenty-five knots a hour! [*Turns his back on* PADDY *scornfully*] Aw,
yuh make me sick! Yuh don't belong!

[*He strides out the door in rear.* PADDY *hums to himself, blinking drowsily*]
[*Curtain*]

Scene Two

Two days out. A section of the promenade deck. MILDRED DOUGLAS *and her*
AUNT *are discovered reclining in deck chairs. The former is a girl of twenty,
slender, delicate, with a pale, pretty face marred by a self-conscious expression
of disdainful superiority. She looks fretful, nervous and discontented, bored by
her own anemia. Her* AUNT *is a pompous and proud—and fat—old lady. She is
a type even to the point of a double chin and lorgnettes. She is dressed preten-
tiously, as if afraid her face alone would never indicate her position in life.*
MILDRED *is dressed all in white.*

The impression to be conveyed by this scene is one of the beautiful, vivid
life of the sea all about—sunshine on the deck in a great flood, the fresh sea
wind blowing across it. In the midst of this, these two incongruous, artificial

figures, inert and disharmonious, the elder like a gray lump of dough touched up with rouge, the younger looking as if the vitality of her stock had been sapped before she was conceived, so that she is the expression not of its life energy but merely of the artificialities that energy had won for itself in the spending.

MILDRED. [*Looking up with affected dreaminess*] How the black smoke swirls back against the sky! Is it not beautiful?

AUNT. [*Without looking up*] I dislike smoke of any kind.

MILDRED. My great-grandmother smoked a pipe—a clay pipe.

AUNT. [*Ruffling*] Vulgar!

MILDRED. She was too distant a relative to be vulgar. Time mellows pipes.

AUNT. [*Pretending boredom but irritated*] Did the sociology you took up at college teach you that—to play the ghoul on every possible occasion, excavating old bones? Why not let your great-grandmother rest in her grave?

MILDRED. [*Dreamily*] With her pipe beside her—puffing in Paradise.

AUNT. [*With spite*] Yes, you are a natural born ghoul. You are even getting to look like one, my dear.

MILDRED. [*In a passionless tone*] I detest you, Aunt. [*Looking at her critically*] Do you know what you remind me of? Of a cold pork pudding against a background of linoleum tablecloth in the kitchen of a—but the possibilities are wearisome. [*She closes her eyes*]

AUNT. [*With a bitter laugh*] Merci for your candor. But since I am and must be your chaperon—in appearance, at least—let us patch up some sort of armed truce. For my part you are quite free to indulge any pose of eccentricity that beguiles you—as long as you observe the amenities—

MILDRED. [*Drawling*] The inanities?

AUNT. [*Going on as if she hadn't heard*] After exhausting the morbid thrills of social service work on New York's East Side—how they must have hated you, by the way, the poor that you made so much poorer in their own eyes! —you are now bent on making your slumming international. Well, I hope Whitechapel [10] will provide the needed nerve tonic. Do not ask me to chaperon you there, however. I told your father I would not. I loathe deformity. We will hire an army of detectives and you may investigate everything— they allow you to see.

MILDRED. [*Protesting with a trace of genuine earnestness*] Please do not mock at my attempts to discover how the other half lives. Give me credit for some sort of groping sincerity in that at least. I would like to help them. I would like to be some use in the world. Is it my fault I don't know how? I would like to be sincere, to touch life somewhere. [*With weary bitterness*] But I'm afraid I have neither the vitality nor integrity. All that was burnt out in our stock before I was born. Grandfather's blast furnaces, flaming to the sky, melting steel, making millions—then father keeping those home fires burning, making more millions—and little me at the tail-end of it all. I'm a waste product in the Bessemer process—like the millions. Or rather, I in-

[10] A part of London somewhat equivalent to New York's lower East Side—where the poor live.

herit the acquired trait of the by-product, wealth, but none of the energy, none of the strength of the steel that made it. I am sired by gold and damned by it, as they say at the race track—damned in more ways than one. [*She laughs mirthlessly*]

AUNT. [*Unimpressed—superciliously*] You seem to be going in for sincerity today. It isn't becoming to you, really—except as an obvious pose. Be as artificial as you are, I advise. There's a sort of sincerity in that, you know. And, after all, you must confess you like that better.

MILDRED. [*Again affected and bored*] Yes, I suppose I do. Pardon me for my outburst. When a leopard complains of its spots, it must sound rather grotesque. [*In a mocking tone*] Purr, little leopard. Purr, scratch, tear, kill, gorge yourself and be happy—only stay in the jungle where your spots are camouflage. In a cage they make you conspicuous.

AUNT. I don't know what you are talking about.

MILDRED. It would be rude to talk about anything to you. Let's just talk. [*She looks at her wrist watch*] Well, thank goodness, it's about time for them to come for me. That ought to give me a new thrill, Aunt.

AUNT. [*Affectedly troubled*] You don't mean to say you're really going? The dirt—the heat must be frightful—

MILDRED. Grandfather started as a puddler. I should have inherited an immunity to heat that would make a salamander[11] shiver. It will be fun to put it to the test.

AUNT. But don't you have to have the captain's—or someone's—permission to visit the stokehole?

MILDRED. [*With a triumphant smile*] I have it—both his and the chief engineer's. Oh, they didn't want to at first, in spite of my social service credentials. They didn't seem a bit anxious that I should investigate how the other half lives and works on a ship. So I had to tell them that my father, the president of Nazareth Steel, chairman of the board of directors of this line, had told me it would be all right.

AUNT. He didn't.

MILDRED. How naïve age makes one! But I said he did, Aunt. I even said he had given me a letter to them—which I had lost. And they were afraid to take the chance that I might be lying. [*Excitedly*] So it's ho! for the stokehole. The second engineer is to escort me. [*Looking at her watch again*] It's time. And here he comes, I think.

[*The* SECOND ENGINEER *enters. He is a husky, fine-looking man of thirty-five or so. He stops before the two and tips his cap, visibly embarrassed and ill-at-ease*]

SECOND ENGINEER. Miss Douglas?

MILDRED. Yes. [*Throwing off her rugs and getting to her feet*] Are we all ready to start?

SECOND ENGINEER. In just a second, ma'am. I'm waiting for the Fourth.[12] He's coming along.

MILDRED. [*With a scornful smile*] You don't care to shoulder this responsibility alone, is that it?

---

[11] A type of small lizard supposed in legend and popular belief to be immune to the destructive power of fire.   [12] Fourth Engineer.

SECOND ENGINEER.   [*Forcing a smile*] Two are better than one. [*Disturbed by her eyes, glances out to sea—blurts out*] A fine day we're having.

MILDRED.   Is it?

SECOND ENGINEER.   A nice warm breeze—

MILDRED.   It feels cold to me.

SECOND ENGINEER.   But it's hot enough in the sun—

MILDRED.   Not hot enough for me. I don't like Nature. I was never athletic.

SECOND ENGINEER.   [*Forcing a smile*] Well, you'll find it hot enough where you're going.

MILDRED.   Do you mean hell?

SECOND ENGINEER.   [*Flabbergasted, decides to laugh*] Ho-ho! No, I mean the stokehole.

MILDRED.   My grandfather was a puddler. He played with boiling steel.

SECOND ENGINEER.   [*All at sea—uneasily*] Is that so? Hum, you'll excuse me, ma'am, but are you intending to wear that dress?

MILDRED.   Why not?

SECOND ENGINEER.   You'll likely rub against oil and dirt. It can't be helped.

MILDRED.   It doesn't matter. I have lots of white dresses.

SECOND ENGINEER.   I have an old coat you might throw over—

MILDRED.   I have fifty dresses like this. I will throw this one into the sea when I come back. That ought to wash it clean, don't you think?

SECOND ENGINEER.   [*Doggedly*] There's ladders to climb down that are none too clean—and dark alleyways—

MILDRED.   I will wear this very dress and none other.

SECOND ENGINEER.   No offense meant. It's none of my business. I was only warning you—

MILDRED.   Warning? That sounds thrilling.

SECOND ENGINEER.   [*Looking down the deck—with a sigh of relief*] There's the Fourth now. He's waiting for us. If you'll come—

MILDRED.   Go on. I'll follow you. [*He goes.* MILDRED *turns a mocking smile on her* AUNT] An oaf—but a handsome, virile oaf.

AUNT.   [*Scornfully*] Poser!

MILDRED.   Take care. He said there were dark alleyways—

AUNT.   [*In the same tone*] Poser!

MILDRED.   [*Biting her lips angrily*] You are right. But would that my millions were not so anemically chaste!

AUNT.   Yes, for a fresh pose I have no doubt you would drag the name of Douglas in the gutter!

MILDRED.   From which it sprang. Good-by, Aunt. Don't pray too hard that I may fall into the fiery furnace.[13]

AUNT.   Poser!

MILDRED.   [*Viciously*] Old hag!

[*She slaps her* AUNT *insultingly across the face and walks off, laughing gaily*]

AUNT.   [*Screams after her*] I said poser!

[*Curtain*]

---

[13] An allusion to the Biblical story of Shadrach, Meshach and Abednego, who were thrown by Nebuchadnezzar into a fiery furnace and emerged unharmed.

Scene Three

The stokehole. In the rear, the dimly outlined bulks of the furnaces and boilers. High overhead one hanging electric bulb sheds just enough light through the murky air laden with coal dust to pile up masses of shadows everywhere. A line of men, stripped to the waist, is before the furnace doors. They bend over, looking neither to right nor left, handling their shovels as if they were part of their bodies, with a strange, awkward, swinging rhythm. They use the shovels to throw open the furnace doors. Then from these fiery round holes in the black a flood of terrific light and heat pours full upon the men who are outlined in silhouette in the crouching, inhuman attitudes of chained gorillas. The men shovel with a rhythmic motion, swinging as on a pivot from the coal which lies in heaps on the floor behind to hurl it into the flaming mouths before them. There is a tumult of noise—the brazen clang of the furnace doors as they are flung open or slammed shut, the grating, teeth-gritting grind of steel against steel, of crunching coal. This clash of sounds stuns one's ears with its rending dissonance. But there is order in it, rhythm, a mechanical regulated recurrence, a tempo. And rising above all, making the air hum with the quiver of liberated energy, the roar of leaping flames in the furnaces, the monotonous throbbing beat of the engines.

As the curtain rises, the furnace doors are shut. The men are taking a breathing spell. One or two are arranging the coal behind them, pulling it into more accessible heaps. The others can be dimly made out leaning on their shovels in relaxed attitudes of exhaustion.

PADDY. [*From somewhere in the line—plaintively*] Yerra, will this divil's own watch nivir end? Me back is broke. I'm destroyed entirely.

YANK. [*From the center of the line—with exuberant scorn*] Aw, yuh make me sick! Lie down and croak, why don't yuh? Always beefin', dat's you! Say, dis is a cinch! Dis was made for me! It's my meat, get me! [*A whistle is blown—a thin, shrill note from somewhere overhead in the darkness.* YANK *curses without resentment*] Dere's de damn engineer crackin' de whip. He tinks we're loafin'.

PADDY. [*Vindictively*] God stiffen him!

YANK. [*In an exultant tone of command*] Come on, youse guys! Git into de game! She's gittin' hungry! Pile some grub in her. Trow it into her belly! Come on now, all of youse! Open her up!

[*At this last all the men, who have followed his movements of getting into position, throw open their furnace doors with a deafening clang. The fiery light floods over their shoulders as they bend round for the coal. Rivulets of sooty sweat have traced maps on their backs. The enlarged muscles form bunches of high light and shadow*]

YANK. [*Chanting a count as he shovels without seeming effort*] One—two—tree— [*His voice rising exultantly in the joy of battle*] Dat's de stuff! Let her have it! All togedder now! Sling it into her! Let her ride! Shoot de piece now! Call de toin on her! Drive her into it! Feel her move! Watch her smoke!

Speed, dat's her middle name! Give her coal, youse guys! Coal, dat's her booze! Drink it up, baby! Let's see yuh sprint! Dig in and gain a lap! Dere she go-o-es.

[*This last in the chanting formula of the gallery gods at the six-day bike race. He slams his furnace door shut. The others do likewise with as much unison as their wearied bodies will permit. The effect is of one fiery eye after another being blotted out with a series of accompanying bangs*]

PADDY. [*Groaning*] Me back is broke. I'm bate out—bate—

[*There is a pause. Then the inexorable whistle sounds again from the dim regions above the electric light. There is a growl of cursing rage from all sides*]

YANK. [*Shaking his fist upward—contemptuously*] Take it easy dere, you! Who d'yuh tink's runnin' dis game, me or you? When I git ready, we move. Not before! When I git ready, git me!

VOICES. [*Approvingly*] That's the stuff!

Yank tal him, py golly!

Yank ain't affeerd.

Goot poy, Yank!

Give him hell!

Tell 'im 'e's a bloody swine!

Bloody slave-driver!

YANK. [*Contemptuously*] He ain't got no noive. He's yellow, get me? All de engineers is yellow. Dey got streaks a mile wide. Aw, to hell wit him! Let's move, youse guys. We had a rest. Come on, she needs it! Give her pep! It ain't for him. Him and his whistle, dey don't belong. But we belong, see! We gotter feed de baby! Come on!

[*He turns and flings his furnace door open. They all follow his lead. At this instant the* SECOND *and* FOURTH ENGINEERS *enter from the darkness on the left with* MILDRED *between them. She starts, turns paler, her pose is crumbling, she shivers with fright in spite of the blazing heat, but forces herself to leave the* ENGINEERS *and take a few steps nearer the men. She is right behind* YANK. *All this happens quickly while the men have their backs turned*]

YANK. Come on, youse guys! [*He is turning to get coal when the whistle sounds again in a peremptory, irritating note. This drives* YANK *into a sudden fury. While the other men have turned full around and stopped dumfounded by the spectacle of* MILDRED *standing there in her white dress,* YANK *does not turn far enough to see her. Besides, his head is thrown back, he blinks upward through the murk trying to find the owner of the whistle, he brandishes his shovel murderously over his head in one hand, pounding on his chest, gorilla-like, with the other, shouting*] Toin off dat whistle! Come down outa dere, yuh yellow, brass-buttoned, Belfast[14] bum, yuh! Come down and I'll knock yer brains out! Yuh lousy, stinkin', yellow mutt of a Catholic-moiderin' bastard! Come down and I'll moider yuh! Pullin' dat whistle on me, huh? I'll show yuh! I'll crash yer skull in! I'll drive yer teet' down yer troat! I'll slam yer nose trou de back of yer head! I'll cut yer guts out for a nickel, yuh lousy boob, yuh dirty, crummy, muck-eatin' son of a— [*Suddenly he becomes conscious of all the other men staring at something directly behind his back. He whirls defensively with a snarling, mur-*

---

[14] Capital of Ulster, center of Protestant Ireland and, on the whole, anti-Catholic.

derous growl, crouching to spring, his lips down back over his teeth, his small eyes gleaming ferociously. He sees MILDRED, *like a white apparition in the full light from the open furnace doors. He glares into her eyes, turned to stone. As for her, during his speech she has listened, paralyzed with horror, terror, her whole personality crushed, beaten in, collapsed, by the terrific impact of this unknown, abysmal brutality, naked and shameless. As she looks at his gorilla face, as his eyes bore into hers, she utters a low, choking cry and shrinks away from him, putting both hands up before her eyes to shut out the sight of his face, to protect her own. This startles* YANK *to a reaction. His mouth falls open, his eyes grow bewildered*]

MILDRED. [*About to faint—to the* ENGINEERS, *who now have her one by each arm—whimperingly*] Take me away! Oh, the filthy beast! [*She faints. They carry her quickly back, disappearing in the darkness at the left, rear. An iron door clangs shut. Rage and bewildered fury rush back on* YANK. *He feels himself insulted in some unknown fashion in the very heart of his pride. He roars*] God damn yuh! [*And hurls his shovel after them at the door which has just closed. It hits the steel bulkhead with a clang and falls clattering on the steel floor. From overhead the whistle sounds again in a long, angry, insistent command*]

[*Curtain*]

Scene Four

The firemen's forecastle. YANK'S *watch has just come off duty and had dinner. Their faces and bodies shine from a soap and water scrubbing but around their eyes, where a hasty dousing does not touch, the coal dust sticks like black make-up, giving them a queer, sinister expression.* YANK *has not washed either face or body. He stands out in contrast to them, a blackened, brooding figure. He is seated forward on a bench in the exact attitude of Rodin's "The Thinker."* [15] *The others, most of them smoking pipes, are staring at* YANK *half-apprehensively, as it fearing an outburst; half-amusedly, as if they saw a joke somewhere that tickled them.*

VOICES. He ain't ate nothin'.
    Py golly, a fallar gat to gat grub in him.
    Divil a lie.
    Yank feeda da fire, no feeda da face.
    Ha-ha.
    He ain't even washed hisself.
    He's forgot.
    Hey, Yank, you forgot to wash.
YANK. [*Sullenly*] Forgot nothin'! To hell wit washin'.
VOICES. It'll stick to you.

[15] Famous statue of a man in a sitting position with his chin on his fist, by Auguste Rodin (1840-1917).

It'll get under your skin.

Give yer the bleedin' itch, that's wot.

It makes spots on you—like a leopard.

Like a piebald nigger, you mean.

Better wash up, Yank.

You sleep better.

Wash up, Yank.

Wash up! Wash up!

YANK. [*Resentfully*] Aw say, youse guys. Lemme alone. Can't youse see I'm tryin' to tink?

ALL. [*Repeating the word after him as one with cynical mockery*] Think! [*The word has a brazen, metallic quality as if their throats were phonograph horns. It is followed by a chorus of hard, barking laughter*]

YANK. [*Springing to his feet and glaring at them belligerently*] Yes, tink! Tink, dat's what I said! What about it?

[*They are silent, puzzled by his sudden resentment at what used to be one of his jokes.* YANK *sits down again in the same attitude of "The Thinker"*]

VOICES. Leave him alone.

He's got a grouch on.

Why wouldn't he?

PADDY. [*With a wink at the others*] Sure I know what's the matther. 'Tis aisy to see. He's fallen in love, I'm telling you.

ALL. [*Repeating the word after him as one with cynical mockery*] Love! [*The word has a brazen, metallic quality as if their throats were phonograph horns. It is followed by a chorus of hard, barking laughter*]

YANK. [*With a contemptuous snort*] Love, hell! Hate, dat's what. I've fallen in hate, get me?

PADDY. [*Philosophically*] 'Twould take a wise man to tell one from the other. [*With a bitter, ironical scorn, increasing as he goes on*] But I'm telling you it's love that's in it. Sure what else but love for us poor bastes in the stokehole would be bringing a fine lady, dressed like a white quane, down a mile of ladders and steps to be havin' a look at us?

[*A growl of anger goes up from all sides*]

LONG. [*Jumping on a bench—hectically*] Hinsultin' us! Hinsultin' us, the bloody cow! And them bloody engineers! What right 'as they got to be exhibitin' us 's if we was bleedin' monkeys in a menagerie? Did we sign for hinsults to our dignity as 'onest workers? Is that in the ship's articles? [16] You kin bloody well bet it ain't! But I knows why they done it. I arsked a deck steward 'oo she was and 'e told me. 'Er old man's a bleedin' millionaire, a bloody Capitalist! 'E's got enuf bloody gold to sink this bleedin' ship! 'E makes arf the bloody steel in the world! 'E owns this bloody boat! And you and me, Comrades, we're 'is slaves! And the skipper and mates and engineers, they're 'is slaves! And she's 'is bloody daughter and we're all 'er slaves, too! And she gives 'er orders as 'ow she wants to see the bloody animals below decks and down they takes 'er! [*There is a roar of rage from all sides*]

YANK. [*Blinking at him bewilderedly*] Say! Wait a moment! Is all dat straight goods?

[16] The regulations to which the men subscribe when they sign up as members of a crew.

LONG. Straight as string! The bleedin' steward as waits on 'em, 'e told me about 'er. And what're we goin' ter do, I arsks yer? 'Ave we got ter swaller 'er hinsults like dogs? It ain't in the ship's articles. I tell yer we got a case. We kin go to law—

YANK. [*With abysmal contempt*] Hell! Law!

ALL. [*Repeating the word after him as one with cynical mockery*] Law! [*The word has a brazen metallic quality as if their throats were phonograph horns. It is followed by a chorus of hard, barking laughter*]

LONG. [*Feeling the ground slipping from under his feet—desperately*] As voters and citizens we kin force the bloody governments—

YANK. [*With abysmal contempt*] Hell! Governments!

ALL. [*Repeating the word after him as one with cynical mockery*] Governments! [*The word has a brazen metallic quality as if their throats were phonograph horns. It is followed by a chorus of hard, barking laughter*]

LONG. [*Hysterically*] We're free and equal in the sight of God—

YANK. [*With abysmal contempt*] Hell! God!

ALL. [*Repeating the word after him as one with cynical mockery*] God! [*The word has a brazen metallic quality as if their throats were phonograph horns. It is followed by a chorus of hard, barking laughter*]

YANK. [*Witheringly*] Aw, join de Salvation Army!

ALL. Sit down! Shut up! Damn fool! Sea-lawyer!

[LONG *slinks back out of sight*]

PADDY. [*Continuing the trend of his thoughts as if he had never been interrupted—bitterly*] And there she was standing behind us, and the Second pointing at us like a man you'd hear in a circus would be saying: In this cage is a queerer kind of baboon than ever you'd find in darkest Africy. We roast them in their own sweat—and be damned if you won't hear some of thim saying they like it! [*He glances scornfully at* YANK]

YANK. [*With a bewildered uncertain growl*] Aw!

PADDY. And there was Yank roarin' curses and turning round wid his shovel to brain her—and she looked at him, and him at her—

YANK. [*Slowly*] She was all white. I tought she was a ghost. Sure.

PADDY. [*With heavy, biting sarcasm*] 'Twas love at first sight, devil a doubt of it! If you'd seen the endearin' look on her pale mug when she shriveled away with her hands over her eyes to shut out the sight of him! Sure, 'twas as if she'd seen a great hairy ape escaped from the Zoo!

YANK. [*Stung—with a growl of rage*] Aw!

PADDY. And the loving way Yank heaved his shovel at the skull of her, only she was out the door! [*A grin breaking over his face*] 'Twas touching, I'm telling you! It put the touch of home, swate home in the stokehole. [*There is a roar of laughter from all*]

YANK. [*Glaring at* PADDY *menacingly*] Aw, choke dat off, see!

PADDY. [*Not heeding him—to the others*] And her grabbin' at the Second's arm for protection. [*With a grotesque imitation of a woman's voice*] Kiss me, Engineer dear, for it's dark down here and me old man's in Wall Street making money! Hug me tight, darlin', for I'm afeerd in the dark and me mother's on deck makin' eyes at the skipper! [*Another roar of laughter*]

YANK. [*Threateningly*] Say! What yuh tryin' to do, kid me, yuh old Harp?

PADDY.   Divil a bit! Ain't I wishin' myself you'd brained her?

YANK.   [*Fiercely*] I'll brain her! I'll brain her yet, wait 'n' see! [*Coming over to* PADDY—*slowly*] Say, is dat what she called me—a hairy ape?

PADDY.   She looked it at you if she didn't say the word itself.

YANK.   [*Grinning horribly*] Hairy ape, huh? Sure! Dat's de way she looked at me, aw right. Hairy ape! So dat's me, huh? [*Bursting into rage—as if she were still in front of him*] Yuh skinny tart! Yuh white-faced bum, yuh! I'll show yuh who's a ape! [*Turning to the others, bewilderment seizing him again*] Say, youse guys. I was bawlin' him out for pullin' de whistle on us. You heard me. And den I seen youse lookin' at somep'n and I tought he'd sneaked down to come up in back of me, and I hopped round to knock him dead wit de shovel. And dere she was wit de light on her! Christ, yuh coulda pushed me over with a finger! I was scared, get me? Sure! I thought she was a ghost, see? She was all in white like dey wrap around stiffs. You seen her. Kin yuh blame me? She didn't belong, dat's what. And den when I come to and seen it was a real skoit and seen de way she was lookin' at me—like Paddy said—Christ, I was sore, get me? I don't stand for dat stuff from nobody. And I flung de shovel—on'y she'd beat it. [*Furiously*] I wished it'd banged her! I wished it'd knocked her block off!

LONG.   And be 'anged for murder or 'lectrocuted? She ain't bleedin' well worth it.

YANK.   I don't give a damn what! I'd be square wit her, wouldn't I? Tink I wanter let her put somep'n over on me? Tink I'm goin' to let her git away wit dat stuff? Yuh don't know me! No one ain't never put nothin' over on me and got away wit it, see!—not dat kind of stuff—no guy and no skoit neither! I'll fix her! Maybe she'll come down again—

VOICE.   No chance, Yank. You scared her out of a year's growth.

YANK.   I scared her? Why de hell should I scare her? Who de hell is she? Ain't she de same as me? Hairy ape, huh? [*With his old confident bravado*] I'll show her I'm better'n her if she on'y knew it. I belong and she don't, see! I move and she's dead! Twenty-five knots a hour, dat's me! Dat carries her but I make dat. She's on'y baggage. Sure! [*Again bewilderedly*] But, Christ, she was funny lookin'! Did yuh pipe her hands? White and skinny. Yuh could see de bones through 'em. And her mush, dat was dead white, too. And her eyes, dey was like dey'd seen a ghost. Me, dat was! Sure! Hairy ape! Ghost, huh? Look at dat arm! [*He extends his right arm, swelling out the great muscles*] I coulda took her wit dat, wit just my little finger even, and broke her in two. [*Again bewilderedly*] Say, who is dat skoit, huh? What is she? What's she come from? Who made her? Who give her de noive to look at me like dat? Dis ting's got my goat right. I don't get her. She's new to me. What does a skoit like her mean, huh? She don't belong, get me! I can't see her. [*With growing anger*] But one ting I'm wise to, aw right, aw right! Youse all kin bet your shoits I'll git even wit her. I'll show her if she tinks she— She grinds de organ and I'm on de string, huh? I'll fix her! Let her come down again and I'll fling her in de furnace! She'll move den! She won't shiver at nothin', den! Speed, dat'll be her! She'll belong den! [*He grins horribly*]

PADDY.   She'll never come. She had her belly-full, I'm telling you. She'll be in bed now, I'm thinking, wid ten doctors and nurses feedin' her salts to clean the fear out of her.

YANK. [*Enraged*] Yuh tink I made her sick, too, do yuh? Just lookin' at me, huh? Hairy ape, huh? [*In a frenzy of rage*] I'll fix her! I'll tell her where to git off! She'll git down on her knees and take it back or I'll bust de face offen her! [*Shaking one fist upward and beating on his chest with the other*] I'll find yuh! I'm comin', d'yuh hear? I'll fix yuh, God damn yuh! [*He makes a rush for the door*]

VOICES. Stop him!
He'll get shot!
He'll murder her!
Trip him up!
Hold him!
He's gone crazy!
Gott, he's strong!
Hold him down!
Look out for a kick!
Pin his arms!

[*They have all piled on him and, after a fierce struggle, by sheer weight of numbers have borne him to the floor just inside the door*]

PADDY. [*Who has remained detached*] Kape him down till he's cooled off. [*Scornfully*] Yerra, Yank, you're a great fool. Is it payin' attention at all you are to the like of that skinny sow widout one drop of rale blood in her?

YANK. [*Frenziedly, from the bottom of the heap*] She done me doit! She done me doit, didn't she? I'll git square wit her! I'll get her some way! Git offen me, youse guys! Lemme up! I'll show her who's a ape!

[*Curtain*]

Scene Five

Three weeks later. A corner of Fifth Avenue in the Fifties on a fine Sunday morning. A general atmosphere of clean, well-tidied, wide street; a flood of mellow, tempered sunshine; gentle, genteel breezes. In the rear, the show windows of two shops, a jewelry establishment on the corner, a furrier's next to it. Here the adornments of extreme wealth are tantalizingly displayed. The jeweler's window is gaudy with glittering diamonds, emeralds, rubies, pearls, etc., fashioned in ornate tiaras, crowns, necklaces, collars, etc. From each piece hangs an enormous tag from which a dollar sign and numerals in intermittent electric lights wink out the incredible prices. The same in the furrier's. Rich furs of all varieties hang there bathed in a downpour of artificial light. The general effect is of a background of magnificence cheapened and made grotesque by commercialism, a background in tawdry disharmony with the clear light and sunshine on the street itself.

Up the side street YANK *and* LONG *come swaggering.* LONG *is dressed in shore clothes, wears a black Windsor tie, cloth cap.* YANK *is in his dirty dun-*

garees. A fireman's cap with black peak is cocked defiantly on the side of his head. He has not shaved for days and around his fierce, resentful eyes—as around those of LONG *to a lesser degree—the black smudge of coal dust still sticks like make-up. They hesitate and stand together at the corner, swaggering, looking about them with a forced, defiant contempt.*

LONG.   [*Indicating it all with an oratorical gesture*] Well, 'ere we are. Fif' Avenoo. This 'ere's their bleedin' private lane, as yer might say. [*Bitterly*] We're trespassers 'ere. Proletarians keep orf the grass!

YANK.   [*Dully*] I don't see no grass, yuh boob. [*Staring at the sidewalk*] Clean, ain't it? Yuh could eat a fried egg offen it. The white wings got some job sweepin' dis up. [*Looking up and down the avenue—surlily*] Where's all de white-collar stiffs yuh said was here—and de skoits—*her* kind?

LONG.   In church, blarst 'em! Arskin' Jesus to give 'em more money.

YANK.   Choich, huh? I useter go to choich onct—sure—when I was a kid. Me old man and woman, dey made me. Dey never went demselves, dough. Always got too big a head on Sunday mornin', dat was dem. [*With a grin*] Dey was scrappers for fair, bot' of dem. On Satiday nights when dey bot' got a skinful dey could put up a bout oughter been staged at de Garden. When dey got trough dere wasn't a chair or table wit a leg under it. Or else dey bot' jumped on me for somep'n. Dat was where I loined to take punishment. [*With a grin and a swagger*] I'm a chip offen de old block, get me?

LONG.   Did yer old man follow the sea?

YANK.   Naw. Worked along shore. I runned away when me old lady croaked wit de tremens.[17] I helped at truckin' and in de market. Den I shipped in de stokehole. Sure. Dat belongs. De rest was nothin'. [*Looking around him*] I ain't never seen dis before. De Brooklyn waterfront, dat was where I was dragged up. [*Taking a deep breath*] Dis ain't so bad at dat, huh?

LONG.   Not bad? Well, we pays for it wiv our bloody sweat, if yer wants to know!

YANK.   [*With sudden angry disgust*] Aw, hell! I don't see no one, see—like her. All dis gives me a pain. It don't belong. Say, ain't dere a back room around dis dump? Let's go shoot a ball. All dis is too clean and quiet and dolled-up, get me! It gives me a pain.

LONG.   Wait and yer'll bloody well see—

YANK.   I don't wait for no one. I keep on de move. Say, what yuh drag me up here for, anyway? Tryin' to kid me, yuh simp, yuh?

LONG.   Yer wants to get back at 'er, don't yer? That's what yer been sayin' every bloomin' hour since she hinsulted yer.

YANK.   [*Vehemently*] Sure ting I do! Didn't I try to get even wit her in Southampton? Didn't I sneak on de dock and wait for her by de gangplank? I was goin' to spit in her pale mug, see! Sure, right in her popeyes! Dat woulda made me even, see? But no chanct. Dere was a whole army of plainclothes bulls around. Dey spotted me and gimme de bum's rush. I never seen her. But I'll git square wit her yet, you watch! [*Furiously*] De lousy tart! She tinks she kin get away wit moider—but not wit me! I'll fix her! I'll tink of a way!

[17] Delirium tremens.

LONG. [*As disgusted as he dares to be*] Ain't that why I brought yer up 'ere—
to show yer? Yer been lookin' at this 'ere 'ole affair wrong. Yer been actin'
an' talkin' 's if it was all a bleedin' personal matter between yer and that
bloody cow. I wants to convince yer she was on'y a representative of 'er
clarss. I wants to awaken yer bloody clarss consciousness. Then yer'll see it's
'er clarss yer've got to fight, not 'er alone. There's a 'ole mob of 'em like 'er,
Gawd blind 'em!

YANK. [*Spitting on his hands—belligerently*] De more de merrier when I gits
started. Bring on de gang!

LONG. Yer'll see 'em in arf a mo', when that church lets out. [*He turns and
sees the window display in the two stores for the first time*] Blimey! Look at
that, will yer? [*They both walk back and stand looking in the jeweler's.*
LONG *flies into a fury*] Just look at this 'ere bloomin' mess! Just look at it!
Look at the bleedin' prices on 'em—more'n our 'ole bloody stokehole makes
in ten voyages sweatin' in 'ell! And they—'er and 'er bloody clarss—buys
'em for toys to dangle on 'em! One of these 'ere would buy scoff [18] for a
starvin' family for a year!

YANK. Aw, cut de sob stuff! T' hell wit de starvin' family! Yuh'll be passin'
de hat to me next. [*With naïve admiration*] Say, dem tings is pretty, huh?
Bet yuh dey'd hock for a piece of change aw right. [*Then turning away,
bored*] But, aw hell, what good are dey? Let her have 'em. Dey don't belong
no more'n she does. [*With a gesture of sweeping the jewelers into oblivion*]
All dat don't count, get me?

LONG. [*Who has moved to the furrier's—indignantly*] And I s'pose this 'ere
don't count neither—skins of poor, 'armless animals slaughtered so as 'er and
'ers can keep their bleedin' noses warm!

YANK. [*Who has been staring at something inside—with queer excitement*]
Take a slant at dat! Give it de once-over! Monkey fur—two t'ousand bucks!
[*Bewilderedly*] Is dat straight goods—monkey fur? What de hell—?

LONG. [*Bitterly*] It's straight enuf. [*With grim humor*] They wouldn't bloody
well pay that for a 'airy ape's skin—no, nor for the 'ole livin' ape with all 'is
'ead, and body, and soul thrown in!

YANK. [*Clenching his fists, his face growing pale with rage as if the skin in the
window were a personal insult*] Trowin' it up in my face! Christ! I'll fix her!

LONG. [*Excitedly*] Church is out. 'Ere they come, the bleedin' swine. [*After a
glance at* YANK's *lowering face—uneasily*] Easy goes, Comrade. Keep yer
bloomin' temper. Remember force defeats itself. It ain't our weapon. We
must impress our demands through peaceful means—the votes of the on-
marching proletarians of the bloody world!

YANK. [*With abysmal contempt*] Votes, hell! Votes is a joke, see. Votes for
women! Let dem do it!

LONG. [*Still more uneasily*] Calm, now. Treat 'em wiv the proper contempt.
Observe the bleedin' parasites but 'old yer 'orses.

YANK. [*Angrily*] Git away from me! Yuh're yellow, dat's what. Force, dat's
me! De punch, dat's me every time, see!

[*The crowd from church enter from the right, sauntering slowly and
affectedly, their heads held stiffly up, looking neither to right nor left, talking in*

---

[18] Food distributed to natives.

toneless, simpering voices. The women are rouged, calcimined, dyed, overdressed to the nth degree. The men are in Prince Alberts, high hats, spats, canes, etc. A procession of gaudy marionettes, yet with something of the relentless horror of Frankensteins in their detached, mechanical unawareness]

VOICES. Dear Doctor Caiaphas! [19] He is so sincere!

What was the sermon? I dozed off.

About the radicals, my dear—and the false doctrines that are being preached.

We must organize a hundred per cent American bazaar.

And let everyone contribute one one-hundredth per cent of their income tax.

What an original idea!

We can devote the proceeds to rehabilitating the veil of the temple.

But that has been done so many times.

YANK. [*Glaring from one to the other of them—with an insulting snort of scorn*] Huh! Huh!

[*Without seeming to see him, they make wide detours to avoid the spot where he stands in the middle of the sidewalk*]

LONG. [*Frightenedly*] Keep yer bloomin' mouth shut, I tells yer.

YANK. [*Viciously*] G'wan! Tell it to Sweeney! [*He swaggers away and deliberately lurches into a top-hatted gentleman, then glares at him pugnaciously*] Say, who d'yuh tink yuh're bumpin'? Tink yuh own de oith?

GENTLEMAN. [*Coldly and affectedly*] I beg your pardon. [*He has not looked at* YANK *and passes on without a glance, leaving him bewildered*]

LONG. [*Rushing up and grabbing* YANK's *arm*] 'Ere! Come away! This wasn't what I meant. Yer'll 'ave the bloody coppers down on us.

YANK. [*Savagely—giving him a push that sends him sprawling*] G'wan!

LONG. [*Picks himself up—hysterically*] I'll pop orf then. This ain't what I meant. And whatever 'appens, yer can't blame me.

[*He slinks off left*]

YANK. T' hell wit youse! [*He approaches a lady—with a vicious grin and a smirking wink*] Hello, Kiddo. How's every little ting? Got anyting on for tonight? I know an old boiler down to de docks we kin crawl into. [*The lady stalks by without a look, without a change of pace.* YANK *turns to others—insultingly*] Holy smokes, what a mug! Go hide yuhself before de horses shy at yuh. Gee, pipe de heine on dat one! Say, youse, yuh look like de stoin of a ferryboat. Paint and powder! All dolled up to kill! Yuh look like stiffs laid out for de boneyard! Aw, g'wan, de lot of youse! Yuh give me de eye-ache. Yuh don't belong, get me! Look at me, why don't youse dare? I belong, dat's me! [*Pointing to a skyscraper across the street which is in process of construction—with bravado*] See dat building goin' up dere? See de steel work? Steel, dat's me! Youse guys live on it and tink yuh're somep'n. But I'm *in* it, see! I'm de hoistin' engine dat makes it go up! I'm it —de inside and bottom of it! Sure! I'm steel and steam and smoke and de rest of it! It moves—speed—twenty-five stories up—and me at de top and bottom—movin'! Youse simps don't move. Yuh're on'y dolls I winds up to see 'm spin. Yuh're de garbage, get me—de leavin's—de ashes we dump over de side! Now, what 'a' yuh gotta say? [*But as they seem neither to see*

[19] Name of the High Priest who presided at the Council of the Sadducees which condemned Jesus.

nor hear him, he flies into a fury] Bums! Pigs! Tarts! Bitches! [*He turns in a rage on the men, bumping viciously into them but not jarring them the least bit. Rather it is he who recoils after each collision. He keeps growling*] Git off de oith! G'wan, yuh bum! Look where yuh're goin', can't yuh? Git outa here! Fight, why don't yuh? Put up yer mitts! Don't be a dog! Fight or I'll knock yuh dead! [*But, without seeming to see him, they all answer with mechanical affected politeness*] I beg your pardon. [*Then at a cry from one of the women, they all scurry to the furrier's window*]

THE WOMAN. [*Ecstatically, with a gasp of delight*] Monkey fur! [*The whole crowd of men and women chorus after her in the same tone of affected delight*] Monkey fur!

YANK. [*With a jerk of his head back on his shoulders, as if he had received a punch full in the face—raging*] I see yuh, all in white! I see yuh, yuh white-faced tart, yuh! Hairy ape, huh? I'll hairy ape yuh!

[*He bends down and grips at the street curbing as if to pluck it out and hurl it. Foiled in this, snarling with passion, he leaps to the lamp-post on the corner and tries to pull it up for a club. Just at that moment a bus is heard rumbling up. A fat, high-hatted, spatted gentleman runs out from the side street. He calls out plaintively*] Bus! Bus! Stop there! [*And runs full tilt into the bending, straining* YANK, *who is bowled off his balance*]

YANK. [*Seeing a fight—with a roar of joy as he springs to his feet*] At last! Bus, huh? I'll bust yuh! [*He lets drive a terrific swing, his fist landing full on the fat gentleman's face. But the gentleman stands unmoved as if nothing had happened*]

GENTLEMAN. I beg your pardon. [*Then irritably*] You have made me lose my bus. [*He claps his hands and begins to scream*] Officer! Officer!

[*Many police whistles shrill out on the instant and a whole platoon of policemen rush in on* YANK *from all sides. He tries to fight but is clubbed to the pavement and fallen upon. The crowd at the window have not moved or noticed this disturbance. The clanging gong of the patrol wagon approaches with a clamoring din*]

[*Curtain*]

Scene Six

Night of the following day. A row of cells in the prison on Blackwells Island.[20] The cells extend back diagonally from right front to left rear. They do not stop, but disappear in the dark background as if they ran on, numberless, into infinity. One electric bulb from the low ceiling of the narrow corridor sheds its light through the heavy steel bars of the cell at the extreme front and reveals part of the interior. YANK can be seen within, crouched on the edge of his cot in the attitude of Rodin's "The Thinker." His face is spotted with black and blue bruises. A blood-stained bandage is wrapped around his head.

[20] Location of the New York city prison, now called Welfare Island.

YANK. [*Suddenly starting as if awakening from a dream, reaches out and shakes the bars—aloud to himself, wonderingly*] Steel. Dis is de Zoo, huh?

[*A burst of hard, barking laughter comes from the unseen occupants of the cells, runs back down the tier, and abruptly ceases*]

VOICES. [*Mockingly*] The Zoo? That's a new name for this coop—a damn good name!

Steel, eh? You said a mouthful. This is the old iron house.

Who is that boob talkin'?

He's the bloke they brung in out of his head. The bulls had beat him up fierce.

YANK. [*Dully*] I musta been dreamin'. I tought I was in a cage at de Zoo—but de apes don't talk, do dey?

VOICES. [*With mocking laughter*] You're in a cage aw right.

A coop!

A pen!

A sty!

A kennel! [*Hard laughter—a pause*]

Say, guy! Who are you? No, never mind lying. What are you?

Yes, tell us your sad story. What's your game?

What did they jug yuh for?

YANK. [*Dully*] I was a fireman—stokin' on de liners. [*Then with sudden rage, rattling his cell bars*] I'm a hairy ape, get me? And I'll bust youse all in de jaw if yuh don't lay off kiddin' me.

VOICES. Huh! You're a hard boiled duck, ain't you!

When you spit, it bounces! [*Laughter*]

Aw, can it. He's a regular guy. Ain't you?

What did he say he was—a ape?

YANK. [*Defiantly*] Sure ting! Ain't dat what youse all are—apes?

[*A silence. Then a furious rattling of bars from down the corridor*]

A VOICE. [*Thick with rage*] I'll show yuh who's a ape, yuh bum!

VOICES. Ssshh! Nix!

Can de noise!

Piano! [21]

You'll have the guard down on us!

YANK. [*Scornfully*] De guard? Yuh mean de keeper, don't yuh?

[*Angry exclamations from all the cells*]

VOICE. [*Placatingly*] Aw, don't pay no attention to him. He's off his nut from the beatin'-up he got. Say, you guy! We're waitin' to hear what they landed you for—or ain't yuh tellin'?

YANK. Sure. I'll tell youse. Sure! Why de hell not? On'y—youse won't get me. Nobody gets me but me, see? I started to tell de Judge and all he says was: "Toity days to tink it over." Tink it over! Christ, dat's all I been doin' for weeks! [*After a pause*] I was tryin' to git even wit someone, see?—someone dat done me doit.

VOICES. [*Cynically*] De old stuff, I bet. Your goil, huh?

Give yuh the double-cross, huh?

[21] Italian for "quiet, low."

That's them every time!

Did yuh beat up de odder guy?

YANK. [*Disgustedly*] Aw, yuh're all wrong! Sure dere was a skoit in it—but not what youse mean, not dat old tripe. Dis was a new kind of skoit. She was dolled up all in white—in de stokehole. I tought she was a ghost. Sure. [*A pause*]

VOICES. [*Whispering*] Gee, he's still nutty.

Let him rave. It's fun listenin'.

YANK. [*Unheeding—groping in his thoughts*] Her hands—dey was skinny and white like dey wasn't real but painted on somep'n. Dere was a million miles from me to her—twenty-five knots a hour. She was like some dead ting de cat brung in. Sure, dat's what. She didn't belong. She belonged in de window of a toy store, or on de top of a garbage can, see! Sure! [*He breaks out angrily*] But would yuh believe it, she had de noive to do me doit. She lamped me like she was seein' somep'n broke loose from de menagerie. Christ, yuh'd oughter seen her eyes! [*He rattles the bars of his cell furiously*] But I'll get back at her yet, you watch! And if I can't find her I'll take it out on de gang she runs wit. I'm wise to where dey hangs out now. I'll show her who belongs! I'll show her who's in de move and who ain't. You watch my smoke!

VOICES. [*Serious and joking*] Dat's de talkin'!

Take her for all she's got!

What was this dame, anyway? Who was she, eh?

YANK. I dunno. First cabin stiff. Her old man's a millionaire, dey says—name of Douglas.

VOICES. Douglas? That's the president of the Steel Trust, I bet.

Sure, I seen his mug in de papers.

He's filthy with dough.

VOICE. Hey, feller, take a tip from me. If you want to get back at that dame, you better join the Wobblies.[22] You'll get some action then.

YANK. Wobblies? What de hell's dat?

VOICE. Ain't you ever heard of the IWW?

YANK. Naw. What is it?

VOICE. A gang of blokes—a tough gang. I been readin' about 'em today in the paper. The guard give me the *Sunday Times*. There's a long spiel about 'em. It's from a speech made in the Senate by a guy named Senator Queen. [*He is in the cell next to* YANK's. *There is a rustling of paper*] Wait'll I see if I got light enough and I'll read you. Listen. [*He reads*]: "There is a menace existing in this country today which threatens the vitals of our fair Republic —as foul a menace against the very life-blood of the American Eagle as was the foul conspiracy of Cataline[23] against the eagles of ancient Rome!"

VOICE. [*Disgustedly*] Aw, hell! Tell him to salt de tail of dat eagle!

VOICE. [*Reading*]. "I refer to that devil's brew of rascals, jailbirds, murderers and cutthroats who libel all honest working men by calling themselves the

---

[22] Name given to members of the Industrial Workers of the World (IWW), an international labor union founded in Chicago in 1905. It was noted for its radical program.

[23] Roman politician and conspirator (108?-62 B.C.), who endeavored unsuccessfully to overthrow the government in 63 B.C.

Industrial Workers of the World; but in the light of their nefarious plots, I call them the Industrious *Wreckers* of the World!"

YANK. [*With vengeful satisfaction*] Wreckers, dat's de right dope! Dat belongs! Me for dem!

VOICE. Ssshh! [*Reading*] "This fiendish organization is a foul ulcer on the fair body of our Democracy—"

VOICE. Democracy, hell! Give him the boid, fellers—the raspberry! [*They do*]

VOICE. Ssshh! [*Reading*] "Like Cato[24] I say to this Senate, the IWW must be destroyed! For they represent an ever-present dagger pointed at the heart of the greatest nation the world has ever known, where all men are born free and equal, with equal opportunities to all, where the Founding Fathers have guaranteed to each one happiness, where Truth, Honor, Liberty, Justice, and the Brotherhood of Man are a religion absorbed with one's mother's milk, taught at our father's knee, sealed, signed, and stamped upon in the glorious Constitution of these United States!"

[*A perfect storm of hisses, catcalls, boos, and hard laughter*]

VOICES. [*Scornfully*] Hurrah for de Fort' of July!

Pass de hat!

Liberty!

Justice!

Honor!

Opportunity!

Brotherhood!

ALL. [*With abysmal scorn*] Aw, hell!

VOICE. Give that Queen Senator guy the bark! All togedder now—one—two—tree— [*A terrific chorus of barking and yapping*]

GUARD. [*From a distance*] Quiet there, youse—or I'll git the hose. [*The noise subsides*]

YANK. [*With growling rage*] I'd like to catch dat senator guy alone for a second. I'd loin him some trut'!

VOICE. Ssshh! Here's where he gits down to cases on the Wobblies. [*Reads*] "They plot with fire in one hand and dynamite in the other. They stop not before murder to gain their en'ds, nor at the outraging of defenseless woman-hood. They would tear down society, put the lowest scum in the seats of the mighty, turn Almighty God's revealed plan for the world topsy-turvy, and make of our sweet and lovely civilization a shambles, a desolation where man, God's masterpiece, would soon degenerate back to the ape!"

VOICE. [*To* YANK] Hey, you guy. There's your ape stuff again.

YANK. [*With a growl of fury*] I got him. So dey blow up tings, do dey? Dey turn tings round, do dey? Hey, lend me dat paper, will yuh?

VOICE. Sure. Give it to him. On'y keep it to yourself, see. We don't wanter listen to no more of that slop.

VOICE. Here you are. Hide it under your mattress.

YANK. [*Reaching out*] Tanks. I can't read much but I kin manage. [*He sits, the paper in the hand at his side, in the attitude of Rodin's "The Thinker." A pause. Several snores from down the corridor. Suddenly* YANK *jumps to his*

---

[24] Roman statesman (234-149 B.C.) whose constant theme was "Carthage must be destroyed."

*feet with a furious groan as if some appalling thought had crashed on him—
bewilderedly*] Sure—her old man—president of de Steel Trust—makes half
de steel in de world—steel—where I tought I belonged—drivin' trou—
movin'—in dat—to make *her*—and cage me in for her to spit on! Christ!
[*He shakes the bars of his cell door till the whole tier trembles. Irritated,
protesting exclamations from those awakened or trying to get to sleep*] He
made dis—dis cage! Steel! *It* don't belong, dat's what! Cages, cells, locks,
bolts, bars—dat's what it means!—holdin' me down wit him at de top! But
I'll drive trou! Fire, dat melts it! I'll be fire—under de heap—fire dat never
goes out—hot as hell—breakin' out in de night—

[*While he has been saying this last he has shaken his cell door to a clanging
accompaniment. As he comes to the "breakin' out" he seizes one bar with both
hands and, putting his two feet up against the others so that his position is
parallel to the floor like a monkey's, he gives a great wrench backwards. The bar
bends like a licorice stick under his tremendous strength. Just at this moment
the prison* GUARD *rushes in, dragging a hose behind him*]

GUARD. [*Angrily*] I'll loin youse bums to wake me up! [*Sees* YANK] Hello, it's
you, huh? Got the D.T.'s, hey? Well, I'll cure 'em. I'll drown your snakes for
yuh! [*Noticing the bar*] Hell, look at dat bar bended! On'y a bug is strong
enough for dat!

YANK. [*Glaring at him*] Or a hairy ape, yuh big yellow bum! Look out! Here
I come! [*He grabs another bar*]

GUARD. [*Scared now—yelling off left*] Toin de hose on, Ben!—full pressure!
And call de others—and a strait jacket!

[*The curtain is falling. As it hides* YANK *from view, there is a splattering
smash as the stream of water hits the steel of* YANK's *cell*]

[*Curtain*]

Scene Seven

*Nearly a month later. An IWW local near the waterfront, showing the
interior of a front room on the ground floor, and the street outside. Moonlight on
the narrow street, buildings massed in black shadow. The interior of the room,
which is general assembly room, office, and reading room, resembles some dingy
settlement boys' club. A desk and high stool are in one corner. A table with
papers, stacks of pamphlets, chairs about it, is at center. The whole is decidedly
cheap, banal, commonplace and unmysterious as a room could well be. The
secretary is perched on the stool making entries in a large ledger. An eye shade
casts his face into shadows. Eight or ten men, longshoremen, iron workers, and
the like, are grouped about the table. Two are playing checkers. One is writing
a letter. Most of them are smoking pipes. A big signboard is on the wall at the
rear, "Industrial Workers of the World—Local No. 57."*

YANK *comes down the street outside. He is dressed as in Scene Five. He moves
cautiously, mysteriously. He comes to a point opposite the door; tiptoes softly up*

to it, listens, is impressed by the silence within, knocks carefully, as if he were guessing at the password to some secret rite. Listens. No answer. Knocks again a bit louder. No answer. Knocks impatiently, much louder.

SECRETARY. [*Turning around on his stool*] What the hell is that—someone knocking? [*Shouts*] Come in, why don't you?

[*All the men in the room look up.* YANK *opens the door slowly, gingerly, as if afraid of an ambush. He looks around for secret doors, mystery, is taken aback by the commonplaceness of the room and the men in it, thinks he may have gotten in the wrong place, then sees the signboard on the wall and is reassured*]

YANK. [*Blurts out*] Hello.

MEN. [*Reservedly*] Hello.

YANK. [*More easily*] I tought I'd bumped into de wrong dump.

SECRETARY. [*Scrutinizing him carefully*] Maybe you have. Are you a member?

YANK. Naw, not yet. Dat's what I come for—to join.

SECRETARY. That's easy. What's your job—longshore?

YANK. Naw. Fireman—stoker on de liners.

SECRETARY. [*With satisfaction*] Welcome to our city. Glad to know you people are waking up at last. We haven't got many members in your line.

YANK. Naw. Dey're all dead to be woild.

SECRETARY. Well, you can help to wake 'em. What's your name? I'll make out your card.

YANK. [*Confused*] Name? Lemme tink.

SECRETARY. [*Sharply*] Don't you know your own name?

YANK. Sure; but I been just Yank for so long—Bob, dat's it—Bob Smith.

SECRETARY. [*Writing*] Robert Smith. [*Fills out the rest of card*] Here you are. Cost you half a dollar.

YANK. Is dat all—four bits? Dat's easy. [*Gives the* SECRETARY *the money*]

SECRETARY. [*Throwing it in drawer*] Thanks. Well, make yourself at home. No introductions needed. There's literature on the table. Take some of those pamphlets with you to distribute aboard ship. They may bring results. Sow the seed, only go about it right. Don't get caught and fired. We got plenty out of work. What we need is men who can hold their jobs—and work for us at the same time.

YANK. Sure. [*But he still stands, embarrassed and uneasy*]

SECRETARY. [*Looking at him—curiously*] What did you knock for? Think we had a coon in uniform to open doors?

YANK. Naw. I thought it was locked—and dat yuh'd wanter give me the once-over trou a peep-hole or somep'n to see if I was right.

SECRETARY. [*Alert and suspicious but with an easy laugh*] Think we were running a crap game? That door is never locked. What put that in your nut?

YANK. [*With a knowing grin, convinced that this is all camouflage, a part of the secrecy*] Dis burg is full of bulls, ain't it?

SECRETARY. [*Sharply*] What have the cops got to do with us? We're breaking no laws.

YANK. [*With a knowing wink*] Sure. Youse wouldn't for woilds. Sure. I'm wise to dat.

SECRETARY. You seem to be wise to a lot of stuff none of us knows about.

YANK. [*With another wink*] Aw, dat's aw right, see. [*Then made a bit resentful by the suspicious glances from all sides*] Aw, can it! Youse needn't put me trou de toid degree. Can't youse see I belong? Sure! I'm reg'lar. I'll stick, get me? I'll shoot de woiks for youse. Dat's why I wanted to join in.

SECRETARY. [*Breezily, feeling him out*] That's the right spirit. Only are you sure you understand what you've joined? It's all plain and above board; still, some guys get a wrong slant on us. [*Sharply*] What's your notion of the purpose of the IWW?

YANK. Aw, I know all about it.

SECRETARY. [*Sarcastically*] Well, give us some of your valuable information.

YANK. [*Cunningly*] I know enough not to speak outa my toin. [*Then resentfully again*] Aw, say! I'm reg'lar. I'm wise to de game. I know yuh got to watch your step wit a stranger. For all youse know, I might be a plain-clothes dick, or somep'n, dat's what yuh're tinkin', huh? Aw, forget it! I belong, see? Ask any guy down to de docks if I don't.

SECRETARY. Who said you didn't?

YANK. After I'm 'nitiated, I'll show yuh.

SECRETARY. [*Astounded*] Initiated? There's no initiation.

YANK. [*Disappointed*] Ain't there no password—no grip nor nothin'?

SECRETARY. What'd you think this is—the Elks—or the Black Hand? [25]

YANK. De Elks, hell! De Black Hand, dey're a lot of yellow back-stickin' Ginees.[26] Naw. Dis is a man's gang, ain't it?

SECRETARY. You said it! That's why we stand on our two feet in the open. We got no secrets.

YANK. [*Surprised but admiringly*] Yuh mean to say yuh always run wide open —like dis?

SECRETARY. Exactly.

YANK. Den yuh sure got your noive wit youse!

SECRETARY. [*Sharply*] Just what was it made you want to join us? Come out with that straight.

YANK. Yuh call me? Well, I got noive, too! Here's my hand. Yuh wanter blow tings up, don't yuh? Well, dat's me! I belong!

SECRETARY. [*With pretended carelessness*] You mean change the unequal conditions of society by legitimate direct action—or with dynamite?

YANK. Dynamite! Blow it offen de oith—steel—all de cages—all de factories, steamers, buildings, jails—de Steel Trust and all dat makes it go.

SECRETARY. So—that's your idea, eh? And did you have any special job in that line you wanted to propose to us? [*He makes a sign to the men, who get up cautiously one by one and group behind* YANK]

YANK. [*Boldly*] Sure, I'll come out wit it. I'll show youse I'm one of de gang. Dere's dat millionaire guy, Douglas—

SECRETARY. President of the Steel Trust, you mean? Do you want to assassinate him?

YANK. Naw, dat don't get yuh nothin'. I mean blow up de factory, de woiks, where he makes de steel. Dat's what I'm after—to blow up de steel, knock all

---

[25] A criminal secret society, composed mainly of Italians and organized in the U.S.A. in the 1890's for the purposes of blackmail and murder.   [26] Slang for Italians.

de steel in de woild up to de moon. Dat'll fix tings! [*Eagerly, with a touch of bravado*] I'll do it by me lonesome! I'll show yuh! Tell me where his woiks is, how to git there, all de dope. Gimme de stuff, de old butter—and watch me do de rest! Watch de smoke and see it move! I don't give a damn if dey nab me—long as it's done! I'll soive life for it—and give 'em de laugh! [*Half to himself*] And I'll write her a letter and tell her de hairy ape done it. Dat'll square tings.

SECRETARY. [*Stepping away from* YANK] Very interesting. [*He gives a signal. The men, huskies all, throw themselves on* YANK *and before he knows it they have his legs and arms pinioned. But he is too flabbergasted to make a struggle, anyway. They feel him over for weapons*]

MAN. No gat, no knife. Shall we give him what's what and put the boots to him?

SECRETARY. No. He isn't worth the trouble we'd get into. He's too stupid. [*He comes closer and laughs mockingly in* YANK'S *face*] Ho-ho! By God, this is the biggest joke they've put up on us yet. Hey, you Joke! Who sent you—Burns or Pinkerton? [27] No, by God, you're such a bonehead I'll bet you're in the Secret Service! Well, you dirty spy, you rotten agent provocator, [28] you can go back and tell whatever skunk is paying you blood-money for betraying your brothers that he's wasting his coin. You couldn't catch a cold. And tell him that all he'll ever get on us, or ever has got, is just his own sneaking plots that he's framed up to put us in jail. We are what our manifesto says we are, neither more nor less—and we'll give him a copy of that any time he calls. And as for you—[*He glares scornfully at* YANK, *who is sunk in an oblivious stupor*] Oh, hell, what's the use of talking? You're a brainless ape.

YANK. [*Aroused by the word to fierce but futile struggles*] What's dat, yuh Sheeny bum, yuh!

SECRETARY. Throw him out, boys.

[*In spite of his struggles, this is done with gusto and éclat. Propelled by several parting kicks,* YANK *lands sprawling in the middle of the narrow cobbled street. With a growl he starts to get up and storm the closed door, but stops bewildered by the confusion in his brain, pathetically impotent. He sits there, brooding, in as near to the attitude of Rodin's "Thinker" as he can get in his position*]

YANK. [*Bitterly*] So dem boids don't tink I belong, neider. Aw, to hell wit 'em! Dey're in de wrong pew—de same old bull—soapboxes and Salvation Army—no guts! Cut out an hour offen de job a day and make me happy! Gimme a dollar more a day and make me happy! Tree square a day, and cauliflowers in de front yard—ekal rights—a woman and kids—a lousy vote —and I'm all fixed for Jesus, huh? Aw, hell! What does dat get yuh? Dis ting's in your inside, but it ain't your belly. Feedin' your face—sinkers and coffee—dat don't touch it. It's way down—at de bottom. Yuh can't grab it, and yuh can't stop it. It moves, and everything moves. It stops and de whole woild stops. Dat's me now—I don't tick, see?—I'm a busted Ingersoll,

---

[27] Detective agencies noted in the past for their antilabor union activity.

[28] An agitator employed to join an organization or a group in order to encourage its members to commit illegal or harmful acts so that they may be liable to punishment.

dat's what. Steel was me, and I owned de woild. Now I ain't steel, and de woild owns me. Aw, hell! I can't see—it's all dark, get me? It's all wrong! [*He turns a bitter mocking face up like an ape gibbering at the moon*] Say, youse up dere, Man in de Moon, yuh look so wise, gimme de answer, huh? Slip me de inside dope, de information right from de stable—where do I get off at, huh?

A POLICEMAN. [*Who has come up the street in time to hear this last—with grim humor*] You'll get off at the station, you boob, if you don't get up out of that and keep movin'.

YANK. [*Looking up at him—with a hard, bitter laugh*] Sure! Lock me up! Put me in a cage! Dat's de on'y answer yuh know. G'wan, lock me up!

POLICEMAN. What you been doin'?

YANK. Enuf to gimme life for! I was born, see? Sure, dat's de charge. Write it in de blotter. I was born, get me!

POLICEMAN. [*Jocosely*] God pity your old woman! [*Then matter-of-fact*] But I've no time for kidding. You're soused. I'd run you in but it's too long a walk to the station. Come on now, get up, or I'll fan your ears with this club. Beat it now! [*He hauls YANK to his feet*]

YANK. [*In a vague mocking tone*] Say, where do I go from here?

POLICEMAN. [*Giving him a push—with a grin, indifferently*] Go to hell.

[*Curtain*]

Scene Eight

Twilight of the next day. The monkey house at the Zoo. One spot of clear gray light falls on the front of one cage so that the interior can be seen. The other cages are vague, shrouded in shadow from which chatterings pitched in a conversational tone can be heard. On the one cage a sign from which the word "gorilla" stands out. The gigantic animal himself is seen squatting on his haunches on a bench in much the same attitude as Rodin's "Thinker." YANK enters from the left. Immediately a chorus of angry chattering and screeching breaks out. The gorilla turns his eyes but makes no sound or move.

YANK. [*With a hard, bitter laugh*] Welcome to your city, huh? Hail, hail, de gang's all here! [*At the sound of his voice the chattering dies away into an attentive silence. YANK walks up to the gorilla's cage and, leaning over the railing, stares in at its occupant, who stares back at him, silent and motionless. There is a pause of dead stillness. Then YANK begins to talk in a friendly confidential tone, half-mockingly, but with a deep undercurrent of sympathy*] Say, yuh're some hard-lookin' guy, ain't yuh? I seen lots of tough nuts dat de gang called gorillas, but yuh're de foist real one I ever seen. Some chest yuh got, and shoulders, and dem arms and mitts! I bet yuh got a punch in eider fist dat'd knock 'em all silly! [*This with genuine admiration.*

The gorilla, as if he understood, stands upright, swelling out his chest and pounding on it with his fist. YANK *grins sympathetically*] Sure, I get yuh. Yuh challenge de whole woild, huh? Yuh got what I was sayin' even if yuh muffed de woids. [*Then bitterness creeping in*] And why wouldn't yuh get me? Ain't we both members of de same club—de Hairy Apes? [*They stare at each other—a pause—then* YANK *goes on slowly and bitterly*] So yuh're what she seen when she looked at me, de white-faced tart! I was you to her, get me? On'y outa de cage—broke out—free to moider her, see? Sure! Dat's what she tought. She wasn't wise dat I was in a cage, too—worser'n yours—sure—a damn sight—'cause you got some chanct to bust loose—but me—[*He grows confused*] Aw, hell! It's all wrong, ain't it? [*A pause*] I s'pose yuh wanter know what I'm doin' here, huh? I been warmin' a bench down to de Battery[29]—ever since last night. Sure. I seen de sun come up. Dat was pretty, too—all red and pink and green. I was lookin' at de skyscrapers—steel—and all de ships comin' in, sailin' out, all over de oith—and dey was steel, too. De sun was warm, dey wasn't no clouds, and dere was a breeze blowin'. Sure, it was great stuff. I got it aw right—what Paddy said about dat bein' de right dope—on'y I couldn't get *in* it, see? I couldn't belong in dat. It was over my head. And I kept tinkin'—and den I beat it up here to see what youse was like. And I waited till dey was all gone to git yuh alone. Say, how d'yuh feel sittin' in dat pen all de time, havin' to stand for 'em comin' and starin' at yuh—de white-faced, skinny tarts and de boobs what marry 'em—makin' fun of yuh, laughin' at yuh, gittin' scared of yuh—damn 'em! [*He pounds on the rail with his fist. The gorilla rattles the bars of his cage and snarls. All the other monkeys set up an angry chattering in the darkness.* YANK *goes on excitedly*] Sure! Dat's de way it hits me, too. On'y yuh're lucky, see? Yuh don't belong wit 'em and yuh know it. But me, I belong wit 'em—but I don't, see? Dey don't belong wit me, dat's what. Get me? Tinkin' is hard— [*He passes one hand across his forehead with a painful gesture. The gorilla growls impatiently.* YANK *goes on gropingly*] It's dis way, what I'm drivin' at. Youse can sit and dope dream in de past, green woods, de jungle and de rest of it. Den yuh belong and dey don't. Den yuh kin laugh at 'em, see? Yuh're de champ of de woild. But me—I ain't got no past to tink in, nor nothin' dat's comin', on'y what's now—and dat don't belong. Sure, you're de best off! Yuh can't tink, can yuh? Yuh can't talk neider. But I kin make a bluff at talkin' and tinkin'—a'most git away wit it—a'most!—and dat's where de joker comes in. [*He laughs*] I ain't on oith and I ain't in heaven, get me? I'm in de middle tryin' to separate 'em, takin' all de woist punches from bot' of 'em. Maybe dat's what dey call hell, huh? But you, yuh're at de bottom. You belong! Sure! Yuh're de on'y one in de woild dat does, yuh lucky stiff! [*The gorilla growls proudly*] And dat's why dey gotter put yuh in a cage, see? [*The gorilla roars angrily*] Sure! Yuh get me. It beats it when you try to tink it or talk it—it's way down—deep—behind—you 'n' me we feel it. Sure! Bot' members of dis club! [*He laughs—then in a savage tone*] What de hell! T' hell with it! A little action, dat's our meat! Dat belongs! Knock 'em down and keep bustin'

---

[29] A park in lower Manhattan facing the Hudson River.

'em till dey croaks yuh with a gat—with steel! Sure! Are yuh game? Dey've looked at youse, ain't dey—in a cage? Wanter git even? Wanter wind up like a sport 'stead of croakin' slow in dere? [*The gorilla roars an emphatic affirmative.* YANK *goes on with a sort of furious exaltation*] Sure! Yuh're reg'lar! Yuh'll stick to de finish! Me 'n' you, huh?—bot' members of this club! We'll put up one last star bout dat'll knock 'em offen deir seats! Dey'll have to make de cages stronger after we're trou! [*The gorilla is straining at his bars, growling, hopping from one foot to the other.* YANK *takes a jimmy from under his coat and forces the lock on the cage door. He throws this open*] Pardon from de governor! Step out and shake hands. I'll take yuh for a walk down Fif' Avenoo. We'll knock 'em offen de oith and croak wit de band playin'. Come on, Brother. [*The gorilla scrambles gingerly out of his cage. Goes to* YANK *and stands looking at him.* YANK *keeps his mocking tone —holds out his hand*] Shake—de secret grip of our order. [*Something, the tone of mockery, perhaps, suddenly enrages the animal. With a spring he wraps his huge arms around* YANK *in a murderous hug. There is a crackling snap of crushed ribs—a gasping cry, still mocking, from* YANK] Hey, I didn't say kiss me! [*The gorilla lets the crushed body slip to the floor; stands over it uncertainly, considering; then picks it up, throws it in the cage, shuts the door, and shuffles off menacingly into the darkness at left. A great uproar of frightened chattering and whimpering comes from the other cages. Then* YANK *moves, groaning, opening his eyes, and there is silence. He mutters painfully*] Say—dey oughter match him—wit Zybszko.[30] He got me, aw right. I'm trou. Even him didn't tink I belonged. [*Then, with sudden passionate despair*] Christ, where do I get off at? Where do I fit in? [*Checking himself as suddenly*] Aw, what de hell! No squawkin', see! No quittin', get me! Croak wit your boots on! [*He grabs hold of the bars of the cage and hauls himself painfully to his feet—looks around him bewilderedly —forces a mocking laugh*] In de cage, huh? [*In the strident tones of a circus barker*] Ladies and gents, step forward and take a slant at de one and only— [*His voice weakening*]—one and original—Hairy Ape from de wilds of— [*He slips in a heap on the floor and dies. The monkeys set up a chattering, whimpering wail. And, perhaps, the Hairy Ape at last belongs*]

[*Curtain*]

---

[30] A champion wrestler of the time.

The Glass Menagerie

Tennessee Williams

Tennessee Williams

Tennessee Williams is a controversial figure in contemporary drama, and it is impossible now to "place" him in the history of dramatic literature. But controversial or no, Williams is a major force in the modern theatre. Although he is best known as the author of plays dealing with violence, sex, and abnormalities, he has also written other plays representing a gentler, more nostalgic side of his dramatic interests. Reprinted here is the one play of the latter group that has had a success equal to the most popular of the former group: *The Glass Menagerie* (1944). It and *A Streetcar Named Desire* (1947), a play of violence, are his most famous dramatic achievements. They are the culmination of his early career and between them nicely illustrate the two dominant sides of his character: his romantic nostalgic view of life and his fascination with brutality and decadence —sides by no means incompatible in a larger view.

Tennessee Williams was born in Mississippi in 1914 to a family originally from Tennessee. When he was 13, he moved with his family to St. Louis where his father found work with a shoe company. The family was beset by poverty and probably lived in a crowded tenement similar to that where his characters, the Wingfields, live. Williams' higher education at the University of Missouri, Washington University, and the University of Iowa was intermittent, punctuated by periods of travel all over the United States and many temporary jobs. He was apparently always interested in writing; in 1939 he won a $100 prize for four one-act plays collectively called the *American Blues*. In 1941 the Theatre Guild bought his *Battle of Angels,* which had a bad reception in Boston on its tryout, leading to its withdrawal before presentation in New York.

During World War II he had two fellowships to continue his writing and worked briefly as a script-writer in Hollywood. He finally won acclaim in Chicago in December, 1944 with *The Glass Menagerie,* which opened in New York March 31, 1945. It had a most successful run of over 550 performances and was eventually filmed. The success of this play "snatched" Williams "out of virtual oblivion" and thrust him "into sudden prominence." "From the precarious tenancy of furnished rooms about the country I was removed to a suite in a first-class Manhattan hotel." Thus has he written of his rise to fame.

A Streetcar Named Desire was an equally popular production. It was produced in 1947 and won a Pulitzer Prize and the New York Drama Critics Circle Award. This triumph was followed by other plays, though not all as successful as the *Menagerie* and *A Streetcar: Summer and Smoke* (1948); *Rose Tattoo* (1950); *Camino Real* (1953); *Cat on a Hot Tin Roof* (1954—this was very successful); *Orpheus Descending* (1957); *Sweet Bird of Youth* (1959);

Suddenly Last Summer (1959). Nor has his productivity flagged during the last few years. Williams is also a poet and writer of short stories, but it is his plays which have brought him fame. They are successful because the author, besides having something to say, has an excellent theatrical sense, a good ear for dialogue, and a taste for melodrama which has a wide appeal, although it is a serious question as to whether he does not at times allow his undoubted gifts to run away with him.

The Glass Menagerie is described by its author as a memory play. It is presented through the thoughts of the character Tom who is the narrator of the events after they occur. Tom escapes at the end of the play's action to the merchant marine, as during the play itself he has predicted he would do. He appears at the beginning in the uniform of a merchant sailor. The play moves from his speeches into direct representation of his memories and back to his speeches in the present. He appears as "the point of view," as the persona-creator of the action and as a commentator and chorus. He is not, however, a detached persona or chorus but one intensely concerned with the action, indeed the very entry into the action, in which he has been heavily involved in the recent past. In the text the stage directions speak of magic-lantern slides, although in the New York production they were omitted. The slides were to carry titles or images which would accent certain values in individual scenes; they were primarily to heighten the sense of recall and of the poignance of the unrecoverable past. The play, then, is presented through the screen of memory and illusion. The action itself, however, is sharp and naturalistic. What is real, the author seems to be saying, becomes something else when viewed through the eyes of memory. The play deals with the effects of illusion and the past upon human beings. Amanda Wingfield, the mother and dominant character, is living in the past just as her son, who is recalling her for the audience, is enmeshed in illusion and the past.

The Glass Menagerie is, thus, another testimony to the interest of our age in memory and its concomitant notions of time, childhood, and dreams. Proust's *Remembrance of Things Past* and Joyce's *Finnegans Wake,* to take only two modern literary examples of memory and dream masterpieces, are thus related in their foundation to *The Glass Menagerie.* What this interest in memory reveals of the state of our culture is uncertain, although one can speculate. But it is certainly one of our major literary themes. Thus the play reflects one aspect of the modern western temper.

This concern with memory and its dominance over us is accompanied in *The Glass Menagerie* by a strong sense of challenge, of waste,' and of nostalgia which may be seen in the reactions of the three main characters to life. Tom, the son, meets the effects of time—the past and the present—by breaking loose, only to realize that one cannot really break free. The very existence of the play testifies to the incompleteness of his break. Laura, the daughter, wastes away in her present among her glass animals. Amanda, the mother, lives in a more glorious past. Yet it is she who best meets the challenge of life and is revealed at the end as the comforter. She is perhaps the only one who really triumphs because of her inner strength.

One may profitably search for symbols and ironies in the play. The storm, the glass menagerie, the lightning are a few examples of symbolic happenings and objects. Ironies may be seen throughout: for example, the irony in Amanda's final words to Tom when she accuses him of being a "dreamer," a term which best describes her. But at least she is not a "selfish dreamer"; she dreams for herself but also for her children, particularly Laura.

The symbols, the setting, the persona all reveal that *The Glass Menagerie* is not a naturalistic play, in spite of its realistic detail. Its fluid quality and its plasticity also emphasize its opposition to the "well-made play" of the past century. It belongs to the Chekhovian, Wagnerian, and Strindbergian tradition rather than to the Ibsenite or Shavian tradition. Yet it is a very American play and a most effective one. Its characters, in spite of a certain sentimentality in their presentation, live for us. The action is pointed; the dialogue, sharp. It holds us and has the power that comes from a unified vision of life.

The Glass Menagerie

Tennessee Williams

Nobody, not even the rain, has such small hands.—E. E. Cummings

CHARACTERS

AMANDA WINGFIELD, *the mother*
LAURA WINGFIELD, *her daughter*
TOM WINGFIELD, *her son*
JIM O'CONNOR, *the gentleman caller*

SCENE: *An Alley in St. Louis*

PART I. *Preparation for a Gentleman Caller.*
PART II. *The Gentleman calls.*

TIME: *Now and the Past.*

Scene One

The Wingfield apartment is in the rear of the building, one of those vast hive-like conglomerations of cellular living-units that flower as warty growths in overcrowded urban centers of lower middle-class population and are sympto-matic of the impulse of this largest and fundamentally enslaved section of American society to avoid fluidity and differentiation and to exist and function as one interfused mass of automatism.

The apartment faces an alley and is entered by a fire-escape, a structure whose name is a touch of accidental poetic truth, for all of these huge buildings are always burning with the slow and implacable fires of human desperation. The fire-escape is included in the set—that is, the landing of it and steps descending from it.

The scene is memory and is therefore nonrealistic. Memory takes a lot of poetic license. It omits some details; others are exaggerated, according to the emotional value of the articles it touches, for memory is seated predominantly in the heart. The interior is therefore rather dim and poetic.

At the rise of the curtain, the audience is faced with the dark, grim rear wall of the Wingfield tenement. This building, which runs parallel to the footlights, is flanked on both sides by dark, narrow alleys which run into murky canyons of tangled clotheslines, garbage cans and the sinister lattice-work of neighboring fire-escapes. It is up and down these side alleys that exterior entrances and exits are made, during the play. At the end of TOM'S *opening commentary, the dark tenement wall slowly reveals (by means of a transparency) the interior of the ground floor Wingfield apartment.*

Downstage is the living room, which also serves as a sleeping room for LAURA, *the sofa unfolding to make her bed. Upstage, center, and divided by a wide arch or second proscenium with transparent faded portieres (or second curtain), is the dining room. In an old-fashioned what-not in the living room are seen scores of transparent glass animals. A blown-up photograph of the father hangs on the wall of the living room, facing the audience, to the left of the archway. It is the face of a very handsome young man in a doughboy's First World War cap. He is gallantly smiling, ineluctably smiling, as if to say, "I will be smiling forever."*

The audience hears and sees the opening scene in the dining room through both the transparent fourth wall of the building and the transparent gauze portieres of the dining-room arch. It is during this revealing scene that the fourth wall slowly ascends, out of sight. This transparent exterior wall is not brought down again until the very end of the play, during TOM'S *final speech.*

The narrator is an undisguised convention of the play. He takes whatever license with dramatic convention as is convenient to his purposes.

TOM *enters dressed as a merchant sailor from alley, stage left, and strolls across the front of the stage to the fire-escape. There he stops and lights a cigarette. He addresses the audience.*

TOM.   Yes, I have tricks in my pocket, I have things up my sleeve. But I am the opposite of a stage magician. He gives you illusion that has the appearance of truth. I give you truth in the pleasant disguise of illusion. To begin with, I turn back time. I reverse it to that quaint period, the thirties, when the huge middle class of America was matriculating in a school for the blind. Their eyes had failed them, or they had failed their eyes, and so they were having their fingers pressed forcibly down on the fiery Braille alphabet of a dissolving economy. In Spain there was revolution. Here there was only shouting and confusion. In Spain there was Guernica.[1] Here there were disturbances of labor, sometimes pretty violent, in otherwise peaceful cities such as Chicago, Cleveland, Saint Louis . . . This is the social background of the play.

---

[1] A town in northern Spain bombed by the Germans in 1937 during the Spanish Civil War and the name of a famous painting by Picasso on the event.

MUSIC

The play is memory. Being a memory play, it is dimly lighted, it is sentimental, it is not realistic. In memory everything seems to happen to music.
That explains the fiddle in the wings. I am the narrator of the play, and also
a character in it. The other characters are my mother, Amanda, my sister,
Laura, and a gentleman caller who appears in the final scenes. He is the most
realistic character in the play, being an emissary from a world of reality that
we were somehow set apart from. But since I have a poet's weakness for
symbols, I am using this character also as a symbol; he is the long delayed
but always expected something that we live for. There is a fifth character in
the play who doesn't appear except in this larger-than-life photograph over
the mantel. This is our father who left us a long time ago. He was a telephone man who fell in love with long distances; he gave up his job with the
telephone company and skipped the light fantastic out of town . . . The
last we heard of him was a picture post-card from Mazatlan, on the Pacific
coast of Mexico, containing a message of two words— "Hello—Good-bye!"
and no address. I think the rest of the play will explain itself. . . .
[AMANDA's *voice becomes audible through the portieres*]

LEGEND ON SCREEN: "OU SONT LES NEIGES" [2]

[*He divides the portieres and enters the upstage area*]

[AMANDA *and* LAURA *are seated at a drop-leaf table. Eating is indicated by
gestures without food or utensils.* AMANDA *faces the audience.* TOM *and*
LAURA *are seated in profile*]

[*The interior has lit up softly and through the scrim we see* AMANDA *and*
LAURA *seated at the table in the upstage area*]

AMANDA. [*Calling*] Tom?
TOM. Yes, Mother.
AMANDA. We can't say grace until you come to the table!
TOM. Coming, Mother. [*He bows slightly and withdraws, reappearing a few
moments later in his place at the table*]
AMANDA. [*To her son*] Honey, don't *push* with your *fingers*. If you have to
push with something, the thing to push with is a crust of bread. And chew
—chew! Animals have sections in their stomachs which enable them to di-
gest food without mastication, but human beings are supposed to chew their
food before they swallow it down. Eat food leisurely, son, and really enjoy
it. A well-cooked meal has lots of delicate flavors that have to be held in the
mouth for appreciation. So chew your food and give your salivary glands a
chance to function!
[TOM *deliberately lays his imaginary fork down and pushes his chair back
from the table*]

---

[2] "Where are the Snows [of Yesteryear]," a famous line from a poem by the medieval French
poet Villon (1431-1480?).

TOM. I haven't enjoyed one bite of this dinner because of your constant directions on how to eat it. It's you that make me rush through meals with your hawk-like attention to every bite I take. Sickening—spoils my appetite—all this discussion of animals' secretion—salivary glands—mastication!

AMANDA. [*Lightly*] Temperament like a Metropolitan star! [*He rises and crosses downstage*] You're not excused from the table.

TOM. I'm getting a cigarette.

AMANDA. You smoke too much.

[*LAURA rises*]

LAURA. I'll bring in the blanc mange.

[*He remains standing with his cigarette by the portieres during the following*]

AMANDA. [*Rising*] No, sister, no, sister—you be the lady this time and I'll be the darky.

LAURA. I'm already up.

AMANDA. Resume your seat, little sister—I want you to stay fresh and pretty —for gentlemen callers!

LAURA. I'm not expecting any gentlemen callers.

AMANDA. [*Crossing out to kitchenette. Airily*] Sometimes they come when they are least expected! Why, I remember one Sunday afternoon in Blue Mountain— [*Enters kitchenette*]

TOM. I know what's coming!

LAURA. Yes. But let her tell it.

TOM. Again?

LAURA. She loves to tell it.

[*AMANDA returns with bowl of dessert*]

AMANDA. One Sunday afternoon in Blue Mountain—your mother received— *seventeen!*—gentlemen callers! Why, sometimes there weren't chairs enough to accommodate them all. We had to send the nigger over to bring in folding chairs from the parish house.

TOM. [*Remaining at portieres*] How did you entertain those gentlemen callers?

AMANDA. I understood the art of conversation!

TOM. I bet you could talk.

AMANDA. Girls in those days *knew* how to talk, I can tell you.

TOM. Yes?

IMAGE: AMANDA AS A GIRL ON A PORCH, GREETING CALLERS

AMANDA. They knew how to entertain their gentlemen callers. It wasn't enough for a girl to be possessed of a pretty face and a graceful figure— although I wasn't slighted in either respect. She also needed to have a nimble wit and a tongue to meet all occasions.

TOM. What did you talk about?

AMANDA. Things of importance going on in the world! Never anything coarse or common or vulgar. [*She addresses TOM as though he were seated in the vacant chair at the table though he remains by portieres. He plays this scene as though he held the book*] My callers were gentlemen—all! Among my callers were some of the most prominent young planters of the Mississippi Delta—planters and sons of planters!

[TOM *motions for music and a spot of light on* AMANDA]

[*Her eyes lift, her face glows, her voice becomes rich and elegiac*]

SCREEN LEGEND: *"OÙ SONT LES NEIGES"*

There was young Champ Laughlin who later became vice-president of the Delta Planters Bank. Hadley Stevenson who was drowned in Moon Lake and left his widow one hundred and fifty thousand in Government bonds. There were the Cutrere brothers, Wesley and Bates. Bates was one of my bright particular beaux! He got in a quarrel with that wild Wainwright boy. They shot it out on the floor of Moon Lake Casino. Bates was shot through the stomach. Died in the ambulance on his way to Memphis. His widow was also well-provided for, came into eight or ten thousand acres, that's all. She married him on the rebound—never loved her—carried my picture on him the night he died! And there was that boy that every girl in the Delta had set her cap for! That beautiful, brilliant young Fitzhugh boy from Greene County!

TOM.   What did he leave his widow?

AMANDA.   He never married! Gracious, you talk as though all of my old admirers had turned up their toes to the daisies!

TOM.   Isn't this the first you've mentioned that still survives?

AMANDA.   That Fitzhugh boy went North and made a fortune—came to be known as the Wolf of Wall Street! He had the Midas touch, whatever he touched turned to gold! And I could have been Mrs. Duncan J. Fitzhugh, mind you! But—I picked your *father!*

LAURA.   [*Rising*] Mother, let me clear the table.

AMANDA.   No, dear, you go in front and study your typewriter chart. Or practice your shorthand a little. Stay fresh and pretty!— It's almost time for our gentlemen callers to start arriving. [*She flounces girlishly toward the kitchenette*] How many do you suppose we're going to entertain this afternoon?

[TOM *throws down the paper and jumps up with a groan*]

LAURA.   [*Alone in the dining room*] I don't believe we're going to receive any, Mother.

AMANDA.   [*Reappearing, airily*]. What? No one—not one? You must be joking! [LAURA *nervously echoes her laugh. She slips in a fugitive manner through the half-open portieres and draws them gently behind her. A shaft of very clear light is thrown on her face against the faded tapestry of the curtains. MUSIC: "THE GLASS MENAGERIE" UNDER FAINTLY. Lightly*] Not one gentleman caller? It can't be true! There must be a flood, there must have been a tornado!

LAURA.   It isn't a flood, it's not a tornado, Mother. I'm just not popular like you were in Blue Mountain. . . . [TOM *utters another groan.* LAURA *glances at him with a faint, apologetic smile. Her voice catching a little]* Mother's afraid I'm going to be an old maid.

THE SCENE DIMS OUT WITH "GLASS MENAGERIE" MUSIC

Scene Two

"Laura, Haven't You Ever Liked Some Boy?"
On the dark stage the screen is lighted with the image of blue roses.
Gradually LAURA'S *figure becomes apparent and the screen goes out.*
The music subsides.
LAURA *is seated in the delicate ivory chair at the small claw-foot table.*
She wears a dress of soft violet material for a kimono—her hair tied back from her forehead with a ribbon.
She is washing and polishing her collection of glass.
AMANDA *appears on the fire-escape steps. At the sound of her ascent,* LAURA *catches her breath, thrusts the bowl of ornaments away and seats herself stiffly before the diagram of the typewriter keyboard as though it held her spellbound. Something has happened to* AMANDA. *It is written in her face as she climbs to the landing: a look that is grim and hopeless and a little absurd.*
She has on one of those cheap or imitation velvety-looking cloth coats with imitation fur collar. Her hat is five or six years old, one of those dreadful cloche hats that were worn in the late twenties and she is clasping an enormous black patent-leather pocketbook with nickel clasps and initials. This is her full-dress outfit, the one she usually wears to the D.A.R.
Before entering she looks through the door.
She purses her lips, opens her eyes wide, rolls them upward and shakes her head.
Then she slowly lets herself in the door. Seeing her mother's expression LAURA *touches her lips with a nervous gesture.*

LAURA. Hello, Mother, I was— [*She makes a nervous gesture toward the chart on the wall.* AMANDA *leans against the shut door and stares at* LAURA *with a martyred look*]
AMANDA. Deception? Deception? [*She slowly removes her hat and gloves, continuing the sweet suffering stare. She lets the hat and gloves fall on the floor—a bit of acting*]
LAURA. [*Shakily*] How was the D.A.R. meeting? [AMANDA *slowly opens her purse and removes a dainty white handkerchief which she shakes out delicately and delicately touches to her lips and nostrils*] Didn't you go to the D.A.R. meeting, Mother?
AMANDA. [*Faintly, almost inaudibly*] —No.—No. [*Then more forcibly*] I did not have the strength—to go to the D.A.R. In fact, I did not have the courage! I wanted to find a hole in the ground and hide myself in it forever!

[*She crosses slowly to the wall and removes the diagram of the typewriter keyboard. She holds it in front of her for a second, staring at it sweetly and sorrowfully—then bites her lips and tears it in two pieces*]

LAURA. [*Faintly*] Why did you do that, Mother? [AMANDA *repeats the same procedure with the chart of the Gregg Alphabet*] Why are you—

AMANDA. Why? Why? How old are you, Laura?

LAURA. Mother, you know my age.

AMANDA. I thought that you were an adult; it seems that I was mistaken. [*She crosses slowly to the sofa and sinks down and stares at* LAURA]

LAURA. Please don't stare at me, Mother.

[AMANDA *closes her eyes and lowers her head. Count ten*]

AMANDA. What are we going to do, what is going to become of us, what is the future?

[*Count ten*]

LAURA. Has something happened, Mother? [AMANDA *draws a long breath and takes out the handkerchief again. Dabbing process*] Mother, has—something happened?

AMANDA. I'll be all right in a minute. I'm just bewildered—[*Count five*]—by life. . . .

LAURA. Mother, I wish that you would tell me what's happened!

AMANDA. As you know, I was supposed to be inducted into my office at the D.A.R. this afternoon. *IMAGE: A SWARM OF TYPEWRITERS*. But I stopped off at Rubicam's Business College to speak to your teachers about your having a cold and ask them what progress they thought you were making down there.

LAURA. Oh. . . .

AMANDA. I went to the typing instructor and introduced myself as your mother. She didn't know who you were. Wingfield, she said. We don't have any such student enrolled at the school! I assured her she did, that you had been going to classes since early in January. "I wonder," she said, "if you could be talking about that terribly shy little girl who dropped out of school after only a few days' attendance?" "No," I said, "Laura, my daughter, has been going to school every day for the past six weeks!" "Excuse me," she said. She took the attendance book out and there was your name, unmistakably printed, and all the dates you were absent until they decided that you had dropped out of school. I still said, "No, there must have been some mistake! There must have been some mix-up in the records!" And she said, "No—I remember her perfectly now. Her hands shook so that she couldn't hit the right keys! The first time we gave a speed-test, she broke down completely—was sick at the stomach and almost had to be carried into the washroom! After that morning she never showed up any more. We phoned the house but never got any answer"—while I was working at Famous and Barr,[3] I suppose, demonstrating those— Oh! I felt so weak I could barely keep on my feet! I had to sit down while they got me a glass of water! Fifty dollars' tuition, all of our plans—my hopes and ambitions for you—just gone up the spout, just gone up the spout like that. [LAURA *draws a long breath*

---

[3] A St. Louis department store.

and gets awkwardly to her feet. She crosses to the victrola and winds it up]
What are you doing?

LAURA. Oh! [*She releases the handle and returns to her seat*]

AMANDA. Laura, where have you been going when you've gone out pretending
that you were going to business college?

LAURA. I've just been going out walking.

AMANDA. That's not true.

LAURA. It is. I just went walking.

AMANDA. Walking? Walking? In winter? Deliberately courting pneumonia in
that light coat? Where did you walk to, Laura?

LAURA. All sorts of places—mostly in the park.

AMANDA. Even after you'd started catching that cold?

LAURA. It was the lesser of two evils, Mother. [*IMAGE: WINTER SCENE IN
PARK*] I couldn't go back up. I—threw up—on the floor!

AMANDA. From half past seven till after five every day you mean to tell me
you walked around in the park, because you wanted to make me think that
you were still going to Rubicam's Business College?

LAURA. It wasn't as bad as it sounds. I went inside places to get warmed up.

AMANDA. Inside where?

LAURA. I went in the art museum and the bird-houses at the Zoo. I visited the
penguins every day! Sometimes I did without lunch and went to the movies.
Lately I've been spending most of my afternoons in the Jewel-box, that big
glass house where they raise the tropical flowers.

AMANDA. You did all this to deceive me, just for deception? [LAURA *looks
down*] Why?

LAURA. Mother, when you're disappointed, you get that awful suffering look
on your face, like the picture of Jesus' mother in the museum!

AMANDA. Hush!

LAURA. I couldn't face it.

[*Pause. A whisper of strings*]

LEGEND: "THE CRUST OF HUMILITY"

AMANDA. [*Hopelessly fingering the huge pocketbook*] So what are we going to
do the rest of our lives? Stay home and watch the parades go by? Amuse
ourselves with the glass menagerie, darling? Eternally play those worn-out
phonograph records your father left as a painful reminder of him? We won't
have a business career—we've given that up because it gave us nervous indigestion! [*Laughs wearily*] What is there left but dependency all our lives?
I know so well what becomes of unmarried women who aren't prepared to
occupy a position. I've seen such pitiful cases in the South—barely tolerated
spinsters living upon the grudging patronage of sister's husband or brother's
wife!—stuck away in some little mouse-trap of a room—encouraged by one
in-law to visit another—little birdlike women without any nest—eating the
crust of humility all their life! Is that the future that we've mapped out for
ourselves? I swear it's the only alternative I can think of! It isn't a very
pleasant alternative, is it? Of course—some girls *do* marry. [LAURA *twists
her hands nervously*] Haven't you ever liked some boy?

LAURA. Yes. I liked one once. [*Rises*] I came across his picture a while ago.

AMANDA. [*With some interest*] He gave you his picture?

LAURA. No, it's in the year-book.

AMANDA. [*Disappointed*] Oh—a high-school boy.

SCREEN IMAGE: JIM AS HIGH-SCHOOL HERO
BEARING A SILVER CUP

LAURA. Yes. His name was Jim. [LAURA *lifts the heavy annual from the claw-foot table*] Here he is in *The Pirates of Penzance*.[4]

AMANDA. [*Absently*] The what?

LAURA. The operetta the senior class put on. He had a wonderful voice and we sat across the aisle from each other Mondays, Wednesdays and Fridays in the Aud. Here he is with the silver cup for debating! See his grin?

AMANDA. [*Absently*] He must have had a jolly disposition.

LAURA. He used to call me— Blue Roses.

IMAGE: BLUE ROSES

AMANDA. Why did he call you such a name as that?

LAURA. When I had that attack of pleurosis—he asked me what was the matter when I came back. I said pleurosis—he thought that I said Blue Roses! So that's what he always called me after that. Whenever he saw me, he'd holler, "Hello, Blue Roses!" I didn't care for the girl that he went out with. Emily Meisenbach. Emily was the best-dressed girl at Soldan. She never struck me, though, as being sincere . . . It says in the Personal Section—they're engaged. That's—six years ago! They must be married by now.

AMANDA. Girls that aren't cut out for business careers usually wind up married to some nice man. [*Gets up with a spark of revival*] Sister, that's what you'll do!

[LAURA *utters a startled, doubtful laugh. She reaches quickly for a piece of glass*]

LAURA. But, Mother—

AMANDA. Yes? [*Crossing to photograph*]

LAURA. [*In a tone of frightened apology*] I'm—crippled!

IMAGE: SCREEN

AMANDA. Nonsense! Laura, I've told you never, never to use that word. Why, you're not crippled, you just have a little defect—hardly noticeable, even! When people have some slight disadvantage like that, they cultivate other things to make up for it—develop charm—and vivacity—and—*charm!* That's all you have to do! [*She turns again to the photograph*] One thing your father had *plenty of*—was *charm!*

[TOM *motions to the fiddle in the wings*]

THE SCENE FADES OUT WITH MUSIC

[4] An operetta by Gilbert and Sullivan (1879).

Scene Three

LEGEND ON SCREEN: "AFTER THE FIASCO—"

[TOM *speaks from the fire-escape landing*]

TOM. After the fiasco at Rubicam's Business College, the idea of getting a gentleman caller for Laura began to play a more important part in Mother's calculations. It became an obsession. Like some archetype of the universal unconscious, the image of the gentleman caller haunted our small apartment. . . . [*IMAGE: YOUNG MAN AT DOOR WITH FLOWERS*] An evening at home rarely passed without some allusion to this image, this spectre, this hope. . . . Even when he wasn't mentioned, his presence hung in Mother's preoccupied look and in my sister's frightened, apologetic manner—hung like a sentence passed upon the Wingfields! Mother was a woman of action as well as words. She began to take logical steps in the planned direction. Late that winter and in the early spring—realizing that extra money would be needed to properly feather the nest and plume the bird—she conducted a vigorous campaign on the telephone, roping in subscribers to one of those magazines for matrons called *The Homemaker's Companion*, the type of journal that features the serialized sublimations of ladies of letters who think in terms of delicate cup-like breasts, slim, tapering waists, rich, creamy thighs, eyes like wood-smoke in autumn, fingers that soothe and caress like strains of music, bodies as powerful as Etruscan sculpture.

SCREEN IMAGE: GLAMOR MAGAZINE COVER

[AMANDA *enters with phone on long extension cord. She is spotted in the dim stage*]

AMANDA. Ida Scott? This is Amanda Wingfield! We *missed* you at the D.A.R. last Monday! I said to myself: She's probably suffering with that sinus condition! How is that sinus condition? Horrors! Heaven have mercy!— You're a Christian martyr, yes, that's what you are, a Christian martyr! Well, I just now happened to notice that your subscription to the *Companion*'s about to expire! Yes, it expires with the next issue, honey!—just when that wonderful new serial by Bessie Mae Hopper is getting off to such an exciting start. Oh, honey, it's something that you can't miss! You remember how *Gone With the Wind* [5] took everybody by storm? You simply couldn't go out if you hadn't read it. All everybody *talked* was Scarlett O'Hara. Well, this is a book that critics already compare to *Gone With the Wind*. It's the *Gone With the Wind* of the post-World War generation!—What?— Burning?— Oh, honey, don't let them burn, go take a look in the oven and I'll hold the wire! Heavens— I think she's hung up!

DIM OUT

[5] An extremely popular novel by Margaret Mitchell (1936).

LEGEND ON SCREEN: "YOU THINK I'M IN LOVE
WITH CONTINENTAL SHOEMAKERS?"

[*Before the stage is lighted, the violent voices of* TOM *and* AMANDA *are heard*]

[*They are quarreling behind the portieres. In front of them stands* LAURA *with clenched hands and panicky expression*]

[*A clear pool of light on her figure throughout this scene*]

TOM. What in Christ's name am I—

AMANDA. [*Shrilly*] Don't you use that—

TOM. Supposed to do!

AMANDA. Expression! Not in my—

TOM. Ohhh!

AMANDA. Presence! Have you gone out of your senses?

TOM. I have, that's true, *driven* out!

AMANDA. What is the matter with you, you—big—big—IDIOT!

TOM. Look—I've got *no thing*, no single thing—

AMANDA. Lower your voice!

TOM. In my life here that I can call my OWN! Everything is—

AMANDA. Stop that shouting!

TOM. Yesterday you confiscated my books! You had the nerve to—

AMANDA. I took that horrible novel back to the library—yes! That hideous book by that insane Mr. Lawrence.[6] [TOM *laughs wildly*] I cannot control the output of diseased minds or people who cater to them—[TOM *laughs still more wildly*] BUT I WON'T ALLOW SUCH FILTH BROUGHT INTO MY HOUSE! No, no, no, no, no!

TOM. House, house! Who pays rent on it, who makes a slave of himself to—

AMANDA. [*Fairly screeching*] Don't you DARE to—

TOM. No, no, I mustn't say things! *I've* got to just—

AMANDA. Let me tell you—

TOM. I don't want to hear any more! [*He tears the portieres open. The upstage area is lit with a turgid smoky red glow*]

[AMANDA'S *hair is in metal curlers and she wears a very old bathrobe, much too large for her slight figure, a relic of the faithless Mr. Wingfield*]

[*An upright typewriter and a wild disarray of manuscripts is on the drop-leaf table. The quarrel was probably precipitated by* AMANDA'S *interruption of his creative labor. A chair lying overthrown on the floor*]

[*Their gesticulating shadows are cast on the ceiling by the fiery glow*]

AMANDA. You *will* hear more, you—

TOM. No, I won't hear more, I'm going out!

AMANDA. You come right back in—

TOM. Out, out out! Because I'm—

AMANDA. Come back here, Tom Wingfield! I'm not through talking to you!

[6] D. H. Lawrence (1885-1930), English poet and novelist.

TOM. Oh, go—

LAURA. [*Desperately*] —Tom!

AMANDA. You're going to listen, and no more insolence from you! I'm at the end of my patience! [*He comes back toward her*]

TOM. What do you think I'm at? Aren't I suppose to have any patience to reach the end of, Mother? I know, I know. It seems unimportant to you, what I'm *doing*—what I *want* to do—having a little *difference* between them! You don't think that—

AMANDA. I think you've been doing things that you're ashamed of. That's why you act like this. I don't believe that you go every night to the movies. Nobody goes to the movies night after night. Nobody in their right minds goes to the movies as often as you pretend to. People don't go to the movies at nearly midnight, and movies don't let out at two A.M. Come in stumbling. Muttering to yourself like a maniac! You get three hours' sleep and then go to work. Oh, I can picture the way you're doing down there. Moping, doping, because you're in no condition.

TOM. [*Wildly*] No, I'm in no condition!

AMANDA. What right have you got to jeopardize your job? Jeopardize the security of us all? How do you think we'd manage if you were—

TOM. Listen! You think I'm crazy *about* the *warehouse*? [*He bends fiercely toward her slight figure*] You think I'm in love with the Continental Shoemakers? You think I want to spend fifty-five *years* down there in that— *celotex interior!* with—*fluorescent*—*tubes!* Look! I'd rather somebody picked up a crowbar and battered out my brains—than go back mornings! I *go!* Every time you come in yelling that God damn *"Rise and Shine!"* *"Rise and Shine!"* I say to myself, "How *lucky dead* people are!" But I get up. I *go!* For sixty-five dollars a month I give up all that I dream of doing and being *ever!* And you say self—*self's* all I ever think of. Why, listen, if self is what I thought of, Mother, I'd be where he is—GONE! [*Pointing to father's picture*] As far as the system of transportation reaches! [*He starts past her. She grabs his arm*] Don't grab at me, Mother!

AMANDA. Where are you going?

TOM. I'm going to the *movies!*

AMANDA. I don't believe that lie!

TOM. [*Crouching toward her, overtowering her tiny figure. She backs away, gasping*] I'm going to opium dens! Yes, opium dens, dens of vice and criminals' hang-outs, Mother. I've joined the Hogan gang, I'm a hired assassin, I carry a Tommy gun in a violin case! I run a string of cat-houses in the Valley! They call me Killer, Killer Wingfield, I'm leading a double-life, a simple, honest warehouse worker by day, by night, a dynamic *czar* of the *underworld, Mother.* I go to gambling casinos, I spin away fortunes on the roulette table! I wear a patch over one eye and a false mustache, sometimes I put on green whiskers. On those occasions they call me—*El Diablo!* Oh, I could tell you things to make you sleepless! My enemies plan to dynamite this place. They're going to blow us all sky-high some night! I'll be glad, very happy, and so will you! You'll go up, up on a broomstick, over Blue Mountain with seventeen gentlemen callers! You ugly—babbling old— *witch. . . .* [*He goes through a series of violent, clumsy movements, seizing his overcoat, lunging to the door, pulling it fiercely open. The women watch him, aghast. His arm catches in the sleeve of the coat as he struggles to pull it on. For a moment he is pinioned by the bulky garment. With an outraged groan he tears the coat off again, splitting the shoulder of it, and hurls it across the room. It strikes against the shelf of* LAURA'S *glass collection, there is a tinkle of shattering glass.* LAURA *cries out as if wounded*]

MUSIC LEGEND: "THE GLASS MENAGERIE"

LAURA. [*Shrilly*] My glass!—menagerie. . . . [*She covers her face and turns away*]

[*But* AMANDA *is still stunned and stupefied by the "ugly witch" so that she barely notices this occurrence. Now she recovers her speech*]

AMANDA. [*In an awful voice*] I won't speak to you—until you apologize! [*She crosses through portieres and draws them together behind her.* TOM *is left with* LAURA. LAURA *clings weakly to the mantel with her face averted.* TOM *stares at her stupidly for a moment. Then he crosses to shelf. Drops awkwardly on his knees to collect the fallen glass, glancing at* LAURA *as if he would speak but couldn't*]

"The Glass Menagerie" steals in as

THE SCENE DIMS OUT

Scene Four

The interior is dark. Faint light in the alley.

A deep-voiced bell in a church is tolling the hour of five as the scene commences.

TOM *appears at the top of the alley. After each solemn boom of the bell in the tower, he shakes a little noise-maker or rattle as if to express the tiny spasm of man in contrast to the sustained power and dignity of the Almighty. This and the unsteadiness of his advance make it evident that he has been drinking.*

As he climbs the few steps to the fire-escape landing light steals up inside. LAURA *appears in nightdress, observing* TOM'S *empty bed in the front room.*

TOM *fishes in his pockets for door key, removing a motley assortment of articles in the search, including a perfect shower of movie-ticket stubs and an empty bottle. At last he finds the key, but just as he is about to insert it, it slips from his fingers. He strikes a match and crouches below the door.*

TOM. [*Bitterly*] One crack—and it falls through!

[LAURA *opens the door.*]

LAURA. Tom! Tom, what are you doing?

TOM. Looking for a door key.

LAURA. Where have you been all this time?

TOM. I have been to the movies.

LAURA. All this time at the movies?

TOM. There was a very long program. There was a Garbo picture and a Mickey Mouse and a travelogue and a newsreel and a preview of coming attractions. And there was an organ solo and a collection for the milk-fund—simultaneously—which ended up in a terrible fight between a fat lady and an usher!

LAURA. [*Innocently*] Did you have to stay through everything?

TOM. Of course! And, oh, I forgot! There was a big stage show! The headliner on this stage show was Malvolio the Magician. He performed wonderful tricks, many of them, such as pouring water back and forth between pitchers. First it turned to wine and then it turned to beer and then it turned to whiskey. I know it was whiskey it finally turned into because he needed somebody to come up out of the audience to help him, and I came up—both shows! It was Kentucky Straight Bourbon. A very generous fellow, he gave souvenirs. [*He pulls from his back pocket a shimmering rainbow-colored scarf*] He gave me this. This is his magic scarf. You can have it, Laura. You wave it over a canary cage and you get a bowl of goldfish. You wave it over the goldfish bowl and they fly away canaries. . . . But the wonderfullest trick of all was the coffin trick. We nailed him into a coffin and he got out of the coffin without removing one nail. [*He has come inside*] There is a trick that would come in handy for me—get me out of this 2 by 4 situation! [*Flops onto bed and starts removing shoes*]

LAURA. Tom—Shhh!

TOM. What're you shushing me for?

LAURA. You'll wake up Mother.

TOM. Goody, goody! Pay 'er back for all those "Rise an' Shines." [*Lies down, groaning*] You know it don't take much intelligence to get yourself into a nailed-up coffin, Laura. But who in hell ever got himself out of one without removing one nail?

[*As if in answer, the father's grinning photograph lights up*]

Scene Dims Out

[*Immediately following: The church bell is heard striking six. At the sixth stroke the alarm clock goes off in AMANDA's room, and after a few moments we hear her calling: "Rise and Shine! Rise and Shine! Laura, go tell your brother to rise and shine!"*]

TOM. [*Sitting up slowly*] I'll rise—but I won't shine.

[*The light increases*]

AMANDA. Laura, tell your brother his coffee is ready.

[LAURA *slips into front room*]

LAURA. Tom it's nearly seven. Don't make Mother nervous. [*He stares at her stupidly. Beseechingly*] Tom, speak to Mother this morning. Make up with her, apologize, speak to her!

TOM. She won't to me. It's her that started not speaking.

LAURA. If you just say you're sorry she'll start speaking.

TOM. Her not speaking—is that such a tragedy?

LAURA. Please—please!

AMANDA. [*Calling from kitchenette*] Laura, are you going to do what I asked you to do, or do I have to get dressed and go out myself?

LAURA. Going, going—soon as I get on my coat! [*She pulls on a shapeless felt hat with nervous, jerky movement, pleadingly glancing at* TOM. *Rushes awkwardly for coat. The coat is one of* AMANDA'S, *inaccurately made-over, the sleeves too short for* LAURA] Butter and what else?

AMANDA. [*Entering upstage*] Just butter. Tell them to charge it.

LAURA. Mother, they make such faces when I do that.

AMANDA. Sticks and stones can break our bones, but the expression on Mr. Garfinkel's face won't harm us! Tell your brother his coffee is getting cold.

LAURA. [*At door*] Do what I asked you, will you, will you, Tom?

[*He looks sullenly away*]

AMANDA. Laura, go now or just don't go at all!

LAURA. [*Rushing out*] Going—going! [*A second later she cries out.* TOM *springs up and crosses to door.* AMANDA *rushes anxiously in.* TOM *opens the door*]

TOM. Laura?

LAURA. I'm all right. I slipped, but I'm all right.

AMANDA. [*Peering anxiously after her*] If anyone breaks a leg on those fire-escape steps, the landlord ought to be sued for every cent he possesses! [*She shuts door. Remembers she isn't speaking and returns to other room.*]

[*As* TOM *enters listlessly for his coffee, she turns her back to him and stands rigidly facing the window on the gloomy gray vault of the areaway. Its light on her face with its aged but childish features is cruelly sharp, satirical as a Daumier print*]

MUSIC UNDER: "AVE MARIA"

[*TOM glances sheepishly but sullenly at her averted figure and slumps at the table. The coffee is scalding hot; he sips it and gasps and spits it back in the cup. At his gasp,* AMANDA *catches her breath and half turns. Then catches herself and turns back to window*]

[*TOM blows on his coffee, glancing sidewise at his mother. She clears her throat.* TOM *clears his. He starts to rise. Sinks back down again, scratches his head, clears his throat again.* AMANDA *coughs.* TOM *raises his cup in both hands to blow on it, his eyes staring over the rim of it at his mother for several moments. Then he slowly sets the cup down and awkwardly and hesitantly rises from the chair*]

TOM. [*Hoarsely*] Mother. I—I apologize, Mother. [AMANDA *draws a quick, shuddering breath. Her face works grotesquely. She breaks into childlike tears*] I'm sorry for what I said, for everything that I said, I didn't mean it.

AMANDA. [*Sobbingly*] My devotion has made me a witch and so I make myself hateful to my children!

TOM. No, you *don't*.

AMANDA. I worry so much, don't sleep, it makes me nervous!

TOM. [*Gently*] I understand that.

AMANDA. I've had to put up a solitary battle all these years. But you're my right-hand bower! Don't fall down, don't fail!

TOM. [*Gently*] I try, Mother.

AMANDA. [*With great enthusiasm*] Try and you will SUCCEED!

[*The notion makes her breathless*] Why, you—you're just *full* of natural endowments! Both of my children—they're *unusual* children! Don't you think I know it? I'm so—*proud!* Happy and—feel I've—so much to be thankful for but— Promise me one thing, son!

TOM. What, Mother?

AMANDA. Promise, son, you'll—never be a drunkard!

TOM. [*Turns to her grinning*] I will never be a drunkard, Mother.

AMANDA. That's what frightened me so, that you'd be drinking! Eat a bowl of Purina!

TOM. Just coffee, Mother.

AMANDA. Shredded wheat biscuit?

TOM. No. No, Mother, just coffee.

AMANDA. You can't put in a day's work on an empty stomach. You've got ten minutes—don't gulp! Drinking too-hot liquids makes cancer of the stomach. . . . Put cream in.

TOM. No, thank you.

AMANDA. To cool it.

TOM. No! No, thank you, I want it black.

AMANDA. I know, but it's not good for you. We have to do all that we can to build ourselves up. In these trying times we live in, all that we have to cling to is—each other. . . . That's why it's so important to— Tom, I— I sent out your sister so I could discuss something with you. If you hadn't spoken I would have spoken to you. [*Sits down*]

TOM. [*Gently*] What is it, Mother, that you want to discuss?

AMANDA. *Laura!*

[TOM *puts his cup down slowly*]

LEGEND ON SCREEN: "LAURA"

MUSIC: "THE GLASS MENAGERIE"

TOM. —Oh.—Laura . . .

AMANDA. [*Touching his sleeve*] You know how Laura is. So quiet but—still water runs deep! She notices things and I think she—broods about them. [TOM *looks up*] A few days ago I came in and she was crying.

TOM. What about?

AMANDA. You.

TOM. Me?

AMANDA. She has an idea that you're not happy here.

TOM. What gave her that idea?

AMANDA. What gives her any idea? However, you do act strangely. I—I'm not criticizing, understand *that!* I know your ambitions do not lie in the warehouse, that like everybody in the whole wide world—you've had to—make

sacrifices, but—Tom—Tom—life's not easy, it calls for—Spartan endurance! There's so many things in my heart that I cannot describe to you! I've
never told you but I—*loved* your father. . . .

TOM. [*Gently*] I know that, Mother.

AMANDA. And you—when I see you taking after his ways! Staying out late—
and—well, you *had* been drinking the night you were in that—terrifying
condition! Laura says that you hate the apartment and that you go out
nights to get away from it! Is that true, Tom?

TOM. No. You say there's so much in your heart that you can't describe to me.
That's true of me, too. There's so much in my heart that I can't describe to
you! So let's respect each other's—

AMANDA. But, why—*why*, Tom—are you always so *restless?* Where do you *go*
to, nights?

TOM. I—go to the movies.

AMANDA. Why do you go to the movies so much, Tom?

TOM. I go to the movies because—I like adventure. Adventure is something I
don't have much of at work, so I go to the movies.

AMANDA. But, Tom, you go to the movies *entirely* too *much!*

TOM. I like a lot of adventure.

[AMANDA *looks baffled, then hurt. As the familiar inquisition resumes he
becomes hard and impatient again.* AMANDA *slips back into her querulous
attitude toward him*]

IMAGE ON SCREEN: SAILING VESSEL WITH JOLLY ROGER

AMANDA. Most young men find adventure in their careers.

TOM. Then most young men are not employed in a warehouse.

AMANDA. The world is full of young men employed in warehouses and offices
and factories.

TOM. Do all of them find adventure in their careers?

AMANDA. They do or they do without it! Not everybody has a craze for adventure.

TOM. Man is by instinct a lover, a hunter, a fighter, and none of those instincts
are given much play at the warehouse!

AMANDA. Man is by instinct! Don't quote instinct to me! Instinct is something
that people have got away from! It belongs to animals! Christian adults don't
want it!

TOM. What do Christian adults want, then, Mother?

AMANDA. Superior things! Things of the mind and the spirit! Only animals
have to satisfy instincts! Surely your aims are somewhat higher than theirs!
Than monkeys—pigs—

TOM. I reckon they're not.

AMANDA. You're joking. However, that isn't what I wanted to discuss.

TOM. [*Rising*] I haven't much time.

AMANDA. [*Pushing his shoulders*] Sit down.

TOM. You want me to punch in red at the warehouse, Mother?

AMANDA. You have five minutes. I want to talk about Laura.

LEGEND: "PLANS AND PROVISIONS"

TOM. All right! What about Laura?

AMANDA. We have to be making plans and provisions for her. She's older than you, two years, and nothing has happened. She just drifts along doing nothing. It frightens me terribly how she just drifts along.

TOM. I guess she's the type that people call home girls.

AMANDA. There's no such type, and if there is, it's a pity! That is unless the home is hers, with a husband!

TOM. What?

AMANDA. Oh, I can see the handwriting on the wall as plain as I see the nose in front of my face! It's terrifying! More and more you remind me of your father! He was out all hours without explanation—Then *left! Good-bye!* And me with the bag to hold. I saw that letter you got from the Merchant Marine. I know what you're dreaming of. I'm not standing here blindfolded. Very well, then. Then *do* it! But not till there's somebody to take your place.

TOM. What do you mean?

AMANDA. I mean that as soon as Laura has got somebody to take care of her, married, a home of her own, independent—why, then you'll be free to go wherever you please, on land, on sea, whichever way the wind blows you! But until that time you've got to look out for your sister. I don't say me because I'm old and don't matter! I say for your sister because she's young and dependent. I put her in business college—a dismal failure! Frightened her so it made her sick to her stomach. I took her over to the Young People's League at the church. Another fiasco. She spoke to nobody, nobody spoke to her. Now all she does is fool with those pieces of glass and play those worn-out records. What kind of a life is that for a girl to lead?

TOM. What can I do about it?

AMANDA. Overcome selfishness! Self, self, self is all that you ever think of! [TOM *springs up and crosses to get his coat. It is ugly and bulky. He pulls on a cap with earmuffs*] Where is your muffler? Put your wool muffler on! [*He snatches it angrily from the closet and tosses it around his neck and pulls both ends tight*] Tom! I haven't said what I had in mind to ask you.

TOM. I'm too late to—

AMANDA. [*Catching his arm—very importunately. Then shyly*] Down at the warehouse, aren't there some—nice young men?

TOM. No!

AMANDA. There *must* be—*some* . . .

TOM. Mother—
[*Gesture*]

AMANDA. Find out one that's clean-living—doesn't drink and—ask him out for Sister!

TOM. What?

AMANDA. For *Sister!* To *meet!* Get *acquainted!*

TOM. [*Stamping to door*]. Oh, my go-osh!

AMANDA. Will you? [*He opens door. Imploringly*] Will you? [*He starts down*] Will you? *Will* you, dear?

TOM. [*Calling back*] YES!

[AMANDA *closes the door hesitantly and with a troubled but faintly hopeful expression*]

SCREEN IMAGE: GLAMOR MAGAZINE COVER

[*Spot* AMANDA *at phone*]

AMANDA. Ella Cartwright? This is Amanda Wingfield! How are you, honey? How is that kidney condition? [*Count five*] Horrors! [*Count five*] You're a Christian martyr, yes, honey, that's what you are, a Christian martyr! Well, I just happened to notice in my little red book that your subscription to the *Companion* has just run out! I knew that you wouldn't want to miss out on the wonderful serial starting in this new issue. It's by Bessie Mae Hopper, the first thing she's written since *Honeymoon for Three*. Wasn't that a strange and interesting story? Well, this one is even lovelier, I believe. It has a sophisticated, society background. It's all about the horsey set on Long Island!

FADE OUT

Scene Five

LEGEND ON SCREEN: "ANNUNCIATION." *Fade with music.*

It is early dusk of a spring evening. Supper has just been finished in the Winfield apartment. AMANDA *and* LAURA *in light-colored dresses are removing dishes from the table, in the upstage area, which is shadowy, their movements formalized almost as a dance or ritual, their moving forms as pale and silent as moths.*

TOM, *in white shirt and trousers, rises from the table and crosses toward the fire-escape.*

AMANDA. [*As he passes her*] Son, will you do me a favor?

TOM. What?

AMANDA. Comb your hair! You look so pretty when your hair is combed! [TOM *slouches on sofa with evening paper. Enormous caption "Franco Triumphs"*] There is only one respect in which I would like you to emulate your father.

TOM. What respect is that?

AMANDA. The care he always took of his appearance. He never allowed himself to look untidy. [*He throws down the paper and crosses to fire-escape*] Where are you going?

TOM. I'm going out to smoke.

AMANDA. You smoke too much. A pack a day at fifteen cents a pack. How much would that amount to in a month? Thirty times fifteen is how much,

Tom? Figure it out and you will be astounded at what you could save. Enough to give you a night-school course in accounting at Washington U! Just think what a wonderful thing that would be for you, son!

[TOM *is unmoved by the thought*]

TOM. I'd rather smoke. [*He steps out on landing, letting the screen door slam*]

AMANDA. [*Sharply*] I know! That's the tragedy of it. . . . [*Alone, she turns to look at her husband's picture*]

DANCE MUSIC: "ALL THE WORLD IS WAITING FOR THE SUN-RISE!"

TOM. [*To the audience*] Across the alley from us was the Paradise Dance Hall. On evenings in spring the windows and doors were open and the music came outdoors. Sometimes the lights were turned out except for a large glass sphere that hung from the ceiling. It would turn slowly about and filter the dusk with delicate rainbow colors. Then the orchestra played a waltz or a tango, something that had a slow and sensuous rhythm. Couples would come outside, to the relative privacy of the alley. You could see them kissing behind ash-pits and telephone poles. This was the compensation for lives that passed like mine, without any change or adventure. Adventure and change were imminent in this year. They were waiting around the corner for all these kids. Suspended in the mist over Berchtesgaden,[7] caught in the folds of Chamberlain's umbrella[8]—In Spain there was Guernica! But here there was only hot swing music and liquor, dance halls, bars, and movies, and sex that hung in the gloom like a chandelier and flooded the world with brief, deceptive rainbows. . . . All the world was waiting for bombardments!

[AMANDA *turns from the picture and comes outside*]

AMANDA. [*Sighing*] A fire-escape landing's a poor excuse for a porch. [*She spreads a newspaper on a step and sits down, gratefully and demurely as if she were settling into a swing on a Mississippi veranda*] What are you looking at?

TOM. The moon.

AMANDA. Is there a moon this evening?

TOM. It's rising over Garfinkel's Delicatessen.

AMANDA. So it is! A little silver slipper of a moon. Have you made a wish on it yet?

TOM. Um-hum.

AMANDA. What did you wish for?

TOM. That's a secret.

AMANDA. A secret, huh? Well, I won't tell mine either. I will be just as mysterious as you.

TOM. I bet I can guess what yours is.

AMANDA. Is my head so transparent?

TOM. You're not a sphinx.

AMANDA. No, I don't have secrets. I'll tell you what I wished for on the moon.

---

[7] Hitler's mountain retreat in southern Bavaria.

[8] A popular symbol of Sir Neville Chamberlain, British Prime Minister in the late thirties who was known as an appeaser of Hitler.

Success and happiness for my precious children! I wish for that whenever there's a moon, and when there isn't a moon, I wish for it, too.

TOM. I thought perhaps you wished for a gentleman caller.

AMANDA. Why do you say that?

TOM. Don't you remember asking me to fetch one?

AMANDA. I remember suggesting that it would be nice for your sister if you brought home some nice young man from the warehouse. I think that I've made that suggestion more than once.

TOM. Yes, you have made it repeatedly.

AMANDA. Well?

TOM. We are going to have one.

AMANDA. *What?*

TOM. A gentleman caller!

THE ANNUNCIATION IS CELEBRATED WITH MUSIC

[AMANDA *rises*]

IMAGE ON SCREEN: CALLER WITH BOUQUET

AMANDA. You mean you have asked some nice young man to come over?

TOM. Yep. I've asked him to dinner.

AMANDA. You really did?

TOM. I did!

AMANDA. You did, and did he—*accept?*

TOM. He did!

AMANDA. Well, well—well, well! That's—lovely!

TOM. I thought that you would be pleased.

AMANDA. It's definite, then?

TOM. Very definite.

AMANDA. Soon?

TOM. Very soon.

AMANDA. For heaven's sake, stop putting on and tell me some things, will you?

TOM. What things do you want me to tell you?

AMANDA. *Naturally* I would like to know when he's *coming!*

TOM. He's coming tomorrow.

AMANDA. *Tomorrow?*

TOM. Yep. Tomorrow.

AMANDA. But, Tom!

TOM. Yes, Mother?

AMANDA. Tomorrow gives me no time!

TOM. Time for what?

AMANDA. Preparations! Why didn't you phone me at once, as soon as you asked him, the minute that he accepted? Then, don't you see, I could have been getting ready!

TOM. You don't have to make any fuss.

AMANDA. Oh, Tom, Tom, Tom, of course I have to make a fuss! I want things nice, not sloppy! Not thrown together. I'll certainly have to do some fast thinking, won't I?

TOM. I don't see why you have to think at all.

AMANDA. You just don't know. We can't have a gentleman caller in a pigsty! All my wedding silver has to be polished, the monogrammed table linen ought to be laundered! The windows have to be washed and fresh curtains put up. And how about clothes? We have to *wear* something, don't we?

TOM. Mother, this boy is no one to make a fuss over!

AMANDA. Do you realize he's the first young man we've introduced to your sister? It's terrible, dreadful, disgraceful that poor little sister has never received a single gentleman caller! Tom, come inside! [*She opens the screen door*]

TOM. What for?

AMANDA. I want to ask you some things.

TOM. If you're going to make such a fuss, I'll call it off, I'll tell him not to come!

AMANDA. You certainly won't do anything of the kind. Nothing offends people worse than broken engagements. It simply means I'll have to work like a Turk! We won't be brilliant, but we will pass inspection. Come on inside. [TOM *follows, groaning*] Sit down.

TOM. Any particular place you would like me to sit?

AMANDA. Thank heavens I've got that new sofa! I'm also making payments on a floor lamp I'll have sent out! And put the chintz covers on, they'll brighten things up! Of course I'd hoped to have these walls re-papered. . . . What is the young man's name?

TOM. His name is O'Connor.

AMANDA. That, of course, means fish—tomorrow is Friday! I'll have that salmon loaf—with Durkee's dressing! What does he do? He works at the warehouse?

TOM. Of course! How else would I—

AMANDA. Tom, he—doesn't drink?

TOM. Why do you ask me that?

AMANDA. Your father *did!*

TOM. Don't get started on that!

AMANDA. He *does* drink, then?

TOM. Not that I know of!

AMANDA. Make sure, be certain! The last thing I want for my daughter's a boy who drinks!

TOM. Aren't you being a little bit premature? Mr. O'Connor has not yet appeared on the scene!

AMANDA. But will tomorrow. To meet your sister, and what do I know about his character? Nothing! Old maids are better off than wives of drunkards!

TOM. Oh, my God!

AMANDA. Be still!

TOM. [*Leaning forward to whisper*] Lots of fellows meet girls whom they don't marry!

AMANDA. Oh, talk sensibly, Tom—and don't be sarcastic! [*She has gotten a hairbrush*]

TOM.   What are you doing?

AMANDA.   I'm brushing that cow-lick down! What is this young man's position at the warehouse?

TOM.   [*Submitting grimly to the brush and the interrogation*] This young man's position is that of a shipping clerk, Mother.

AMANDA.   Sounds to me like a fairly responsible job, the sort of a job *you* would be in if you just had more *get-up*. What is his salary? Have you any idea?

TOM.   I would judge it to be approximately eighty-five dollars a month.

AMANDA.   Well—not princely, but—

TOM.   Twenty more than I make.

AMANDA.   Yes, how well I know! But for a family man, eighty-five dollars a month is not much more than you can just get by on. . . .

TOM.   Yes, but Mr. O'Connor is not a family man.

AMANDA.   He might be, mightn't he? Some time in the future?

TOM.   I see. Plans and provisions.

AMANDA.   You are the only young man that I know of who ignores the fact that the future becomes the present, the present the past, and the past turns into everlasting regret if you don't plan for it!

TOM.   I will think that over and see what I can make of it.

AMANDA.   Don't be supercilious with your mother! Tell me some more about this—what do you call him?

TOM.   James D. O'Connor. The D. is for Delaney.

AMANDA.   Irish on *both* sides! *Gracious!* And doesn't drink?

TOM.   Shall I call him up and ask him right this minute?

AMANDA.   The only way to find out about those things is to make discreet inquiries at the proper moment. When I was a girl in Blue Mountain and it was suspected that a young man drank, the girl whose attentions he had been receiving, if any girl *was*, would sometimes speak to the minister of his church, or rather her father would if her father was living, and sort of feel him out on the young man's character. That is the way such things are discreetly handled to keep a young woman from making a tragic mistake!

TOM.   Then how did you happen to make a tragic mistake?

AMANDA.   That innocent look of your father's had everyone fooled! He *smiled*, the world was *enchanted*! No girl can do worse than put herself at the mercy of a handsome appearance! I hope that Mr. O'Connor is not too good-looking.

TOM.   No, he's not too good-looking. He's covered with freckles and hasn't too much of a nose.

AMANDA.   He's not right-down homely, though?

TOM.   Not right-down homely. Just medium homely, I'd say.

AMANDA.   Character's what to look for in a man.

TOM.   That's what I've always said, Mother.

AMANDA.   You've never said anything of the kind and I suspect you would never give it a thought.

TOM.   Don't be so suspicious of me.

AMANDA.   At least I hope he's the type that's up and coming.

TOM.   I think he really goes in for self-improvement.

AMANDA.   What reason have you to think so?

TOM. He goes to night school.

AMANDA. [*Beaming*] Splendid! What does he do, I mean study?

TOM. Radio engineering and public speaking!

AMANDA. Then he has visions of being advanced in the world! Any young man who studies public speaking is aiming to have an executive job some day! And radio engineering? A thing for the future! Both of these facts are very illuminating. Those are the sort of things that a mother should know concerning any young man who comes to call on her daughter. Seriously or—not.

TOM. One little warning. He doesn't know about Laura. I didn't let on that we had dark ulterior motives. I just said, why don't you come and have dinner with us? He said okay and that was the whole conversation.

AMANDA. I bet it was! You're eloquent as an oyster. However, he'll know about Laura when he gets here. When he sees how lovely and sweet and pretty she is, he'll thank his lucky stars he was asked to dinner.

TOM. Mother, you mustn't expect too much of Laura.

AMANDA. What do you mean?

TOM. Laura seems all those things to you and me because she's ours and we love her. We don't even notice she's crippled any more.

AMANDA. Don't say crippled! You know that I never allow that word to be used!

TOM. But face facts, Mother. She is and—that's not all—

AMANDA. What do you mean "not all"?

TOM. Laura is very different from other girls.

AMANDA. I think the difference is all to her advantage.

TOM. Not quite all—in the eyes of others—strangers—she's terribly shy and lives in a world of her own and those things make her seem a little peculiar to people outside the house.

AMANDA. Don't say peculiar.

TOM. Face the facts. She is.

The Dance-Hall Music Changes to a Tango That Has a Minor and Somewhat Ominous Tone

AMANDA. In what way is she peculiar—may I ask?

TOM. [*Gently*] She lives in a world of her own—a world of—little glass ornaments, Mother. . . . [*Gets up.* AMANDA *remains holding brush, looking at him, troubled*] She plays old phonograph records and—that's about all—[*He glances at himself in the mirror and crosses to door*]

AMANDA. [*Sharply*] Where are you going?

TOM. I'm going to the movies. [*Out screen door*]

AMANDA. Not to the movies, every night to the movies! [*Follows quickly to screen door*] I don't believe you always go to the movies! [*He is gone.* AMANDA *looks worriedly after him for a moment. Then vitality and optimism return and she turns from the door. Crossing to portieres*] Laura! Laura! [LAURA *answers from kitchenette*]

LAURA. Yes, Mother.

AMANDA. Let those dishes go and come in front! [LAURA *appears with dish towel. Gaily*] Laura, come here and make a wish on the moon!

LAURA. [*Entering*] Moon—moon?

AMANDA. A little silver slipper of a moon. Look over your left shoulder, Laura, and make a wish! [LAURA *looks faintly puzzled as if called out of sleep.* AMANDA *seizes her shoulders and turns her at an angle by the door*] No! Now, darling, *wish!*

LAURA. What shall I wish for, Mother?

AMANDA. [*Her voice trembling and her eyes suddenly filling with tears*] Happiness! Good Fortune!

[*The violin rises and the stage dims out*]

Scene Six

IMAGE: HIGH SCHOOL HERO

TOM. And so the following evening I brought Jim home to dinner. I had known Jim slightly in high school. In high school Jim was a hero. He had tremendous Irish good nature and vitality with the scrubbed and polished look of white chinaware. He seemed to move in a continual spotlight. He was a star in basketball, captain of the debating club, president of the senior class and the glee club and he sang the male lead in the annual light operas. He was always running or bounding, never just walking. He seemed always at the point of defeating the law of gravity. He was shooting with such velocity through his adolescence that you would logically expect him to arrive at nothing short of the White House by the time he was thirty. But Jim apparently ran into more interference after his graduation from Soldan. His speed had definitely slowed. Six years after he left high school he was holding a job that wasn't much better than mine.

IMAGE: CLERK

He was the only one at the warehouse with whom I was on friendly terms. I was valuable to him as someone who could remember his former glory, who had seen him win basketball games and the silver cup in debating. He knew of my secret practice of retiring to a cabinet of the washroom to work on poems when business was slack in the warehouse. He called me Shakespeare. And while the other boys in the warehouse regarded me with suspicious hostility, Jim took a humorous attitude toward me. Gradually his attitude affected the others, their hostility wore off and they also began to smile at me as people smile at an oddly fashioned dog who trots across their path at some distance.

I knew that Jim and Laura had known each other at Soldan, and I had heard Laura speak admiringly of his voice. I didn't know if Jim remembered her or not. In high school Laura had been as unobtrusive as Jim had been astonishing. If he did remember Laura, it was not as my sister, for when I asked him to dinner, he grinned and said, "You know, Shakespeare, I never thought of you as having folks!"

He was about to discover that I did. . . .

LIGHT UP STAGE

LEGEND ON SCREEN: "THE ACCENT OF A COMING FOOT"

[*Friday evening. It is about five o'clock of a late spring evening which comes "scattering poems in the sky"*]

[*A delicate lemony light is in the Wingfield apartment*]

[AMANDA *has worked like a Turk in preparation for the gentleman caller. The results are astonishing. The new floor lamp with its rose-silk shade is in place, a colored paper lantern conceals the broken light fixture in the ceiling, new billowing white curtains are at the windows, chintz covers are on chairs and sofa, a pair of new sofa pillows make their initial appearance*]

[*Open boxes and tissue paper are scattered on the floor*]

[LAURA *stands in the middle with lifted arms while* AMANDA *crouches before her, adjusting the hem of the new dress, devout and ritualistic. The dress is colored and designed by memory. The arrangement of* LAURA'S *hair is changed; it is softer and more becoming. A fragile, unearthly prettiness has come out in* LAURA: *she is like a piece of translucent glass touched by light, given a momentary radiance, not actual, not lasting*]

AMANDA.   [*Impatiently*] Why are you trembling?

LAURA.   Mother, you've made me so nervous!

AMANDA.   How have I made you nervous?

LAURA.   By all this fuss! You make it seem so important!

AMANDA.   I don't understand you, Laura. You couldn't be satisfied with just sitting home, and yet whenever I try to arrange something for you, you seem to resist it. [*She gets up*] Now take a look at yourself. No, wait! Wait just a moment—I have an idea!

LAURA.   What is it now?

[AMANDA *produces two powder puffs which she wraps in handkerchiefs and stuffs in* LAURA's *bosom*]

LAURA.   Mother, what are you doing?

AMANDA.   They call them "Gay Deceivers"!

LAURA.   I won't wear them!

AMANDA.   You will!

LAURA.   Why should I?

AMANDA.   Because, to be painfully honest, your chest is flat.

LAURA.   You make it seem like we were setting a trap.

AMANDA.   All pretty girls are a trap, a pretty trap, and men expect them to be. *LEGEND: "A PRETTY TRAP."* Now look at yourself, young lady. This is the prettiest you will ever be! I've got to fix myself now! You're going to be surprised by your mother's appearance! [*She crosses through portieres, humming gaily*]

[LAURA *moves slowly to the long mirror and stares solemnly at herself*]

[*A wind blows the white curtains inward in a slow, graceful motion and with a faint, sorrowful sighing*]

AMANDA. [*Off stage*] It isn't dark enough yet. [*She turns slowly before the mirror with a troubled look.*]

LEGEND ON SCREEN: "THIS IS MY SISTER: CELEBRATE HER WITH STRINGS!" MUSIC.

AMANDA. [*Laughing, off*] I'm going to show you something. I'm going to make a spectacular appearance!
LAURA. What is it, Mother?
AMANDA. Possess your soul in patience—you will see! Something I've resurrected from that old trunk! Styles haven't changed so terribly much after all. . . . [*She parts the portieres*] Now just look at your mother! [*She wears a girlish frock of yellowed voile with a blue silk sash. She carries a bunch of jonquils—the legend of her youth is nearly revived. Feverishly*] This is the dress in which I led the cotillion. Won the cakewalk twice at Sunset Hill, wore one spring to the Governor's ball in Jackson! See how I sashayed around the ballroom, Laura? [*She raises her skirt and does a mincing step around the room*] I wore it on Sundays for my gentlemen callers! I had it on the day I met your father—I had malaria fever all that spring. The change of climate from East Tennessee to the Delta[9]—weakened resistance—I had a little temperature all the time—not enough to be serious—just enough to make me restless and giddy! Invitations poured in—parties all over the Delta!—"Stay in bed," said Mother, "you have fever!"—but I just wouldn't.—I took quinine but kept on going, going!—Evenings, dances!—Afternoons, long, long rides! Picnics—lovely!—So lovely, that country in May.—All lacy with dogwood, literally flooded with jonquils!—That was the spring I had the craze for jonquils. Jonquils became an absolute obsession. Mother said, "Honey, there's no more room for jonquils." And still I kept on bringing in more jonquils. Whenever, wherever I saw them, I'd say, "Stop! Stop! I see jonquils!" I made the young men help me gather the jonquils! It was a joke, Amanda and her jonquils! Finally there were no more vases to hold them, every available space was filled with jonquils. No vases to hold them? All right, I'll hold them myself! And then I—[*She stops in front of the picture.* MUSIC] met your father! Malaria fever and jonquils and then—this—boy. . . . [*She switches on the rose-colored lamp*] I hope they get here before it starts to rain. [*She crosses upstage and places the jonquils in bowl on table*] I gave your brother a little extra change so he and Mr. O'Connor could take the service car home.
LAURA. [*With altered look*] What did you say his name was?
AMANDA. O'Connor.
LAURA. What is his first name?

[9] The rich cotton-growing area of the state of Mississippi.

AMANDA. I don't remember. Oh, yes, I do. It was—Jim!
[LAURA *sways slightly and catches hold of a chair*]

LEGEND ON SCREEN: "NOT JIM!"

LAURA. [*Faintly*] Not—Jim!
AMANDA. Yes, that was it, it was Jim! I've never known a Jim that wasn't nice!

MUSIC: OMINOUS

LAURA. Are you sure his name is Jim O'Connor?
AMANDA. Yes. Why?
LAURA. Is he the one that Tom used to know in high school?
AMANDA. He didn't say so. I think he just got to know him at the warehouse.
LAURA. There was a Jim O'Connor we both knew in high school—[*Then, with effort*] If that is the one that Tom is bringing to dinner—you'll have to excuse me, I won't come to the table.
AMANDA. What sort of nonsense is this?
LAURA. You asked me once if I'd ever liked a boy. Don't you remember I showed you this boy's picture?
AMANDA. You mean the boy you showed me in the year book?
LAURA. Yes, that boy.
AMANDA. Laura, Laura, were you in love with that boy?
LAURA. I don't know, Mother. All I know is I couldn't sit at the table if it was him!
AMANDA. It won't be him! It isn't the least bit likely. But whether it is or not, you will come to the table. You will not be excused.
LAURA. I'll have to be, Mother.
AMANDA. I don't intend to humor your silliness. Laura. I've had too much from you and your brother, both! So just sit down and compose yourself till they come. Tom has forgotten his key so you'll have to let them in, when they arrive.
LAURA. [*Panicky*] Oh, Mother—*you* answer the door!
AMANDA. [*Lightly*] I'll be in the kitchen—busy!
LAURA. Oh, Mother, please answer the door, don't make me do it!
AMANDA. [*Crossing into kitchenette*] I've got to fix the dressing for the salmon. Fuss, fuss—silliness!—over a gentleman caller!
[*Door swings shut.* LAURA *is left alone*]

LEGEND: "TERROR!"

[*She utters a low moan and turns off the lamp—sits stiffly on the edge of the sofa, knotting her fingers together*]

LEGEND ON SCREEN: "THE OPENING OF A DOOR!"

[TOM *and* JIM *appear on the fire-escape steps and climb to landing. Hearing their approach,* LAURA *rises with a panicky gesture. She retreats to the portieres*]

[*The doorbell.* LAURA *catches her breath and touches her throat. Low drums*]

AMANDA. [*Calling*] Laura, sweetheart! The door!

[LAURA *stares at it without moving*]

JIM. I think we just beat the rain.

TOM. Uh-huh. [*He rings again, nervously.* JIM *whistles and fishes for a cigarette*]

AMANDA. [*Very, very gaily*] Laura, that is your brother and Mr. O'Connor! Will you let them in, darling?

[LAURA *crosses toward kitchenette door*]

LAURA. [*Breathlessly*] Mother—you go to the door!

[AMANDA *steps out of kitchenette and stares furiously at* LAURA. *She points imperiously at the door*]

LAURA. Please, please!

AMANDA. [*In a fierce whisper*] What is the matter with you, you silly thing?

LAURA. [*Desperately*] Please, you answer it, *please!*

AMANDA. I told you I wasn't going to humor you, Laura. Why have you chosen this moment to lose your mind?

LAURA. Please, please, please, you go!

AMANDA. You'll have to go to the door because I can't!

LAURA. [*Despairingly*] I can't either!

AMANDA. *Why?*

LAURA. I'm *sick!*

AMANDA. I'm sick, too—of your nonsense! Why can't you and your brother be normal people? Fantastic whims and behavior! [TOM *gives a long ring.*] Preposterous goings on! Can you give me one reason—[*Calls out lyrically*] COMING! JUST ONE SECOND!—why you should be afraid to open a door? Now you answer it, Laura!

LAURA. Oh, oh, oh . . . [*She returns through the portieres. Darts to the victrola and winds it frantically and turns it on*]

AMANDA. Laura Wingfield, you march right to that door!

LAURA. Yes—yes, Mother!

[*A faraway, scratchy rendition of "Dardanella" softens the air and gives her strength to move through it. She slips to the door and draws it cautiously open*]

[TOM *enters with the caller,* JIM O'CONNOR]

TOM. Laura, this is Jim. Jim, this is my sister, Laura.

JIM. [*Stepping inside*] I didn't know that Shakespeare had a sister!

LAURA. [*Retreating stiff and trembling from the door*] How—how do you do?

JIM. [*Heartily extending his hand*] Okay!

[LAURA *touches it hesitantly with hers*]

JIM. Your hand's *cold,* Laura!

LAURA. Yes, well—I've been playing the victrola. . . .

JIM. Must have been playing classical music on it! You ought to play a little hot swing music to warm you up!

LAURA. Excuse me—I haven't finished playing the victrola. . . .

[*She turns awkwardly and hurries into the front room. She pauses a second by the victrola. Then catches her breath and darts through the portieres like a frightened deer*]

JIM.   [*Grinning*] What was the matter?

TOM.   Oh—with Laura? Laura is—terribly shy.

JIM.   Shy, huh? It's unusual to meet a shy girl nowadays. I don't believe you ever mentioned you had a sister.

TOM.   Well, now you know. I have one. Here is the *Post Dispatch*. You want a piece of it?

JIM.   Uh-huh.

TOM.   What piece? The comics?

JIM.   Sports! [*Glances at it*] Ole Dizzy Dean[10] is on his bad behavior.

TOM.   [*Disinterest*] Yeah? [*Lights cigarette and crosses back to fire-escape door*]

JIM.   Where are *you* going?

TOM.   I'm going out on the terrace.

JIM.   [*Goes after him*] You know, Shakespeare—I'm going to sell you a bill of goods!

TOM.   What goods?

JIM.   A course I'm taking.

TOM.   Huh?

JIM.   In public speaking! You and me, we're not the warehouse type.

TOM.   Thanks—that's good news. But what has public speaking got to do with it?

JIM.   It fits you for—executive positions!

TOM.   Awww.

JIM.   I tell you it's done a helluva lot for me.

IMAGE: EXECUTIVE AT DESK

TOM.   In what respect?

JIM.   In every! Ask yourself what is the difference between you an' me and men in the office down front? Brains?—No!—Ability?—No! Then what? Just one little thing—

TOM.   What is that one little thing?

JIM.   Primarily it amounts to—social poise! Being able to square up to people and hold your own on any social level!

AMANDA.   [*Off stage*] Tom?

TOM.   Yes, Mother?

AMANDA.   Is that you and Mr. O'Connor?

TOM.   Yes, Mother.

AMANDA.   Well, you just make yourselves comfortable in there.

TOM.   Yes, Mother.

AMANDA.   Ask Mr. O'Connor if he would like to wash his hands.

JIM.   Aw, no—no—thank you—I took care of that at the warehouse. Tom—

TOM.   Yes?

JIM.   Mr. Mendoza was speaking to me about you.

TOM.   Favorably?

JIM.   What do you think?

TOM.   Well—

[10] A well-known baseball pitcher of the St. Louis Cardinals.

JIM. You're going to be out of a job if you don't wake up.

TOM. I am waking up—

JIM. You show no signs.

TOM. The signs are interior.

IMAGE ON SCREEN: THE SAILING VESSEL WITH JOLLY ROGER
AGAIN

TOM. I'm planning to change. [*He leans over, the rail speaking with quiet exhilaration. The incandescent marquees and signs of the first-run movie houses light his face from across the alley. He looks like a voyager*] I'm right at the point of committing myself to a future that doesn't include the warehouse and Mr. Mendoza or even a night-school course in public speaking.

JIM. What are you gassing about?

TOM. I'm tired of the movies.

JIM. Movies!

TOM. Yes, movies! Look at them— [*A wave toward the marvels of Grand Avenue*] All of those glamorous people—having adventures—hogging it all, globbling the whole thing up! You know what happens? People go to the *movies* instead of *moving!* Hollywood characters are supposed to have all the adventures for everybody in America, while everybody in America sits in a dark room and watches them have them! Yes, until there's a war. That's when adventure becomes available to the masses! *Everyone's* dish, not only Gable's! [11] Then the people in the dark room come out of the dark room to have some adventures themselves—Goody, goody!—It's our turn now, to go to the South Sea Island—to make a safari—to be exotic, far-off!—But I'm not patient. I don't want to wait till then. I'm tired of the *movies* and I am *about* to *move!*

JIM. [*Incredulously*] Move?

TOM. Yes.

JIM. When?

TOM. Soon!

JIM. Where? Where?

THEME THREE MUSIC SEEMS TO ANSWER THE QUESTION,
WHILE TOM THINKS IT OVER. HE SEARCHES AMONG HIS
POCKETS

TOM. I'm starting to boil inside. I know I seem dreamy, but inside—well, I'm boiling! Whenever I pick up a shoe, I shudder a little thinking how short life is and what I am doing!—Whatever that means, I know it doesn't mean shoes—except as something to wear on a traveler's feet! [*Finds paper*] Look—

JIM. What?

TOM. I'm a member.

JIM. [*Reading*] The Union of Merchant Seamen.

[11] Clark Gable, well-known motion picture actor.

TOM.   I paid my dues this month, instead of the light bill.

JIM.   You will regret it when they turn the lights off.

TOM.   I won't be here.

JIM.   How about your mother?

TOM.   I'm like my father. The bastard son of a bastard! See how he grins? And he's been absent going on sixteen years!

JIM.   You're just talking, you drip. How does your mother feel about it?

TOM.   Shhh!—Here comes Mother! Mother is not acquainted with my plans!

AMANDA.   [*Enters portieres*] Where are you all?

TOM.   On the terrace, Mother.

[*They start inside. She advances to them.* TOM *is distinctly shocked at her appearance. Even* JIM *blinks a little. He is making his first contact with girlish Southern vivacity and in spite of the night-school course in public speaking is somewhat thrown off the beam by the unexpected outlay of social charm*]

[*Certain responses are attempted by* JIM *but are swept aside by* AMANDA'S *gay laughter and chatter.* TOM *is embarrassed but after the first shock* JIM *reacts very warmly. Grins and chuckles, is altogether won over*]

IMAGE: AMANDA AS A GIRL

AMANDA.   [*Coyly smiling, shaking her girlish ringlets*] Well, well, well, so this is Mr. O'Connor. Introductions entirely unnecessary. I've heard so much about you from my boy. I finally said to him, Tom—good gracious!—why don't you bring this paragon to supper? I'd like to meet this nice young man at the warehouse!—Instead of just hearing him sing your praises so much! I don't know why my son is so standoffish—that's not Southern behavior! Let's sit down and—I think we could stand a little more air in here! Tom, leave the door open. I felt a nice fresh breeze a moment ago. Where has it gone to? Mmm, so warm already! And not quite summer, even. We're going to burn up when summer really gets started. However, we're having—we're having a very light supper. I think light things are better fo' this time of year. The same as light clothes are. Light clothes an' light food are what warm weather calls fo'. You know our blood gets so thick during th' winter—it takes a while fo' us to *adjust* ou'selves! —when the season changes . . . It's come so quick this year. I wasn't pre-pared. All of a sudden—heavens! Already summer!—I ran to the trunk an' pulled out this light dress— Terribly old! Historical almost! But feels so good—so good an' co-ol, y'know. . . .

TOM.   Mother—

AMANDA.   Yes, honey?

TOM.   How about—supper?

AMANDA.   Honey, you go ask Sister if supper is ready! You know that Sister is in full charge of supper! Tell her you hungry boys are waiting for it. [*To* JIM] Have you met Laura?

JIM.   She—

AMANDA.   Let you in? Oh, good, you've met already! It's rare for a girl as sweet an' pretty as Laura to be domestic! But Laura is, thank heavens, not only pretty but also very domestic. I'm not at all. I never was a bit. I never could make a thing but angel-food cake. Well, in the South we had so many servants. Gone, gone, gone. All vestige of gracious living! Gone completely! I wasn't prepared for what the future brought me. All of my gentlemen callers were sons of planters and so of course I assumed that I would be married to one and raise my family on a large piece of land with plenty of servants. But man proposes—and woman accepts the proposal!—To vary that old, old saying a little bit—I married no planter! I married a man who worked for the telephone company!—That gallantly smiling gentleman over there! [*Points to the picture*] A telephone man who—fell in love with long-distance!— Now he travels and I don't even know where!— But what am I going on for about my—tribulations? Tell me yours—I hope you don't have any! Tom?

TOM. [*Returning*] Yes, Mother?

AMANDA. Is supper nearly ready?

TOM. It looks to me like supper is on the table.

AMANDA. Let me look— [*She rises prettily and looks through portieres*] Oh, lovely!— But where is Sister?

TOM. Laura is not feeling well and she says that she thinks she'd better not come to the table.

AMANDA. What?—Nonsense!—Laura? Oh, Laura!

LAURA. [*Off stage, faintly*] Yes, Mother.

AMANDA. You really must come to the table. We won't be seated until you come to the table! Come in, Mr. O'Connor. You sit over there, and I'll— Laura? Laura Wingfield! You're keeping us waiting, honey! We can't say grace until you come to the table!

[*The back door is pushed weakly open and* LAURA *comes in. She is obviously quite faint, her lips trembling, her eyes wide and staring. She moves unsteadily toward the table*]

LEGEND: "TERROR!"

[*Outside a summer storm is coming abruptly. The white curtains billow inward at the windows and there is a sorrowful murmur and deep blue dusk*]

[LAURA *suddenly stumbles—she catches at a chair with a faint moan*]

TOM. Laura!

AMANDA. Laura! [*There is a clap of thunder*] [LEGEND: "AH!"] [*Despairingly*] Why, Laura, you *are* sick, darling! Tom, help your sister into the living room, dear! Sit in the living room, Laura—rest on the sofa. Well! [*To the gentleman caller*] Standing over the hot stove made her ill!—I told her that it was just too warm this evening, but— [TOM *comes back in.* LAURA *is on the sofa*] Is Laura all right now?

TOM. Yes.

AMANDA. What *is* that? Rain? A nice cool rain has come up! [*She gives the gentleman caller a frightened look*] I think we may—have grace—now . . . [TOM *looks at her stupidly*] Tom, honey—you say grace!

TOM. Oh . . . "For these and all thy mercies—" [*They bow their heads,* AMANDA *stealing a nervous glance at* JIM. *In the living room* LAURA, *stretched on the sofa, clenches her hand to her lips, to hold back a shuddering sob*] God's Holy Name be praised—

THE SCENE DIMS OUT

Scene Seven

A SOUVENIR.

Half an hour later. Dinner is just being finished in the upstage area which is concealed by the drawn portieres.

As the curtain rises LAURA *is still huddled upon the sofa, her feet drawn under her, her head resting on a pale blue pillow, her eyes wide and mysteriously watchful. The new floor lamp with its shade of rose-colored silk gives a soft, becoming light to her face, bringing out the fragile, unearthly prettiness which usually escapes attention. There is a steady murmur of rain, but it is slackening and stops soon after the scene begins; the air outside becomes pale and luminous as the moon breaks out.*

A moment after the curtain rises, the lights in both rooms flicker and go out.]

JIM. Hey, there, Mr. Light Bulb!
     [AMANDA *laughs nervously*]

LEGEND: "SUSPENSION OF A PUBLIC SERVICE"

AMANDA. Where was Moses when the lights went out? Ha-ha. Do you know the answer to that one, Mr. O'Connor?
JIM. No, Ma'am, what's the answer?
AMANDA. In the dark! [JIM *laughs appreciatively*] Everybody sit still. I'll light the candles. Isn't it lucky we have them on the table? Where's a match? Which of you gentlemen can provide a match?
JIM. Here.
AMANDA. Thank you, sir.
JIM. Not at all, Ma'am!
AMANDA. I guess the fuse has burnt out. Mr. O'Connor, can you tell a burnt-out fuse? I know I can't and Tom is a total loss when it comes to mechanics. [*SOUND: GETTING UP: VOICES RECEDE A LITTLE TO KITCH-ENETTE*] Oh, be careful you don't bump into something. We don't want our gentleman caller to break his neck. Now wouldn't that be a fine howdy-do?
JIM. Ha-ha! Where is the fuse-box?
AMANDA. Right here next to the stove. Can you see anything?
JIM. Just a minute.

AMANDA. Isn't electricity a mysterious thing? Wasn't it Benjamin Franklin who tied a key to a kite? We live in such a mysterious universe, don't we? Some people say that science clears up all the mysteries for us. In my opinion it only creates more! Have you found it yet?

JIM. No, Ma'am. All these fuses look okay to me.

AMANDA. Tom!

TOM. Yes, Mother?

AMANDA. That light bill I gave you several days ago. The one I told you we got the notices about?

TOM. Oh—Yeah.

LEGEND: "HA!"

AMANDA. You didn't neglect to pay it by any chance?

TOM. Why, I—

AMANDA. Didn't! I might have known it!

JIM. Shakespeare probably wrote a poem on that light bill, Mrs. Wingfield.

AMANDA. I might have known better than to trust him with it! There's such a high price for negligence in this world!

JIM. Maybe the poem will win a ten-dollar prize.

AMANDA. We'll just have to spend the remainder of the evening in the nineteenth century, before Mr. Edison made the Mazda lamp!

JIM. Candlelight is my favorite kind of light.

AMANDA. That shows you're romantic! But that's no excuse for Tom. Well, we got through dinner. Very considerate of them to let us get through dinner before they plunged us into everlasting darkness, wasn't it, Mr. O'Connor?

JIM. Ha-ha!

AMANDA. Tom, as a penalty for your carelessness you can help me with the dishes.

JIM. Let me give you a hand.

AMANDA. Indeed you will not!

JIM. I ought to be good for something.

AMANDA. Good for something? [*Her tone is rhapsodic*] You? Why, Mr. O'Connor, nobody, *nobody's* given me this much entertainment in years—as you have!

JIM. Aw, now, Mrs. Wingfield!

AMANDA. I'm not exaggerating, not one bit! But Sister is all by her lonesome. You go keep her company in the parlor! I'll give you this lovely old candelabrum that used to be on the altar at the church of the Heavenly Rest. It was melted a little out of shape when the church burnt down. Lightning struck it one spring. Gypsy Jones was holding a revival at the time and he intimated that the church was destroyed because the Episcopalians gave card parties.

JIM. Ha-ha.

AMANDA. And how about you coaxing Sister to drink a little wine? I think it would be good for her! Can you carry both at once?

JIM. Sure. I'm Superman!

AMANDA. Now, Thomas, get into this apron!

[*The door of kitchenette swings closed on* AMANDA'S *gay laughter; the flickering light approaches the portieres*]

[LAURA *sits up nervously as he enters. Her speech at first is low and breathless from the almost intolerable strain of being alone with a stranger*]

THE LEGEND. *"I DON'T SUPPOSE YOU REMEMBER ME AT ALL!"*

[*In her first speeches in this scene, before* JIM'S *warmth overcomes her paralyzing shyness,* LAURA'S *voice is thin and breathless as though she has just run up a steep flight of stairs*]

[JIM'S *attitude is gently humorous. In playing this scene it should be stressed that while the incident is apparently unimportant, it is to* LAURA *the climax of her secret life*]

JIM. Hello, there, Laura.

LAURA. [*Faintly*] Hello. [*She clears her throat*]

JIM. How are you feeling now? Better?

LAURA. Yes. Yes, thank you.

JIM. This is for you. A little dandelion wine. [*He extends it toward her with extravagant gallantry*]

LAURA. Thank you.

JIM. Drink it—but don't get drunk! [*He laughs heartily.* LAURA *takes the glass uncertainly; laughs shyly*] Where shall I set the candles?

LAURA. Oh—oh, anywhere . . .

JIM. How about here on the floor? Any objections?

LAURA. No.

JIM. I'll spread a newspaper under to catch the drippings. I like to sit on the floor. Mind if I do?

LAURA. Oh, no.

JIM. Give me a pillow?

LAURA. What?

JIM. A pillow!

LAURA. Oh . . . [*Hands him one quickly*]

JIM. How about you? Don't you like to sit on the floor?

LAURA. Oh—yes.

JIM. Why don't you, then?

LAURA. I—will.

JIM. Take a pillow! [LAURA *does. Sits on the other side of the candelabrum.* JIM *crosses his legs and smiles engagingly at her*] I can't hardly see you sitting way over there.

LAURA. I can—see you.

JIM. I know, but that's not fair, I'm in the limelight. [LAURA *moves her pillow closer*] Good! Now I can see you! Comfortable?

LAURA. Yes.

JIM. So am I. Comfortable as a cow. Will you have some gum?

LAURA. No, thank you.

JIM. I think that I will indulge, with your permission. [*Musingly unwraps it and holds it up*] Think of the fortune made by the guy that invented the first piece of chewing gum. Amazing, huh? The Wrigley Building is one of the sights of Chicago.—I saw it summer before last when I went up to the Century of Progress.[12] Did you take in the Century of Progress?

LAURA. No, I didn't.

JIM. Well, it was quite a wonderful exposition. What impressed me most was the Hall of Science. Gives you an idea of what the future will be in America, even more wonderful than the present time is! [*Pause. Smiling at her*] Your brother tells me you're shy. Is that right, Laura?

LAURA. I—don't know.

JIM. I judge you to be an old-fashioned type of girl. Well, I think that's a pretty good type to be. Hope you don't think I'm being too personal—do you?

LAURA. [*Hastily, out of embarrassment*] I believe I *will* take a piece of gum, if you—don't mind. [*Clearing her throat*] Mr. O'Connor, have you—kept up with your singing?

JIM. Singing? Me?

LAURA. Yes. I remember what a beautiful voice you had.

JIM. When did you hear me sing?

VOICE OFF STAGE IN THE PAUSE

VOICE. [*Off stage*]

> O blow, ye winds, heigh-ho,
> A-roving I will go!
>   I'm off to my love
>   With a boxing glove—
> Ten thousand miles away!

JIM. You say you've heard me sing?

LAURA. Oh, yes! Yes, very often . . . I—don't suppose you remember me—at all?

JIM. [*Smiling doubtfully*] You know I have an idea I've seen you before. I had that idea soon as you opened the door. It seemed almost like I was about to remember your name. But the name that I started to call you—wasn't a name! And so I stopped myself before I said it.

LAURA. Wasn't it—Blue Roses?

JIM. [*Springs up. Grinning*] Blue Roses! My gosh, yes—Blue Roses! That's what I had on my tongue when you opened the door! Isn't it funny what tricks your memory plays? I didn't connect you with high school somehow or other. But that's where it was; it was high school. I didn't even know you were Shakespeare's sister! Gosh, I'm sorry.

LAURA. I didn't expect you to. You—barely knew me!

JIM. But we did have a speaking acquaintance, huh?

LAURA. Yes, we—spoke to each other.

JIM. When did you recognize me?

LAURA. Oh, right away!

---

[12] The title given to the theme of the Chicago World's Fair of 1933.

JIM. Soon as I came in the door?

LAURA. When I heard your name I thought it was probably you. I knew that Tom used to know you a little in high school. So when you came in the door— Well, then I was—sure.

JIM. Why didn't you *say* something, then?

LAURA. [*Breathlessly*] I didn't know what to say, I was—too surprised!

JIM. For goodness' sakes! You know, this sure is funny!

LAURA. Yes! Yes, isn't it, though . . .

JIM. Didn't we have a class in something together?

LAURA. Yes, we did.

JIM. What class was that?

LAURA. It was—singing—Chorus!

JIM. Aw!

LAURA. I sat across the aisle from you in the Aud.

JIM. Aw.

LAURA. Mondays, Wednesdays and Fridays.

JIM. Now I remember—you always came in late.

LAURA. Yes, it was so hard for me, getting upstairs. I had that brace on my leg—it clumped so loud!

JIM. I never heard any clumping.

LAURA. [*Wincing at the recollection*] To me it sounded like—thunder!

JIM. Well, well, well, I never even noticed.

LAURA. And everybody was seated before I came in. I had to walk in front of all those people. My seat was in the back row. I had to go clumping all the way up the aisle with everyone watching!

JIM. You shouldn't have been self-conscious.

LAURA. I know, but I was. It was always such a relief when the singing started.

JIM. Aw, yes, I've placed you now! I used to call you Blue Roses. How was it that I got started calling you that?

LAURA. I was out of school a little while with pleurosis. When I came back you asked me what was the matter. I said I had pleurosis—you though I said Blue Roses. That's what you always called me after that!

JIM. I hope you didn't mind.

LAURA. Oh, no—I liked it. You see, I wasn't acquainted with many—people. . . .

JIM. As I remember you sort of stuck by yourself.

LAURA. I—I—never have had much luck at—making friends.

JIM. I don't see why you wouldn't.

LAURA. Well, I—started out badly.

JIM. You mean being—

LAURA. Yes, it sort of—stood between me—

JIM. You shouldn't have let it!

LAURA. I know, but it did, and—

JIM. You were shy with people!

LAURA. I tried not to be but never could—

JIM. Overcome it?

LAURA. No, I—I never could!

JIM. I guess being shy is something you have to work out of kind of gradually.

LAURA. [*Sorrowfully*] Yes—I guess it—

JIM. Takes time!

LAURA. Yes—

JIM. People are not so dreadful when you know them. That's what you have to remember! And everybody has problems, not just you, but practically everybody has got some problems. You think of yourself as having the only problems, as being the only one who is disappointed. But just look around you and you will see lots of people as disappointed as you are. For instance, I hoped when I was going to high school that I would be further along at this time, six years later, than I am now— You remember that wonderful write-up I had in the *Torch*?

LAURA. Yes! [*She rises and crosses to table*]

JIM. It said I was bound to succeed in anything I went into! [LAURA *returns with the annual*] Holy Jeez! The *Torch*! [*He accepts it reverently. They smile across it with mutual wonder.* LAURA *crouches beside him and they begin to turn through it.* LAURA's *shyness is dissolving in his warmth*]

LAURA. Here you are in *Pirates of Penzance*!

JIM. [*Wistfully*] I sang the baritone lead in that operetta.

LAURA. [*Rapidly*] So—*beautifully*!

JIM. [*Protesting*] Aw—

LAURA. Yes, yes—beautifully—beautifully!

JIM. You heard me?

LAURA. All three times!

JIM. No!

LAURA. Yes!

JIM. All three performances?

LAURA. [*Looking down*] Yes.

JIM. Why?

LAURA. I—wanted to ask you to—autograph my program.

JIM. Why didn't you ask me to?

LAURA. You were always surrounded by your own friends so much that I never had a chance to.

JIM. You should have just—

LAURA. Well, I—thought you might think I was—

JIM. Thought I might think you was—what?

LAURA. Oh—

JIM. [*With reflective relish*] I was beleaguered by females in those days.

LAURA. You were terribly popular!

JIM. Yeah—

LAURA. You had such a—friendly way—

JIM. I was spoiled in high school.

LAURA. Everybody—liked you!

JIM. Including you?

LAURA. I—yes, I—I did, too— [*She gently closes the book in her lap*]

JIM. Well, well, well!—Give me that program, Laura. [*She hands it to him. He signs it with a flourish*] There you are—better late than never!

LAURA. Oh, I—what a—surprise!

JIM. My signature isn't worth very much right now. But some day—maybe—

it will increase in value! Being disappointed is one thing and being discouraged is something else. I am disappointed but I am not discouraged. I'm twenty-three years old. How old are you?

LAURA. I'll be twenty-four in June.

JIM. That's not old age!

LAURA. No, but—

JIM. You finished high school?

LAURA. [*With difficulty*] I didn't go back.

JIM. You mean you dropped out?

LAURA. I made bad grades in my final examinations. [*She rises and replaces the book and the program. Her voice strained*] How is—Emily Meisenbach getting along?

JIM. Oh, that kraut-head!

LAURA. Why do you call her that?

JIM. That's what she was.

LAURA. You're not still—going with her?

JIM. I never see her.

LAURA. It said in the Personal Section that you were—engaged!

JIM. I know, but I wasn't impressed by that—propaganda!

LAURA. It wasn't—the truth?

JIM. Only in Emily's optimistic opinion!

LAURA. Oh—

LEGEND. "WHAT HAVE YOU DONE SINCE HIGH SCHOOL?"

[JIM *lights a cigarette and leans indolently back on his elbows smiling at* LAURA *with a warmth and charm which lights her inwardly with altar candles. She remains by the table and turns in her hands a piece of glass to cover her tumult*]

JIM. [*After several reflective puffs on a cigarette*] What have you done since high school? [*She seems not to hear him*] Huh? [LAURA *looks up*] I said what have you done since high school, Laura?

LAURA. Nothing much.

JIM. You must have been doing something these six long years.

LAURA. Yes.

JIM. Well, then, such as what?

LAURA. I took a business course at business college—

JIM. How did that work out?

LAURA. Well, not very—well—I had to drop out, it gave me—indigestion— [JIM *laughs gently*]

JIM. What are you doing now?

LAURA. I don't do anything—much. Oh, please don't think I sit around doing nothing! My glass collection takes up a good deal of time. Glass is something you have to take good care of.

JIM. What did you say—about glass?

LAURA. Collection I said—I have one— [*She clears her throat and turns away again, acutely shy*]

JIM. [*Abruptly*] You know what I judge to be the trouble with you? Inferiority complex! Know what that is? That's what they call it when someone low-rates himself! I understand it because I had it, too. Although my case was not so aggravated as yours seems to be. I had it until I took up public speaking, developed my voice, and learned that I had an aptitude for science. Before that time I never thought of myself as being outstanding in any way whatsoever! Now I've never made a regular study of it, but I have a friend who says I can analyze people better than doctors that make a profession of it. I don't claim that to be necessarily true, but I can sure guess a person's psychology, Laura! [*Takes out his gum*] Excuse me, Laura. I always take it out when the flavor is gone. I'll use this scrap of paper to wrap it in. I know how it is to get it stuck on a shoe. Yep—that's what I judge to be your principal trouble. A lack of confidence in yourself as a person. You don't have the proper amount of faith in yourself. I'm basing that fact on a number of your remarks and also on certain observations I've made. For instance that clumping you thought was so awful in high school. You say that you even dreaded to walk into class. You see what you did? You dropped out of school, you gave up an education because of a clump, which as far as I know was practically non-existent! A little physical defect is what you have. Hardly noticeable even! Magnified thousands of times by imagination! You know what my strong advice to you is? Think of yourself as *superior* in some way?

LAURA.   In what way would I think?

JIM.   Why, man alive, Laura! Just look about you a little. What do you see? A world full of common people! All of 'em born and all of 'em going to die! Which of them has one-tenth of your good points! Or mine! Or anyone else's, as far as that goes— Gosh! Everybody excels in some one thing. Some in many! [*Unconsciously glances at himself in the mirror*] All you've got to do is discover in *what!* Take me, for instance. [*He adjusts his tie at the mirror*] My interest happens to lie in electro-dynamics. I'm taking a course in radio engineering at night school, Laura, on top of a fairly responsible job at the warehouse. I'm taking that course and studying public speaking.

LAURA.   Ohhhh.

JIM.   Because I believe in the future of television! [*Turning back to her*] I wish to be ready to go up right along with it. Therefore I'm planning to get in on the ground floor. In fact I've already made the right connections and all that remains is for the industry itself to get under way! Full steam— [*His eyes are starry*] Knowledge—Zzzzzp! Money—Zzzzzzp!—Power! That's the cycle democracy is built on! [*His attitude is convincingly dynamic.* LAURA *stares at him, even her shyness eclipsed in her absolute wonder. He suddenly grins*] I guess you think I think a lot of myself!

LAURA.   No—o-o-o, I—

JIM.   Now how about you? Isn't there something you take more interest in than anything else?

LAURA.   Well, I do—as I said—have my—glass collection—
[*A peal of girlish laughter from the kitchen*]

JIM.   I'm not right sure I know what you're talking about. What kind of glass is it?

LAURA.   Little articles of it, they're ornaments mostly! Most of them are little animals made out of glass, the tiniest little animals in the world. Mother calls them a glass menagerie! Here's an example of one, if you'd like to see it! This one is one of the oldest. It's nearly thirteen. [*MUSIC: "THE GLASS MENAGERIE"*] [*He stretches out his hand*] Oh, be careful—if you breathe, it breaks!

JIM. I'd better not take it. I'm pretty clumsy with things.

LAURA. Go on, I trust you with him! [*Places it in his palm*] There now— you're holding him gently! Hold him over the light, he loves the light! You see how the light shines through him?

JIM. It sure does shine!

LAURA. I shouldn't be partial, but he is my favorite one.

JIM. What kind of a thing is this one supposed to be?

LAURA. Haven't you noticed the single horn on his forehead?

JIM. A unicorn, huh?

LAURA. Mmm-hmmm!

JIM. Unicorns, aren't they extinct in the modern world?

LAURA. I know!

JIM. Poor little fellow, he must feel sort of lonesome.

LAURA. [*Smiling*] Well, if he does he doesn't complain about it. He stays on a shelf with some horses that don't have horns and all of them seem to get along nicely together.

JIM. How do you know?

LAURA. [*Lightly*] I haven't heard any arguments among them!

JIM. [*Grinning*] No arguments, huh? Well, that's a pretty good sign! Where shall I set him?

LAURA. Put him on the table. They all like a change of scenery once in a while!

JIM. [*Stretching*] Well, well, well, well— Look how big my shadow is when I stretch!

LAURA. Oh, oh, yes—it stretches across the ceiling!

JIM. [*Crossing to door*] I think it's stopped raining. [*Opens fire-escape door*] Where does the music come from?

LAURA. From the Paradise Dance Hall across the alley.

JIM. How about cutting the rug a little, Miss Wingfield?

LAURA. Oh, I—

JIM. Or is your program filled up? Let me have a look at it. [*Grasps imaginary card*] Why, every dance is taken! I'll just have to scratch some out. [*WALTZ MUSIC: "LA GOLONDRINA"*] Ahhh, a waltz! [*He executes some sweeping turns by himself then holds his arms toward* LAURA]

LAURA. [*Breathlessly*] I—can't dance!

JIM. There you go, that inferiority stuff!

LAURA. I've never danced in my life!

JIM. Come on, try!

LAURA. Oh, but I'd step on you!

JIM. I'm not made out of glass.

LAURA. How—how—how do we start?

JIM. Just leave it to me. You hold your arms out a little.

LAURA. Like this?

JIM. A little bit higher. Right. Now don't tighten up, that's the main thing about it—relax.

LAURA. [*Laughing breathlessly*] It's hard not to.

JIM. Okay.

LAURA. I'm afraid you can't budge me.

JIM. What do you bet I can't? [*He swings her into motion*]

LAURA. Goodness, yes, you can!

JIM. Let yourself go, now, Laura, just let yourself go.

LAURA. I'm—

JIM. Come on!

LAURA. Trying!

JIM. Not so stiff— Easy does it!

LAURA. I know but I'm—

JIM. Loosen th' backbone! There now, that's a lot better.

LAURA. Am I?

JIM. Lots, lots better! [*He moves her about the room in a clumsy waltz*]

LAURA. Oh, my!

JIM. Ha-ha!

LAURA. Oh, my goodness!

JIM. Ha-ha-ha! [*They suddenly bump into the table. JIM stops*] What did we hit on?

LAURA. Table.

JIM. Did something fall off it? I think—

LAURA. Yes.

JIM. I hope that it wasn't the little glass horse with the horn!

LAURA. Yes.

JIM. Aw, aw, aw. Is it broken?

LAURA. Now it is just like all the other horses.

JIM. It's lost its—

LAURA. Horn! It doesn't matter. Maybe it's a blessing in disguise.

JIM. You'll never forgive me. I bet that that was your favorite piece of glass.

LAURA. I don't have favorites much. It's no tragedy, Freckles. Glass breaks so easily. No matter how careful you are. The traffic jars the shelves and things fall off them.

JIM. Still I'm awfully sorry that I was the cause.

LAURA. [*Smiling*] I'll just imagine he had an operation. The horn was removed to make him feel less—freakish! [*They both laugh*] Now he will feel more at home with the other horses, the ones that don't have horns . . .

JIM. Ha-ha, that's very funny! [*Suddenly serious*] I'm glad to see that you have a sense of humor. You know—you're—well—very different! Surprisingly different from anyone else I know! [*His voice becomes soft and hesitant with a genuine feeling*] Do you mind me telling you that? [LAURA *is abashed beyond speech*] I mean it in a nice way . . . [LAURA *nods shyly, looking away*] You make me feel sort of—I don't know how to put it! I'm usually pretty good at expressing things, but— This is something that I don't know how to say! [LAURA *touches her throat and clears it—turns the broken unicorn in her hands*] [*Even softer*] Has anyone ever told you that you were pretty? [*PAUSE: MUSIC*] [LAURA *looks up slowly, with wonder, and shakes her head*] Well, you are! In a very different way from anyone else. And all the nicer because of the difference, too. [*His voice becomes low and husky.* LAURA *turns away, nearly faint with the novelty of her emotions*] I wish that you were my sister. I'd teach you to have some confidence in yourself. The different people are not like other people, but being different is nothing to be ashamed of. Because other people are not such wonderful people. They're one hundred times one thousand. You're one times one! They walk all over the earth. You just stay here. They're common as—weeds, but —you—well, you're—*Blue Roses!*

IMAGE ON SCREEN: BLUE ROSES

MUSIC CHANGES

LAURA. But blue is wrong for—roses . . .
JIM. It's right for you— You're—pretty!
LAURA. In what respect am I pretty?
JIM. In all respects—believe me! Your eyes—your hair—are pretty! Your hands are pretty! [*He catches hold of her hand*] You think I'm making this up because I'm invited to dinner and have to be nice. Oh, I could do that! I could put on an act for you, Laura, and say lots of things without being very sincere. But this time I am. I'm talking to you sincerely. I happened to notice you had this inferiority complex that keeps you from feeling comfortable with people. Somebody needs to build your confidence up and make you proud instead of shy and turning away and—blushing— Somebody ought to— Ought to—*kiss* you, Laura! [*His hand slips slowly up her arm to her shoulder*] [*MUSIC SWELLS TUMULTUOUSLY*] [*He suddenly turns her about and kisses her on the lips*] [*When he releases her* LAURA *sinks on the sofa with a bright, dazed look*] [JIM *backs away and fishes in his pocket for a cigarette*] [*LEGEND ON SCREEN: "SOUVENIR"*] Stumble-john! [*He lights the cigarette, avoiding her look*] [*There is a peal of girlish laughter from* AMANDA *in the kitchen*] [LAURA *slowly raises and opens her hand. It still contains the little broken glass animal. She looks at it with a tender, bewildered expression*] Stumble-john! I shouldn't have done that— That was way off the beam. You don't smoke, do you? [*She looks up, smiling, not hearing the question*] [*He sits beside her a little gingerly. She looks at him speechlessly—waiting*] [*He coughs decorously and moves a little farther aside as he considers the situation and senses her feelings, dimly, with perturbation*] [*Gently*] Would you—care for a—mint? [*She doesn't seem to hear him but her look grows brighter even*] Peppermint—Life Saver? My pocket's a regular drug store—wherever I go . . . [*He pops a mint in his mouth. Then gulps and decides to make a clean breast of it. He speaks slowly and gingerly*] Laura, you know, if I had a sister like you, I'd do the same thing as Tom. I'd bring out fellows and—introduce her to them. The right type of boys of a type to—appreciate her. Only—well—he made a mistake about me. Maybe I've got no call to be saying this. That may not

have been the idea in having me over. But what if it was? There's nothing wrong about that. The only trouble is that in my case—I'm not in a situation to—do the right thing. I can't take down your number and say I'll phone. I can't call up next week and—ask for a date. I thought I had better explain the situation in case you misunderstood it and—hurt your feelings. . . . [*Pause*] [*Slowly, very slowly,* LAURA's *look changes, her eyes returning slowly from his to the ornament in her palm*] [AMANDA *utters another gay laugh in the kitchen*]

LAURA. [*Faintly*] You—won't—call again?

JIM. No, Laura, I can't. [*He rises from the sofa*] As I was just explaining, I've —got strings on me, Laura, I've—been going steady! I go out all the time with a girl named Betty. She's a home-girl like you, and Catholic, and Irish, and in a great many ways we—get along fine. I met her last summer on a moonlight boat trip up the river to Alton, on the *Majestic*. Well—right away from the start it was—love! [*LEGEND: LOVE!*] [LAURA *sways slightly forward and grips the arm of the sofa. He fails to notice, now enrapt in his own comfortable being*] Being in love has made a new man of me! [*Leaning stiffly forward, clutching the arm of the sofa,* LAURA *struggles visibly with her storm. But* JIM *is oblivious, she is a long way off*] The power of love is really pretty tremendous! Love is something that—changes the whole world, Laura! [*The storm abates a little and* LAURA *leans back. He notices her again*] It happened that Betty's aunt took sick, she got a wire and had to go to Centralia. So Tom—when he asked me to dinner—I naturally just accepted the invitation, not knowing that you—that he—that I— [*He stops awkwardly*] Huh—I'm a stumble-john! [*He flops back on the sofa*] [*The holy candles in the altar of* LAURA's *face have been snuffed out. There is a look of almost infinite desolation*] [JIM *glances at her uneasily*] I wish that you would—say something. [*She bites her lip which was trembling and then bravely smiles. She opens her hand again on the broken glass ornament. Then she gently takes his hand and raises it level with her own. She carefully places the unicorn in the palm of his hand, then pushes his fingers closed upon it*] What are you—doing that for? You want me to have him?—Laura? [*She nods*] What for?

LAURA. A—souvenir . . .

[*She rises unsteadily and crouches beside the victrola to wind it up*]

LEGEND ON SCREEN: "THINGS HAVE A WAY OF TURNING OUT SO BADLY!"

OR IMAGE: "GENTLEMAN CALLER WAVING GOODBYE!—GAILY"

[*At this moment* AMANDA *rushes brightly back in the front room. She bears a pitcher of fruit punch in an old-fashioned cut-glass pitcher and a plate of macaroons. The plate has a gold border and poppies painted on it*]

AMANDA. Well, well, well! Isn't the air delightful after the shower? I've made you children a little liquid refreshment. [*Turns gaily to the gentleman caller*] Jim, do you know that song about lemonade?

> "Lemonade, lemonade
> Made in the shade and stirred with a spade—
> Good enough for any old maid!"

JIM. [*Uneasily*] Ha-ha! No—I never heard it.

AMANDA. Why, Laura! You look so serious!

JIM. We were having a serious conversation.

AMANDA. Good! Now you're better acquainted!

JIM. [*Uncertainly*] Ha-ha! Yes.

AMANDA. You modern young people are much more serious-minded than my generation. I was so gay as a girl!

JIM. You haven't changed, Mrs. Wingfield.

AMANDA. Tonight I'm rejuvenated! The gaiety of the occasion, Mr. O'Connor! [*She tosses her head with a peal of laughter. Spills lemonade*] Oooo! I'm baptizing myself!

JIM. Here—let me—

AMANDA. [*Setting the pitcher down*] There now. I discovered we had some maraschino cherries. I dumped them in, juice and all!

JIM. You shouldn't have gone to that trouble, Mrs. Wingfield.

AMANDA. Trouble, trouble? Why it was loads of fun! Didn't you hear me cutting up in the kitchen? I bet your ears were burning! I told Tom how outdone with him I was for keeping you to himself so long a time! He should have brought you over much, much sooner! Well, now that you've found your way, I want you to be a very frequent caller! Not just occasional but all the time. Oh, we're going to have a lot of gay times together! I see them coming! Mmm, just breathe that air! So fresh, and the moon's so pretty! I'll skip back out—I know where my place is when young folks are having a—serious conversation!

JIM. Oh, don't go out, Mrs. Wingfield. The fact of the matter is I've got to be going.

AMANDA. Going, now? You're joking! Why, it's only the shank of the evening, Mr. O'Connor!

JIM. Well, you know how it is.

AMANDA. You mean you're a young workingman and have to keep workingmen's hours. We'll let you off early tonight. But only on the condition that next time you stay later. What's the best night for you? Isn't Saturday night the best night for you workingmen?

JIM. I have a couple of time-clocks to punch, Mrs. Wingfield. One at morning, another one at night!

AMANDA. My, but you *are* ambitious! You work at night, too?

JIM. No, Ma'am, not work but—Betty! [*He crosses deliberately to pick up his hat. The band at the Paradise Dance Hall goes into a tender waltz*]

AMANDA. Betty? Betty? Who's—Betty! [*There is an ominous cracking sound in the sky*]

JIM. Oh, just a girl. The girl I go steady with! [*He smiles charmingly. The sky falls*]

LEGEND: "THE SKY FALLS"

AMANDA. [*A long-drawn exhalation*] Ohhhh . . . Is it a serious romance, Mr. O'Connor?

JIM. We're going to be married the second Sunday in June.

AMANDA. Ohhhh—how nice! Tom didn't mention that you were engaged to be married.

JIM. The cat's not out of the bag at the warehouse yet. You know how they are. They call you Romeo and stuff like that. [*He stops at the oval mirror to put on his hat. He carefully shapes the brim and the crown to give a discreetly dashing effect*] It's been a wonderful evening, Mrs. Wingfield. I guess this is what they mean by Southern hospitality.

AMANDA. It really wasn't anything at all.

JIM. I hope it don't seem like I'm rushing off. But I promised Betty I'd pick her up at the Wabash depot, an' by the time I get my jalopy down there her train'll be in. Some women are pretty upset if you keep 'em waiting.

AMANDA. Yes, I know— The tyranny of women! [*Extends her hand*] Goodbye, Mr. O'Connor. I wish you luck—and happiness—and success! All three of them, and so does Laura!— Don't you, Laura?

LAURA. Yes!

JIM. [*Taking her hand*] Good-bye, Laura. I'm certainly going to treasure that souvenir. And don't you forget the good advice I gave you. [*Raises his voice to a cheery shout*] So long, Shakespeare! Thanks again, ladies— Good night!

[*He grins and ducks jauntily out*]

[*Still bravely grimacing,* AMANDA *closes the door on the gentleman caller. Then she turns back to the room with a puzzled expression. She and* LAURA *don't dare to face each other.* LAURA *crouches beside the victrola to wind it*]

AMANDA. [*Faintly*] Things have a way of turning out so badly. I don't believe that I would play the victrola. Well, well—well— Our gentleman caller was engaged to be married! Tom!

TOM. [*From back*] Yes, Mother?

AMANDA. Come in here a minute. I want to tell you something awfully funny.

TOM. [*Enters with macaroon and a glass of the lemonade*] Has the gentleman caller gotten away already?

AMANDA. The gentleman caller has made an early departure. What a wonderful joke you played on us!

TOM. How do you mean?

AMANDA. You didn't mention that he was engaged to be married.

TOM. Jim? Engaged?

AMANDA. That's what he just informed us.

TOM. I'll be jiggered! I didn't know about that.

AMANDA. That seems very peculiar.

TOM. What's peculiar about it?

AMANDA. Didn't you call him your best friend down at the warehouse?

TOM. He is, but how did I know?

AMANDA. It seems extremely peculiar that you wouldn't know your best friend was going to be married!

TOM. The warehouse is where I work, not where I know things about people!

AMANDA. You don't know things anywhere! You live in a dream; you manufacture illusions! [*He crosses to door*] Where are you going?

TOM. I'm going to the movies.

AMANDA. That's right, now that you've had us make such fools of ourselves. The effort, the preparations, all the expense! The new floor lamp, the rugs, the clothes for Laura! All for what? To entertain some other girl's fiancé! Go to the movies, go! Don't think about us, a mother deserted, an unmarried sister who's crippled and has no job! Don't let anything interfere with your selfish pleasure! Just go, go, go—to the movies!

TOM. All right, I will! The more you shout about my selfishness to me the quicker I'll go, and I won't go to the movies!

AMANDA. Go, then! Then go to the moon—you selfish dreamer!

[TOM *smashes his glass on the floor. He plunges out on the fire-escape, slamming the door.* LAURA *screams—cut by door*]

[*Dance-hall music up.* TOM *goes to the rail and grips it desperately, lifting his face in the chill white moonlight penetratng the narrow abyss of the alley*]

LEGEND ON SCREEN: "AND SO GOOD-BYE . . ."

[TOM'S *closing speech is timed with the interior pantomime. The interior scene is played as though viewed through soundproof glass.* AMANDA *appears to be making a comforting speech to* LAURA *who is huddled upon the sofa. Now that we cannot hear the mother's speech, her silliness is gone and she has dignity and tragic beauty.* LAURA'S *dark hair hides her face until at the end of the speech she lifts it to smile at her mother.* AMANDA'S *gestures are slow and graceful, almost dancelike, as she comforts the daughter. At the end of her speech she glances a moment at the father's picture—then withdraws through the portieres. At close of* TOM'S *speech,* LAURA *blows out the candles, ending the play*]

TOM. I didn't go to the moon, I went much further—for time is the longest distance between two places— Not long after that I was fired for writing a poem on the lid of a shoe-box. I left Saint Louis. I descended the steps of this fire-escape for a last time and followed, from then on, in my father's footsteps, attempting to find in motion what was lost in space— I traveled around a great deal. The cities swept about me like dead leaves, leaves that were brightly colored but torn away from the branches. I would have stopped, but I was pursued by something. It always came upon me unawares, taking me altogether by surprise. Perhaps it was a familiar bit of music. Perhaps it was only a piece of transparent glass— Perhaps I am walking along a street at night, in some strange city, before I have found companions. I pass the lighted window of a shop where perfume is sold. The window is filled with pieces of colored glass, tiny transparent bottles in delicate colors, like bits of a shattered rainbow. Then all at once my sister touches my shoulder. I turn around and look into her eyes . . . Oh, Laura, Laura, I tried to leave you behind me, but I am more faithful than I intended to be! I reach for a cigarette, I cross the street, I run into the movies or a bar, I buy a drink, I speak to the nearest stranger—anything that can blow your candles out! [LAURA *bends over the candles*]—for nowadays the world is lit by lightning! Blow out your candles, Laura—and so good-bye. . . .

[*She blows the candles out*]

THE SCENE DISSOLVES

Production Notes

Being a "memory play," *The Glass Menagerie* can be presented with unusual freedom of convention. Because of its considerably delicate or tenuous material, atmospheric touches and subtleties of direction play a particularly important part. Expressionism and all other unconventional techniques in drama have only one valid aim, and that is a closer approach to truth. When a play employs unconventional techniques, it is not, or certainly shouldn't be, trying to escape its responsibility of dealing with reality, or interpreting experience, but is actually or should be attempting to find a closer approach, a more penetrating and vivid expression of things as they are. The straight realistic play with its genuine frigidaire and authentic ice-cubes, its characters that speak exactly as its audience speaks, corresponds to the academic landscape and has the same virtue of a photographic likeness. Everyone should know nowadays the unimportance of the photographic in art: that truth, life, or reality is an organic thing which the poetic imagination can represent or suggest, in essence, only through transformation, through changing into other forms than those which were merely present in appearance.

These remarks are not meant as comments only on this particular play. They have to do with a conception of a new, plastic theatre which must take the place of the exhausted theatre of realistic conventions if the theatre is to resume vitality as a part of our culture.

The Screen Device

There is *only one important difference between the original and acting version of the play* and that is the *omission* in the latter of the device which I tentatively included in my *original* script. This device was the use of a screen on which were projected magic-lantern slides bearing images or titles. I do not regret the omission of this device from the present Broadway production. The extraordinary power of Miss Taylor's[13] performance made it suitable to have the utmost simplicity in the physical production. But I think it may be interesting to some readers to see how this device was conceived. So I am putting it

---

[13] Who first played the part of Amanda.

into the published manuscript. These images and legends, projected from behind, were cast on a section of wall between the front-room and dining-room areas, which should be indistinguishable from the rest when not in use.

The purpose of this will probably be apparent. It is to give accent to certain values in each scene. Each scene contains a particular point (or several) which is structurally the most important. In an episodic play, such as this, the basic structure or narrative line may be obscured from the audience; the effect may seem fragmentary rather than architectural. This may not be the fault of the play so much as a lack of attention in the audience. The legend or image upon the screen will strengthen the effect of what is merely allusion in the writing and allow the primary point to be made more simply and lightly than if the entire responsibility were on the spoken lines. Aside from this structural value, I think the screen will have a definite emotional appeal, less definable but just as important. An imaginative producer or director may invent many other uses for this device than those indicated in the present script. In fact the possibilities of the device seem much larger to me than the instance of this play can possibly utilize.

The Music

Another extra-literary accent in this play is provided by the use of music. A single recurring tune, "The Glass Menagerie," is used to give emotional emphasis to suitable passages. This tune is like circus music, not when you are on the grounds or in the immediate vicinity of the parade, but when you are at some distance and very likely thinking of something else. It seems under those circumstances to continue almost interminably and it weaves in and out of your preoccupied consciousness; then it is the lightest, most delicate music in the world and perhaps the saddest. It expresses the surface vivacity of life with the underlying strain of immutable and inexpressible sorrow. When you look at a piece of delicately spun glass you think of two things: how beautiful it is and how easily it can be broken. Both of those ideas should be woven into the recurring tune, which dips in and out of the play as if it were carried on a wind that changes. It serves as a thread of connection and allusion between the narrator with his separate point in time and space and the subject of his story. Between each episode it returns as reference to the emotion, nostalgia, which is the first condition of the play. It is primarily Laura's music and therefore comes out most clearly when the play focuses upon her and the lovely fragility of glass which is her image.

The Lighting

The lighting in the play is not realistic. In keeping with the atmosphere of memory, the stage is dim. Shafts of light are focused on selected areas or actors, sometimes in contradistinction to what is the apparent center. For instance, in the quarrel scene between Tom and Amanda, in which Laura has no active part, the clearest pool of light is on her figure. This is also true of the supper scene, when her silent figure on the sofa should remain the visual center. The light upon Laura should be distinct from the others, having a peculiar pristine clarity such as light used in early religious portraits of female saints or madonnas. A certain correspondence to light in religious paintings, such as El Greco's, where the figures are radiant in atmosphere that is relatively dusky, could be effectively used throughout the play. (It will also permit a more effective use of the screen.) A free, imaginative use of light can be of enormous value in giving a mobile, plastic quality to plays of a more or less static nature.

T.W.

The Caucasian Chalk Circle

Bertolt Brecht

Bertolt Brecht

O ne of the most interesting and important of twentieth-century dramatists and theoreticians of drama is Bertolt Brecht (1898-1956) whose life story was much affected by the violence and upheavals of his time—nazism and communism, and two world wars. He was born in Germany, served briefly in the first World War, and participated in the political rebellions and the experiments of the artistic avant-garde in Berlin in the twenties. Upon Hitler's accession to power in 1933, Brecht, who was a *persona non grata* to the regime, fled to Denmark and later to the United States. After the second World War he returned to Switzerland and finally went to East Germany where he lived his last years under the Communists. He was a restless experimenter in drama and tried to revivify the theatre by breaking away from the established conventions of even the newer playwrights like Ibsen, Strindberg, and Shaw, though he was indebted to these writers, especially to Shaw.

Brecht introduced a new approach to drama necessitating a special vocabulary that attempted, not always successfully, to express what he was trying to do. His powerful impact has led to a cult of Brecht in recent times which makes of him the apostle of the theatre of the future and elevates his theories into dogmas. In spite of some of the exaggerations of this movement, it testifies in solid fashion to the great importance his plays and his thinking have had upon our age. His technical and dramatic innovations may very well be pointers to the future.

The term most intimately connected with Brecht's achievements is "epic theatre," which he first used in 1926 in opposing his methods to "dramatic theatre." The phrase is hard to define briefly since his own comments on the subject are not particularly lucid or extensive. In some ways the phrase may be best presented in terms of what it opposes. Brecht believed that the spectator and actor must not be too closely involved in the dramatic action but rather be distanced from it. This notion of alienation (the "V-effect" 'as he called it from the German word *Verfremdung*) is essential to the "epic theatre." The actor is not so much King Lear as a man presenting King Lear. He must never forget that he is an actor. Brecht was much opposed to the identification theory of acting, the Stanislavsky "method" approach. The spectator, too, must not lose himself in the play but must be aware that he is watching a play and be stimulated in his reason as much as in his emotions as he contemplates the action before him.

Brecht was against psychological and mood drama in which the emphasis is upon character. Instead, he wished to make the story or plot primary, but the story was to be episodic and truly narrative. He was opposed to the well-made plot with its central climax and preferred that each scene be self-contained and carried over into the next largely by the natural flow of time, by the continuity of the characters or by ideas. In this emphasis on the plot, Brecht shows his indebtedness to the classical novel and the picaresque tale. *The Caucasian Chalk Circle*, however, does have a climax, and in this it is somewhat uncharacteristic. Besides his indebtedness to the forms of fiction, Brecht's style, with its emphasis on episode, was influenced by the action movies of Hollywood and by writers such as Kipling, who exalted action. He also used music, song, projectors, masks, choruses, and commentators to bring every possible effect to the stage. Gesture and movement are emphasized. Perhaps one may sum it all up by saying that Brecht rebelled against the traditional limitations of the stage and of Western theatrical conventions and strove to extend the boundaries of the theatre to bring in effects and themes never before attempted in Western drama. He hoped to transcend the normal dramatic means of expression by giving his plays some of the freedom of the novel.

Brecht was born into a respectable bourgeois family in Augsburg, Germany, and was brought up as a Protestant. His ancestors on both sides were of Baden peasant stock. He went to school in Augsburg and, in 1916, moved on to Munich where he studied science and medicine at the university. He was called up as a medical orderly and served in the forces until the end of the war. The experience of war made him a revolutionary, and he participated in a November 1918 uprising in his native town. Shortly thereafter he returned to medical school in Munich and began to write plays.

He drifted into the literary world, lost interest in his medical studies, and lived a bohemian life in Munich until he moved to Berlin in 1924. In 1922 his first play, *Drums in the Night,* was produced, and by the time he came to live permanently in Berlin he had won some fame. There he came under the influence of the left-wing theatrical director Erwin Piscator who had used the term "epic drama" for some of his productions. However, for him the term primarily meant a large dose of what we would today call socialist realism with its mass scenes, simplified moral judgments, imitations of "real" life. Brecht was to infuse new meaning into the term.

Various plays were produced in succession as Brecht's reputation gradually grew: *Baal* in 1926 (actually the first play he wrote), *The Threepenny Opera* (his most famous play) in 1928, and *The Rise and Fall of the City of Mahagonny* in 1930, to mention only a few. Some of these Berlin plays are adaptations, rather than original compositions. Hašek's *Good Soldier Schweik,* Marlowe's *Edward II* and Gay's *The Beggar's Opera* (the basis of *The Threepenny Opera*) are some of the works he adapted. *The Caucasian Chalk Circle* itself is based on an old Chinese play. All his plays, original in plot or not, show the hand of an inventive and imaginative writer.

Exile came with Hitler and return with the end of the war, but the intense sense of expectation and the spirit of rebellion in the Berlin atmosphere of the twenties had vanished. Brecht continued to write plays and poetry which fed the great interest of the world in him. His last years were spent in Berlin in a more or less uneasy truce with the Communists. He had his own theatrical company, the Berlin Ensemble, which under his supervision produced his plays with great care and thought. His plays upset both the Communist and the non-

Communist worlds, for they attacked many of the routine ideals cherished by both, and they made men think. He was, in his later years, somewhat ambiguous about his attitude to the Communist party, but he certainly never broke his external loyalty to it. He died a loyal Marxist, if not a good Communist. He never could resolve the conflict between his heart and his head in the matter of communism. Although he was well aware that the Communists would never produce a perfect society, he refused to give up his idealistic views entirely. Fundamentally, he hated injustice and favored the poor and oppressed. These were the springs of his social views.

His dramatic fertility continued until the end, although his last great plays were written before his return to Germany. Among them are *The Caucasian Chalk Circle* (1944-1945), *Mother Courage* (1939), *The Life of Galileo* (1938-1939), and *The Good Woman of Setzuan* (1938-1940). Some of his dramas, including the *Circle*, have been excellently translated into English by Professor Eric Bentley who has captured in English a good deal of the force and power of Brecht's extraordinary language. Professor Bentley has been a tireless protagonist of Brecht in Anglo-Saxon countries.

Although, as indicated above, *The Caucasian Chalk Circle* is not entirely characteristic of Brecht, it is nonetheless one of his great plays and reveals in some important ways the Brechtian technique. In it there is a singer or storyteller who presents the play to us and makes comments on the action. Some of the comments fill in time gaps, some explain the action, some tell us what the characters are thinking: they are like the comments of a *persona* in a novel. There are also songs and a prologue in the present, although the action of the play itself is laid in the past. The movement of the plot is episodic, as in a narrative, even though it culminates in a climax. In Scene 4, where Azdak the judge is introduced, the plot moves back in time, as a novel might. There is much action and movement on the stage.

The impersonality of the language, which is especially notable in the love scenes between Simon and Grusha, helps the viewer to attain that distancing or alienation which Brecht considered so important. The shifts in time, the intrusion of the singer, the episodic quality also create this effect.

The central episode, the story of the chalk circle, is based on an old folk tale, which also occurs in a slightly different form in the story of Solomon's judgment in the Old Testament. It serves to underline the importance of real, as opposed to nominal, relationships. Grusha deserves the child, even if by blood she is not Michael's mother, because she, unlike the real mother, treats him as a mother should. This general point is also made in the Prologue: the collective farm which uses the land best is to have it. Yet there is more than a suggestion of injustice here, and some Communist critics have repudiated this interpretation of the Prologue. Although there is much satire on power and authority in the play, it should be noticed that the peasants and commoners are, in general, as hard as their masters.

The characterization, especially of Adzak, is vivid. The judge is a kind of rogue hero like those found in picaresque novels. Grusha is a lovely character of great strength, and her final victory elicits release and satisfaction in the audience. The language is rich and at times actually vulgar, but it seems always to be appropriate. To read, or even more to see, this play is to participate in a rich and satisfying experience, comic and tragic at once, and to experience both entertainment and enlightenment in a triumphant manner.

The first performance was in English at Carleton College, Northfield, Minnesota, in 1948. In the original language it was first publicly performed in Berlin in 1954. In the next year, it was put on in Paris by the Berlin Ensemble. It has been a notable success in the theatre.

The Caucasian Chalk Circle

Bertolt Brecht

ADAPTED BY ERIC BENTLEY

This adaptation, commissioned and approved by Bertolt Brecht, is based on the German MS of 1946. A German version very close to this MS was published in a supplement to *Sinn und Form,* 1949. My English text has now appeared in three versions. Maja Apelman collaborated on the first one (copyrighted 1947, 1948). The second and third were respectively copyrighted in 1961 and 1963.—E.B., New York, 1963

CHARACTERS

OLD MAN, *on the right*
PEASANT WOMAN, *on the right*
YOUNG PEASANT
A VERY YOUNG WORKER
OLD MAN, *on the left*
PEASANT WOMAN, *on the left*
AGRICULTURIST KATO
GIRL TRACTORIST
WOUNDED SOLDIER
THE DELEGATE *from the capital*
THE SINGER
GEORGI ABASHWILI, *the Governor*
NATELLA, *the Governor's wife*
MICHAEL, *their son*
SHALVA, *an adjutant*
ARSEN KAZBEKI, *a fat prince*
MESSENGER, *from the capital*
NIKO MIKADZE *and* MIKA LOLADZE, *doctors*
SIMON SHASHAVA, *a soldier*
GRUSHA VASHNADZE, *a kitchen maid*
OLD PEASANT, *with the milk*
CORPORAL *and* PRIVATE
PEASANT *and his wife*
LAVRENTI VASHNADZE, *Grusha's brother*

ANIKO, *his wife*
PEASANT WOMAN, *for a while Grusha's mother-in-law*
JUSSUP, *her son*
MONK
AZDAK, *village recorder*
SHAUWA, *a policeman*
GRAND DUKE
DOCTOR
INVALID
LIMPING MAN
BLACKMAILER
LUDOVICA
INNKEEPER, *her father-in-law*
STABLEBOY
POOR OLD PEASANT WOMAN
IRAKLI, *her brother-in-law, a bandit*
THREE WEALTHY FARMERS
ILLO SHUBOLADZE *and* SANDRO OBOLADZE, *lawyers*
OLD MARRIED COUPLE
SOLDIERS, SERVANTS,
PEASANTS, BEGGARS,
MUSICIANS, MERCHANTS,
NOBLES, ARCHITECTS

PROLOGUE

Among the ruins of a war-ravaged Caucasian village the members of two Kolkhoz[1] villages, mostly women and older men, are sitting in a circle, smoking and drinking wine. With them is a delegate of the state reconstruction commission from Nuka, the capital.

PEASANT WOMAN [*Left*]

[*Pointing*] In those hills over there we stopped three Nazi tanks, but the apple orchard was already destroyed.

OLD MAN [*Right*]

Our beautiful dairy farm: a ruin.

GIRL TRACTORIST

I laid the fire, Comrade. [*Pause*]

THE DELEGATE

Now listen to the report. Delegates from the goat-breeding Kolkhoz "Rosa Luxemburg" have been to Nuka. When Hitler's armies approached, the Kolkhoz had moved its goat-herds further east on orders from the authorities. They are now thinking of returning. Their delegates have investigated the village and the land and found a lot of it destroyed. [DELEGATES *on right nod*] The neighboring fruit-culture Kolkhoz [*To the left*] "Galinsk" is proposing to use the former grazing land of Kolkhoz "Rosa Luxemburg," a valley with scanty growth of grass, for orchards and vineyards. As a delegate of the Reconstruction Commission, I request that the two Kolkhoz villages decide between themselves whether Kolkhoz "Rosa Luxemburg" shall return here or not.

OLD MAN [*Right*]

First of all, I want to protest against the restriction of time for discussion. We of Kolkhoz "Rosa Luxemburg" have spent three days and three nights getting here. And now discussion is limited to half a day.

WOUNDED SOLDIER [*Left*]

Comrade, we haven't as many villages as we used to have. We haven't as many hands. We haven't as much time.

GIRL TRACTORIST

All pleasures have to be rationed. Tobacco is rationed, and wine. Discussion should be rationed.

OLD MAN [*Right*]

[*Sighing*] Death to the fascists! But I will come to the point and explain why we want our valley back. There are a great many reasons, but I'll begin with one of the simplest. Makina Abakidze, unpack the goat cheese. [A PEASANT WOMAN *from right takes from a basket an enormous cheese wrapped in a cloth. Applause and laughter*] Help yourselves, Comrades, start in!

[1] A collective farm in the Soviet Union.

OLD MAN [*Left*]

[*Suspiciously*] Is this a way of influencing us?

OLD MAN [*Right*]

[*Amid laughter*] How could it be a way of influencing you, Surab, you valley-thief? Everyone knows you will take the cheese and the valley, too. [*Laughter*] All I expect from you is an honest answer. Do you like the cheese?

OLD MAN [*Left*]

The answer is: yes.

OLD MAN [*Right*]

Really. [*Bitterly*] I ought to have known you know nothing about cheese.

OLD MAN [*Left*]

Why not? When I tell you I like it?

OLD MAN [*Right*]

Because you can't like it. Because it's not what it was in the old days. And why not? Because our goats don't like the new grass as they did the old. Cheese is not cheese because grass is not grass, that's the thing. Please put that in your report.

OLD MAN [*Left*]

But your cheese is excellent.

OLD MAN [*Right*]

It isn't excellent. It's just passable. The new grazing land is no good, whatever the young people may say. One can't live there. It doesn't even smell of morning in the morning. [SEVERAL PEOPLE *laugh*]

THE DELEGATE

Don't mind their laughing: they understand you. Comrades, why does one love one's country? Because the bread tastes better there, the air smells better, voices sound stronger, the sky is higher, the ground is easier to walk on. Isn't that so?

OLD MAN [*Right*]

The valley has belonged to us from all eternity.

SOLDIER [*Left*]

What does *that* mean—from all eternity? Nothing belongs to anyone from all eternity. When you were young you didn't even belong to yourself. You belonged to the Kazbeki[2] princes.

OLD MAN [*Right*]

Doesn't it make a difference, though, what kind of trees stand next to the house you are born in? Or what kind of neighbors you have? Doesn't that make a difference? We want to go back just to have you as our neighbors, valley-thieves! Now you can all laugh again.

OLD MAN [*Left*]

[*Laughing*] Then why don't you listen to what your neighbor, Kato Wachtang, our agriculturist, has to say about the valley?

PEASANT WOMAN [*Right*]

We've not said all there is to be said about our valley. By no means. Not all the houses are destroyed. As for the dairy farm, at least the foundation wall is still standing.

[2] A Caucasian district.

DELEGATE

You can claim State support—here and there—you know that. I have suggestions here in my pocket.

PEASANT WOMAN [*Right*]

Comrade Specialist, we haven't come here to bargain. I can't take your cap and hand you another, and say "This one's better." The other one might *be* better; but you *like* yours better.

GIRL TRACTORIST

A piece of land is not a cap—not in our country, Comrade.

DELEGATE

Don't get angry. It's true we have to consider a piece of land as a tool to produce something useful, but it's also true that we must recognize love for a particular piece of land. As far as I'm concerned, I'd like to find out more exactly what you [*To those on the left*] want to do with the valley.

OTHERS

Yes, let Kato speak.

DELEGATE

Comrade Agriculturist!

KATO [*Rising*, SHE'S *in military uniform*]

Comrades, last winter, while we were fighting in these hills here as Partisans, we discussed how, after the expulsion of the Germans, we could build up our fruit culture to ten times its original size. I've prepared a plan for an irrigation project. By means of a cofferdam on our mountain lake, 300 hectares of unfertile land can be irrigated. Our Kolkhoz could not only cultivate more fruit, but also have vineyards. The project, however, would pay only if the disputed valley of Kolkhoz "Galinsk" were also included. Here are the calculations. [SHE *hands the* DELEGATE *a briefcase*]

OLD MAN [*Right*]

Write into a report that our Kolkhoz plans to start a new stud farm.

GIRL TRACTORIST

Comrades, the project was conceived during days and nights when we had to take cover in the mountains. We were often without ammunition for our half-dozen rifles. Even getting a pencil was difficult. [*Applause from both sides*]

OLD MAN [*Right*]

Our thanks to the Comrades of Kolkhoz "Galinsk" and all who have defended our country! [THEY *shake hands and embrace*]

PEASANT WOMAN [*Left*]

In doing this our thought was that our soldiers—both your men and our men —should return to a still more productive homeland.

GIRL TRACTORIST

As the poet Mayakovsky[3] said: "The home of the Soviet people shall also be the home of Reason"!

[*The* DELEGATES *including the* OLD MAN *have got up, and with the* DELEGATE *specified proceed to study the Agriculturist's drawings . . . exclamations such as:* "Why is the altitude of all 22 meters?"—"This rock must be

---

[3] Vladimir Mayakovsky (1894-1930) was one of the greatest Russian poets of this century.

blown up"—"Actually, all they need is cement and dynamite"—"They force the water to come down here, that's clever!"]

A VERY YOUNG WORKER [*Right*]

[*To* OLD MAN, *right*] They're going to irrigate all the fields between the hills, look at that, Aleko!

OLD MAN [*Right*]

I'm not going to look. I knew the project would be good. I won't have a revolver aimed at my chest.

DELEGATE

But they only want to aim a pencil at your chest. [*Laughter*]

OLD MAN [*Right*]

[*Gets up gloomily, and walks over to look at the drawings*] These valley-thieves know only too well that we can't resist machines and projects in this country.

PEASANT WOMAN [*Right*]

Aleko Bereshwili, you have a weakness for new projects. That's well known.

DELEGATE

What about my report? May I write that you will all support the cession of your old valley in the interests of this project when you get back to your Kolkhoz?

PEASANT WOMAN [*Right*]

I will. What about you, Aleko?

OLD MAN [*Right*]

[*Bent over drawings*] I suggest that you give us copies of the drawings to take along.

PEASANT WOMAN [*Right*]

Then we can sit down and eat. Once he has the drawings and he's ready to discuss them, the matter is settled. I know him. And it will be the same with the rest of us. [DELEGATES *laughingly embrace again*]

OLD MAN [*Left*]

Long live the Kolkhoz "Rosa Luxemburg" and much luck to your horse-breeding project!

PEASANT WOMAN [*Left*]

In honor of the visit of the delegates from Kolkhoz "Rosa Luxemburg" and of the Specialist, the plan is that we all hear a presentation of the Singer Arkadi Tscheidse. [*Applause.* GIRL TRACTORIST *has gone off to bring the* SINGER]

PEASANT WOMAN [*Right*]

Comrades, your entertainment had better be good. We're going to pay for it with a valley.

PEASANT WOMAN [*Left*]

Arkadi Tscheidse knows about our discussion. He's promised to perform something that has a bearing on the problem.

KATO

We wired to Tiflis[4] three times. The whole thing nearly fell through at the last minute because his driver had a cold.

[4] Capital of the Georgian Republic of the U.S.S.R.

PEASANT WOMAN [*Left*]

Arkadi Tscheidse knows 21,000 lines of verse.

OLD MAN [*Left*]

It's very difficult to get him. You and the Planning Commission should see to it that you get him to come North more often, Comrade.

DELEGATE

We are more interested in economics, I'm afraid.

OLD MAN [*Left*]

[*Smiling*] You arrange the redistribution of vines and tractors, why not of songs?

[*Enter the* SINGER ARKADI TSCHEIDSE, *led by* GIRL TRACTORIST. HE *is a well-built man of simple manners, accompanied by* FOUR MUSICIANS *with their instruments. The* ARTISTS *are greeted with applause*]

GIRL TRACTORIST

This is the Comrade Specialist, Arkadi. [*The* SINGER *greets them all*]

DELEGATE

I'm honored to make your acquaintance. I heard about your songs when I was a boy at school. Will it be one of the old legends?

THE SINGER

A very old one. It's called The Chalk Circle and comes from the Chinese. But we'll do it, of course, in a changed version. Comrades, it's an honor for me to entertain you after a difficult debate. We hope you will find that the voice of the old poet also sounds well in the shadow of Soviet tractors. It may be a mistake to mix different wines, but old and new wisdom mix admirably. Now I hope we'll get something to eat before the performance begins—it would certainly help.

VOICES

Surely. Everyone into the Club House! [*While* EVERYONE *begins to move, the* DELEGATE *turns to the* GIRL TRACTORIST]

DELEGATE

I hope it won't take long. I've got to get back tonight.

GIRL TRACTORIST

How long will it last, Arkadi? The Comrade Specialist must get back to Tiflis tonight.

THE SINGER

[*Casually*] It's actually two stories. An hour or two.

GIRL TRACTORIST

[*Confidentially*] Couldn't you make it shorter?

THE SINGER

No.

VOICE

Arkadi Tscheidse's performance will take place here in the square after the meal. [*And* THEY ALL *go happily to eat*]

1. The Noble Child

As the lights go up, THE SINGER *is seen sitting on the floor, a black sheepskin cloak round his shoulders, and a little well-thumbed notebook in his hand. A small group of listeners—the* CHORUS—*sits with him. The manner of his recitation makes it clear that* HE *has told his story over and over again.* HE *mechanically fingers the pages, seldom looking at them. With appropriate gestures,* HE *gives the signal for each scene to begin.*

THE SINGER

In olden times, in a bloody time,
There ruled in a Caucasian city—
Men called it City of the Damned—
A governor.
His name was Georgi Abashwili.
He was rich as Croesus
He had a beautiful wife
He had a healthy baby.
No other governor in Grusinia
Had so many horses in his stable
So many beggars on his doorstep
So many soldiers in his service
So many petitioners in his courtyard.
Georgi Abashwili—how shall I describe him to you?
He enjoyed his life.
On the morning of Easter Sunday
The governor and his family went to church.
[*At the left a large doorway, at the right an even larger gateway.* BEGGARS *and* PETITIONERS *pour from the gateway, holding up thin* CHILDREN, *crutches, and petitions.* THEY *are followed by* IRONSHIRTS, *and then, expensively dressed, the* GOVERNOR'S FAMILY]

BEGGARS AND PETITIONERS

Mercy! Mercy, Your Grace! The taxes are too high.
—I lost my leg in the Persian War, where can I get . . .
—My brother is innocent, Your Grace, a misunderstanding . . .
—The child is starving in my arms!
—Our petition is for our son's discharge from the army, our last remaining son!
—Please, Your Grace, the water inspector takes bribes.
[ONE SERVANT *collects the petitions,* ANOTHER *distributes coins from a purse.* SOLDIERS *push the* CROWD *back, lashing at them with thick leather whips*]
THE SOLDIER

Get back! Clear the church door! [*Behind the* GOVERNOR, HIS WIFE, *and the* ADJUTANT, *the* GOVERNOR'S CHILD *is brought through the gateway in an ornate carriage*]

THE CROWD
—The baby!
—I can't see it, don't shove so hard!
—God bless the child, Your Grace!

THE SINGER [*While the* CROWD *is driven back with whips*]
For the first time on that Easter Sunday, the people saw the Governor's heir. Two doctors never moved from the noble child, apple of the Governor's eye. Even the mighty Prince Kazbeki bows before him at the church door. [A FAT PRINCE *steps forward and greets the family*]

THE FAT PRINCE
Happy Easter, Natella Abashwili! What a day! When it was raining last night, I thought to myself, gloomy holidays! But this morning the sky was gay. I love a gay sky, a simple heart, Natella Abashwili. And little Michael is a governor from head to foot! Tititi! [HE *tickles the* CHILD]

THE GOVERNOR'S WIFE
What do you think, Arsen, at last Georgi has decided to start building the wing on the east side. All those wretched slums are to be torn down to make room for the garden.

THE FAT PRINCE
Good news after so much bad! What's the latest on the war, Brother Georgi? [*The* GOVERNOR *indicates a lack of interest*]

THE FAT PRINCE
Strategical retreat, I hear. Well, minor reverses are to be expected. Sometimes things go well, sometimes not. Such is war. Doesn't mean a thing, does it?

THE GOVERNOR'S WIFE
He's coughing. Georgi, did you hear? [SHE *speaks sharply to the* DOCTORS, *two dignified men standing close to the little carriage*] He's coughing!

THE FIRST DOCTOR [*To the* SECOND]
May I remind you, Niko Mikadze, that I was against the lukewarm bath? [*To the* GOVERNOR'S WIFE]
There's been a little error over warming the bath water, Your Grace.

THE SECOND DOCTOR [*Equally polite*] Mika Loladze, I'm afraid I can't agree with you. The temperature of the bath water was exactly what our great, beloved Mishiko Oboladze prescribed. More likely a slight draft during the night, Your Grace.

THE GOVERNOR'S WIFE
But do pay more attention to him. He looks feverish, Georgi.

THE FIRST DOCTOR [*Bending over the* CHILD] No cause for alarm, Your Grace. The bath water will be warmer. It won't occur again.

THE SECOND DOCTOR [*With a venomous glance at the* FIRST]
I won't forget that, my dear Mika Loladze. No cause for concern, Your Grace.

THE FAT PRINCE
Well, well, well! I always say: "A pain in my liver? Then the doctor gets fifty strokes on the soles of his feet." We live in a decadent age. In the old days one said: "Off with his head!"

THE GOVERNOR'S WIFE
Let's go into church. Very likely it's the draft here.

[*The procession of* FAMILY *and* SERVANTS *turns into the doorway. The* FAT PRINCE *follows, but the* GOVERNOR *is kept back by the* ADJUTANT, *a handsome young man. When the crowd of* PETITIONERS *has been driven off, a young dust-stained* RIDER, *his arm in a sling, remains behind*]

THE ADJUTANT [*Pointing at the* RIDER, *who steps forward*]

Won't you hear the messenger from the capital, your Excellency? He arrived this morning. With confidential papers.

THE GOVERNOR

Not before Service, Shalva. But did you hear Brother Kazbeki wish me a happy Easter? Which is all very well, but I don't believe it did rain last night.

THE ADJUTANT [*Nodding*]

We must investigate.

THE GOVERNOR

Yes, at once. Tomorrow.

[THEY *pass through the doorway. The* RIDER, *who has waited in vain for an audience, turns sharply round and, muttering a curse, goes off. Only one of the palace guards—*SIMON SHASHAVA—*remains at the door*]

THE SINGER

The city is still.

Pigeons strut in the church square.

A soldier of the Palace Guard

Is joking with a kitchen maid

As she comes up from the river with a bundle.

[*A girl—*GRUSHA VASHADZE—*comes through the gateway with a bundle made of large green leaves under her arm*]

SIMON

What, the young lady is not in church? Shirking?

GRUSHA

I was dressed to go. But they needed another goose for the banquet. And they asked me to get it. I know about geese.

SIMON

A goose? [HE *feigns suspicion*] I'd like to see that goose. [GRUSHA *does not understand*] One has to be on one's guard with women. "I only went for a fish," they tell you, but it turns out to be something else.

GRUSHA [*Walking resolutely toward him and showing him the goose*]

There! If it isn't a fifteen-pound goose stuffed full of corn, I'll eat the feathers.

SIMON

A queen of a goose! The Governor himself will eat it. So the young lady has been down to the river again?

GRUSHA

Yes, at the poultry farm.

SIMON

Really? At the poultry farm, down by the river . . . not higher up maybe? Near those willows?

GRUSHA

I only go to the willows to wash the linen.

SIMON [*Insinuatingly*]

Exactly.

GRUSHA

Exactly what?

SIMON [*Winking*]

Exactly that.

GRUSHA

Why shouldn't I wash the linen by the willows?

SIMON [*With exaggerated laughter*]

"Why shouldn't I wash the linen by the willows!" That's good, really good!

GRUSHA

I don't understand the soldier. What's so good about it?

SIMON [*Slyly*]

"If something I know someone learns, she'll grow hot and cold by turns!"

GRUSHA

I don't know what I could learn about those willows.

SIMON

Not even if there was a bush opposite? That one could see everything from? Everything that goes on there when a certain person is—"washing linen"?

GRUSHA

What does go on? Won't the soldier say what he means and have done?

SIMON

Something goes on. And something can be seen.

GRUSHA

Could the soldier mean I dip my toes in the water when it is hot? There is nothing else.

SIMON

More. Your toes. And more.

GRUSHA

More what? At most my foot?

SIMON

Your foot. And a little more. [HE *laughs heartily*]

GRUSHA [*Angrily*]

Simon Shashava, you ought to be ashamed of yourself! To sit in a bush on a hot day and wait till someone comes and dips her leg in the river! And I bet you bring a friend along too! [SHE *runs off*]

SIMON [*Shouting after her*]

I didn't bring any friend along! [As *the* SINGER *resumes his tale, the* SOLDIER *steps into the doorway as though to listen to the service*]

THE SINGER

The city lies still

But why are there armed men?

The Governor's palace is at peace

But why is it a fortress?

And the Governor returned to his palace

And the fortress was a trap

And the goose was plucked and roasted

But the goose was not eaten this time

And noon was no longer the hour to eat:
Noon was the hour to die.

[*From the doorway at the left the* FAT PRINCE *quickly appears, stands still, looks around. Before the gateway at the right* TWO IRONSHIRTS *are squatting and playing dice. The* FAT PRINCE *sees them, walks slowly past, making a sign to them.* THEY *rise:* ONE *goes through the gateway, the* OTHER *goes off at the right. Muffled voices are heard from various directions in the rear: "To your posts!" The palace is surrounded. The* FAT PRINCE *quickly goes off. Church bells in the distance. Enter, through the doorway, the* GOVERNOR'S FAMILY *and* PROCESSION, *returning from church*]

THE GOVERNOR'S WIFE [*Passing the* ADJUTANT]

It's impossible to live in such a slum. But Georgi, of course, will only build for his little Michael. Never for me! Michael is all! All for Michael!

[*The* PROCESSION *turns into the gateway. Again the* ADJUTANT *lingers behind.* HE *waits. Enter the* WOUNDED RIDER *from the doorway.* TWO IRONSHIRTS *of the palace guard have taken up positions by the gateway*]

THE ADJUTANT [*To the* RIDER]

The Governor does not wish to receive military reports before dinner—especially if they're depressing, as I assume. In the afternoon His Excellency will confer with prominent architects. They're coming to dinner too. And here they are! [*Enter* THREE GENTLEMEN *through the doorway*] Go in the kitchen and get yourself something to eat, my friend. [*As the* RIDER *goes, the* ADJUTANT *greets the* ARCHITECTS] Gentlemen, His Excellency expects you at dinner. He will devote all his time to you and your great new plans. Come!

ONE OF THE ARCHITECTS

We marvel that His Excellency intends to build. There are disquieting rumors that the war in Persia has taken a turn for the worse.

THE ADJUTANT

All the more reason to build! There's nothing to those rumors anyway. Persia is a long way off, and the garrison here would let itself be hacked to bits for its Governor. [*Noise from the palace. The shrill scream of a woman. Someone is shouting orders. Dumbfounded, the* ADJUTANT *moves toward the gateway. An* IRONSHIRT *steps out, points his lance at him*] What's this? Put down that lance, you dog.

ONE OF THE ARCHITECTS

It's the Princes! Don't you know the Princes met last night in the capital? And they're against the Grand Duke and his Governors? Gentlemen, we'd better make ourselves scarce. [*THEY* *rush off. The* ADJUTANT *remains helplessly behind*]

THE ADJUTANT [*Furiously to the* PALACE GUARD]

Down with those lances! Don't you see the Governor's life is threatened?

[*The* IRONSHIRTS *of the Palace Guard refuse to obey.* THEY *stare coldly and indifferently at the* ADJUTANT *and follow the next events without interest*]

THE SINGER

O blindness of the great!

They go their way like gods,
Great over bent backs,
Sure of hired fists,
Trusting in the power
Which has lasted so long.
But long is not forever.
O change from age to age!
Thou hope of the people!
[*Enter the* GOVERNOR, *through the gateway, between* TWO SOLDIERS *armed to the teeth.* HE *is in chains. His face is gray*]
Up, great sir, deign to walk upright!
From your palace the eyes of many foes follow you!
And now you don't need an architect, a carpenter will do.
You won't be moving into a new palace
But into a little hole in the ground.
Look about you once more, blind man!
[*The arrested man looks round*]
Does all you had please you?
Between the Easter Mass and the Easter meal
You are walking to a place whence no one returns.
[*The* GOVERNOR *is led off. A horn sounds an alarm. Noise behind the gateway*]
When the house of a great one collapses
Many little ones are slain.
Those who had no share in the *good* fortunes of the mighty
Often have a share in their *mis*fortunes.
The plunging wagon
Drags the sweating oxen down with it
Into the abyss.
[*The* SERVANTS *come rushing through the gateway in panic*]
THE SERVANTS [*Among themselves*]
—The baskets!
—Take them all into the third courtyard! Food for five days!
—The mistress has fainted! Someone must carry her down.
—She must get away.
—What about us? We'll be slaughtered like chickens, as always.
—Goodness, what'll happen? There's bloodshed already in the city, they say.
—Nonsense, the Governor has just been asked to appear at a Princes' meeting. All very correct. Everything'll be ironed out. I heard this on the best authority . . .
[*The* TWO DOCTORS *rush into the courtyard*]
THE FIRST DOCTOR [*Trying to restrain the other*]
Niko Mikadze, it is your duty as a doctor to attend Natella Abashwili.
THE SECOND DOCTOR
My duty! It's yours!
THE FIRST DOCTOR
Whose turn is it to look after the child today, Niko Mikadze, yours or mine?

THE SECOND DOCTOR

Do you really think, Mika Loladze, I'm going to stay a minute longer in this accursed house on that little brat's account?

[THEY *start fighting. All one hears is: "You neglect your duty!" and "Duty, my foot!" Then the* SECOND DOCTOR *knocks the* FIRST *down*]

Go to hell!

[*Exit*]

[*Enter the* SOLDIER, SIMON SHASHAVA. HE *searches in the crowd for* GRUSHA]

SIMON

Grusha! There you are at last! What are you going to do?

GRUSHA

Nothing. If worst comes to worst, I've a brother in the mountains. How about you?

SIMON

Forget about me. [*Formally again*] Grusha Vashnadze, your wish to know my plans fills me with satisfaction. I've been ordered to accompany Madam Natella Abashwili as her guard.

GRUSHA

But hasn't the Palace Guard mutinied?

SIMON [*Seriously*]

That's a fact.

GRUSHA

Isn't it dangerous to go with her?

SIMON

In Tiflis, they say: Isn't the stabbing dangerous for the knife?

GRUSHA

You're not a knife, you're a man, Simon Shashava, what has that woman to do with you?

SIMON

That woman has nothing to do with me. I have my orders, and I go.

GRUSHA

The soldier is pigheaded: he is getting himself into danger for nothing— nothing at all. I must get into the third courtyard, I'm in a hurry.

SIMON

Since we're both in a hurry we shouldn't quarrel. You need time for a good quarrel. May I ask if the young lady still has parents?

GRUSHA

No, just a brother.

SIMON

As time is short—my second question is this: Is the young lady as healthy as a fish in water?

GRUSHA

I may have a pain in the right shoulder once in a while. Otherwise I'm strong enough for my job. No one has complained. So far.

SIMON

That's well-known. When it's Easter Sunday, and the question arises who'll

run for the goose all the same, she'll be the one. My third question is this:
Is the young lady impatient? Does she want apples in winter?

GRUSHA

Impatient? No. But if a man goes to war without any reason and then no
message comes—that's bad.

SIMON

A message will come. And now my final question . . .

GRUSHA

Simon Shashava, I must get to the third courtyard at once. My answer is yes.

SIMON [*Very embarrassed*]

Haste, they say, is the wind that blows down the scaffolding. But they also
say: The rich don't know what haste is. I'm from . . .

GRUSHA

Kutsk . . .

SIMON

So the young lady has been inquiring about me? I'm healthy, I have no
dependants, I make ten piasters a month, as paymaster twenty piasters, and
I'm asking—very sincerely—for your hand.

GRUSHA

Simon Shashava, it suits me well.

SIMON [*Taking from his neck a thin chain with a little cross on it*]

My mother gave me this cross, Grusha Vashnadze. The chain is silver. Please
wear it.

GRUSHA

Many thanks, Simon.

SIMON [*Hangs it round her neck*]

It would be better for the young lady to go to the third courtyard now. Or
there'll be difficulties. Anyway, I must harness the horses. The young lady
will understand?

GRUSHA

Yes, Simon. [THEY *stand undecided*]

SIMON

I'll just take the mistress to the troops that have stayed loyal. When the
war's over, I'll be back. In two weeks. Or three. I hope my intended won't
get tired, awaiting my return.

GRUSHA

Simon Shashava, I shall wait for you.
Go calmly into battle, soldier
The bloody battle, the bitter battle
From which not everyone returns:
When you return I shall be there.
I shall be waiting for you under the green elm
I shall be waiting for you under the bare elm
I shall wait until the last soldier has returned
And longer.
When you come back from the battle
No boots will stand at my door

The pillow beside mine will be empty
And my mouth will be unkissed.
When you return, when you return
You will be able to say: It is just as it was.

SIMON

I thank you, Grusha Vashnadze. And goodbye! [HE *bows low before her.*
SHE *does the same before him. Then* SHE *runs quickly off without looking
round. Enter the* ADJUTANT *from the gateway*]

THE ADJUTANT [*Harshly*]

Harness the horses to the carriage! Don't stand there doing nothing, louse!
[SIMON SHASHAVA *stands to attention and goes off*]

[TWO SERVANTS *crowd from the gateway, bent low under huge trunks.
Behind them, supported by her* WOMEN, *stumbles* NATELLA ABASHWILI. SHE
is followed by a WOMAN *carrying the* CHILD]

THE GOVERNOR'S WIFE

I hardly know if my head's still on. Where's Michael? Don't hold him so
clumsily. Pile the trunks onto the carriage. Shalva, is there no news from
the city?

THE ADJUTANT

None. All's quiet so far, but there's not a minute to lose. No room for all
these trunks in the carriage. Pick out what you need.

[*Exit quickly*]

THE GOVERNOR'S WIFE

Only essentials! Quick, open the trunks! I'll tell you what I need. [*The
trunks are lowered and opened.* SHE *points at some brocade dresses*] The
green one! And, of course, the one with the fur trimming. Where are Niko
Mikadze and Mika Loladze? I've suddenly got the most terrible migraine
again. It always starts in the temples.
[*Enter* GRUSHA]
Taking your time, eh? Go at once and get the hot water bottles! [GRUSHA
runs off, returns later with hot water bottles; the GOVERNOR'S WIFE *orders
her about by signs*] Don't tear the sleeves.

A YOUNG WOMAN

Pardon, madam, no harm has come to the dress.

THE GOVERNOR'S WIFE

Because I stopped you. I've been watching you for a long time. Nothing in
your head but making eyes at Shalva Tzereteli. I'll kill you, you bitch! [SHE
beats the woman]

THE ADJUTANT [*Appearing in the gateway*]

Please make haste, Natella Abashwili. Firing has broken out in the city.

[*Exit*]

THE GOVERNOR'S WIFE [*Letting go of the* YOUNG WOMAN]

Oh dear, do you think they'll lay hands on us? Why should they? Why? [SHE
herself begins to rummage in the trunks] How's Michael? Asleep?

THE WOMAN WITH THE CHILD

Yes, madam.

THE GOVERNOR'S WIFE

Then put him down a moment and get my little saffron-colored boots from the bedroom. I need them for the green dress. [*The* WOMAN *puts down the* CHILD *and goes off*] Just look how these things have been packed! No love! No understanding! If you don't give them every order yourself . . . At such moments you realize what kind of servants you have! They gorge themselves at your expense, and never a word of gratitude! I'll remember this.

THE ADJUTANT [*Entering, very excited*]

Natella, you must leave at once!

THE GOVERNOR'S WIFE

Why? I've got to take this silver dress—it cost a thousand piasters. And that one there, and where's the wine-colored one?

THE ADJUTANT [*Trying to pull her away*]

Riots have broken out! We must leave at once. Where's the baby?

THE GOVERNOR'S WIFE [*Calling to the* YOUNG WOMAN *who was holding the baby*]

Maro, get the baby ready! Where on earth are you?

THE ADJUTANT [*Leaving*]

We'll probably have to leave the carriage behind and go ahead on horseback.

[*The* GOVERNOR'S WIFE *rummages again among her dresses, throws some onto the heap of chosen clothes, then takes them off again. Noises, drums are heard. The* YOUNG WOMAN *who was beaten creeps away. The sky begins to grow red*]

THE GOVERNOR'S WIFE [*Rummaging desperately*]

I simply cannot find the wine-colored dress. Take the whole pile to the carriage. Where's Asja? And why hasn't Maro come back? Have you all gone crazy?

THE ADJUTANT [*Returning*]

Quick! Quick!

THE GOVERNOR'S WIFE [*To the* FIRST WOMAN]

Run! Just throw them into the carriage!

THE ADJUTANT

We're not taking the carriage. And if you don't come now, I'll ride off on my own.

THE GOVERNOR'S WIFE [*As the* FIRST WOMAN *can't carry everything*]

Where's that bitch Asja? [*The* ADJUTANT *pulls her away*] Maro, bring the baby! [*To the* FIRST WOMAN]

Go and look for Masha. No, first take the dresses to the carriage. Such nonsense! I wouldn't dream of going on horseback!

[*Turning round,* SHE *sees the red sky, and starts back rigid. The fire burns.* SHE *is pulled out by the* ADJUTANT. *Shaking, the* FIRST WOMAN *follows with the dresses*]

MARO [*From the doorway with the boots*]

Madam! [SHE *sees the trunks and dresses and runs toward the* BABY, *picks it up, and holds it a moment*] They left it behind, the beasts. [SHE *hands it to* GRUSHA] Hold it a moment. [SHE *runs off, following the* GOVERNOR'S WIFE]

[*Enter* SERVANTS *from the gateway*]

THE COOK

Well, so they've actually gone. Without the food wagons, and not a minute too early. It's time for us to clear out.

A GROOM

This'll be an unhealthy neighborhood for quite a while. [*To one of the* WOMEN] Suliko, take a few blankets and wait for me in the foal stables.

GRUSHA

What have they done with the governor?

THE GROOM [*Gesturing throat cutting*]

Ffffft.

A FAT WOMAN [*Seeing the gesture and becoming hysterical*]

Oh dear, oh dear, oh dear, oh dear! Our master Georgi Abashwili! A picture of health he was, at the Morning Mass—and now! Oh, take me away, we're all lost, we must die in sin like our master, Georgi Abashwili!

THE OTHER WOMAN [*Soothing her*]

Calm down, Nina! You'll be taken to safety. You've never hurt a fly.

THE FAT WOMAN [*Being led out*]

Oh dear, oh dear, oh dear! Quick! Let's all get out before they come, before they come!

A YOUNG WOMAN

Nina takes it more to heart than the mistress, that's a fact. They even have to have their weeping done for them.

THE COOK

We'd better get out, all of us.

ANOTHER WOMAN [*Glancing back*]

That must be the East Gate burning.

THE YOUNG WOMAN [*Seeing the* CHILD *in* GRUSHA'S *arms*]

The baby! What are you doing with it?

GRUSHA

It got left behind.

THE YOUNG WOMAN

She simply left it there. Michael, who was kept out of all the drafts!

[*The* SERVANTS *gather round the* CHILD]

GRUSHA

He's waking up.

THE GROOM

Better put him down, I tell you. I'd rather not think what'd happen to anybody who was found with that baby.

THE COOK

That's right. Once they get started, they'll kill each other off, whole families at a time. Let's go.

[*Exeunt all but* GRUSHA, *with the* CHILD *on her arm, and* TWO WOMEN]

THE TWO WOMEN

Didn't you hear? Better put him down.

GRUSHA

The nurse asked me to hold him a moment.

THE OLDER WOMAN

She's not coming back, you simpleton.

THE YOUNGER WOMAN

Keep your hands off it.

THE OLDER WOMAN [*Amiably*]

Grusha, you're a good soul, but you're not very bright, and you know it. I
tell you, if he had the plague he couldn't be more dangerous.

GRUSHA [*Stubbornly*]

He hasn't got the plague. He looks at me! He's human!

THE OLDER WOMAN

Don't look at *him*. You're a fool—the kind that always gets put upon. A
person need only say, "Run for the salad, you have the longest legs," and
you run. My husband has an ox cart—you can come with us if you hurry!
Lord, by now the whole neighborhood must be in flames.

[BOTH WOMEN *leave, sighing. After some hesitation,* GRUSHA *puts the sleeping* CHILD *down, looks at it for a moment, then takes a brocade blanket from
the heap of clothes and covers it. Then* BOTH WOMEN *return, dragging bun-
dles.* GRUSHA *starts guiltily away from the* CHILD *and walks a few steps to one
side*]

THE YOUNGER WOMAN

Haven't you packed anything yet? There isn't much time, you know. The
Ironshirts will be here from the barracks.

GRUSHA

Coming. [SHE *runs through the doorway.* BOTH WOMEN *go to the gateway
and wait. The sound of horses is heard.* THEY *flee, screaming*]

[*Enter the* FAT PRINCE *with drunken* IRONSHIRTS. *One of them carries the
governor's head on a lance*]

THE FAT PRINCE

Here! In the middle! [ONE SOLDIER *climbs onto the other's back, takes the
head, holds it tentatively over the door*] That's not the middle. Farther to
the right. That's it. What I do, my friends, I do well.

[*While, with hammer and nail, the* SOLDIER *fastens the head to the wall by
its hair*]

This morning at the church door I said to Georgi Abashwili: "I love a clear
sky." Actually, I prefer the lightning that comes out of a clear sky. Yes,
indeed. It's a pity they took the brat along, though, I need him, urgently.

[*Exit with* IRONSHIRTS *through the gateway. Trampling of horses again.
Enter* GRUSHA *through the doorway looking cautiously about her. Clearly* SHE
has waited for the IRONSHIRTS *to go. Carrying a bundle,* SHE *walks toward the
gateway. At the last moment,* SHE *turns to see if the* CHILD *is still there. Catching sight of the head over the doorway,* SHE *screams. Horrified,* SHE *picks up
her bundle again, and is about to leave when the* SINGER *starts to speak.* SHE
stands rooted to the spot]

THE SINGER

As she was standing between courtyard and gate,
She heard or she thought she heard a low voice calling.
The child called to her,
Not whining, but calling quite sensibly,
Or so it seemed to her.
"Woman," it said, "help me."
And it went on, not whining, but saying quite sensibly:
"Know, woman, he who hears not a cry for help
But passes by with troubled ears will never hear

The gentle call of a lover nor the blackbird at dawn
Nor the happy sigh of the tired grape-picker as the Angelus rings."
[SHE *walks a few steps toward the* CHILD *and bends over it*]
Hearing this she went back for one more look at the child:
Only to sit with him for a moment or two,
Only till someone should come,
His mother, or anyone.
[*Leaning on a trunk,* SHE *sits facing the* CHILD]
Only till she would have to leave, for the danger was too great,
The city was full of flame and crying.
[*The light grows dimmer, as though evening and night were coming on*]
Fearful is the seductive power of goodness!
[GRUSHA *now settles down to watch over the* CHILD *through the night.
Once,* SHE *lights a small lamp to look at it. Once,* SHE *tucks it in with a coat.
From time to time* SHE *listens and looks to see whether someone is coming*]
And she sat with the child a long time,
Till evening came, till night came, till dawn came.
She sat too long, too long she saw
The soft breathing, the small clenched fists,
Till toward morning the seduction was complete
And she rose, and bent down and, sighing, took the child
And carried it away.
[SHE *does what the* SINGER *says as* HE *describes it*]
As if it was stolen goods she picked it up.
As if she was a thief she crept away.

2. The Flight into the Northern Mountains

THE SINGER

When Grusha Vashnadze left the city
On the Grusinian highway
On the way to the Northern Mountains
She sang a song, she bought some milk.

THE CHORUS

How will this human child escape
The bloodhounds, the trap-setters?
Into the deserted mountains she journeyed
Along the Grusinian highway she journeyed
She sang a song, she bought some milk.

[GRUSHA VASHNADZE *walks on. On her back* SHE *carries the* CHILD *in a sack,
in one hand is a large stick, in the other a bundle.* SHE *sings*]

THE SONG OF THE FOUR GENERALS

Four generals
Set out for Iran.

With the first one, war did not agree.
The second never won a victory.
For the third the weather never was right.
For the fourth the men would never fight.
Four generals
And not a single man!

Sosso Robakidse
Went marching to Iran
With him the war did so agree
He soon had won a victory.
For him the weather was always right.
For him the men would always fight.
Sosso Robakidse,
He is our man!

[*A peasant's cottage appears*]

GRUSHA [*To the* CHILD]

Noontime is meal time. Now we'll sit hopefully in the grass, while the good Grusha goes and buys a little pitcher of milk. [SHE *lays the* CHILD *down and knocks at the cottage door. An* OLD MAN *opens it*] Grandfather, could I have a little pitcher of milk? And a corn cake, maybe?

THE OLD MAN

Milk? We have no milk. The soldiers from the city have our goats. Go to the soldiers if you want milk.

GRUSHA

But grandfather, you must have a little pitcher of milk for a baby?

THE OLD MAN

And for a God-bless-you, eh?

GRUSHA

Who said anything about a God-bless-you? [SHE *shows her purse*] We'll pay like princes. "Head in the clouds, backside in the water." [*The* PEASANT *goes off, grumbling, for milk*] How much for the milk?

THE OLD MAN

Three piasters. Milk has gone up.

GRUSHA

Three piasters for this little drop? [*Without a word the* OLD MAN *shuts the door in her face*] Michael, did you hear that? Three piasters! We can't afford it! [SHE *goes back, sits down again, and gives the* CHILD *her breast*] Suck. Think of the three piasters. There's nothing there, but you *think* you're drinking, and that's something. [*Shaking her head,* SHE *sees that the* CHILD *isn't sucking any more.* SHE *gets up, walks back to the door, and knocks again*] Open grandfather, we'll pay. [*Softly*] May lightning strike you! [*When the* OLD MAN *appears*] I thought it would be half a piaster. But the baby must be fed. How about one piaster for that little drop?

THE OLD MAN

Two.

GRUSHA

Don't shut the door again. [SHE *fishes a long time in her bag*]
Here are two piasters. The milk better be good. I still have two days' journey
ahead of me. It's a murderous business you have here—and sinful, too!

THE OLD MAN

Kill the soldiers if you want milk.

GRUSHA [*Giving the* CHILD *some milk*]

This is an expensive joke. Take a sip, Michael, it's a week's pay. Around
here they think we earned our money just sitting around. Oh, Michael, Michael, you're a nice little load for a girl to take on! [*Uneasy*, SHE *gets up,
puts the* CHILD *on her back, and walks on. The* OLD MAN, *grumbling, picks
up the pitcher and looks after her unmoved*]

THE SINGER

As Grusha Vashnadze went northward
The Princes' Ironshirts went after her.

THE CHORUS

How will the barefoot girl escape the Ironshirts,
The bloodhounds, the trap-setters?
They hunt even by night.
Pursuers never tire.
Butchers sleep little.
[TWO IRONSHIRTS *are trudging along the highway*]

THE CORPORAL

You'll never amount to anything, blockhead, your heart's not in it. Your
senior officer sees this in little things. Yesterday, when I made the fat gal,
yes, you grabbed her husband as I commanded, and you did kick him in the
stomach, at my request, but did you *enjoy* it, like a loyal Private, or were
you just doing your duty? I've kept an eye on you blockhead, you're a hollow reed and a tinkling cymbal, you won't get promoted. [THEY *walk a
while in silence*] Don't think I've forgotten how insubordinate you are,
either. Stop limping! I forbid you to limp! You limp because I sold the
horses, and I sold the horses because I'd never have got that price again.
You limp to show me you don't like marching. I know you. It won't help.
You wait. Sing!

THE TWO IRONSHIRTS [*Singing*]

Sadly to war I went my way
Leaving my loved one at her door.
My friends will keep her honor safe
Till from the war I'm back once more.

THE CORPORAL

Louder!

THE TWO IRONSHIRTS [*Singing*]

When 'neath a headstone I shall be
My love a little earth will bring:
"Here rest the feet that oft would run to me
And here the arms that oft to me would cling." [THEY *begin to walk again
in silence*]

THE CORPORAL

A good soldier has his heart and soul in it. When he receives an order, he gets a hard on, and when he drives his lance into the enemy's guts, he comes. [HE *shouts for joy*] He lets himself be torn to bits for his superior officer, and as he lies dying he takes note that his corporal is nodding approval, and that is reward enough, it's his dearest wish. *You* won't get any nod of approval, but you'll croak all right. Christ, how'm I to get my hands on the Governor's bastard with the help of a fool like you! [THEY *stay on stage behind*]

THE SINGER

When Grusha Vashnadze came to the River Sirra
Flight grew too much for her, the helpless child too heavy.
In the cornfields the rosy dawn
Is cold to the sleepless one, only cold.
The gay clatter of the milk cans in the farmyard where the smoke rises
Is only a threat to the fugitive.
She who carries the child feels its weight and little more.

[GRUSHA *stops in front of a farm. A* FAT PEASANT WOMAN *is carrying a milk can through the door.* GRUSHA *waits until* SHE *has gone in, then approaches the house cautiously*]

GRUSHA [*To the* CHILD]

Now you've wet yourself again, and you know I've no linen. Michael, this is where we part company. It's far enough from the city. They wouldn't want you *so* much that they'd follow you all *this* way, little good-for-nothing. The peasant woman is kind, and can't you just smell the milk? [SHE *bends down to lay the* CHILD *on the threshold*] So farewell, Michael, I'll forget how you kicked me in the back all night to make me walk faster. And you can forget the meager fare—it was meant well. I'd like to have kept you—your nose is so tiny—but it can't be. I'd have shown you your first rabbit, I'd have trained you to keep dry, but now I must turn around. My sweetheart the soldier might be back soon, and suppose he didn't find me? You can't ask that, can you?

[SHE *creeps up to the door and lays the* CHILD *on the threshold. Then, hiding behind a tree,* SHE *waits until the* PEASANT WOMAN *opens the door and sees the bundle*]

THE PEASANT WOMAN

Good heavens, what's this? Husband!

THE PEASANT

What is it? Let me finish my soup.

THE PEASANT WOMAN [*To the* CHILD]

Where's your mother then? Haven't you got one? It's a boy. Fine linen. He's from a good family, you can see that. And they just leave him on our doorstep. Oh, these are times!

THE PEASANT

If they think we're going to feed it, they're wrong. You can take it to the priest in the village. That's the best we can do.

THE PEASANT WOMAN

What'll the priest do with him? He needs a mother. There, he's waking up. Don't you think we could keep him, though?

THE PEASANT [*Shouting*]

No!

THE PEASANT WOMAN

I could lay him in the corner by the armchair. All I need is a crib. I can take him into the fields with me. See him laughing? Husband, we have a roof over our heads. We can do it. Not another word out of you!

[SHE *carries the* CHILD *into the house. The* PEASANT *follows protesting.* GRUSHA *steps out from behind the tree, laughs, and hurries off in the opposite direction*]

THE SINGER

Why so cheerful, making for home?

THE CHORUS

Because the child has won new parents with a laugh,
Because I'm rid of the little one, I'm cheerful.

THE SINGER

And why so sad?

THE CHORUS

Because I'm single and free, I'm sad
Like someone who's been robbed
Someone who's newly poor.

[SHE *walks for a short while, then meets the* TWO IRONSHIRTS, *who point their lances at her*]

THE CORPORAL

Lady, you are running straight into the arms of the Armed Forces. Where are you coming from? And when? Are you having illicit relations with the enemy? Where is he hiding? What movements is he making in your rear? How about the hills? How about the valleys? How are your stockings fastened? [GRUSHA *stands there frightened*] Don't be scared, we always stage a retreat, if necessary . . . what, blockhead? I always stage retreats. In that respect at least, I can be relied on. Why are you staring like that at my lance? In the field no soldier drops his lance, that's a rule. Learn it by heart, blockhead. Now, lady, where are you headed?

GRUSHA

To meet my intended, one Simon Shashava, of the Palace Guard in Nuka.

THE CORPORAL

Simon Shashava? Sure, I know him. He gave me the key so I could look you up once in a while. Blockhead, we are getting to be unpopular. We must make her realize we have honorable intentions. Lady, behind apparent frivolity I conceal a serious nature, so let me tell you officially: I want a child from you. [GRUSHA *utters a little scream*] Blockhead, she understood me. Uh-huh, isn't it a sweet shock? "Then first I must take the noodles out of the oven, Officer. Then first I must change my torn shirt, Colonel." But away with jokes, away with my lance! We are looking for a baby. A baby from a good family. Have you heard of such a baby, from the city, dressed in fine linen, and suddenly turning up here?

GRUSHA

No, I haven't heard a thing.

[*Suddenly* SHE *turns round and runs back, panic-stricken. The* IRONSHIRTS *glance at each other, then follow her, cursing*]

THE SINGER

Run, kind girl! The killers are coming!

Help the helpless babe, helpless girl!

And so she runs!

THE CHORUS

In the bloodiest times

There are kind people.

[*As* GRUSHA *rushes into the cottage, the* PEASANT WOMAN *is bending over the* CHILD's *crib*]

GRUSHA

Hide him. Quick! The Ironshirts are coming! I laid him on your doorstep. But he isn't mine. He's from a good family.

THE PEASANT WOMAN

Who's coming? What Ironshirts?

GRUSHA

Don't ask questions. The Ironshirts that are looking for it.

THE PEASANT WOMAN

They've no business in my house. But I must have a little talk with you, it seems.

GRUSHA

Take off the fine linen. It'll give us away.

THE PEASANT WOMAN

Linen, my foot! In this house I make the decisions! "*You* can't vomit in *my* room!" Why did you abandon it? It's a sin.

GRUSHA [*Looking out of the window*]

Look, they're coming out from behind those trees! I shouldn't have run away, it made them angry. Oh, what shall I do?

THE PEASANT WOMAN [*Looking out of the window and suddenly starting with fear*] Gracious! Ironshirts!

GRUSHA

They're after the baby.

THE PEASANT WOMAN

Suppose they come in!

GRUSHA

You mustn't give him to them. Say he's yours.

THE PEASANT WOMAN

Yes.

GRUSHA

They'll run him through if you hand him over.

THE PEASANT WOMAN

But suppose they ask for it? The silver for the harvest is in the house.

GRUSHA

If you let them have him, they'll run him through, right here in this room! You've got to say he's yours!

THE PEASANT WOMAN

Yes. But what if they don't believe me?

GRUSHA

You must be firm.

THE PEASANT WOMAN

They'll burn the roof over our heads.

GRUSHA

That's why you must say he's yours. His name's Michael. But I shouldn't have told you. [*The* PEASANT WOMAN *nods*] Don't nod like that. And don't tremble—they'll notice.

THE PEASANT WOMAN

Yes.

GRUSHA

And stop saying yes, I can't stand it. [SHE *shakes the* WOMAN] Don't you have any children?

THE PEASANT WOMAN [*Muttering*]

He's in the war.

GRUSHA

Then maybe *he's* an Ironshirt? Do you want *him* to run children through with a lance? You'd bawl him out. "No fooling with lances in *my* house!" you'd shout, "is that what I've reared you for? Wash your neck before you speak to your mother!"

THE PEASANT WOMAN

That's true, he couldn't get away with anything around here!

GRUSHA

So you'll say he's yours?

THE PEASANT WOMAN

Yes.

GRUSHA

Look! They're coming!

[*There is a knocking at the door. The* WOMEN *don't answer. Enter* IRON-SHIRTS. *The* PEASANT WOMAN *bows low*]

THE CORPORAL

Well, here she is. What did I tell you? What a nose I have! I *smelt* her. Lady, I have a question for you. Why did you run away? What did you think I would do to you? I'll bet it was something dirty. Confess!

GRUSHA [*While the* PEASANT WOMAN *bows again and again*]

I'd left some milk on the stove, and I suddenly remembered it.

THE CORPORAL

Or maybe you imagined I looked at you in a dirty way? Like there could be something between us? A lewd sort of look, know what I mean?

GRUSHA

I didn't see it.

THE CORPORAL

But it's possible, huh? You admit that much. After all, I might be a pig. I'll be frank with you: I could think of all sorts of things if we were alone. [*To the* PEASANT WOMAN] Shouldn't you be busy in the yard? Feeding the hens?

THE PEASANT WOMAN [*Falling suddenly to her knees*]
Soldier, I didn't know a thing about it. Please don't burn the roof over our heads.

THE CORPORAL
What are you talking about?

THE PEASANT WOMAN
I had nothing to do with it. She left it on my doorstep, I swear it!

THE CORPORAL [*Suddenly seeing the* CHILD *and whistling*]
Ah, so there's a little something in the crib! Blockhead, I smell a thousand piasters. Take the old girl outside and hold on to her. It looks like I have a little cross-examining to do.

[*The* PEASANT WOMAN *lets herself be led out by the* PRIVATE, *without a word*]
So, you've got the child I wanted from you! [HE *walks toward the crib*]

GRUSHA
Officer, he's mine. He's not the one you're after.

THE CORPORAL
I'll just take a look. [HE *bends over the crib.* GRUSHA *looks round in despair*]

GRUSHA
He's mine! He's mine!

THE CORPORAL
Fine linen!
[GRUSHA *dashes at him to pull him away.* HE *throws her off and again bends over the crib. Again looking round in despair,* SHE *sees a log of wood, seizes it, and hits the* CORPORAL *over the head from behind. The* CORPORAL *collapses.* SHE *quickly picks up the* CHILD *and rushes off*]

THE SINGER
And in her flight from the Ironshirts
After twenty-two days of journeying
At the foot of the Janga-Tu Glacier
Grusha Vashnadze decided to adopt the child.

THE CHORUS
The helpless girl adopted the helpless child.
[GRUSHA *squats over a half-frozen stream to get the* CHILD *water in the hollow of her hand*]

GRUSHA
Since no one else will take you, son,
I must take you.
Since no one else will take you, son,
You must take me.
O black day in a lean, lean year,
The trip was long, the milk was dear,
My legs are tired, my feet are sore:
But I wouldn't be without you any more.
I'll throw your silken shirt away
And dress you in rags and tatters.
I'll wash you, son, and christen you in glacier water.
We'll see it through together.

[SHE *has taken off the* CHILD's *fine linen and wrapped it in a rag*]

THE SINGER

When Grusha Vashnadze
Pursued by the Ironshirts
Came to the bridge on the glacier
Leading to the villages of the Eastern Slope
She sang the Song of the Rotten Bridge
And risked two lives.

[*A wind has risen. The bridge on the glacier is visible in the dark. One rope is broken and half the bridge is hanging down the abyss.* MERCHANTS, TWO MEN *and a* WOMAN, *stand undecided before the bridge as* GRUSHA *and the* CHILD *arrive.* ONE MAN *is trying to catch the hanging rope with a stick*]

THE FIRST MAN

Take your time, young woman. You won't get across here anyway.

GRUSHA

But I *have* to get the baby to the east side. To my brother's place.

THE MERCHANT WOMAN

Have to? How d'you mean, "have to"? I have to get there, too—because I have to buy carpets in Atum[5]—carpets a woman had to sell because her husband had to die. But can *I* do what I have to? Can she? Andrei's been fishing for that rope for hours. And I ask you, how are we going to fasten it, even if he gets it up?

THE FIRST MAN [*Listening*]

Hush, I think I hear something.

GRUSHA

The bridge isn't quite rotted through. I think I'll try it.

THE MERCHANT WOMAN

I wouldn't—if the devil himself were after me. It's suicide.

THE FIRST MAN [*Shouting*]

Hi!

GRUSHA

Don't shout! [*To the* MERCHANT WOMAN] Tell him not to shout.

THE FIRST MAN

But there's someone down there calling. Maybe they've lost their way.

THE MERCHANT WOMAN

Why shouldn't he shout? Is there something funny about you? Are they after you?

GRUSHA

All right, I'll tell. The Ironshirts are after me. I knocked one down.

THE SECOND MAN

Hide our merchandise! [*The* WOMAN *hides a sack behind a rock*]

THE FIRST MAN

Why didn't you say so right away? [*To the* OTHERS] If they catch her they'll make mincemeat out of her!

GRUSHA

Get out of my way. I've got to cross that bridge.

[5] A trading center.

THE SECOND MAN
  You can't. The precipice is two thousand feet deep.

THE FIRST MAN
  Even with the rope it'd be no use. We could hold it up with our hands. But then we'd have to do the same for the Ironshirts.

GRUSHA
  Go away.
  [*There are calls from the distance: "Hi, up there!"*]

THE MERCHANT WOMAN
  They're getting near. But you can't take the child on that bridge. It's sure to break. And look!
  [GRUSHA *looks down into the abyss. The* IRONSHIRTS *are heard calling again from below*]

THE SECOND MAN
  Two thousand feet!

GRUSHA
  But those men are worse.

THE FIRST MAN
  You can't do it. Think of the baby. Risk your life but not a child's.

THE SECOND MAN
  With the child she's that much heavier!

THE MERCHANT WOMAN
  Maybe she's *really* got to get across. Give *me* the baby. I'll hide it. Cross the bridge alone!

GRUSHA
  I won't. We belong together. [*To the* CHILD] "Live together, die together."
  [SHE *sings*]

THE SONG OF THE ROTTEN BRIDGE

Deep is the abyss, son,
I see the weak bridge sway
But it's not for us, son,
To choose the way.

The way I know
Is the one you must tread,
And all you will eat
Is my bit of bread.

Of every four pieces
You shall have three.
Would that I knew
How big they will be!

Get out of my way, I'll try it without the rope.

THE MERCHANT WOMAN
  You are tempting God!
  [*There are shouts from below*]

GRUSHA

Please, throw that stick away, or they'll get the rope and follow me.

[*Pressing the* CHILD *to her,* SHE *steps onto the swaying bridge. The* MER-CHANT WOMAN *screams when it looks as though the bridge is about to collapse. But* GRUSHA *walks on and reaches the far side*]

THE FIRST MAN

She made it!

THE MERCHANT WOMAN [*Who has fallen on her knees and begun to pray, angrily*]

I still think it was a sin.

[*The* IRONSHIRTS *appear; the* CORPORAL'S *head is bandaged*]

THE CORPORAL

Seen a woman with a child?

THE FIRST MAN [*While the* SECOND MAN *throws the stick into the abyss*]

Yes, there! But the bridge won't carry you!

THE CORPORAL

You'll pay for this, blockhead!

[GRUSHA, *from the far bank, laughs and shows the* CHILD *to the* IRONSHIRTS. SHE *walks on. The wind blows*]

GRUSHA [*Turning to the* CHILD]

You mustn't be afraid of the wind. He's a poor thing too. He has to push the clouds along and he gets quite cold doing it. [*Snow starts falling*] And the snow isn't so bad, either, Michael. It covers the little fir trees so they won't die in winter. Let me sing you a little song. [SHE *sings*]

THE SONG OF THE CHILD

Your father is a bandit
A harlot the mother who bore you.
Yet honorable men
Shall kneel down before you.

Food to the baby horses
The tiger's son will take.
The mothers will get milk
From the son of the snake.

3. In the Northern Mountains

THE SINGER

Seven days the sister, Grusha Vashnadze,
Journeyed across the glacier
And down the slopes she journeyed.
"When I enter my brother's house," she thought
"He will rise and embrace me."
"Is that you, sister?" he will say,

"I have long expected you.
This is my dear wife,
And this is my farm, come to me by marriage,
With eleven horses and thirty-one cows. Sit down.
Sit down with your child at our table and eat."
The brother's house was in a lovely valley.
When the sister came to the brother,
She was ill from walking.
The brother rose from the table.

[*A* FAT PEASANT COUPLE *rise from the table.* LAVRENTI VASHNADZE *still has a napkin round his neck, as* GRUSHA, *pale and supported by a* SERVANT, *enters with the* CHILD]

LAVRENTI
Where've *you* come from, Grusha?

GRUSHA [*Feebly*]
Across the Janga-Tu Pass, Lavrenti.

THE SERVANT
I found her in front of the hay barn. She has a baby with her.

THE SISTER-IN-LAW
Go and groom the mare.

[*Exit the* SERVANT]

LAVRENTI
This is my wife Aniko.

THE SISTER-IN-LAW
I thought you were in service in Nuka.

GRUSHA [*Barely able to stand*]
Yes, I was.

THE SISTER-IN-LAW
Wasn't it a good job? We were told it was.

GRUSHA
The Governor got killed.

LAVRENTI
Yes, we heard there were riots. Your aunt told us. Remember, Aniko?

THE SISTER-IN-LAW
Here with us, it's very quiet. City people always want something going on. [SHE *walks toward the door, calling*] Sosso, Sosso, don't take the cake out of the oven yet, d'you hear? Where on earth are you?

[*Exit, calling*]

LAVRENTI [*Quietly, quickly*]
Is there a father? [*As* SHE *shakes her head*] I thought not. We must think up something. She's religious.

THE SISTER-IN-LAW [*Returning*]
Those servants! [*To* GRUSHA] You have a child.

GRUSHA
It's mine.

[SHE *collapses.* LAVRENTI *rushes to her assistance*]

THE SISTER-IN-LAW
Heavens, she's ill—what are we going to do?

LAVRENTI [*Escorting her to a bench near the stove*]

Sit down, sit. I think it's just weakness, Aniko.

THE SISTER-IN-LAW

As long as it's not scarlet fever!

LAVRENTI

She'd have spots if it was. It's only weakness. Don't worry, Aniko. [*To* GRUSHA] Better, sitting down?

THE SISTER-IN-LAW

Is the child hers?

GRUSHA

Yes, mine.

LAVRENTI

She's on her way to her husband.

THE SISTER-IN-LAW

I see. Your meat's getting cold. [LAVRENTI *sits down and begins to eat*] Cold food's not good for you, the fat mustn't get cold, you know your stomach's your weak spot. [*To* GRUSHA] If your husband's not in the city, where is he?

LAVRENTI

She got married on the other side of the mountain, she says.

THE SISTER-IN-LAW

On the other side of the mountain. I see. [SHE *also sits down to eat*]

GRUSHA

I think I should lie down somewhere, Lavrenti.

THE SISTER-IN-LAW

If it's consumption we'll all get it. [SHE *goes on cross-examining her*] Has your husband got a farm?

GRUSHA

He's a soldier.

LAVRENTI

But he's coming into a farm—a small one—from his father.

THE SISTER-IN-LAW

Isn't he in the war? Why not?

GRUSHA [*With effort*]

Yes, he's in the war.

THE SISTER-IN-LAW

Then why d'you want to go to the farm?

LAVRENTI

When he comes back from the war, he'll return to his farm.

THE SISTER-IN-LAW

But you're going there now?

LAVRENTI

Yes, to wait for him.

THE SISTER-IN-LAW [*Calling shrilly*]

Sosso, the cake!

GRUSHA [*Murmuring feverishly*]

A farm—a soldier—waiting—sit down, eat.

THE SISTER-IN-LAW
  It's scarlet fever.
GRUSHA [*Starting up*]
  Yes, he's got a farm!
LAVRENTI
  I think it's just weakness, Aniko. Would you look after the cake yourself,
  dear?
THE SISTER-IN-LAW
  But when will he come back if war's broken out again as people say? [SHE
  waddles off, shouting] Sosso! Where on earth are you? Sosso!
LAVRENTI [*Getting up quickly and going to* GRUSHA]
  You'll get a bed in a minute. She has a good heart. But wait till after supper.
GRUSHA [*Holding out the* CHILD *to him*]
  Take him.
LAVRENTI [*Taking it and looking around*]
  But you can't stay here long with the child. She's religious, you see.
  [GRUSHA *collapses.* LAVRENTI *catches her*]
THE SINGER
  The sister was so ill,
  The cowardly brother had to give her shelter.
  Summer departed, winter came.
  The winter was long, the winter was short
  People mustn't know anything,
  Rats mustn't bite,
  Spring mustn't come.
  [GRUSHA *sits over the weaving loom in a workroom.* SHE *and the* CHILD,
who is squatting on the floor, are wrapped in blankets.]

[SHE *sings*]

THE SONG OF THE CENTER

  And the lover started to leave
  And his betrothed ran pleading after him
  Pleading and weeping, weeping and teaching:
  "Dearest mine, dearest mine
  When you go to war as now you do
  When you fight the foe as soon you will
  Don't lead with the front line
  And don't push with the rear line
  At the front is red fire
  In the rear is red smoke
  Stay in the war's center
  Stay near the standard bearer
  The first always die
  The last are also hit
  Those in the center come home."

Michael, we must be clever. If we make ourselves as small as cockroaches,
the sister-in-law will forget we're in the house, and then we can stay till
the snow melts.

[*Enter* LAVRENTI. HE *sits down beside his* SISTER]

LAVRENTI

Why are you sitting there muffled up like coachmen, you two? Is it too cold in the room?

GRUSHA [*Hastily removing one shawl*]

It's not too cold, Lavrenti.

LAVRENTI

If it's too cold, you shouldn't be sitting here with the child. Aniko would never forgive herself! [*Pause*] I hope our priest didn't question you about the child?

GRUSHA

He did, but I didn't tell him anything.

LAVRENTI

That's good. I wanted to speak to you about Aniko. She has a good heart but she's very, very sensitive. People need only mention our farm and she's worried. She takes everything hard, you see. One time our milkmaid went to church with a hole in her stocking. Ever since, Aniko has worn two pairs of stockings in church. It's the old family in her. [HE *listens*] Are you sure there are no rats around? If there are rats, you couldn't live here.

[*There are sounds as of dripping from the roof*] What's that, dripping?

GRUSHA

It must be a barrel leaking.

LAVRENTI

Yes, it must be a barrel. You've been here six months, haven't you? Was I talking about Aniko? [THEY *listen again to the snow melting*] You can't imagine how worried she gets about your soldier-husband. "Suppose he comes back and can't find her!" she says and lies awake. "He can't come before the spring," I tell her. The dear woman! [*The drops begin to fall faster*] When d'you think he'll come? What do *you* think? [GRUSHA *is silent*] Not before the spring, you agree? [GRUSHA *is silent*] You don't believe he'll come at all? [GRUSHA *is silent*]

But when the spring comes and the snow melts here and on the passes, you can't stay on. They may come and look for you. There's already talk of an illegitimate child. [*The "glockenspiel" of the falling drops has grown faster and steadier*] Grusha, the snow is melting on the roof. Spring is here.

GRUSHA

Yes.

LAVRENTI [*Eagerly*]

I'll tell you what we'll do. You need a place to go, and, because of the child, [HE *sighs*] you have to have a husband, so people won't talk. Now I've made cautious inquiries to see if we can find you a husband. Grusha, I *have* one. I talked to a peasant woman who has a son. Just the other side of the mountain. A small farm. And she's willing.

GRUSHA

But I *can't* marry! I must wait for Simon Shashava.

LAVRENTI

Of course. That's all been taken care of. You don't need a man in bed— you need a man on paper. And I've found you one. The son of this peasant woman is going to die. Isn't that wonderful? He's at his last gasp. And all in line with our story—a husband from the other side of the mountain! And when you met him he was at the last gasp. So you're a widow. What do you say?

GRUSHA

It's true I could use a document with stamps on it for Michael.

LAVRENTI

Stamps make all the difference. Without something in writing the Shah couldn't prove he's a Shah. And you'll have a place to live.

GRUSHA

How much does the peasant woman want?

LAVRENTI

Four hundred piasters.

GRUSHA

Where will you find it?

LAVRENTI [*Guiltily*]

Aniko's milk money.

GRUSHA

No one would know us there. I'll do it.

LAVRENTI [*Getting up*]

I'll let the peasant woman know.

[*Quick exit*]

GRUSHA

Michael, you cause a lot of fuss. I came to you as the pear tree comes to the sparrows. And because a Christian bends down and picks up a crust of bread so nothing will go to waste. Michael, it would have been better had I walked quickly away on that Easter Sunday in Nuka in the second courtyard. Now I *am* a fool.

THE SINGER

The bridegroom was lying on his deathbed when the bride arrived.
The bridegroom's mother was waiting at the door, telling her to hurry.
The bride brought a child along.
The witness hid it during the wedding.

[*On one side the bed. Under the mosquito net lies a very* SICK MAN. GRUSHA *is pulled in at a run by her future* MOTHER-IN-LAW. THEY *are followed by* LAVRENTI *and the* CHILD]

THE MOTHER-IN-LAW

Quick! Quick! Or he'll die on us before the wedding. [*To* LAVRENTI] I was never told she had a child already.

LAVRENTI

What difference does it make? [*Pointing toward the* DYING MAN] It can't matter to him—in his condition.

THE MOTHER-IN-LAW

To him? But *I'll* never survive the shame! We are honest people. [SHE *begins to weep*] My Jussup doesn't have to marry a girl with a child!

LAVRENTI

All right, make it another two hundred piasters. You'll have it in writing that the farm will go to you: but she'll have the right to live here for two years.

THE MOTHER-IN-LAW [*Drying her tears*]

It'll hardly cover the funeral expenses. I hope she'll really lend a hand with the work. And what's happened to the monk? He must have slipped out through the kitchen window. We'll have the whole village round our necks when they hear Jussup's end is come! Oh dear! I'll run and get the monk. But he mustn't see the child!

LAVRENTI

I'll take care he doesn't. But why only a monk? Why not a priest?

THE MOTHER-IN-LAW

Oh, he's just as good. I only made one mistake: I paid half his fee in advance. Enough to send him to the tavern. I only hope . . . [SHE *runs off*]

LAVRENTI

She saved on the priest, the wretch! Hired a cheap monk.

GRUSHA

You *will* send Simon Shashava over to see me if he turns up after all?

LAVRENTI

Yes. [*Pointing at the* SICK MAN] Won't you take a look at him?

[GRUSHA, *taking* MICHAEL *to her, shakes her head*]

He's not moving an eyelid. I hope we aren't too late.

[THEY *listen. On the opposite side enter* NEIGHBORS *who look around and take up positions against the walls, thus forming another wall near the bed, yet leaving an opening so that the bed can be seen.* THEY *start murmuring prayers. Enter the* MOTHER-IN-LAW *with a* MONK. *Showing some annoyance and surprise,* SHE *bows to the* GUESTS]

THE MOTHER-IN-LAW

I hope you won't mind waiting a few moments? My son's bride has just arrived from the city. An emergency wedding is about to be celebrated. [*To the* MONK *in the bedroom*] I might have known you couldn't keep your trap shut. [*To* GRUSHA] The wedding can take place at once. Here's the license. I myself and the bride's brother [LAVRENTI *tries to hide in the background, after having quietly taken* MICHAEL *back from* GRUSHA. *The* MOTHER-IN-LAW *waves him away*], who will be here in a moment, are the wittnesses.

[GRUSHA *has bowed to the* MONK. THEY *go to the bed. The* MOTHER-IN-LAW *lifts the mosquito net. The* MONK *starts reeling off the marriage ceremony in Latin. Meanwhile, the* MOTHER-IN-LAW *beckons to* LAVRENTI *to get rid of the* CHILD, *but fearing that it will cry* HE *draws its attention to the ceremony.* GRUSHA *glances once at the* CHILD, *and* LAVRENTI *waves the* CHILD'S *hand in a greeting*]

THE MONK

Are you prepared to be a faithful, obedient, and good wife to this man, and to cleave to him until death you do part?

GRUSHA [*Looking at the* CHILD]

I am.

THE MONK [*To the* SICK PEASANT]

And are you prepared to be a good and loving husband to your wife until death you do part?

[*As the* SICK PEASANT *does not answer, the* MONK *looks inquiringly around*]

THE MOTHER-IN-LAW

Of course he is! Didn't you hear him say yes?

THE MONK

All right. We declare the marriage contracted! How about extreme unction?

THE MOTHER-IN-LAW

Nothing doing! The wedding cost quite enough. Now I must take care of the mourners. [*To* LAVRENTI] Did we say seven hundred?

LAVRENTI

Six hundred. [HE *pays*] Now I don't want to sit with the guests and get to know people. So farewell, Grusha, and if my widowed sister comes to visit me, she'll get a welcome from my wife, or I'll show my teeth. [*Nods, gives the* CHILD *to* GRUSHA, *and leaves*]

[*The* MOURNERS *glance after him without interest*]

THE MONK

May one ask where this child comes from?

THE MOTHER-IN-LAW

Is there a child? I don't see a child. And you don't see a child either—you understand? Or it may turn out I saw all sorts of things in the tavern! Now come on.

[*After* GRUSHA *has put the* CHILD *down and told him to be quiet,* THEY *move over left,* GRUSHA *is introduced to the* NEIGHBORS]

This is my daughter-in-law. She arrived just in time to find dear Jussup still alive.

ONE WOMAN

He's been ill now a whole year, hasn't he? When our Vassili was drafted he was there to say goodbye.

ANOTHER WOMAN

Such things are terrible for a farm. The corn all ripe and the farmer in bed! It'll really be a blessing if he doesn't suffer too long, I say.

THE FIRST WOMAN [*Confidentially*]

You know why we thought he'd taken to his bed? Because of the draft! And now his end is come!

THE MOTHER-IN-LAW

Sit yourselves down, please! And have some cakes!

[SHE *beckons to* GRUSHA *and* BOTH WOMEN *go into the bedroom, where* THEY *pick up the cake pans off the floor. The* GUESTS, *among them the* MONK, *sit on the floor and begin conversing in subdued voices*]

ONE PEASANT [*To whom the* MONK *has handed the bottle which* HE *has taken from his soutane*]

There's a child, you say! How can that have happened to Jussup?

A WOMAN

She was certainly lucky to get herself hitched, with him so sick!

THE MOTHER-IN-LAW

They're gossiping already. And gorging themselves on the funeral cakes at the same time! If he doesn't die today, I'll have to bake some more tomorrow!

GRUSHA

I'll bake them for you.

THE MOTHER-IN-LAW

Yesterday some horsemen rode by, and I went out to see who it was. When I came in again he was lying there like a corpse! So I sent for you. It can't take much longer. [SHE *listens*]

THE MONK

Dear wedding and funeral guests! Deeply touched, we stand before a bed of death and marriage. The bride gets a veil; the groom, a shroud: how varied, my children, are the fates of men! Alas! One man dies and has a roof over his head, and the other is married and the flesh turns to dust from which it was made. Amen.

THE MOTHER-IN-LAW

He's getting his own back. I shouldn't have hired such a cheap one. It's what you'd expect. A more expensive monk would behave himself. In Sura there's one with a real air of sanctity about him, but of course he charges a fortune. A fifty-piaster monk like that has no dignity, and as for piety, just fifty piasters' worth and no more! When I came to get him in the tavern he'd just made a speech, and he was shouting: "The war is over, beware of the peace!" We must go in.

GRUSHA [*Giving* MICHAEL *a cake*]

Eat this cake, and keep nice and still, Michael.

[*The* TWO WOMEN *offer cakes to the* GUESTS. *The* DYING MAN *sits up in bed.* HE *puts his head out from under the mosquito net, stares at the* TWO WOMEN, *then sinks back again. The* MONK *takes two bottles from his soutane and offers them to the* PEASANT *beside him. Enter* THREE MUSICIANS *who are greeted with a sly wink by the* MONK]

THE MOTHER-IN-LAW [*To the* MUSICIANS]

What are you doing here? With instruments?

ONE MUSICIAN

Brother Anastasius here [*Points at the* MONK] told us there was a wedding on.

THE MOTHER-IN-LAW

What? You brought them? Three more on my neck! Don't you know there's a dying man in the next room?

THE MONK

A very tempting assignment for a musician: something that could be either a subdued Wedding March or a spirited Funeral Dance.

THE MOTHER-IN-LAW

Well, you might as well play. Nobody can stop you eating in any case.

[*The* MUSICIANS *play a potpourri. The* WOMEN *serve cakes*]

THE MONK

The trumpet sounds like a whining baby. And you, little drum, what have you got to tell the world?

THE DRUNKEN PEASANT [*Beside the* MONK, *sings*]

Miss Roundass took the old old man
And said that marriage was the thing
To everyone who met 'er.

She later withdrew from the contract because
Candles are better.
[*The* MOTHER-IN-LAW *throws the* DRUNKEN PEASANT *out. The music stops. The* GUESTS *are embarrassed*]

THE GUESTS [*Loudly*]
—Have you heard? The Grand Duke is back! But the Princes are against him.
—They say the Shah of Persia has lent him a great army to restore order in Grusinia.
—But how is that possible? The Shah of Persia is the enemy . . .
—The enemy of Grusinia, you donkey, not the enemy of the Grand Duke!
—In any case, the war's over, so our soldiers are coming back.
[GRUSHA *drops a cake pan.* GUESTS *help her pick up the cake*]

AN OLD WOMAN [*To* GRUSHA]
Are you feeling bad? It's just excitement about dear Jussup. Sit down and rest a while, my dear. [GRUSHA *staggers*]

THE GUESTS
Now everything'll be the way it was. Only the taxes'll go up because now we'll have to pay for the war.

GRUSHA [*Weakly*]
Did someone say the soldiers are back?

A MAN
I did.

GRUSHA
It can't be true.

THE FIRST MAN [*To a* WOMAN]
Show her the shawl. We bought it from a soldier. It's from Persia.

GRUSHA [*Looking at the shawl*]
They are here.
[SHE *gets up, takes a step, kneels down in prayer, takes the silver cross and chain out of her blouse, and kisses it*]

THE MOTHER-IN-LAW [*While the* GUESTS *silently watch* GRUSHA]
What's the matter with you? Aren't you going to look after our guests? What's all this city nonsense got to do with us?

THE GUESTS [*Resuming conversation while* GRUSHA *remains in prayer*]
—You can buy Persian saddles from the soldiers too. Though many want crutches in exchange for them.
—The big shots on one side can win a war, the soldiers on both sides lose it.
—Anyway, the war's over. It's something they can't draft you any more.
[*The* DYING MAN *sits bolt upright in bed.* HE *listens*]
—What we need is two weeks of good weather.
—Our pear trees are hardly bearing a thing this year.

THE MOTHER-IN-LAW [*Offering cakes*]
Have some more cakes and welcome! There are more!
[*The* MOTHER-IN-LAW *goes to the bedroom with the empty cake pans. Unaware of the* DYING MAN, SHE *is bending down to pick up another tray when* HE *begins to talk in a hoarse voice*]

THE PEASANT

How many more cakes are you going to stuff down their throats? Think I'm a fucking goldmine?

[*The* MOTHER-IN-LAW *starts, stares at him aghast, while* HE *climbs out from behind the mosquito net*]

THE FIRST WOMAN [*Talking kindly to* GRUSHA *in the next room*]

Has the young wife got someone at the front?

A MAN

It's good news that they're on their way home, huh?

THE PEASANT

Don't stare at me like that! Where's this wife you've hung round my neck?

[*Receiving no answer,* HE *climbs out of bed and in his nightshirt staggers into the other room. Trembling,* SHE *follows him with the cake pan*]

THE GUESTS [*Seeing him and shrieking*]

Good God! Jussup!

[EVERYONE *leaps up in alarm. The* WOMEN *rush to the door.* GRUSHA, *still on her knees, turns round and stares at the* MAN]

THE PEASANT

A funeral supper! You'd enjoy that, wouldn't you? Get out before I throw you out! [*As the* GUESTS *stampede from the house, gloomily to* GRUSHA] I've upset the apple cart, huh? [*Receiving no answer,* HE *turns round and takes a cake from the pan which his* MOTHER *is holding*]

THE SINGER

O confusion! The wife discovers she has a husband.
By day there's the child, by night there's the husband.
The lover is on his way both day and night.
Husband and wife look at each other.
The bedroom is small.

[*Near the bed the* PEASANT *is sitting in a high wooden bathtub, naked, the* MOTHER-IN-LAW *is pouring water from a pitcher. Opposite* GRUSHA *cowers with* MICHAEL, *who is playing at mending straw mats*]

THE PEASANT [*To his* MOTHER]

That's her work, not yours. Where's she hiding out now?

THE MOTHER-IN-LAW [*Calling*]

Grusha! The peasant wants you!

GRUSHA [*To* MICHAEL]

There are still two holes to mend.

THE PEASANT [*When* GRUSHA *approaches*]

Scrub my back!

GRUSHA

Can't the peasant do it himself?

THE PEASANT

"Can't the peasant do it himself?" Get the brush! To hell with you! Are you the wife here? Or are you a visitor? [*To the* MOTHER-IN-LAW] It's too cold!

THE MOTHER-IN-LAW

I'll run for hot water.

GRUSHA

Let me go.

THE PEASANT

You stay here. [*The* MOTHER-IN-LAW *exits*] Rub harder. And no shirking. You've seen a naked fellow before. That child didn't come out of thin air.

GRUSHA

The child was not conceived in joy, if that's what the peasant means.

THE PEASANT [*Turning and grinning*]

You don't look the type. [GRUSHA *stops scrubbing him, starts back*]
[*Enter the* MOTHER-IN-LAW]

THE PEASANT

A nice thing you've hung around my neck! A simpleton for a wife!

THE MOTHER-IN-LAW

She just isn't co-operative.

THE PEASANT

Pour—but go easy! Ow! Go easy, I said. [*To* GRUSHA] Maybe you did something wrong in the city . . . I wouldn't be surprised. Why else should you be here? But I won't talk about that. I've not said a word about the illegitimate object you brought into my house either. But my patience has limits! It's against nature. [*To the* MOTHER-IN-LAW] More! [*To* GRUSHA] And even if your soldier does come back, you're married.

GRUSHA

Yes.

THE PEASANT

But your soldier won't come back. Don't you believe it.

GRUSHA

No.

THE PEASANT

You're cheating me. You're my wife and you're not my wife. Where you lie, nothing lies, and yet no other woman can lie there. When I go to work in the morning I'm tired—when I lie down at night I'm awake as the devil. God has given you sex—and what d'you do? I don't have ten piasters to buy myself a woman in the city. Besides, it's a long way. Woman weeds the fields and opens up her legs, that's what our calendar says. D'you hear?

GRUSHA [*Quietly*]

Yes. I didn't mean to cheat you out of it.

THE PEASANT

She didn't mean to cheat me out of it! Pour some more water! [*The* MOTHER-IN-LAW *pours*] Ow!

THE SINGER

As she sat by the stream to wash the linen
She saw his image in the water
And his face grew dimmer with the passing moons.
As she raised herself to wring the linen
She heard his voice from the murmuring maple
And his voice grew fainter with the passing moons.
Evasions and sighs grew more numerous,
Tears and sweat flowed.
With the passing moons the child grew up.
[GRUSHA *sits by a stream, dipping linen into the water. In the rear, a few*

CHILDREN *are standing*]

GRUSHA [*To* MICHAEL]

You can play with them, Michael, but don't let them boss you around just because you're the littlest.

[MICHAEL *nods and joins the* CHILDREN. THEY *start playing*]

THE BIGGEST BOY

Today it's the Heads-Off Game. [*To a* FAT BOY] You're the Prince and you laugh. [*To* MICHAEL] You're the Governor. [*To a* GIRL] You're the Governor's wife and you cry when his head's cut off. And I do the cutting. [HE *shows his wooden sword*] With this. First, they lead the Governor into the yard. The Prince walks in front. The Governor's wife comes last.

[THEY *form a procession. The* FAT BOY *is first and laughs. Then comes* MICHAEL, *then the* BIGGEST BOY, *and then the* GIRL, *who weeps*]

MICHAEL [*Standing still*]

Me cut off head!

THE BIGGEST BOY

That's my job. You're the littlest. The Governor's the easy part. All you do is kneel down and get your head cut off—simple.

MICHAEL

Me want sword!

THE BIGGEST BOY

It's mine! [HE *gives him a kick*]

THE GIRL [*Shouting to* GRUSHA]

He won't play his part!

GRUSHA [*Laughing*]

Even the little duck is a swimmer, they say.

THE BIGGEST BOY

You can be the Prince if you can laugh.

[MICHAEL *shakes his head*]

THE FAT BOY

I laugh best. Let him cut off the head just once. Then you do it, then me.

[*Reluctantly, the* BIGGEST BOY *hands* MICHAEL *the wooden sword and kneels down. The* FAT BOY *sits down slaps his thigh, and laughs with all his might. The* GIRL *weeps loudly.* MICHAEL *swings the big sword and "cuts off" the head. In doing so,* HE *topples over*]

THE BIGGEST BOY

Hey! I'll show you how to cut heads off!

[MICHAEL *runs away. The* CHILDREN *run after him.* GRUSHA *laughs, following them with her eyes. On looking back,* SHE *sees* SIMON SHASHAVA *standing on the opposite bank.* HE *wears a shabby uniform*]

GRUSHA

Simon!

SIMON

Is that Grusha Vashnadze?

GRUSHA

Simon!

SIMON [*Formally*]

A good morning to the young lady. I hope she is well.

GRUSHA [*Getting up gaily and bowing low*]

A good morning to the soldier. God be thanked he has returned in good health.

SIMON

They found better fish, so they didn't eat me, said the haddock.

GRUSHA

Courage, said the kitchen boy. Good luck, said the hero.

SIMON

How are things here? Was the winter bearable? The neighbor considerate?

GRUSHA

The winter was a trifle rough, the neighbor as usual, Simon.

SIMON

May one ask if a certain person still dips her foot in the water when rinsing the linen?

GRUSHA

The answer is no. Because of the eyes in the bushes.

SIMON

The young lady is speaking of soldiers. Here stands a paymaster.

GRUSHA

A job worth twenty piasters?

SIMON

And lodgings.

GRUSHA [*With tears in her eyes*]

Behind the barracks under the date trees.

SIMON

Yes, there. A certain person has kept her eyes open.

GRUSHA

She has, Simon.

SIMON

And has not forgotten [GRUSHA *shakes her head*] So the door is still on its hinges as they say? [GRUSHA *looks at him in silence and shakes her head again*] What's this? Is something not as it should be?

GRUSHA

Simon Shashava, I can never return to Nuka. Something has happened.

SIMON

What can have happened?

GRUSHA

For one thing, I knocked an Ironshirt down.

SIMON

Grusha Vashnadze must have had her reasons for that.

GRUSHA

Simon Shashava, I am no longer called what I used to be called.

SIMON [*After a pause*]

I do not understand.

GRUSHA

When do women change their names, Simon? Let me explain. Nothing stands between us. Everything is just as it was. You must believe that.

SIMON

Nothing stands between us and yet there's something?

GRUSHA

How can I explain it so fast and with the stream between us? Couldn't you cross the bridge there?

SIMON

Maybe it's no longer necessary.

GRUSHA

It is very necessary. Come over on this side, Simon. Quick!

SIMON

Does the young lady wish to say someone has come too late?

[GRUSHA *looks up at him in despair, her face streaming with tears.* SIMON *stares before him.* HE *picks up a piece of wood and starts cutting it*]

THE SINGER

So many words are said, so many left unsaid.

The soldier has come.

Where he comes from, he does not say.

Hear what he thought and did not say:

"The battle began, gray at dawn, grew bloody at noon.

The first man fell in front of me, the second behind me, the third at my side.

I trod on the first, left the second behind, the third was run through by the captain.

One of my brothers died by steel, the other by smoke.

My neck caught fire, my hands froze in my gloves, my toes in my socks.

I fed on aspen buds, I drank maple juice, I slept on stone, in water."

SIMON

I see a cap in the grass. Is there a little one already?

GRUSHA

There is, Simon. There's no keeping that from you. But please don't worry, it is not mine.

SIMON

When the wind once starts to blow, they say, it blows through every cranny. The wife need say no more.

[GRUSHA *looks into her lap and is silent*]

THE SINGER

There was yearning but there was no waiting.

The oath is broken. Neither could say why.

Hear what she thought but did not say:

"While you fought in the battle, soldier,

The bloody battle, the bitter battle

I found a helpless infant

I had not the heart to destroy him

I had to care for a creature that was lost

I had to stoop for breadcrumbs on the floor

I had to break myself for that which was not mine

That which was other people's.

Someone must help!

For the little tree needs water

The lamb loses its way when the shepherd is asleep
And its cry is unheard!"

SIMON

Give me back the cross I gave you. Better still, throw it in the stream. [HE *turns to go*]

GRUSHA [*Getting up*]

Simon Shashava, don't go away! He isn't mine! He isn't mine! [SHE *hears the* CHILDREN *calling*] What's the matter, children?

VOICES

Soldiers! And they're taking Michael away!

[GRUSHA *stands aghast as* TWO IRONSHIRTS, *with* MICHAEL *between them, come toward her*]

ONE OF THE IRONSHIRTS

Are you Grusha? [SHE *nods*] Is this your child?

GRUSHA

Yes.

[SIMON *goes*]

Simon!

THE IRONSHIRT

We have orders, in the name of the law, to take this child, found in your custody, back to the city. It is suspected that the child is Michael Abashwili, son and heir of the late Governor Georgi Abashwili, and his wife, Natella Abashwili. Here is the document and the seal. [THEY *lead the* CHILD *away*]

GRUSHA

[*Running after them, shouting*]
Leave him here. Please! He's mine!

THE SINGER

The Ironshirts took the child, the beloved child.
The unhappy girl followed them to the city, the dreaded city.
She who had borne him demanded the child.
She who had raised him faced trial.
Who will decide the case?
To whom will the child be assigned?
Who will the judge be? A good judge? A bad?
The city was in flames.
In the judge's seat sat Azdak.[6]

4. The Story of the Judge

THE SINGER

Hear the story of the judge
How he turned judge, how he passed judgment, what kind of judge he was.
On that Easter Sunday of the great revolt, when the Grand Duke was overthrown

---

[6] The name Azdak should be accented on the second syllable.

And his Governor Abashwili, father of our child, lost his head

The Village Scrivener Azdak found a fugitive in the woods and hid him in his hut.

[AZDAK, *in rags and slightly drunk, is helping an* OLD BEGGAR *into his cottage*]

AZDAK

Stop snorting, you're not a horse. And it won't do you any good with the police, to run like a snotty nose in April. Stand still, I say. [HE *catches the* OLD MAN, *who has marched into the cottage as if* HE'D *like to go through the walls*] Sit down. Feed. Here's a hunk of cheese. [*From under some rags, in a chest,* HE *fishes out some cheese, and the* OLD MAN *greedily begins to eat*] Haven't eaten in a long time, huh? [*The* OLD MAN *growls*] Why were you running like that, asshole? The cop wouldn't even have seen you.

THE OLD MAN

Had to! Had to!

AZDAK

Blue Funk? [*The* OLD MAN *stares, uncomprehending*] Cold feet? Panic? Don't lick your chops like a Grand Duke. Or an old sow. I can't stand it. We have to accept respectable stinkers as God made them, but not you! I once heard of a senior judge who farted at a public dinner to show an independent spirit! Watching you eat like that gives me the most awful ideas. Why don't you say something? [*Sharply*] Show me your hand. Can't you hear? [*The* OLD MAN *slowly puts out his hand*] White! So you're not a beggar at all! A fraud, a walking swindle! And I'm hiding you from the cops as though you were an honest man! Why were you running like that if you're a landowner? For that's what you are. Don't deny it! I see it in your guilty face! [HE *gets up*] Get out! [*The* OLD MAN *looks at him uncertainly*] What are you waiting for, peasant-flogger?

THE OLD MAN

Pursued. Need undivided attention. Make proposition . . .

AZDAK

Make what? A proposition? Well, if that isn't the height of insolence. He's making me a proposition! The bitten man scratches his fingers bloody, and the leech that's biting him makes him a proposition! Get out, I tell you!

THE OLD MAN

Understand point of view! Persuasion! Pay hundred thousand piasters one night! Yes?

AZDAK

What, you think you can buy me? For a hundred thousand piasters? Let's say a hundred and fifty thousand. Where are they?

THE OLD MAN

Have not them here. Of course. Will be sent. Hope do not doubt.

AZDAK

Doubt very much. Get out!

[*The* OLD MAN *gets up, waddles to the door. A* VOICE *is heard off stage*]

A VOICE

Azdak!

[*The* OLD MAN *turns, waddles to the opposite corner, stands still*]

AZDAK [*Calling out*]

I'm not in! [HE *walks to door*] So you're sniffing around here again, Shauwa?

POLICEMAN SHAUWA [*Reproachfully*]

You've caught another rabbit, Azdak. And you promised me it wouldn't happen again!

AZDAK [*Severely*]

Shauwa, don't talk about things you don't understand. The rabbit is a dangerous and destructive beast. It feeds on plants, especially on the species of plants known as weeds. It must therefore be exterminated.

SHAUWA

Azdak, don't be so hard on me. I'll lose my job if I don't arrest you. I know you have a good heart.

AZDAK

I do not have a good heart! How often must I tell you I'm a man of intellect?

SHAUWA [*Slyly*]

I know, Azdak. You're a superior person. You say so yourself. I'm just a Christian and an ignoramus. So I ask you: When one of the Prince's rabbits is stolen, and I'm a policeman, what should I do with the offending party?

AZDAK

Shauwa, Shauwa, shame on you. You stand and ask me a question, than which nothing could be more seductive. It's like you were a woman—let's say that bad girl Nunowna, and you showed me your thigh—Nunowna's thigh, that would be—and asked me: "What shall I do with my thigh, it itches?" Is she as innocent as she pretends? Of course not. I catch a rabbit, but you catch a man. Man is made in God's image. Not so a rabbit, you know that. I'm a rabbit-eater, but you're a man-eater, Shauwa. And God will pass judgment on you. Shauwa, go home and repent. No, stop, there's something . . . [HE *looks at the* OLD MAN *who stands trembling in the corner*] No, it's nothing. Go home and repent.

[HE *slams the door behind* SHAUWA]

Now you're surprised, huh? Surprised I didn't hand you over? I couldn't hand over a bedbug to that animal. It goes against the grain. Now don't tremble because of a cop! So old and still so scared? Finish your cheese, but eat it like a poor man, or else they'll still catch you. Must I even explain how a poor man behaves?

[HE *pushes him down, and then gives him back the cheese*]

That box is the table. Lay your elbows on the table. Now, encircle the cheese on the plate like it might be snatched from you at any moment—what right have you to be safe, huh?—now, hold your knife like an undersized sickle, and give your cheese a troubled look because, like all beautiful things, it's already fading away.

[AZDAK *watches him*]

They're after you, which speaks in your favor, but how can we be sure they're not mistaken about you? In Tiflis one time they hanged a landowner, a Turk, who could prove he quartered his peasants instead of merely cutting them in half, as is the custom, and he squeezed twice the usual amount of taxes out of them, his zeal was above suspicion. And yet they hanged him like a common criminal—because he was a Turk—a thing he couldn't do much about. What injustice! He got onto the gallows by a sheer fluke. In short, I don't trust you.

THE SINGER

Thus Azdak gave the old beggar a bed,
And learned that old beggar was the old butcher, the Grand Duke himself,
And was ashamed.
He denounced himself and ordered the policeman to take him to Nuka, to court, to be judged.

[*In the court of justice* THREE IRONSHIRTS *sit drinking. From a beam hangs a man in judge's robes. Enter* AZDAK, *in chains, dragging* SHAUWA *behind him*]

AZDAK [*Shouting*]

I've helped the Grand Duke, the Grand Thief, the Grand Butcher, to escape! In the name of justice I ask to be severely judged in public trial!

THE FIRST IRONSHIRT

Who's this queer bird?

SHAUWA

That's our Village Scrivener, Azdak.

AZDAK

I am contemptible! I am a traitor! A branded criminal! Tell them, flat-foot, how I insisted on being chained up and brought to the capital. Because I sheltered the Grand Duke, the Grand Swindler, by mistake. And how I found out afterwards. See the marked man denounce himself! Tell them how I forced you to walk with me half the night to clear the whole thing up.

SHAUWA

And all by threats. That wasn't nice of you, Azdak.

AZDAK

Shut your mouth, Shauwa. You don't understand. A new age is upon us! It'll go thundering over you. You're finished. The police will be wiped out— poof! Everything will be gone into, everything will be brought into the open. The guilty will give themselves up. Why? They couldn't escape the people in any case. [*To* SHAUWA] Tell them how I shouted all along Shoemaker Street: [*With big gestures, looking at the* IRONSHIRTS] "In my ignorance I let the Grand Swindler escape! So tear me to pieces, brothers! I wanted to get it in first.

THE FIRST IRONSHIRT

And what did your brothers answer?

SHAUWA

They comforted him in Butcher Street, and they laughed themselves sick in Shoemaker Street. That's all.

AZDAK

But with you it's different. I can see you're men of iron. Brothers, where's the judge? I must be tried.

THE FIRST IRONSHIRT [*Points at the hanged man*]

There's the judge. And please stop "brothering" us. It's rather a sore spot this evening.

AZDAK

"There's the judge." An answer never heard in Grusinia before. Townsman, where's His Excellency the Governor? [*Pointing to the floor*] There's His

Excellency, stranger. Where's the Chief Tax Collector? Where's the official Recruiting Officer? The Patriarch? The Chief of Police? There, there, there —all there. Brothers, I expected no less of you.

THE SECOND IRONSHIRT
What? *What* was it you expected, funny man?

AZDAK
What happened in Persia, brother, what happened in Persia?

THE SECOND IRONSHIRT
What did happen in Persia?

AZDAK
Everybody was hanged. Viziers, tax collectors. Everybody. Forty years ago now. My grandfather, a remarkable man by the way, saw it all. For three whole days. Everywhere.

THE SECOND IRONSHIRT
And who ruled when the Vizier was hanged?

AZDAK
A peasant ruled when the Vizier was hanged.

THE SECOND IRONSHIRT
And who commanded the army?

AZDAK
A soldier, a soldier.

THE SECOND IRONSHIRT
And who paid the wages?

AZDAK
A dyer. A dyer paid the wages.

THE SECOND IRONSHIRT
Wasn't it a weaver, maybe?

THE FIRST IRONSHIRT
And why did all this happen, Persian?

AZDAK
Why did all this happen? Must there be a special reason? Why do you scratch yourself, brother? War! Too long a war! And no justice! My grandfather brought back a song that tells how it was. I will sing it for you. With my friend the policeman. [*To* SHAUWA] And hold the rope tight. It's very suitable.

[HE *sings, with* SHAUWA *holding the rope tight around him*]

THE SONG OF INJUSTICE IN PERSIA

Why don't our sons bleed any more? Why don't our daughters weep?
Why do only the slaughter-house cattle have blood in their veins?
Why do only the willows shed tears on Lake Urmi?

The king must have a new province, the peasant must give up his savings.
That the roof of the world might be conquered, the roof of the cottage is torn down.
Our men are carried to the ends of the earth, so that great ones can eat at home.
The soldiers kill each other, the marshals salute each other.
They bite the widow's tax money to see if it's good, their swords break.

The battle was lost, the helmets were paid for.
[*Refrain*]
Is it so? Is it so?
[*Refrain*] [*By* SHAUWA]
Yes, yes, yes, yes, yes it's so.

AZDAK

Do you want to hear the rest of it?
[*The* FIRST IRONSHIRT *nods*]

THE SECOND IRONSHIRT [*To* SHAUWA]

Did he teach you that song?

SHAUWA

Yes, only my voice isn't very good.

THE SECOND IRONSHIRT

No. [*To* AZDAK] Go on singing.

AZDAK

The second verse is about the peace.

[HE *sings*]

The offices are packed, the streets overflow with officials.
The rivers jump their banks and ravage the fields.
Those who cannot let down their own trousers rule countries.
They can't count up to four, but they devour eight courses.
The corn farmers, looking round for buyers, see only the starving.
The weavers go home from their looms in rags.
[*Refrain*]
Is it so? Is it so?
[*Refrain*] [*By* SHAUWA]
Yes, yes, yes, yes, yes it's so.

AZDAK

That's why our sons don't bleed any more, that's why our daughters don't weep.
That's why only the slaughter-house cattle have blood in their veins,
And only the willows shed tears by Lake Urmi toward morning.

THE FIRST IRONSHIRT

Are you going to sing that song here in town?

AZDAK

Sure. What's wrong with it?

THE FIRST IRONSHIRT

Have you noticed that the sky's getting red? [*Turning round,* AZDAK *sees the sky red with fire*] It's the people's quarters. On the outskirts of town. The carpet weavers have caught the "Persian Sickness," too. And they've been asking if Prince Kazbeki isn't eating too many courses. This morning they strung up the city judge. As for us we beat them to pulp. We were paid one hundred piasters per man, you understand?

AZDAK [*After a pause*]

I understand.

[HE *glances shyly round and, creeping away, sits down in a corner, his head in his hands*]

THE IRONSHIRTS [*To each other*]

—If there ever was a trouble-maker it's him.

—He must've come to the capital to fish in the troubled waters.

SHAUWA

Oh, I don't think he's a really bad character, gentlemen. Steals a few chickens here and there. And maybe a rabbit.

THE SECOND IRONSHIRT [*Approaching* AZDAK]

Came to fish in the troubled waters, huh?

AZDAK [*Looking up*]

I don't know why I came.

THE SECOND IRONSHIRT

Are you in with the carpet weavers maybe? [AZDAK *shakes his head*] How about that song?

AZDAK

From my grandfather. A silly and ignorant man.

THE SECOND IRONSHIRT

Right. And how about the dyer who paid the wages?

AZDAK [*Muttering*]

That was in Persia.

THE FIRST IRONSHIRT

And this denouncing of yourself? Because you didn't hang the Grand Duke with your own hands?

AZDAK

Didn't I tell you I let him run? [HE *creeps farther away and sits on the floor*]

SHAUWA

I can swear to that: he let him run.

[*The* IRONSHIRTS *burst out laughing and slap* SHAUWA *on the back.* AZDAK *laughs loudest.* THEY *slap* AZDAK *too, and unchain him.* THEY ALL *start drinking as the* FAT PRINCE *enters with a* YOUNG MAN]

THE FIRST IRONSHIRT [*To* AZDAK, *pointing at the* FAT PRINCE]

There's your "new age" for you! [*More laughter*]

THE FAT PRINCE

Well, my friends, what is there to laugh about? Permit me a serious word. Yesterday morning the Princes of Grusinia overthrew the war-mongering government of the Grand Duke and did away with his Governors. Unfortunately the Grand Duke himself escaped. In this fateful hour our carpet weavers, those eternal trouble-makers, had the effrontery to stir up a rebellion and hang the universally loved city judge, our dear Illo Orbeliani. Ts-ts-ts. My friends, we need peace, peace, peace in Grusinia! And Justice! So I've brought along my dear nephew Bizergan Kazbeki. He'll be the new judge, hm? A very gifted fellow. What do you say? I want your opinion. Let the people decide!

THE SECOND IRONSHIRT

Does this mean *we* elect the judge?

THE FAT PRINCE

Precisely. Let the people propose some very gifted fellow! Confer among yourselves, my friends. [*The* IRONSHIRTS *confer*] Don't worry, my little fox. The job's yours. And when we catch the Grand Duke we won't have to kiss this rabble's ass any longer.

THE IRONSHIRTS [*Between themselves*]

—Very funny: they're wetting their pants because they haven't caught the Grand Duke.

—When the outlook isn't so bright, they say: "My friends!" and "Let the people decide!"

—Now he even wants justice for Grusinia! But fun is fun as long as it lasts! [*Pointing at* AZDAK]

—*He* knows all about justice. Hey, rascal, would you like this nephew fellow to be the judge?

AZDAK

Are you asking me? You're not asking *me*?!

THE FIRST IRONSHIRT

Why not? Anything for a laugh!

AZDAK

You'd like to test him to the marrow, correct? Have you a criminal on hand? An experienced one? So the candidate can show what he knows?

THE SECOND IRONSHIRT

Let's see. We do have a couple of doctors downstairs. Let's use them.

AZDAK

Oh, no, that's no good, we can't take real criminals till we're sure the judge will be appointed. He may be dumb, but he must be appointed, or the Law is violated. And the Law is a sensitive organ. It's like the spleen, you mustn't hit it—that would be fatal. Of course you can hang those two without violating the Law, because there was no judge in the vicinity. But Judgment, when pronounced, must be pronounced with absolute gravity—it's all such nonsense. Suppose, for instance, a judge jails a woman—let's say she's stolen a corncake to feed her child—and this judge isn't wearing his robes— or maybe he's scratching himself while passing sentence and half his body is uncovered—a man's thigh *will* itch once in a while—the sentence this judge passes is a disgrace and the Law is violated. In short it would be easier for a judge's robe and a judge's hat to pass judgment than for a man with no robe and no hat. If you don't treat it with respect, the Law just disappears on you. Now you don't try out a bottle of wine by offering it to a dog; you'd only lose your wine.

THE FIRST IRONSHIRT

Then what do you suggest, hair-splitter?

AZDAK

I'll be the defendant.

THE FIRST IRONSHIRT

You? [HE *bursts out laughing*]

THE FAT PRINCE

What have you decided?

THE FIRST IRONSHIRT

We've decided to stage a rehearsal. Our friend here will be the defendant. Let the candidate be the judge and sit there.

THE FAT PRINCE

It isn't customary, but why not? [*To the* NEPHEW] A mere formality, my little fox. What have I taught you? Who got there first—the slow runner or the fast?

THE NEPHEW

The silent runner, Uncle Arsen.

[*The* NEPHEW *takes the chair. The* IRONSHIRTS *and the* FAT PRINCE *sit on the steps. Enter* AZDAK, *mimicking the gait of the Grand Duke*]

AZDAK [*In the Grand Duke's accent*]

Is any here knows me? Am Grand Duke.

THE IRONSHIRTS

—What is he?

—The Grand Duke. He knows him, too.

—Fine. So get on with the trial.

AZDAK

Listen! Am accused instigating war? Ridiculous! Am saying ridiculous! That enough? If not, have brought lawyers. Believe five hundred. [HE *points behind him, pretending to be surrounded by lawyers*] Requisition all available seats for lawyers!

[*The* IRONSHIRTS *laugh, the* FAT PRINCE *joins in*]

THE NEPHEW [*To the* IRONSHIRTS]

You really wish me to try this case? I find it rather unusual. From the taste angle, I mean.

THE FIRST IRONSHIRT

Let's go!

THE FAT PRINCE [*Smiling*]

Let him have it, my little fox!

THE NEPHEW

All right. People of Grusinia versus Grand Duke. Defendant, what have you got to say for yourself?

AZDAK

Plenty. Naturally, have read war lost. Only started on the advice of patriots. Like Uncle Arsen Kazbeki. Call Uncle Arsen as witness.

THE FAT PRINCE [*To the* IRONSHIRTS, *delightedly*]

What a screw-ball!

THE NEPHEW

Motion rejected. One cannot be arraigned for declaring a war, which every ruler has to do once in a while, but only for running a war badly.

AZDAK

Rubbish! Did not run it at all! Had it run! Had it run by Princes! Naturally, they messed it up.

THE NEPHEW

Do you by any chance deny having been commander-in-chief?

AZDAK

Not at all! Always *was* commander-in-chief. At birth shouted at wet nurse. Was trained drop turds in toilet, grew accustomed to command. Always commanded officials rob my cash box. Officers flog soldiers only on command.

Landowners sleep with peasants' wives only on strictest command. Uncle Arsen here grew his belly at *my* command!

THE IRONSHIRTS [*Clapping*]

He's good! Long live the Grand Duke!

THE FAT PRINCE

Answer him, my little fox. I'm with you.

THE NEPHEW

I shall answer him according to the dignity of the law. Defendant, preserve the dignity of the law!

AZDAK

Agreed. Command you to proceed with the trial!

THE NEPHEW

It is not your place to command me. You claim that the Princes forced you to declare war. How can you claim, then, that they—er—"messed it up"?

AZDAK

Did not send enough people. Embezzled funds. Sent sick horses. During attack, drinking in whorehouse. Call Uncle Arsen as witness.

THE NEPHEW

Are you making the outrageous suggestion that the Princes of this country did not fight?

AZDAK

No. Princes fought. Fought for war contracts.

THE FAT PRINCE [*Jumping up*]

That's too much! This man talks like a carpet weaver!

AZDAK

Really? I told nothing but the truth.

THE FAT PRINCE

Hang him! Hang him!

THE FIRST IRONSHIRT [*Pulling the* PRINCE *down*]

Keep quiet! Go on, Excellency!

THE NEPHEW

Quiet! I now render a verdict: You must be hanged! By the neck! Having lost war!

AZDAK

Young man, seriously advise not fall publicly into jerky clipped manner of speech. Cannot be employed as watchdog if howl like wolf. Got it? If people realize Princes speak same language as Grand Duke, may hang Grand Duke *and Princes*, huh? By the way, must overrule verdict. Reason? War lost, but not for Princes. Princes won their war. Got 3,863,000 piasters for horses not delivered, 8,240,000 piasters for food supplies not produced. Are therefore victors. War lost only for Grusinia, which as such is not present in this court.

THE FAT PRINCE

I think that will do, my friends. [*To* AZDAK] You can withdraw, funny man. [*To the* IRONSHIRTS] You may now ratify the new judge's appointment, my friends.

THE FIRST IRONSHIRT

Yes, we can. Take down the judge's gown.

[ONE IRONSHIRT *climbs on the back of the* OTHER, *pulls the gown off the hanged man*]

THE FIRST IRONSHIRT [*To the* NEPHEW]

> Now you run away so the right ass can get on the right chair. [*To* AZDAK]
> Step forward! Go to the judge's seat! Now sit in it!
> [AZDAK *steps up, bows, and sits down*]
> The judge was always a rascal! Now the rascal shall be a judge!
> [*The judge's gown is placed round his shoulders, the hat on his head*]
> And what a judge!

THE SINGER

> And there was civil war in the land.
> The mighty were not safe.
> And Azdak was made a judge by the Ironshirts.
> And Azdak remained a judge for two years.

THE SINGER AND CHORUS

> When the towns were set afire
> And rivers of blood rose higher and higher,
> Cockroaches crawled out of every crack.
> And the court was full of schemers
> And the church of foul blasphemers.
> In the judge's cassock sat Azdak.

[AZDAK *sits in the judge's chair, peeling an apple.* SHAUWA *is sweeping out the hall. On one side an* INVALID *in a wheelchair. Opposite, a* YOUNG MAN *accused of blackmail. An* IRONSHIRT *stands guard, holding the Ironshirt's banner*]

AZDAK

> In consideration of the large number of cases, the Court today will hear two cases at a time. Before I open the proceedings, a short announcement—I accept.
> [HE *stretches out his hand. The* BLACKMAILER *is the only one to produce any money.* HE *hands it to* AZDAK]
> I reserve the right to punish one of the parties for contempt of court. [HE *glances at* THE INVALID] You [*To the* DOCTOR] are a doctor, and you [*To the* INVALID] are bringing a complaint against him. Is the doctor responsible for your condition?

THE INVALID

> Yes. I had a stroke on his account.

AZDAK

> That would be professional negligence.

THE INVALID

> Worse than negligence. I gave this man money for his studies. So far, he hasn't paid me back a cent. It was when I heard he was treating a patient free that I had my stroke.

AZDAK

> Rightly. [*To a* LIMPING MAN] And what are *you* doing here?

THE LIMPING MAN

> I'm the patient, your honor.

AZDAK

> He treated your leg for nothing?

THE LIMPING MAN

The wrong leg! My rheumatism was in the left leg, and he operated on the right. That's why I limp now.

AZDAK

And you were treated free?

THE INVALID

A five-hundred-piaster operation free! For nothing! For a God-bless-you! And I paid for this man's studies! [*To the* DOCTOR] Did they teach you to operate free?

THE DOCTOR

Your Honor, it is actually the custom to demand the fee before the operation, as the patient is more willing to pay before an operation than after. Which is only human. In the case in question I was convinced, when I started the operation, that my servant had already received the fee. In this I was mistaken.

THE INVALID

He was mistaken! A good doctor doesn't make mistakes! He examines before he operates!

AZDAK

That's right. [*To* SHAUWA] Public Prosecutor, what's the other case about?

SHAUWA [*Busily sweeping*]

Blackmail.

THE BLACKMAILER

High Court of Justice, I'm innocent. I only wanted to find out from the landowner concerned if he really *had* raped his niece. He informed me very politely that this was not the case, and gave me the money only so I could pay for my uncle's studies.

AZDAK

Hm. [*To the* DOCTOR] You, on the other hand, can cite no extenuating circumstances for your offense, huh?

THE DOCTOR

Except that to err is human.

AZDAK

And you are aware that in money matters a good doctor is a highly responsible person? I once heard of a doctor who got a thousand piasters for a sprained finger by remarking that sprains have something to do with blood circulation, which after all a less good doctor might have overlooked, and who, on another occasion made a real gold mine out of a somewhat disordered gall bladder, he treated it with such loving care. You have no excuse, Doctor. The corn merchant, Uxu, had his son study medicine to get some knowledge of trade, our medical schools are so good. [*To the* BLACKMAILER] What's the landowner's name?

SHAUWA

He doesn't want it mentioned.

AZDAK

In that case I will pass judgment. The Court considers the blackmail proved. And you [*To the* INVALID] are sentenced to a fine of one thousand piasters. If you have a second stroke, the doctor will have to treat you free. Even if he has to amputate. [*To the* LIMPING MAN] As compensation, you will receive a bottle of rubbing alcohol. [*To the* BLACKMAILER] You are sentenced to hand over half the proceeds of your deal to the Public Prosecutor to keep the landowner's name secret. You are advised, moreover, to study medicine—you seem well suited to that calling. [*To the* DOCTOR] You have perpetrated an unpardonable error in the practice of your profession: you are acquitted. Next cases!

THE SINGER AND CHORUS

Men won't do much for a shilling.
For a pound they may be willing.
For 20 pounds the verdict's in the sack.
As for the many, all too many,
Those who've only got a penny—
They've one single, sole recourse: Azdak.

[*Enter* AZDAK *from the caravansary on the highroad, followed by an old bearded* INNKEEPER. *The judge's chair is carried by a* STABLEMAN *and* SHAUWA. *An* IRONSHIRT, *with a banner, takes up his position*]

AZDAK

Put me down. Then we'll get some air, maybe even a good stiff breeze from the lemon grove there. It does justice good to be done in the open: the wind blows her skirts up and you can see what she's got. Shauwa, we've been eating too much. These official journeys are exhausting. [*To the* INN-KEEPER] It's a question of your daughter-in-law?

THE INNKEEPER

Your Worship, it's a question of the family honor. I wish to bring an action on behalf of my son, who's on business on the other side of the mountain. This is the offending stableman, and here's my daughter-in-law.

[*Enter the* DAUGHTER-IN-LAW, *a voluptuous wench.* SHE *is veiled*]

AZDAK [*Sitting down*]

I accept.

[*Sighing, the* INNKEEPER *hands him some money*]

Good. Now the formalities are disposed of. This is a case of rape?

THE INNKEEPER

Your Honor, I caught the fellow in the act. Ludovica was in the straw on the stable floor.

AZDAK

Quite right, the stable. Lovely horses! I specially liked the little roan.

THE INNKEEPER

The first thing I did, of course, was to question Ludovica. On my son's behalf.

AZDAK [*Seriously*]

I said I specially liked the little roan.

THE INNKEEPER [*Coldly*]

Really? Ludovica confessed the stableman took her against her will.

AZDAK

Take your veil off, Ludovica. [SHE *does so*] Ludovica, you please the Court. Tell us how it happened.

LUDOVICA [*Well-schooled*]

When I entered the stable to see the new foal the stableman said to me on his own accord: "It's hot today!" and laid his hand on my left breast. I said to him: "Don't do that!" But he continued to handle me indecently, which provoked my anger. Before I realized his sinful intentions, he got much closer. It was all over when my father-in-law entered and accidentally trod on me.

THE INNKEEPER [*Explaining*]
On my son's behalf.

AZDAK [*To the* STABLEMAN]
You admit you started it?

THE STABLEMAN
Yes.

AZDAK
Ludovica, you like to eat sweet things?

LUDOVICA
Yes, sunflower seeds!

AZDAK
You like to lie a long time in the bathtub?

LUDOVICA
Half an hour or so.

AZDAK
Public Prosecutor, drop your knife—there—on the ground. [SHAUWA *does so*] Ludovica, pick up that knife.
[LUDOVICA, *swaying her hips, does* so] See that? [HE *points at her*] The way it moves? The rape is now proven. By eating too much—sweet things, especially—by lying too long in warm water, by laziness and too soft a skin, you have raped that unfortunate man. Think you can run around with a behind like that and get away with it in court? This is a case of intentional assault with a dangerous weapon! You are sentenced to hand over to the Court the little roan which your father liked to ride "on his son's behalf." And now, come with me to the stables, so the Court may inspect the scene of the crime, Ludovica.

THE SINGER AND CHORUS
When the sharks the sharks devour
Little fishes have their hour.
For a while the load is off their back.
On Grusinia's highways faring
Fixed-up scales of justice bearing
Strode the poor man's magistrate: Azdak.

And he gave to the forsaken
All that from the rich he'd taken.
And a bodyguard of roughnecks was Azdak's.
And our good and evil man, he
Smiled upon Grusinia's Granny.
His emblem was a tear in sealing wax.

All mankind should love each other
But when visiting your brother

Take an ax along and hold it fast.
Not in theory but in practice
Miracles are wrought with axes
And the age of miracles is not past.

[AZDAK'S *judge's chair is in a tavern.* THREE RICH FARMERS *stand before* AZDAK. SHAUWA *brings him wine. In a corner stands an* OLD PEASANT WOMAN. *In the open doorway, and outside, stand* VILLAGERS *looking on. An* IRONSHIRT *stands guard with a banner*]

AZDAK

The Public Prosecutor has the floor.

SHAUWA

It concerns a cow. For five weeks the defendant has had a cow in her stable, the property of the farmer Suru. She was also found to be in possession of a stolen ham, and a number of cows belonging to Shutoff were killed after he asked the defendant to pay the rent on a piece of land.

THE FARMERS

—It's a matter of my ham, Your Honor.
—It's a matter of my cow, Your Honor.
—It's a matter of my land, Your Honor.

AZDAK

Well, Granny, what have *you* got to say to all this?

THE OLD WOMAN

Your Honor, one night toward morning, five weeks ago, there was a knock at my door, and outside stood a bearded man with a cow. "My dear woman," he said, "I am the miracle-working Saint Banditus and because your son has been killed in the war, I bring you this cow as a souvenir. Take good care of it."

THE FARMERS

—The robber, Irakli, Your Honor!
—Her brother-in-law, Your Honor!
—The cow-thief!
—The incendiary!
—He must be beheaded!

[*Outside, a* WOMAN *screams. The* CROWD *grows restless, retreats. Enter the* BANDIT IRAKLI *with a huge ax*]

THE BANDIT

A very good evening, dear friends! A glass of vodka!

THE FARMERS [*Crossing themselves*]

Irakli!

AZDAK

Public Prosecutor, a glass of vodka for our guest. And who are you?

THE BANDIT

I'm a wandering hermit, Your Honor. Thanks for the gracious gift.

[HE *empties the glass which* SHAUWA *has brought*]

Another!

AZDAK

I am Azdak. [HE *gets up and bows. The* BANDIT *also bows*] The Court welcomes the foreign hermit. Go on with your story, Granny.

THE OLD WOMAN

Your Honor, that first night I didn't yet know Saint Banditus could work miracles, it was only the cow. But one night, a few days later, the farmer's servants came to take the cow away again. Then they turned round in front of my door and went off without the cow. And bumps as big as a fist sprouted on their heads. So I knew that Saint Banditus had changed their hearts and turned them into friendly people. [*The* BANDIT *roars with laughter*]

THE FIRST FARMER

I know what changed them.

AZDAK

That's fine. You can tell us later. Continue.

THE OLD WOMAN

Your Honor, the next one to become a good man was the farmer Shutoff—a devil, as everyone knows. But Saint Banditus arranged it so he let me off the rent on the little piece of land.

THE SECOND FARMER

Because my cows were killed in the field. [*The* BANDIT *laughs*]

THE OLD WOMAN [*Answering* AZDAK'S *sign to continue*]

Then one morning the ham came flying in at my window. It hit me in the small of the back. I'm still lame, Your Honor, look. [SHE *limps a few steps*] [*The* BANDIT *laughs*]

Your Honor, was there ever a time when a poor old woman could get a ham *without* a miracle?

[*The* BANDIT *starts sobbing*]

AZDAK [*Rising from his chair*]

Granny, that's a question that strikes straight at the Court's heart. Be so kind as to sit here.

[*The* OLD WOMAN, *hesitating, sits in the judge's chair*]

AZDAK [*Sits on the floor, glass in hand, reciting*]

Granny
We could almost call you Granny Grusinia
The Woebegone
The Bereaved Mother
Whose sons have gone to war
Receiving the present of a cow
She bursts out crying.
When she is beaten
She remains hopeful.
When she's not beaten
She's surprised.
On us
Who are already damned
May you render a merciful verdict
Granny Grusinia!
[*Bellowing at the* FARMERS]

Admit you don't believe in miracles, you atheists! Each of you is sentenced to pay five hundred piasters! For godlessness! Get out!

[*The* FARMERS *slink out*]

And you Granny, and you [*To the* BANDIT] pious man, empty a pitcher of wine with the Public Prosecutor and Azdak!

THE SINGER AND CHORUS

And he broke the rules to save them.
Broken law like bread he gave them,
Brought them to shore upon his crooked back.
At long last the poor and lowly
Had someone who was not too holy
To be bribed by empty hands: Azdak.

For two years it was his pleasure
To give the beasts of prey short measure:
He became a wolf to fight the pack.
From All Hallows to All Hallows
On his chair beside the gallows
Dispensing justice in his fashion sat Azdak.

THE SINGER

But the era of disorder came to an end.
The Grand Duke returned.
The Governor's wife returned.
A trial was held.
Many died.
The people's quarters burned anew.
And fear seized Azdak.

[AZDAK's *judge's chair stands again in the court of justice.* AZDAK *sits on the floor, shaving and talking to* SHAUWA. *Noises outside. In the rear the* FAT PRINCE's *head is carried by on a lance*]

AZDAK

Shauwa, the days of your slavery are numbered, maybe even the minutes. For a long time now I have held you in the iron curb of reason, and it has torn your mouth till it bleeds. I have lashed you with reasonable arguments, I have manhandled you with logic. You are by nature a weak man, and if one slyly throws an argument in your path, you *have* to snap it up, you can't resist. It is your nature to lick the hand of some superior being. But superior beings can be of very different kinds. And now, with your liberation, you will soon be able to follow your natural inclinations, which are low. You will be able to follow your infallible instinct, which teaches you to plant your fat heel on the faces of men. Gone is the era of confusion and disorder, which I find described in the Song of Chaos. Let us now sing that song together in memory of those terrible days. Sit down and don't do violence to the music. Don't be afraid. It sounds all right. And it has a fine refrain.

[HE *sings*]

THE SONG OF CHAOS

Sister, hide your face! Brother, take your knife!
The times are out of joint!

Big men are full of complaint
And small men full of joy.
The city says:
"Let us drive the strong ones from our midst!"
Offices are raided. Lists of serfs are destroyed.
They have set Master's nose to the grindstone.
They who lived in the dark have seen the light.
The ebony poor box is broken.
Magnificent sesnem wood is sawed up for beds.
Who had no bread have barns full.
Who begged for alms of corn now mete it out.

SHAUWA [*Refrain*]
Oh, oh, oh, oh.

AZDAK [*Refrain*]
Where are you, General, where are you?
Please, please, please, restore order!

The nobleman's son can no longer be recognized;
The lady's child becomes the son of her slave.
The councilors meet in a shed.
Once, this man was barely allowed to sleep on the wall;
Now, he stretches his limbs in a bed.
Once, this man rowed a boat; now, he owns ships.
Their owner looks for them, but they're his no longer.
Five men are sent on a journey by their master.
"Go yourself," they say, "we have arrived."

SHAUWA [*Refrain*]
Oh, oh, oh, oh.

AZDAK [*Refrain*]

Where are you, General, where are you?
Please, please, please, restore order!

Yes, So it might have been, had order been neglected much longer. But now the Grand Duke has returned to the capital, and the Persians have lent him an army to restore order with. The suburbs are already aflame. Go and get me the big book I always sit on.
[SHAUWA *brings the big book from the judge's chair.* AZDAK *opens it*]
This is the Statute Book and I've always used it, as you can testify. Now I'd better look in this book and see what they can do to me. I've let the down-and-outs get away with murder, and I'll have to pay for it. I helped poverty onto its skinny legs, so they'll hang me for drunkenness. I peeped into the rich man's pocket, which is bad taste. And I can't hide anywhere—everybody knows me because I've helped everybody.

SHAUWA
Someone's coming!

AZDAK [*In panic,* HE *walks trembling to the chair*]
It's the end. And now they'd enjoy seeing what a Great Man I am. I'll de-

prive them of that pleasure. I'll beg on my knees for mercy. Spittle will slobber down my chin. The fear of death is in me.

[*Enter* NATELLA ABASHWILI, *the* GOVERNOR'S WIFE, *followed by the* ADJUTANT *and an* IRONSHIRT]

THE GOVERNOR'S WIFE

What sort of a creature is that, Shalva?

AZDAK

A willing one, Your Highness, a man ready to oblige.

THE ADJUTANT

Natella Abashwili, wife of the late Governor, has just returned. She is looking for her two-year-old son, Michael. She has been informed that the child was carried off to the mountains by a former servant.

AZDAK

The child will be brought back, Your Highness, at your service.

THE ADJUTANT

They say that the person in question is passing it off as her own.

AZDAK

She will be beheaded, Your Highness, at your service.

THE ADJUTANT

That is all.

THE GOVERNOR'S WIFE [*Leaving*]

I don't like that man.

AZDAK [*Following her to door, bowing*]

At your service, Your Highness, it will all be arranged.

5. The Chalk Circle

THE SINGER

Hear now the story of the trial
Concerning Governor Abashwili's child
And the establishing of the true mother
By the famous test of the Chalk Circle.

[*The court of justice in Nuka.* IRONSHIRTS *lead* MICHAEL *across stage and out at the back.* IRONSHIRTS *hold* GRUSHA *back with their lances under the gateway until the* CHILD *has been led through. Then* SHE *is admitted.* SHE *is accompanied by the former governor's* COOK. *Distant noises and a fire-red sky*]

GRUSHA [*Trying to hide*]

He's brave, he can wash himself now.

THE COOK

You're lucky. It's not a real judge. It's Azdak, a drunk who doesn't know what he's doing. The biggest thieves have got by through him. Because he gets everything mixed up and the rich never offer him big enough bribes, the likes of us sometimes do pretty well.

GRUSHA

I *need* luck right now.

THE COOK

Touch wood. [SHE *crosses herself*] I'd better offer up another prayer that the judge may be drunk.

[SHE *prays with motionless lips, while* GRUSHA *looks around, in vain, for the* CHILD]

Why must you hold on to it at any price if it isn't yours? In days like these?

GRUSHA

He's mine. I brought him up.

THE COOK

Have you never thought what'd happen when she came back?

GRUSHA

At first I thought I'd give him to her. Then I thought she wouldn't come back.

THE COOK

And even a borrowed coat keeps a man warm, hm? [GRUSHA *nods*] I'll swear to anything for you. You're a decent girl. [SHE *sees the soldier* SIMON SHASHAVA *approaching*] You've done wrong by Simon, though. I've been talking with him. He just can't understand.

GRUSHA [*Unaware of* SIMON's *presence*]

Right now I can't be bothered whether he understands or not!

THE COOK

He knows the child isn't yours, but you married and not free "til death you do part"—he can't understand *that*.

[GRUSHA *sees* SIMON *and greets him*]

SIMON [*Gloomily*]

I wish the lady to know I will swear I am the father of the child.

GRUSHA [*Low*]

Thank you, Simon.

SIMON

At the same time I wish the lady to know my hands are not tied—nor are hers.

THE COOK

You needn't have said that. You know she's married.

SIMON

And it needs no rubbing in.

[*Enter an* IRONSHIRT]

THE IRONSHIRT

Where's the judge? Has anyone seen the judge?

ANOTHER IRONSHIRT [*Stepping forward*]

The judge isn't here yet. Nothing but a bed and a pitcher in the whole house!

[*Exeunt* IRONSHIRTS]

THE COOK

I hope nothing has happened to him. With any other judge you'd have about as much chance as a chicken has teeth.

GRUSHA [*Who has turned away and covered her face*]

Stand in front of me. I shouldn't have come to Nuka. If I run into the Ironshirt, the one I hit over the head . . .

[SHE *screams. An* IRONSHIRT *had stopped and, turning his back, had been listening to her.* HE *now wheels around. It is the* CORPORAL, *and* HE *has a huge scar across his face*]

THE IRONSHIRT [*In the gateway*]

What's the matter, Shotta? Do you know her?

THE CORPORAL [*After staring for some time*]

No.

THE IRONSHIRT

She's the one who stole the Abashwili child, or so they say. If you know anything about it you can make some money, Shotta. [*Exit the* CORPORAL, *cursing*]

THE COOK

Was it him? [GRUSHA *nods*] I think he'll keep his mouth shut, or he'd be admitting he was after the child.

GRUSHA

I'd almost forgotten him.

[*Enter* THE GOVERNOR'S WIFE, *followed by the* ADJUTANT *and* TWO LAW-YERS]

THE GOVERNOR'S WIFE

At least there are no common people here, thank God. I can't stand their smell. It always gives me migraine.

THE FIRST LAWYER

Madam, I must ask you to be careful what you say until we have another judge.

THE GOVERNOR'S WIFE

But I didn't say anything, Illo Shuboladze. I love the people with their sim-ple straightforward minds. It's only that their smell brings on my migraine.

THE SECOND LAWYER

There won't be many spectators. The whole population is sitting at home behind locked doors because of the riots on the outskirts of town.

THE GOVERNOR'S WIFE [*Looking at* GRUSHA]

Is that the creature?

THE FIRST LAWYER

Please, most gracious Natella Abashwili, abstain from invective until it is certain the Grand Duke has appointed a new judge and we're rid of the present one, who's about the lowest fellow ever seen in judge's gown. Things are all set to move, you see.

[*Enter* IRONSHIRTS *from the courtyard*]

THE COOK

Her Grace would pull your hair out on the spot if she didn't know Azdak is for the poor. He goes by the face.

[IRONSHIRTS *begin fastening a rope to a beam.* AZDAK, *in chains, is led in, followed by* SHAUWA, *also in chains. The* THREE FARMERS *bring up the rear*]

AN IRONSHIRT

Trying to run away, were you? [HE *strikes* AZDAK]

ONE FARMER

Off with his judge's gown before we string him up!

[IRONSHIRTS *and* FARMERS *tear off* AZDAK'S *gown. His torn underwear is visible. Then someone kicks him*]

AN IRONSHIRT [*Pushing him into someone else*]

 If you want a heap of justice, here it is!

[*Accompanied by shouts of "You take it!" and "Let me have him, Brother!"*]
THEY *throw* AZDAK *back and forth until* HE *collapses. Then* HE *is lifted up and
dragged under the noose*]

THE GOVERNOR'S WIFE [*Who, during this "Ball-game," has clapped her hands
 hysterically*]

 I disliked that man from the moment I first saw him.

AZDAK [*Covered with blood, panting*]

 I can't see. Give me a rag.

AN IRONSHIRT

 What is it you want to see?

AZDAK

 You, you dogs!

 [HE *wipes the blood out of his eyes with his shirt*]

 Good morning, dogs! How goes it, dogs! How's the dog world? Does it smell
 good? Got another boot for me to lick? Are you back at each other's throats,
 dogs?

[*Accompanied by a* CORPORAL, *a dust-covered* RIDER *enters.* HE *takes some
documents from a leather case, looks at them, then interrupts*]

THE RIDER

 Stop! I bring a dispatch from the Grand Duke, containing the latest ap-
 pointments.

THE CORPORAL [*Bellowing*]

 Atten-shun!

THE RIDER

 Of the new judge it says: "We appoint a man whom we have to thank for
 saving a life indispensable to the country's welfare—a certain Azdak of
 Nuka." Which is he?

SHAUWA [*Pointing*]

 That's him, Your Excellency.

THE CORPORAL [*Bellowing*]

 What's going on here?

AN IRONSHIRT

 I beg to report that His Honor Azdak was already His Honor Azdak, but
 on these farmers' denunciation was pronounced the Grand Duke's enemy.

THE CORPORAL [*Pointing at the* FARMERS]

 March them off!

 [THEY *are marched off.* THEY *bow all the time*]

 See to it that His Honor Azdak is exposed to no more violence.

                                         [*Exeunt* RIDER *and* CORPORAL]

THE COOK [*To* SHAUWA]

 She clapped her hands! I hope he saw it!

THE FIRST LAWYER

 It's a catastrophe.

 [AZDAK *has fainted. Coming to,* HE *is dressed again in judge's robes.* HE
walks, swaying, toward the IRONSHIRTS]

AN IRONSHIRT

What does Your Honor desire?

AZDAK

Nothing, fellow dogs, or just an occasional boot to lick. [*To* SHAUWA] I pardon you. [HE *is unchained*] Get me some red wine, the sweet kind.

[SHAUWA *stumbles off*]

Get out of here, I've got to judge a case.

[*Exeunt* IRONSHIRTS. SHAUWA *returns with a pitcher of wine.* AZDAK *gulps it down*]

AZDAK

Something for my backside.

[SHAUWA *brings the Statute Book, puts it on the judge's chair.* AZDAK *sits on it*]

I accept.

[*The* PROSECUTORS, *among whom a worried council has been held, smile with relief.* THEY *whisper*]

THE COOK

Oh dear!

SIMON

A well can't be filled with dew, they say.

THE LAWYERS [*Approaching* AZDAK, *who stands up, expectantly*]

A quite ridiculous case, Your Honor. The accused has abducted a child and refuses to hand it over.

AZDAK [*Stretching out his hand, glancing at* GRUSHA]

A most attractive person. [HE *fingers the money, then sits down, satisfied*] I declare the proceedings open and demand the whole truth. [*To* GRUSHA] Especially from you.

THE FIRST LAWYER

High Court of Justice! Blood, as the popular saying goes, is thicker than water. This old adage . . .

AZDAK [*Interrupting*]

The Court wants to know the lawyers' fee.

THE FIRST LAWYER [*Surprised*]

I beg your pardon?

[AZDAK, *smiling, rubs his thumb and index finger*]

Oh, I see. Five hundred piasters, Your Honor, to answer the Court's somewhat unusual question.

AZDAK

Did you hear? The question is unusual. I ask it because I listen in quite a different way when I know you're good.

THE FIRST LAWYER [*Bowing*]

Thank you, Your Honor. High Court of Justice, of all ties the ties of blood are strongest. Mother and child—is there a more intimate relationship? Can one tear a child from its mother? High Court of Justice, she has conceived it in the holy ecstasies of love. She has carried it in her womb. She has fed it with her blood. She has borne it with pain. High Court of Justice, it has been observed that even the wild tigress, robbed of her young, roams restless through the mountains, shrunk to a shadow. Nature herself . . .

AZDAK [*Interrupting, to* GRUSHA]

What's your answer to all this and anything else that lawyer might have to say?

GRUSHA

He's mine.

AZDAK

Is that all? I hope you can prove it. Why should I assign the child to you in any case?

GRUSHA

I brought him up like the priest says "according to my best knowledge and conscience." I always found him something to eat. Most of the time he had a roof over his head. And I went to such trouble for him. I had expenses too. I didn't look out for my own comfort. I brought the child up to be friendly with everyone, and from the beginning taught him to work. As well as he could, that is. He's still very little.

THE FIRST LAWYER

Your Honor, it is significant that the girl herself doesn't claim any tie of blood between her and the child.

AZDAK

The Court takes note of that.

THE FIRST LAWYER

Thank you, Your Honor. And now permit a woman bowed in sorrow—who has already lost her husband and now has also to fear the loss of her child— to address a few words to you. The gracious Natella Abashwili is . . .

THE GOVERNOR'S WIFE [*Quietly*]

A most cruel fate, Sir, forces me to describe to you the tortures of a bereaved mother's soul, the anxiety, the sleepless nights, the . . .

THE SECOND LAWYER [*Bursting out*]

It's outrageous the way this woman is being treated! Her husband's palace is closed to her! The revenue of her estates is blocked, and she is cold-bloodedly told that it's tied to the heir. She can't do a thing without that child. She can't even pay her lawyers!!

[*To the* FIRST LAWYER, *who, desperate about this outburst, makes frantic gestures to keep him from speaking*]

Dear Illo Shuboladze, surely it can be divulged now that the Abashwili estates are at stake?

THE FIRST LAWYER

Please, Honored Sandro Oboladze! We agreed . . . [*To* AZDAK] Of course it is correct that the trial will also decide if our noble client can dispose of the Abashwili estates, which are rather extensive. I say "also" advisedly, for in the foreground stands the human tragedy of a mother, as Natella Abashwili very properly explained in the first words of her moving statement. Even if Michael Abashwili were not heir to the estates, he would still be the dearly beloved child of my client.

AZDAK

Stop! The Court is touched by the mention of estates. It's a proof of human feeling.

THE SECOND LAWYER

Thanks, Your Honor. Dear Illo Shuboladze, we can prove in any case that the woman who took the child is not the child's mother. Permit me to lay before the Court the bare facts. High Court of Justice, by an unfortunate chain of circumstances, Michael Abashwili was left behind on that Easter Sunday while his mother was making her escape. Grusha, a palace kitchen maid, was seen with the baby . . .

THE COOK

All her mistress was thinking of was what dresses she'd take along!

THE SECOND LAWYER [*Unmoved*]

Nearly a year later Grusha turned up in a mountain village with a baby and there entered into the state of matrimony with . . .

AZDAK

How did you get to that mountain village?

GRUSHA

On foot, Your Honor. And it was mine.

SIMON

I am the father, Your Honor.

THE COOK

I used to look after it for them, Your Honor. For five piasters.

THE SECOND LAWYER

This man is engaged to Grusha, High Court of Justice: his testimony is not trustworthy.

AZDAK

Are you the man she married in the mountain village?

SIMON

No, Your Honor, she married a peasant.

AZDAK [*To* GRUSHA]

Why? [*Pointing at* SIMON] Is he no good in bed? Tell the truth.

GRUSHA

We didn't get that far. I married because of the baby. So it'd have a roof over his head. [*Pointing at* SIMON] He was in the war, Your Honor.

AZDAK

And now he wants you back again, huh?

SIMON

I wish to state in evidence . . .

GRUSHA [*Angrily*]

I am no longer free, Your Honor.

AZDAK

And the child, you claim, comes from whoring?

[GRUSHA *doesn't answer*]

I'm going to ask you a question: What kind of child is it? Is it a ragged little bastard or from a well-to-do family?

GRUSHA [*Angrily*]

He's just an ordinary child.

AZDAK

I mean—did he have refined features from the beginning?

GRUSHA

He had a nose on his face.

AZDAK

A very significant comment! It has been said of me that I went out one time and sniffed at a rosebush before rendering a verdict—tricks like that are needed nowadays. Well, I'll make it short, and not listen to any more lies. [*To* GRUSHA] Especially not yours. [*To* ALL *the accused*] I can imagine what you've cooked up to cheat me! I know you people. You're swindlers.

GRUSHA [*Suddenly*]

I can understand your wanting to cut it short, now I've seen what you accepted!

AZDAK

Shut up! Did I accept anything from you?

GRUSHA [*While the* COOK *tries to restrain her*]

I haven't got anything.

AZDAK

True. Quite true. From starvelings I never get a thing. I might just as well starve, myself. You want justice, but do you want to pay for it, hm? When you go to a butcher you know you have to pay, but you people go to a judge as if you were going to a funeral supper.

SIMON [*Loudly*]

When the horse was shod, the horse-fly held out its leg, as the saying is.

AZDAK [*Eagerly accepting the challenge*]

Better a treasure in manure than a stone in a mountain stream.

SIMON

A fine day. Let's go fishing, said the angler to the worm.

AZDAK

I'm my own master, said the servant, and cut off his foot.

SIMON

I love you as a father, said the Czar to the peasants, and had the Czarevitch's head chopped off.

AZDAK

A fool's worst enemy is himself.

SIMON

However, a fart has no nose.

AZDAK

Fined ten piasters for indecent language in court! That'll teach you what justice is.

GRUSHA [*Furiously*]

A fine kind of justice! You play fast and loose with us because we don't talk as refined as that crowd with their lawyers!

AZDAK

That's true. You people are too dumb. It's only right you should get it in the neck.

GRUSHA

You want to hand the child over to her, and she wouldn't even know how to keep it dry, she's so "refined"! You know about as much about justice as I do!

AZDAK

There's something in that. I'm an ignorant man. Haven't even a decent pair of pants on under this gown. Look! With me, everything goes for food and drink—I was educated at a convent. Incidentally, I'll fine you ten piasters for contempt of court. And you're a very silly girl, to turn me against you, instead of making eyes at me and wiggling your backside a little to keep me in a good temper. Twenty piasters!

GRUSHA

Even if it was thirty, I'd tell you what I think of your justice, you drunken onion! [*Incoherently*] How dare you talk to me like the cracked Isaiah on the church window? As if you were somebody? For you weren't born to this. You weren't born to rap your own mother on the knuckles if she swipes a little bowl of salt someplace. Aren't you ashamed of yourself when you see how I tremble before you? You've made yourself their servant so no one will take their houses from them—houses they had stolen! Since when have houses belonged to the bedbugs? But you're on the watch, or they couldn't drag our men into their wars! You bribe-taker!

[AZDAK *half gets up, starts beaming. With his little hammer* HE *half-heartedly knocks on the table as if to get silence. As* GRUSHA'S *scolding continues,* HE *only beats time with his hammer*]

I've no respect for you. No more than for a thief or a bandit with a knife! You can do what you want. You can take the child away from me, a hundred against one, but I tell you one thing: only extortioners should be chosen for a profession like yours, and men who rape children! As punishment! Yes, let *them* sit in judgment on their fellow creatures. It is worse than to hang from the gallows.

AZDAK [*Sitting down*]

Now it'll be thirty! And I won't go on squabbling with you—we're not in a tavern. What'd happen to my dignity as a judge? Anyway, I've lost interest in your case. Where's the couple who wanted a divorce? [*To* SHAUWA] Bring 'em in. This case is adjourned for fifteen minutes.

THE FIRST LAWYER [*To the* GOVERNOR'S WIFE]

Even without using the rest of the evidence, Madam, we have the verdict in the bag.

THE COOK [*To* GRUSHA]

You've gone and spoiled your chances with him. You won't get the child now.

THE GOVERNOR'S WIFE

Shalva, my smelling salts!

[*Enter a* VERY OLD COUPLE]

AZDAK

I accept. [*The* OLD COUPLE *don't understand*] I hear you want to be divorced. How long have you been together?

THE OLD WOMAN

Forty years, Your Honor.

AZDAK

And why do you want a divorce?

THE OLD MAN
  We don't like each other, Your Honor.
AZDAK
  Since when?
THE OLD WOMAN
  Oh, from the very beginning, Your Honor.
AZDAK
  I'll think about your request and render my verdict when I'm through with
  the other case.
  [SHAUWA *leads them back*]
  I need the child. [HE *beckons* GRUSHA *to him and bends not unkindly toward
  her*] I've noticed you have a soft spot for justice. I don't believe he's your
  child, but if he *were* yours, woman, wouldn't you want him to be rich?
  You'd only have to say he wasn't yours, and he'd have a palace and many
  horses in his stable and many beggars on his doorstep and many soldiers in
  his service and many petitioners in his courtyard, wouldn't he? What do you
  say—don't you want him to be rich?
  [GRUSHA *is silent*]
THE SINGER
  Hear now what the angry girl thought but did not say:

> Had he golden shoes to wear
> He'd be cruel as a bear.
> Evil would his life disgrace.
> He'd laugh in my face.
> Carrying a heart of flint
> Is too troublesome a stint.
> Being powerful and bad
> Is hard on a lad.
>
> Then let hunger be his foe!
> Hungry men and women, no.
> Let him fear the darksome night
> But not daylight!

AZDAK
  I think I understand you, woman.
GRUSHA [*Suddenly and loudly*]
  I won't give him up. I've raised him, and he knows me.
  [*Enter* SHAUWA *with the* CHILD]
THE GOVERNOR'S WIFE
  It's in rags!
GRUSHA
  That's not true. But I wasn't given time to put his good shirt on.
THE GOVERNOR'S WIFE
  It must have been in a pigsty.
GRUSHA [*Furiously*]
  I'm not a pig, but there are some who are! Where did you leave your baby?
THE GOVERNOR'S WIFE
  I'll show you, you vulgar creature!

[SHE *is about to throw herself on* GRUSHA, *but is restrained by her* LAWYERS]
She's a criminal, she must be whipped. Immediately!

THE SECOND LAWYER [*Holding his hand over her mouth*]
Natella Abashwili, your promised . . . Your Honor, the plaintiff's nerves . . .

AZDAK
Plaintiff and defendant! The Court has listened to your case, and has come to no decision as to who the real mother is, therefore, I, the judge, am obliged to *choose* a mother for the child. I'll make a test. Shauwa, get a piece of chalk and draw a circle on the floor.

[SHAUWA *does so*]

AZDAK
Now place the child in the center.

[SHAUWA *puts* MICHAEL, *who smiles at* GRUSHA, *in the center of the circle*]
Stand near the circle, both of you.

[THE GOVERNOR'S WIFE *and* GRUSHA *step up to the circle*]
Now each of you take the child by one hand.

[THEY *do so*]
The true mother is she who can pull the child out of the circle.

THE SECOND LAWYER [*Quickly*]
High Court of Justice, I object! The fate of the great Abashwili estates, which are tied to the child, as the heir, should not be made dependent on such a doubtful duel. In addition, my client does not command the strength of this person, who is accustomed to physical work.

AZDAK
She looks pretty well fed to me. Pull!

[GOVERNOR'S WIFE *pulls the* CHILD *out of the circle on her side;* GRUSHA *has let go and stands aghast*]
What's the matter with you? You didn't pull!

GRUSHA
I didn't hold on to him.

THE FIRST LAWYER [*Congratulating the* GOVERNOR'S WIFE]
What did I say! The ties of blood!

GRUSHA [*Running to* AZDAK]
Your Honor, I take back everything I said against you. I ask your forgiveness. But could I keep him till he can speak all the words? He knows a few.

AZDAK
Don't influence the Court. I bet you only know about twenty words yourself. All right, I'll make the test once more, just to be certain.

[*The* TWO WOMEN *take up their positions again*] Pull! [*Again* GRUSHA *lets go of the* CHILD]

GRUSHA [*In despair*]
I brought him up! Shall I also tear him to pieces? I can't!

AZDAK [*Rising*]
And in this manner the Court has established the true mother. [*To* GRUSHA] Take your child and be off. I advise you not to stay in the city with him. [*To the* GOVERNOR'S WIFE] And you disappear before I fine you for fraud. Your estates fall to the city. They'll be converted into a playground for the

children. They need one, and I've decided it shall be called after me: Azdak's Garden.

[THE GOVERNOR'S WIFE *has fainted and is carried out by the* LAWYERS *and the* ADJUTANT. GRUSHA *stands motionless.* SHAUWA *leads the* CHILD *toward her*]
Now I'll take off this judge's gown—it's grown too hot for me. I'm not cut out for a hero. In token of farewell I invite you all to a little dance outside on the meadow. Oh, I'd almost forgotten something in my excitement . . . to sign the divorce decree.

[*Using the judge's chair as a table,* HE *writes something on a piece of paper, and prepares to leave. Dance music has started*]
SHAUWA [*Having read what is on the paper*]
But that's not right. You've not divorced the old people. You've divorced Grusha!

AZDAK
Have I divorced the wrong couple? What a pity! And I never retract! If I did, how could we keep order in the land? [*To the* OLD COUPLE] I'll invite you to my party instead. You don't mind dancing with each other, do you? [*To* GRUSHA *and* SIMON] I've got forty piasters coming from you.

SIMON [*Pulling out his purse*]
Cheap at the price, Your Honor. And many thanks.

AZDAK [*Pocketing the cash*]
I'll be needing this.

GRUSHA [*To* MICHAEL]
So we'd better leave the city tonight, Michael. [*To* SIMON] You like him?

SIMON
With my respects, I like him.

GRUSHA
Now I can tell you: I took him because on that Easter Sunday I got engaged to you. So he's a child of love. Michael, let's dance.

[SHE *dances with* MICHAEL, SIMON *dances with the* COOK, *the* OLD COUPLE *with each other.* AZDAK *stands lost in thought. The* DANCERS *soon hide him from view. Occasionally* HE *is seen, but less and less as* MORE COUPLES *join the dance*]
THE SINGER
And after that evening Azdak vanished and was never seen again.
The people of Grusinia did not forget him but long remembered
The period of his judging as a brief golden age,
Almost an age of justice.

[ALL THE COUPLES *dance off.* AZDAK *has disappeared*]

THE SINGER
But you, you who have listened to the Story of the Chalk Circle,
Take note what men of old concluded:
That what there is shall go to those who are good for it,
Children to the motherly, that they prosper,
Carts to good drivers, that they be driven well,
The valley to the waterers, that it yield fruit.

The Firebugs

Max Frisch

Max Frisch

In his diary, Max Frisch wrote, "As a playwright, I would consider my task to have been thoroughly fulfilled if one of my plays could succeed in so posing a question that from that moment on the audience could not go on living without an answer—without their own answer, which they can give only through their own lives." And although Frisch knows that he can never conceivably fulfill his ambition, he continues to try, his plays one after another putting the most searching questions to a world that not only has few answers but is unwilling to sacrifice in a search for them.

Max Frisch was born in Zurich, Switzerland, in 1911. He studied at the University of Zurich but in 1933 was forced to leave for financial reasons and became a free-lance journalist. From his early youth Frisch had a compulsion to write. At the age of sixteen he sent off a play to the famous director Max Reinhardt in Berlin, hoping for encouragement; when the play was gently rejected, he simply shifted genres and turned to the novel. His first book, *Jüng Reinhart*, was published in 1934. It was not long before Frisch realized that journalism, from either an artistic or a financial point of view, was not an appropriate career for him; and when a wealthy friend offered to send him to architectural school, he accepted. Frisch became a serious and successful architect, but he did not allow his new profession to interfere with his writing. Following a dual career, he found, had benefits as well as hardships; and as long as he did his work well, his professional colleagues, he said wryly, did not hold his literary life against him.

Frisch had his first literary success with his novels and a journal that he kept while serving with the Swiss Army in the late 1930s: Guard duty on the Swiss border at a time when the surrounding nations were about to be at each other's throats was a remarkable stimulus to thought. Shortly after the end of World War II, Frisch became known as a dramatist. *Now They Sing Again* (*Nun singen sie wieder*), a surrealistic fantasy written as a requiem for the victims of Hitler's madness; *The Chinese Wall* (*Die chinesische Mauer*), another dramatic fantasy in which characters from history (Cleopatra, Napoleon) and literature (Don Quixote, Romeo and Juliet) meet in ancient China and discuss the atom bomb with a Man of Today; *When the War Was Over* (*Als der Krieg zu Ende war*), a grim play in "epic" style based on an anecdote of the war Frisch had heard on a visit to Berlin in 1947—these plays and others brought Frisch a major European reputation and sufficient income so that he was able to drop the practice of architecture and devote his energies to literature. International renown came with the novel *Stiller* (1954)—the English title is *I'm Not Stiller*—a philosophical novel probing the question of the individual's identity, and *Andorra* (1961), a play again about identity, about anti-Semitism, about the moral complacency that says, It can't happen here. *Andorra* had major success all over Europe, but for complex reasons was not well received in New York.

Frisch has been a continuously experimental writer. When asked on one occasion to name his favorite literary genre, he replied, "I am primarily interested in changing the medium." Not that he would go so far as some recent dramatic explorations in the United States, such as those of The Living Theatre, for example, that try to break down the distinction between actors and audience. Frisch thinks this a fatal misconception of the nature of theatre. "Any gesture that ignores the footlights," he writes, "loses some of its magic . . . and the playwright who altogether removes this barrier signs his own death warrant." Otherwise, however, no holds are barred in what Frisch calls his "dialectical wrestling match" with the dramatic. Bertolt Brecht, whom Frisch came to know well after the war, was a major influence in Frisch's theatrical technique as well as ideas; and Thornton Wilder, too, particularly in *The Skin of Our Teeth*, affected Frisch's work. It is possible to see both influences in *The Firebugs* (*Herr Biedermann und die Brandstifter*), the original idea for which was sketched in Frisch's diary in 1948. The idea was fleshed out into a radio play in 1953 and then expanded into a play for the theatre, first produced in Zurich in 1958.

Like many of the plays of Brecht, *The Firebugs* is a parable for our time. Although the original idea was apparently suggested by the Communist take-over in Czechoslovakia in 1948, the basic situation of the play is unhappily applicable to political and social crises endemic in our world, the ascension to power of Hitler being only the most obvious. Gottlieb Biedermann, who has made a fortune out of selling worthless hair tonic, and who has forced into suicide the employee who made his fortune possible, invites into his home two obvious thugs who quite openly intend to destroy him. The act is irrational: Why should this rich, "respectable" Biedermann (the name in German indicates a complacent Babbitt) thus solicit his own downfall? At the most obvious level, why doesn't he simply call the police? Willi, one of the thugs, understands very well: "Because he's guilty himself—that's why. Above a certain income every citizen is guilty one way or another." If Biedermann were to call the police, an inquiry might be made into a number of things; Biedermann might lose his hair tonic and any risk is preferable to that. Sepp and Willi have a fine instinct for vulnerability; they know that the last thing Biedermann can face is the truth. Though the two men are gangsters—engaging gangsters in their way—there is an unpleasant justice in the way they induce Biedermann to hand over the matches for his own destruction. When at the end Sepp calls Biedermann by the name EVERYMAN (the reference is to the medieval morality play of that name), the allegory is painfully clear.

But if the moral of *The Firebugs* is grim, the way it is presented is very funny indeed. Biedermann is a comic figure and the major mode of the play is comic, including the pontifications of the fire-brigade chorus. Frisch is nowhere more contemporary than in his disposition to represent a desperately hopeless social situation in comic, even burlesque, terms. One implication is that there are times when all one can do is laugh.

The version of *Herr Biedermann und die Brandstifter* printed here is an adaptation by Mordecai Gorelik; it does not include an Epilogue that Frisch composed for a performance in Frankfurt in 1959.

The Firebugs

Max Frisch

TRANSLATED BY MORDECAI GORELIK

CHARACTERS

GOTTLIEB BIEDERMANN
BABETTE, *his wife*
ANNA, *a maidservant*
SEPP SCHMITZ, *a wrestler*
WILLI EISENRING, *a waiter*

A POLICEMAN
A PH.D.
MRS. KNECHTLING
THE CHORUS OF FIREMEN

SCENE: *A simultaneous setting, showing the living room and the attic of* BIEDERMANN's *house.*
TIME: *Now.*

Scene One

The stage is dark; then a match flares, illuminating the face of GOTTLIEB BIEDERMANN. *He is lighting a cigar, and as the stage grows more visible he looks about him. He is surrounded by firemen wearing their helmets.*

BIEDERMANN.   You can't even light a cigar any more without thinking of houses on fire. . . . It's disgusting! [*He throws away the burning cigar and exits.*]

The firemen come forward in the manner of an antique CHORUS. *The town clock booms the quarter-hour.*

CHORUS.   Fellow citizens, we,
    Guardians of the city.

Watchers, listeners,
Friends of the friendly town.
LEADER.   Which pays our salaries.
CHORUS.   Uniformed, equipped,
We guard your homes,
Patrol your streets,
Vigilant, tranquil.
LEADER.   Resting from time to time,
But alert, unsleeping.
CHORUS.   Watching, listening,
Lest hidden danger
Come to light
Too late.

The clock strikes half-hour.

LEADER.   Much goes up in flames,
But not always
Because of fate.
CHORUS.   Call it fate, they tell you,
And ask no questions.
But mischief alone
Can destroy whole cities.
LEADER.   Stupidity alone——
CHORUS.   Stupidity, all-too-human——
LEADER.   Can undo our citizens,
Our all-too-mortal citizens.

The clock strikes three-quarters.

CHORUS.   Use your head;
A stitch in time saves nine.
LEADER.   Exactly.
CHORUS.   Just because it happened,
Don't put the blame on God,
Nor on our human nature,
Nor on our fruitful earth,
Nor on our radiant sun . . .
Just because it happened,
Must you call the damned thing Fate?

The clock strikes four-quarters.

LEADER.   Our watch begins.

The CHORUS *sits. The clock strikes nine o'clock.*

Scene Two

The Living Room. BIEDERMANN *is reading the paper and smoking a cigar.*
ANNA, *the maidservant, in a white apron, brings him a bottle of wine.*

ANNA.   Mr. Biedermann? [*No answer.*] Mr. Biedermann——

> BIEDERMANN *puts down his paper.*

BIEDERMANN.   They ought to hang them! I've said so all along! Another fire!
And always the same story: another peddler shoe-horning his way into
somebody's attic—another "harmless" peddler—— [*He picks up the bottle.*]
They ought to hang every one of them! [*He picks up the corkscrew.*]
ANNA.   He's still here, Mr. Biedermann. The peddler. He wants to talk to you.
BIEDERMANN.   I'm not in!
ANNA.   Yes, sir, I told him—an hour ago. He says he knows you. I can't throw
him out, Mr. Biedermann.
BIEDERMANN.   Why not?
ANNA.   He's too strong.
BIEDERMANN.   Let him come to the office tomorrow.
ANNA.   Yes sir. I told him three times. He says he's not interested. He doesn't
want any hair tonic.
BIEDERMANN.   What *does* he want?
ANNA.   Kindness, he says. Humanity.
BIEDERMANN [*sniffs at the cork*].   Tell him I'll throw him out myself if he
doesn't get going at once. [*He fills his glass carefully.*] Humanity! [*He
tastes the wine.*] Let him wait in the hall for me. If he's selling suspenders or
razor blades . . . I'm not inhuman, you know, Anna. But they mustn't come
into the house—I've told you that a hundred times! Even if we have three
vacant beds, it's out of the question! Anybody knows what this sort of thing
can lead to, these days——

> ANNA *is about to go, when* SCHMITZ *enters. He is athletic, in a costume rem-*
iniscent partly of the prison, partly of the circus; his arms are tattooed and there
are leather straps on his wrists. ANNA *edges out.* BIEDERMANN *sips his wine, un-*
aware of SCHMITZ, *who waits until he turns around.*

SCHMITZ.   Good evening. [BIEDERMANN *drops his cigar in surprise.*] Your cigar,
Mr. Biedermann. [*He picks up the cigar and hands it to* BIEDERMANN.]
BIEDERMANN.   Look here——
SCHMITZ.   Good evening.
BIEDERMANN.   What is this? I told the girl distinctly to have you wait in the
hall.
SCHMITZ.   My name is Schmitz.
BIEDERMANN.   Without even knocking!
SCHMITZ.   Sepp Schmitz. [*Silence*] Good evening.
BIEDERMANN.   What do you want?

SCHMITZ.   You needn't worry, Mr. Biedermann. I'm not a peddler.

BIEDERMANN.   No?

SCHMITZ.   I'm a wrestler. I mean I *used* to be.

BIEDERMANN.   And now?

SCHMITZ.   Unemployed. [*Pause.*] Don't worry, sir, I'm not looking for a job—
I'm fed up with wrestling. I came in here because it's raining hard outside.
[*Pause.*] It's warm in here. [*Pause.*] I hope I'm not intruding . . . [*Pause.*]

BIEDERMANN.   Cigar? [*He offers one.*]

SCHMITZ.   You know, it's awful, Mr. Biedermann—with a build like mine,
everybody gets scared. . . . Thank you. [BIEDERMANN *gives him a light.*]
Thank you. [*They stand there, smoking.*]

BIEDERMANN.   Get to the point.

SCHMITZ.   My name is Schmitz.

BIEDERMANN.   You've said that . . . Delighted.

SCHMITZ.   I have no place to sleep. [*He holds the cigar to his nose, enjoying the
aroma.*] No place to sleep.

BIEDERMANN.   Would you like—some bread?

SCHMITZ.   If that's all there is.

BIEDERMANN.   A glass of wine?

SCHMITZ.   Bread and wine . . . If it's no trouble, sir; if it's no trouble. [BIE-
DERMANN *goes to the door.*]

BIEDERMANN.   Anna! [*He comes back.*]

SCHMITZ.   The girl said you were going to throw me out personally, Mr. Biedermann, but I knew you didn't mean it. [ANNA *has entered.*]

BIEDERMANN.   Anna, bring another glass.

ANNA.   Yes sir.

BIEDERMANN.   And some bread.

SCHMITZ.   And if you don't mind, miss, a little butter. Some cheese or cold
cuts. Only don't go to any trouble. Some pickles, a tomato or something,
some mustard—whatever you have, miss.

ANNA.   Yes sir.

SCHMITZ.   If it's no trouble.

ANNA *exits.*

BIEDERMANN.   You told the girl you know me.

SCHMITZ.   That's right, sir.

BIEDERMANN.   How do you know me?

SCHMITZ.   I know you at your best, sir. Last night at the pub—you didn't see
me; I was sitting in the corner. The whole place liked the way you kept
banging the table.

BIEDERMANN.   What did I say?

SCHMITZ.   Exactly the right thing, Mr. Biedermann! [*He takes a puff at his
cigar.*] "They ought to hang them all! The sooner the better—the whole
bunch! All those firebugs!"

BIEDERMANN *offers him a chair.*

BIEDERMANN.   Sit down. [SCHMITZ *sits.*]

SCHMITZ.   This country needs men like you, sir.

BIEDERMANN.   I know, but——

SCHMITZ.   No buts, Mr. Biedermann, no buts. You're the old-time type of solid citizen. That's why your slant on things——

BIEDERMANN.   Certainly, but——

SCHMITZ.   That's why.

BIEDERMANN.   Why what?

SCHMITZ.   You have a conscience. Everybody in the pub could see that. A solid conscience.

BIEDERMANN.   Naturally, but——

SCHMITZ.   Mr. Biedermann, it's not natural at all. Not these days. In the circus, where I did my wrestling, for instance—before it burned down, the whole damned circus—our manager, for instance; you know what he told me? "Sepp," he says, "You know me. They can shove it. What do I need a conscience for?" Just like that! "What my animals need is a whip," he says. That's the sort of guy he is! "A conscience!" [*He sneers.*] "If anybody has a conscience, you can bet it's a bad one." [*Enjoying his cigar.*] God rest him!

BIEDERMANN.   Is he dead?

SCHMITZ.   Burned to a cinder, with everything he owned. [*A pendulum clock strikes nine.*]

BIEDERMANN.   I don't know what's keeping that girl so long.

SCHMITZ.   I've got time. [*Their eyes meet*] You haven't an empty bed in the house, Mr. Biedermann. The girl told me.

BIEDERMANN.   Why do you laugh?

SCHMITZ.   "Sorry, no empty bed." That's what they all say. . . . What's the result? Somebody like me, with no place to sleep—— Anyway I don't want a bed.

BIEDERMANN.   No?

SCHMITZ.   Oh, I'm used to sleeping on the floor. My father was a miner. I'm used to it. [*He puffs at his cigar.*] No apologies necessary, sir. You're not one of those birds who sounds off in public—when *you* say something I believe it. What are things coming to if people can't believe each other any more? Nothing but suspicion all over! Am I right? But *you* still believe in yourself and others. Right? You're about the only man left in this town who doesn't say right off that people like us are firebugs.

BIEDERMANN.   Here's an ash tray.

SCHMITZ   Or am I wrong? [*He taps the ash off his cigar carefully.*] People don't believe in God any more—they believe in the Fire Department.

BIEDERMANN.   What do you mean by that?

SCHMITZ.   Nothing but the truth.

ANNA *comes in with a tray.*

ANNA.   We have no cold cuts.

SCHMITZ.   This will do, miss, this will do fine. Only you forgot the mustard.

ANNA.   Excuse me.   [*Exits.*]

BIEDERMANN.   Eat. [*He fills the glasses.*]

SCHMITZ.   You don't get a reception like this every place you go, Mr. Biedermann, let me tell you! I've had some experiences! Somebody like me comes to the door—no necktie, no place to stay, hungry; "Sit down," they say, "have a seat"—and meanwhile they call the police. How do you like that? All I ask for is a place to sleep, that's all. A good wrestler who's wrestled all his life—and some bird who never wrestled at all grabs me by the collar! "What's this?" I ask myself. I turn around just to look, and first thing you know he's broken his shoulder! [*Picks up his glass.*] Prosit! [*They drink, and* SCHMITZ *starts eating.*]

BIEDERMANN.   That's how it goes, these days. You can't open a newspaper without reading about another arson case. The same old story: another peddler asking for a place to sleep, and next morning the house is in flames. I mean to say . . . well, frankly, I can understand a certain amount of distrust . . . [*Reaches for his newspaper.*] Look at this! [*He lays the paper next to* SCHMITZ's *plate.*]

SCHMITZ.   I saw it.

BIEDERMANN.   A whole district in flames. [*He gets up to show it to* SCHMITZ.] Just read that! [SCHMITZ *eats, reads, and drinks.*]

SCHMITZ.   Is this wine Beaujolais?

BIEDERMANN.   Yes.

SCHMITZ.   Could be a little warmer. [*He reads, over his plate.*] "Apparently the fire was planned and executed in the same way as the previous one." [*They exchange a glance.*]

BIEDERMANN.   Isn't that the limit?

SCHMITZ.   That's why I don't care to read newspapers. Always the same thing.

BIEDERMANN.   Yes, yes, naturally . . . But that's no answer to the problem, to stop reading the papers. After all, you have to know what you're up against.

SCHMITZ.   What for?

BIEDERMANN.   Why, because.

SCHMITZ.   It'll happen anyway, Mr. Biedermann, it'll happen anyway. [*He sniffs the sausage.*] God's will. [*He slices the sausage.*]

BIEDERMANN.   You think so?

ANNA *brings the mustard.*

SCHMITZ.   Thank you, miss, thank you.

ANNA.   Anything else you'd like?

SCHMITZ.   Not today. [ANNA *stops at the door.*] Mustard is my favorite dish. [*He squeezes mustard out of the tube.*]

BIEDERMANN.   How do you mean, God's will?

SCHMITZ.   God knows . . . [*He continues to eat with his eye on the paper.*] "Expert opinion is that apparently the fire was planned and executed in the same way as the previous one." [*He laughs shortly, and fills his glass.*]

ANNA.   Mr. Biedermann?

BIEDERMANN.   What is it now?

ANNA.   Mr. Knechtling would like to speak to you.

BIEDERMANN.   Knechtling? Now? Knechtling?

ANNA.   He says——

BIEDERMANN.   Out of the question.

ANNA.   He says he simply can't understand you.

BIEDERMANN.   Why must he understand me?

ANNA.   He has a sick wife and three children, he says——

BIEDERMANN.   Out of the question! [*He gets up impatiently.*] Mr. Knechtling. Mr. Knechtling! Let Mr. Knechtling leave me alone, dammit! Or let
him get a lawyer! Please—let him! I'm through for the day. . . . Mr.
Knechtling! All this to-do because I gave him his notice! Let him get a
lawyer, by all means! I'll get one, too. . . . Royalties on his invention! Let
him stick his head in the gas stove or get a lawyer! If Mr. Knechtling can
afford indulging in lawyers! Please—let him! [*Controlling himself, with a
glance at* SCHMITZ.] Tell Mr. Knechtling I have a visitor. [ANNA *exits.*]
Excuse me.

SCHMITZ.   This is your house, Mr. Biedermann.

BIEDERMANN.   How is the food? [*He sits, observing* SCHMITZ, *who attacks his
food with enthusiasm.*]

SCHMITZ.   Who'd have thought you could still find it, these days?

BIEDERMANN.   Mustard?

SCHMITZ.   Humanity! [*He screws the top of the mustard tube back on.*]
Here's what I mean: you don't grab me by the collar and throw me out in
the rain, Mr. Biedermann. *That's* what we need, Mr. Biedermann! Humanity! [*He pours himself a drink.*] God will reward you! [*He drinks with
gusto.*]

BIEDERMANN.   You mustn't think I'm inhuman, Mr. Schmitz.

SCHMITZ.   Mr. Biedermann!

BIEDERMANN.   That's what Mrs. Knechtling thinks.

SCHMITZ.   Would you be giving me a place to sleep tonight if you were inhuman?—Ridiculous!

BIEDERMANN.   Of course!

SCHMITZ.   Even if it's a bed in the attic. [*He puts down his glass.*] Now our
wine's the right temperature. [*The doorbell rings.*] Police?

BIEDERMANN.   My wife. [*The doorbell rings again.*] Come along, Mr. Schmitz.
. . . But mind you, no noise! My wife has a heart condition——

Women's voices are heard offstage. BIEDERMANN *motions to* SCHMITZ *to
hurry. They pick up the tray, bottles, and glasses and tiptoe toward stage right,
where the* CHORUS *is sitting.*

BIEDERMANN.   Excuse me! [*He steps over the bench.*]

SCHMITZ.   Excuse me! [*He steps over the bench. He and* BEIDERMANN *disappear.*]

BABETTE BIEDERMANN *enters, left, accompanied by* ANNA, *who takes her
packages.*

BABETTE.   Where's my husband?—You know, Anna, we're not narrow-minded,
and I don't mind your having a boy friend. But if you're going to park
him in the house——

ANNA.   But I don't have a boy friend, Mrs. Biedermann.

BABETTE.   Then whose rusty bicycle is that, outside the front door? It scared me to death!

The Attic. BIEDERMANN *switches on the light and gestures for* SCHMITZ *to come in. They speak in whispers.*

BIEDERMANN.   Here's the light switch. If you get cold, there's an old sheep-skin around here somewhere. Only for heaven's sake be quiet! Take off your shoes! [SCHMITZ *puts down the tray, takes off one shoe.*] Mr. Schmitz?

SCHMITZ.   Mr. Biedermann?

BIEDERMANN.   You promise me, though, you're not a firebug? [SCHMITZ *starts to laugh.*] Sh!! [*He nods good night and exits, closing the door.* SCHMITZ *takes off his other shoe.*]

The Living Room. BABETTE *has heard something; she listens, frightened. Then, relieved, she turns to the audience.*

BABETTE.   Gottlieb, my husband, promised to go up to the attic every evening, personally, to see if there is any firebug up there. I'm so thankful! Other-wise I'd lie awake half the night.   [BABETTE *exits.*]

The Attic. SCHMITZ, *now in his socks, goes to the light switch and snaps out the light.*

Below.

CHORUS.   Fellow citizens, we,
　　Shield of the innocent,
　　Guardians ever-tranquil,
　　Shield of the sleeping city.
　　Standing or
　　Sitting,
　　Ever on guard.

LEADER.   Taking a quiet smoke, now and again, to pass the time.

CHORUS.   Watching,
　　Listening,
　　Lest malignant fire leap out
　　Above these cozy rooftops
　　To undo our city.

The town clock strikes three.

LEADER.   Everyone knows we're here,
　　Ready on call. [*He fills his pipe.*]

CHORUS.   Who turns the light on at this wee, small hour?
　　Woe!
　　Nerve-shattered,

Uncomforted by sleep,
The wife appears.

BABETTE *enters in a bathrobe.*

BABETTE.   Somebody coughed! [*A snore.*] Gottlieb, did you hear that? [*A cough.*] Somebody's there! [*A snore.*] That's men for you! A sleeping pill is all they need!

The town clock strikes four.

LEADER.   Four o'clock. [BABETTE *turns off the light again.*]
      We were not called. [*He puts away his pipe. The stage lightens.*]
CHORUS.   O radiant sun!
      O godlike eye!
      Light up the day above our cozy roofs!
      Thanks be!
      No harm has come to our sleeping town.
      Not yet.
      Thanks be! [*The* CHORUS *sits.*]

Scene Three

The Living Room. BIEDERMANN, *his hat and coat on, his brief case under his arm, is drinking a cup of coffee standing up, and is speaking to* BABETTE, *who is offstage.*

BIEDERMANN.   For the last time—he's not a firebug!
BABETTE'S VOICE.   How do you know?
BIEDERMANN.   I asked him myself, point blank—— Can't you think of anything else in this world, Babette? You and your firebugs—you're enough to drive a man insane!

BABETTE *enters with the cream pitcher.*

BABETTE.   Don't yell at me.
BIEDERMANN.   I'm not yelling at you, Babette, I'm merely yelling. [*She pours cream into his cup.*] I have to go. [*He drinks his coffee. It's too hot.*] If everybody goes around thinking everybody else is an arsonist—— You've got to have a little trust in people, Babette, just a little! [*He looks at his watch.*]
BABETTE.   I don't agree. You're too good-hearted, Gottlieb. You listen to the promptings of your heart, but I'm the one who can't sleep all night. . . . I'll give him some breakfast and then I'll send him on his way, Gottlieb.
BIEDERMANN.   Do that.
BABETTE.   In a nice way, of course, without offending him.
BIEDERMANN.   Do that. [*He puts his cup down.*] I have to see my lawyer.

[*He gives* BABETTE *a perfunctory kiss. They do not notice* SCHMITZ, *who enters, the sheepskin around his shoulders.*]

BABETTE.   Why did you give Knechtling his notice?

BIEDERMANN.   I don't need him any more.

BABETTE.   But you were always so pleased with him!

BIEDERMANN.   That's just what he's presuming on, now! Royalties on his invention—that's what he wants! Invention! Our Hormotone hair tonic is merchandise, that's all—it's no invention! All those good folk who pour our tonic on their domes could use their own piss for all the good it does them!

BABETTE.   Gottlieb!

BIEDERMANN.   It's true, though. [*He checks to see if he has everything in his brief case.*] I'm too good-hearted—you're right. But I'll take care of this Knechtling! [*He is about to go when he sees* SCHMITZ.]

SCHMITZ.   Good morning, everybody.

BIEDERMANN.   Mr. Schmitz—— [SCHMITZ *offers his hand.*]

SCHMITZ.   Call me Sepp.

BIEDERMANN [*ignores his hand*].   My wife will speak with you, Mr. Schmitz. I have to go, I'm sorry. Good luck. . . . [*Changes his mind and shakes hands.*] Good luck, Sepp.   [BIEDERMANN *exits.*]

SCHMITZ.   Good luck, Gottlieb. [BABETTE *looks at him.*] That's your husband's name, isn't it—Gottlieb?

BABETTE.   How did you sleep?

SCHMITZ.   Thank you, madam—kind of freezing. But I made use of this sheepskin. Reminded me of old days in the mines. I'm used to the cold.

BABETTE.   Your breakfast is ready.

SCHMITZ.   Really, madam! [*She motions for him to sit.*] No, really, I—— [*She fills his cup.*]

BABETTE.   You must pitch in, Sepp. You have a long way to go, I'm sure.

BIEDERMANN.   Mr. Schmitz——[SCHMITZ *offers his hand.*]

SEPP.   How do you mean? [*She points to the chair again.*]

BABETTE.   Would you care for a soft-boiled egg?

SCHMITZ.   Two.

BABETTE.   Anna!

SCHMITZ.   I feel right at home, madam. [*He sits.*]

ANNA *enters.*

BABETTE.   Two soft-boiled eggs.

ANNA.   Yes, ma'am.

SCHMITZ.   Three and a half minutes.

ANNA *starts to leave.*

SCHMITZ.   Miss—— [ANNA *stops at the door.*] Good morning.

ANNA.   Morning.   [*She exits.*]

SCHMITZ.   The look she gave me! If it was up to her I'd still be out there in the pouring rain. [BABETTE *fills his cup.*]

BABETTE.   Mr. Schmitz——

SCHMITZ.   Yeah?

BABETTE.   If I may speak frankly——
SCHMITZ.   Your hands are shaking, madam.
BABETTE.   Mr. Schmitz——
SCHMITZ.   What's troubling you?
BABETTE.   Here's some cheese.
SCHMITZ.   Thank you.
BABETTE.   Marmalade.
SCHMITZ.   Thank you.
BABETTE.   Honey.
SCHMITZ.   One at a time, madam, one at a time. [*He leans back, eating his bread and butter; attentively.*] Well?
BABETTE.   Frankly, Mr. Schmitz——
SCHMITZ.   Just call me Sepp.
BABETTE.   Frankly——
SCHMITZ.   You'd like to get rid of me.
BABETTE.   No, Mr. Schmitz, no! I wouldn't put it that way——
SCHMITZ.   How would you put it? [*He takes some cheese.*] Tilsit cheese is my dish. [*He leans back, eating; attentively.*] Madam thinks I'm a firebug.
BABETTE.   Please don't misunderstand me. What did I say? The last thing I want to do is hurt your feelings, Mr. Schmitz. . . . You've got me all confused now. Who ever mentioned firebugs? Even your manners, Mr. Schmitz; I'm not complaining.
SCHMITZ.   I know. I have no manners.
BABETTE.   That's not it, Mr. Schmitz——
SCHMITZ.   I smack my lips when I eat.
BABETTE.   Nonsense.
SCHMITZ.   That's what they used to tell me at the orphanage: "Schmitz, don't smack your lips when you eat!" [BABETTE *is about to pour more coffee.*]
BABETTE.   You don't understand me. Really, you don't in the least! [SCHMITZ *places his hand over his cup.*]
SCHMITZ.   I'm going.
BABETTE.   Mr. Schmitz.
SCHMITZ.   I'm going.
BABETTE.   Another cup of coffee? [*He shakes his head.*] Half a cup? [*He shakes his head.*] You mustn't take it like that, Mr. Schmitz. I didn't mean to hurt your feelings. I didn't say a single word about you making noises while you eat. [*He gets up.*] Have I hurt your feelings? [*He folds his napkin.*]
SCHMITZ.   It's not your lookout, madam, if I have no manners. My father was a coal miner. Where would people like us get any manners? Starving and freezing, madam—that's something I don't mind; but no education, madam, no manners, madame, no refinement——
BABETTE.   I understand.
SCHMITZ.   I'm going.
BABETTE.   Where?
SCHMITZ.   Out in the rain.
BABETTE.   Oh, no!

SCHMITZ. I'm used to it.

BABETTE. Mr. Schmitz . . . don't look at me like that. Your father was a miner—I can understand it. You had an unfortunate childhood——

SCHMITZ. No childhood at all, madam. [*He looks down at his fingers.*] None at all. My mother died when I was seven. . . . [*He turns away to wipe his eyes.*]

BABETTE. Sepp!— But Sepp——

ANNA *brings the soft-boiled eggs.*

ANNA. Anything else you'd like? [*She gets no answer; exits.*]

BABETTE. I haven't ordered you to leave, Mr. Schmitz. I never said that. After all, what did I say? You misunderstand me, Mr. Schmitz. Really, I mean it—won't you believe me? [*She takes his sleeve—with some hesitation.*] Come, Sepp—finish eating! [SCHMITZ *sits down again.*] What do you take us for? I haven't even noticed that you smack your lips. Honestly! Even if I did—we don't care a bit about external things. We're not like that at all, Mr. Schmitz. . . . [*He cracks his egg.*]

SCHMITZ. God will reward you.

BABETTE. Here's the salt. [*He eats the egg with a spoon.*]

SCHMITZ. It's true, madam, you didn't order me away. You didn't say a word about it. That's true. Pardon me, madam, for not understanding.

BABETTE. Is the egg all right?

SCHMITZ. A little soft . . . Do pardon me, won't you? [*He has finished the egg.*] What were you going to say, madam, when you started to say, very frankly——

BABETTE. Well, I was going to say . . . [*He cracks the second egg.*] My friend Willi says you can't find it any more, he says. Private charity. No fine people left; everything State-controlled. No real people left, these days . . . he says. The world is going to the dogs—that's why! [*He salts his egg.*] Wouldn't he be surprised to get a breakfast like this! Wouldn't he open his eyes, my friend, Willi! [*The doorbell rings.*] That could be him. [*It rings again.*]

BABETTE. Who is Willi?

SCHMITZ. You'll see, madam. Willi's refined. Used to be a waiter at the Metropol. Before it burned down . . .

BABETTE. Burned down?

SCHMITZ. Headwaiter.

ANNA *enters.*

BABETTE. Who is it?

ANNA. A gentleman.

BABETTE. What does he want?

ANNA. From the fire insurance, he says. To look over the house. [BABETTE *gets up.*] He's wearing a frock coat——

SCHMITZ. My friend Willi!

CHORUS. Now two of them dismay us——

Two bicycles, both rusty.
To whom do they belong?
LEADER.   One yesterday's arrival.
One today's.
CHORUS.   Woe!
LEADER.   Night once again, and our watch.

The town clock strikes.

CHORUS.   How much the coward fears where nothing threatens!
Dreading his own shadow,
Whirling at each sound,
Until his fears overtake him
At his own bedside!

The town clock strikes.

LEADER.   They never leave their room, these two.
What is the reason?

The town clock strikes.

CHORUS.   Blind, ah, blind is the weakling!
Trembling, expectant of evil,
Yet hoping somehow to avoid it!
Defenseless!
Ah, weary of menacing evil,
With open arms he receives it!

The town clock strikes.

Woe! [*The* CHORUS *sits.*]

Scene Four

The Attic. SCHMITZ *is dressed as before.* EISENRING *has removed the jacket of his frock coat and is in a white vest and shirt sleeves. He and* SCHMITZ *are rolling tin barrels into a corner of the attic. The barrels are the type used for storing gasoline. Both vagabonds are in their socks and are working as quietly as they can.*

EISENRING.   Quiet! Quiet!
SCHMITZ.   Suppose he calls the police?
EISENRING.   Keep going.
SCHMITZ.   What then?
EISENRING.   Easy! Easy!

They roll the barrels up to those already stacked in the shadows. EISENRING *wipes his fingers with some cotton waste.*

EISENRING. Why would he call the police?
SCHMITZ. Why not?
EISENRING. Because he's guilty himself—that's why. [*He throws away the rag.*] Above a certain income every citizen is guilty one way or another. Have no fear. [*Doves are heard cooing.*] It's morning. Bedtime! [*There is a sudden knocking on the locked door.*]
BIEDERMANN'S VOICE. Open up! Open up, there! [*He pounds on the door and shakes it.*]
EISENRING. That's no call for breakfast.
BIEDERMANN'S VOICE. Open, I say! Immediately!
SCHMITZ. He was never like that before.

The banging on the door gets louder. Without haste, but briskly, EISENRING *puts on his jacket, straightens his tie and flicks the dust from his trousers. Then he opens the door.* BIEDERMANN *enters. He is in his bathrobe. He does not see* EISENRING, *who is now behind the open door.*

BIEDERMANN. Mr. Schmitz!
SCHMITZ. Good morning, sir. I hope this noise didn't wake you.
BIEDERMANN. Mr. Schmitz——
SCHMITZ. It won't happen again, I assure you.
BIEDERMANN. Leave this house! [*Pause.*] I say leave this house!
SCHMITZ. When?
BIEDERMANN. At once!
SCHMITZ. But——
BIEDERMANN. Or my wife will call the police. And I can't and won't stop her.
SCHMITZ. Hm . . .
BIEDERMANN. I said right away, and I mean it. What are you waiting for? [SCHMITZ *picks up his shoes.*] I'll have no discussion about it!
SCHMITZ. Did I say anything?
BIEDERMANN. If you think you can do as you like here because you're a wrestler—— A racket like that, all night—— [*Points to the door.*] Out, I say! Get out! [SCHMITZ *turns to* EISENRING.]
SCHMITZ. He was never like that before. . . . [BIEDERMANN *sees* EISENRING *and is speechless.*]
EISENRING. My name is Eisenring.
BIEDERMANN. What's the meaning of this?
EISENRING. Willi Maria Eisenring.
BIEDERMANN. Why are there two of you suddenly? [SCHMITZ *and* EISENRING *look at each other.*] Without even asking!
EISENRING. There, you see!
BIEDERMANN. What's going on here?

EISENRING [*to* SCHMITZ]. Didn't I tell you? Didn't I say it's no way to act, Sepp? Where are your manners? Without even asking! Suddenly two of us!

BIEDERMANN.   I'm beside myself!

EISENRING.   There, you see! [*He turns to* BIEDERMANN.] That's what I told him! [*Back to* SCHMITZ.] Didn't I?

SCHMITZ *hangs his head.*

BIEDERMANN.   Where do you think you are? Let's get one thing clear, gentlemen—I'm the owner of this house! I ask you—where do you think you are? [*Pause.*]

EISENRING.   Answer when the gentleman asks you something! [*Pause.*]

SCHMITZ.   Willi is a friend of mine. . . .

BIEDERMANN.   And so?

SCHMITZ.   We were schoolmates together.

BIEDERMANN.   And so?

SCHMITZ.   And so I thought . . .

BIEDERMANN.   What?

SCHMITZ.   I thought . . . [*Pause.*]

EISENRING.   You didn't think! [*He turns to* BIEDERMANN.] I understand fully, Mr. Biedermann. All you want to do is what's right—let's get that clear! [*He shouts at* SCHMITZ.] You think the owner of this house is going to be pushed around? [*He turns to* BIEDERMANN *again.*] Sepp didn't consult you at all?

BIEDERMANN.   Not a word!

EISENRING.   Sepp——

BIEDERMANN.   Not one word!

EISENRING [*to* SCHMITZ].   And then you're surprised when people throw you out in the street! [*He laughs contemptuously.*]

BIEDERMANN.   There's nothing to laugh at, gentlemen! I'm serious! My wife has a heart condition——

EISENRING.   There, you see!

BIEDERMANN.   She didn't sleep half the night because of your noise. And anyway, what are you doing here? [*He looks around.*] What the devil are these barrels doing here? [SCHMITZ *and* EISENRING *look hard where there are no barrels.*] If you don't mind—what are these? [*He raps on a barrel.*]

SCHMITZ.   Barrels . . .

BIEDERMANN.   Where did *they* come from?

SCHMITZ.   Do you know, Willi? Where they came from?

EISENRING.   It says "Imported" on the label.

BIEDERMANN.   Gentlemen——

EISENRING.   It says so on them somewhere! [EISENRING *and* SCHMITZ *look for a label.*]

BIEDERMANN.   I'm speechless! What do you think you're doing? My whole attic is full of barrels—floor to ceiling! All the way from floor to ceiling!

EISENRING.   I knew it! [EISENRING *swings around.*] Sepp had it figured all wrong. [*To* SCHMITZ.] Six by eight meters, you said. There's not twenty square meters in this attic—I couldn't leave my barrels in the street, Mr. Biedermann; you can understand that——

BIEDERMANN.   I don't understand a thing! [SCHMITZ *shows him a label.*]

SCHMITZ.   Here, Mr. Biedermann—here's the label.

BIEDERMANN.   I'm speechless.

SCHMITZ.   Here it says where they come from. Here.

BIEDERMANN.   Simply speechless. [*He inspects the label.*]

The Living Room. ANNA *leads a* POLICEMAN *in.*

ANNA.   I'll call him. What's it about, officer?

POLICEMAN.   Official business. [ANNA *exits. The* POLICEMAN *waits.*]

The Attic.

BIEDERMANN.   Is it true? Is it true?

EISENRING.   Is what true?

BIEDERMANN.   What's printed on this label? [*He shows them the label.*] What do you take me for? I've never in my life seen anything like this! Do you think I can't read? [*They look at the label.*] Just look! [*He laughs sarcastically.*] Gasoline! [*In the voice of a district attorney.*] What is in those barrels?

EISENRING.   Gasoline!

BIEDERMANN.   Never mind your jokes! I'm asking you for the last time— what's in those barrels? You know as well as I do—attics are no place for gasoline! [*He runs his finger over one of the barrels.*] If you don't mind— just smell that for yourselves! [*He waves a finger under their noses.*] Is that gasoline or isn't it? [*They sniff and exchange glances.*]

EISENRING.   It is.

SCHMITZ.   It is.

BOTH.   No doubt whatever.

BIEDERMANN.   Are you insane? My whole attic full of gasoline——

SCHMITZ.   That's just why we don't smoke up here, Mr. Biedermann.

BIEDERMANN.   What do you think you're doing? A thing like that—when every single newspaper is warning people to watch out for fires! My wife will have a heart attack!

EISENRING.   There, you see!

BIEDERMANN.   Don't keep saying, "There, you see!"

EISENRING.   You can't do that to a lady, Sepp. Not to a housewife. I know housewives. [ANNA *calls up the stairs.*]

ANNA.   Mr. Biedermann! Mr. Biedermann! [BIEDERMANN *shuts the door.*]

BIEDERMANN.   Mr. Schmitz! Mr.——

EISENRING.   Eisenring.

BIEDERMANN.   If you don't get these barrels out of the house this instant— and I mean this instant——

EISENRING.   You'll call the police.

BIEDERMANN.   Yes!

SCHMITZ.   There, you see! [ANNA *calls up the stairs.*]

ANNA.   Mr. Biedermann!

BIEDERMANN [*lowers his voice*].   That's my last word.

EISENRING.   Which word?

BIEDERMANN.   I won't stand for it! I won't stand for gasoline in my attic!

Once and for all! [*There is a knock at the door.*] I'm coming! [*He opens the door.*]

The POLICEMAN *enters.*

POLICEMAN.   Ah, there you are, Mr. Biedermann! You don't have to come down; I won't take much of your time.

BIEDERMANN.   Good morning!

POLICEMAN.   Good morning!

EISENRING.   Morning!

SCHMITZ.   Morning!

SCHMITZ *and* EISENRING *nod courteously.*

POLICEMAN.   There's been an accident.

BIEDERMANN.   Good Heavens!

POLICEMAN.   An elderly man. His wife says he used to work for you. . . . An inventor. Put his head inside his kitchen stove last night. [*He consults his notebook.*] Knechtling, Johann. Number 11 Rossgasse. [*He puts his notebook away.*] Did you know anybody by that name?

BIEDERMANN.   I——

POLICEMAN.   Maybe you'd rather we talked about this privately, Mr. Biedermann?

BIEDERMANN.   Yes.

POLICEMAN.   It doesn't concern these employees of yours.

BIEDERMANN.   No . . . [*He stops at the door.*] If anyone wants me, gentlemen, I'll be at the police station. I'll be right back.

SCHMITZ *and* EISENRING *nod.*

POLICEMAN.   Mr. Biedermann——

BIEDERMANN.   Let's go.

POLICEMAN.   What have you got in those barrels?

BIEDERMANN.   These?

POLICEMAN.   If I may ask?

BIEDERMANN.   . . . Hair tonic . . . [*He looks at* SCHMITZ *and* EISENRING.]

EISENRING.   Hormotone. Science's gift to the well-groomed.

SCHMITZ.   Try a bottle today.

EISENRING.   You won't regret it.

BOTH.   Hormotone. Hormotone. Hormotone. [*The* POLICEMAN *laughs.*]

BIEDERMANN.   Is he dead? [*He and the* POLICEMAN *exit.*]

EISENRING.   A real sweetheart!

SCHMITZ.   Didn't I tell you?

EISENRING.   But he didn't mention breakfast.

SCHMITZ.   He was never like that before. . . .

EISENRING [*reaching in his pocket*].   Have you got the detonator?

SCHMITZ [*feeling in his pocket*].   He was never like that before.

Downstairs.

CHORUS.   O radiant sun!
   O godlike eye!

Light up the day again above our cozy roofs!
LEADER.   Today same as yesterday.
CHORUS.   Hail!
LEADER.   No harm has come to our sleeping city.
CHORUS.   Hail!
LEADER.   Not yet . . .
CHORUS.   Hail!

Traffic noises offstage; honking, streetcars.

LEADER.   Wise is man,
  And able to ward off most perils,
  If, sharp of mind and alert,
  He heeds signs of coming disaster
  In time.
CHORUS.   And if he does not?
LEADER.   He, who
  Attentive to possible dangers,
  Studies his newspaper daily—
  Is daily, at breakfast, dismayed
  By distant tidings, whose meaning
  Is daily digested to spare him
  Fatigue of his own muddled brain work—
  Learning daily what's happened, afar—
  Can he so quickly discern
  What is happening under his roof?
  Things that are——
CHORUS.   Unpublished!
LEADER.   Disgraceful!
CHORUS.   Inglorious!
LEADER.   Real!
CHORUS.   Things not easy to face!
  For, if he——

The LEADER *interrupts with a gesture.*

LEADER.   He's coming.

The CHORUS *breaks formation.*

CHORUS.   No harm has come to the sleeping city.
  No harm yesterday or today.
  Ignoring all omens,
  The freshly shaven citizen
  Speeds to his office. . . .

Enter BIEDERMANN *in hat and coat, his brief case under his arm.*

BIEDERMANN.   Taxi! . . . Taxi! . . . Taxi! [*The* CHORUS *is in his way.*]
  What's the trouble?

CHORUS. Woe!

BIEDERMANN. What's up?

CHORUS. Woe!

BIEDERMANN. You've said that already!

CHORUS. Three times woe!

BIEDERMANN. But why?

LEADER. All-too-strangely a fiery prospect
Unfolds to our eyes.
And to yours.
Shall I be plainer?
Gasoline in your attic——

BIEDERMANN [*shouts*]. Is that *your* business? [*Silence.*] Let me through—I have to see my lawyer—— What do you want of me? I'm not guilty. . . . [*Unnerved.*] What's this—an inquisition? [*Masterfully.*] Let me through, please!

The CHORUS *remains motionless.*

CHORUS. Far be it from us, the Chorus,
To judge a hero of drama——

LEADER. But we *do* see the oncoming peril,
See clearly the menacing danger!

CHORUS. Making a simple inquiry
About an impending disaster—
Uttering, merely, a warning—
Civic-minded, the Chorus comes forward,
Bathed, alas, in cold sweat,
In half-fainting fear of that moment
That calls for the hoses of firemen!

BIEDERMANN *looks at his wrist watch.*

BIEDERMANN. I'm in a hurry.

CHORUS. Woe!

LEADER. All that gasoline, Gottlieb
Biedermann!
How could you take it?

BIEDERMANN. Take it?

LEADER. You know very well,
The world is a brand for the burning!
Yet, knowing it, what did you think?

BIEDERMANN. Think? [*He appraises the* CHORUS.] My dear sirs, I am a free and independent citizen. I can think anything I like. What are all these questions? I have the right, my dear sirs, not to think at all if I feel like it! Aside from the fact that whatever goes on under my own roof—— Let's get one thing clear, gentlemen: I am the owner of the house!

CHORUS. Sacred, sacred to us
Is property,
Whatever befall!
Though we be scorched,

Though we be cindered—
Sacred, sacred to us!

BIEDERMANN.   Well, then—— [*Silence.*] Why can't I go through? [*Silence.*]
Why must you always imagine the worst? Where will that get you? All I
want is some peace and quiet, not a thing more. . . . As for those two
gentlemen—aside from the fact that I have other troubles right now . . .
[BABETTE *enters in street clothes.*] What do *you* want here?

BABETTE.   Am I interrupting?

BIEDERMANN.   Can't you see I'm in conference? [BABETTE *nods to the* CHORUS,
then whispers in BIEDERMANN'S *ear.*] With ribbons, of course. Never mind
the cost. As long as it's a wreath. [BABETTE *nods to the* CHORUS.]

BABETTE.   Excuse me, sirs.   [*She exits.*]

BIEDERMANN.   To cut it short, gentlemen, I'm fed up! You and your firebugs! I don't even go to the pub any more—that's how fed up I am! Is there
nothing else to talk about these days? Let's get one thing straight—if you go
around thinking everybody except yourself is an arsonist, how are things
ever going to improve? A little trust in people, for heaven's sake. A little
good will! Why keep looking at the bad side? Why go on the assumption
that everybody else is a firebug? A little confidence, a little—— [*Pause.*]
You can't go on living in fear! [*Pause.*] You think I closed my eyes last
night for one instant? I'm not an imbecile, you know! Gasoline is gasoline!
I had the worst kind of thoughts running through my head last night. . . .
I climbed up on the table to listen—even got up on the bureau and put my
ear to the ceiling! They were snoring, mind you—snoring! At least four
times I climbed up on that bureau. Peacefully snoring! Just the same I got
as far as the stairs, once—believe it or not—in my pajamas—and frantic,
I tell you—frantic! I was all ready to wake up those two scoundrels and
throw them out in the street, along with their barrels. Single-handedly,
without compunction, in the middle of the night!

CHORUS.   Single-handedly?

BIEDERMANN.   Yes.

CHORUS.   Without compunction?

BIEDERMANN.   Yes.

CHORUS.   In the middle of the night?

BIEDERMANN.   Just about to! If my wife hadn't come after me, afraid I'd
catch cold—— [*Embarrassed, he reaches for a cigar.*]

LEADER.   How shall I put it?
Sleepless he passed the night.
That they'd take advantage of a man's good nature—
Was that conceivable?
Suspicion came over him. Why?

BIEDERMANN *lights his cigar.*

CHORUS.   No, it's not easy for the citizen,
Tough in business
But really soft of heart,
Always ready,
Ready always to do good.

LEADER.   If that's how he happens to feel.

CHORUS.   Hoping that goodness
   Will come of goodness.
   How mistaken can you be?

BIEDERMANN.   What are you getting at?

CHORUS.   It seems to us there's a stink of gasoline.

BIEDERMANN sniffs.

BIEDERMANN.   I don't smell anything.

CHORUS.   Woe to us!

BIEDERMANN.   Not a thing.

CHORUS.   Woe to us!

LEADER.   How soon he's got accustomed to bad smells!

CHORUS.   Woe to us!

BIEDERMANN.   And don't keep giving us that defeatism, gentlemen. Don't keep saying, "Woe to us!" [*A car honks offstage.*] Taxi!—Taxi! [*A car stops offstage.*] If you'll excuse me——   [*He hurries off.*]

CHORUS.   Citizen—where to?

The car drives off.

LEADER.   What is his recourse, poor wretch?
   Forceful, yet fearful,
   Milk-white of face,
   Fearful yet firm—
   Against what?

The car is heard honking.

CHORUS.   So soon accustomed to bad smells!

The car is heard distantly honking.

Woe to us!

LEADER.   Woe to you!

The CHORUS retires. All but the LEADER, who takes out his pipe.

He who dreads action
More than disaster,
How can he fight
When disaster impends?   [*He follows the CHORUS out.*]

Scene Five

The Attic. EISENRING is alone, unwinding cord from a reel and singing "Lily Marlene" while he works. He stops, wets his forefinger, and holds it up to the dormer window to test the wind.

The Living Room. BIEDERMANN *enters, cigar in mouth, followed by* BA-
BETTE. *He takes off his coat and throwns down his brief case.*

BIEDERMANN.   Do as I say.

BABETTE.   A goose?

BIEDERMANN.   A goose! [*He takes off his tie without removing his cigar.*]

BABETTE.   Why are you taking off your necktie, Gottlieb?

BIEDERMANN.   If I report those two guys to the police, I'll make them my
enemies. What good will that do me? Just one match and the whole house
is up in flames! What good will that do us? On the other hand, if I go up
there and invite them to dinner, why——

BABETTE.   Why, what?

BIEDERMANN.   Why, then we'll be friends. [*He takes off his jacket, hands it to*
BABETTE, *and exits.*]

BABETTE [*speaking to* ANNA, *offstage.*]   Just so you'll know Anna: you can't
get off this evening—we're having company. Set places for four.

The Attic. EISENRING *is singing "Lily Marlene." There is a knock at the
door.*

EISENRING.   Come in! [*He goes on singing. No one enters.*] Come in! [BIEDER-
MANN *enters in shirt sleeves, holding his cigar.*] Good day, Mr. Biedermann!

BIEDERMANN [*tactfully*].   May I come in?

EISENRING.   I hope you slept well last night?

BIEDERMANN.   Thank you—miserably.

EISENRING.   So did I. It's this wind. [*He goes on working with the reel.*]

BIEDERMANN.   If I'm not disturbing you——

EISENRING.   This is your house, Mr. Biedermann.

BIEDERMANN.   If I'm not in the way—— [*The cooing of doves is heard.*]
Where is our friend?

EISENRING.   Sepp? He went to work this morning. The lazy dog—he didn't
want to go without breakfast! I sent him out for some sawdust.

BIEDERMANN.   Sawdust?

EISENRING.   It helps spread the fire. [BIEDERMANN *laughs politely at what
sounds like a poor joke.*]

BIEDERMANN.   I came up to say, Mr. Eisenring——

EISENRING.   That you still want to kick us out?

BIEDERMANN.   In the middle of the night—I'm out of sleeping pills—it suddenly struck me: you folks have no toilet facilities up here.

EISENRING.   We have the roof gutter.

BIEDERMANN.   Well, just as you like, of course. It merely struck me you
might like to wash or take a shower—I kept thinking of that all night. . . .
You're very welcome to use my bathroom. I told Anna to hang up some
towels for you there. [EISENRING *shakes his head.*] Why do you shake your
head?

EISENRING.   Where on earth did he put it?

BIEDERMANN.   What?

EISENRING.   You haven't seen a detonator cap? [*He searches around.*] Don't trouble yourself, Mr. Biedermann. In jail, you know, we had no bathrooms either.

BIEDERMANN.   In jail?

EISENRING.   Didn't Sepp tell you I just came out of prison?

BIEDERMANN.   No.

EISENRING.   Not a word about it?

BIEDERMANN.   No.

EISENRING.   All he likes to talk about is himself. There *are* such people!—— Is it our fault, after all, if his youth was tragic? Did *you* have a tragic youth, Mr. Biedermann? *I* didn't. I could have gone to college; my father wanted me to be a lawyer. . . . [*He stands at the attic window murmuring to the doves.*] Grrr! Grrr! Grrr! [BIEDERMANN *relights his cigar.*]

BIEDERMANN.   Frankly, Mr. Eisenring, I couldn't sleep all night. Is there really gasoline in those barrels?

EISENRING.   You don't trust us.

BIEDERMANN.   I'm merely asking.

EISENRING.   Mr. Biedermann, what do you take us for? Frankly, what sort of people——

BIEDERMANN.   Mr. Eisenring, you mustn't think I have no sense of humor. Only your idea of a joke—well——

EISENRING.   That's something we've learned.

BIEDERMANN.   What is?

EISENRING.   A joke is good camouflage. Next best comes sentiment: like when Sepp talks about childhood in the coal mines, orphanages, circuses, and so forth. But the best camouflage of all—in my opinion—is the plain and simple truth. Because nobody ever believes it.

The Living Room. ANNA *shows in the* WIDOW KNECHTLING, *dressed in black.*

ANNA.   Take a seat, please. [*The* WIDOW *sits.*] But if you are Mrs. Knechtling, it's no use. Mr. Biedermann wants nothing to do with you, he said. [*The* WIDOW *gets up.*] Do sit down, please! [*The* WIDOW *sits down again.*] But don't get up any hopes.   [ANNA *exits.*]

The Attic. EISENRING *busies himself stringing out the fuse.* BIEDERMANN *is smoking.*

EISENRING.   I wonder what's keeping Sepp. Sawdust can't be so hard to find. I hope they haven't nabbed him.

BIEDERMANN.   Nabbed?

EISENRING.   Why do you smile?

BIEDERMANN.   When you use words like that, Mr. Eisenring, it's as though you came from another world. Nab him! Like another world! *Our* kind of people seldom get nabbed!

EISENRING. Because your kind of people seldom steal sawdust. That's obvious, Mr. Biedermann. That's the class difference.

BIEDERMANN. Nonsense!

EISENRING. You don't mean to say, Mr. Biedermann——

BIEDERMANN. I don't hold with class differences—you must have realized that by now, Mr. Eisenring. I'm not old-fashioned—just the opposite, in fact. And I regret that the lower classes still talk about class differences. Aren't we all of us—rich or poor—the creation of one Creator? The middle class, too. Are we not—you and I—human beings, made of flesh and blood? . . . I don't know, sir, whether you smoke cigars—— [*He offers one, but* EISENRING *shakes his head.*] I don't mean reducing people to a common level, understand me. There will always be rich and poor, thank heaven—but why can't we just shake hands? A little good will, for heaven's sake, a little idealism, a little—and we'd all have peace and quiet, both the poor and the rich. Don't you agree?

EISENRING. If I may speak frankly, Mr. Biedermann——

BIEDERMANN. Please do.

EISENRING. You won't take it amiss?

BIEDERMANN. The more frankly the better.

EISENRING. Frankly speaking, you oughtn't to smoke here. [BIEDERMANN, *startled, puts out his cigar.*] I can't make rules for you here, Mr. Biedermann. After all, it's your house. Still and all——

BIEDERMANN. Of course.

EISENRING [*looking down*]. There it is! [*He takes something off the floor and blows it clean before attaching it to the fuse. He starts whistling "Lily Marlene."*]

BIEDERMANN. Tell me, Mr. Eisenring, what is that you're doing? If I may ask? What is that thing?

EISENRING. A detonator.

BIEDERMANN. A ——?

EISENRING. And this is a fuse.

BIEDERMANN. A ——?

EISENRING. Sepp says they've developed better ones lately. But they're not for sale to the public. Anyway buying them's out of the question for us. Anything that has to do with war is frightfully expensive. Always the best quality . . .

BIEDERMANN. A fuse, you say?

EISENRING. A time fuse. [*He hands* BIEDERMANN *one end of the cord.*] If you'd be kind enough, Mr. Biedermann, to hold this end—— [BIEDERMANN *holds it for him.*]

BIEDERMANN. All joking aside, my friend——

EISENRING. One second—— [*He whistles "Lily Marlene," measuring the fuse.*] Thank you, Mr. Biedermann. [BIEDERMANN *suddenly laughs.*]

BIEDERMANN. Ha, ha! You can't put a scare into me, Willi! Though I must say, you do count on people's sense of humor. The way you talk, I can understand your getting arrested now and then. You know, not everybody has my sense of humor!

EISENRING.   You have to find the right man.

BIEDERMANN.   At the pub, for instance—just say you believe in the natural goodness of man, and they have you marked down.

EISENRING.   Ha! [*He puts down the fuse.*] Those who have no sense of humor get what's coming to them just the same when the time comes—so don't let *that* worry you. [BIEDERMANN *sits down on a barrel. He has broken into a sweat.*] What's the trouble, Mr. Biedermann? You've gone quite pale. [*He claps him on the shoulder.*] It's the smell. I know, if you're not used to it . . . I'll open the window for you, too. [*He opens the door.*]

BIEDERMANN.   Thanks . . . [ANNA *calls up the stairs.*]

ANNA'S VOICE.   Mr. Biedermann! Mr. Biedermann!

EISENRING.   The police again? It's a Police State!

ANNA'S VOICE.   Mr. Biedermann——

BIEDERMANN.   I'm coming! [*They both whisper from here on.*] Mr. Eisenring, do you like goose?

EISENRING.   Goose?

BIEDERMANN.   Roast goose.

EISENRING.   Why?

BIEDERMANN.   Stuffed with chestnuts?

EISENRING.   And red cabbage?

BIEDERMANN.   Yes . . . I was going to say: my wife and I—I, especially— if we may have the pleasure . . . I don't mean to intrude, Mr. Eisenring, but if you'd care to join us at a little supper, you and Sepp——

EISENRING.   Today?

BIEDERMANN.   Or tomorrow, if you prefer——

EISENRING.   We probably won't stay until tomorrow. But today—of course, Mr. Biedermann, with pleasure.

BIEDERMANN.   Shall we say seven o'clock? [*They shake hands.* BIEDERMANN *at the door.*] Is it a date? [*He nods genially, then stares once more at the barrels and the fuse.*]

EISENRING.   It's a date.

BIEDERMANN *exits.* EISENRING *goes to work again, whistling. The* CHORUS *enters below as if for the end of the scene. They are interrupted by the sound of of a crash, of something falling in the attic.*

EISENRING.   You can come out, Professor. [*A* PH.D., *wearing horn-rimmed glasses, crawls out from behind the barrels.*] You heard: we're invited to dinner, Sepp and me. You'll keep an eye on things. Nobody's to come in here and smoke, understand? Not before we're ready. [*The* PH.D. *polishes his glasses.*] I often ask myself, Professor, why in hell you hang around with us. You don't enjoy a good-crackling fire, or flames, or sparks. Or sirens that go off too late—or dogs barking—or people shrieking—or smoke. Or ashes . . . [*The* PH.D. *solemnly adjusts his glasses.* EISENRING *laughs.*] Do-gooder! [*He whistles gently to himself, surveying the professor.*] I don't like you eggheads—I've told you that before, Professor. You get no real fun out of anything. You're all so idealistic, so solemn. . . .

Until you're ready to betray. That's no fun either, Professor. [*He goes back to his work, whistling.*]

Downstairs.

CHORUS. Ready for action,
Axes and fire hose;
Polished and oiled,
Every brass fitting.
Every man of us tested and ready.
LEADER. We'll be facing a high wind.
CHORUS. Every man of us tested and ready.
Our brass fire pump
Polished and oiled,
Tested for pressure.
LEADER. And the fire hydrants?
CHORUS. Everything ready.
LEADER. Tested and ready for action.

Enter BABETTE *with a goose, and the* PH.D.

BABETTE. Yes, Professor, I know, but my husband . . . Yes, I understand it's urgent, Professor. I'll tell him—— [*She leaves the professor and comes to the footlights.*] My husband ordered a goose. See, this is it. And I have to roast it, so we can be friends with those people upstairs. [*Churchbells ring.*] It's Saturday night—you can hear the bells ringing. I have an odd feeling, somehow, that it may be the last time we'll hear them. [BIEDERMANN *calls*, "Babette!"] I don't know, ladies, if Gottlieb is always right. . . . You know what he says? "Certainly they're scoundrels, Babette, but if I make enemies of them, it's goodbye to our hair tonic!" [BIEDERMANN *calls*, "Babette!"] Gottlieb's like that. Good-hearted. Always too good-hearted! [*She exits with the goose.*]
CHORUS. This son of good family,
A wearer of glasses,
Pale, studious, trusting,
But trusting no longer
In power of goodness,
Will do anything now, for
Ends justify means.
(So he hopes.)
Ah, honest-dishonest!
Now wiping his glasses
To see things more clearly,
He sees no barrels—
No gasoline barrels!
Its an idea he sees—
An abstract conception—
Until it explodes!
PH.D. Good evening . . .

LEADER.   To the pumps!
  The ladders!
  The engines!

The firemen rush to their posts.

LEADER.   Good evening. [*To the audience, as shouts of* "Ready!" *echo through the theatre.*]
  We're ready.

Scene Six

The Living Room. The WIDOW KNECHTLING *is still there waiting. Outside, the bells are ringing loudly.* ANNA *is setting the table.* BIEDERMANN *brings in two chairs.*

BIEDERMANN.   You can see, can't you, Mrs. Knechtling? I haven't time now—no time to think about the dead. . . . I told you, go see my lawyer. [*The* WIDOW KNECHTLING *leaves.*] You can't hear yourself think, with that noise. Close the window. [ANNA *shuts the window. The sound of the bells is fainter.*] I said a simple, informal dinner. What are those idiotic candelabra for?

ANNA.   But, Mr. Biedermann, we always have those!

BIEDERMANN.   I said simple, informal—no ostentation. Fingerbowls! Knife-rests! Nothing but crystal and silver! What are you trying to do? [*He picks up the knife-rests and shoves them into his pants pocket.*] Can't you see I'm wearing my oldest jacket? And you . . . leave the carving knife, Anna—we'll need it; but away with the rest of this silver! Those two gentlemen must feel at home!—— Where's the corkscrew?

ANNA.   Here.

BIEDERMANN.   Don't we have anything simpler?

ANNA.   In the kitchen. But that one is rusty.

BIEDERMANN.   Bring it here. [*He takes a silver ice bucket off the table.*] What's this for?

ANNA.   For the wine.

BIEDERMANN.   Silver! [*He glares at the bucket, then at* ANNA.] Do we always use that, too?

ANNA.   We're going to need it, Mr. Biedermann.

BIEDERMANN.   Humanity, brotherhood—that's what we need here! Away with that thing! And what are those, will you tell me?

ANNA.   Napkins.

BIEDERMANN.   Damask napkins!

ANNA.   We don't have any others. [BIEDERMANN *shoves the napkins into the silver bucket.*]

BIEDERMANN.   There are whole nations, Anna, that live without napkins!

[BABETTE *enters with a large wreath.* BIEDERMANN, *standing in front of the table, does not see her come in.*] And why a cloth on the table?

BABETTE.   Gottlieb?

BIEDERMANN.   Let's have no class distinctions! [*He sees* BABETTE.] What is that wreath?

BABETTE.   It's what we ordered—— Gottlieb, what do you think? They sent the wreath here by mistake! And I gave them the address myself—Knechtling's address—I wrote it down, even! And the ribbon and everything—they've got it all backward!

BIEDERMANN.   What's wrong with the ribbon?

BABETTE.   And the clerk says they sent the bill to Mrs. Knechtling! [*She shows him the ribbon.*] "To Our Dear, Departed Gottlieb Biedermann." [*He considers the ribbon.*]

BIEDERMANN.   We won't accept it, that's all! I should say not! They've got to exchange it! [*He goes back to the table.*] Don't upset me, will you Babette? I can't think of everything——

BABETTE exits.

BIEDERMANN.   Take the tablecloth away. Help me, Anna. And remember—no serving! You come in and put the pan on the table.

ANNA.   The roasting pan? [*He takes off the tablecloth.*]

BIEDERMANN.   That's better! Just a bare table, for a plain and simple supper. [*He hands* ANNA *the tablecloth.*]

ANNA.   You mean that, Mr. Biedermann—just bring in the goose in the pan? [*She folds up the tablecloth.*] What wine shall I bring?

BIEDERMANN.   I'll get it myself.

ANNA.   Mr. Biedermann!

BIEDERMANN.   What now?

ANNA.   I don't have any sweater, sir—any old sweater, as if I belonged to the family.

BIEDERMANN.   Borrow one of my wife's.

ANNA.   The yellow or the red one?

BIEDERMANN.   Don't make a fuss! No apron or cap, understand? And get rid of these candelabra. And make sure especially, Anna, that everything's not so neat!—I'll be in the cellar.   [BIEDERMANN *exits.*]

ANNA.   "Make sure especially, Anna, that everything's not so neat!" [*She throws the tablecloth down on the floor and stomps on it with both feet.*] How's that?

SCHMITZ and EISENRING *enter, each holding a rose.*

BOTH.   Good evening, miss.

ANNA exits without looking at them.

EISENRING.   Why no sawdust?

SCHMITZ.   Confiscated. Police measure. Precaution. They're picking up anybody who sells or owns sawdust without written permission. Precautions all over the place. [*He combs his hair.*]

EISENRING.   Have you got matches?

SCHMITZ.   No.

EISENRING.   Neither have I. [SCHMITZ *blows his comb clean.*]

SCHMITZ.   We'll have to ask him for them.

EISENRING.   Biedermann?

SCHMITZ.   Don't forget. [*He puts away his comb and sniffs.*] Mmm! That smells good!

Scene Seven

BIEDERMANN *comes to the foolights with a bottle.*

BIEDERMANN.   You can think what you like about me, gentlemen. But just answer one question—— [*Laughter and loud voices offstage.*] I say to my-self: as long as they're laughing and drinking, we're safe. The best bottles out of my cellar! I tell you, if anybody had told me a week ago . . . When did *you* guess they were arsonists, gentlemen? This sort of thing doesn't happen the way you think. It comes on you slowly—slowly, at first—then sudden suspicion! Though I was suspicious at once—one's always suspicious! But tell me the truth, sirs—what would *you* have done? If you were in my place, for God's sake? And when? *When* would you have done it? At what point? [*He waits for an answer. Silence.*] I must go back up. [*He leaves the stage quickly.*]

Scene Eight

The Living Room. The dinner is in full swing. Laughter. BIEDERMANN, *es-pecially, cannot contain himself at the joke he's just heard. Only* BABETTE *is not laughing.*

BIEDERMANN.   Oil waste! Did you hear that, Babette? Oil waste, he says! Oil waste burns better!

BABETTE.   I don't see what's funny.

BIEDERMANN.   Oil waste! You know what that is?

BABETTE.   Yes.

BIEDERMANN.   You have no sense of humor, Babette. [*He puts the bottle on the table.*]

BABETTE.   All right, then, explain it.

BIEDERMANN.   Okay!—— This morning Willi told Sepp to go out and steal some sawdust. Sawdust—get it? And just now, when I asked Sepp if he got any, he said he couldn't find any sawdust—he found some oil waste instead. Get it? And Willi says, "Oil waste burns better!"

BABETTE.   I understood all that.

BIEDERMANN.   You did?

BABETTE.   What's funny about it? [BIEDERMANN *gives up.*]

BIEDERMANN.   Let's drink, men! [BIEDERMANN *removes the cork from the bottle.*]

BABETTE.   Is that the truth, Mr. Schmitz? Did you bring oil waste up to our attic?

BIEDERMANN.   This will kill you, Babette! This morning we even measured the fuse together, Willi and I!

BABETTE.   The fuse?

BIEDERMANN.   The time fuse. [*He fills the glasses.*]

BABETTE.   Seriously—what does that mean? [BIEDERMANN *laughs.*]

BIEDERMANN.   Seriously! You hear that? Seriously! . . . Don't let them kid you, Babette. I told you—our friends have their own way of kidding! Different company, different jokes—that's what I always say. . . . All we need now is to have them ask me for matches! [SCHMITZ *and* EISENRING *exchange glances.*] These gentlemen took me for some Milquetoast, for some dope without humor—— [*He lifts his glass.*] Prosit!

EISENRING.   *Prosit!*

SCHMITZ.   *Prosit!*

BIEDERMANN.   To our friendship! [*They drink the toast standing up, then sit down again.*] We're not doing any serving. Just help yourselves, gentlemen.

SCHMITZ.   I can't eat any more.

EISENRING.   Don't restrain yourself, Sepp, you're not at the orphanage. [*He helps himself to more goose.*] Your goose is wonderful, madam.

BABETTE.   I'm glad to hear it.

EISENRING.   Roast goose and stuffing! Now all we need is a tablecloth.

BABETTE.   You hear that, Gottlieb?

EISENRING.   We don't have to have one. But one of those tablecloths, white damask, with silverware on it——

BIEDERMANN [*loudly*].   Anna!

EISENRING.   Damask, with flowers all over it—a white flower pattern—we don't have to have one. We didn't have any in prison.

BABETTE.   In prison?

BIEDERMANN.   Where is that girl?

BABETTE.   Have you been in prison?

ANNA *enters. She is wearing a bright red sweater.*

BIEDERMANN.   A tablecloth here—immediately!

ANNA.   Yes sir.

BIEDERMANN.   And if you have some fingerbowls or something——

ANNA.   Yes sir.

EISENRING.   Madam, you may think it's childish, but that's how the little man is. Take Sepp, for instance—he grew up in the coal mines, but it's the dream of his miserable life, a table like this, with crystal and silver! Would you believe it? He never heard of a knife-rest!

BABETTE.   But, Gottlieb, we have all those things!

EISENRING.   Of course we don't *have* to have them here——

ANNA.   Very well.

EISENRING.   If you have napkins, miss, out with them!

ANNA.   But Mr. Biedermann said——

BIEDERMANN.   Out with them!

ANNA.   Yes sir. [*She starts to bring back the table service.*]

EISENRING.   I hope you won't take it amiss, madam, but when you're just out of prison—months at a time with no refinement whatever—— [*He shows the tablecloth to* SCHMITZ.] You know what this is? [*To* BABETTE.] He never saw one before! [*He turns back to* SCHMITZ.] This is damask!

SCHMITZ.   What do you want me to do with it? [EISENRING *ties the tablecloth around* SCHMITZ's *neck.*]

EISENRING.   There—— [BIEDERMANN *tries to find this amusing. He laughs.*]

BABETTE.   Where are the knife-rests, Anna?

ANNA.   Mr. Biedermann——

BIEDERMANN.   Out with them!

ANNA.   But you said "Take them away!" before!

BIEDERMANN.   Bring them here, I tell you! Where are they, goddammit?

ANNA.   In your pants pocket. [BIEDERMANN *reaches in his pants pocket and finds them.*]

EISENRING.   Don't get excited.

ANNA.   I can't help it!

EISENRING.   No excitement, now miss—— [ANNA *bursts into sobs and runs out.*]

EISENRING.   It's this wind. [*Pause.*]

BIEDERMANN.   Drink up, friends! [*They drink. A silence.*]

EISENRING.   I ate roast goose every day when I was a waiter. I used to flit down those corridors holding a platter like this. . . . How do you suppose, madam, waiters clean off their hands? In their hair, that's how—while there's others who use crystal fingerbowls. That's something I'll never forget. [*He dips his fingers in the fingerbowl.*] Have you ever heard of a trauma?

BIEDERMANN.   No.

EISENRING.   I learned all about it in jail. [*He wipes his fingers dry.*]

BABETTE.   And how did you happen to be there, Mr. Eisenring?

BIEDERMANN.   Babette!

EISENRING.   How did I get into jail?

BIEDERMANN.   One doesn't ask questions like that!

EISENRING.   I wonder at that myself. . . . I was a waiter—a little headwaiter. Suddenly they made me out a great arsonist.

BIEDERMANN.   Hm.

EISENRING.   They called for me at my own home.

BIEDERMANN.   Hm.

EISENRING.   I was so amazed, I played along.

BIEDERMANN.   Hm.

EISENRING.   I had luck, madam—seven really charming policemen. I said, "I have no time—I have to go to work." They answered, "Your restaurant's burned to the ground."

BIEDERMANN.   Burned to the ground?

EISENRING. Overnight, apparently.

BABETTE. Burned to the ground?

EISENRING. "Fine," I said. "Then I *have* time. . . ." Just a black, smoking hulk—that's all that was left of that place. I saw it as we drove by. Through those windows, you know, the little barred windows they have in those prison vans—— [*He sips his wine delicately.*]

BIEDERMANN. And then? [EISENRING *studies the wine label.*]

EISENRING. We used to keep this, too: '49, Cave de l'Echanon . . . And then? Let Sepp tell you the rest—— As I was sitting in that police station, playing with my handcuffs, who do you think they brought in?—— That one, there! [SCHMITZ *beams.*] Prosit, Sepp!

SCHMITZ. Prosit, Willi! [*They drink.*]

BIEDERMANN. And then?

SCHMITZ. "Are you a firebug?" they asked him, and offered him cigarettes. He said, "Excuse me, I have no matches, Mr. Commissioner, although you think I'm a firebug——" [*They laugh uproariously and slap each other's thighs.*]

BIEDERMANN. Hm.

ANNA *enters, in cap and apron again. She hands* BIEDERMANN *a visiting card.*

ANNA. It's urgent, he says.

BIEDERMANN. When I have visitors—— [SCHMITZ *and* EISENRING *clink glasses again.*]

SCHMITZ. Prosit, Willi!

EISENRING. Prosit, Sepp! [*They drink.* BIEDERMANN *studies the visiting card.*]

BABETTE. Who is it, Gottlieb?

BIEDERMANN. It's some Ph.D. . . . [ANNA *is busy at the sideboard.*]

EISENRING. And what are those other things, miss—those silver things?

ANNA. The candlesticks?

EISENRING. Why do you hide them?

BIEDERMANN. Bring them here!

ANNA. But you said, yourself, Mr. Biedermann——

BIEDERMANN. I say bring them here! [ANNA *places the candelabra on the table.*]

EISENRING. What do you say to that, Sepp? They have candlesticks and they hide them! Real silver candlesticks—what more do you want?—— Have you a match? [*He reaches into his pants pocket.*]

SCHMITZ. Me? No. [*He reaches into his pants pocket.*]

EISENRING. Sorry, no matches, Mr. Biedermann.

BIEDERMANN. I have some.

EISENRING. Let's have them.

BIEDERMANN. I'll light the candles. Let me—I'll do it. [*He begins lighting the candles.*]

BABETTE [*to* ANNA]. What does the visitor want?

ANNA. I don't know, ma'am. He says he can no longer be silent. And he's waiting on the stoop.

BABETTE. It's private, he says?

ANNA. Yes ma'am. He says he wants to expose something.

BABETTE. Expose something?!

ANNA. That's what he keeps saying. I don't understand him. He wants to dissociate himself, he says. . . . [BIEDERMANN *is still lighting candles.*]

EISENRING. It creates an atmosphere, doesn't it, madam? Candlelight, I mean.

BABETTE. Yes, it does.

EISENRING. I'm all for atmosphere. Refined, candlelight atmosphere——

BIEDERMANN. I'm happy to know that. [*All the candles are lit.*]

EISENRING. Schmitz, don't smack your lips when you eat! [BABETTE *takes* EISENRING *aside.*]

BABETTE. Let him alone!

EISENRING. He has no manners, madam. Excuse me—it's awful. But where could he have picked up any manners? From the coal mines to the orphanage——

BABETTE. I know.

EISENRING. From the orphanage to the circus.

BABETTE. I know.

EISENRING. From the circus to the theatre——

BABETTE. I didn't know.

EISENRING. A football of fate, madam. [BABETTE *turns to* SCHMITZ.]

BABETTE. In the theatre! Were you, really? [SCHMITZ *gnaws on a drumstick and nods.*] Where?

SCHMITZ. Upstage.

EISENRING. Really talented, too! Sepp as a ghost! Can you imagine it?

SCHMITZ. Not any more, though.

EISENRING. Why not?

SCHMITZ. I was in the theatre only a week, madam, before it burned to the ground.

BABETTE. Burned to the ground?

EISENRING [*to* SCHMITZ]. Don't be diffident!

BIEDERMANN. Burned to the ground?

EISENRING. Don't be so diffident! [*He unties the tablecloth* SCHMITZ *has been wearing and throws it over* SCHMITZ's *head.*] Come on! [SCHMITZ *gets up with the tablecloth over him.*] Doesn't he look like a ghost?

ANNA. I'm frightened!

EISENRING. Come here, little girl! [*He pulls* ANNA *onto his lap. She hides her face in her hands.*]

SCHMITZ. Who calleth?

EISENRING. That's theatre language, madam. They call that a cue. He learned it in less than a week, before the theatre burned down.

BABETTE. Please don't keep talking of fires!

SCHMITZ. Who calleth?

EISENRING. Ready—— [*Everybody waits expectantly.* EISENRING *has a tight grip on* ANNA.]

SCHMITZ. EVERYMAN! EVERYMAN!

BABETTE. Gottlieb?

BIEDERMANN. Quiet!

BABETTE. We saw that in Salzburg!

SCHMITZ. BIEDERMANN! BIEDERMANN!

EISENRING. He's terrific!

SCHMITZ. BIEDERMANN! BIEDERMANN!

EISENRING. You must say, "Who are you?"

BIEDERMANN. Me?

EISENRING. Or he can't say his lines.

SCHMITZ. EVERYMAN! BIEDERMANN!

BIEDERMANN. All right, then—who am I?

BABETTE. No! You must ask him who *he* is.

BIEDERMANN. I see.

SCHMITZ. DOST THOU HEAR ME?

EISENRING. No, no, Sepp—start it again. [*They change their positions.*]

SCHMITZ. EVERYMAN! BIEDERMANN!

BABETTE. Are you the Angel of Death, maybe?

BIEDERMANN. Nonsense!

BABETTE. What else *could* he be?

BIEDERMANN. Ask him. He might be the ghost in *Hamlet*. Or that other one—what's-his-name—in *Macbeth*.

SCHMITZ. WHO CALLS ME?

EISENRING. Go on.

SCHMITZ. GOTTLIEB BIEDERMANN!

BABETTE. Go ahead, ask him. He's talking to you.

SCHMITZ. DOST THOU HEAR ME?

BIEDERMANN. Who are you?

SCHMITZ. I AM THE GHOST OF—KNECHTLING. [*He throws the tablecloth over* BIEDERMANN. BABETTE *jumps up with a scream.*]

EISENRING. Stop! [*He pulls the tablecloth off* BIEDERMANN.] Idiot! How could you do such a thing? Knechtling was buried today!

SCHMITZ. That's why I thought of him. [BABETTE *hides her face in her hands.*]

EISENRING. He's not Knechtling, madam. [*He shakes his head over* SCHMITZ.] What crudeness!

SCHMITZ. He was on my mind.

EISENRING. Of all things—Knechtling! Mr. Biedermann's best old employee! Imagine it: buried today—cold and stiff—not yet moldy—pale as this tablecloth—white and shiny as damask—— To go and act Knechtling—— [*He takes* BABETTE *by the shoulder.*] Honest to God, madam, it's Sepp—it's not Knechtling at all. [SCHMITZ *wipes off his sweat.*]

SCHMITZ. I'm sorry. . . .

BIEDERMANN. Let's sit down again.

ANNA. Is it over?

BIEDERMANN. Would you care for cigars, sirs? [*He offers a box of cigars.*]

EISENRING [*to* SCHMITZ]. Idiot! You see how Mr. Biedermann is shaking! . . . Thank you, Mr. Biedermann!—— You think that's funny, Sepp? When you know very well that Knechtling put his head inside the gas stove? After everything Gottlieb did for him? He gave this Knechtling a job for fourteen years—and this is his thanks!

BIEDERMANN. Let's not talk about it.

EISENRING [*to* SCHMITZ]. And that's your thanks for the goose! [*They attend to their cigars.*]

SCHMITZ. Would you like me to sing something?

EISENRING. What?

SCHMITZ. "Fox, you stole that lovely goosie . . . [*He sings loudly.*]
Fox, you stole that lovely goosie,
Give it back again!"

EISENRING. That's enough.

SCHMITZ. "Give it back again!
Or they'll get you in the shnoosie———"

EISENRING. He's drunk.

SCHMITZ. "With their shooting gun!"

EISENRING. Pay no attention to him.

SCHMITZ. "Give it back again!
Or they'll get you in the shnoosie
With their shooting gun!"

BIEDERMANN. "Shooting gun!" That's good!

THE MEN *all join in the song.*

THE MEN. "Fox, you stole that lovely goosie . . ."

They harmonize, now loudly, now softly. Laughter and loud cheer. There is a pause, and BIEDERMANN *picks up again, leading the hilarity until they've all had it.*

BIEDERMANN. So—— Prosit! [*They raise their glasses. Fire sirens are heard nearby.*] What was that?

EISENRING. Sirens.

BIEDERMANN. Joking aside——

BABETTE. Firebugs! Firebugs!

BIEDERMANN. Don't yell like that!

BABETTE *runs to the window and throws it open. The sound of the sirens comes nearer, with a howl that goes to the marrow. The fire engines roar past.*

BIEDERMANN. At least it's not here.

BABETTE. I wonder where?

EISENRING. From where the wind is blowing.

BIEDERMANN. Not here, anyway.

EISENRING. That's how we generally work it. Lure the Fire Department out to some suburb or other, and then, when things really let loose, they find their way back blocked.

BIEDERMANN. No, gentlemen—all joking aside——

SCHMITZ. That's how we do it—joking aside——

BIEDERMANN. Please—enough of this nonsense! Don't overdo it! Look at my wife—white as chalk!

BABETTE.   And you too!

BIEDERMANN.   Besides, a fire alarm is nothing to laugh at, gentlemen. Somewhere some place is burning, or the Fire Department wouldn't be rushing there. [EISENRING *looks at his watch.*]

EISENRING.   We've got to go now.

BIEDERMANN.   Now?

EISENRING.   Sorry.

SCHMITZ.   "Or they'll get you in the shnoosie . . ." [*The sirens are heard again.*]

BIEDERMANN.   Bring us some coffee, Babette! [BABETTE *goes out.*] And you, Anna—do you have to stand there and gape? [ANNA *goes out.*] Just between us, gentlemen: enough is enough. My wife has a heart condition. Let's have no more joking about fires.

SCHMITZ.   We're not joking, Mr. Biedermann.

EISENRING.   We're firebugs.

BIEDERMANN.   No, gentlemen, quite seriously——

EISENRING.   Quite seriously.

SCHMITZ.   Yeah, quite seriously. Why don't you believe us?

EISENRING.   Your house is very favorably situated, Mr. Biedermann, you must admit that. Five villas like yours around the gasworks. . . . It's true they keep a close watch on the gasworks. Still, there's a good stiff wind blowing——

BIEDERMANN.   It can't be——

SCHMITZ.   Let's have plain talk! You think we're firebugs——

BIEDERMANN [*like a whipped dog*].   No, no, I don't think you are! You do me an injustice, gentlemen—I don't think you're firebugs. . . .

EISENRING.   You swear you don't?

BIEDERMANN.   No! No! No! I don't believe it!

SCHMITZ.   What *do* you think we are?

BIEDERMANN.   You're my friends. . . . [*They clap him on the shoulder and start to leave.*]

EISENRING.   It's time to leave.

BIEDERMANN.   Gentlemen, I swear to you by all that's holy——

EISENRING.   By all that's holy?

BIEDERMANN.   Yes. [*He raises his hand as though to take an oath.*]

SCHMITZ.   Willi doesn't believe in anything holy, Mr. Biedermann. Any more than you do. You'll waste your time swearing. [*They go to the door.*]

BIEDERMANN.   What can I do to make you believe me? [*He blocks the doorway.*]

EISENRING.   Give us some matches.

BIEDERMANN.   Some——

EISENRING.   We have no more matches.

BIEDERMANN.   You want me to——

EISENRING.   If you don't think we're firebugs.

BIEDERMANN.   Matches——

SCHMITZ.   To show your belief in us, he means. [BIEDERMANN *reaches in his pocket.*]

EISENRING.   See how he hesitates?

BIEDERMANN.   Sh! Not in front of my wife . . .

BABETTE *returns.*

BABETTE.   Your coffee will be ready in a minute. [*Pause.*] Must you go?

BIEDERMANN [*formally*].   At least you've felt, while here, my friends . . . I don't want to make a speech on this occasion, but may we not drink, before you go, to our eternal friendship? [*He picks up a bottle and the corkscrew.*]

EISENRING.   Tell your very charming husband, madam, that he needn't open any more bottles on our account. It isn't worth the trouble any more.

BIEDERMANN.   It's no trouble, my friends, no trouble at all. If there's anything else you'd like—anything at all—— [*He fills the glasses once more and hands them out.*] My friends! [*They clink glasses.*] Sepp—— Willi—— [*He kisses them each on the cheek. All drink.*]

EISENRING.   Just the same, we must go now.

SCHMITZ.   Unfortunately.

EISENRING.   Madam—— [*Sirens.*]

BABETTE.   It's been such a nice evening. [*Alarm bells.*]

EISENRING.   Just one thing, now, Gottlieb——

BIEDERMANN.   What is it?

EISENRING.   I've mentioned it to you before.

BIEDERMANN.   Anything you like. Just name it.

EISENRING.   The matches.

ANNA *has entered with coffee.*

BABETTE.   Why, what is it, Anna?

ANNA.   The coffee.

BABETTE.   You're all upset, Anna!

ANNA.   Back there—Mrs. Biedermann—the sky! You can see it from the kitchen—the whole sky is burning, Mrs. Biedermann!

The scene is turning red as SCHMITZ *and* EISENRING *make their bows and exit.* BIEDERMANN *is left pale and shaken.*

BIEDERMANN.   Not our house, fortunately . . . Not our house . . . Not our . . . [*The* PH.D. *enters.*] Who are you, and what do you want?

PH.D.   I can no longer be silent. [*He takes out a paper and reads.*] "Cognizant of the events now transpiring, whose iniquitous nature must be readily apparent, the undersigned submits to the authorities the subsequent statement . . ." [*Amid the shrieking of sirens he reads an involved statement, of which no one understands a word. Dogs howl, bells ring, there is the scream of departing sirens and the crackling of flames. The* PH.D. *hands* BIEDERMANN *the paper.*] I disassociate myself. . . .

BIEDERMANN.   But——

PH.D.   I have said my say. [*He takes off and folds up his glasses.*] You see, Mr. Biedermann, I was intent on improving the world; I knew about everything they were doing in your attic, everything. The one thing I didn't know was this: They—they are doing it for the pure joy of it.

BIEDERMANN.   Professor—— [*The* PH.D. *removes himself.*] What will I do with this, Professor?

The PH.D. *climbs over the footlights and takes a seat in the audience.*

BABETTE.   Gottlieb——
BIEDERMANN.   He's gone.
BABETTE.   What did you give them? Matches? Not matches?
BIEDERMANN.   Why not?
BABETTE.   Not matches?
BIEDERMANN.   If they really were firebugs, do you think they wouldn't have matches? Don't be foolish, Babette!

The clock strikes. Silence. The red light onstage begins deepening into blackness. Sirens. Bells ring. Dogs howl. Cars honk. . . . A crash of collapsing buildings. A crackling of flames. Screams and outcries . . . fading. The CHORUS *comes on again.*

CHORUS.   Useless, quite useless.
   And nothing more useless
   Than this useless story.
   For arson, once kindled,
   Kills many,
   Leaves few,
   And accomplishes nothing.

First detonation.

LEADER.   That was the gasworks.

Second detonation.

CHORUS.   Long foreseen, disaster
   Has reached us at last.
   Horrendous arson!
   Unquenchable fire.
   Fate—so they call it!

Third detonation.

LEADER.   More gas tanks.

There is a series of frightful explosions.

CHORUS.   Woe to us! Woe to us! Woe!

The house lights go up.

[*Curtain*]

The American Dream

Edward Albee

Edward Albee

Recent developments in the theatre and in drama have raised important questions about their future. The rise of the so-called theatre of the absurd; the increase of spectacle, the visual element, and "stage business"; and experiments in audience participation have called in question some of the established dramatic verities of the first part of the twentieth century and in some cases have reintroduced notions and habits of the medieval festivals and theatre and of Spanish drama of the "Golden Age," especially that of Calderon. These developments are no doubt the result of certain social changes going on around us—the new orality, the emphasis on concern and authenticity, the increase in speed of communication, the importance of film, the new media, and so forth. It is hard, indeed impossible, to evaluate what will persist and what will not; what will lead to lasting changes and what will vanish. In any case, persistent or not, such changes are bound to interest any lover of the stage.

Because of the increased nonverbal element in the contemporary theatre, many plays cannot be properly captured in print. Furthermore, judgments on very contemporary drama are hard to make. *The American Dream*, by Albee, although it is basically within the tradition and because of that most suitable for an anthology such as this, does show, however, a few of the new dramatic elements. In particular, the vague sense of menace and incomprehensibility, a feature of modern plays by such men as Beckett, Ionesco, and Pinter, with emphasis on man's alienation, is manifested here. The sense of impending doom and meaninglessness—of absurdity—especially in the first part of this play, is excellently conveyed in the sparse and slightly puzzling dialogue. Furthermore, the nonrealistic quality of some of the action and speech indicates the strong use of symbolism. The symbolism here can be profitably compared with that used by O'Neill in *The Hairy Ape* (pp. 445-479), a comparison that reveals interesting differences from and similarities with the experimental theatre of the twenties.

Albee was born in 1928 and adopted when very young. He was brought up in the Westchester community of Larchmont, New York, just north of New York City. His foster parents were wealthy, part owners of the Keith-Albee theatre chain that operated theatres in many cities across the country. Albee was sent to good preparatory schools and for a while attended Trinity College, Hartford, Connecticut. He was never very successful in academic work, and we may presume he was not very happy in school or college. In 1949 he settled in Greenwich Village, living off a trust fund left to him by one of his grandparents and doing odd jobs here and there. In 1953 he began to think of himself as a playwright, and five years later wrote his first successful play, *The Zoo Story*, which was produced in German in Berlin in 1959. His next major play was *The American Dream*; the two plays brought him increasing success and renown in the early sixties.

With *Who's Afraid of Virginia Woolf?* (1962) came international fame—performances in many countries of the world and the final accolade: a highly successful film made from the play, with Elizabeth Taylor and Richard Burton acting the principal roles. Throughout the sixties Albee continued writing plays, but none of them gained quite the acclaim of *Virginia Woolf*. The best known of these were *Tiny Alice* (1964) and *A Delicate Balance* (1966). His most recent play, *All Over* (1971), was not well received in the United States but was an enormous success in Europe.

It is clear that Albee is a foremost contemporary dramatist whose future is still open to all kinds of possibilities. That he will continue to write valuable plays seems guaranteed by his intelligence, his sense of audience, his ability to write exciting dialogue, and his feeling for dramatic structure. These virtues come out in *The American Dream*. Albee in his preface writes that this play "is an examination of the American Scene, an attack on the substitution of artificial for real values in our society, a condemnation of complacency, cruelty, emasculation, and vacuity; it is a stand against the fiction that everything in this slipping land of ours is peachy-keen." It attacks American false values through the pieties of the family. Mommy is a cruel woman, superficial and stupid, although she possesses a certain drive that enables her to be mistress of the household. Daddy is a pathetic character dominated by Mommy but brighter than he seems. Grandma, however, stands for the sound and traditional American values (which Albee obviously favors): honesty, decency, self-respect, mixed with a certain shrewdness. Her faith in the Young Man who embodies the future of America and who appears toward the end of the play ("it will all become clear" she says) sounds a basically optimistic note. At the conclusion of the play Grandma stands outside the action and explains matters to us with characteristic shrewdness. It is not only the young who are trying to say something to the old, but the old who are trying to say something to the young. A basic trust in humanity in spite of Albee's cynical realism runs through this and his other plays.

The movement of *The American Dream* is fast, the dialogue impressive in its capturing of human vacuities and human interactions; the characterization is sure—even with the enigmatic Mrs. Barker who precipitates the climax. In its lack of historical detail, in its exaggerations to create symbolic overtones, in its satire, it represents much that is characteristic of contemporary America and contemporary literature.

The American Dream

Edward Albee

THE PLAYERS

MOMMY
DADDY
GRANDMA
MRS. BARKER
YOUNG MAN

THE SCENE: *A living room. Two armchairs, one toward either side of the stage, facing each other diagonally out toward the audience. Against the rear wall, a sofa. A door, leading out from the apartment, in the rear wall, far stage-right. An archway, leading to other rooms, in the side wall, stage-left.*

At the beginning, MOMMY *and* DADDY *are seated in the armchairs,* DADDY *in the armchair stage-left,* MOMMY *in the other.*

Curtain up. A silence. Then:

MOMMY
I don't know what can be keeping them.
DADDY
They're late, naturally.
MOMMY
Of course, they're late; it never fails.
DADDY
That's the way things are today, and there's nothing you can do about it.
MOMMY
You're quite right.

DADDY

When we took this apartment, they were quick enough to have me sign the lease; they were quick enough to take my check for two months' rent in advance . . .

MOMMY

And one month's security . . .

DADDY

. . . and one month's security. They were quick enough to check my references; they were quick enough about all that. But now! But now, try to get the icebox fixed, try to get the doorbell fixed, try to get the leak in the johnny fixed! Just try it . . . they aren't so quick about *that*.

MOMMY

Of course not; it never fails. People think they can get away with anything these days . . . and, of course they can. I went to buy a new hat yesterday.
(*Pause*)
I said, I went to buy a new hat yesterday.

DADDY

Oh! Yes . . . yes.

MOMMY

Pay attention.

DADDY

I *am* paying attention, Mommy.

MOMMY

Well, be sure you do.

DADDY

Oh, I am.

MOMMY

All right, Daddy; now listen.

DADDY

I'm listening, Mommy.

MOMMY

You're sure!

DADDY

Yes . . . yes, I'm sure, I'm all ears.

MOMMY

(*Giggles at the thought; then*)
All right, now. I went to buy a new hat yesterday and I said, "I'd like a new hat, please." And so, they showed me a few hats, green ones and blue ones, and I didn't like any of them, not one bit. What did I say? What did I just say?

DADDY

You didn't like any of them, not one bit.

MOMMY

That's right; you just keep paying attention. And then they showed me one that I did like. It was a lovely little hat, and I said, "Oh, this is a lovely little hat; I'll take this hat; oh my, it's lovely. What color is it?" And they said, "Why, this is beige; isn't it a lovely little beige hat?" And I said, "Oh, it's just lovely." And so, I bought it.

(*Stops, looks at* DADDY)

DADDY

(*To show he is paying attention*)

And so you bought it.

MOMMY

And so I bought it, and I walked out of the store with the hat right on my head, and I ran spang into the chairman of our woman's club, and she said, "Oh, my dear, isn't that a lovely little hat? Where did you get that lovely little hat? It's the loveliest little hat; I've always wanted a wheat-colored hat *myself*." And, I said, "Why, no, my dear; this hat is beige; beige." And she laughed and said, "Why no, my dear, that's a wheat-colored hat . . . wheat. I know beige from wheat." And I said, "Well, my dear, I know beige from wheat, too." What did I say? What did I just say?

DADDY

(*Tonelessly*)

Well, my dear, I know beige from wheat, too.

MOMMY

That's right. And she laughed, and she said, "Well, my dear, they certainly put one over on you. That's wheat if I ever saw wheat. But it's lovely, just the same." And then she walked off. She's a dreadful woman, you don't know her; she has dreadful taste, two dreadful children, a dreadful house, and an absolutely adorable husband who sits in a wheel chair all the time. You don't know him. You don't know anybody, do you? She's just a dreadful woman, but she *is* chairman of our woman's club, so naturally I'm terribly fond of her. So, I went right back into the hat shop, and I said, "Look here; what do you mean selling me a hat that you say is beige, when it's wheat all the time . . . wheat! I can tell beige from wheat any day in the week, but not in this artificial light of yours." They have artificial light, Daddy.

DADDY

Have they!

MOMMY

And I said, "The minute I got outside I could tell that it wasn't a beige hat at all; it was a wheat hat." And they said to me, "How could you tell that when you had the hat on the top of your head?" Well, that made me angry, and so I made a scene right there; I screamed as hard as I could; I took my hat off and I threw it down on the counter, and oh, I made a terrible scene. I said, I made a terrible scene.

DADDY

(*Snapping to*)

Yes . . . yes . . . good for you!

MOMMY

And I made an absolutely terrible scene; and they became frightened, and they said, "Oh, madam; oh, madam." But I kept right on, and finally they admitted that they might have made a mistake; so they took my hat into the back, and then they came out again with a hat that looked exactly like it. I took one look at it, and I said, "This hat is wheat-colored; wheat." Well, of course, they said, "Oh, no, madam, this hat is beige; you go outside and see." So, I went outside, and lo and behold, it *was* beige. So I bought it.

DADDY

(*Clearing his throat*)
I would imagine that it was the same hat they tried to sell you before.

MOMMY

(*With a little laugh*)
Well, of course it was!

DADDY

That's the way things are today; you just can't get satisfaction; you just try.

MOMMY

Well, *I* got satisfaction.

DADDY

That's right, Mommy. *You did* get satisfaction, didn't you?

MOMMY

Why are they so late? I don't know what can be keeping them.

DADDY

I've been trying for two weeks to have the leak in the johnny fixed.

MOMMY

You can't get satisfaction; just try. *I* can get satisfaction, but you can't.

DADDY

I've been trying for two weeks and it isn't so much for my sake; I can always go to the club.

MOMMY

It isn't so much for my sake, either; I can always go shopping.

DADDY

It's really for Grandma's sake.

MOMMY

Of course it's for Grandma's sake. Grandma cries every time she goes to the johnny as it is; but now that it doesn't work it's even worse, it makes Grandma think she's getting feeble-headed.

DADDY

Grandma *is* getting feeble-headed.

MOMMY

Of course Grandma is getting feeble-headed, but not about her johnny-do's.

DADDY

No; that's true. I must have it fixed.

MOMMY

WHY are they so late? I don't know what can be keeping them.

DADDY

When they came here the first time, they were ten minutes early; they were quick enough about it then.

(*Enter* GRANDMA *from the archway, stage-left. She is loaded down with boxes, large and small, neatly wrapped and tied.*)

MOMMY

Why Grandma, look at you! What *is* all that you're carrying?

GRANDMA

They're boxes. What do they look like?

MOMMY

Daddy! Look at Grandma; look at all the boxes she's carrying!

DADDY

My goodness, Grandma; look at all those boxes.

GRANDMA

Where'll I put them?

MOMMY

Heavens! I don't know. Whatever are they for?

GRANDMA

That's nobody's damn business.

MOMMY

Well, in that case, put them down next to Daddy; there.

GRANDMA

(*Dumping the boxes down, on and around* DADDY'S *feet*)
I sure wish you'd get the john fixed.

DADDY

Oh, I do wish they'd come and fix it. We hear you . . . for hours . . .
whimpering away. . . .

MOMMY

Daddy! What a terrible thing to say to Grandma!

GRANDMA

Yeah. For shame, talking to me that way.

DADDY

I'm sorry, Grandma.

MOMMY

Daddy's sorry, Grandma.

GRANDMA

Well, all right. In that case I'll go get the rest of the boxes. I suppose I deserve being talked to that way. I've gotten so old. Most people think that
when you get so old, you either freeze to death, or you burn up. But you
don't. When you get so old, all that happens is that people talk to you that
way.

DADDY

(*Contrite*)
I said I'm sorry, Grandma.

MOMMY

Daddy said he was sorry.

GRANDMA

Well, that's all that counts. People being sorry. Makes you feel better; gives
you a sense of dignity, and that's all that's important . . . a sense of dignity. And it doesn't matter if you don't care, or not, either. You got to
have a sense of dignity, even if you don't care, 'cause, if you don't have that,
civilization's doomed.

MOMMY

You've been reading my book club selections again!

DADDY

How dare you read Mommy's book club selections, Grandma!

GRANDMA

Because I'm old! When you're old you gotta do something. When you get old, you can't talk to people because people snap at you. When you get so old, people talk to you that way. That's why you become deaf, so you won't be able to hear people talking to you that way. And that's why you go and hide under the covers in the big soft bed, so you won't feel the house shaking from people talking to you that way. That's why old people die, eventually. People talk to them that way. I've got to go and get the rest of the boxes.

(GRANDMA *exits*)

DADDY

Poor Grandma, I didn't mean to hurt her.

MOMMY

Don't you worry about it; Grandma doesn't know what she means.

DADDY

She knows what she says, though.

MOMMY

Don't you worry about it; she won't know that soon. I love Grandma.

DADDY

I love her, too. Look how nicely she wrapped these boxes.

MOMMY

Grandma has always wrapped boxes nicely. When I was a little girl, I was very poor, and Grandma was very poor, too, because Grandpa was in heaven. And every day, when I went to school, Grandma used to wrap a box for me, and I used to take it with me to school; and when it was lunchtime, all the little boys and girls used to take out their boxes of lunch, and they weren't wrapped nicely at all, and they used to open them and eat their chicken legs and chocolate cakes; and I used to say, "Oh, look at my lovely lunch box; it's so nicely wrapped it would break my heart to open it." And so, I wouldn't open it.

DADDY

Because it was empty.

MOMMY

Oh no. Grandma always filled it up, because she never ate the dinner she cooked the evening before; she gave me all her food for my lunch box the next day. After school, I'd take the box back to Grandma, and she'd open it and eat the chicken legs and chocolate cake that was inside. Grandma used to say, "I love day-old cake." That's where the expression day-old cake came from. Grandma always ate everything a day late. I used to eat all the other little boys' and girls' food at school, because they thought my lunch box was empty. They thought my lunch box was empty, and that's why I wouldn't open it. They thought I suffered from the sin of pride, and since that made them better than me, they were very generous.

DADDY

You were a very deceitful little girl.

MOMMY

We were very poor! But then I married you, Daddy, and now we've very rich.

DADDY

Grandma isn't rich.

MOMMY

No, but you've been so good to Grandma she feels rich. She doesn't know you'd like to put her in a nursing home.

DADDY

I wouldn't!

MOMMY

Well, heaven knows, *I* would! I can't stand it, watching her do the cooking and the housework, polishing the silver, moving the furniture. . . .

DADDY

She likes to do that. She says it's the least she can do to earn her keep.

MOMMY

Well, she's right. You can't live off people. I can live off you, because I married you. And aren't you lucky all I brought with me was Grandma. A lot of women I know would have brought their whole families to live off you. All I brought was Grandma. Grandma is all the family I have.

DADDY

I feel very fortunate.

MOMMY

You should. I have a right to live off of you because I married you, and because I used to let you get on top of me and bump your uglies; and I have a right to all your money when you die. And when you do, Grandma and I can live by ourselves . . . if she's still here. Unless you have her put away in a nursing home.

DADDY

I have no intention of putting her in a nursing home.

MOMMY

Well, I wish somebody would do something with her!

DADDY

At any rate, you're very well provided for.

MOMMY

You're my sweet Daddy; that's very nice.

DADDY

I love my Mommy.

(*Enter* GRANDMA *again, laden with more boxes*)

GRANDMA

(*Dumping the boxes on and around* DADDY's *feet*)

There; that's the lot of them.

DADDY

They're wrapped so nicely.

GRANDMA

(*To* DADDY)

You won't get on my sweet side that way . . .

MOMMY

Grandma!

GRANDMA

. . . telling me how nicely I wrap boxes. Not after what you said: how I whimpered for hours. . . .

MOMMY

Grandma!

GRANDMA

(*To* MOMMY)

Shut up!

(*To* DADDY)

You don't have any feelings, that's what's wrong with you. Old people make all sorts of noises, half of them they can't help. Old people whimper, and cry, and belch, and make great hollow rumbling sounds at the table; old people wake up in the middle of the night screaming, and find out they haven't even been asleep; and when old people *are* asleep, they try to wake up, and they can't . . . not for the longest time.

MOMMY

Homilies, homilies!

GRANDMA

And there's more, too.

DADDY

I'm really very sorry, Grandma.

GRANDMA

I know you are, Daddy; it's Mommy over there makes all the trouble. If you'd listened to me, you wouldn't have married her in the first place. She was a tramp and a trollop and a trull to boot, and she's no better now.

MOMMY

Grandma!

GRANDMA

(*To* MOMMY)

Shut up!

(*To* DADDY)

When she was no more than eight years old she used to climb up on my lap and say, in a sickening little voice, "When I gwo up, I'm going to mahwy a wich old man; I'm going to set my wittle were end right down in a tub o' butter, that's what I'm going to do." And I warned you, Daddy; I told you to stay away from her type. I told you to. I did.

MOMMY

You stop that! You're my mother, not his!

GRANDMA

I am?

DADDY

That's right, Grandma. Mommy's right.

GRANDMA

Well, how would you expect somebody as old as I am to remember a thing like that? You don't make allowances for people. I want an allowance. I want an allowance!

DADDY

All right, Grandma; I'll see to it.

MOMMY

Grandma! I'm ashamed of you.

GRANDMA

Humf! It's a fine time to say that. You should have gotten rid of me a long time ago if that's the way you feel. You should have had Daddy set me up in business somewhere . . . I could have gone into the fur business, or I could have been a singer. But no; not you. You wanted me around so you could sleep in my room when Daddy got fresh. But now it isn't important, because Daddy doesn't want to get fresh with you any more, and I don't blame him. You'd rather sleep with me, wouldn't you, Daddy?

MOMMY

Daddy doesn't want to sleep with anyone. Daddy's been sick.

DADDY

I've been sick. I don't even want to sleep in the apartment.

MOMMY

You see? I told you.

DADDY

I just want to get everything over with.

MOMMY

That's right. Why are they so late? Why can't they get here on time?

GRANDMA

(*An owl*)

Who? Who? . . . Who? Who?

MOMMY

You know, Grandma.

GRANDMA

No, I don't.

MOMMY

Well, it doesn't really matter whether you do or not.

DADDY

Is that true?

MOMMY

Oh, more or less. Look how pretty Grandma wrapped these boxes.

GRANDMA

I didn't really like wrapping them; it hurt my fingers, and it frightened me. But it had to be done.

MOMMY

Why, Grandma?

GRANDMA

None of your damn business.

MOMMY

Go to bed.

GRANDMA

I don't want to go to bed. I just got up. I want to stay here and watch. Besides . . .

MOMMY
   Go to bed.
DADDY
   Let her stay up, Mommy; it isn't noon yet.
GRANDMA
   I want to watch; besides . . .
DADDY
   Let her watch, Mommy.
MOMMY
   Well all right, you can watch; but don't you dare say a word.
GRANDMA
   Old people are very good at listening; old people don't like to talk; old people
   have colitis and lavender perfume. Now I'm going to be quiet.
DADDY
   She never mentioned she wanted to be a singer.
MOMMY
   Oh, I forgot to tell you, but it was ages ago.
   (*The doorbell rings*)
   Oh, goodness! Here they are!
GRANDMA
   Who? Who?
MOMMY
   Oh, just some people.
GRANDMA
   The van people? Is it the van people? Have you finally done it? Have you
   called the van people to come and take me away?
DADDY
   Of course not, Grandma!
GRANDMA
   Oh, don't be too sure. She'd have you carted off too, if she thought she could
   get away with it.
MOMMY
   Pay no attention to her, Daddy.
   (*An aside to* GRANDMA)
   My God, you're ungrateful!
   (*The doorbell rings again*)
DADDY
   (*Wringing his hands*)
   Oh dear; oh dear.
MOMMY
   (*Still to* GRANDMA)
   Just you wait; I'll fix your wagon.
   (*Now to* DADDY)
   Well, go let them in, Daddy. What are you waiting for?
DADDY
   I think we should talk about it some more. Maybe we've been hasty . . . a
   little hasty, perhaps.

(*Doorbell rings again*)
I'd like to talk about it some more.

MOMMY

There's no need. You made up your mind; you were firm; you were mascu-line and decisive.

DADDY

We might consider the pros and the . . .

MOMMY

I won't argue with you; it has to be done; you were right. Open the door.

DADDY

But I'm not sure that . . .

MOMMY

Open the door.

DADDY

Was I firm about it?

MOMMY

Oh, so firm; so firm.

DADDY

And was I decisive?

MOMMY

SO decisive! Oh, I shivered.

DADDY

And masculine? Was I really masculine?

MOMMY

Oh, Daddy, you were so masculine; I shivered and fainted.

GRANDMA

Shivered and fainted, did she? Humf!

MOMMY

You be quiet.

GRANDMA

Old people have a right to talk to themselves; it doesn't hurt the gums, and it's comforting.
(*Doorbell rings again*)

DADDY

I shall now open the door.

MOMMY

WHAT a masculine Daddy! Isn't he a masculine Daddy?

GRANDMA

Don't expect me to say anything. Old people are obscene.

MOMMY

Some of your opinions aren't so bad. You know that?

DADDY

(*Backing off from the door*)
Maybe we can send them away.

MOMMY

Oh, look at you! You're turning into jelly; you're indecisive; you're a woman.

DADDY

All right. Watch me now; I'm going to open the door. Watch. Watch!

MOMMY

We're watching; we're watching.

GRANDMA

I'm not.

DADDY

Watch now; it's opening.

(*He opens the door*)

It's open!

(MRS. BARKER *steps into the room*)

Here they are!

MOMMY

Here they are!

GRANDMA

Where?

DADDY

Come in. You're late. But, of course, we expected you to be late; we were saying that we expected you to be late.

MOMMY

Daddy, don't be so rude! We were saying that you just can't get satisfaction these days, and we were talking about you, of course. Won't you come in?

MRS. BARKER

Thank you. I don't mind if I do.

MOMMY

We're very glad that you're here, late as you are. You do remember us, don't you? You were here once before. I'm Mommy, and this is Daddy, and that's Grandma, doddering there in the corner.

MRS. BARKER

Hello, Mommy; hello, Daddy; and hello there, Grandma.

DADDY

Now that you're here, I don't suppose you could go away and maybe come back some other time.

MRS. BARKER

Oh no; we're much too efficient for that. I said, hello there, Grandma.

MOMMY

Speak to them, Grandma.

GRANDMA

I don't see them.

DADDY

For shame, Grandma; they're here.

MRS. BARKER

Yes, we're here, Grandma. I'm Mrs. Barker. I remember you; don't you remember me?

GRANDMA

I don't recall. Maybe you were younger, or something.

MOMMY

Grandma! What a terrible thing to say!

MRS. BARKER

Oh now, don't scold her, Mommy; for all she knows she may be right.

DADDY

Uh . . . Mrs. Barker, is it? Won't you sit down?

MRS. BARKER

I don't mind if I do.

MOMMY

Would you like a cigarette, and a drink, and would you like to cross your legs?

MRS. BARKER

You forget yourself, Mommy; I'm a professional woman. But I will cross my legs.

DADDY

Yes, make yourself comfortable.

MRS. BARKER

I don't mind if I do.

GRANDMA

Are they still here?

MOMMY

Be quiet, Grandma.

MRS. BARKER

Oh, we're still here. My, what an unattractive apartment you have!

MOMMY

Yes, but you don't know what a trouble it is. Let me tell you . . .

DADDY

I was saying to Mommy . . .

MRS. BARKER

Yes, I know. I was listening outside.

DADDY

About the icebox, and . . . the doorbell . . . and the . . .

MRS. BARKER

. . . and the johnny. Yes, we're very efficient; we have to know everything in our work.

DADDY

Exactly what do you do?

MOMMY

Yes, what is your work?

MRS. BARKER

Well, my dear, for one thing, I'm chairman of your woman's club.

MOMMY

Don't be ridiculous. I was talking to the chairman of my woman's club just yester— Why, so you are. You remember, Daddy, the lady I was telling you about? The lady with the husband who sits in the *swing*? Don't you remember?

DADDY

No . . . no . . .

MOMMY

Of course you do. I'm so sorry, Mrs. Barker. I would have known you anywhere, except in this artificial light. And look! You have a hat just like the one I bought yesterday.

MRS. BARKER

(*With a little laugh*)

No, not really; this hat is cream.

MOMMY

Well, my dear, that may look like a cream hat to you, but I can . . .

MRS. BARKER

Now, now; you seem to forget who I am.

MOMMY

Yes, I do, don't I? Are you sure you're comfortable? Won't you take off your dress?

MRS. BARKER

I don't mind if I do.

(*She removes her dress*)

MOMMY

There. You must feel a great deal more comfortable.

MRS. BARKER

Well, I certainly *look* a great deal more comfortable.

DADDY

I'm going to blush and giggle.

MOMMY

Daddy's going to blush and giggle.

MRS. BARKER

(*Pulling the hem of her slip above her knees*)

You're lucky to have such a man for a husband.

MOMMY

Oh, don't I know it!

DADDY

I just blushed and giggled and went sticky wet.

MOMMY

Isn't Daddy a caution, Mrs. Barker?

MRS. BARKER

Maybe if I smoked . . . ?

MOMMY

Oh, that isn't necessary.

MRS. BARKER

I don't mind if I do.

MOMMY

No; no, don't. Really.

MRS. BARKER

I don't mind . . .

MOMMY

I won't have you smoking in my house, and that's that! You're a professional woman.

DADDY

Grandma drinks AND smokes; don't you, Grandma?

GRANDMA
No.

MOMMY
Well, now, Mrs. Barker; suppose you tell us why you're here.

GRANDMA
(As MOMMY *walks through the boxes*)
The boxes . . . the boxes . . .

MOMMY
Be quiet, Grandma.

DADDY
What did you say, Grandma?

GRANDMA
(As MOMMY *steps on several of the boxes*)
The boxes, damn it!

MRS. BARKER
Boxes; she said boxes. She mentioned the boxes.

DADDY
What about the boxes, Grandma? Maybe Mrs. Barker is here because of the boxes. Is that what you meant, Grandma?

GRANDMA
I don't know if that's what I meant or not. It's certainly not what I *thought* I meant.

DADDY
Grandma is of the opinion that . . .

MRS. BARKER
Can we assume that the boxes are for us? I mean, can we assume that you had us come here for the boxes?

MOMMY
Are you in the habit of receiving boxes?

DADDY
A very good question.

MRS. BARKER
Well, that would depend on the reason we're here. I've got my fingers in so many little pies, you know. Now, I can think of one of my little activities in which we are in the habit of receiving *baskets;* but more in a literary sense than really. We *might* receive boxes, though, under very special circumstances. I'm afraid that's the best answer I can give you.

DADDY
It's a very interesting answer.

MRS. BARKER
I thought so. But, does it help?

MOMMY
No; I'm afraid not.

DADDY
I wonder if it might help us any if I said I feel misgivings, that I have definite qualms.

MOMMY
Where, Daddy?

DADDY

Well, mostly right here, right around where the stitches were.

MOMMY

Daddy had an operation, you know.

MRS. BARKER

Oh, you poor Daddy! I didn't know; but then, how could I?

GRANDMA

You might have asked; it wouldn't have hurt you.

MOMMY

Dry up, Grandma.

GRANDMA

There you go. Letting your true feelings come out. Old people aren't dry enough, I suppose. My sacks are empty, the fluid in my eyeballs is all caked on the inside edges, my spine is made of sugar candy, I breathe ice; but you don't hear me complain. Nobody hears old people complain because people think that's all old people do. And *that's* because old people are gnarled and sagged and twisted into the shape of a complaint.

(*Signs off*)

That's all.

MRS. BARKER

What was wrong, Daddy?

DADDY

Well, you know how it is: the doctors took out something that was there and put in something that wasn't there. An operation.

MRS. BARKER

You're very fortunate, I should say.

MOMMY

Oh, he is; he is. All his life, Daddy has wanted to be a United States Senator; but now . . . why now he's changed his mind, and for the rest of his life he's going to want to be Governor . . . it would be nearer the apartment, you know.

MRS. BARKER

You *are* fortunate, Daddy.

DADDY

Yes, indeed; except that I get these qualms now and then, definite ones.

MRS. BARKER

Well, it's just a matter of things settling; you're like an old house.

MOMMY

Why Daddy, thank Mrs. Barker.

DADDY

Thank you.

MRS. BARKER

Ambition! That's the ticket. I have a brother who's very much like you, Daddy . . . ambitious. Of course, he's a great deal younger than you; he's even younger than I am . . . if such a thing is possible. He runs a little newspaper. Just a little newspaper . . . but he runs it. He's chief cook and bottle washer of that little newspaper, which he calls *The Village*

Idiot. He has such a sense of humor; he's so self-deprecating, so modest. And he'd never admit it himself, but he *is* the Village Idiot.

MOMMY

Oh, I think that's just grand. Don't you think so, Daddy?

DADDY

Yes, just grand.

MRS. BARKER

My brother's a dear man, and he has a dear little wife, whom he loves, dearly. He loves her so much he just can't get a sentence out without mentioning her. He wants everybody to know he's married. He's really a stickler on that point; he can't be introduced to anybody and say hello without adding, "Of course, I'm married." As far as I'm concerned, he's the chief exponent of Woman Love in this whole country; he's even been written up in psychiatric journals because of it.

DADDY

Indeed!

MOMMY

Isn't that lovely.

MRS. BARKER

Oh, I think so. There's too much woman hatred in this country, and that's a fact.

GRANDMA

Oh, I don't know.

MOMMY

Oh, I think that's just grand. Don't you think so, Daddy?

DADDY

Yes, just grand.

GRANDMA

In case anybody's interested . . .

MOMMY

Be quiet, Grandma.

GRANDMA

Nuts!

MOMMY

Oh, Mrs. Barker, you *must* forgive Grandma. She's rural.

MRS. BARKER

I don't mind if I do.

DADDY

Maybe Grandma has something to say.

MOMMY

Nonsense. Old people have nothing to say; and if old people *did* have something to say, nobody would listen to them.

(*To* GRANDMA)

You see? I can pull that stuff just as easy as you can.

GRANDMA

Well, you got the rhythm, but you don't really have the quality. Besides, you're middle-aged.

MOMMY

    I'm proud of it!

GRANDMA

    Look. I'll show you how it's really done. Middle-aged people think they can do anything, but the truth is that middle-aged people can't do most things as well as they used to. Middle-aged people think they're special because they're like everybody else. We live in the age of deformity. You see? Rhythm *and* content. You'll learn.

DADDY

    I do wish I weren't surrounded by women; I'd like some men around here.

MRS. BARKER

    You can say that again!

GRANDMA

    I don't hardly count as a woman, so can I say my piece?

MOMMY

    Go on. Jabber away.

GRANDMA

    It's very simple; the fact is, these boxes don't have anything to do with why this good lady is come to call. Now, if you're interested in knowing why these boxes *are* here . . .

DADDY

    I'm sure that must be all very true, Grandma, but what does it have to do with why . . . pardon me, what is that name again?

MRS. BARKER

    Mrs. Barker.

DADDY

    Exactly. What does it have to do with why . . . that name again?

MRS. BARKER

    Mrs. Barker.

DADDY

    Precisely. What does it have to do with why what's-her-name is here?

MOMMY

    They're here because we asked them.

MRS. BARKER

    Yes. That's why.

GRANDMA

    Now if you're interested in knowing why these boxes *are* here . . .

MOMMY

    Well, nobody *is* interested!

GRANDMA

    You can be as snippety as you like for all the good it'll do you.

DADDY

    You two will have to stop arguing.

MOMMY

    I don't argue with her.

DADDY

    It will just have to stop.

MOMMY

Well, why don't you call a van and have her taken away?

GRANDMA

Don't bother; there's no need.

DADDY

No, now, perhaps I can go away myself. . . .

MOMMY

Well, one or the other; the way things are now it's impossible. In the first place, it's too crowded in this apartment.

(*To* GRANDMA)

And it's you that takes up all the space, with your enema bottles, and your Pekinese, and God-only-knows-what-else . . . and now all these boxes. . . .

GRANDMA

These boxes are . . .

MRS. BARKER

I've never heard of enema *bottles*. . . .

GRANDMA

She means enema bags, but she doesn't know the difference. Mommy comes from extremely bad stock. And besides, when Mommy was born . . . well, it was a difficult delivery, and she had a head shaped like a banana.

MOMMY

You ungrateful— Daddy? Daddy, you see how ungrateful she is after all these years, after all the things we've done for her?

(*To* GRANDMA)

One of these days you're going away in a van; that's what's going to happen to you!

GRANDMA

Do tell!

MRS. BARKER

Like a banana?

GRANDMA

Yup, just like a banana.

MRS. BARKER

My word!

MOMMY

You stop listening to her; she'll say anything. Just the other night she called Daddy a hedgehog.

MRS. BARKER

She didn't!

GRANDMA

That's right, baby; you stick up for me.

MOMMY

I don't know where she gets the words; on the television, maybe.

MRS. BARKER

Did you really call him a hedgehog?

GRANDMA

Oh look; what difference does it make whether I did or not?

DADDY

Grandma's right. Leave Grandma alone.

MOMMY

(*To* DADDY)

How dare you!

GRANDMA

Oh, leave her alone, Daddy; the kid's all mixed up.

MOMMY

You see? I told you. It's all those television shows. Daddy, you go right into Grandma's room and take her television and shake all the tubes loose.

DADDY

Don't mention tubes to me.

MOMMY

Oh! Mommy forgot!

(*To* MRS. BARKER)

Daddy has tubes now, where he used to have tracts.

MRS. BARKER

Is that a fact!

GRANDMA

I know why this dear lady is here.

MOMMY

You be still.

MRS. BARKER

Oh, I do wish you'd tell me.

MOMMY

No! No! That wouldn't be fair at all.

DADDY

Besides, she knows why she's here; she's here because we called them.

MRS. BARKER

La! But that still leaves me puzzled. I know I'm here because you called us, but I'm such a busy girl, with this committee and that committee, and the Responsible Citizens Activities I indulge in.

MOMMY

Oh my; busy, busy.

MRS. BARKER

Yes, indeed. So I'm afraid you'll have to give me some help.

MOMMY

Oh, no. No, you must be mistaken. I can't believe we asked you here to give you any help. With the way taxes are these days, and the way you can't get satisfaction in ANYTHING . . . no, I don't believe so.

DADDY

And if you need help . . . why, I should think you'd apply for a Fulbright Scholarship. . . .

MOMMY

And if not that . . . why, then a Guggenheim Fellowship. . . .

GRANDMA

Oh, come on; why not shoot the works and try for the Prix de Rome.

(*Under her breath to* MOMMY *and* DADDY)
Beasts!

MRS. BARKER

Oh, what a jolly family. But let me think. I'm knee-deep in work these days; there's the Ladies' Auxiliary Air Raid Committee, for one thing; how do you feel about air raids?

MOMMY

Oh, I'd say we're hostile.

DADDY

Yes, definitely; we're hostile.

MRS. BARKER

Then, you'll be no help there. There's too much hostility in the world these days as it is; but I'll not badger you! There's a surfeit of badgers as well.

GRANDMA

While we're at it, there's been a run on old people, too. The Department of Agriculture, or maybe it wasn't the Department of Agriculture—anyway, it was some department that's run by a girl—put out figures showing that ninety percent of the adult population of the country is over eighty years old . . . or eighty percent is over ninety years old . . .

MOMMY

You're such a liar! You just finished saying that everyone is middle-aged.

GRANDMA

I'm just telling you what the government says . . . that doesn't have anything to do with what . . .

MOMMY

It's that television! Daddy, go break her television.

GRANDMA

You won't find it.

DADDY

(*Wearily getting up*)
If I must . . . I must.

MOMMY

And don't step on the Pekinese; it's blind.

DADDY

It may be blind, but Daddy isn't.
(*He exits, through the archway, stage-left*)

GRANDMA

You won't find *it*, either.

MOMMY

Oh, I'm so fortunate to have such a husband. Just think; I could have a husband who was poor, or argumentative, or a husband who sat in a wheel chair all day . . . OOOOHHHH! *What* have I said? What *have* I said?

GRANDMA

You said you could have a husband who sat in a wheel . . .

MOMMY

I'm mortified! I could die! I could cut my tongue out! I could . . .

MRS. BARKER

(*Forcing a smile*)

Oh, now . . . now . . . don't think about it . . .

MOMMY

I could . . . why, I could . . .

MRS. BARKER

. . . don't think about it . . . really. . . .

MOMMY

You're quite right. I won't think about it, and that way I'll forget that I ever said it, and that way it will be all right.

(*Pause*)

There . . . I've forgotten. Well, now, now that Daddy is out of the room we can have some girl talk.

MRS. BARKER

I'm not sure that I . . .

MOMMY

You *do* want to have some girl talk, don't you?

MRS. BARKER

I was going to say I'm not sure that I wouldn't care for a glass of water. I feel a little faint.

MOMMY

Grandma, go get Mrs. Barker a glass of water.

GRANDMA

Go get it yourself. I quit.

MOMMY

Grandma loves to do little things around the house; it gives her a false sense of security.

GRANDMA

I quit! I'm through!

MOMMY

Now, you be a good Grandma, or you know what will happen to you. You'll be taken away in a van.

GRANDMA

You don't frighten me. I'm too old to be frightened. Besides . . .

MOMMY

WELL! I'll tend to you later. I'll hide your teeth . . . I'll . . .

GRANDMA

Everything's hidden.

MRS. BARKER

I *am* going to faint. I *am*.

MOMMY

Good heavens! I'll go myself.

(*As she exits, through the archway, stage-left*)

I'll fix you Grandma. I'll take care of you later.

(*She exits*)

GRANDMA

Oh, go soak your head.

(*To* MRS. BARKER)
Well, dearie, how do you feel?

MRS. BARKER
A little better, I think. Yes, much better, thank you, Grandma.

GRANDMA
That's good.

MRS. BARKER
But . . . I feel so lost . . . not knowing why I'm here . . . and, on top of it, they say I was here before.

GRANDMA
Well, you were. You weren't *here*, exactly, because we've moved around a lot, from one apartment to another, up and down the social ladder like mice, if you like similes.

MRS. BARKER
I don't . . . particularly.

GRANDMA
Well, then, I'm sorry.

MRS. BARKER
(*Suddenly*)
Grandma, I feel I can trust you.

GRANDMA
Don't be too sure; it's every man for himself around this place. . . .

MRS. BARKER
Oh . . . is it? Nonetheless, I really do feel that I can trust you. *Please* tell me why they called and asked us to come. I implore you!

GRANDMA
Oh my; that feels good. It's been so long since anybody implored me. Do it again. Implore me some more.

MRS. BARKER
You're your daughter's mother, all right!

GRANDMA
Oh, I don't mean to be hard. If you won't implore me, then beg me, or ask me, or entreat me . . . just anything like that.

MRS. BARKER
You're a dreadful old woman!

GRANDMA
You'll understand some day. Please!

MRS. BARKER
Oh, for heaven's sake! . . . I implore you . . . I beg you . . . I beseech you!

GRANDMA
Beseech! Oh that's the nicest word I've heard in ages. You're a dear, sweet woman. . . . You . . . beseech . . . me. I can't resist that.

MRS. BARKER
Well, then . . . please tell me why they asked us to come.

GRANDMA
Well, I'll give you a hint. That's the best I can do, because I'm a muddle-headed old woman. Now listen, because it's important. Once upon a time,

not too very long ago, but a long enough time ago . . . oh, about twenty years ago . . . there was a man very much like Daddy, and a woman very much like Mommy, who were married to each other, very much like Mommy and Daddy are married to each other; and they lived in an apartment very much like one that's very much like this one, and they lived there with an old woman who was very much like yours truly, only younger, because it was some time ago; in fact, they were all somewhat younger.

MRS. BARKER

How fascinating!

GRANDMA

Now, at the same time, there was a dear lady very much like you, only younger then, who did all sorts of Good Works. . . . And one of the Good Works this dear lady did was in something very much like a volunteer capacity for an organization very much like the Bye-Bye Adoption Service, which is nearby and which was run by a terribly deaf old lady very much like the Miss Bye-Bye who runs the Bye-Bye Adoption Service nearby.

MRS. BARKER

How enthralling!

GRANDMA

Well, be that as it may. Nonetheless, one afternoon this man, who was very much like Daddy, and this woman who was very much like Mommy, came to see this dear lady who did all the Good Works, who was very much like you, dear, and they were very sad and very hopeful, and they cried and smiled and bit their fingers, and they said all the most intimate things.

MRS. BARKER

How spellbinding! What did they say?

GRANDMA

Well, it was very sweet. The woman, who was very much like Mommy, said that she and the man who was very much like Daddy had never been blessed with anything very much like a bumble of joy.

MRS. BARKER

A what?

GRANDMA

A bumble; a bumble of joy.

MRS. BARKER

Oh, like bundle.

GRANDMA

Well, yes; very much like it. Bundle, bumble; who cares? At any rate, the woman, who was very much like Mommy, said that they wanted a bumble of their own, but that the man, who was very much like Daddy, couldn't have a bumble; and the man, who was very much like Daddy, said that yes, they had wanted a bumble of their own, but that the woman, who was very much like Mommy, couldn't have one, and that now they wanted to buy something very much like a bumble.

MRS. BARKER

How engrossing.

GRANDMA

Yes. And the dear lady, who was very much like you, said something that was very much like, "Oh, what a shame; but take heart . . . I think we have just the bumble *for* you." And, well, the lady, who was very much like Mommy, and the man, who was very much like Daddy, cried and smiled and bit their fingers, and said some more intimate things, which were totally irrelevant but which were pretty hot stuff, and so the dear lady, who was very much like you, and who had something very much like a penchant for pornography, listened with something very much like enthusiasm. "Whee," she said. "Whoooopeeeeee!" But that's beside the point.

MRS. BARKER

I suppose *so*. But how gripping!

GRANDMA

Anyway . . . they *bought* something very much like a bumble, and they took it away with them. But . . . things didn't work out very well.

MRS. BARKER

You mean there was trouble?

GRANDMA

You got it.

(*With a glance through the archway*)

But, I'm going to have to speed up now because I think I'm leaving soon.

MRS. BARKER

Oh. Are you really?

GRANDMA

Yup.

MRS. BARKER

But old people don't go anywhere; they're either taken places, or put places.

GRANDMA

Well, this old person is different. Anyway . . . things started going badly.

MRS. BARKER

Oh yes. Yes.

GRANDMA

Weeeeellll . . . in the first place, it turned out that the bumble didn't look like either one of its parents. That was enough of a blow, but things got worse. One night, it cried its heart out, if you can imagine such a thing.

MRS. BARKER

Cried its heart out! Well!

GRANDMA

But that was only the beginning. Then it turned out it only had eyes for its Daddy.

MRS. BARKER

For its Daddy! Why, any self-respecting woman would have gouged those eyes right out of its head.

GRANDMA

Well, she did. That's exactly what she did. But then, it kept its nose up in the air.

MRS. BARKER

Ufggh! How disgusting!

GRANDMA

That's what they thought. But *then*, it began to develop an interest in its you-know-what.

MRS. BARKER

In its you-know-what! Well! I hope they cut its hands off at the wrists!

GRANDMA

Well, yes, they did that eventually. But first, they cut off its you-know-what.

MRS. BARKER

A much better idea!

GRANDMA

That's what they thought. But after they cut off its you-know-what, it *still* put its hand under the covers, *looking* for its you-know-what. So, finally, they *had* to cut off its hands at the wrists.

MRS. BARKER

Naturally!

GRANDMA

And it was such a resentful bumble. Why, one day it called its Mommy a dirty name.

MRS. BARKER

Well, I hope they cut its tongue out!

GRANDMA

Of course. And then, as it got bigger, they found out all sorts of terrible things about it, like: it didn't have a head on its shoulders, it had no guts, it was spineless, its feet were made of clay . . . just dreadful things.

MRS. BARKER

Dreadful!

GRANDMA

So you can understand how they became discouraged.

MRS. BARKER

I certainly can! And what did they do?

GRANDMA

What did they do? Well, for the last straw, it finally up and died; and you can imagine how *that* made them feel, their having paid for it, and all. So, they called up the lady who sold them the bumble in the first place and told her to come right over to their apartment. They wanted satisfaction; they wanted their money back. That's what they wanted.

MRS. BARKER

My, my, my.

GRANDMA

How do you like *them* apples?

MRS. BARKER

My, my, my.

DADDY

(*Offstage*)

Mommy! I can't find Grandma's television, and I can't find the Pekinese, either.

MOMMY

(*Offstage*)

Isn't that funny! And I can't find the water.

GRANDMA

Heh, heh, heh. I told them everything was hidden.

MRS. BARKER

Did you hide the water, too?

GRANDMA

(*Puzzled*)

No. No, I didn't do *that*.

DADDY

(*Offstage*)

The truth of the matter is, I can't even find Grandma's room.

GRANDMA

Heh, heh, heh.

MRS. BARKER

My! You certainly did hide things, didn't you?

GRANDMA

Sure, kid, sure.

MOMMY

(*Sticking her head in the room*)

Did you ever hear of such a thing, Grandma? Daddy can't find your television, and he can't find the Pekinese, and the truth of the matter is he can't even find your room.

GRANDMA

I told you. I hid everything.

MOMMY

Nonsense, Grandma! Just wait until I get my hands on you. You're a troublemaker . . . that's what you are.

GRANDMA

Well, I'll be out of here pretty soon, baby.

MOMMY

Oh, you don't know how right you are! Daddy's been wanting to send you away for a long time now, but I've been restraining him. I'll tell you one thing, though . . . I'm getting sick and tired of this fighting, and I might just let him have his way. Then you'll see what'll happen. Away you'll go; in a van, too. I'll let Daddy call the van man.

GRANDMA

I'm way ahead of you.

MOMMY

How can you be so old and so smug at the same time? You have no sense of proportion.

GRANDMA

You just answered your own question.

MOMMY

Mrs. Barker, I'd much rather you came into the kitchen for that glass of water, what with Grandma out here, and all.

MRS. BARKER

I don't see what Grandma has to do with it; and besides, I don't think you're very polite.

MOMMY

You seem to forget that you're a guest in this house . . .

GRANDMA

Apartment!

MOMMY

Apartment! And that you're a professional woman. So, if you'll be so good as to come into the kitchen, I'll be more than happy to show you where the water is, and where the glass is, and then you can put two and two together, if you're clever enough.
(*She vanishes*)

MRS. BARKER

(*After a moment's consideration*)
I suppose she's right.

GRANDMA

Well, that's how it is when people call you up and ask you over to do something for them.

MRS. BARKER

I suppose you're right, too. Well, Grandma, it's been very nice talking to you.

GRANDMA

And I've enjoyed listening. Say, don't tell Mommy or Daddy that I gave you that hint, will you?

MRS. BARKER

Oh, dear me, the hint! I'd forgotten about it, if you can imagine such a thing. No, I won't breathe a word of it to them.

GRANDMA

I don't know if it helped you any . . .

MRS. BARKER

I can't tell, yet. I'll have to . . . what *is* the word I want? . . . I'll have to relate it . . . that's it . . . I'll have to relate it to certain things that I *know*, and . . . draw . . . conclusions. . . . What I'll really have to do is to see if it applies to anything. I mean, after all, I *do* do volunteer work for an adoption service, but it isn't very much *like* the Bye-Bye Adoption Service . . . it *is* the Bye-Bye Adoption Service . . . and while I can remember Mommy and Daddy coming to see me, oh, about twenty years ago, about buying a bumble, I can't quite remember anyone very much *like* Mommy and Daddy coming to see me about buying a bumble. Don't you see? It really presents quite a problem. . . . I'll have to think about it . . . mull it . . . but at any rate, it was truly first-class of you to try to help me. Oh, will you still be here after I've had my drink of water?

GRANDMA

Probably . . . I'm not as spry as I used to be.

MRS. BARKER

Oh. Well, I won't say good-by then.

GRANDMA

No. Don't

(MRS. BARKER *exits through the archway*)

People don't say good-by to old people because they think they'll frighten
them. Lordy! If they only knew how awful "hello" and "my, you're looking chipper" sounded, they wouldn't say those things either. The truth is,
there isn't much you *can* say to old people that doesn't sound just terrible.

(*The doorbell rings*)

Come on in!

(*The* YOUNG MAN *enters.* GRANDMA *looks him over*)

Well, now, aren't you a breath of fresh air!

YOUNG MAN

Hello there.

GRANDMA

My, my, my. Are you the van man?

YOUNG MAN

The what?

GRANDMA

The van man. The van man. Are you come to take me away?

YOUNG MAN

I don't know what you're talking about.

GRANDMA

Oh.

(*Pause*)

Well.

(*Pause*)

My, my, aren't you something!

YOUNG MAN

Hm?

GRANDMA

I said, my, my, aren't you something.

YOUNG MAN

Oh. Thank you.

GRANDMA

You don't sound very enthusiastic.

YOUNG MAN

Oh, I'm . . . I'm used to it.

GRANDMA

Yup . . . yup. You know, if I were about a hundred and fifty years
younger I could go for you.

YOUNG MAN

Yes, I imagine so.

GRANDMA

Unh-hunh . . . will you look at those muscles!

YOUNG MAN
  (*Flexing his muscles*)
  Yes, they're quite good, aren't they?

GRANDMA
  Boy, they sure are. They natural?

YOUNG MAN
  Well the basic structure was there, but I've done some work, too . . . you know, in a gym.

GRANDMA
  I'll bet you have. You ought to be in the movies, boy.

YOUNG MAN
  I know.

GRANDMA
  Yup! Right up there on the old silver screen. But I suppose you've heard that before.

YOUNG MAN
  Yes, I have.

GRANDMA
  You ought to try out for them . . . the movies.

YOUNG MAN
  Well, actually, I may have a career there yet. I've lived out on the West Coast almost all my life . . . and I've met a few people who . . . might be able to help me. I'm not in too much of a hurry, though. I'm almost as young as I look.

GRANDMA
  Oh, that's nice. And will you look at that face!

YOUNG MAN
  Yes, it's quite good, isn't it? Clean-cut, midwest farm boy type, almost insultingly good-looking in a typically American way. Good profile, straight nose, honest eyes, wonderful smile . . .

GRANDMA
  Yup. Boy, you know what you are, don't you? You're the American Dream, that's what you are. All those other people, they don't know what they're talking about. You . . . *you* are the American Dream.

YOUNG MAN
  Thanks.

MOMMY
  (*Offstage*)
  Who rang the doorbell?

GRANDMA
  (*Shouting offstage*)
  The American Dream!

MOMMY
  (*Offstage*)
  What? What was that, Grandma?

GRANDMA
  (*Shouting*)
  The American Dream! The American Dream! Damn it!

DADDY
> (*Offstage*)
> How's that, Mommy?

MOMMY
> (*Offstage*)
> Oh, some gibberish; pay no attention. Did you find Grandma's room?

DADDY
> (*Offstage*)
> No. I can't even find Mrs. Barker.

YOUNG MAN
> What was all that?

GRANDMA
> Oh, that was just the folks, but let's not talk about them, honey; let's talk about you.

YOUNG MAN
> All right.

GRANDMA
> Well, let's see. If you're not the van man, what are you doing here?

YOUNG MAN
> I'm looking for work.

GRANDMA
> Are you! Well, what kind of work?

YOUNG MAN
> Oh, almost anything . . . almost anything that pays. I'll do almost anything for money.

GRANDMA
> Will you . . . will you? Hmmmm. I wonder if there's anything you could do around here?

YOUNG MAN
> There might be. It looked to be a likely building.

GRANDMA
> It's always looked to be a rather unlikely building to me, but I suppose you'd know better than I.

YOUNG MAN
> I can sense these things.

GRANDMA
> There *might* be something you could do around here. Stay there! Don't come any closer.

YOUNG MAN
> Sorry.

GRANDMA
> I don't mean I'd *mind*. I don't know whether I'd mind, or not. . . . But it wouldn't look well; it would look just *awful*.

YOUNG MAN
> Yes; I suppose so.

GRANDMA
> Now, stay there, let me concentrate. What could you do? The folks have

been in something of a quandary around here today, sort of a dilemma, and I wonder if you mightn't be some help.

YOUNG MAN
I hope so . . . if there's money in it. Do you have any money?

GRANDMA
Money! Oh, there's more money around here than you'd know what to do with.

YOUNG MAN
I'm not so sure.

GRANDMA
Well, maybe not. Besides, I've got money of my own.

YOUNG MAN
You have?

GRANDMA
Sure. Old people quite often have lots of money; more often than most people expect. Come here, so I can whisper to you . . . not too close. I might faint.

YOUNG MAN
Oh, I'm sorry.

GRANDMA
It's all right, dear. Anyway . . . have you ever heard of that big baking contest they run? The one where all the ladies get together in a big barn and bake away?

YOUNG MAN
I'm . . . not . . . sure. . . .

GRANDMA
Not so close. Well, it doesn't matter whether you've heard of it or not. The important thing is—and I don't want anybody to hear this . . . the folks think I haven't been out of the house in eight years—the important thing is that I won first prize in that baking contest this year. Oh, it was in all the papers; not under my own name, though. I used a *nom de boulangère;* I called myself Uncle Henry.

YOUNG MAN
Did you?

GRANDMA
Why not? I didn't see any reason not to. I look just as much like an old man as I do like an old woman. And you know what I called it . . . what I won for?

YOUNG MAN
No. What did you call it?

GRANDMA
I called it Uncle Henry's Day-Old Cake.

YOUNG MAN
That's a very nice name.

GRANDMA
And it wasn't any trouble, either. All I did was go out and get a store-bought cake, and keep it around for a while, and then slip it in, unbeknownst to anybody. Simple.

YOUNG MAN

You're a very resourceful person.

GRANDMA

Pioneer stock.

YOUNG MAN

Is all this true? Do you want me to believe all this?

GRANDMA

Well, you can believe it or not . . . it doesn't make any difference to me. All *I* know is, Uncle Henry's Day-Old Cake won me twenty-five thousand smackerolas.

YOUNG MAN

Twenty-five thou—

GRANDMA

Right on the old loggerhead. Now . . . how do you like them apples?

YOUNG MAN

Love 'em.

GRANDMA

I thought you'd be impressed.

YOUNG MAN

Money talks.

GRANDMA

Hey! You look familiar.

YOUNG MAN

Hm? Pardon?

GRANDMA

I said, you look familiar.

YOUNG MAN

Well, I've done some modeling.

GRANDMA

No . . . no. I don't mean that. You look familiar.

YOUNG MAN

Well, I'm a type.

GRANDMA

Yup; you sure are. Why do you say you'd do anything for money . . . if you don't mind my being nosy?

YOUNG MAN

No, no. It's part of the interviews. I'll be happy to tell you. It's that I have no talents at all, except what you see . . . my person; my body, my face. In every other way I am incomplete, and I must therefore . . . compensate.

GRANDMA

What do you mean, incomplete? You look pretty complete to me.

YOUNG MAN

I think I can explain it to you, partially because you're very old, and very old people have perceptions they keep to themselves, because if they expose them to other people . . . well, you know what ridicule and neglect are.

GRANDMA

I do, child, I do.

YOUNG MAN

Then listen. My mother died the night that I was born, and I never knew my father; I doubt my mother did. But, I wasn't alone, because lying with me . . . in the placenta . . . there was someone else . . . my brother . . . my twin.

GRANDMA

Oh, my child.

YOUNG MAN

We were identical twins . . . he and I . . . not fraternal . . . identical; we were derived from the same ovum; and in *this*, in that we were twins not from separate ova but from the same one, we had a kinship such as you cannot imagine. We . . . we felt each other breathe . . . his heartbeats thundered in my temples . . . mine in his . . . our stomachs ached and we cried for feeding at the same time . . . are you old enough to understand?

GRANDMA

I think so, child; I think I'm nearly old enough.

YOUNG MAN

I hope so. But we were separated when we were still very young, my brother, my twin and I . . . inasmuch as you can separate one being. We were torn apart . . . thrown to opposite ends of the continent. I don't know what became of my brother . . . to the rest of myself . . . except that, from time to time, in the years that have passed, I have suffered losses . . . that I can't explain. A fall from grace . . . a departure of innocence . . . loss . . . loss. How can I put it to you? All right; like this: Once . . . it was as if all at once my heart . . . became numb . . . almost as though I . . . almost as though . . . just like that . . . it had been wrenched from my body . . . and from that time I have been unable to love. Once . . . I was asleep at the time . . . I awoke, and my eyes were burning. And since that time I have been unable to see anything, *anything*, with pity, with affection . . . with anything but . . . cool disinterest. And my groin . . . even there . . . since one time . . . one specific agony . . . since then I have not been able to *love* anyone with my body. And even my hands . . . I cannot touch another person and feel love. And there is more . . . there are more losses, but it all comes down to this: I no longer have the capacity to feel anything. I have no emotions. I have been drained, torn asunder . . . disemboweled. I have, now, only my person . . . my body, my face. I use what I have . . . I let people love me . . . I accept the syntax around me, for while I know I cannot relate . . . I know I must be related *to*. I let people love me . . . I let people touch me . . . I let them draw pleasure from my groin . . . from my presence . . . from the fact of me . . . but, that is all it comes to. As I told you, I am incomplete . . . I can feel nothing. I can feel nothing. And so . . . here I am . . . as you see me. I am . . . but this . . . what you see. And it will always be thus.

GRANDMA

Oh, my child; my child.

(*Long pause; then*)

I was mistaken. . . before. I don't know you from somewhere, but I knew . . . once . . . someone very much like you . . . or, very much as perhaps you were.

YOUNG MAN

Be careful; be very careful. What I have told you may not be true. In my profession . . .

GRANDMA

Shhhhhh.

(*The* YOUNG MAN *bows his head, in acquiescence*)

Someone . . . to be more precise . . . who might have turned out to be very much like you might have turned out to be. And . . . unless I'm terribly mistaken . . . you've found yourself a job.

YOUNG MAN

What are my duties?

MRS. BARKER

(*Offstage*)

Yoo-hoo! Yoo-hoo!

GRANDMA

Oh-oh. You'll . . . you'll have to play it by ear, my dear . . . unless I get a chance to talk to you again. I've got to go into my act, now.

YOUNG MAN

But, I . . .

GRANDMA

Yoo-hoo!

MRS. BARKER

(*Coming through archway*)

Yoo-hoo . . . oh, there you are, Grandma. I'm glad to see somebody. I can't find Mommy or Daddy.

(*Double takes*)

Well . . . who's this?

GRANDMA

This? Well . . . un . . . oh, this is the . . . uh . . . the van man. That's who it is . . . the van man.

MRS. BARKER

So! It's true! They *did* call the van man. They *are* having you carted away.

GRANDMA

(*Shrugging*)

Well, you know. It figures.

MRS. BARKER

(*To* YOUNG MAN)

How dare you cart this poor old woman away!

YOUNG MAN

(*After a quick look at* GRANDMA, *who nods*)

I do what I'm paid to do. I don't ask any questions.

MRS. BARKER

(*After a brief pause*)

Oh.

(*Pause*)
Well, you're right, of course, and I shouldn't meddle.

GRANDMA

(*To* YOUNG MAN)
Dear, will you take my things out to the van?
(*She points to the boxes*)

YOUNG MAN

(*After only the briefest hesitation*)
Why certainly.

GRANDMA

(*As the* YOUNG MAN *takes up half the boxes, exits by the front door*)
Isn't that a nice young van man?

MRS. BARKER

(*Shaking her head in disbelief, watching the* YOUNG MAN *exit*)
Unh-hunh . . . some things have changed for the better. I remember
when I had *my* mother carted off . . . the van man who came for her
wasn't anything near as nice as this one.

GRANDMA

Oh, did you have your mother carted off, too?

MRS. BARKER

(*Cheerfully*)
Why certainly! Didn't you?

GRANDMA

(*Puzzling*)
No . . . no, I didn't. At least, I can't remember. Listen dear; I got to talk
to you for a second.

MRS. BARKER

Why certainly, Grandma.

GRANDMA

Now, listen.

MRS. BARKER

Yes, Grandma. Yes.

GRANDMA

Now listen carefully. You got this dilemma here with Mommy and
Daddy . . .

MRS. BARKER

Yes! I wonder where they've gone to?

GRANDMA

They'll be back in. Now, LISTEN!

MRS. BARKER

Oh, I'm sorry.

GRANDMA

Now, you got this dilemma here with Mommy and Daddy, and I think I
got the way out for you.
(*The* YOUNG MAN *reenters through the front door*)
Will you take the rest of my things out now, dear?
(*To* MRS. BARKER, *while the* YOUNG MAN *takes the rest of the boxes, exits
again by the front door*)

Fine. Now listen, dear.
(*She begins to whisper in* MRS. BARKER'S *ear*)

MRS. BARKER

Oh! Oh! Oh! I don't think I could . . . do you really think I could? Well, why not? What a wonderful idea . . . what an absolutely wonderful idea!

GRANDMA

Well, yes, I thought it was.

MRS. BARKER

And you so old!

GRANDMA

Heh, heh, heh.

MRS. BARKER

Well, I think it's absolutely marvelous, anyway. I'm going to find Mommy and Daddy right now.

GRANDMA

Good. You do that.

MRS. BARKER

Well, now. I think I will say good-by. I can't thank you enough.
(*She starts to exit through the archway*)

GRANDMA

You're welcome. Say it!

MRS. BARKER

Huh? What?

GRANDMA

Say good-by.

MRS. BARKER

Oh. Good-by.
(*She exits*)
Mommy! I say, Mommy! Daddy!

GRANDMA

Good-by.
(*By herself now, she looks about*)
Ah me.
(*Shakes her head*)
Ah me.
(*Takes in the room*)
Good-by.
(*The* YOUNG MAN *reenters*)

GRANDMA

Oh, hello, there.

YOUNG MAN

All the boxes are outside.

GRANDMA

(*A little sadly*)
I don't know why I bother to take them with me. They don't have much in them . . . some old letters, a couple of regrets . . . Pekinese . . .

blind at that . . . the television . . . my Sunday teeth . . . eighty-six
years of living . . . some sounds . . . a few images, a little garbled by
now . . . and, well . . .
(*She shrugs*)
. . . you know . . . the things one accumulates.

YOUNG MAN

Can I get you . . . a cab, or something?

GRANDMA

Oh no, dear . . . thank you just the same. I'll take it from here.

YOUNG MAN

And what shall I do now?

GRANDMA

Oh, you stay here, dear. It will all become clear to you. It will be explained.
You'll understand.

YOUNG MAN

Very well.

GRANDMA

(*After one more look about*)
Well . . .

YOUNG MAN

Let me see you to the elevator.

GRANDMA

Oh . . . that *would* be nice, dear.

(*They both exit by the front door, slowly*)

(*Enter* MRS. BARKER *followed by* MOMMY *and* DADDY)

MRS. BARKER

. . . and I'm happy to tell you that the whole thing's settled. Just like
that.

MOMMY

Oh, we're so glad. We were afraid there might be a problem, what with
delays, and all.

DADDY

Yes, we're very relieved.

MRS. BARKER

Well, now; that's what professional women are for.

MOMMY

Why . . . where's Grandma? Grandma's not here! Where's Grandma?
And look! The boxes are gone, too. Grandma's gone, and so are the boxes.
She's taken off, and she's stolen something! Daddy!

MRS. BARKER

Why, Mommy, the van man was here.

MOMMY

(*Startled*)
The what?

MRS. BARKER

The van man. The van man was here.
(*The lights might dim a little, suddenly*)

MOMMY

(*Shakes her head*)

No, that's impossible.

MRS. BARKER

Why, I saw him with my own two eyes.

MOMMY

(*Near tears*)

No, no, that's impossible. No. There's no such thing as the van man. There is no van man. We . . . we made him up. Grandma? Grandma?

DADDY

(*Moving to* MOMMY)

There, there, now.

MOMMY

Oh Daddy . . . where's Grandma?

DADDY

There, there, now.

(*While* DADDY *is comforting* MOMMY, GRANDMA *comes out, stage right, near the footlights*)

GRANDMA

(*To the audience*)

Shhhhhh! I want to watch this.

(*She motions to* MRS. BARKER *who, with a secret smile, tiptoes to the front door and opens it. The* YOUNG MAN *is framed therein. Lights up full again as he steps into the room*)

MRS. BARKER

Surprise! Surprise! Here we are!

MOMMY

What? What?

DADDY

Hm? What?

MOMMY

(*Her tears merely sniffles now*)

What surprise?

MRS. BARKER

Why, I told you. The surprise I told you about.

DADDY

You . . . you know, Mommy.

MOMMY

Sur . . . prise?

DADDY

(*Urging her to cheerfulness*)

You remember, Mommy; why we asked . . . uh . . . what's-her-name to come here?

MRS. BARKER

Mrs. Barker, if you don't mind.

DADDY

Yes. Mommy? You remember now? About the bumble . . . about wanting satisfaction?

MOMMY

(*Her sorrow turning into delight*)

Yes. Why yes! Of course! Yes! Oh, how wonderful!

MRS. BARKER

(*To the* YOUNG MAN)

This is Mommy.

YOUNG MAN

How . . . how do you do?

MRS. BARKER

(*Stage whisper*)

Her name's Mommy.

YOUNG MAN

How . . . how do you do, Mommy?

MOMMY

Well! Hello there!

MRS. BARKER

(*To the* YOUNG MAN)

And that is Daddy.

YOUNG MAN

How do you do, sir?

DADDY

How do you do?

MOMMY

(*Herself again, circling the* YOUNG MAN, *feeling his arm, poking him*)

Yes, sir! Yes, sirree! Now this is more like it. Now this is a great deal more like it! Daddy! Come see. Come see if this isn't a great deal more like it.

DADDY

I . . . I can see from here, Mommy. It does look a great deal more like it.

MOMMY

Yes, sir. Yes sirree! Mrs. Barker, I don't know *how* to thank you.

MRS. BARKER

Oh, don't worry about that. I'll send you a bill in the mail.

MOMMY

What this really calls for is a celebration. It calls for a drink.

MRS. BARKER

Oh, what a nice idea.

MOMMY

There's some sauterne in the kitchen.

YOUNG MAN

I'll go.

MOMMY

Will you? Oh, how nice. The kitchen's through the archway there.

(*As the* YOUNG MAN *exits: to* MRS. BARKER)

He's very nice. Really top notch; much better than the other one.

MRS. BARKER

I'm glad you're pleased. And I'm glad everything's all straightened out.

MOMMY

Well, at least we know why we sent for you. We're glad that's cleared up. By the way, what's his name?

MRS. BARKER

Ha! Call him whatever you like. He's yours. Call him what you called the other one.

MOMMY

Daddy? What did we call the other one?

DADDY

(*Puzzles*)

Why . . .

YOUNG MAN

(*Reentering with a tray on which are a bottle of sauterne and five glasses*)

Here we are!

MOMMY

Hooray! Hooray!

MRS. BARKER

Oh, good!

MOMMY

(*Moving to the tray*)

So, let's— Five glasses? Why five? There are only four of us. Why five?

YOUNG MAN

(*Catches* GRANDMA's *eye;* GRANDMA *indicates she is not there*)

Oh, I'm sorry.

MOMMY

You must learn to count. We're a wealthy family, and you must learn to count.

YOUNG MAN

I will.

MOMMY

Well, everybody take a glass.

(*They do*)

And we'll drink to celebrate. To satisfaction! Who says you can't get satisfaction these days!

MRS. BARKER

What dreadful sauterne!

MOMMY

Yes, isn't it?

(*To* YOUNG MAN, *her voice already a little fuzzy from the wine*)

You don't know how happy I am to see you! Yes sirree. Listen, that time we had with . . . with the other one. I'll tell you about it some time.

(*Indicates* MRS. BARKER)

After she's gone. She was responsible for all the trouble in the first place. I'll tell you all about it.

(*Sidles up to him a little*)

Maybe . . . maybe later tonight.

YOUNG MAN

(*Not moving away*)

Why yes. That would be very nice.

MOMMY

(*Puzzles*)

Something familiar about you . . . you know that? I can't quite place it. . . .

GRANDMA

(*Interrupting . . . to audience*)

Well, I guess that just about wraps it up. I mean, for better or for worse, this is a comedy, and I don't think we'd better go any further. No, definitely not. So, let's leave things as they are right now . . . while everybody's happy . . . while everybody's got what he wants . . . or everybody's got what he thinks he wants. Good night, dears.

[*Curtain*]